FORECASTING IN INTERNATIONAL RELATIONS
Theory, Methods, Problems, Prospects

Edited by

Nazli Choucri

Massachusetts Institute of Technology

and

Thomas W. Robinson

National Defense University

W. H. Freeman and Company
San Francisco

Library of Congress Cataloging in Publication Data

Main entry under title:

Forecasting in international relations.
Bibliography: p.
Includes index.

1.   International relations—Research.
2.   Twentieth century—Forecasts.   I.   Choucri,
Nazli.   II.   Robinson, Thomas W.
JX1291.F64   327'.07'2   78-19169
ISBN 0-7167-0059-X

Printed in the United States of America

10   9   8   7   6   5   4   3   2   1

CONTENTS

PREFACE

This volume represents the first collective effort by an international group of scholars to sketch out the boundaries and the content of forecasting as applied to international relations. A number of individual works have been published previously, but for the most part students in the field have concentrated on demonstrating some particular forecasting method or have been concerned with specific forecasts of a particular set of events or with a particular country or region. Moreover, most previous efforts have not attempted to overcome the inevitable bias that results from the national perspective of the forecaster, or they have not focused on the different viewpoints of the scholar-as-forecaster versus the policy maker-as-forecaster. The present undertaking represents an initial summary of the field at a preliminary state of development. It seeks to be representative of the main directions of research in the field as of the middle 1970's.

The volume is divided into five parts. The first, comprising Chapters 1 and 2, lays out some of the general issues commonly met in international relations forecasting and warns of the many pitfalls that await the serious scholar or policy maker. Part II integrates forecasting efforts and theory in international relations, an indispensable task because every forecast must be linked with a particular view of international relations, explicitly noted or not. All of the authors of this part agree that theory and forecasting are symbiotic: A workable theory must include a forecasting component—it must dare to forecast—just as a serious forecast must depend on an explicit theory, however controversial.

Part III is the longest of the volume, but not merely because there is a plenitude of forecasting methods that needs to be utilized in international relations forecasting. The choice of what method to utilize determines, perhaps even more than the type of theory involved, the level of effort, money, and time invested in the forecast. As such, it heavily influences the probability that the forecast will be "successful," however one wishes to define that term. Some of the methods discussed are, in fact, being applied to the field for the first time in these chapters. In several cases, applications are merely suggested, because the methods in question have been utilized in other fields of forecasting. In others, extensive experience has been obtained, such as in the cases of expert opinion, gaming, and computer simulation. All told, Part III presents a broad review of a rapidly expanding field.

Part IV inspects particular aspects of international relations forecasting that stem from the question of what time perspective interests the forecaster. Both purpose and procedure will vary greatly, depending on whether one adopts a short-, medium-, or long-term time-frame. Retrospective forecasting has also been used as a powerful tool to improve the quality of forecasting and of theory. The authors of this part indicate that much remains to be done by way of differentiating the period of the forecast and its effect on the method of forecasting.

The last part has two purposes. The first is to demonstrate how forecasts vary according to the purpose of the exercise and the organization doing the work. Particularly germane are forecasts that have a high policy content or that are conducted by governments. These quickly become enmeshed in the political process and become different instruments and serve different purposes than forecasts made by scholars operating without immediate time pressures. The second purpose is to show how forecasts vary across national boundaries and among different cultures.

Today a number of centers and projects, as well as many scholars, are working in international relations forecasting. The editors have attempted to draw together what they consider most representative of these efforts, which are now worldwide. There are undoubtedly omissions. We are aware, for instance, that West European thinking, in particular, recent French and Italian efforts, is underrepresented. We are also painfully cognizant that many of the authors of the twenty-eight chapters do not make a single forecast. This book is devoted chiefly to the intellectual and methodological underpinnings of international relations forecast-ing, largely as they have been developed in the United States. It will remain for subsequent volumes to treat these omissions, as well as to record the rate of progress and failure of existing modes of looking into the future.

This endeavor had its origins in December, 1971, in a Conference on International Relations Forecasting at the San Ysidro Ranch, Santa Barbara, California, chaired by Professor Gerald Shure of the University of California, Los Angeles. One result of that meeting was a conviction by both the editors and some of the contributors that a pressing need existed for an overall examination of the status of international relations forecasting that would be comprehensive, authoritative, and international in scope. The editors therefore sent out a call for papers to a wide range of authors, most of whose responses are contained in the present volume. In order to facilitate scholarly interchange, the Institute for World Order generously agreed to fund, together with the Center for International Studies at the Massachusetts Institute of Technology, a conference on the subject at the American Academy of Arts and Sciences. That conference, organized by the staff of the Center for International Studies (MIT), took place in October, 1973, and was attended, in addition to most of the authors, by a number of academic and government leaders from the Boston and Washington, DC, areas. During the two years surrounding the conference, the editors convened panels at several academic meetings—the American Association for the Advancement of Science, the American Political Science Association, the International Studies Association, and the Peace Research Society—to expose the ideas contained therein to further scrutiny. The final manuscript took shape during 1975 and 1976, when revised drafts were submitted and W. H. Freeman and Company undertook to publish the results.

This volume would not have been possible without the combined efforts of a substantial number of people. The editors would like to take this occasion to convey their appreciation to all of them, whether mentioned here by name or not. The volume would not exist at all, of course, without the contributory efforts of the chapter authors. They deserve recognition not merely for their work but for their patience and understanding during the long gestation period of the book. In addition, there would have been no published output, at least in the present form, were it not for the assistance of several individuals and institutions. The Institute for World Order, its president, Saul Mendlowitz, and, in particular, A. Michael Washburn were instrumental in encouraging the editors to move ahead with the project. Mr. Washburn took a constant, direct, and personal interest in the success of the volume, even to the extent of becoming one of the contributors. The Institute provided major funding. Dr. Dennis Pirages, then Social Science Editor at W. H. Freeman and Company, encouraged us further. Professor Ithiel de Sola Pool, Professor of Political Science at the Massachusetts Institute of Technology, chaired the 1973 conference and provided order and coherence during the entire proceedings. Richard Lamb, Political Science Editor at W. H. Freeman and Company, was instrumental in taking the enterprise through the long and complicated process of publishing and provided a great deal of sage advice at every stage. Patricia Brewer, Project Editor at W. H. Freeman and Company, also deserves much credit for her perspicacity and professionalism. Mimi Fellores, a (now graduated) student at the University of Washington, went far beyond her duties in retyping the manuscript, in pointing out and correcting errors, and in preparing the combined bibliography. Finally, we would like to express our appreciation to Naomi Tschoegl and Phoebe Green at MIT for their careful review of the manuscript at various stages of production— from typescript to galleys and page proofs.

Mention should also be made of the institutional support to the editors directly. Nazli Choucri is indebted to the National Science Foundation for support on basic research in international relations forecasting and to the Center for International Studies at the Massachusetts Institute of Technology for assistance throughout the project. Thomas Robinson would like to convey his thanks for support rendered by the Rand Corporation, the Council on Foreign Relations, and the Institute for Comparative and Foreign Areas Studies at the University of Washington.

Nazli Choucri
Thomas W. Robinson

May 1978

THE EDITORS

Nazli Choucri, Professor of Political Science at MIT, has written extensively on theory and methods in international relations and has completed several studies forecasting future outcomes. She is the author of *International Politics of Energy Interdependence: The Case of Petroleum* (1976) and *Population Dynamics and International Violence: Propositions, Insights, and Evidence* (1974). With Robert C. North, she has written *Nations in Conflict: National Growth and International Violence* (1975), a study that undertakes retrospective forecasts and policy analyses. Professor Choucri is currently completing a study forecasting the effects of alternative prices on the world petroleum exchanges to the year 2000.

Thomas W. Robinson, Professor of International Relations, the National War College, National Defense University, has written and taught widely in the fields of international relations, Chinese and Soviet politics and foreign policies, and security studies. His doctoral dissertation was entitled "Hans J. Morgenthau's Theory of International Relations." He is editor and co-author of *The Cultural Revolution in China* and author of *Chinese Foreign Policy* and *Lin Piao: A Chinese Military Politician* (both forthcoming). He was a member of the Social Science Department research staff at the Rand Corporation, Visiting Fellow at the Council on Foreign Relations, and Associate Professor at the University of Washington. Additionally, he has taught at Dartmouth, the University of California at Los Angeles, and Princeton University, and he has been consultant to a number of government and private institutions.

THE CONTRIBUTORS

Richard K. Ashley
School of International Relations
University of Southern California

Edward E. Azar
Department of Political Science
University of North Carolina, Chapel Hill

Igor V. Bestuzhev-lada
Institute for Sociological Research
Moscow

Lincoln P. Bloomfield
Department of Political Science
Massachusetts Institute of Technology

Davis B. Bobrow
Bureau of Governmental Research
and Department of Government and Politics
University of Maryland

Marie V. Bousfield
Department of Development and Planning
City of Chicago

Garry D. Brewer
School of Organization and Management
and Department of Political Science
Yale University

Nazli Choucri
Department of Political Science
Massachusetts Institute of Technology

Cheryl Christensen
Department of Government and Politics
University of Maryland

Chester L. Cooper
Institute for Energy, Washington, DC
Former Fellow at the Woodrow Wilson
International Center for Scholars

Vladimir P. Filatov
Institute for Sociological Research
Moscow

G. Robert Franco
International Monetary Fund
Washington, DC

Alexander L. George
Department of Political Science
Stanford University

Olaf Helmer
Graduate School of Business Administration
University of Southern California

Charles F. Hermann
Department of Political Science
and Mershon Center
Ohio State University

Thomas E. Jones
New School for Social Research
and Graduate School of Management
Polytechnic Institute of New York

M. R. Leavitt
Research Division, Federal Judicial Center
Washington, DC

Ali A. Mazrui
Department of Political Science
University of Michigan

Thomas W. Milburn
Mershon Center
Ohio State University

Robert C. North
Department of Political Science
Stanford University

Warren R. Phillips
Department of Government and Politics
University of Maryland

Ithiel de Sola Pool
Department of Political Science
Massachusetts Institute of Technology

Thomas W. Robinson
National War College
National Defense University
Washington, DC

David Scott Ross
Department of Political Science
University of Minnesota

John Gerard Ruggie
Department of Political Science
and School of International Affairs
Columbia University

Yoshikazu Sakamoto
Faculty of Law
University of Tokyo

Hiroharu Seki
Institute of Oriental Culture
University of Tokyo

Alexander Szalai
Karl Marx University of Economics
Budapest

Stuart J. Thorson
Department of Political Science
and Polimetrics Laboratory
Ohio State University

A. Michael Washburn
Independent Consultant
Formerly of the Institute for World Order

Robert A. Young
International Research & Development, Inc.
Washington, DC
Formerly of the Cybernetics Technology Office
Defense Advanced Research Projects Agency

PART I

INTRODUCTION

CHAPTER ONE

KEY ISSUES IN INTERNATIONAL RELATIONS FORECASTING

Nazli Choucri

I. INTRODUCTION: FORECASTING AND THE IMPERATIVES OF INTERNATIONAL RELATIONS

Forecasting is a problem of reasoning, of reducing uncertainty, and of bounded and disciplined speculation. Exploring the unknown, identifying possibilities associated with different outcomes, and isolating likelihoods of occurrences constitute the essence of forecasting. In the social sciences, the problem is defined as one of minimizing uncertainty. Reducing variances around alternative estimates of the unknown provides the lowest common denominator among different modes and techniques of forecasting. Beyond that, the range of approaches to forecasting are as numerous as they are varied. It is a truism—but important—that what one sees depends on how one looks at it: In the same vein, the methodologies one employs, the assumptions one holds, and the values one espouses are all critical in determining how one will look at the future and what one will see. This chapter examines key issues in international relations forecasting and specifies the ways by which we might increase our ability to develop reliable views of future outcomes.

Reality comes in many guises: It is at the same time the actual, the possible, the potential, the

I am particularly grateful to Hayward Alker for incisive comments and suggestions. I am also grateful to Richard Ashley, Daniel Bell, Michael Leavitt, Amy Leiss, Ithiel Pool, Thomas Robinson, Scott Ross, John Ruggie, and Alexander Szalai for comments on an earlier draft of this article. An earlier version of this chapter was prepared for the annual meeting of the American Association for the Advancement of Science, Washington, DC, December, 1972 and appeared as "Forecasting in International Relations: Problems and Prospects," *International Interactions*, Vol. 1, 1974, pp. 63–86. It appears with the permission of the publisher, Gordon and Breach.

probable, or the preferable. Reality may also be the undesirable, the negative, the chiliastic, or the apocalyptical. Although many other views of reality undoubtedly exist, we tend to view and define futures in terms of "goods" and "bads." However, if we interject probabilities, contingencies, and conscious specification of alternatives, we will obtain a more enlightened view of possible futures than if we adopt such simplistic and dichotomous views. Indeed, the critical distinction between prediction and forecasting involves contingencies and probabilities.

A prediction usually dispenses with probabilistic interpretations; a forecast is always conceived within a certain probability range. A prediction is generally made in terms of a point or event; a forecast is made in terms of alternatives. A prediction focuses upon one outcome; a forecast involves contingencies. The composite distinction between prediction and forecasting—in terms of probabilities, contingent outcomes and on conscious specification of alternatives—lies at the core of existing approaches to the future.

The major issues of international relations involve the following: (1) the different roles of nations, their positions in global politics, and the means by which they conduct their relations with other states; (2) the determinants of power and weakness, the global implications of imbalances in capability and military inequalities; (3) the imperatives of resource scarcities, availabilities, and usages; (4) the political implications of technological development and the distribution of knowledge and skills; (5) the political consequences of demographic profiles, the implications of added numbers, and the consequences of increasing loads upon the surface of the earth; (6) the configuration of national perceptions, attitudes, and cognitions; (7) the global implications of nonterritorial actors, multinational corporations, international institutions, and transnational organizations; and (8) the relation of international politics to international society and the interdependence between international politics and international economics.

These issues all converge around the causes of war and the preconditions for peace. Each of these questions bears directly upon propensities and probabilities of violence. For forecasting purposes, therefore, we must obtain some reliable means of gauging changes and developments along every one of these critical issue areas and of assessing the extent to which systems are war-prone or peace-prone. Different forecasting methodologies are appropriate for examining different problems. And the time frame within which the forecast is undertaken is a critical determinant of the methodology selected and of the type of forecast obtained.

When forecasting international outcomes, we are concerned with the ranges of possibilities and contingencies and probabilities associated with each. A successful forecast must account for at least the following: the direction of the activity modeled, the direction of sharp breaks or reversals, the extent of change, the period over which change is likely to persist, the points in the system most amenable to manipulation, and the costs of manipulation.

Forecasting in international relations is particularly challenging in view of the large number of variables in question, the magnitudes of the unknowns, and the propensities for random or exogenous shocks. All the complexities associated with forecasting are compounded by the uncertainties of tomorrow's international realities. This chapter addresses five key issues in international relations forecasting: (1) the prophecy implications of forecasting; (2) the role of theory; (3) alternative modes of forecasting; (4) the purposes and time perspective of a forecast; and (5) the policy implications of forecasting. By way of conclusion we shall note some requisites for viewing the future more successfully than has been done to date.

II. FORECASTING AS SCIENTIFIC PROPHECY: ALTERNATIVE MOTIVATIONS AND THE ROLE OF VALUES

In this technocratic age of ours forecasting is sometimes viewed as scientific prophecy, and controlling the unknown emerges as a necessary corollary. Together, prophecy and control converge to make forecasting an important aspect of today's scientific perspective. The roots of this perspective involve technocratic hermaneutics and liberative prediction.[1] In forecasting parlance, the former refers to disciplined empathy for the structure of the unknown in providing some understanding of futures, and the latter to the result and liberation from the conceptual constraints of the present.

The function of prophecy is complex and involves an epistemology for creating images of the future that implies possible "goods" or "bads." The possible/desirable becomes the domain of policy planning which, in turn, results in some institutionalized imperative for forecasting. Viewing the future involves, to some extent, creating it: The forecasters and the theorists of the last generation frequently become the realists of the present. Forecasting thus serves as an orienting device between the past and the future. And the exercise of forecasting involves creating new outcomes that are not bound by present information. It is in this sense that forecasting becomes prophecy and becomes an important requisite for planning.

Our conception of future realities rests almost exclusively on our understanding of the past and the present. The various motivations for forecasting can operationally justify linking our conception of the present with our expectations of preferred future. The utopian and the strategist represent two poles of a continuum seeking to impose order upon the unknown and to provide some framework for the assessment of information, observation, and data. Whatever objective information each draws upon, the interpretation of this information is truth.

The forecaster who views forecasting as scientific prophecy seeks, like all scientific inquirers, greater understanding of the unknown; he emphasizes the procedures of forecasting. The forecaster interested in controlling future outcomes seeks to manipulate, develop, and implement policy; he emphasizes identification of sensitive points in a system and of areas in which critical decisions might lead to different choices and to different outcomes. The forecaster interested in long-range futures seeks to understand the overall dynamics under consideration in order to better appreciate present conditions; he emphasizes long-term system behavior. The forecaster interested in tomorrow morning's outcomes seeks to plan for immediate contingencies; he emphasizes the decision-making process.

Each of these motivations entails different procedures of forecasting with associated costs and benefits. Forecasting forces us to think of *alternatives*. "Goods" and "bads" assume the same theoretical importance in the forecasting design: The distinction between them is imposed upon future realities by the motivations, preferences, and expectations of the forecaster.

The value-neutral posture of science is sometimes confused with the value-driven imperatives of prophecy, resulting in an undifferentiated and often methodologically unsound use of both theory and method. So, too, we tend also to confound what *is* with what *ought* to be, without appreciating that the discrepancy between the "is" and the "ought" is an important datum bearing directly upon the results of the forecast. For these reasons the forecaster must make explicit his beliefs about the past and the present, the relationship of the individual to society, the relationship of societies to each other, and the nature of the decision-systems governing interactions among societies. These underlying beliefs—or theories—inevitably affect the nature of the forecast, and when investigations differ in their underlying beliefs about each of these considerations, the forecasting outcomes will almost certainly differ.[2] And for forecasting purposes, systematic structuring of negative images (or prophecies) is as important as systematic structuring of positive ones. Our underlying values differentiate the positive from the negative; there is nothing absolutely good or bad. How we interpret data, observations, and present or past facts depends largely upon our theories of presents and pasts, and upon the ways we employ theory to guide our search and understanding of alternative futures.

III. THE ROLE OF THEORY IN INTERNATIONAL RELATIONS FORECASTING

Theory generally performs several functions in the course of empirical investigation: It provides a coding scheme for storing and retrieving information, and it serves as a search instrument that guides the investigator toward the relevant questions and appropriate data. Theory preserves and facilitates inspection of data; theory also preserves and focuses upon what the theorist sees as relevant. Through its built-in capabilities for dissociating and recombining information (in terms of first- and higher-order symbols), theory provides a means of accommodating new information and new combinations of ideas and concepts.[3]

The formalized and semi-formalized tenets of social science theory provide important clues for thinking about global futures and for developing appropriate frameworks within which the forecast may be undertaken and the results interpreted meaningfully. More specifically, theory performs two specific tasks: (1) it provides guidelines and propositions, and in some cases, validates findings concerning the relationships among critical variables or among components of the system investigated, and (2) it provides criteria for evaluating the performance of the forecast and assessing its outcome. These criteria also bear upon the forecaster's understanding of the "realities" at hand, an understanding that is made explicit through a series of theoretical statements, and then made to relate, also explicitly, to other people's understanding of these realities and to empirical findings emerging from previous analysis or from the conventional wisdom on the issue at hand.

In short, theory orients thinking and thinking directs the forecast. Without theory, forecasting becomes crude prophecy. With theory, forecasting assumes scientific proportions. And the methodological question of *how to forecast* is then placed in proper perspective. There are at least five levels of analysis in international relations where social science theory yields important clues for forecasting and where existing theory can provide a systematic framework for a forecasting design.

We know something about the behavior of *individuals* under a variety of conditions, and psychological theory is rich with propositions regarding cognitive processes and mechanisms of psychological adaptation to the external environment. We know something about the operation of groups and of *social systems*, including social behavior, group behavior, economic behavior, and political behavior. We also know something about interactions along large units termed *nation-states*. And we know something about the societal implications of large numbers of entities harbored in *ecological* systems, demographic systems, and so forth. Finally, we have some initial theoretical developments concerning the means by which these levels interrelate, given some *meta-level* of analysis, such as general systems theory or, more operationally, system dynamics.

At each of these levels, social science theory has made considerable inroads toward the development of formalized tenets of human behavior. But much yet remains to be done. For forecasting purposes, such formalized thinking is imperative. But forecasting may also be employed as a means of testing and developing theory. In many ways a symbiotic relationship exists between forecasting as

scientific prophecy and social science theory as formalized understanding and explanation of individual and social behavior.

When viewed in the context of international relations, social science theory provides important clues toward understanding intersocietal interactions. These clues are conventionally thought of as *international relations theory*. But this is a misnomer; the most significant theoretical developments in international relations have come not from scholars engaged in the analysis of international "realities" in the context of conventional and traditional wisdom, but from scholars actively engaged in breaking down the barriers among the social sciences and employing international relations as a laboratory within which to test propositions about human behavior and intersocietal relations. From these concentrated efforts emerge several "islands of theory" that yield important insight into the international relations—past, present, and future.[4]

There is a modicum of international relations theory about the political implications of national attributes and capabilities, about modes of international relations, about systematic constraints on national behavior, about national goals and objectives, about armament competitions and other forms of competition, about system change, and so forth. Such theory, though far from polished, sets forth some partial findings and assessments. Much more needs to be done, however, before we can rely upon international relations theory for valid guidance in thinking about the future.[5]

The *operational* statement of theory in a research design is made in terms of a model. The most important purpose of a model is to structure the inquiry, but its actual relevance depends upon the purpose of the forecast and the desired rigor of the research design. Verbal and functional models are the least systematic. Statistical, mathematical, and simulation models all represent more complex statements of theory and greater precision for thinking about the future.

Perhaps the most important theoretical problem for forecasting involves causal relations. One's beliefs about causality determine in large part the methodologies one adopts for forecasting and the types of values one chooses to accommodate. There are five different concepts of causation, each with an attendant interpretation of international realities. The most common view involves *time prece-dence*, one thing followed by another. But this is a rather simplistic notion, and philosophers of science tend to agree that causality in terms of *asymmetrical relations* is more realistic. Others maintain that causal relations involve *unidirectional* or recursive relations and that causality cannot, by definition, accommodate mutual dependencies. Conversely, still others argue that *simultaneous* relations are not inconsistent with causal notions that the "real" world is of this nature. And, by way of accommodating such differing perspectives, some attempts have been made to think of causality both in terms of mutual dependencies and in terms of unidirectional relations. This compromise is based upon a *block recursive systems* view of reality. This perspective assumes that, within a localized domain, causal relations are unidirectional, but that these localized systems of relations are imbedded in larger structures characterized by simultaneous dependencies.[6] Thus, according to this last view, in international relations, one can think of the domestic sources of foreign policy as a localized system composed of unidirectional influences— from the system to the leadership and eventually to the external environment—but these localized relations are influenced by external considerations (international alliances, ongoing armament competitions, and so forth) which themselves are fairly independent from the internal determinants of foreign policy. In this way, a block recursive view of international realities accommodates a unidirectional concept of causation as well as one that stresses mutual and simultaneous dependencies.

These different views of causation dictate different ways of structuring the research problem and of approaching the forecast design which, in turn, determines the choice of methodology. But causality is also related to the purpose of forecasting and to the time perspective involved. If one were interested in tomorrow morning's outcomes, it would not be wise to opt for a block recursive view of causation, nor to employ an associated methodology. The outcomes of tomorrow might best be viewed through a unidirectional perspective, or through one that stresses time precedence, rather than one that involves an unnecessarily complex view of reality.

In sum, then, different models and different perspectives upon causality serve different purposes, and since what we see depends upon how we look at something, the forecaster must appreciate the consequences of selecting one type of model or one view of causal relations rather than another as the basis of the forecasting design. A realistic appraisal of what can in fact be done given the tools at our disposal amounts to a necessary prerequisite for forecasting in international relations. The following section indicates the range of forecasting methodologies available. Further along, we shall pull the pieces together and illustrate the convergence between different problems in international relations and different types of forecasting methodology.

IV. ALTERNATIVE FORECASTING METHODOLOGIES: MULTIPLE REALITIES AND MULTIPLE PERSPECTIVES

A first step in the development of a forecasting design is an assessment of the implications of different methodologies. Our conception of reality is often misleading, and perceptions that seem objective may often be subjective. The distortions imposed upon our understanding of futures are transmitted through our use of methodology, unless sufficient care is taken to render the assumptions underlying the forecasting mode employed as explicit as possible. Often, too, an unrecognized but symbiotic relationship exists between personal values and biases, on the one hand, and the assumptions of methodology on the other.

At the most general level of abstraction, one can distinguish among forecasting methodologies in terms of the degree of explicit theory employed, the use of systematic procedures, the use of empirical data, and the purposes of the forecast. Again, how we look at the future determines in large part what we see. Ranging from the least to the most systematic, alternative forecasting methodologies include (1) normative forecasts, (2) exploratory projections, (3) methods employing formal models, (4) simulation methodologies, and (5) artificial intelligence. The more precise the methodology is, the greater are the probabilities of obtaining valid forecasts, but at the same time, the greater are the forecaster's inputs into the forecasting design. And, when reducing uncertainty itself involves working with uncertainty, precision becomes a liability and not an asset.

Normative forecasts involve specifying the "ought" rather than the "is." They are based on implicit theory, little or no use of formalized methodology, and almost no resort to systematically collected data. Such forecasts amount to little more than undisciplined speculation about futures, and as yet, no formalized procedures exist by which such forecasts can be undertaken systematically and their reliability increased. The purpose of normative forecasts is to identify those conditions that lead to desired outcomes rather than to develop and use models for systematically investigating intervening processes. The result is often in the nature of self-fulfilling prophecies. A group-opinion procedure to obtain images of such futures—known as the Delphi method—contains a built-in regression toward the mean, in that consensus is obtained at the expense of precision and verification through a reality check.[7]

Slightly more systematic forecasting methods include *exploratory projections*, trend extrapolations, or heuristic forecasts. Such forecasting modes represent a step in the direction of explicit theorizing and the use of systematic methodology. But they are appropriate for forecasting only those conditions that do not change or change very gradually and as such are relevant only to a very small subset of international relations. Such forecasting modes cannot account for reversals, system change, or the identification of points at which critical decisions may contribute to system change. Demographic trends, ecological factors, and international transactions such as trade, business factors, and the like, can be forecasted in such manner, but micro factors, such as the nature of tomorrow morning's decisions, or macro factors, such as the probabilities of war and violence, cannot be satisfactorily investigated with trend projections or exploratory forecasts.[8]

Forecasting methodologies predicated upon the *explicit use of formal models*—descriptive, explanatory, or predictive—represent further development in the direction of precision and reliability.[9] Such models may be statistical or functional, based on parameter selection rather than parameter estimation, based upon empirical data, or based on decision analysis and Bayesian algorithms. Each type of model alerts the forecaster to different aspects of reality.

Statistical models, based upon explicit theory, formalized methodology, and empirical data, accommodate a primarily unidirectional view of reality and of causality, although in some cases mutual causation can also be accommodated. *Functional models*, where the purpose is to identify the interrelationship among components of a system rather than its stochastic properties or the probabilistic interdependence of its components, are based on a view of reality that explicitly rejects simultaneous causation and incorporates only the unidirectional causal perspective. Such forecasting modes also make little use of empirical data for the development of the underlying model (the emphasis being upon obtaining a stable system structure), and empirical data are therefore not a necessary requisite for the forecast. Statistical and functional forecasting models are complementary, although most investigators tend to employ one method or the other rather than employing them in supplementary fashion, and for this reason their joint use for forecasting is yet to be explored.[10]

Decision analysis (Bayesian statistics), another approach to uncertainty, confronts the unknown directly rather than through inferences based upon conventional probability distributions, but it involves some *a priori* specification of the structure of the problem. In the Bayesian view of causality, conditionality prevails, and mutual dependencies are accommodated within a context of contingencies that serves to provide bounds and constraints upon uncertainty.[11] The same general assessment may be made of *Markov processes*, which are statistically based and involve explicit use of theory, empirical data, and systematic methodology. The Markov view of causality, also unidirectional, holds that movements from one state or condition to another can be specified; and the probabilities associated with such movements and transitions become the purpose of the forecast. But that movement is only in one direction. Reversals and sharp changes cannot be taken into account. Thus, if the forecasting problem at hand can be meaningfully investigated within such bounds, Markov processes are likely to be a reliable mode of forecasting. To date, however, little or no work has been done employing either Bayesian or Markov models explicitly in a forecasting mode.[12]

Simulation analysis for forecasting purposes is a

sophisticated complex approach to uncertainty analysis and to alternative futures. There are many modes of simulation, and they all involve some explicit use of theory, some formal model, and some systematic procedure for drawing inferences about the nature and behavior of the system in question. All-man simulations are particularly useful for the analysis of decision making under crisis conditions; considerable inroads have been made in such simulations.[13] All-computer simulations are most appropriate for highly analytical approaches to the unknown, but by their very nature they abstract from reality that which is generic and systematic, and there is almost no way to incorporate or account for the idiosyncratic or erratic. Unfortunately, the erratic often governs outcomes of international realities. At one level of analysis, however, all-computer simulations are extremely useful for forecasting, but at another, their relevance is less apparent. The more immediate the problem, the higher the costs associated with an erroneous forecast; and the more idiosyncratic a system's characteristics, the less advisable it is to rely upon an all-computer forecast. In the last analysis, however, the type of simulation-based model for forecasting depends upon the purpose of the forecast: Without a clear statement of purpose, it is difficult to determine which of the approaches to forecasting is most suitable to the issues at hand.

The most recent addition to the repertoire of systematic analysis in the social sciences is *artificial intelligence*, a mode of all-computer simulation developed for the analysis of adaptive behavior and learning, for investigating endogenous system change and self-changing structures, for the analysis of the influence of precedence upon behavior and decision making, and for the analysis of the implications of accumulating experience in any environment. So far almost no attempts at employing artificial intelligence in the forecasting mode have been made. Such a venture would require a successful adaptation of systematic modes of analysis to forecasting—particularly those noted here—so as to generate self-changing probabilities associated with system behavior and system adaptation. Methodologically, at least, artificial intelligence is a challenging approach to forecasting, particularly when applied to macro-level questions concerning system behavior and long-range forecasting, as well

as to the ambiguities associated with tomorrow's outcomes. But much work remains to be done before we can reliably evaluate the usefulness of artificial intelligence in international relations forecasting. This is undoubtedly the most probable of investigations for expanding our knowledge of forecasting modes and methodologies.[14]

The phenomenological critique of the social sciences can aid the assessment of alternative approaches to forecasting by pointing to the complexities at hand. This critique assumes that what we often view as objective within the social science context is little more than the projection of subjectivity, projection and cognition upon external realities, and that such projection in itself creates that reality which we so judiciously seek to investigate through "objectives" and "reliable" modes of analysis. To date the conventional wisdom in the behavioral and social sciences has not deemed it necessary to confront the phenomenological critique directly nor to specify the ways by which we might counter such charges. The fact remains, however, that all respectable social scientists do indeed claim to guard against such distortions specified in the phenomenological assessment, but little is in fact done.[15]

The phenomenologists levy against the most systematic social scientists the same kind of criticism that methodologists raise against normative forecasters, descriptive scholars, or traditional analysts. This formalized reaction to conventional social science raises two issues that are central to any forecasting exercise. One involves anchoring the forecast, and the other pertains to the extent to which forecasting is a reality-creating enterprise.

V. ANCHORING A FORECAST: THE CHOICE OF AXIAL PRINCIPLE[16]

The realities we perceive are very much conditioned by the methodologies we employ, and for operational purposes the forecast is always anchored in some initial conditions. The anchor provides the operational bounds and limitations of the forecast, as well as the expected range of permissible behavior of the system investigated. The choice of anchor is thus the first step in the actual conduct of a forecast.

Anchoring a forecast involves holding constant at

least one—perhaps more—critical dimensions of the future while allowing the others to vary accordingly and observing the implications of the forecast. A special case of anchoring involves holding all relevant aspects of the future constant and allowing one to vary. The actual selection of an anchor depends almost entirely upon the purpose of the forecast.

In practice, forecasts can be anchored in at least four different types of initial conditions. First, with *structural anchors* a forecast is predicated upon careful specification of the structural attributes of the system in question and then the research design observes the implications of these structural characteristics under different sets of contingencies. In international relations, such structural factors include demographic and ecological considerations, aggregate resource profiles and flows, institutional and governmental factors, and so forth. The purpose of forecasting in such cases is to inquire into the alternative behavioral correlates that might accompany these structural factors under different conditions. Second, the forecast may be anchored in *probabilities and degrees of possibilities.* The inquiry would then be grounded in alternative probability structures or distributions, and the objective would be to inquire into the behavioral or structural correlates associated with outcomes of different probabilities. The focus here would be the possible, or the likely, as opposed to the desirable. Third, a forecast can be anchored in *preference structures.* When the forecaster's purposes are normative, the anchor is in the nature of preference ordering, where the "ought" is specified as the initial anchoring condition, and the object is to identify the behavioral correlates of such preferred outcomes and, hopefully, the means by which these might be realized. Under ideal research situations, a combination of preference specification and an identification of the paths to make the "ought" congruent with the "is" would be a feasible research objective. Another more conventional anchor involves *trends and projections* of some aggregate systematic factor, which is generally characterized by linear attributes; the forecast is then assigned to observe the implications of the trends in question. By far the greatest thrust of contemporary forecasting is of this nature. United Nations projections regarding future population involve projections of this kind. The task of inter-

national relations forecasting is to specify the implications of such projections for global and regional politics, or for particular structural, political, or behavioral conditions.

In sum, then, forecasts anchored differently look different and say different things. The choice of an anchor is difficult to make, for often one is interested in more than one anchor, thus complicating considerably the task at hand. Nonetheless, the selection of an anchor is a necessary step toward assigning a specific meaning to the realities we seek to forecast.

Are some anchors better than others? It depends. One's purpose in forecasting determines the selection of anchor. In the last analysis, however, a judicious choice of anchor is critical to the forecasting enterprise, and the forecaster should be prepared to defend his choice. Without sound justification for its anchor, the forecast loses much of its critical validity.

VI. PULLING THE PIECES TOGETHER: THE TIME PERSPECTIVE AND THE PURPOSE OF THE FORECAST

The plethora of issues discussed so far raises further queries. How can we make use of these different types of forecasting methodologies and different anchoring principles in ways that would enhance our abilities to forecast? Are some forecasting modes more applicable to certain problems than others? How can different forecasting methodologies be employed in complementary fashion? In short, how do the pieces fit together?

To answer these questions, we must consider (1) the purpose of the forecast, and (2) the time frame within which the forecast is undertaken. The purpose of the forecast determines the initial requirements of the design and identifies the variables of interest. A forecast aimed at planning and policy making will focus primarily upon manipulable variables that can be controlled by the policy maker. A forecast that aims to gain insights into the structure of international systems in the next century will focus primarily upon aggregate structural conditions that are stable over the long term and therefore not readily amenable to manipulation. In the first case, the emphasis is upon short-term forecasting; in the second, it is upon the long range. The methodologies and the requirements of the forecast differ, as do the criteria employed for assessing its outcome. The variable of time can serve as an important organizing device around which different forecasting modes converge. An analysis of the past through retrospective forecasting helps us think about the future and about ways to orient our analysis of short-range and long-range futures. Different forecasting methodologies suit different time frames. Figure 1.1 indicates the relationships of forecasting mode to time perspective, and the following discussion illustrates how different forecasting methods apply to different time frames and different forecasting purposes.

Restrospective forecasting (or forecasting over known data) has great import for international relations, where the past represents a rich laboratory of experience and data for thinking about futures. For forecasting large-scale system change and development, the history of international relations over the past several centuries contains myriad examples of system breaks (such as wars), integrative processes (such as nation-building, alliances,

and overall community formation), global transactions (such as international trade and investments), global confrontation and cultural clashes (such as colonialism, classical imperialism, or ethnic hostilities), and so forth. The past may not hold the key to the future, but the past once was the future. Viewed in this fashion, therefore, retrospective forecasting assumes paramount importance.

Long-range forecasting (for futures in the time frame of 15 to 50 or 100 years from now) can best be approached through system dynamics or econometric analysis. Both of these methods can also be employed for analysis of short-range outcomes but their capabilities particularly suit long-range forecasting. System dynamics, a functional approach to the study of nonlinear, large-scale social systems, is based on feedback loops and the interdependence of levels and rates of change. By contrast, econometric analysis, a statistical approach to modeling, is based primarily upon linear approximations of complex systems and parameter estimations as a prerequisite of forecasting. Each

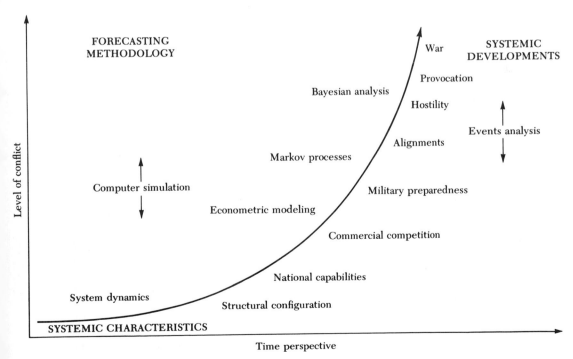

Figure 1.1 Integrating forecasting methodologies: an illustration from conflict analysis.

has advantages and disadvantages; the choice depends upon the problem at hand, the investigator's conception of causality, his familiarity with the system in question, how much data are needed and what kind, and finally, how robust the coefficients are to be. These queries all assume that the investigator wishes to employ explicit theory, systematic procedure, and empirical analysis. Normative forecasting, or Delphi procedures, provides nonrigorous alternatives for long-range forecasting.

For *short-range forecasting* (from tomorrow morning to 3 or 5 years from now) decision analysis, Markov processes, and events analysis are three appropriate techniques. These methods can also be used for long-range forecasting—the algorithms do not preclude this possibility—but their capabilities (noted below) are uniquely suited to analysis of short-range outcomes.[17] If the problem at hand involves reducing uncertainty associated with decision making, the Bayesian approach to short-range forecasting, which accommodates idiosyncratic factors directly in the research design through analysis of subjective conditions, will serve best. If the problem at hand involves depicting changes over the short range, the Markov models approach to forecasting, which is designed to assist in identifying the probabilities associated with transitions from one state to another, is the more appropriate.

A third approach to short-range forecasting, events analysis, enables the forecaster to develop reliable early warning systems that generate signals of future events long before the events come to pass. Early warnings with respect to the outbreak of international violence are aided by tensionometers or conflict barometers. If we develop reliable measurements of international scope we could forecast future outcomes more systematically than has been done so far. This kind of forecasting is still very experimental, but recent developments suggest its potential promise.[18]

One of the most frequently used instruments for early warning is a generic inter-nation interaction scale designed to tap the implications for violence imbedded in actions and interactions among nations. There are many versions of the scale. The most commonly used one has interval properties that greatly facilitate statistical analysis, and has been employed in analysis of events and actions for forecasting purposes involving systematic identification of the line of normal relations among states to identify significant departures from normality. Because normal relations among states are situation specific, this approach to forecasting takes into account the uniqueness of the situation and related idiosyncrasies. For example, the line of normal relations between Canada and the United States is probably around level 2 or 5 on the 13-point conflict scale (with 1 indicating cooperation and 13 violence), while that between Israel and the Arab states is undoubtedly closer to 11 or 12. We cannot therefore apply the same criteria for forecasting probability of conflict between the opposing parties, and the forecast must take into account the difference in these two situations. If United States-Canada interactions were to jump to a mean of 8 on a 13-point conflict scale the implications would be quite different than if Arab-Israeli interactions were to converge around a mean of 8. In the first case, the forecast would point to greater propensities for violence; in the second, to a reduction of hostilities.[19] Although forecasting international events can be undertaken for analysis in the long run as well as in the short run, events analysis is perhaps best suited to short-range forecasting. It is possible, in this time frame, to acquire fairly sensitive indicators of subtle shifts in national behavior.

How then do we link short-range and long-term forecasting? How can we forecast tomorrow's outcomes while still keeping an eye upon longer range outcomes? No one has satisfactorily demonstrated the operational linkage between the two. We do, however, have some operational clues to this problem of *intersection between time perspectives*. The problem involves: (1) defining the parameters of a situation and determining when variables become parameters and the reverse, and (2) identifying nonlinearities in the system and determining when nonlinearities become breakpoints and signal system change. We know immediate short-range factors are imbedded in a larger societal context, which is invariably conditioned as much by time as by habit, inertia, and social history. These conditions become the *parameters* of a situation in the shorter range. But in the long run, over years and decades, they are *variables;* they change over time and take on new attributes and characteristics. Today's idiosyncracies invariably become tomorrow's parameters. The forecasting problem is this: If we can identify the conditions under which variables become parameters and if we can determine how it is, and why it is, that this change takes place, then we would in effect resolve the problem of moving from short-range considerations to long-range imperatives. The methodology task is to incorporate this information in a forecasting design the purpose of which would be to alert us to the probabilities of change in the system under consideration.[20] The second aspect of the intersection problem, *identification of nonlinearities and breakpoints*, involves the analysis of system breaks. A breakpoint represents a sharp change (which, in regression analysis is exemplified by a change in the regression slope), but a nonlinearity indicates a gentler departure from linearity, the nature of which can often be captured by conventional nonlinear functions. Nonlinearities generally represent the functional relationship among variables. Complex systems are invariably nonlinear. If we expect linearities, and we sensitize our forecasting tools to search for linearities, then we almost certainly will generate invalid forecasts. The world around us is complex and nonlinear, and cannot be reduced to the simplistic approximations imposed by conventional statistical or intellectual tools. If we look only for linearities we may observe nonlinearities, and we are likely to draw the erroneous inference that a system break has occurred, when the system may in fact be nonlinear but stable, regular, and exhibiting orthodox behavior. When it comes to the identification of breakpoints, the situation is much the same; because there is a tendency in the social sciences to confuse breakpoints with nonlinearities when observing system breaks, we must guard against the erroneous inference that it is a system break. It may be so, but it may not.[21]

In international relations we tend to view a large-scale war as a system break. On the other hand, we consider change in diplomatic representation, modification of trade patterns, or change in alliance structures more appropriately as nonlinearities or, alternatively, as discontinuities. But there are no hard and fast rules governing the assignment of meaning to these factors. In the last analysis, breaks and nonlinearities are situation bound, and monitoring for breaks or for non-

linearities becomes crucial to forecasting. The critical international sectors where *monitoring for breaks* has important implications for forecasting include demography and ecology, technological development and innovations, economic change, social and political departures from current patterns, cultural change, and religious or ethical conditions. These are all large-scale macro characteristics that, in the long run, are variables in any particular situation, but in the short range, when change is imminent, become the parameters in question. It is also true, however, that when change is imminent, or when a break emerges, these factors are variable also in the short range.

It is desirable to distinguish between breaks due to quantitative changes and those due to qualitative change. For example, changes resulting from sudden increases or decreases in population may well have different effects upon a social order than breaks originating from a significant qualitative change, such as a new invention or technological innovation. This is an important distinction. The conjunction of qualitative and quantitative change is extremely challenging to the forecaster since the unknowns converge, thus compounding uncertainty. Where one looks for breaks depends almost entirely upon the problem at hand and the anchor of the forecast. It is also true that breaks in such systems characteristics tend to have spill-over effects in that their consequences are rarely contained, and the forecaster must take the ramifications into account.

Undoubtedly the most difficult problem for forecasting purposes involves the nature of the system *beyond* the break. For example, recent studies in quantitative international politics have traced the origins of conflict and warfare to increases in levels and rates of population growth in conjunction with imbalances in levels and rates of growth in technological development and access to critical resources. These aggregate societal factors provide the context within which day-to-day politics unfold and, in the long run, the parameters of a conflict situation where the belligerents confront each other in hostile stance. A large-scale war represents a system break. And the question is, how does the system change following such a break?

If we look carefully at population, resources, and technology, we might be able to put together the alternative scenarios upon which politics, governance, and structural considerations would be predicted. Students of political demography are beginning to investigate the demographic consequences of wars upon population dynamics in order to determine the probable nature of systems following large-scale breaks and to construct alternative futures based upon such analyses.

Since we know, for instance, that wars often affect the demographic composition of a state, which in turn affects the structure of the social order, we can introduce into our forecasting design some consideration for potential changes in demographic characteristics. The same must be done for the other parameters of a situation. If we developed some systematic procedures for recording expected departures from system behavior, and if this procedure were generalized to issue-areas other than population, resources, and technology, we might begin to construct forecasts of probable outcomes beyond system breaks.[22]

By combining the information and insights obtained through long- and short-range forecasting and through their intersection, we can infer the types of decisions that would be made in different situations. By recording forecasting information along each of these time frames and according to the issue-areas of interest, we can then develop a two-dimensional matrix summarizing the relevant data and related inferences. In this way, a cross-impact method of identifying cumulative or interactive effects of departures from trends or expectations can systematically explicate some of the forecast's potential implications.

Comprehensive forecasting design along those lines would allow us to account for endogenous system change without any external intervention. The forecast itself would adapt to different time frames and to different levels of analysis; the design would, by its very nature, incorporate those decision points at which a system change is likely to take place. Forecasting capabilities of this nature would be predicated upon the least amount of intervention by the forecaster. This simple consideration will enhance the internal validity of the forecasting design in that factors exogenous to the forecast could not contaminate its outcome. It would then be easier to identify weaknesses in the forecasting design and isolate problems resulting from intervention by the forecaster.

Figure 1.1 shows the critical factors for different stages in the development of a conflict situation and, by inference, the transformation of variables as long-range determinants of conflict to parameters in the short term. Also included in Figure 1.1 are the "islands" of international relations theory that most aid the understanding of each stage in a conflict situation. This illustration pertains to conflict dynamics. But the same rationale is relevant to any other issue or problem in international relations. When variables, theory, and methodology are juxtaposed, a more comprehensive picture of a design for forecasting international violence emerges. To date we have approached the different time frames separately but the intersection problem is yet to be solved. More remains to be done.

VII. VALIDATION, SALIENT DANGERS, AND RECURRING ERRORS

When is a forecast good enough? How do we gauge the reliability of a forecast? What criteria do we employ for evaluating its performance? When reality is unknown, the success of a forecast rests upon some *a priori* set of criteria determined partly by theory and partly by the purpose of the forecast.

Despite our increasing methodological sophistication, certain dangers are common to all forecasting efforts. Some of these problems are particularly striking in international relations where we have insufficient expertise to guard against common errors. An overcommitment to existing situations often means a refusal to evaluate unexpected findings and a tendency to place evidence upon data or upon problems and solutions of the recent past; a short memory appears to be one of the most serious problems characteristic of many forecasters.[23] Other recurring errors include a disregard for potential sources of change and an implicit assumption that all crucial innovations in international relations have already occurred. Most forecasters tend to adopt a position of persistent pessimism, or persistent optimism, or a random mixture of the two, without a solid underlying rationale. This situation amounts to the introduction of systematic bias in the forecast, a danger that even the most sophisticated analysts finds difficult to avoid.

Not unrelated are the distortions that arise from adopting a narrow focus upon specific issues without regard for possible ramifications. But the most common error of all is a tendency among forecasters to adopt a parochial view of their subject, resulting in an *a priori* emphasis upon certain variables that appear critical in one's own context—without adequate validation or reality check. This problem is especially pertinent in Delphi and normative forecasts.

At least three general sets of procedures exist for evaluating the performance of a forecast: (1) interrogation processes, (2) validation processes, and (3) comparisons of forecast outcome with empirical data. The first is more appropriate for technological forecasting; the second for forecasts based on statistical or empirical models, quantitative data, and systematic procedures; and the third for retrospective forecasting.

Interrogation processes of evaluation are based upon systematic queries concerning (1) the purpose or need of the forecast, (2) the underlying causes in terms of the forecast's objective and its basic causal network, (3) the extent of reliability of the information processed by the forecasting design, and (4) the general reliability of the forecasting enterprise itself.[24] Inferences about the validity of the forecast design can be drawn from the responses to these queries. This is a "soft" procedure in the sense that few external criteria of validity are involved in drawing inferences concerning the extent of built-in errors or biases. Nonetheless, such interrogation allows us to determine the extent to which the forecast is subject to the dangers noted above.

Evaluating forecasts through *validation procedures* involves comparing outcomes with some *a priori* set of criteria for determining the extent to which outcomes result from the research design or built-in biases or errors.[25] *Face validity* means the extent to which the outcome of the forecast appears reasonable to the educated public. Conventional wisdom, the only external judge, is often not the best source of validation. *Internal validity* means the degree to which the forecasting outcome coincides with the process and structure that has produced the results. Great inconsistencies or incongruities between outcome and research design should be suspect, although such discrepancies might provide important clues for further research.

Still other forms of validation involve classical *statistical methods* for evaluating the parameters of a model and the relative strength of determining variables. The criteria employed include a comparison of the outcomes of the analysis with the probability distribution to determine significant departures from chance. The more statistically significant the results, the greater the validity of the forecast, and the sounder the inferences about the future are likely to be. Statistical validation is particularly applicable to the structure of a research design, interconnections among critical variables, and the causal network or underlying relationships. Conventional validation tools are fairly well established for model building and estimation, but much needs still to be done regarding the validity of a forecast.

The third major type of validation involves *comparing the forecasting outcome with empirical data,* a procedure that applies only to retrospective forecasting. History is a rich laboratory for forecasting over known data. Systematic comparisons of forecasts based on different methodologies—with different costs and different benefits—allow us to evaluate the extent to which forecasting outcomes are conditioned by the methodology in question.

Systematic assessment of the forecasting outcome requires strict noninterference with the forecasting process; otherwise it is not possible to isolate the inferences drawn on the basis of the forecast *outcome* from those based on the effects we have imposed upon the forecasting *process* itself. The two are interconnected. But we must then validate both the process and the outcome. However, in the last analysis, the question "valid for what?" depends upon the purpose of the forecast. And the type of validation employed depends upon the nature of the problem and the extent of reliability needed.[26]

VIII. THE PROBABLE AND THE POSSIBLE: SOME POLICY IMPLICATIONS OF FORECASTING

For policy purposes we must identify the manipulables in social and international systems, the costs of manipulation and social intervention, and the choice points or the sensitive areas in a system. The relevance of a policy forecast to decision making is directly proportional to the extent to which we take these three issues into account.

The *manipulables* in social and international systems are those factors that can be changed by policy intervention. Some variables can be manipulated on short order, others cannot. And the *cost* of manipulation is generally related to the ease with which effective intervention can take place. Accurate assessment of the *choice points* in a system involves identifying those areas most sensitive to manipulation—given the constraints of *a priori* cost. Obviously it is more difficult to change aggregate societal factors like population than variables like a budgetary allocation and the assignment of national priorities. And the costs of intervention always directly affect the type of policy adopted.

Forecasting must precede planning; a good plan requires a good forecast. Forecasting assigns likelihoods and probabilities to alternative futures, and planning defines parameters of future action. Planning is an attempt to confront alternative risks and to assure that any risks taken are the right risks, while forecasting involves reducing uncertainty around the implications or consequences of planning. Thus, for the forecaster concerned with the accuracy of the forecast, related policy implications become apparent when alternative outcomes crystallize. However, the unanticipated consequences of planning may often have implications not identified by the forecast. *Operationally*, both forecasting and planning aim to reduce uncertainty and specify risks. A society's allocations to research and development indicate its degree of concern for converting uncertainty into potential risk and potential risk into desired risk.

There are at least two types of forecasting for policy analysis. One involves *alternative budgeting*, that is, examining ways to pursue national priorities through different allocation systems. This type of inquiry assists us in looking at the implication of alternative allocation formats and alternative structures of national priorities. When viewed in a forecasting mode, alternative budgeting processes provide an operational handle on critical manipulables. The most readily manipulable factors in any society are budgetary allocations.[27] The other mode of forecasting for policy analysis involves *alternative contingency analysis*, that is, systematic confrontation of "what if . . . ?" questions by "if . . . then. . . ." answers and associated costs and benefits. The higher the costs associated with alternative risks, the greater likelihood that policy will involve contingency analysis. These "if . . . then. . . ." queries are also central to forecasting

and policy analysis in econometrics, system dynamics, or subjective probability modes.

Once the forecasts are made, the task is to identify possible ways to realize them. The paths that are associated with alternative contingencies or alternative allocations of national priorities are a critical aspect of forecasting for policy purposes. Strategic analysis and defense policy are generally of this nature.

One of the most pressing problems of forecasting for policy and planning involves bureaucratic politics. Deviation from norms and expectations are not encouraged in bureaucracies, and a built-in regression toward the mean gives rise to many of the forecasting errors and salient dangers noted above. These errors generate distortions that invariably affect the outcome of the forecast and, by extension, the planning process. The bureaucratic politics of forecasting reflect the tensions between the policy planner-bureaucrat and the forecaster-scientist generated by the structural characteristics of bureaucracies. Those in government who need forecasting most, often are least willing to accommodate to the requirements of forecasting or to acknowledge the implications of a forecast.[28]

IX. INTERNATIONAL PERSPECTIVES AND GLOBAL POLITICS: THE ROLE OF FORECASTING IN SHAPING THE FUTURE

Many of the theoretical and methodological issues noted above can be reduced to a choice between forecasting trends versus forecasting events. The two are not mutually exclusive; often forecasting one assists us in forecasting the other. Some interdependencies in international relations allow us to forecast events through trend analysis just as we can forecast trends through the analysis of discrete actions and events.

Trends analysis assists in reducing uncertainty surrounding the probabilities and implications of particular outcomes. Trends provide the context within which events gain meaning in the short range. Patterns of events eventually become trends and constitute the context within which new events take place in the long run. Because of this interdependence, the distinction between trends and events loses much of its significance. When discrete political, economic, and social events are placed within an international context, trends and events provide complementary approaches to the unknown. And when the forecast is anchored in one particular aspect of reality, the entire exercise is then brought to bear more sharply upon the purpose of the forecast.

All this is to suggest that contingent explanations of alternative futures are not only possible but scientifically desirable. The "what if . . . ?" question is thus endemic to every forecast, and the forecaster must confront it directly (theoretically and methodologically) to produce a sound design.

In conceptual terms at least, forecasting involves creating the future or making forecasted outcomes more probable. Reality begins in our minds; policies that make this reality increasingly probable begin in the forecasts we make about the unknown. The mere act of forecasting does not make the forecasting outcome likely, but that the probabilities of the outcomes becoming realities of the future increase, particularly if that reality appears desirable and/or is predicated upon today's unknowns. And when this importation of today onto tomorrow is undertaken as a matter of course, the probabilities of erroneous forecasts and the occurrence of salient dangers increase accordingly. The use of *a priori* criteria for evaluating the forecasting design, albeit for its development in the first place, becomes critical to the forecasting exercise, and the role of international relations theory assumes paramount importance in highlighting the issue areas of potential interest and providing some guidelines for the development of the forecasting design.

Five substantive issue-areas have critical political implications for forecasting global futures: (1) the characteristics and attributes of dominant actors in the international system; (2) the conditions under which international systems change and transform; (3) the role of nonterritorial actors in international politics; (4) the dictates and imperatives of territorial actors, and (5) the view of the international perspectives from below as perceived by the poor and the nonprivileged. In addition, any forecasting design that focuses upon any of the international questions noted at the onset must recognize demography and ecology, governance, technology, resources, politics and culture—all critical structural dimensions of international systems.[29]

The *dominant actors* of today include the United States, the Soviet Union, China, Japan, and some West European states—depending upon one's criteria. Since it is a truism that "might makes right," forecasting the membership of the dominant actor group in future international politics amounts to more than simply a numerative exercise. Dominant powers tend to control the rules of the game, just as they control the structure of the international system and draw the bounds of permissible behavior. Dominant actors set the pace for world culture and institutionalize its attributes and characteristics. Who the dominant actors of tomorrow will be can be inferred from current levels and rates of population growth, from levels and rates of economic growth, and from the extent to which they are today engaged in violent behavior that depletes resources and taxes overall capabilities. The simple ratio between the loads upon a system and its capabilities provides important clues into the probabilities of attaining (or maintaining) dominant-power status in years to come.[30]

The dominant *world culture* of today is a Western-scientific one. The characteristics of tomorrow's world culture can be inferred from past and present cultural attributes. Without the benefit of a sophisticated forecast, one could anticipate the persistence of scientific values, but it would be foolish to assume that such values would not change and adapt to emerging world problems and global realities. Change is already apparent, given current queries about the wisdom of continued growth. Further reassessments will undoubtedly continue.[31]

Forecasting the *transformation of the international system* is always one of the major concerns to theorists of international relations. Although we can successfully explain changes in the international system after they have occurred, we cannot as yet identify clues of potential transformation. Again, careful monitoring of changes in the critical international dimensions noted above provides important insights into possible structures and future outcomes, but these insights must be formalized and incorporated systematically in a forecasting design.[32]

The prevalence of *nonterritorial actors* in today's international system—and of proliferating structures and functions—is one of the most distinguishing characteristics of the present global system. We now define certain problems as being global in nature—such as environmental control and human rights—and approach them from a global perspective. If such developments continue, nonterritorial actors will invariably assume an even greater international role than they do today. The prevalence of such actors depends upon the extent to which they can avoid threatening territorial actors and national security. The wider the definition of "national security," the less probable it is that nonterritorial actors will assume permanent status in the international system. Nonterritorial actors are becoming institutionalized, but this process will not necessarily persist in years to come.[33]

Despite the high degree of penetration among states and the increasing importance of nonterritorial actors, *national sovereignty* remains the guiding principle of the day. The effect of dominant actors on all other actors in the international system is becoming increasingly pervasive (reinforced no doubt by increasing communication and military technology and by control over resource extractive techniques), providing a paradoxical situation in a system dominated by the contrast between the myth and the reality of national sovereignty for nondominant actors. In the last analysis, the effective exercise of sovereignty depends upon the capabilities of a state in question, upon the issue-area, and upon the extent to which other states honor conventional sovereignty. In practical terms, therefore, the effective sovereignty of dominant powers is always more extensive and more institutionalized than the sovereignty attributed to nondominant actors. Again the explanation is simple: In international politics, might does indeed make right.[34]

The view from below—the international system as perceived by nondominant actors—provides important sources of insights and information into the potentials for system change and transformation. The issue is conventionally treated as involving a conflict of interest between the *status-quo* and non-*status-quo* powers, and between the satisfied and less-satisfied states, not to mention the common dichotomy between rich and poor.[35] The critical question for forecasting is not whether such differentials are likely to persist, but what the implications of these differentials are likely to be, for whom, in what manner and why. We can obtain some initial answers to these queries by looking at the international system from the perspective of less privileged actors, while taking into account their attributes and characteristics, and their role

in shaping the major international questions (as noted in the first section of this chapter).

An analysis of the view from below may be anchored in either (1) preferences and values, such as liberal humanitarian values, greater equality, justice, and so forth, or (2) hard realities of power politics. In the first instance, the inquiry may be motivated by the search for better patterns of international relations, ones that might distribute scarce goods more equitably, perhaps on a per-capita basis rather than on a per-power-unit basis. In the second instance, the hard reality that most of the mineral and energy resources critical to industrial processes are located in less developed countries spurs new interests in examining the societal and political contexts within which deposits of needed resources are located. Whatever the anchor may be, the view from below will become increasingly important to international relations forecasting.

X. CRITICAL IMPERATIVES FOR INTERNATIONAL RELATIONS FORECASTING

The most critical imperatives for forecasting involve managing social complexity and the explosion of knowledge, and incorporating existing data about social and political systems in ways that are parsimonious, theoretically useful, and methodologically sound. We must now formulate developmental constructs for thinking about futures and for orienting our inquiries into the unknown.

Many years ago, Harold Lasswell presented a verbal model of technological society in a military stance, which he termed the "garrison state." Lasswell depicted the characteristics of such a society and suggested ways by which we might think about the military implications of complex social systems (see Lasswell, 1941). Years later, Christian Bay presented an analysis of some of the conceptual requisites of human freedom and presented ways by which we might think about the significance of freedom in complex systems.[36] Later still, Arthur Stinchcombe put forth a summary of the ways in which we might think of the organizations and complexities of social orders and human behavior.[37] And many others have added important insights to the existing repertoire of constructs for thinking about human societies and social behavior. There have even been some attempts to apply such constructs to the analysis of international politics. But these have been disparate and disjointed. We have barely begun to scratch the surface.

Perhaps the most useful contributions in terms of systematic thinking about complex systems and potential applications for international relations forecasting have been made by Hayward R. Alker, Jr. and J. W. Forrester. Each, in his own way, has presented us with novel ways of thinking about international relations and has put forth a set of analytical constructs that undoubtedly will have great effect upon forecasting efforts for years to come.

Alker has summarized the costs and benefits of different statistical approaches to social behavior (Alker, 1969). His survey was not carried explicitly to cover the forecasting capabilities of various statistical algorithms, but the implications are clear and the groundwork has been laid for extending this analysis to forecasting. The same may be said of Alker's first major effort of this sort, in which he attempted to explicate the mathematical implications of integration theory and various strands thereof (Alker, 1970). Again, the groundwork for extending our thinking about integration to forecasting analysis of future outcomes has been laid. We are now confronted with the task of developing forecasting designs predicated upon these meticulous expositions. Hayward Alker's papers highlighted directions for further research. We must now extend such work into forecasting.

The controversial volume by Jay Forrester entitled *World Dynamics* represents another important contribution in thinking about, and forecasting, social and complex systems (Forrester, 1971). Forrester's work represents a nonstatistical approach to the analysis of complex systems predicated on functional relationships and based on feedback loops and delay structures, ranging from simple to complex lags. The shortcomings of this approach to complex systems have been discussed extensively elsewhere.[38] Here we note only that the nonstatistical nature of the analysis provides a drawback of major importance: for forecasting purposes explicit recognition of the role of chance and of uncertainty is critical. We must now introduce a statistical perspective within this system dynamics framework—one that would allow the analyst to generate critical functions from empirical data, validate these by application of the conventional statistical tools, and then proceed to project the interdependencies into the future, real or retrospective as the case may be.

In a methodological vein, therefore, the critical imperatives in international relations forecasting involve pulling the pieces together, assessing the costs and benefits of alternative ways of viewing the future, and identifying those problems that are best examined by one methodology rather than another and one mode of forecasting rather than another. Analytical and methodological integration is yet to be done.

On a theoretical vein, the task is one of imagination, exploration, and disciplined speculation about future outcomes—much as Lasswell, Bay, and Stinchcombe, among others, have done. These are steps in the right direction, however incomplete, tentative, and preliminary they now appear to be. But where do we go from here?

We now realize that certain theoretical, methodological, and substantive requisites for forecasting in international relations must be attended to in any forecasting design. The following requisites provide sound direction for further developments in the area of forecasting.[39]

1. We must always adopt a dynamic orientation toward the future, and not a static structural orientation. Change is unquestionably difficult to think about and account for, but the real world is ever changing, and we must confront this reality directly. The present provides intellectual blinders when thinking about futures. But these blinders are not insurmountable.

2. We must be aware of the implications of the questions we raise, the methodologies we employ, the assumptions upon which they are grounded, and the values we hold. Often the definition of the problem is made in terms of implicit values and premises. An essential prerequisite to forecasting is a clear explication of underlying premises and preferences.

3. We must consciously try to clarify the nature of the gap between things as they are (or will be) and things as they ought to be (or should be). We commonly confuse the "is" with the "ought." A sound analysis of potential futures will not be served by this confusion.

4. We must recognize that the images of the future, as well as the models we employ to think about futures, are both constrained and conditioned by our understanding of the present and

the past. Our positions in social and international stratification condition in large part our definition of problems and our view of the world. We would be mistaken to assume that our perceptions mirror reality.

5. We must attempt to maximize the relevance of the intellectual tools at our disposal. Substitution of space for time may assist us in coping with the issues of change, development, and adaptation to structural or systematic transformation. The past or the present at one point, location, or issue-area may serve as a model for the future at another point, location, or issue-area. Substitution of space for time is common practice upon development analysis, but we have not yet begun to exploit this possibility for thinking about futures.

6. We must consciously seek to import the future into the present. Social designs and assessments of the implications for the present if certain futures were realized, and of the implications of the future if certain presents persist, must be actively considered as part of the forecasting exercise as adapted to the particular problem at hand or issue-area of concern.

7. We must be willing to make "possidictions,"[40] that is, prophesying the possible. Possidictions involve systematic evaluations of what present trends are likely to produce, assessments of ranges in expected outcomes, and expectations of the alternatives associated with each potential outcome. We must begin to specify how we get from here to there. Making possidictions can also be viewed as a means of preventing things from happening. Possidiction is the forecaster's contribution to planning. The planner's contribution to forecasting lies in the area of problem solving. The conscious selection of alternative (or preferred) futures and a systematic explication of the road from here to there is the essence of planning. The planner suggests how preferred futures might be realized; the forecaster delineates the structure of alternative futures.

NOTES

1. See Habermas (1968) for a discussion of issues revolving around the notion of technocratic hermaneutics. The notion of liberative prediction comes from the classical behavioral and social science literature.
2. See especially Bell, Mau, Huber, and Boldt in Bell and Mau (1971) concerning the interconnections among these sets of beliefs. Their discussion of these factors is more elaborate than noted here, but there is very little analysis of the implications of the *contents* of these beliefs.
3. The most recent and complete synthesis of the role of theory in social science research is found in Deutsch (1972). The following paragraph draws upon Deutsch's survey of the role of theory and the discussion in this section extends the arguments further.
4. The idea of "islands of theory" is common in international relations, and is attributable to Harold Guetzkow who argued many years ago that the most profitable approach to theory building in international relations is through an empirically based, piecemeal analysis of empirical relationships, and that through limited efforts of this nature "islands" of verifiable knowledge will develop. This view of theory building is now part of the orthodox behavioral approach to systematic study of international relations. See Guetzkow (1950 and 1969).
5. See Rosenau (1969b) and Alker and Bock (1973) for a survey of recent thinking in international relations; and Bobrow (1972a), Whiting (1972), and Young (1972) for a critique of novel approaches to the analysis of international politics.
6. The entire volume edited by Ando, *et al.* (1963) is devoted to issues of this nature. It is surprising that few students of international relations have seized upon these ideas in the course of systematic inquiry.
7. See Dalkey (1969) as one example of the Delphi method. There are many others as exemplified primarily in RAND publications. In the last analysis, it may well be that this approach to forming group opinion is more an exercise in the dynamics of group behavior than it is a systematic approach to forecasting. For applications of Delphi procedures to technological forecasting, see especially Martino (1972), Chapter 2. The references in Martino (1972) indicate the extensive literature on this subject.
8. For a survey of trend analysis techniques, see particularly Bell (1964) and Brown (1963). For applications to technological forecasting, see Martino (1972), Chapter 5.
9. See especially Christ (1966) and Laponce and Smoker (1972), among others.
10. See Choucri, *et al.* (1972) for a system dynamics formulation of theoretical relations which were specified initially in statistical terms in Choucri and North (1972), and in econometric terms in Choucri (1972).
11. See Ashley and Choucri (1973) for the application of Bayesian analysis to forecasting in international relations, especially to the analysis of conflict situations, and Ashley, *et al.* (1973) for a summary of these arguments. See also Ben-Dak and Mihalka (1972) for applications of Bayesian analysis to peace research. For a general survey, see Holstein (1970).
12. Zinnes and Wilkenfeld (1971) have provided some initial illustrations of applications of Markov processes to the study of international conflict. See chapter below for adaptation of Markov modeling to forecasting in international relations.

13. See Laponce and Smoker (1972) and Inbar and Stoll (1972). Also see Leavitt (1974) for a critical survey of applications of computer simulation to forecasting. For a combination of man-computer simulations, see Guetzkow (1972), Smoker (1968a), and Hermann and Hermann (1967). For recent applications of simulation approaches to political analysis, also see Coplin (1968); and for application to crises in foreign policy, see Hermann (1969). For an extensive compilation of recent works on simulation in the social and administrative sciences, see Guetzkow, *et al.* (1972).

14. See Alker and Christensen (1972) for the first application of artificial intelligence thinking to forecasting in international relations.

15. See Habermas (1968) for extensive treatment of such issues.

16. I am grateful to Michael Washburn for clarification of the role of an anchor in the forecasting design. Implicit references to anchor conditions are found in Bell and Mau (1971). I am indebted to Daniel Bell for the notion of "axial principle" and am grateful for his drawing to my attention its implication for forecasting.

17. See Azar (1970a) for a summary of events analysis and Azar (1973) and McClelland (1973) for applications of events analysis to forecasting in international relations. Choucri and North (1975) and Choucri (1972) provide applications of events analysis to retrospective forecasting in international relations within the context of econometric modeling and simulation.

18. The idea of an early warning system was first put forth operationally by Edward Azar, with particular reference to the Middle East conflict. See Azar (1970a and 1973).

19. See Moses, *et al.* (1967) for the first inter-nation interaction scale and Azar (1973) for subsequent developments.

20. For an initial operational perspective upon this problem, see Choucri (1972) and Choucri and North (1972 and 1975). See also Azar (1973) for approaches to this problem in the context of events analysis.

21. It is instructive to note that a table function in system dynamics plays the same role in empirical analysis as does a coefficient in statistical inquiry or econometric modeling; however, the identification of breakpoints necessitates different procedures in each case. It is easier to isolate a breakpoint in statistical inquiry predicated upon assumptions of nonlinearity in variables and parameters than it is in functional analysis of dynamics systems where the entire modeling exercise is predicated upon the isolation of nonlinear, complex relationships.

22. See Choucri and North (1975) for empirical and philosophical approaches to these questions. Professor Organski of the University of Michigan, Ann Arbor, is currently examining the demographic implications of conflict and warfare. This investigation should clarify the conditions under which violence results in significant demographic changes, and the implications of these changes for society, polity, and international relations.

23. These observations are based upon Martino (1972), Chapters 19 and 20.

24. See Martino (1972), Chapter 21, for a discussion of the interrogation model for evaluating the performance of a forecast, particularly with respect to technological forecasting.

25. See Blalock (1960) and Blalock and Blalock (1968); see also Christ (1966), Johnston (1972), and Rao and Miller (1971). For a critical appraisal of the validation problem in international relations forecasting, see Hermann, *et al.* (1973) and Hermann (1967); and for criteria for evaluating forecasts, see Bobrow (1973).

26. Different validation procedures are applicable to different forecasting modes and different computer-based approaches to complex systems. The contrasts in validation procedures employed for forecasting based on econometrics and forecasting based on system dynamics are indicative of the issues in question.

27. See especially Schultze, *et al.* (1971) and Rivlin (1971) as illustrations of this type of analysis and associated imperatives.

28. See Allison (1969) and Allison and Halperin (1972) for evidence and analysis regarding bureaucratic politics and the organizational imperatives of institutions and organizations.

29. See Choucri (1972a) for a critical analysis of the implications of population, resources, and technology for future international orders and related cultural considerations. See also North and Choucri (1972) concerning the implications of these dimensions for United States policy and planning. The relations of population, resources, and technology to international conflict and violence are discussed theoretically in Choucri and North (1972) and a critical survey of the literature is presented in Choucri (1972). These are first thrusts into systematic exposition of the interconnections of political and nonpolitical considerations for thinking about global dynamics and international futures. See also the World Order Studies sponsored by the World Law Fund for institutional structural aspects of alternative futures. Bell and Mau (1971) provide insights into ways of thinking about futures.

30. The merging power configuration in the changing relationship between the United States and Japan is indicative of such developments as is the apparent rapprochement between China and the United States. Global politics among super-powers might increasingly involve a four-power international system: the United States, the USSR, China, and Japan.

31. The recent volume, *Civilization and Science* (1971) provides a philosophical perspective upon the critical issues at hand and highlights some of the more intricate philosophical and scientific dilemmas of our time, particularly as related to alternative futures.

32. Rosecrance (1963) and Bozeman (1960) illustrate alternative approaches to systematic treatment of large-scale transformations of international systems.

33. See especially Nye and Keohane (1972) and Kay and Skolnikoff (1972) for insights into these impending developments. Ruggie (1972) presents a different

perspective upon future developments in global politics.

34. This statement is in tribute to Hans Morgenthau, who has long been ignored by behavioral scientists concerned with international politics. This oversight on their part is a testimony to the theoretical and intellectual paucity of the behavioral "revolution" in international politics. Greater attention to more traditional writings might provide the behavioral scientists with valuable insights into real-world dynamics.

35. To date little exists concerning the view from below other than the naive literature on political development that emerged from the structural-functional literature of the fifties and early sixties. One notable exception is the volume edited by Bhagwati (1972) and, to a much lesser extent, the series on political development sponsored by the Center for International Studies at Princeton University.

36. See Bay (1958), which stands as a landmark in the political theory literature.

37. Stinchcombe (1968) combines empirical and theoretical approaches to social systems. See also Russett (1972).

38. The most notable critique of the conventional wisdom in the social sciences from a phenomenological perspective include Thevenaz (1962), Husserl (1965), and Natanson (1963).

39. These observations draw upon Bell and Mau (1971), pp. 6–44.

40. The term "possidiction" is employed by Bell and Mau (1971) and attributed to Wascow (1969).

CHAPTER TWO

THE ART OF THE
SOCIAL SCIENCE SOOTHSAYER

Ithiel de Sola Pool

I. FORECASTING AS SOPHISM

Around 1951 when the Rand Corporation was first being formed, Abraham Girshick and Abraham Kaplan launched as one of the first activities of that organization a study on what makes a good forecaster in international relations. The new organization was to help policy makers understand better what was going in the world. What could be more important than to determine whose recorded forecasts had proved reliable and why? They collected past forecasts with an eye to scoring them. But the study had to be abandoned. It turned out that even after the passage of some time, there were practically no forecasts that they could score as having proved right or wrong. Social scientists, journalists, and statesmen alike talked with such equivocation that no one could say with certainty whether their forecasts had been right or wrong.

Now, social science is not forecasting, and forecasting is not necessarily specific prediction; we shall develop these points below. But the ability to make a specific prediction under some appropriate circumstances is a legitimate test of the power of a science. It is also true that society often views social scientists as soothsayers, from whom it expects anticipations of the future. Such soothsayers use many devices to avoid the hard test of empirical confirmation:

1. There are predictions without date. "It's going to rain" is a prototype of such predictions. Implicitly that means it's going to rain "soon," but what is soon? Sooner or later it will certainly rain. So it is with any cyclical or periodic phenomenon. All wars must end, so those who predict the end of a war are eventually proven right. In the American political system one may predict that the public will become dissatisfied with the performance of

the incumbent party and will vote it out of office. Some day it will. One can predict the end of the bull market or the end of the bear market, but without a date such a prediction will not make one rich. Nor are such predictions a contribution to knowledge.

2. There are forecasts that are really statements of intent. The teacher who grades on a curve "predicts" that there will be 15 percent A's, if that is his norm. He is really announcing his intent. He is forecasting that which is within his power. Such statements, however, do contain an element of forecast; it is not the forecast of the grades, for about that he is making a current statement of intent. The forecast is: "I will not change my mind." That is indeed a legitimate forecast about one man's psyche, but one for which the relevant evidence and prior probabilities are different than a forecast about grades on a curve.

So, too, in politics and world affairs, when a statesman forecasts that colony X will be freed next year, or that there will be continuing terrorism in some disputed area, only to a small degree is he making a forecast. Rather he may be saying something about his present intentions regarding something within his power.

Of course there are mixed cases. When the President of the United States says that South Vietnam will not be overrun, and when Hanoi says the imperialists will be driven out of South Vietnam, each is making a statement about its present intent. But since the outcome is not fully under either's control, each is also making a genuine forecast that his side will in fact succeed in doing what it intends to do. At the same time, the outcome rests, to a substantial degree, on the intensity of the intent. If the President of the United States were to say he will use any weapon in his arsenal to achieve his goal in Vietnam, he would presumably no longer be making a prediction, but rather a threat, for he did have it in his physical power to impose his will. If, however, his intent is limited to achieve what he can achieve only with more moderate means, then to that degree he is making a prediction if he forecasts success. No wonder that Girshick and Kaplan, reading texts of past statements, found it impossible to extricate unambiguous predictions in the mass of forecasting statements. When statesmen talk it is a matter of exegesis to

sort out how much is prediction and how much is intent.

3. There are apparent forecasts that are really scoops. A columnist writes that cabinet minister John Doe will resign next week. That is again a prediction only of the fact that the decision already made about which the journalist got a leak will not be changed in the next week. The statement is primarily an assertion of a current but secret fact. It differs from above-discussed statements of intent in that here we are dealing with statements made by third parties who *report* the intent of a decision maker rather than with statements of intent by the decision maker himself. But the statements still report current facts more than it forecasts. Most forecasts in the news media are of that character. They may start as a trial balloon, a deliberate leak, or an investigative discovery, but they are reporting rather than forecasting.

4. There are "either-or" forecasts. Either there will be detente or the strain between the great powers will be exhausting. That example says very little more than that there will either be detente or there won't be. It is a particularly vapid example, because the "either" and the "or" between them cover the whole possibility space. Quite different would be the statement that either X or Y will be the next President of the General Assembly. That is a significant forecast, for presumably there are many other possible presidents, and the forecast that it will be one of only two people narrows the possibility space considerably.

Thus, "either-or" statements found in the literature cannot casually be dismissed as illegitimate or vapid. Many of them may be significant conveyors of large amounts of information. However, the very fact that they may be sensible makes them attractive camouflage for vacuity. The "either-or" statements that appear in public print are often nearly, if not totally, vapid.

5. There are "if . . . then . . ." forecasts, which, to the extent that they are assertions of functional relations, are really propositions rather than predictions. Nonetheless, they are another kind of forecast, in some instances directly translatable into "either-or" forecasts, but also sometimes different.

For instance, those cases where the "if" statement does not come true leave it indeterminate whether the prediction is confirmed or not. Consider the prediction "If China and the Soviet Union reconcile their differences, then Japan will draw closer to the United States." It is ambiguous whether the converse is also being asserted, namely that if China and the Soviet Union remain at odds, then Japan will draw away from the United States. Since it is this latter situation that actually emerged as the reality, the original prediction must be regarded as untested.

For soothsayers, such ambiguity provides an easy gambit. There are many forecasts in which the "if" condition is almost certain not to happen leaving the soothsayer's ability as a pundit virtually untested. The assertion that "if nuclear war occurs, then civilization will be destroyed" is a highly plausible piece of punditry that hopefully and probably will never be tested. Another example in the large class of disaster forecasts are those of catastrophe from continued exponential growth: "If we don't do something about it, the population explosion will make the world unlivable." Perhaps so, but it is virtually certain that we will do something about it, perhaps not before there are painful consequences to motivate us, but well before the world becomes unlivable.

Clearly, the disaster forecasts are not nonsense. On the contrary, the two examples given are both plausible and wise statements. But those of us who believe such statements must do so not on the basis of empirical tests, for the test situation will probably never occur, but on the basis of theoretical inference. Often, however, sheer faith rather than rigorous theory constitutes the basis for such forecasts.

6. There are forecasts where confirmation may well be pure chance. A particularly troublesome case is the unique event forecast. Religions have been founded because a prophet predicted correctly that a war would start or a plague break out at a particular time, and then it happened as foretold. The forecast was right no doubt, and the forecaster deserves whatever kudos go with being right. But was it luck or inspiration? That is clearly what underlies the debate between true believers and skeptics.

Even where a forecaster maintains a record of repeated success over time, it is sometimes obscure, in the absence of careful analysis, whether his performance is better than chance. Where an outcome is highly probable, the forecaster who consistently sticks to predicting that outcome will succeed more often than he will fail. Medicine men have practiced that from time eternal. Most illnesses are not fatal, so if the doctor promises you recovery if you do what he prescribes, he will be proven right more often than not, regardless of whether his treatment was causal. Most international crises do not lead to war. A soothsayer who practiced optimism would have a pretty good batting average. Almost any politician could defend the wisdom of his government's foreign policy or the effectiveness of the United Nations by such an argument; they have avoided a myriad of potential wars. Currently, for example, detente can be defended by asserting that it will assure continued avoidance of war between the great powers. Perhaps that is so, but the mere continuation of the most probable state, no war, is hardly proof.

Of the various high probability outcomes that soothsayers forecast, the most common one is the condition of no change. If one predicts that tomorrow's weather will be the same as today's, more often than not you will be right. Slightly more subtle, but just as arbitrary as the prediction of no change is the prediction of no change in trend. Some years ago it was found that one could have done as well on the stock market as the average of the advisory services if one simply assumed that whichever way the market had moved today it would move tomorrow. Swings tend to last for several days, so on most days the trend continues. Of course, that is no panacea for making money, since the few days when the market reverses its trend can wipe out profits made on most previous days. But if the moral satisfaction of being right more often than wrong is what is wanted there is an easy way to have it: predict the continuation of a trend.

In the literature on international relations, predictions of continuity are the most common of all. Pundits make their reputations by repeatedly prognosticating that developing countries will suffer the toils of underdevelopment, that the Third World nations will object to great power policies, that the Soviet Union will resist tendencies toward decomposition of its bloc, that movements of dissent and for cultural openness will be repressed there, that the United States will resist growth in communist power, and that Europe will object to withdrawal of American support. Like trend predictions on the stock market, such predictions are safe day after day, and indeed in this instance year after year. But how much wisdom do they really show on the part of the pundit? The risk takers are the pundits who forecast the rare revolutionary breaks in these continuities. Any pundit who makes many specific forecasts of such very low-probability turns of events is almost sure to be wrong much more often than the pseudo-prophet who simply predicts continuity each time. Predicting low-probability events may be more important, but it is more difficult and riskier than predicting continuity.

7. Finally, the most common gambit of all for making predictions untestable is the use of vagueness. Examples abound: "The international system is becoming decreasingly viable"; "the nationalist spirit will not be quenched"; "the conflict between the classes will grow ever more intense." None of these statements is meaningless, yet all are vague enough so that even after the fact observers will continue to disagree as to whether the event forecast happened or not.

Vagueness in forecast need not depend on the kind of literary flourishes in the above examples. There were forecasts before the 1972 United States elections that the Republicans would win and forecasts that the Democrats would win. Which occurred? The Republican President won in a landslide, but the Democrats carried the Congress. Many predictions had been vague as to the indicators of party victory. Or consider the American military intervention in Vietnam. For years, if not forever, there will be debate as to whether it was a victory or defeat. If the criterion chosen is the formal statements of purpose of the Johnson and Nixon administrations, the American intervention was successful, for the goal was never stated to be anything more than permitting the survival of the regime in the South for an unspecified time period. If the goal is taken as establishing the credibility among anticommunist regimes of American guarantees, or encouraging the development of stable, noncommunist regimes in Asia, the question is clearly unresolved. If price is entered into the equation, the war can easily be argued to have been a failure for the United States. But neither those who were forecasting victory at various times over the years nor those who kept calling the conflict an "unwinnable" war specified their predictions well enough so that in retrospect one can make them admit to error.

In "if . . . then . . ." forecasts, either term or both may be vague. "If the underprivileged are not given a sense of stake in the system, then there will be civil war." Civil war is presumably a recognizable state, and perhaps one can expect some intersubjective agreement among judges as to whether it occurred or not. But is there likely to be any agreement on the evidence as to whether the underprivileged (whoever they are) had or had not acquired a sense of stake in the system? Perhaps even civil war is not a clear term. Certainly a prediction that one side or another will break a cease fire is predictably obscure. There are violations to any cease fire. How many violations breaks it?

In short, the language in which public affairs is discussed and in which international relations predictions are made is so inadequately specified that one can rarely say that a forecast has been confirmed or disconfirmed. That was the disconcerting finding of Girshick and Kaplan.

II. PREDICTION AND FORECASTING: A DIGRESSION ON WORD USAGE

Forecasting, it is often argued, is not prediction. Even if we are quite unable to predict future outcomes, it may well be possible to exercise intelligence in regard to their future. If we call the latter forecasting, then inability to predict may be no indictment of forecasting.

Part of the exercise of intelligence in regard to the future is the identification of dangers to be avoided. A forecaster, for example, might analyze the proposal for a multiethnic Palestine. He would do so in the light of events in other areas where attempts have been made to include very disparate hostile populations within the same borders. The Indian subcontinent, Canada, South Africa, Ireland, and Cyprus are cases in point. A forecast of the consequences need not include a prediction that such a national unit would actually be set up, the date of it, or its form. The forecast might well be so negative that the predicted event would never be tried.

Forecasting, in short, can be defined as the identification of alternatives in a stochastic world, the estimation of their probabilities, the tracing out of the consequences (e.g., payoff) of each, and the giving of policy guidance about how to realize a chosen alternative.

Various writers use the terms "prediction" and "forecasting" in different ways but if one accepts that formulation of forecasting, then prediction might seem no part of it, and the failures of public figures, journalists, and social scientists when they try to act as soothsayers is irrelevant. It would be testimony to their sophistication, not their sophism, that one rarely finds specific predictions in their writings. It would only mean that they were not attempting the impossible as they applied their intelligence to the future.

I cannot accept that view. It is in part valid, but in part false. What is valid is that the exercise of intelligence about the future is not *just* prediction. Identification of possibilities, if-then statements, either-or statements, or advocacy of policy choices are all valid and meaningful ways of thinking. What is invalid in the separation of forecasting from prediction is the argument that prediction is not even part of forecasting. Indeed, I would argue that forecasting is impossible if one cannot to some degree predict. In every forecast there are hidden predictions. They can be glossed over, as we have illustrated above. But the forecast is not improved by that. On the contrary, understanding requires that we force the predictions out into the glaring light of day.

A forecast that does not imply a prediction that under some specified circumstances some specified outcome will happen, at least probabilistically, is meaningless. There may be all sorts of qualifications about uncertainty, *ceteris paribus*, etc., but however deeply embedded, a vague or qualified prediction is part of every forecast.

III. FORECASTING AS INTERPRETATION

There are good reasons for the vagueness with which historical trends in society are forecast. Nonconfirmable forecasts are not merely the result of sloppiness or deliberate sophistry. The scholar who is careful enough to make his language precise enough for testing, who attaches dates to his forecasts, who specifies the turning points when trends will reverse themselves, would almost certainly be wrong so often as to amuse his colleagues. I have tried such an exercise in precision and I know.

In 1965 I decided to experiment with violating all the Girshick-Kaplan gambits. The American Academy of Arts and Sciences issued a volume of forecasting papers (Bell, 1968). I decided to make the predictions in mine specific and testable. I knew perfectly well that that would make them wrong. I said:

Those of us whose profession is the search for understanding, however, must learn to live with self-exposure. Just as understanding is gained by unrelenting exposure of one's unconscious, so also can understanding be aided by exposure of one's unconscious assumptions.

The predictions are not stated in arrogant confidence, for the results are certain to be proved wrong. The only thing of which one can be confident is that reality will depart radically from these predictions. Such predictions may be taken to be the modal items on subjective probability distributions. If forced to bet between each prediction and alternatives to it of comparable detail, the predictions chosen are those on which the author would prefer to bet. This is not to say that the predictions made are probable. (Bell, p. 318)

Since I presented what I believed to be the modal probabilities, but ones below 0.5, most of them turned out wrong—as I predicted they would. My first forecast, for example, was that by 1970 both DeGaulle and Mao would be dead. Given their ages, the probability in each case was substantial that in a 5-year period they would pass on. In point of fact, of course, one died and one survived. It would be sheer pedantry to argue that one forecast proved "better" than the other. It would be far more sensible to say that chance made one right and one wrong between essentially equally valid forecasts. What happened after that in France and China was conditioned by that chance, and thus the contingencies of history built upon each other. Clearly, picking the most probable path along a tree with many branches, no one of which approaches 0.5, is a route to a large number of errors, whatever uses the procedure may have.

Even though the limitations on the forecasts and the inevitability of error in them were flagged in the introduction to the essay, various authors have written about them since, holding them up to satire because reality diverged from the course laid out in my essay. William Thompson devoted considerable space in his book, *At the Edge of History,* to picking the predictions apart (1971). So did a Soviet author.

My point is not to protest a critic's barbs. Ideologues have the right to pick a rhetorically convenient target, which my piece was, because of its specificity. The point I prefer to make is to show how difficult it is, even afterwards, to evaluate forecasts. In detail the 1965 forecasts were clearly wrong—as it was forecasted they would be. But how far they were wrong in their basic perspective remains a subtle issue into which point of view enters almost as strongly now as it would have in 1965.

Take, for example, the statement:

> By 1970 the central civil rights issues will be the introduction into the South of certain federally-financed, special opportunity programs in education and small-business loans. The major areas around which social protest movements will be organized will be matters of personal self-expression—for example, demands for sexual freedom or for less conformity in school systems. (Bell, p. 320)

Was that a good forecast? I don't know. Certainly the statement about civil rights is a good description of the Nixon program of 1970, but did that make his programmatic choices "the central civil rights issues"? I do not think so, but even with hindsight that is not a matter of simple perceptual fact about which any objective observer could agree. What the central issues were is a matter of evaluative interpretation.

The statement about the character of protest in the schools I would call a bull's-eye hit, but was I right in calling these "the major areas" of social protest movements? No mention is made in that passage of protests against the Vietnam War, since on that I had made a blooper by expecting major fighting to fade out in 1967, not 1973. But even in retrospect, was the dominant feature of the worldwide protest movement of 1970 its pacifism (certainly a significant factor in the United States)

or was it personal self-expression? I do not know the answer with any better certainty now than I did when I made the forecast in 1965. It remains in aftcast, as well as forecast, a matter of arguable opinion. It is a muddy and unsatisfactory state of affairs when, even with hindsight and even with regard to unusually specific predictions, the evaluation of the predictions is not an obvious or self-evident fact, but a matter of point of view, emphasis, ideology, and judgment.

To recognize that fact is the beginning of wisdom about forecasting of social trends. We must abandon the overly simple notion that the only reason that forecasts are hard to evaluate is that demagogic writers use those tricks that Girshick and Kaplan identified to fuzz up their texts and make them invulnerable to testing. They often do that, but, in addition, there are profound problems in matching even carefully made statements with reality. These problems are much the same whether the statement is made at a date earlier than the observation (i.e., forecasting) or whether the statement is about current affairs, or whether the statement is made at a date later than the reality referred to (i.e., history). The logical problems of empirical confirmation or disconfirmation of interpretive statements about the world are substantially the same in all of these time frames.

In principle, "postdiction" is just as hard as "prediction"; "aftcasts" are as hard as "forecasts." Consider the "what if . . ." questions of history (Vaihinger, 1925). What if Oswald's bullet had missed? In that event, would America have become involved in land warfare in Vietnam in 1965? If that question had been raised in 1964, the answer would have been a prediction. To answer it now is a postdiction, but logically there is no difference. Very little of what we have learned since 1965 has much bearing on the question of what would have happened if history had taken a different turn on November 22, 1963. The "what if . . ." questions about the counterfactual past are usually just as uncertain as the "what if" questions we ask today about the future.

The fact of uncertainty is a fact of the human condition, in the face of which we still must act. Even if incapable of firm validation, both forecasting and aftcasting are legitimate activities. The historian who attempts to interpret the significance of an event in the past, the news commentator talking about today, or the forecaster looking to the future all suffer from limitations on knowledge. If the forecaster has any greater problem it is only that a wider range of relevant items are as yet unknown. The historian starts with a few more contemporaneous givens that for the forecaster are still unknowns. The unknowns of the forecaster and the aftcaster are, however, not logically different.

Consider an historian trying to explain the outcome of the Cuban missile crisis. He can take it as given that the Soviets tried to place missiles in Cuba, but it is a pure act of aftcasting for him to speculate about *what* would have happened *if* Kennedy's reaction to that move had been to bomb the missile sites. An historian could not write intelligently about what actually happened without taking note of what might have happened under that counterfactual alternative. For someone writing before the crisis, it would have a quite similar act of interpretation to forecast what would happen *if* the Soviets put missiles into Cuba and Kennedy reacted by bombing them. Logically it is hard to see any difference in the logic of speculation involved in the predictive or the historical statement, even though one more fact would be a given for the historian.

Let us now formalize the points we have been making. Descriptive statements about the world may either describe an alleged counterfactual condition or a condition alleged to have actually occurred. These two classes of statements are validated in different ways.

Statements about conditions that have actually occurred can be tested in the same way and in addition can be tested by empirical observation of the real world. The statement that is compared with data about the real world may have been made before the condition came into being (in a prediction), contemporaneously with the condition, or after the condition had passed (in historical assertions).

Since observations and statements are different orders of things, however, there is always an intuitive leap of inference whenever we say that what is observed is like (or is different from) what is described in the statement. The uncertainty involved in the leap varies in degree as between highly theoretical statements (e.g., "This society is anomic.") and highly empirical statements (e.g.,

"That is a dog."), but it is always there. Even a category as concrete as a dog has fuzzy margins. Is a dead dog a dog? Is a cross between wolf and dog a dog? Was what was seen a coyote or a dog? Or is it an optical illusion or hallucination? So the mere fact that the statement is about an empirical and present fact does not eliminate uncertainty in testing its descriptive validity. The criteria we use in international relations are very fuzzy; when is fighting describable as a war?

Social interpretation consists only in part of statements about the alleged actual facts in the real world. Social interpretation is very largely the comparison of such facts with counterfactual alternatives: What would happen or what will happen if different alternative courses are followed. Thus, forecasts that are interpretations of society cannot be evaluated by just holding them up to the facts. The notion that with the passage of time we will know by looking at hard facts whether the forecast was right or wrong turns out to be a myth. The forecast can be evaluated only in a context of theory that takes into account the counterfactual alternatives.

The recognition of the ambiguity of forecasts is not to denigrate the effort to forecast, any more than asserting that historical interpretations are like forecasts is an attempt to denigrate history. Forecasting, aftcasting, and concurrent interpretation of alternatives other than the actual one are all important activities. When well done they help us to understand the branching tree of history.

IV. FORECASTS AS EXPERIMENTS

So far we have examined forecasting and prediction as they occur in the mass media and in public affairs, often sophistically and sometimes as serious interpretation. We turn now to a use of prediction and forecasting in science. Scientists, just as other scholars, interpret reality by theoretical evaluation of counterfactual alternatives. But empirical scientists also engage in the more hard-headed but difficult task of inventing predictions that can be tested by matching them to actual events. That is what the scientist does when he works in a rigorous hypothesis-testing mode. He uses ingenuity to design a prediction so well defined that there will be agreement in calling it confirmed or disconfirmed. That is a hard thing to do. The great scientist is clever in inventing such testable predictions that bear on important matters.

The basic empirical activity of science is controlled observation. The scientist systematically manipulates the objects that he observes so as to be able to say with some confidence whether the resulting data confirm or disconfirm some statement about the empirical world. The name we give to that kind of controlled observation is "experiment" although sometimes the word "experiment" is reserved for a special subclass of extremely controlled observations that we can usually conduct only in a laboratory. Experimentation in a narrow sense is a manipulation that allows us at will to vary one variable while physically holding others constant. But in the broader sense we may also call it an experiment if we merely control the observation—for example, measuring rainfall under a fixed, well defined procedure, even if we cannot physically control the environment that brings the rain. Forecasting outside the laboratory is much like forecasting the outcome of a laboratory experiment except that one waits for nature to produce the desired conditions for observation rather than producing them by manipulation. Forecasting, done with careful, replicable, explicit procedures, is thus one kind of scientific experimentation, at least in the broad sense of the word "experiment."

In the most rigorous, most definitive experiments the forecast that is tested is a single-point prediction, but in much of science one settles for a looser forecast. When the astronauts brought rocks back from the moon, there was no single prediction as to what the rocks would be. On the moon, as on earth, rocks are mixes that vary from spot to spot. Yet the distribution of the moon rocks, when interpreted through statistical models, fits one alternative forecast better than another. The experimental scientist tries to make as explicit as he can the predictions implicit in his forecasts, but one should not exaggerate the extent to which he can normally do so.

There are many ways of manipulating the environment so as to increase our confidence in the meaning of the data produced. One way is to systematize the sample of observations. When we draw a scientific sample we gain confidence that the observed pattern of results is a valid representation of the world.[1] When we use reliable instruments of observation, we are also increasing our confidence in the interpretation of the world. When, in a laboratory, we apply systematic variation of the conditions of observation and use controls to prevent unintended variations, we are again increasing our confidence in what we are observing.

Another control device used by scientists to increase their confidence in a statement about a process in the real world is to put a prediction on record before observing. The point is to avoid peeking. The complex and inferential statement that "as Sino-Soviet tensions grow China *will* become more friendly to the United States" may *ex post facto* prove as difficult to confirm or disconfirm with certainty as the statement that "as Sino-Soviet tensions grew, China became more friendly to the United States," but the social scientist who makes the former statement has less chance for fudging. If one makes an empirical observation first, and then interprets it, there are generally a myriad of alternative interpretations that can account for the facts. If one chooses one's hypothesis first without peeking, it is generally far less likely that the observation that is later made will correspond to it. Therefore, predicting an observation in advance is a rigorous control.

Note that scientific forecasting is the forecasting of observations. Often, the world itself may already have been in the forecast state at the time that the forecast was made. In that case, the forecast is not a forecast about the world but about the act of observing. An analyst may forecast, for example, where a reconnaissance satellite will find a missile site. He is not forecasting that it will be put there after his forecast; it is already there. He is forecasting the result of the observation.

A scientific forecast of an observation of something that has not yet transpired at the moment of the forecast can also be made. One may forecast, for example, that the population of China will be 1 billion by 1990. As a scientific testing operation, there is no significant difference between that prediction and a prediction that a contemporary world census would show a population of 800 million. They are both forecasts of an observation as to what one will find, whether or not the condition has as yet come into existence. From a scientific point of view, one important thing about a prediction is that it be a rigorous test that prevents peeking and *post hoc* interpretations. The forecast that deals with something not yet in existence does indeed have a rhetorical or aesthetic merit in that peeking is impossible, so the audience may be more easily satisfied that the test was a valid one, but that is all. In either case one is predicting an observation not yet made. For the scientist then, predicting is just one of a series of available devices for subjecting observation to control. It goes along with many other devices, such as the rigorous use of language, the specification of the extensional limits of the generalization, and the adding of detail. The vague forecast (in 1971) that 1972 would be a Republican year is a less good scientific test than the prediction that the Republicans would sweep the Presidency and the Democrats the Congress, or than the prediction that the Republicans would carry twenty-nine states. And since controls can be applied to many dimensions of an observation, there is no simple preference to be expressed between the vague forecast that 1972 would be a Republican year (made without peeking) and the *post hoc* explanation that an analyst might give of the reasons for the difference in the Presidential and Congressional results. One of these interpretive procedures has the merit of a control against peeking, and the other has the merit of specificity and detail. As an intellectual operation each has its strengths and weaknesses on different dimensions. Best of all would be a test that would apply controls on both dimensions.

What the scientist tries to do, with all possible ingenuity, is to formulate a prediction that is both testable, specific, detailed, and that (either by the scientist's own manipulations or naturally) has a chance to become the factual state of affairs. Forecasts that can be tested do not just happen. They have to be designed for the purpose.

V. FORECASTING IN POLICY SCIENCE

In the last two sections we considered uses of forecasting where, at least proximately, the knowledge was an end in itself. Now we consider forecasting in applied policy sciences. The politician or the analyst who makes a formal or implicit cost/benefit analysis of policy alternatives is forecasting. He asks such questions as: Will expenditure on education promote equality? Will deployment of more missiles deter an opponent? Will a negotiatory offer be accepted?

Forecasting in the policy sciences involves all of the dilemmas already discussed. The politician deliberating about alternatives is likely to indulge in all the sophisticated devices of futuristic rhetoric that we find in any public debate. He raises "what if . . ." questions about the counterfactual alternatives that could be chosen. Unless there is a chance to try different policies in different times and places, history is going to allow only one choice to be realized and evaluated empirically. Whether other choices would have worked better or worse will remain a matter of interpretation. And even the one branch of the tree of historical alternatives that actually gets tried may be hard to assess empirically because of all of the problems of matching empirical facts to verbal statements.

There is one more difficulty that is particularly harassing to the predictor of policy consequences: the forecaster, by his forecast, himself changes the future about which he is forecasting. That is the classic observer/observed problem in the social sciences.[2]

Consider the case of a defense planner predicting that failure to install some border defenses will result in aggressive action by an unfriendly neighbor. Suppose no special action is taken and border clashes do occur, and then 10 years later he returns to do an evaluation study. He will have all of the analytic problems listed previously plus this last one. He will not know what would have happened if defenses had been built; perhaps border clashes would have gone up just as much. He may have trouble evaluating whether aggressive action has in fact gone up, for aggression is not an unambiguous concept. Finally, there is the new difficulty that we are now considering. Did the prediction, rather than lack of defenses as such, produce the increase in border clashes? The prediction was perhaps read in the neighboring country and interpreted as a threat. In short, the prediction could have been a self-fulfilling one.

The world of social behavior is full of self-fulfilling and self-defeating prophecies. Optimism and self-confidence are often keys to success, and pessimism and defeatism the sources of failure.

Thus, the belief that one will succeed is a self-fulfilling prophecy of success and the expectation that there is no use trying because one cannot succeed is a self-fulfilling prophecy of failure. In international affairs a prevailing belief that one country is stronger than another is an important element in its being stronger. So, too, in the stock market, when most speculators believe that prices will go up, they do go up.

There are also self-defeating prophecies in the stock market. No one could invent a successful, but public scheme for predicting the market. Suppose that some super-economist of the future proposed a scheme for precisely predicting what the market would do the day after tomorrow. And suppose that his theory was proved by success over a period of time. Soon, if he predicted that the market would go up the day after tomorrow, people would buy tomorrow and the market would rise before the day he forecast. His predictions would be defeated by the fact that he made them.

That phenomenon of self-defeating prophecies is one reason why we should not expect that the social sciences will ever get to forecast as well as the natural sciences. A certain amount of naive literature on the social sciences argues that they are young sciences that have not yet had the time to reach the predictive excellence of such sciences as physics or even meteorology. Some day, according to this thesis, the Newton of the social sciences will come along and give us better theories that will enable us to forecast with accuracy. This is probably fantasy. In the first place, the social sciences are no younger than the natural sciences. They both had early foreshadowings in Aristotle, and then a spurt of original thought in the Renaissance (e.g., Galileo and Machiavelli), new great writings in the period of Newton and Hobbes, and the institutionalization of empirical research in the nineteenth and twentieth centuries. If the social sciences have not succeeded as rapidly as the natural sciences, it is because of the inherently greater difficulty of their subject matter. The strength of the observer/observed problem is one aspect of that difficulty. The problem exists in the natural sciences, too. A thermometer affects the temperature of the object it touches, whose temperature it is trying to measure. But the problem is of enormously greater intensity in the social sciences. One of the features of the social sciences is

that they predict the behavior of entities, that is, humans, one of whose most salient features is their ability and interest in hearing the forecasts.

Above we noted a very important class of self-defeating forecasts—the forecasts of catastrophe. Every road sign that says "Caution, dangerous intersection" is hopefully a self-defeating forecast. With the sign, the intersection may become no more dangerous than the average one. We noted above the forecast that a nuclear war will destroy civilization. If statesmen believe this then there will be no nuclear war.

Indeed, one of the reasons why the social sciences seem to be poor in prediction is the prevalence in the social world of self-defeating forecasts of catastrophe. Consider how poor we are as forecasters on urban problems. Why do we seem so incapable of designing programs that will work in reducing crime or in maintaining the quality of life? One reason why we seem to be poor at such forecasts, although we are in fact rather good at them, is that whenever we are able to make good forecasts of undesired results we act on our knowledge and defeat these forecasts. Sometime in the evolution of modern cities we realized that unless fire departments were organized in a certain way, cities would burn down. We realized, too, that unless refuse was removed, we would be consumed in contagion. Unless police and courts were organized, violence would be out of control. Society acted on these and many other forecasts, and made the life of the modern city possible. What remained after the easy problems were solved were the hard problems. If we do not know how to solve the residue of crime that remains after police and courts have been created, it is because there are no simple and obvious predictions about how to control the high tail of the criminal distribution without imposing excessive restraints and costs on the rest of the population. In short, it is not that the social sciences do not forecast well. They forecast all of the time and most of their forecasts are so persuasive that people act to defeat them. The situation in which people do not act to defeat the forecast is likely to be that in which there is considerable uncertainty. The forecasts on which social scientists are judged are the ones that are most likely to be wrong.

These considerations apply strongly to forecasting in international relations. Why are we so poor at forecasting the outcome of wars? One reason is that wars whose outcome is easily predictable seldom occur, since the weaker side sees that fighting would be futile. Wars typically occur in those impasses in negotiations when each side believes it can perhaps successfully insist on its views. Analysts on both sides can easily forecast what the outcome would be if a country in Eastern Europe went to war against the Soviet Union or if Cuba went to war against the United States. Such a war will not occur, even though the felt grievances in each case are adequate. It is thus only the crises where the forces are relatively evenly balanced that flare up and come to the center of attention of the social scientist. In those situations his forecasts will be in demand; however, in those situations his forecasts may not be very good.

Some of the above examples of self-defeating forecasts have an important trait in common—namely, that the forecast fails by becoming known. It is sometimes mistakenly assumed that if social forecasts were not revealed, they could be objectively tested and would not run into the observer/observed problem. That is true for a large class of forecasts but not for all. It is true that if one neglected to put up a "dangerous intersection" sign, and merely predicted that there would be a high accident rate at the crossing, one could test one's forecast over time. However, there is also a large class of cases in which the success of social science forecasts depend upon the forecast being known. Examples are game theory and the classical economics of the free market. In those theories, the forecast takes the form of asserting that if people have full knowledge they will act in a certain way. Most theories of rational behavior are of that character. They assert the existence of a Pareto optimum condition from which no player will want to deviate if all players know that that is the nature of the condition and know what will happen if they move away from the point of stability. The forecast that Cuba and the United States will not go to war depends on both nations knowing and understanding that forecast and the reasons for it.

Thus, in one way or another, in forecasting the consequences of public policy actions, one's analysis must take account of the iterative feedback loop between the forecast and the external world about which the forecast is made. That loop may take a variety of forms, either reinforcing and thus helping to fulfill the predicted outcome, or inhibiting and perhaps defeating it.

VI. SUMMARY

The general tenor of this chapter has been to emphasize the limitations on the possibility of forecasting but not on its usefulness. The social sciences do have contributions to make in improving our ability to forecast. They are, first of all, substantive social science propositions and theories that we can use in our forecasts—theories, for example, such as those on the causes of war. There are, in the second place, social science insights into the conditions of our own knowledge—insights in the sociology and psychology of science. Awareness of such matters as group influences, pressure toward conformity, wish fulfillment, distortions of judgment that occur under stress, and cognitive processes of concept formation can help us to evaluate the conditions that make for or restrict objective judgment. In the third place, there are models of human decision that the social sciences have developed. Models of rationality, "satisficing," utility, bargaining, and information processing help us to predict what people will do in decision situations. Nonetheless the possibilities of forecasting are limited.

We have considered some difficulties of forecasting in four different kinds of social and political discourse. First, we considered how forecasting is done in ordinary political discussion; we noted the hopeless ambiguity of such forecasts. But when we turned to examining the problems of forecasting in more serious and careful political and historical interpretation, we found that the difficulties in evaluating forecasts did not go away; they were much the same. The third kind of discourse we examined was that of rigorous science that could be described as a systematic attempt to make the predictions testable both by applying rigid canons to the formulation of the forecasts and by controlling the conditions of observation. In this way validation of predictions becomes possible, but even here deep logical problems remain. Finally, we considered forecasts as used in deliberations about policy alternatives, and we noted the added dilemma that the forecast itself affects the outcome.

All of this suggests a certain reserve about a

naive view that exists as an ideal type, even though no intelligent social scientist defends the view. That naive view affirms that the measure of success of the social sciences is their ability to predict. They may not predict very well right now, but, that view asserts, the time will come when social scientists will be able to anticipate what will happen in society. For the present (it asserts) we should measure how good different social sciences and social scientists are by their batting averages in forecasts. The argument of this paper is that those views are wrong on all points. We argue, to the contrary, that there are inherent limitations on the ability to forecast, that uncertainty is inherent in the nature of knowledge, and that forecasting and aftcasting share that uncertainty in the same way. Useful as forecasting may be, it is not the measure of the quality of social science.

NOTES

1. That is, it has "external validity" in the language of Campbell and Stanley (1963).
2. Cf. Henshel and Kennedy (1973), pp. 119–126.

PART II

FORECASTING IN INTERNATIONAL RELATIONS: REQUIREMENTS OF THEORY

CHAPTER THREE

CONSIDERATIONS FOR EFFECTIVE FORECASTING

Davis B. Bobrow

If yet to words relating to the future, there shall some other signes be added, they may become as valid, as if they had been spoken of the present.

HOBBES, *Philosophical Rudiments
Concerning Government and Society*

I. INTRODUCTION

The modest and hopefully realizable purpose of this essay is to provide a frame of reference for evaluative decisions about forecasts and forecasting methods by those who produce, consume, and allocate resources to forecasts. The major sections of the paper discuss, first, considerations applicable to forecasts regardless of technique or purpose to

assess their effectiveness and, second, the different purposes that forecasts may be intended to serve as these affect the role of the considerations raised in the first section.

Before we turn to those subjects, it seems useful to clarify the perspective that underlies this essay with respect to two common perceptions. I refer to the views that the effectiveness of forecasts depends critically on their predictive accuracy, and that forecasting capability primarily serves *status quo* and oppressive elites.

The Limited Pertinence of Predictive Accuracy

Karl Schuessler suggests that people make predictions of two kinds (1968, pp. 418–425). The first is cross-sectional. When we know some characteristics of a given entity at a particular point in time, we predict other attributes of the entity despite our lack of knowledge about them. The second is

An earlier version of one part of this paper was presented at the Annual Meeting of the American Association for the Advancement of Science, Washington, DC, December 26–31, 1972 and of another at a symposium on "Assessing the Future and Policy Planning," sponsored by the Institute of Management Sciences, the World Future Society, and the National Bureau of Standards, Gaithersburg, Md., March 9–10, 1970. I am indebted for their comments to the editors, Alexander George, Robert Kudrle, Joseph Martino, Martin Shubik, and Ralph Strauch.

longitudinal. When we know some or all characteristics of a given entity at a particular time, we predict the value of all or some of its characteristics at a future time. Schuessler defines forecasting as the latter, longitudinal set of predictive operations.

As will become clear, it is insufficient and often unwise to reply on the considerations pertinent to cross-sectional predictions for those of a longitudinal kind. Perhaps the most important reason for distinguishing between the two kinds of predictions lies in why we search for longitudinal anticipatory knowledge at all. Quite simply, the reason is control. Through forecasts we seek the opportunity to make our personal or collective future different from what it otherwise might be. We seek to determine or mitigate the consequences of situations yet to come and to plan effectively to achieve wanted states of affairs. Predictive accuracy is then a poor measure of effectiveness in and of itself. That is, we would not judge a forecast to be ineffective simply because the predictive statement— for example, an assertion in 1960 about the number of nuclear powers in 1965—did not match the eventual historical reality—that is, the number of nuclear powers found in 1965. We would not be on sound ground to dub a forecast of runaway inflation as ineffective if it triggered preventive fiscal and monetary policy. The occurrence of self-fulfilling and self-denying forecasts poses a problem in the formulation of criteria but it often is a socially desirable aspect of forecasting.[1] The problem for our understanding of forecasting, therefore, is to take social purpose and possibility into account. We need a set of considerations that embody the values or preferences that people pursue and the means available to them to aid their own pursuits and block those of others.

Accuracy is often used inappropriately in another sense. We are all familiar with arguments that treat a correlation as a causal demonstration. For example, a prediction is made that a depression will occur if present trends continue. Advocates of a particular policy argue that its use will avert depression. Their argument is accepted and the recommended policy adopted and applied. The depression does not occur. Obviously, the information in the example does not justify any conclusion about *why* the depression did not occur. Perhaps it was not coming; perhaps it was and other changes in

the world prevented it; perhaps the advocated policy did have the claimed impact. To illustrate, few of us would find compelling the view of the H-bomb offered to me by a distinguished natural scientist. He argued that nuclear war seemed likely in the late 1940's and early 1950's. Proponents of the H-bomb claimed that it would deter war. The H-bomb was procured and nuclear war has yet to happen. Therefore, the predictions that the H-bomb would prevent nuclear war were accurate forecasts. In sum, inaccuracy does not make forecasts ineffective nor does accuracy necessarily make them effective.

If we decide not to rely solely on accuracy, how shall we assess how effective different forecasts and forecasting methods are? We need to answer this question in a manner congruent with our emphasis on the social context and decision-making implications of forecasting. Accordingly, the considerations cannot be restricted solely to the forecast itself, either to its substance or apparatus. Our framework must enable us to relate forecast characteristics to the attributes of their intended and unintended consumers. In part, forecasts are increments to the existing store of information. And they are increments whose effects depend on the existing content and structure of information and the ways in which it is used.

It seems clear that we will have to bring a number of considerations to bear to assess the effectiveness of forecasts and forecasting methods. It seems inherently unlikely that forecasts can optimize on all the considerations simultaneously. Also, it may be well beyond the current or likely state of the art to be able to achieve the characteristics called for by any consideration perfectly. Accordingly, it seems important to try and operationalize the considerations in a manner that allows us to compare their relative degree of realization across forecasts and forecasting methods. We shall try to do so subsequently. In the attempt to specify and operationalize pertinent considerations, it is important to keep in mind that we are seeking guidance for anticipatory assessment. We do not want to have to hold assessment of forecasts in abeyance until the end of the forecast period. To do so nullifies the initial reason for making the forecast. This need for evaluative foresight about forecasts applies to their consumers (who may need to act in accordance with the implications of the forecast), and to their producers (who must make numerous substantive and methodological choices).

Why Invest in Forecasting?

There are those who assert that technical improvements in forecasting inevitably favor *status quo* power elites (Dencik, 1973). This position seems to me to confuse who stands to benefit from better forecasting with who currently procures and seems to use forecasts. In the United States and other industrialized societies, it is generally true that current producers and consumers primarily are large establishment institutions, such as intelligence and military bureaucracies and multinational corporations. While historical explanation of this fact has little relevance to us, a summary of the basic reasons for it will readily suggest that change-oriented groups have at least an equal need for information about the future.

The large institutions currently involved with international relations forecasting have been motivated by several considerations. First, they recognize that the future is partially controllable and is contingent in part on their own actions. Second, they recognize the substantial lead-time required to design, procure, and deploy complex systems. Accordingly, they attribute substantial opportunity costs to failure to plan ahead. Third, they recognize the need to formulate and disseminate a portrait of the future so that the numerous and semiautonomous elements of their complex organizations act in ways that complement rather than cancel out the actions of other elements. These motivating considerations seem at least equally germane to those who would substantially alter international relations both with regard to war and peace and welfare distributions. Indeed, without a step-function advantage in their comprehension of possible futures and roads to them, how can those who seek new forms of international relations possibly be successful?

II. GENERAL CONSIDERATIONS FOR EFFECTIVE FORECASTING

Although forecasts differ in their purposes, it seems useful to introduce some considerations that apply regardless of purpose and to state them in an appropriately generalized way. These considerations are not limited to predictive accuracy but instead reflect the social purpose noted previously. We do not mean to present the considerations as exhaustive or logically exclusive—numerous mixes are conceivable and others may have additional considerations to suggest. Our discussion deals with six considerations: (1) importance, (2) utility, (3) timeliness, (4) reduction of uncertainty, (5) relevance, and (6) durability. We will present and briefly explore each consideration with respect to two kinds of forecasts. *End-state forecasts* present estimates of what some attribute, in this case of international relations, will be like at a future point in time. *Contingent forecasts* explore the implications of different "if" statements with reference to a selected "then" statement.

Importance

Our first consideration is that of importance (IF). To what extent does the forecast more or less explicitly identify actions by the policy system which will produce substantially different international outcomes (OF) than would otherwise occur (O)? That is, $IF = f(OF - O)$. In the case of end-state forecasts, this consideration tends to be achieved when the forecast shows that outcome values are the function of initial conditions which are clearly manipulable. In the case of contingent forecasts, this consideration tends to be achieved when the forecast identifies courses of policy system action different from those currently planned which are associated with substantially different probabilities of an outcome. One may conceive of forecasts as stimuli to choices about interventions or treatments to apply to the ongoing structures and processes of international relations. One subset choices involves doing nothing. Our importance consideration leads us to seek forecasts and forecasting methodologies conducive to choices that will, in effect, break trend lines or shift the locations of expected breakpoints in trend lines.[2]

Some highly abbreviated examples may be helpful at this point. Let us consider two end-state forecasts about nuclear proliferation. One suggests that the broad flow of the world situation will lead to a world of numerous nuclear-armed states. The other argues that assuming no substantial disarmament by the current nuclear powers and continuation of present plans to acquire nuclear power capacity, we will enter into a world of numerous nuclear-armed states. The latter forecast fares better in terms of our importance consideration in that it identifies potentially manipulable factors. Let us also consider two contingent forecasts. One identifies certain intervening conditions of international economic sanctions and incentives to which governments will be highly sensitive in deciding on whether or not to acquire a nuclear capability at all. The other only identifies international economic practices that will retard by less than a decade the speed of acquisition. The former seems more important.

Utility

Our previous consideration, importance, dealt with the magnitude of the difference between probable outcomes with and without the information provided by the forecast. Utility, our second consideration, deals with the direction of that difference in a normative sense. That is, forecasts have positive utility when they present information conducive to the pursuit of outcomes that are preferred to those that are otherwise probable. Forecasts have negative utility when use of their information tends to produce outcomes that are less desirable than those that otherwise are probable. Utility is the degree of attainment of preferred outcomes by means of responsiveness to the forecast. Accordingly, forecasts may be important but may not have positive utility. We can bring this consideration to bear in assessing forecasts and forecasting methodology without having to consider the degree to which the policy system(s) is in fact responsive. Application does require a judicious degree of thinking through the implications were the policy system to be responsive to the forecast.

More formally, the utility of forecasts (UF) depends on the extent to which the gap between the desired state of affairs (DS) and that achieved by responding to the forecast (OF) is less than that between the desired state and what would have occurred without the forecast (O). $UF = f[(DS - O) - (DS - OF)]$. What about the possible case where the desired state is exceeded because of responsiveness to the forecast? Technically, the

problem is easily handled by specifying that $(DS - OF) \leq O$. More substantively, in a world of scarce resources and incompatible utilities, such overshooting probably imposes costs on other items of value and thus is disfunctional.

Weak performance on our utility consideration often is associated with a failure to spell out (and examine carefully) assumptions and second and third order effects (Bauer, 1969). Some international relations examples will illustrate this point. Forecasts that predict that substantial military expenditures will result in national superiority often leave implicit the ability of other governments to respond competitively. Forecasts that contend that pursuit of nuclear power will produce energy interdependence may not deal with the net cost/benefit ratios for given time periods of alternatives such as coal which do not involve the distribution of long-lived hazardous materials and the potential to produce more.

In practice, foreign affairs policy operators have been particularly eager to secure warning forecasts. Accordingly, it is important to note that application of this consideration may suggest that some warning forecasts have negative utility. Three types of instances that share this negative property merit explicit recognition. First, warnings that make a possible negative future situation seem overwhelming may create a generalized feeling of powerlessness and arouse so much fear as to make any coping action seem fruitless (see the report by Janis and Feshback, 1953, pp. 78–92). Second, well-known warning forecasts that have not come true in fact may reduce vigilance and thus responsiveness to subsequent warnings (the so-called cry-wolf phenomenon) (Wolfenstein, 1957). Third, warning forecasts may generate an exaggerated response which itself produces the negative future situation it was designed to avoid. For example, some analysts treat forecasts of adversary weapons-build-ups with resulting missile gaps as triggers for military procurements which in turn produce increased weapons-build-ups by the adversary.[3]

Timeliness

We are used to treating the element of time in forecasting as the time perspective of the prediction, for example, short-term, mid-range, long-term. In this usage, time refers to the chronological interval between the time at which the forecast is made and the time at which the forecast is supposed to be realized. The consideration of timeliness refers to a different concern. Forecasts are timely when they suggest actions sufficiently far ahead of time that, if carried out, they will alter the otherwise probable future. Timeliness is a necessary condition for importance and thus for utility. The extent to which a forecast is effective in the sense of timely depends on a number of factors. The timeliness of a forecast (TF) depends on the extent to which the time interval between the outcome being forecast (OBF) less the time to choose an action (ACT) to affect that outcome exceeds or equals the length of time required for that action to have the desired impact (AIT). Thus,

$$TF = f[(OBF - ACT) - AIT].$$

Forecasts cannot be timely unless $(OBF - ACT) \leq AIT$.

One can increase the timeliness of a forecast by affecting any of the three terms in the definition. Forecasts can be made to cover increasingly distant points in the future, thus raising the value of OBF. One can reduce the time required to secure resources and authorization to make forecasts, to produce forecasts, to disseminate their results, and to select actions responsive to the results, thus decreasing the value of ACT. Finally, one can reduce the time required for actions to have impact on the future as one gains in causal understanding of the situation to be affected. To the extent that one can count on quick implementation of chosen courses of action, the value of AIT will decrease accordingly. Note that many of the determinants of timeliness are properties of the forecast producers and consumers and their relationships more than of the forecast content and methodology *per se*. Given our view of forecasts as purposeful social actions, these properties enter into judgments about how effective a particular forecast has been or will be.

We cannot apply this consideration at all to forecasts with no specified time horizon—for example, the forecast that the world will become more interdependent, or more hungry, etc. End-state forecasts do little to clarify how timely are their implications since actions bearing on outcomes are not directly addressed. Accordingly, if we value highly the timeliness consideration, we are led to prefer contingent forecasts that are quite specific

about the components in each path to the values of the outcome variables. For example, the timeliness consideration is served less well by an end-state forecast of massive famines in the decade 1985–1995 than by a contingent forecast that shows the impact on the degree of famine of alternative combinations of weather, seed strains, fertilizer production, distribution of food production inputs and of food harvested, and timetables for each combination.

Reduction of Uncertainty

We view reduction of uncertainty as the fourth consideration central to appraising the effectiveness of forecasts and forecasting methodologies. Forecasts can reduce uncertainty in at least two major ways. First, they can differentiate the likelihood of one future relative to other possible futures. What we have referred to earlier as end-state forecasting reduces uncertainty to the extent that different probabilities are assigned to different conceivable futures. Betting on international outcomes, like horse-racing outcomes, benefits from odds that differentiate the probability of each outcome from every other outcome as contrasted with lumping the likelihoods together. Accordingly, an appropriate summary of uncertainty reduction for end-state forecasts ($UREF$) is the average difference in probabilities between each end state considered. To get this estimate, we need to calculate the difference in probabilities assigned to the members of every pair of outcomes under consideration divided by the number of possible pairs. The formalism is:

$$UREF = f \left(\frac{\displaystyle\sum_{i=1}^{n} \sum_{j=1}^{n} |P_i - P_j|}{\dfrac{n(n-1)}{m}} \right)$$

where P = probability assigned to an **end-state**
   n = number of end-states to which probabilities are assigned in the forecast
   m = 2.

Under this formula, end-state forecasts do more to reduce uncertainty when they deal with a small number of possible outcomes and discriminate their probabilities sharply—for example, that the nuclear club will or will not have a South American and an African member by 1980—than when they deal with numerous possible outcomes that are not differentiated according to likelihood—for example, by 1980, the nuclear club may include Brazil, and/or Israel, and/or Egypt, and/or South Africa, etc.

Second, forecasts can reduce uncertainty as they differentiate the extent to which the probabilities of a particular future being realized change as different courses of action are taken and different circumstances evolve prior to the forecast time point. This is what contingent forecasts seek to do. End-state forecasts are transformed into our contingent type when the analyst shows how outcome probabilities vary (i.e., are sensitive to) alternative circumstances. The logic for an assessment of the reduction of uncertainty by contingent forecasts resembles that for end-state forecasts with the difference that we focus on how the probabilities of a given outcome vary with different courses of action.

$$URCF = f \left(\frac{\sum\limits_{i=1}^{n} \sum\limits_{j=1}^{n} |R_i - R_j|}{\frac{n(n-1)}{m}} \right)$$

where R = probability assigned to the end-state under a particular course of action
n = number of distinct courses of action for which probabilities assigned to the end-state
m = 2.

Again, the reduction of uncertainty is best served by discriminating the probability of the alternatives considered rather than by an undifferentating extension of the set of possibilities. For example, uncertainty does not decline very much if a forecast states that lots of different occurrences may improve the economic welfare of the poor peoples of the globe—resource cartels, economic interdependence, R&D breakthroughs, humanitarianism, revolution, etc. Uncertainty is reduced to a greater extent by a forecast which with regard to the future economic welfare of the global poor shows that a uniform "what-the-market-will-bear" pricing policy by a petroleum cartel is substantially more likely to depress the prospects for the global

poor than a two-price policy by that same cartel in which the poor do not have to meet the market competition of the rich.

It seems useful to emphasize our view that forecasting of both the end-state and contingent types should produce a set of comparative probability statements. Even if these are implicit, they must be present if we are to work intelligently with the results. When only one end-state or only one intervening course of action receives attention, the consumer of the forecast is left to infer either that the probability of that one possibility discussed is extremely high relative to all others or, more critically, that the forecaster does not know the probabilities of others or does not care to reveal them. In the latter instances, the consumer is unlikely to find his uncertainty reduced appreciably (except perhaps in his opinion of the forecaster!).

Relevance

Forecasts are effective, among other considerations, to the extent to which they are relevant. In the cast of end-state forecasting, relevance means the extent to which the aspects of the future addressed are of interest to the intended consumers. In the case of contingent forecasting, relevance means the extent to which the alternative courses of action lie within the set of behavioral opportunities available to the intended consumers. Relevance for both types may be thought of in set-theory terms. The relevance of end-state forecasting (REF) depends on the intersection $(\cap)$ between futures of interest to consumers (FIC) and futures addressed in the forecast (FF).

$$REF = f\left(\frac{FF \cap FIC}{FF}\right) .$$

The relevance of contingent forecasting (RCF) depends on the intersection between courses of action open to consumers (CAI) and courses of action addressed in the forecast (CAF).

$$RCF = f\left(\frac{CAF \cap CAI}{CAF}\right)$$

Recognition of relevance as a consideration with regard to effectiveness does not imply that forecasters should only deal with matters of interest to consumers. It does imply that when they do not, the effectiveness of the forecast as a social intervention will suffer. To argue otherwise would be to assert, for example, that the effectiveness of weather forecasts is not affected by the extent to which economic decision makers understand the implications of the phenomena predicted for their sector of economic performance (the analogy is drawn from Monin, 1972, pp. 174–175).

In this formulation the relevance of a forecast can be altered either by changes in forecast content or by changes in the identity, interests, and authority of consumers. The heterogeneity of consumers argues against those who offer the same forecast to all—president and generals, peasants and workers. Some interdependencies with our timeliness, importance, and reduction of uncertainty considerations can usefully be made explicit. The set of futures of interest depends on the time horizon involved both for end-states and courses of action. The extent to which persons and institutions have the authority to engage in unusual and far-reaching courses of action does depend in large part on the importance of the consequences involved. And we know that individuals and institutions often tend to set aside possible futures and options for dealing with them when the whole situation seems highly uncertain. To go one step further, if we are dealing with forecasts with unspecified time horizons, whose importance is moot, and which do little to reduce uncertainty, we cannot meaningfully estimate their relevance. However, if time horizons are clear and their importance substantial, the inability to reduce uncertainty may not deprive the forecast of relevance. Decision makers can conclude that they had best move cautiously and hedge their choices.

Durability

Finally, forecasts tend to be effective also as they are durable, that is, relatively invulnerable to particular items of new information. The durability consideration tends to be met when the arrival of new information incompatible with some element of the forecast does not thereby imply that the whole forecast should be discarded. An obvious, and regretably familiar way of achieving durability is to make forecasts so vague and all-encompassing that it becomes difficult to find any information item incompatible with them. This tactic, however, runs counter to the reduction of uncertainty and

the timeliness considerations. A more suitable adaptation is to make the forecast modular so that parts of it can be changed in response to additional information without having to discard the whole. Forecasts clearly have this property to the extent that they are decomposable into relatively autonomous elements. Another, less restrictive adaption is to incorporate in the forecast an explicit predictive structure that can be used to recalculate forecast conclusions using values and relational statements warranted by new information. One wants to make iteration easy rather than difficult.

The type of forecasting methodology in which all relationships and variable positions are stipulated explicitly lends itself to the sort of adjustment and salvage compatible with our durability consideration. A methodology that is extremely implicit about the relationships and data points used to arrive at an estimate about the future does not allow for facile adjustment. We would, for example, expect a computer simulation of the dynamics of NATO cohesion and disintegration to be more durable in our sense than a verbal discussion in which much of the forecaster's reasoning and data are essentially private.

In sum, we suggest that forecasts are effective as they perform well in terms of six considerations: importance, utility, timeliness, reduction of uncertainty, relevance, and durability. We also contend that performance on any one of our considerations is sensitive to performance on others. Trade-offs are, of course, necessary. The next section suggests the relative importance of our different considerations according to the nature and weight of the purposes that a forecaster or those who allocate resources for a forecast may have. Before turning to those varied purposes, it seems well to emphasize that our commitment to the considerations discussed above does not imply that we regard all forecasts that do not do well on them as ineffective or worthless. After all, we may still respect a .250 batter in baseball even though we would prefer a .400 hitter, but we will have different expectations of and strategies for the use of each.

III. PURPOSE-SPECIFIC CONSIDERATIONS FOR EFFECTIVE FORECASTING

With due respect for the dangers and aridness of categorization schemes, some gross distinctions as to purpose can help us point out the varying importance of our general considerations and suggest considerations that are specific to a subset of purposes. We will treat forecasts in terms of seven nonexclusive, and not exhaustive, purposes: (1) social mobilization, (2) system replacement, (3) warning, (4) adaptive planning, (5) group perquisites, (6) efficient resource allocation, and (7) administrative control. Hopefully, the discussion will contribute to more critical consumption and evaluation of forecasts prepared by others.

Social Mobilization

Forecasts with a social mobilization purpose try to generate support to place some matter of concern on the agenda for collective action. The forecast may take one of two forms. In the first, it portrays a dire future as almost inevitable unless remedial actions are taken quickly. In the second, the forecast portrays a golden opportunity to reach an attractive future quickly slipping away. In either case, now is not too soon to start; it may even be too late. Common techniques include straight forward trend extrapolation and macro relationships (recently, these are being expressed in equations) whose scope conditions are not always stipulated. Such forecasts have been made with regard to population growth, the destructive power of weapons, and the population–natural resources balance (see Malthus, 1967; Meadows, *et al.*, 1972; Ogburn, 1972; Cole, *et al.*, 1973). Usually, all futures other than the black and white extremes are assigned extremely low probabilities. Just as the spectrum of futures often is very limited, so too is the discussion of the sensitivity of the future to alternative courses of action. Negative social mobilization forecasts usually assert a need for general, across-the-board actions to reverse trends but do not deal with the specific content of those actions in a comprehensive manner nor with the issue of "how much is enough." Positive social mobilization forecasts tend to assert that one course of action will achieve the desired end-state and that all others will fall markedly short.

Since the purpose of forecasts of this type is primarily agitational, the extent and nature of arousal they produce determines their success. Accordingly, the extent to which they are effective depends primarily on the perceptions they generate among different groups in the social system.

Since the point is to change the existing agenda, such forecasts must appeal to groups not fully committed to the existing agenda of the established system but in a political position to influence that agenda. In order to achieve social mobilization, such forecasts must be perceived as important, have strong and clear utility implications, and obviously must meet our timeliness criterion. To do so, they often invoke symbols such as "crisis"—for example, of energy or food supply—and "revolution"—for example, of rising expectations or national liberation. Since they are usually addressed to a broad constituency, and are imprecise about the contingencies that might intervene between the prediction and the time horizon of the forecast, durability is usually insured by vagueness about what would be incompatible events. Indeed, the trick is to reinforce durability by interpreting salient events as confirming evidence. In order to maximize relevance, the producers of social mobilization forecasts seek to make the problem or opportunity under discussion as broad as possible, where appropriate actions are available to ordinary citizens as well as to elites.

An additional consideration must be brought into play for us to assess adequately the effectiveness of social mobilization forecasts. And that consideration is the legitimacy, in the sense of knowledge and disinterestedness, of the source. Parties with no economic or political benefit to gain but with some appropriate professional credentials are often seen as legitimate sources—for example, academics, sages, theologians. Of course, as the gospel spreads, the newest recruits become sources for others not yet convinced of or familiar with the forecast. Social mobilization forecasts are likely to meet the legitimacy consideration to the extent that their visible adherents also possess legitimacy. To the extent that the initial adherents are from low-credibility social elements or from groups seen as threatening for other reasons—such as "black militants," "long-haired kids," "fellow travelers," "right-wing deviationists,"—the forecast loses legitimacy and may even trigger a countermobilization.

System Replacement

Forecasts with a system replacement purpose put forward the high probability that a fundamental and inclusive future state of affairs differing radically from the present will occur. Furthermore, it is presumed that the new system will be a substantial improvement over the current state of affairs. The new system contrasts sharply with other possibilities and a gross outline sketches the transition from the present to the future, for example, Marx, Charles Reich (Marx and Engels, 1948; Marx, 1936; Reich, 1970). However, the precise timing and the priority of alternative specific actions is left open. The forecast claims explicitly that some types of present and future events mark progress toward the replacement of the current by the new system.

With reference to our general consideration, timeliness is met by keeping the end-state time of occurrence open. As a result, the forecast can never literally become discredited for timeliness reasons. System replacement forecasts seek to be effective by putting forward an important future, in the sense that the social relationships will be very different, and by establishing a certainty of positive utility to the vast majority of the population.

The role of utility does have some additional aspects that merit our attention. One common way of buttressing imputed positive utility is by arguing that the new system will have negative utility for certain fractions of the social system who are hurting the majority—for example, imperialists, rich ethnic minorities. Hopefully, the bad elements will notice the forecasts and express hostility to its sources, thus catalyzing the "my enemy's enemy is my friend" pattern. Such expressions of hostility buttress the utility of the forecast. However, they also can make the forecast less effective in terms of reduction of uncertainty and durability.

It is crucial for the new system to seem certain of realization and in order to do that it must not be discredited by intervening events. That is, it must be durable in terms of withstanding two sorts of shocks. The first is from the occurrence of actions that imply movement away from the posited endstate. For example, if the forecast asserts linear development toward a world of socialist governments, a threat is posed by the occasional replacement of those governments by less socialist regimes—for example, the fate of Allende in Chile. The second type of shock is from actions that proponents of the forecast hail as progress toward the end-state but which for many others cast doubt on its desirability. For example, the elimination of "hostile social elements" following a revolution may raise doubts about the net benefits of the new system of the

withering away of the state hailed in the forecast. As another example, a forecast of economic interdependence as a new system may seem less attractive if steps toward interdependence seem to lead to massive power on the part of multinational corporations that are unrepresentative of different groups in the world and under less than complete control by any group of political officials. In sum, when opponents mobilize, they may be able to take actions that seem to be "setbacks" and that make the whole forecast less convincing unless those events can be deprived of significance or transformed into signs of progress. When proponents believe that opponents are or are likely to become capable of imposing setbacks, they may take preemptive actions apparently at odds with the portrayed replacement system.

Warning

Forecasts with a warning purpose seek to provide explicit, highly reliable statements that a negative event of a specific kind will or will not occur at a specified time (or within a specified and narrow range of time) in the future. At a minimum, they are effective to the extent that they provide notice that the probability of the event occurring or not occurring has changed substantially since the last forecast.

Before we discuss warning forecasts in terms of our general considerations, it is important to emphasize the seriousness of many of the international relations occurrences for which statesmen and citizens would like to have warnings. The nature of the predicted events—such as war, famine, revolution—are such that measures to ameliorate their consequences involve major disruptions of routine and therefore carry with them substantial costs. This inherent costliness may or may not also be true of actions in response to warning to avert the unwanted event. It varies with the nature of contingency plans and the dynamic effects that different actions may produce—for example, the inherent costs of using the Washington–Moscow hotline are substantially less directly and possibly less indirectly than raising military alert status. To return to the courses of action to ameliorate consequences, the relationships of costs to the correctness of warning forecasts tend to be in the following order. The costs of ameliorative measures if the warning is warranted tend to be less than the costs of not taking such steps under that condition. However, they tend to be greater than the costs of not taking the ameliorative steps should a warning that an unwanted event will occur turn out to be wrong. While the costs of false warning are a product of many factors, it is important to note that for an important subset of international events of a military character they jump sharply as actions to ameliorate consequences take the form of irrevocable hostile acts. For example, in the case of warning of a nuclear attack, the actions taken might emphasize population dispersal or launching intercontinental ballistic missiles. The latter is more irrevocable and the costs of erroneous warning are likely to be greater.

When we turn to our general considerations for effective forecasts, we find that warnings must be important to be at all effective. If the notice given does not have implications for possible ways of ameliorating the consequences or changing the likelihood of the unwanted event, the forecast has little worth. Importance for warning forecasts is closely associated with their timeliness. Sufficient lead-time to avoid or ameliorate outcomes turns importance in principle into importance in practice. Timeliness requires that the dynamics of international relations producing the event do not have such momentum as to outrun feedback. In this context, efforts to build pauses into escalation scenarios and to invent more and more steps short of irrevocable actions represent attempts to decrease momentum and thus increase the chances that warnings of impending hostilities will be timely. The negative or positive utility of warning forecasts depends significantly, as we have noted, on their accuracy. This is particularly true in tense international relationships in which inaccurate warning forecasts may be seen by a suspicious foreign government or domestic opposition as attempts to create an excuse for serious and otherwise unwarranted measures. The relevance consideration interacts with that of timeliness in that the effectiveness of warning depends on quick communication between he who hears the forecast and he who can act on it. In practice, this assessment rule is relatively well understood and warning forecasts, more than those of many other types, are preprogramed into specified chains of communication, command, and control. Forecasts with a warning purpose are particularly apt illustrations of

the extent to which how effective a forecast is depends on factors outside of the forecast itself.

Given the costs of accepting many warnings, producers and consumers of warning forecasts often are impelled to define the future dichotomously (the event will occur or will not), and to try to drive the probability of one side of the dichotomy as close to zero or unity as possible. Parenthetically, this tendency is reinforced by the relative difficulty of confirming whether forecasts that seek to reveal changes in probabilities are or are not sound. Especially in matters of cardinal importance, warning forecasts tend to become burdened (wisely or not) with the task of refuting all alternative explanations of the information that leads to issuing warning. This is particularly true because, given the "bad news" nature of warning, strong motivations are at work to find alternative explanations and thus deny the probable occurrence of the unwanted event. This desire to reject warning is familiar to students of foreign policy processes whether the event involves penetration of a sphere of influence, loss of dominance in a technology sector, or the failure of an attempt to bargain through and resolve a chronic conflict (for example, see Knorr, 1964, pp. 455–467; Whaley, 1973).

Accordingly, warning forecasts and forecasting methodologies have to be durable in a demanding manner to be effective. First, independent sets of information must converge on the same conclusion—for example, troop movements, the activities of political leaders, and diplomatic communications that draw on different sets of collection and reporting systems. Second, the data that point to the negative event occurring must be inherently more trustworthy indicators of what is to come than all other sets of available information. For example, if human sources suggest that the unwanted event will occur and satellite reconnaissance does not, it is critical that satellite collections are not almost automatically thought to be informative. Third, the forecasts must have a well-established record for not providing false warning. Otherwise, the extent to which they meet the durability consideration becomes degraded by doubts based on previous shortcomings. For example, if a warning system predicts an attack by a persistent adversary based on observing a substantial set of military deployments which turned out to be only an exercise, that system will have less credibility in the future should it predict attacks based on observed actions compatible with a military exercise. Fourth, if false warnings reduce confidence in a warning system, substantiated warnings build confidence. This poses a particularly difficult challenge to those who seek effective warning forecasts of as yet unexperienced events. To build confidence, they must find relevant fragments of those events that have a sufficient contemporary incidence to establish warning forecast accuracy. They must build a record of success in forecasting fragments necessary for the unexperienced negative event while at the same time demonstrating that the forecast did not go to the point of attaching an unwarrantedly high probability to the complete event.

To close, the need to use especially credible indicators again emphasizes the significance for effective forecasting of the beliefs of consumers and how well they fit with the beliefs of those who construct and operate the forecasting apparatus.[4] For example, a warning of world food shortages based on satellite photography and other instrumentation will not be deemed credible, except possibly after the fact, by consumers who distrust elaborate technology.

Adaptive Planning

Forecasts that try to aid in adaptive planning provide a complex contingency structure, which maps the period from the time at which the forecast is made to the time at which the forecast will come to pass.[5] The forecast usually presents a number of alternatives as possible, none of which carry a probability approaching unity. The power of such forecasts is in their ability to envision the chain of developments associated with particular probabilities for alternative end-states. With such knowledge, planners gain the following benefits. First, they are able to relate the choice of courses of action to different end-states and alter those choices as the preference for or probability of particular end-states changes. Second, the fleshed out contingency structure reveals the calculus of expectations on which probabilities were initially assigned to the end-states considered. Fresh information can readily be matched with those expectations, and the relational statements on which they were

based, and the forecast can be modified appropriately in an incremental fashion. Forecasts to serve adaptive planning attempt to provide the structure for a continuing process whose specific conclusions will change over time, rather than providing a more rigid conclusion that warrants an unswerving course of action. The capability for iterative forecasting well serves incremental decision making, a dominant decision-making style in policy systems faced with complex and uncertain futures.

How do we relate our general considerations for effective forecasts to those with an adaptive planning purpose? Such forecasts have to be important but not necessarily to a large proportion of the population. Adaptive forecasts are consumed by those who wish to steer a social system and devote large fractions of their time to that activity. The message of adaptive planning forecasts is that there are multiple possible futures rather than any one which is relatively certain and that inaction as well as action determines the eventual outcome. The chances for negative utility are minimized and those for positive utility maximized under most conditions because of the two benefits noted in the previous paragraph. The exceptions occur when the very complexity and multiple contingencies of the forecast impede necessary decisive actions. When this happens, the process of working with the forecast interferes with the conclusions necessary for our timeliness criterion to be met. Timeliness is difficult for yet another reason. Adaptive planning forecasts are extremely difficult and time consuming to construct for large scale problems. The difficulties multiply when numerous actors are involved where their relationships are sensitive to many diverse factors—diverse in substance, units of measurement, and time constants. For example, it is immensely more difficult to engage in adaptive forecasting about conventional military forces than it is to do so about strategic nuclear forces. The lead-time for the construction of adaptive forecasts in a technically sound fashion may, first, exceed the time for which an underlying conceptual model remains valid, and, second, sharply reduce the time interval available for selecting certain options and for those options to impact on the problem of interest.

Given the complexity and open system view central to adaptive planning forecasts, it seems paradoxical to note that they can notably reduce and identify uncertainty and indeed must demonstrate that capacity for anyone to bother with the work which their use involves. However, the paradox is of less concern when we recognize that the uncertainty reduction, if any, deals with the effects of alternative courses of action on a particular end-state's probabilities more than with the probability distribution across the set of considered end-states. For example, with regard to the management of ocean resources, we are more likely to reduce our uncertainty about the relative viability of a strategy that relies on the evolution of some new, authoritative international organization *versus* one that features specific agreements between heads of state, than we are to reduce uncertainty about the relative probability of international management *versus* the current situation. The relevance consideration is likely to be met to the extent that: (1) a wide range of contingent events and actions are incorporated into the model; (2) the technical approach used is congenial to planners; and (3) responsibility for the dimension(s) of the future dealt with in the forecast have been institutionalized as the responsibility of an identifiable group of planners. It is thus not surprising to find that adaptive forecasts are more effective with regard to more customary aspects of international affairs—for example, military, trade—than issue areas so fresh as to be lacking in mission organizations—for example, environment, ocean resources. Finally, the developed infrastructure of adaptive planning forecasts makes them almost invulnerable to blanket disconfirmation. Instead, even if an unexpected piece of information comes to light, the forecasters are in a good position to adjust their construct.

Group Perquisites

Forecasts whose purpose is the protection or expansion of group perquisites, or "perks," seek to make the case that collective success in dealing with the future depends on providing sufficient "goodies," be they money, deference, or authority, to the group producing the forecast. Otherwise, the outcome will be bleak. The hallmarks of such forecasts include great vagueness about courses of action, future end-states (other than the "worst case"), and time terms. Vagueness may be achieved by references to special information—for

example, technically esoteric or highly classified material, or by the use of concepts with no clear and common referent, such as national interest.[6]

Group perquisite forecasts have a rather easily recognizable pattern in terms of our general considerations. They claim important differences will be made by allocations to the favored group but do not discuss the sensitivity of the outcomes to different increases in allocation levels—for example, the sensitivity of national security outcomes to 10 or 20 percent increments to a budget or order of magnitude increases in research and development programs. The utility they claim emphasizes avoiding negative states. Forecasts with this predominant purpose have the knack of somehow sounding urgent, but reappearing periodically at resource allocation time and soon become hardy perennials ("light at the end of the tunnel"). In terms of our reduction of uncertainty consideration, group perquisite forecasts tend to do badly because all alternatives other than support of group perks are lumped together. They are relevant to all those who stand to benefit from resource allocation to the group and confirmation of its prescience. For example, different weapons scientists may disagree on particulars, but so long as the conflicting positions support the importance of weapons science expertise, the forecasts have common relevance (Wohlstetter, 1964, pp. 174–239). Such forecasts also have obvious relevance to direct competitors for resources. Accordingly, skillful perks forecasters go to considerable lengths to frame the forecast so that its implications appear to be public goods, such as national security, independence. With regard to durability, the forecasts use vagueness to make it difficult to identify disconfirming events. Indeed, the principle vulnerability of perks forecasts lies in the discovery of behaviors that shed doubt on the efficacy of the group to do well what it tries—for example, cost-over-runs on military systems, inconclusive results from prolonged diplomatic negotiations.

Efficient Resource Allocation

Forecasts whose purpose is to effect efficient resource allocation are attempts to specify the future, to pin it down, in order to decide on allocations in the present. They are frequently used when long lead-time items are involved that are useful for only a narrow subset of possible policies and when situations are examined and assigned costs and benefits in relation to a single or weighed set of future situations. The options are usually spelled out in great detail and often involve different mixes of the same set of hardware or program alternatives. Accordingly, resource allocation forecasts are usually contingent forecasts. They take the general form of comparisons between the consequences for a future situation if the course of action chosen in the present is X_1 rather than X_2. Producers of efficient resource allocation forecasts wish to assume that, or are bureaucratically compelled to act as if, they can choose the most desirable course of action at one point in time and that their choice will retain its value despite events beyond the control of the institutions whose resources are being allocated. If adaptive planning forecasts are attempts to maintain flexibility in an on-going process, resource allocation forecasts are anticipatory evaluations of alternative courses of action to prescribe some substantive commitments and foreclose others.

With reference to our general considerations, forecasts of this type seek to show that different volumes and distributions of resources will produce substantially different future situations. Since resources are always finite, positive utility must be established superior to that offered by alternative resource uses. The extent to which resource allocation forecasts are really effective with regard to utility depends in large measure on the breadth of options considered. Also, it matters whether or not the future whose consequences are to be altered has any significant probability of occurrence. The utility of this type of forecast depends, like that of warning forecasts, on accuracy. Inaccuracy will make the use of resources at best inefficient and at worst disfunctional. Since we are usually talking about resource allocations by large organizations with scheduled budgetary processes, timeliness is substantially affected by the extent to which the forecast meshes properly with the budgetary cycle and receives priority for implementation. We are confronted with lags that may well be on the order of several years before implementation of the recommended option actually begins, for example, military force structure.

The reduction of uncertainty sought by resource allocation forecasts is highly appropriate for our formal measure stated earlier. An effective forecast usually does not establish that one alternative has a probability close to unity but instead tends to discriminate well between the probabilities associated with each member of a sizeable set of alternative courses of action. The uncertainty reduced in this case concerns estimates of relative costs and benefits. Efforts to be effective in terms of our relevance consideration may take either of two forms. In the first, the forecaster examines alternatives within the problem definition supplied by the client, that is, options tied clearly to policy instruments and choices available to the officials of that institution. The result tends to be a narrow "operations-analysis" type of cost-effectiveness study. In the second, the forecaster analyzes the problem of his client for himself rather than being bound by the client's statement of the problem and allocation alternatives. Perhaps the best known example of the latter type is the strategic basing study by the Rand Corporation (Wohlstetter, *et al.*, 1954).

It is important to note that neither form usually considers fundamentally different missions including some beyond the jurisdiction of the client as resource allocation alternatives for dealing with an international relations problem. In the example just mentioned, analysts would consider many alternatives for maintaining deterrence but not diplomacy. Similarly, many resource allocation forecasts addressed to the problem of strategic stability which are sponsored by force management bureaucracies do not entertain the possibility of shifting resources to accelerate economic interdependence. The mission structures of existing bureaucracies often constrain the set of allocation alternatives examined.

Resource allocation forecasts may lack durability for several reasons. The first is that the future whose consequences were dealt with comes to seem extremely improbable. In this case, all the fine-grain comparisons of options against it seem trivial. The second is that an option arises that was not considered and is obviously superior to those which were examined. Perhaps the least vulnerable to these problems are those efficient resource allocation forecasts that explicitly recognize that the future situation of interest is extremely improbable but tremendously important should it come to pass. Since the probability of the future initially is pegged very low, the forecasts are not vulnerable to general rejection on the first ground mentioned above. Resource allocation forecasts about general nuclear war have had this advantage—which may be why a set of forecasting methodologies gained a reputation in this area which has not been sustained in applications to more probable, if perhaps less important, futures for which experience has provided a harsh set of tests.

Administrative Control

For administrative control, our final purpose, forecasts are devices to induce subordinates to engage in desired behaviors. They basically serve to establish what should be achieved within some specified time period and what resources will be available for achieving it. Unlike adaptive planning forecasts, those for administrative control try to confine the latitude of behavior open to subordinates. Accordingly, they are usually very specific, tend to state explicit measures that will be used to evaluate performance, and, once the forecasts are approved, make it clear that subordinates will be held accountable for failures to achieve stated targets on those measures. Examples include forecasts that a given foreign aid program will produce so many classrooms or highway miles by a given year, or that a certain foreign information program will result in the use of X number of stories based on copy provided by the foreign information office in Y number of indigenous newspapers over a specified time period.

Administrative control forecasts are important only when the state of affairs differs from that which would have occurred through bureaucratic inertia. That is, they are effective to the extent that they refer to some departure from the norm in administrative output. The utility of such forecasts becomes negative when they depress performance by providing unduly low targets or ones that seem impossible to attain. The timeliness problems resemble those for resource allocation forecasts. That is, the forecast must assert control in ways that mesh with the scheduled decision processes of the institution and must be made before those parts of the process that come earliest in any decision cycle. To the extent that administrative control forecasts leave substantial uncertainty about what is

expected of subordinates or fail to deal with courses of action within their control, they tend to be ineffective. Durability, our last general consideration, depends on the absence of doubt about the stability of the program preferences and authority of the superior officials. If these are seen as highly changeable, the utility of the forecast suffers.

IV. SUMMARY

We have argued that forecasts in international relations are purposeful behaviors that should be assessed as effective or ineffective in terms of considerations different from those applied to predictions made primarily as part of the pursuit of scientific knowledge. The principal reason for forecasting work in international relations or in any other area of collective concern is less Comte's to "know in order to foresee" than to know in order to achieve or prevent (Rolbiecki, 1970, p. 280). Some general considerations have across-the-board pertinence to forecasts (importance, utility, timeliness, reduction of uncertainty, relevance, and durability). However, the application and weight of these considerations must be adjusted in the light of the purpose of any particular forecasting activity. The seven purposes discussed call for substantially different adjustments. If we are to judge how effective forecasts made by others are, we must be prepared to first determine what their purpose was. And if as producers of forecasts we are to make our own choices wisely, we had best be clear on precisely what purpose we hope to serve.

NOTES

1. The classic discussion of self-fulfilling prophecies is that of Merton (1967), pp. 421–436. For a differently oriented discussion of the inadequacy of the predictive accuracy criterion, see Martino (1972), pp. 11–44.
2. Campbell and Stanley (1966); Caporoso and Roos, Jr. (1973). For an international relations example, see Caporoso and Pelowski (1971), pp. 418–433.
3. The arms-spiral dynamic occurs frequently in discussions of arms races and how to control them. The alleged phenomenon is inherent in, for example, the formulations of Lewis Frye Richardson. See Rashevsky and Trucco (1960).
4. For discussion of this and other factors dependent on the identity of producers and consumers, see

Wilensky (1967); Webb (1969); Rosenthal and Weiss (1966), pp. 302–340; Wohlstetter (1962).

5. Forrester states the problem well: ". . . the complex system is even more deceptive than merely hiding causes. In the complex system, when we look for a cause near in time and space to a symptom we usually find what appears to be a plausible cause. The complex system presents apparent causes that are in fact coincident symptoms . . . . In the complex system the cause of a difficulty may lie far back in time from the symptoms, or in a completely different and remote part of the system. (Forrester, 1969, pp. 9–10; Brunner and Brewer, 1972).

6. For example, see the discussion of the use of the term "national interest" in Rothstein (1972).

CHAPTER FOUR

THE FORECASTING POTENTIAL
OF INTERNATIONAL RELATIONS THEORIES

Cheryl Christensen

I. INTRODUCTION: REALITY TESTING
AND THE MAGIC OF FORECASTING

Freud once characterized primitive magic as a form of narcissism where the self-importance and self-infatuation of the magician prevented him from seeing that his wishes were insufficient to alter himself or his environment (Freud, 1918). Armed with a partial knowledge of the empirical regularities of nature and a pre-scientific understanding of human psychology, the magician attempted to fulfill much larger needs and desires: the need to control and exorcise the terrors of nature and the desire to be in fact what he was in psychic experience—the center of the universe. As a system for manipulating nature, primitive magic failed. The pressing needs to which magicians responded psychologically could not be genuinely met with the knowledge and skills at hand. While primitive magic brought a partially satisfying illusion of control, and the perpetual hope of greater success, the practices and attitudes it enshrined did not help produce more genuinely effective knowledge.

Less than charitable critics of social forecasting could easily raise the charge that forecasting, like primitive magic, is driven more by desire than capability. Few would deny that avoiding social and political crises appears to depend more upon developing better ways of steering complex modern societies, or that such steering in turn apparently requires greater insight into and attention toward the future.[1] Yet it can be argued that contemporary attempts to forecast by extrapolation, expert consensus, curve fitting, or imaginative insight are woefully inadequate tools with which to consciously and deliberately shape the future. The standard reply to such criticisms is that more *theory-based* forecasts are required. Whether this reply is a self-deluding platitude or an exciting social and intellectual challenge depends on how the forecasting potential of social science theories is evaluated.

The purpose of this chapter is to examine the forecasting potential of international relations theory (or theories). It is a difficult task, for as an exercise in reality testing it requires specifying what theory might contribute to forecasting, what it takes to make the contribution, and whether international relations theory has what it takes. The task is made more compelling by the wide-spread sense that the present era is a key transitional period in international relations, and that the choices made in the next few years will strongly shape the image of the future. Unrealistically downgrading the forecasting potential of international relations theory may justify short-sighted choices whose unanticipated consequences could be the roots of deeper future problems. Overplaying the capabilities of existing theory, when most attempts at building scientific theories occur in nations with strong international interests, could encourage both self-deception about the future consequences of present actions and pseudo-scientific rationalizations of political positions. The present demand for international forecasts, in the context of genuinely competing visions of future international orders, makes it imperative to address the normative dimensions of theory-based international forecasts. To fail to consider the interaction among theory, forecasts, and norms would be politically and intellectually naive.

The entire scope of international relations cannot be adequately discussed in a chapter of this length. For this reason, the assessment of theoretical forecasting potential will be made primarily in the context of international political economy and the political demands for a new international economic order. Because of the heavy concern with scarcities of resources and food, and the need to ascertain the long-term significance of recent economic crises, this issue-area is also substantively important to international forecasters. Sharp normative differences make it possible to examine the interplay between political norms and forecasts, while the emergence of new approaches focusing on concepts such as interdependence, linkage, and *de-pendencia* invite assessments of theoretical richness.

Within its established focus, this chapter will attempt to develop three central points. First, there is a basic tension between the aims and standards of forecasting, as it relates to scientific theory building, and decision-oriented forecasting. This tension is reflected both in different standards for "good" forecasts and in the manner in which errors in forecasting are identified and corrected. Overly simplistic conceptions of the dynamics of theory construction can disguise some of the political costs of incorporating theoretical forecasts into policy planning. Second, while no contemporary international relations theories are sufficiently elaborated or corroborated to contribute "detailed, precise, high-confidence prescriptions for action in any contingency," some have potential for making insightful contingent predictions, while others because of their theoretical incompleteness cannot make even this limited contribution.[2] Third, forecasts that are intellectually well grounded may still remain ineffective in catalyzing political discussion, affecting goals, or contributing to policy planning. Attempts to increase the salience of forecasts are frequently influence attempts in some political arena. Like "sophisticated voting," "sophisticated forecasting" may involve judging the significance of the expectations and interests of others for one's own position. Having *effective* forecasting potential may depend as much on the structure of the forecasting relationship as upon the intellectual quality of the forecast. It is worth remembering in this context that many failures in technological forecasting arose not because forecasters misjudged the potential for scientific innovation, but rather because they neglected to correctly assess the commitment of the socio-political milieu to developing that potential.[3]

II. ORIENTATIONS TOWARD FORECASTING

A forecast is a statement about possible situations, actions, or outcomes (future or counterfactual) that have not occurred, based on knowledge of what has happened and a specified connection between known occurrences and other possibilities. Time itself is a crucial variable in some forecasts. Technological forecasting and futurology are exclusively concerned with making statements about unknown outcomes whose location in time ("the future") is their most salient feature.[4] In other forecasts, the future *per se* may be less important. A scientist may forecast that under some experimental conditions not yet created, a particular outcome may occur. Generally the fact that the experiment will be undertaken "in the future" is far less salient than the way in which the experimental situation differs from what has already been observed. Substantive theory is generally required to specify explicitly the conditions under which a forecast is expected to hold. The utility of forecasts, either to decision makers or to academic investigators, is **generally greater when the forecasts are explicitly conditional, have well defined domains of application**, and provide estimates of the probability associated with them under specified conditions.

Forecasting has been undertaken within the context of different analytical perspectives, implying different perspectives on both formulating and evaluating forecasts. While in the final analysis most forecasting will have implications for human choice and action, in some forecasting perspectives the central focus of forecasters is to make direct and immediate inputs into human decision making; in others, forecasts are seen as the products emerging from more general processes of substantive inquiry. Oversimplifying considerably, from the *technical perspective*, forecasting is primarily concerned with finding techniques for specifying a connection between known occurrences and a narrow range of future possibilities. Forecasts are justified in terms of the methods that produce them. From the *decision (or policy) perspective*, forecasting is concerned with generating information to improve decision making. Specifying technical estimates is only one way to achieve this. It may be equally important to develop ways of expanding the number of alternatives considered in decisions, systematizing informal judgments about the possible effects of different factors, providing organizational methods for identifying unanticipated consequences, lengthening the time horizon of decision makers, and removing the element of surprise to permit smoother planning. Some technological forecasting and most business forecasting has this orientation. Forecasts are justified in terms of the consequences they have for decision-making procedures and outputs.[5] From the *academic perspective*, forecasting is embedded in substantive inquiry. Forecasts are both the products of inquiry and a means for assessing the correctness of theories and explanations. Forecasts are generally undertaken with a view toward expanding knowledge and finding theoretically meaningful connections between known occurrences and other possibilities. Improvements in decision making are conceived to be primarily the product of increased knowledge. Hence, forecasts are useful to the extent one can be reasonably confident that they are valid. Forecasts are justified in terms of the results obtained in testing them, and the corroboration that can be provided for the body of knowledge from which they are derived.

Differences in aims and goals among the three perspectives have important implications for attempts to define the role of theory in forecasting or the potential a particular theory has for filling that role. The most important tensions are those between forecasting directed primarily at affecting human decision-making processes and orientations that focus primarily on producing corroborated bodies of knowledge that may *at some point* yield forecasts that are salient to decision makers. Individuals within the decision perspective, aware of the necessity to make a decision even without explicitly formulated and defended forecasts, examine forecasting methodologies and substantive theories in terms of their ability to contribute, even marginally, to current decision making.[6] Academic forecasters are frequently sensitive to the fact that even marginal contributions depend on the corroboration of theories and the assumptions of methodologies. Dramatic failures can result from attempts to apply empirically untested formal theories in a perscriptive forecasting mode.[7]

The Academic Perspective

Academic forecasts are generated in the process of exploring theories, or in Lakatos' terms, formulating and exploring research programs. Forecasting is not simply the *product* of a mature scientific theory, but an integral part of theory development as well. Testing and validation are paramount concerns of academic forecasters for two reasons. First, attempts to test forecasts and use the results of tests to corroborate or falsify competing theoretical perspectives are necessary to the growth and cumulation of scientific knowledge. Second, the confidence scholars place in applied forecasts rests on the extent to which they emerge from well corroborated theories. Unless forecasting, as defined in the academic perspective, occurs within research programs, hopes for high-confidence, applied forecasts are simply wishful thinking.

Examined from this perspective, forecasting has several important features. First, forecasts are formulated and tested within the context of research programs. What is interesting or important to forecast is defined with respect to the unsolved problems of a theoretical perspective, and the guidelines (positive and negative heuristics) that focus scientific investigation.[8] Lakatos suggests that the cumulation of scientific research stems in part from the fact that forecasting and testing are organized around a hard core of basic theoretical concerns (Lakatos, 1970, p. 132). As some international relations theorists have observed, there may be trade-offs between making forecasts that are "relevant" to cumulative knowledge accumulation and making forecasts that are "relevant" to applied problem solving.[9]

A second feature of academic forecasting is that it stimulates a dynamic adjustment of measurement theories as well as theoretical models. On the basis of a theoretical model, forecasts about an as yet unobserved situation or outcome may be made. The forecast is conditional in two ways. First, it suggests the theoretical conditions under which a result is expected. Second, it suggests the conditions under which the measurement theory employed is expected to be correct. Hence, *if the theoretical model is correctly specified and complete and if the underlying measurement theory is correct, then* a certain result is expected (Lakatos, 1970, pp. 116–132). Obtaining a different result (forecast failure) suggests that *either* the theoretical *relationships were incorrectly specified or* the measurement theory was incorrect. The dynamics of science often involve attempting to establish which of these possibilities is correct. The scientist may, for example, add another factor to the model or suggest more appropriate measurements. The logic of the research program suggests that the scientist explore these alternatives before concluding that the basic premises of the theoretical approach (its hard core) is wrong.

Within this perspective, there is no single test, no critical experiment, that allows the scientist to judge how much confidence ought to be put in a particular theory (Lakatos, pp. 154–159). Judgments about theoretical completeness and measurement procedures emerge over time as the result of a series of forecasts and test. Only as more and more potentially promising adjustments fail to produce new, corroborated, empirical findings does it become "rational" to give up a research program. Only as more and more attempts to test a theory strongly yield positive results do scientists develop confidence in its corroboration.

It is clear, then, why testing and validation remain primary concerns of academic forecasters. There is no point at which it is safe to say that a theory is proved, and hence, open to uncritical application. Application cannot be divorced from the continuing investigation process. In most engineering fields, practical techniques are adjusted to reflect progress in related theoretical knowledge. As this chapter will demonstrate shortly, it may be extremely difficult to achieve such an adjustment in the context of international decision making.

Under what circumstances could international relations theories have applied forecasting potential? By implication, a nontrivial elaboration of a theoretical hard core must occur. This, in turn, requires that a theory be capable of being formulated in a testable manner, that observation or measurement theories exist to relate the theory to an empirical base, and that methods for corroborating or rejecting forecasts be developed. In addition, it must be possible to identify some of the assumptions contained in *ceteris paribus* clauses, and be able to explore them rigorously enough to provide corroborating or falsifying evidence for the theory itself. The potential for making applied forecasts not directly motivated by theoretical concerns rests on being able to ground them in relatively well-corroborated theoretical models. In addition, the forecaster needs to apply the same rigorous testing of measurement assumptions and careful analysis of conditions to the forecasting model.

The Decision Perspective

Decision-oriented forecasts frequently assess the importance of validity in forecasting quite differently (Martino, 1973, pp. 26–52). How a forecast is evaluated depends in part on the situation in which it is applied. The most important variable in defining the situation is the amount of control the decision maker has in the milieu in which he operates (Martino, 1973, pp. 26–28). Where a decision maker has complete control, there is no practical need for forecasts. In situations where the decision maker has no control over the environment, the purpose of a forecast must be to aid in adapting to expected situation. For such cases, a "bad forecast" is one that does not accurately predict what will occur. Incorrect forecasts are useless, or worse, because the decision maker may be mislead into foregoing other adaptive options that might have minimized his losses or taken better advantage of the situation as it actually emerged.

Most decision situations, however, are situations in which there is partial control. In these circumstances, decision makers generally want to do more than passively adapt. They want to tailor actions to make maximum use of their resources. In order to do this, they need to know the probable outcomes of various courses of action open to them. What is required is a collection of contingent, counterfactual predictions.[10] As Martino correctly notes, the correctness of forecasts, defined in terms of whether or not they came true, is not the best standard for evaluating them. Forecasts of "evils" that become self-negating once made may be successful forecasts, as would be self-fulfilling forecasts of achievable "goods." In addition, forecasts that are incorrect may still be useful. Forecasts warning of dangers that do not materialize may catalyze preparations that reduce risks in other areas. Hence, Martino argues the forecast user is not interested in whether the forecast came true, or even whether it might have come true; his real concern is with whether the forecast given as information for making a decision is useful in doing so, and whether it is likely to contribute to making a good decision.

When the term "validity" is used in this context, it often implies a judgment about whether a forecast can validly be used as an input into a specific decision process, something an academic forecaster might call appropriateness. The attempt is made to match the informational needs (who needs to know what, how badly, over what time period) with the factors (variables) relevant to the need. Attempts are made to produce a check list of important variables (relevance tree), to determine if all relevant variables have been taken into account, and finally, to ascertain the reliability of the information pre-

sented in forecasts.[11] The predominance of forecasting techniques that are essentially means for ordering information to assist in planning (relevance trees, morphological approaches, cross-impact matrices) suggest the paramount importance of defining and evaluating relevant variables. Quite often the actual estimation of importance, interaction effects, or probability are left to subjective judgment, either individual or collective (Delphi techniques, brainstorming, scenario construction).

Under what circumstances could international relations theories have decision-oriented forecasting potential? By implication, theories should contain variables that are relevant to on-going decision processes. At a minimum, the theory should be able to provide a consistent ordering of variables, a means for assessing the direction of their effect, and a method for identifying interaction effects. Beyond this, theories must identify politically manipulable variables and establish theoretical links to action. Beyond this, theories should be able to suggest *theoretically grounded* contingencies that need consideration, and ideally should be rich enough in their structure to produce conditional, counterfactual assessments of the likely results of specific decision alternatives. This might be possible if theories were *complete,* and formulated *schedules* of capabilities in the context of theoretically based models of probabilistic outcomes.[12]

Even this brief discussion of forecasting perspectives should suggest several points. First, in both the academic and the decision-oriented orientations, the *completeness* of a theory is of paramount importance. The ability to produce counterfactual conditional statements depends upon the *ordering* of theoretical relationships, and hence upon the structure of a theory, not simply on its proposition considered individually (Simon and Resher, 1966, pp. 323–340). To have a genuinely theory-based forecasting capability, theory development must be sufficiently advanced to either permit forecasting technically complex enough to include all salient relationships or to make theoretically based judgments about the distortions arising from omissions. Second, in both orientations, explicitly conditional forecasts are critical. Forecasts made without specifying conditions contribute little new knowledge in an academic context, while providing little practical guidance in decision-making contexts.

Achieving forecasts that are themselves genuinely conditional (not simply given conditional interpretations by those using them) implies the need to develop forecasts from theoretical models capable of producing different estimates of parameters and outcomes under varying conditions. The attempt to seriously build policy-relevant forecasting models, however, may well make clear some of the trade-offs between academic forecasting procedures and decision-oriented requirements. If the purpose of forecasting models is to provide alternatives to the process of judging intuitively how situations are likely to develop or what is likely to be effective, a great deal of emphasis must be placed on assessing the theoretical structure of forecasting models.

There is good reason for this. Simon and Resher have demonstrated that the properties we commonly associate with the concept of "cause" are not properties of one specific relationship (a causal operator) but instead emerge from the ordering of functional relationships (1966, pp. 323–340). Each of the relationships, taken alone, may have properties we reject as properties of a causal connection—for example, they may be reversible. Yet the ordering of the relationships imposes the asymmetry we associate with the idea of cause. Significantly, if key relationships are omitted, the ordering will be different—producing an incorrect causal hierarchy. Since the ability to make accurate counterfactual conditional statements, essential to the evaluation of alternative hypothetical courses of action, depends upon the causal hierarchy (the ordering of functional relationships), an incomplete model will produce incorrect forecasts (Simon and Resher, pp. 329–330). In a convergent analysis of causal explanation, von Wright has demonstrated that when key elements of a theoretical system are excluded, judgments about necessary and sufficient conditions may similarly be in error (1971, pp. 34–82).

There are thus two possible dangers in forecasting from incomplete theoretical models. Not only will the range of available options for action be too small, but it is possible that even within the constricted range, the action prescriptions based on the model will be wrong.

As a forecasting model becomes more complex, it is increasingly difficult for decision makers to separate surprising forecasts that are genuinely counterintuitive possibilities from surprising results that arise from model incompleteness or mis-specification. If complex forecasts are to serve any useful purpose, decision makers must seriously consider the possibility of counterintuitive results. Yet forecasting models accepted uncritically may introduce serious errors into decision-making processes. This is particularly acute since (if philosophers of science like Lakatos are at all correct), scientific investigation produces no single test, no "instant rationality" that allows us to judge how much confidence ought to be put in a particular theory. Judgments about its completeness, and the accurateness of its measurement assumptions, emerge over time, as the result of a series of forecasts and tests. Indeed, Lakatos maintains that attempting to identify a particular theory as scientific is operating at the wrong unit of analysis. What must be evaluated in judging scientificalness is the relationship among successive theories (Lakatos, 1970, pp. 118–122). We cannot know for sure if a theory is complete, and the observations supporting it validly observed, but we can know if our learning proceeds in the direction of more comprehensive, powerful formulations.

This analysis suggests that scientists or philosophers of science will not be able to specify an objective point at which one might, with certainty of its correctness, apply a theory. This has particularly acute implications for the social sciences, for application cannot be divorced from the continuing investigation process. In most engineering fields, practical techniques are adjusted to reflect progress in their related theoretical science. The same may not be easy to assure in social engineering, where, for example, bureaucratic structures established on the basis of theoretical knowledge at one point in time may be difficult to adjust to new knowledge.

A dilemma then arises for forecasting that attempts to integrate developing theoretical knowledge and continuing political practice. The instances in which theoretically based forecasts are most necessary are those in which discontinuities with existing trends may be emerging, or systemic behavior is likely to exhibit counterintuitive behavior. Yet forecasting such situations puts an extremely heavy demand on theory. Not only must the *content* of theory be developed to the point where nontrival insights into politics emerge, but the philosophy of science underlying theory development must also be meshed with decision-oriented forecasting attempts. This means (minimally) models that are open to adjustment, and may be subject to frequent changes, must also be able to make consistent enough forecasts to have their recommendations seriously considered in a political decision milieu. As the earlier discussion of academic forecasting implied, such intellectual requirements of forecasting efforts may clash with features of the political environment in which they operate. In an environment where continuous experimenting and updating is possible at relatively small social cost, such a program is feasible. In an environment where policies are difficult to readjust to forecasting modifications, forecasting programs may become self-encapsulated, or even worse, positively maladaptive. Furthermore, competing perspectives and frequent model modification, central to the confidence scientists place in their work, may detract from political confidence in forecasting models. This will be especially true where policy changes are not politically easy to implement, or where the realities of adjusting competing interests dictate compromise policies including only some of the theoretically relevant provisions. Hence, features of forecasting most desirable and essential from an academic prospective (sufficient complexity, openness to continual testing, and adjustments from competing intellectual perspectives) may detract from the potential utility forecasts may have in decision-making contents.

III. FORECASTING IN THE CONTEMPORARY INTERNATIONAL MILIEU

While it remains difficult to ascertain which theories have forecasting potentials, and *when* the potential could (and *should*) be used, it is less difficult to identify theoretical, structural weaknesses in approaches that deny theories forecasting potential. It is conventionally asserted that an inability to operationalize concepts, formulate relationships, or obtain enough empirically founded relations denies contemporary international relations approaches forecasting potential. This may be true but it remains only part of the problem. Even more basically, the theoretical structure upon which projections are made may suggest they have little potential for making sound forecasts, even if they can be operationalized and linked to over-time relationships. The purpose of this section is to provide two examples of theoretical structures that

have been inadequate to support sound forecasts for conceptual reasons: (1) neo-Malthusian theories of the population-food interaction, and (2) classical models of international economic transactions that are predicated upon the assumption that natural economics may be treated as relatively "closed" entities. In both cases, conceptual readjustments, not better measurements, are required for additional forecasting potential.

In 1789 Thomas Malthus provided a dramatic analysis of the relationship between population growth and food supply. He suggested that while human population had the potential to grow at a geometric rate, food production was limited (by a finite stock of cultivatable land and diminishing returns) to an arithmetic rate of growth (Malthus, 1963). It is widely recognized that Malthus made a major error in assuming that technological change was not possible in the agricultural sector. Along this dimension, contemporary neo-Malthusians improve upon Malthus by suggesting that rather than being rigidly constrained, agricultural output is subject to both increases due to technological innovation and corresponding limitations to growth under those technologies. Most neo-Malthusians do no better than Malthus in assessing realistic potentials for population growth and control. Like Malthus, they recognize both positive (death-rate increasing) and preventive (birth-rate decreasing) measures to limit population growth, and like Malthus, they hold little hope for voluntary restraints on births. Here they may be faulted, for there is increasing evidence that under favorable socio-economic conditions, such methods may be highly effective. In one respect, most neo-Malthusians are more short sighted than Malthus himself. It is not widely recognized that Malthus' later work attempted to include a system of economic distribution in his conception of the relationship between population growth, food supply, and industrial growth (Malthus, 1951). Contemporary neo-Malthusian analyses theoretically neglect explicit treatments of distribution systems, hence in effect assume them to be neutral and unalterable. This is a major conceptual error, and one which limits both the understanding of the global food crisis which can emerge from this perspective, and the policy options available for coping with it.

Almost all neo-Malthusian models fail to incorporate systems of distribution explicitly in their models. Some analysts, like Lester Brown, are sensitive to the fact that redistribution of food resources, conditional on a change in dietary tastes in advanced industrial states, would dramatically alter the world food prospects—and perhaps even the prospect for population control (Brown, 1973). Yet because Brown discusses the structure and genesis of the "food crisis" without making clear how distribution contributes to it, policy recommendations on redistribution are theoretically *ad hoc*. This is so because the system of distribution defines what constitutes effective demand, and it is *effective demand* that will condition what will be supplied. We shall attempt to demonstrate that part of the world food problem stems from problems in the international distribution system, the international food market, both in the way effective demand is defined and in the way in which the market structures and supplies dietary tastes.

It is initially instructive to examine Malthus' own analysis of the distribution system—the classical market. In his later economic work, Malthus translated his earlier assumption of an absence of technological change in agriculture into a simple two-sector model of the economy, and tried to specify the relationship between the sectors (see the discussion in Higgins, 1968, pp. 34–52). He postulated an industrial sector, characterized by technological progress and "increasing returns," and an agricultural sector, without technological progress, characterized by unmitigated diminishing returns. Capital was invested in the agricultural sector until all available land was brought under cultivation and improved (e.g., enclosed, supplied with basic equipment for production). After this point, there were no more profitable opportunities for agricultural investment. In a mature economy, then, agricultural output depended only upon the amount of agricultural labor and the stock of improved land. Changes in agricultural output would, then, depend only on the marginal productivity of agricultural labor (positive but diminishing) and the rate of growth in the agricultural force. (There will be no changes in the amount of improved land in a mature system; this is the maximum realizable amount.) The agricultural labor force will grow until net investment in agriculture disappears— when agricultural profits have dropped too low, as a result of falling output per man-year. Diminishing returns to increased employment in agriculture

can be avoided only by rapid technological progress in the industrial sector, where investment is enough to absorb population growth in the industrial sector and reduce the cost of living (hence the amount they must be paid) of workers on the land, which would permit additional, relatively profitable employment on the land.

The industrial sector is crucial in determining the effective demand for agricultural goods, and hence, also affecting the amount produced. Effective demand is the ability to purchase goods—not just the need for them. For workers, this means basically being employed. Malthus assumes that workers' wages are minimal subsistence wages, sufficient to sustain life but not to save. Malthus also assumes that the amount of investment determines the level of employment; this investment comes from the savings of capitalist landlords. They not only have enough income to save but enough to consume above subsistence levels, and hence, to create an effective demand for the luxuries of the industrial sector. When this class can generate both enough effective demand to consume the industrial products and enough savings to continue to absorb the population into the industrial sector, economic growth takes place.

In an immature economy, more workers (who do not grow their own food) will create an effective demand for food, and make it profitable for the landowner to bring all his land into an improved state, and hire more laborers. Malthus suggests, however, that without effective demand, land that could produce will not be brought into production and improved because it is not profitable. Hence, a maximum production effort need not be made, and hunger may exist among those with no effective demand because it is not profitable to alleviate it.

The upper limits of supportable population come, then, either because starvation occurs where there is no effective demand to stimulate greater production, or where production has revealed its maximum (a linear growth rate for Malthus because no technological improvement is possible, and hence, diminishing returns exist.) This is, even in its error, a more sophisticated understanding of how the process for distributing agricultural output (effective demand through the market) affects the production of food and the existence of hunger— and ultimately, the food population balance.

Food problems cannot be conceptualized as

races between production and consumption, no matter how sophisticated definitions and measures of each become. The flaw in forecasts taking that perspective is that their model is misspecified—it omits a crucial variable and in so doing, implies an incorrect causal dynamics. While such forecasts may be used as projections of what may result if current distribution methods are maintained, they cannot present a range of possible outcomes, nor can they be used to evaluate the impact of policy options (even those having to do only with population or food production). From a theoretical perspective, the neo-Malthusian approach lacks forecasting potential. A similar situation prevails in attempts to forecast key aspects of contemporary international political economy.

Despite increasing rhetoric about global interdependence, most economic analysis treats national economies as closed economies. A serious consideration of interdependence would suggest a different initial perspective—that the world is a closed economy, the context within which national economies must be studied. Traditional analyses of international economic relations, especially those among relatively equal nations, view them as closed economies with international relations grafted on.[13] But, as a few economists now argue:

> . . . the US economy is not a closed economy; nor is that of any other nation. The only closed economy it makes sense to talk about is the world economy. One cannot understand the American economy within an American perspective; it must be viewed from the perspective of the world economy. (Wanniski, 1975, p. 34)

Taking this perspective, several features of the contemporary relationships among industrialized nations become theoretically intelligible, especially the wide range of mutual sensitivities that analysts have detailed (cf. Cooper, 1968).

The importance of viewing major industrial nations as part of a closed world economy becomes apparent when two issues are considered: (1) how "international effects" are passed to domestic economies; and (2) the role unilateral governmental actions may plan in adjusting domestic economies.

It is generally assumed that insofar as economies experience fluctuations in the rates of inflation as a result of other governments, these disturbances are limited in scope by the volume of trade with the

rest of the world. Thus, conventional wisdom asserts that the United States is in large part independent of the economies of the rest of the world, especially since its monetary policies are no longer linked to other countries through fixed exchange rates. International connections are assumed to be relatively small, since the United States trades only 5 percent of its GNP. Thus, it is argued that the United States economy is less vulnerable to the effects of international disturbances than more trade-oriented nations (such as the European Community and Japan). Robert Mundell and Arthur Laffer present both theoretical and empirical arguments to the contrary. In doing so, they also challenge the assumption that devaluation or revaluation of currencies can genuinely affect the international terms of trade.

Assuming that the effects of international changes in the value of the dollar would affect domestic prices only in proportion to the volume of US foreign trade,

> In 1971 when the dollar was devalued by 13% virtually the entire economics profession in the United States calculated that because US trade was only 5% of GNP, the effect of the devaluation on the level of US prices would merely be 13% of five, or a little more than a half-point on the Consumer Price Index. (Wanniski, 1975, p. 34)

Mundell and Laffer assume, however, that prices are tied together around the world not only by the volume of goods traded, but by rapid communication of price changes. If this is true, then a small trade volume does not reduce the impact of price changes on a domestic economy. Instead, it suggests that if a country devalues its currency by 13 percent against other international currencies, it can expect to experience higher inflation than those countries, *ceteris paribus,* until its prices have risen by 13 percent more than those of the other countries.[14] An initial period of "confusion" over relative purchasing power may arise, during which exports from the nation devaluing may appear cheaper, but this is a short-term effect, which will disappear as accurate information about relative purchasing power becomes available.

Within this theoretical context, the role of the multinational corporation may be seen differently. Under international arrangements where production was basically national, there was a rather substantial "foreign trade lag." It took some time for supply and demand changes to be transmitted among societies. In addition, public sector institutions within nations had more comprehensive information about economic conditions, and hence could reasonably expect at least partially to mitigate domestic effects by anticipating the response of national businesses and financial institutions, and moving to regulate them. In the case of multinational corporations with genuinely global outlooks and foreign branches that are fully integrated into the firm's production process, corporations are in an excellent position to reap profits from expected price increases. The corporate structure does not *create* the price increases; it is simply efficient in shifting the costs of international changes to others while acquiring some benefits. Regulation might reduce the advantage-taking, but it would not reduce the transmitted price increases.

Moving beyond this, Mundell claims that money, like goods, is subject to these international forces of supply and demand (Wanniski, 1975, pp. 35–37). Or, stated differently, given the contemporary facilities for private international monetary changes, interest rates in one country are a function of the demand for capital throughout the industrialized nations.[15] Models of international monetary transactions can no longer treat national interest rates as exogenous—they are now endogenous.[16] Nations are linked together not only by the prices of shipped goods and information about those prices, but also by short-term capital rates and information about them. The Eurocurrency market developed as a kind of private international clearing house, a feature of the international economic system that is likely to grow in importance as a means for making short-term adjustments in international capital flows. These features of international economic relations suggest governmental efforts to stabilize, or stimulate domestic economies are increasingly difficult.

It has frequently been suggested that the multinational corporation and the vehicles for private international money markets are threats to the sovereignty of nation-states and politically ought to be handled as such. There is no doubt that multinational banking and multinational corporations have reduced the ease with which national governments can cope with economic policies. Focusing on them as potential political threats, however,

obscures the extent to which they are simply one set of possible institutions for operating in an internationalized economic environment. The fact that that environment currently exists is as much the result of political and security choices as it is of private economic innovation. Rather than focusing on the possibility for regulating multinational corporations, this perspective would suggest concern for developing institutions to cope with the increasing international chaos likely to result if multinational corporations cease to perform functions that have become crucial in an international system where truly international financial links (e.g., private monetary transactions) are not luxuries but fundamental to international economic processes.

From this perspective, international relations theory may considerably increase its forecasting potential if it continues to construct more nearly complete theories and make more realistic assessments of the roles of actors and processes. Thus, theories should deal with political-economic, and not merely political-military, variables and should include analysis of the role of transnational actors other than states and of international transactions other than state bureaucracies. Clearly from the perspective of achieved forecasting ability, the "interdependence" approach is woefully inadequate. However, careful micro studies of actors, processes, and channels could produce far better, conceptually adequate forecasts than have come from nation-state oriented, "realist" perspectives. Similarly, conceptual advances in understanding the limits of international political action provide greater forecasting potential. Theories that can incorporate natural, environmental constraints into models that detail actor constraints (interdependence, dominance, deterrence, bargaining, etc.) seem crucial for adequate long-term forecasting.

IV. NORMS AND FORECASTS

Normative issues impinge on theoretical forecasting at several levels. First, it is necessary to consider whether forecasts emerging from specific theoretical perspectives themselves reflect particular social or political values. Second, it is necessary to examine the relationship between forecasts and the clientele they serve, being especially sensitive to the second-order value consequences of forecasts. Finally, it is necessary to consider the impact of the different value hierarchies of the scientific, academic milieu where enlightenment is a *primary* value, and political contexts where values like power, respect, and rectitude may be more basic values, with enlightenment serving as an instrumental value. Each point will be considered in turn.

1. The structure of a theory from which forecasts are developed may introduce subtle (sometimes blatant) normative biases. As has been demonstrated, incomplete theories or misspecified models (omitting key variables or important theoretical relationships) may lead to incorrect causal inferences. Where the variables included in theories reflect the definition of international political reality that prevails in some subset of the international system, the forecasts generated from incomplete systems may also become imbedded in value-laden political perspectives. It is not simply a matter of forecasts becoming "politicized" as actors in the international milieu respond to them, but more fundamentally, the possibility that theoretical forecasts are themselves carriers of political values. While the conceptual inadequacy of incomplete theories or misspecified models can be uncovered through continued testing, normative perspectives may be more difficult to adjust. This point will be developed by two contemporary illustrations of the problem: (1) the explicitly forecasting-oriented *Limits to Growth* tradition and (2) the less operationalized *dependencía* tradition.

The original *Limits to Growth* model was in many ways a very sophisticated forecasting attempt that made a number of contributions to international forecasting (Meadows, *et al.*, 1972). Instead of employing methodologies tied to assumptions of linear growth, the authors employed methods capable of handling the exponential patterns that appeared to characterize the data. The significance of exponential growth was explained and linked to a dynamic process model (positive, or self-amplifying feedback). Interactions among variables and processes were explicitly formulated. Relationships were structured. The model was rich enough to systematically explore counterfactual possibilities and generate a range of possible outcomes. On the other hand, as critics have noted, data were simply aggregated to yield a "global" model without providing a global structure, the model was closed and deterministic, and several subsystems were designed under unrealistic assumptions (Cole, *et al.*, 1973). Any one of these could invalidate the model as a predictive-evaluative tool.

Particularly significant for the present discussion is the model's level of aggregation, and two features that flow from it: the omission of the politico-economic relationships that allocate resources among international "actors," and the focus on scarcity rather than distribution as the definition of the problem. By beginning at the global level, without attempting to characterize the global system, the model proceeds as though the dynamics of population, agricultural production, industrial growth, and pollution were globally salient by virtue of the interrelationships specified by the model. Yet this is not the case. One of the most striking features of the global system is the extent to which population growth, industrial capacity, pollution, and agricultural productivity are unequally distributed. Even a regional disaggregation yields substantially different forecasts.[17] If the model had focused on the interactions, sensitivities, and channels (ecological-politico-economic) through which dynamics of population growth, industrial dynamics, agricultural production, and pollution linked the relevant "actors," the spectre of general resource scarcity, declining life expectancy, or starvation might well have been remote.

The normative implications of the initial *Limits to Growth* model were significant. First, by aggregating to a global level, and suggesting a global catastrophe, the model implied a general, common interest in acting to avoid catastrophe. From this perspective, the political question is one of providing a collective good, and the problem becomes one of coordinating political actors and policies in time to permit effective action.[18] Unwillingness to move toward this end can only be seen as the triumph of short-run, particular interests over long-run common interests. Given the contemporary international political economy, however, there is a real possibility that for some actors (nations, regions, classes) an assessment of long-run interests would not dictate a shared interest in preserving the global order. In addition, the causal dynamics of the model suggest that slowing population growth and industrial expansion are key to avoiding global catastrophe. Within the context of contemporary global patterns, this places the heaviest burden of adjustment on poorer, less developed states, whose population must be controlled and whose prospects for greater well being may be most seriously mortaged by serious attempts to slow new industrial expansion. Formulations that explicitly analyzed inequalities in resource utilization, in the context of measures of quality of life, might arrive at substantially different perscriptions. Finally, by focusing on the future as the domain of catastrophe, the model suggests (tacitly) that contemporary needs and demands may be less crucial. While not advocating triage-like analyses of "hard trade-offs," the model forecasts that such tradeoffs may be necessary to a "realistic" assessment of global prospects. There is no corresponding pressure to consider analyses pushing for radical redistributions of international wealth as similarly necessary or "realistic." It is hardly surprising, therefore, that the forecasts have generated normative controversy in the context of genuinely competing assessments of alternate futures.

Normative complexities are also evident in the contemporary controversy over the academic worth of "dependency" approaches to international relations. Dependency (*dependencía*) approaches focus primarily on explaining the phenomena of *underdevelopment*, and as such, rarely attempt to characterize international relations *in toto*. What distinguishes dependence approaches from most other perspectives on development, and makes them of interest to international relations scholars, is their focus on the international system, not the nation-state, as the unit of analysis. For *dependencía* scholars, the international milieu is not a neutral medium linking national economies and politics nor an arena that simply reflects and transmits the consequences of different national levels of development. The transsocietal relationships whose structure characterize the international system are posited to contribute to both generating and sustaining underdevelopment.

Dependencía theories emerged in the 1960's out of an intellectual and political milieu which challenged the prevailing social scientific approaches to development.[19] As development programs predicated upon Western models faltered, scholars became more aware of the extent to which linkages with the international system conditioned political and economic development prospects.[20] Yet the normative connotations of investigation development from a perspective which suggests that underdevelopment may have been at least partially created by international exchanges are as important as problems of operationalization and testability in explaining the slowness with which *dependencía* and interdependence perspectives are simultaneously explored. Investigations within the *dependencía* tradition (Marxist or non-Marxist) carry connotations of responsibility for underdevelopment, while interdependence approaches suggest accepting mutual sensitivities and managing them as emergent properties of a new, more complex international milieu. Although conceptually convergent on many points (the salience of nonnation-state actors, the need to include political economy in discussions of international relations, the importance of transsocietal linkages), *dependencía* approaches continue to conceptualize international relations in terms of the international reality of less-developed states, while interdependence approaches incorporate the central concerns of great power perspectives (the nuclear balance, crisis management, mutual adjustment, technologically conditioned sensitivities). Neither framework is sufficiently developed to test the theoretical merit of its focus. Hence, for the present at least, formal or informal forecasts from each perspective are likely to carry important value connotations.

2. The availability of forecasts within political and economic contexts characterized by differential access to information and varying capabilities to adjust behavior on the basis of forecasts may raise somewhat different normative issues. As international relations theorists become more aware of the "meta-structuring" capabilities of key international actors (nation-states, multinational corporations, specialized financial agencies), it becomes possible to be more attentive internationally to questions raised in the context of the "policy science" literature—including the political consequences of providing specified clientele with additional information. Forecasts that are not linked to value positions may operate (intentionally or unintentionally) to affect value trade-offs. Contemporary proposals to upgrade forecasting of international crop failures, and speed dissemination of these forecasts, provide a concrete basis for exploring some "record-order" normative implications of international forecasting.

Those involved in international famine relief programs have long recognized that advance warning of impending famine is crucial to organizing successful relief efforts (Mayer, 1975, pp. 571–577). With better international crop monitoring and forecasting, the resources available for famine relief could be more effectively utilized. In addition, attempts to institute programs for international coordination of food "reserves" and relief allocations require better forecasts of both production and acute need. The United States experience in the 1972 Soviet wheat sale further underlined the need for more accurate forecasts of shortfall to guide international food transactions. It might, then, appear that proposals to make possible more accurate forecasts and disseminate them would be generally advantageous, and might serve to promote a more rational international food system.

When such proposals are analyzed in the context of the structure of the international food market, some additional complications emerge. The markets for all major grains are highly concentrated, in terms of both the nations that export and the number of firms handling export-import transactions. A few nations, and a few firms within those nations, can make decisions that will affect market conditions for a large number of buyers. These actors also tend to have greater capabilities to use new information to achieve their goals, for they have: (1) the capabilities to take advantage of action opportunities to make positive gains in the international system, as well as to control or prevent negative effects; (2) the meta-power to internally restructure to increase productive and exchange advantages and/or overcome disadvantages; and (3) the meta-power to shape the external environment to gain advantages and/or limit disadvantageous consequences (Baumgartner, 1975, p. 9). Where this is the case, better forecasting may make some values—especially those the existing structure does not strongly attempt to realize—more difficult to actualize.

In this context, it is worth examining prevalent hopes that better forecasts of food production would contribute to a better matching of nutritional needs and food supplies of a more stable international food environment, while providing a starting point for creating a more rational international food system. While it is clear that advance notice of impending famine in an area might make relief efforts more effective, it is worth remembering that famine relief is a peripheral part of international food transactions. More information on shortages might be valuable if it led to a greater willingness and ability to commit resources to that area in advance. This may not be the consequence of such information, however. With better knowledge of the market possibilities (including possibilities for food sales to richer states with crop shortfalls), it is equally likely that more information might result in fewer resources being committed to politically peripheral famine areas, given the opportunity costs of such commitments.

Similarly, while it is clear that better information about the 1972 Soviet crop failure might have prevented American errors in the massive Soviet wheat sale, it is not clear that better information would work to stabilize prices. Reports of possible shortages are likely to set off waves of speculation, during which prices may rise. Such speculation is particularly damaging to small, relatively poor, politically peripheral states that genuinely need food imports. Unlike larger, more politically influential states whose position makes it possible for them to affect the market price for grains, smaller purchasers face prices that are essentially "given" by the market. Rising prices, reflecting speculation, will be reflected in the contracts such states make for future delivery. Even if shortages do not emerge, such nations may be committed to contracts specifying higher prices. Unlike more politically significant states, marginal purchasers cannot cancel contracts, refuse to pay penalty clauses, and expect their ability to purchase to remain unaffected. Better knowledge of global food needs will lead to a better allocation of food to meet needs only if sufficient reserves exist to meet annual needs *and* policies for allocating such reserves are oriented toward responding to food needs that may not be backed by effective demand.

3. A more subtle normative issue stems from the difference in the value hierarchies that govern scientific theory construction and political action. Most visions of policy science or future-oriented programs for anticipatory policy planning assume that theoretical insights could be used in designing forecasting and monitoring networks linked to action possibilities predicated on theoretical relation-

ships.[21] The assumption that theoretical disagreements could be "bracketed" for practical applications in turn reflects two tacit assumptions about theory construction and academic forecasting. First, there is the presumption that theoretical relationships that have been supported by some testing will not later be found to be fundamentally wrong, or at least have an identifiably low probability of being fundamentally wrong. Second, it is presumed that, except for "extraordinary" periods, theory building will go on within a paradigm characterized by agreement on theoretical fundamentals. Such agreement is seen as helping to guarantee a cumulation of scientific knowledge. Many philosophers of science now reject both assumptions. In place of critical tests that establish results, they see findings that may be reversed by theoretical reinterpretations or changes in observation or measurement theories. In place of a unified paradigm that brings "order" to theoretical investigations and reflects basic consensus, they see competition as one of the key dynamics of scientific investigation (Lakatos, 1970, pp. 154–188). Hence, as students of science and public policy know well, any scientific discipline is likely to contain substantially different theoretical assessments which cannot be theoretically eliminated.

Within the scientific milieu, competition among research programs and the process of reformulating theoretical models and observation theories within research programs serve to generate new knowledge and direct its cumulation. Exploring *ceteris paribus* clauses (challenging and testing assumptions), forecasting outcomes, testing the forecasts, and reformulating theories on the basis of inferences from tests are activities that characterize a social milieu in which *enlightenment* (knowledge generation and confirmation) is the paramount value. Prestige, respect, and power flow from achievements in generating knowledge, and cannot long be sustained without corroboration of alleged achievements. Scientific activity is value free only in the sense that it attempts to create an environment where the social, political, religious, or cultural values of a scientist do not distort attempts to gain and test knowledge. Scientific activity is committed to knowledge advancement as a value.

In part, scientific investigation is "kept honest" by the social milieu in which it occurs. An openness to knowledge challenges, while not perfectly achieved, supports a wide variety of investigations, and makes tolerable and even exciting major adjustments of perspectives. If, as many philosophers of science contend, the confidence placed in knowledge developed in scientific disciplines is partly founded in the processes that produce and correct it, attempts to employ theoretical forecasting in milieus not characterized by these features may need special attention.

Three features set forecasts used in policy decision making apart from the norms of academic forecasting. First, the costs of making changes in models is slight in the academic context. In the political arena, they may be more substantial. Forecasting models that are subject to periodic, substantial changes may lose their political credibility. Especially if models are used to provide long-range forecasts, supporting claims that programs must be begun to avoid future, undesirable consequences or achieve greater gains, substantial changes in the model's projections may make decision makers less willing to commit resources to such programs. In addition, if resources are committed to programs (e.g., developing alternate sources of energy on the basis of forecasts of scarcity or continuing high prices for oil), it may be difficult to alter programs easily if forecasts are later shown to be oversimplified. Second, when a range of plausible options are produced in the context of forecasting efforts, it may be difficult to find people willing to advocate the appropriate range of options in the political milieu. As Alex George has noted, the political costs involved in advocating unpleasant or unpopular options frequently produce a narrower range of options and possibilities (George, 1972, pp. 751–785). In addition, having committed political resources (prestige, influence, channels of access, etc.) to a particular option, it may be much more difficult to "shift gears" as theoretical issues suggest new conclusions. Finally, differences in the political domain are more often resolved by adjusting interests than submitting differences to knowledge-oriented testing procedures. Thus, it is likely that political realities will produce action programs different from those that might flow from available forecasts. Current attempts to forge a "national energy policy" or form an OECD (Organization for Economic Cooperation and Development) common stance on energy illustrate the situation. In this context, competing forecasts made under different assumptions feed into the political process. Political resolutions of differences among forecasts may not produce self-correcting, cumulative bodies of knowledge. Under such conditions, hopes for linking forecasts to steering mechanisms seems less promising than assessments of some advocates of "social engineering."

V. FORECASTING "STRATEGIES"

Several alternative approaches to constructing theoretical forecasts exist, with different demands on theory and different links to political action. Perhaps the most desirable strategy, from the perspective of academic standards is to develop simulation models, ideally based upon theoretically grounded process models, complex enough to permit systematic counterfactual conditional evaluations ("what if . . .") as well as projections of the outcomes or conditions that might result if identified relationships continued without substantial change. Theoretically identified interactions should be represented. A variety of methodologies are available for constructing simulation models, including econometric techniques for estimating single equations or systems of simultaneous equations, path analysis, information processing models, and artificial intelligence approaches.[22] Some such models are presently available.[23] In addition, a wide range of techniques for providing formal representations of data is needed in such models, making crucial measurements and at least partially validating measurement models (see Alker, 1975). Such available methods, more fully applied, could produce better formal representations of international relations theories.

Yet a more crucial limitation to forecasting potential may lie in the theoretical perspectives being developed. Most forecasting models are framed in terms of *national* actors, despite increasing realizations that such perspectives are inadequate. But being able to generate complex models of transnational processes, including transnational and transbureaucratic processes requires both better theoretical formulations of key concepts such as interdependence, linkage, sensitivity, and dependence. Such advances are likely to depend upon

much better studies of the channels through which "interdependence" is transmitted; that is, how general statements about growing interdependence are linked to the behavior of an expanded range of internationally significant actors. With this information, process models could be developed, as could schedules of the capabilities of actors.

Constructing well-tested, relatively complete forecasting models is costly and time consuming. They tend to be developed within an academic context (where they may have payoffs for theorizing) or in the context of serving as resources for specific governmental agencies. The implicit forecasting strategy is to make an input into planning or political decision making by providing a general resource for some policy-making or policy-evaluating agency. Whether this strategy depends crucially on political access to key decision arenas, is something Cooper (Chapter 23) suggests is relatively rare outside the defense establishment.

Several other alternative strategies are possible. Forecasting models may be used to focus public attention (and perhaps the attention of salient policy-making institutions) on a key problem. It has been argued that Food and Agricultural Organization forecasts of starvation served this function. This was clearly the result of the publication of *The Limits to Growth*. In this context, it may be more important that forecasts suggest clear, dramatic outcomes than that models constitute finely tuned, theoretically perfected instruments. When attention is focused on an area, criticism and attempts to improve (or challenge) forecasts may produce continued academic research that stimulates theoretically improved models at the same time political attention may be focused on new problems, perhaps generating pressures for better assessments of the issue. There are obvious limits to this process, and trade-offs between dramatic findings and carefully stated *ceteris paribus* assumptions. Yet such forecasting models may at least partially overcome problems of access and decision makers' attention.

Less ambitious attempts may include using forecasting models (or selected conditional forecasts) to contribute to policy debates. Given a set of current policy issues, limited forecasting models may be contructed to provide a vehicle for making judgments about the likely effect of different policy options. This seems to be the role George (Chapter 22) suggests for policy-science relevant "contingent predictions." Because specific policy issues may be "live" for a relatively short time, there may be a trade-off between formalizing and testing forecasting models and drawing upon theory to make less formalized (but still contingent) assessments.

Yet another forecasting strategy is to attempt to simply improve the day-to-day operation of policy relevant agencies. Here the interests of decision-oriented forecasting predominate. It is possible that existing theoretical perspectives could make contributions in this regard—suggesting key factors that decisions should include, drawing attention to the need to consider impacts in medium- and long-run as well as immediate consequences, making more systematic the process of generating possibilities to consider, and identifying interactions to observe. Such attempts may either take as given the focus and goals of the clientele and suggest ways to better realize these or attempt to change the focus and perspective of potential clients. Many social science forecasting efforts in effect fall into the latter category, constituting attempts to change the perspective of some clientele by expanding their range of considered options or sensitizing them to potentially significant theoretical points.

Discussing this range of strategies is important for several reasons. First, forecasters have a wider range of options than is frequently acknowledged in the academic literature. Where forecasts are based on strongly tested, well-corroborated forecasting models, it may be appropriate to make claims to theory-based forecasts. In other cases, however, forecasting may offer insights, provide inputs into multiple advocacy procedures, or support well-reasoned attempts to provoke greater attention to key issues. It is possible to engage in such forecasting strategies without making invalid claims about theoretical backing for forecasts, or compromising the aims of academic theory construction. Second, they highlight the range of different tasks to which forecasting might be expected to contribute. If the task of theoretically self-conscious forecasting is to contribute to improving generally accepted decision-making procedures, there may be a substantial potential for even pres-

ent theoretical perspectives. If, on the other hand, the aim is to transform decision-making procedures radically, present potential is quite low. More careful attention to the aims of forecasting might contribute to a better matching of capabilities, needs, and potentials.

NOTES

1. For an elaborate development of this thesis, see Bell (1973).
2. The quotation is drawn from George and Smoke (1974), p. 627.
3. For a technological forecaster's realization of this point, see Suk (1969). A more general treatment of the interplay between forecasting and the socio-political milieu is Iklé (1971b), pp. 142–150.
4. For examples of this orientation, see Gabor (1963); Jantsch (1972); de Jouvenel (1967); Jungk (1969); Jungk and Galtung (1968); Kuhn and Wener (1967); Prehoda (1967).
5. For samples of literature from this perspective, see Ayres (1969); Bright (1968); Bright and Schoeman (1973). Martino (1973), makes this position explicit. Also cf. Martino (1972); Pyke (1970).
6. For an example of techniques from academic-oriented forecasting applied to policy-arena formulations, see O'Leary and Coplin (1976).
7. For an excellent example, see George and Smoke (1974), which details problems in the policy applications of deterrence.
8. Lakatos (1970), pp. 132–138. A similar focus for forecasting is suggested in Kuhn (1970).
9. Young (1972), argues for concentrating research on theoretically significant problems and delaying attempts to make policy applications until theory is more fully developed.
10. Martino (1973) pp. 28–30. The following discussion draws on Martino's analysis of decision-oriented validity.
11. This is the final item Martino presents in his evaluation scheme, which is intended to be a sequential process. See pp. 35–52.
12. For the concept of a "schedule" for political action, cf. Alker (1973).
13. The analysis draws on Wanniski (1975), pp. 31–52.
14. The Wanniski article states that research by one of Laffer's students, Moon Hoe Lee, found this relationship to hold empirically in his study of nine countries, 1900–1972. No formal citation was provided, however, and I have been unable to verify this empirical claim.
15. Hewson and Sakakibara (1975), pp. 13–37, develop a theoretical model for this situation. They see the market as a product of private innovation, adding new parameters to more traditional international economic models.

16. The consequences of this are demonstrated in Hewson and Sakakibara (1975), pp. 22–27.

17. See the more recent Club of Rome publication, Mesarović (1974).

18. There is a growing tendency to examine international relations in this context. The original impetus was Olson (1965). For a recent development of the theme, see Ruggie (1972), 874–894.

19. For examples of this extensive literature, see Alavi (1973); Bodenheimer (1971), pp. 155–182; Cockroft, *et al.* (1972); Furtado (1973); Galofre (1973); Sunkel (1973). Much of the initial impulse came from Prebish (1950).

20. Rosenau's initial formulation of "linkage politics," while not a theoretical formulation, was an attempt to provide an explicit scheme for considering such relationships. See Rosenau (1969). His argument for the need for linkage theory (pp. 3–7) is perceptive, although the scheme (pp. 49–56) is *ad hoc* and flawed. The need remains, as Rosenau suggests in his *Theorizing Across Systems: Linkage Politics Revisited* (1973). More well-articulated approaches, through interdependence approaches are presented in Koehane and Nye (1972); Cooper (1968); Huntington (1973), pp. 333–368; Kaiser (1969), pp. 726–750; and "Transnational Politics: Toward a Theory of Multinational Politics" *International Organization*, Vol. 24, No. 4 (Autumn, 1971); Morse (1972), pp. 123–150 and

(1969). An explicit attempt to relate this perspective to conflicts is Nye (1974), pp. 961–998. Some qualifications are offered in Rosecrance (1973), pp. 1–27; Waltz (1970); and Wagner (1974). Recent attempts to further advance the approach include Koehane and Nye (1974); Alker, *et al.* (1974) and the attempt to specify concrete examples for United States-Canadian relations in *International Organization*, Vol. 28, No. 4 (Autumn, 1974), pp. 595–607.

21. A variety of forecasting programs are tied to attempts to selectively monitor the environment. See Bright (1973), pp. 238–256. Comparable efforts in political science include Azar's conflict monitoring system (discussed in this volume), the "social indicators" movement, and many conceptions of emerging "policy science." See, for example, Burgess and Lawton (1972) and Hermann, *et al.* (1973).

22. Good treatments of these techniques are found in Blalock and Blalock (1968); Malinvaud (1966); and Shank and Colby (1973), and the bibliographies contained in these works.

23. For an attempt to move from causal modeling to more artificial-intelligence-like models, see Alker and Christensen (1972). For an excellent example of a dynamic, simultaneous equation model for which validation has been attempted, see Choucri and North (1975).

CHAPTER FIVE

VALIDATING INTERNATIONAL RELATIONS FORECASTS TO DEVELOP THEORY

Charles F. Hermann, Warren R. Phillips, & Stuart J. Thorson

I. INTRODUCTION

Periodically, policy makers, the public, and other scholars urge international relations researchers to cast the results of their studies in terms of forecasts or expectations about the future. The reasons seem clear enough. We all have an interest in anticipating aspects of future global politics. Because everyone is concerned with the future, the ability to produce accepted forecasts confers power upon their makers. Another reason for urging more forecasting is the effect on policy. If an individual or collectivity accepts the projected results of a forecast, it becomes the basis for prescriptive action.

The authors acknowledge the support of the Mershon Center and the Project for Theoretical Politics at the Ohio State University in the preparation of this chapter. They are grateful for the constructive comments of Nazli Choucri on an earlier draft.

Humans thus participate consciously to shape their future and to engage in self-fulfilling or self-denying forecasting ("If certain occurrences will happen, we need to undertake the actions to promote, obstruct, or take advantage of them."). In addition to the value accruing to forecasters who are believed and the policy implications of forecasts, certain types of forecasting lead to the expansion of knowledge. If the forecasts have involved articulate calculations or other explicit methods, investigators can presumably use forecasts that prove inadequate to revise their procedures. New estimates of future developments can be made using the revisions and these in turn can subsequently be checked to provide a further round of modifications in the underlying forecasting procedures. Such a cyclical process produces successive approximations that hopefully achieve a gradually improved fit between forecast and subsequent observation. With improved forecasts derived in this fashion should come improvement in the explanatory base that generated them.

Perhaps few proponents of greater forecasting in international relations would state their case in such unqualified terms, but the reasons advanced above appear to capture the core of such advocacy. Notice that all the arguments for more forecasting in international relations assume that someone can eventually determine their accuracy. A forecast that is stated in such a way as to permit its verification against the unfolding future or previously uninvestigated historical events (retrospective forecasts) introduces the problem of forecast validity, which is the subject of this chapter.

The difficulties arise in moving from these simple statements of aspiration to the development of insights and procedures that can be applied in research. At the point of actually validating forecasts a host of philosophical and practical questions arise. What does a forecast represent? Or, put a different way, assuming that a forecast could be validated, what does it mean? How does purpose affect the validation of a forecast? What validation procedures can be employed? What about inconsistencies between the results of forecasts and other means of validating insights or a theory? How can one confidently know (and measure) the future reference system about which a·forecast has been made? These questions alert the reader to the conclusions to be found at the end of this chapter. Using forecasts as a validation procedure is much more complex and the results less certain than appears at first glance. Nevertheless, it is an important, if insufficient, operation for improving our knowledge of international relations. For that reason, this chapter seeks to provide some exploration of the issues posed by the questions above and, where possible, to suggest procedures for dealing with them.

II. THEORY AS THE GENERATOR OF FORECASTS

Assume for the moment that by some means a forecast has been validated, by which we mean the state of affairs it asserts as transpiring in a given system has been confirmed as having occurred. One question that remains is what do we know when we have such a validated forecast? In such circumstances, we would know that a particular estimate made at some prior time has been confirmed to some degree by subsequent developments. This confirmation of forecasts can be variously referred to as validation, goodness of fit, verisimilitude, verification, or accuracy. A validated forecast can be used to bestow blame or praise. (Who failed to act upon Senator Keating's warning in the autumn of 1962 that there were missiles in Cuba?) Usually, the accuracy of a single forecast in and of itself is an issue for works of history and biography. Beyond this use of the confirmed relationship between the forecast and actual events, we frequently want to infer something about the means and the source by which the forecast was generated. More specifically, we wish to determine the ability of that source to generate other valid forecasts. Take the following example: "Carl was correct in anticipating the outcome of this week's soccer game, but will his judgment be as good for next week's match?" In this case, the inquiry is about the ability of an individual to make a forecast. Unless he was making an ungrounded guess, the forecaster performed some calculations that formed the basis for his estimate. Thus, one of the fundamental uses of validated forecast is to assess the utility of the calculations by which it was made in order that the calculations can be used again.

As several chapters in this book make clear, numerous ways exist to generate forecasts. When the purpose of one or more forecasts is to determine the utility of an explanatory source for subsequent forecasts and explanations, the components of the forecasting system and their logical relationships to one another must be explicit. Otherwise, what can be inferred about the validity of any future performances of the system will be quite limited.[1] In short, we assert that in order to use forecast validation as a means for inferring the future predictive capability of the source, the source should have the characteristics of a deductive theory. That is, a series of the statements and the logical relationships between them are necessary to derive the forecast. In some instances a given theory may be incomplete in the sense that not all the statements and their connections may be identified, but the closer it comes to approximating the requirements for deductive theory, the greater the value of forecasts as a validating technique.

This theory requirement certainly limits the range of sources that can be evaluated through forecast validation. Nevertheless, the requirement of a deductive theory as the source of forecasts seems appropriate, if our validity studies must take into account the following considerations:

1. Forecasts are used to estimate the utility of the source for future forecasts.

2. The forecast source is to be adjusted or altered to attempt to improve subsequent forecasts based upon its previous performance.

3. It is necessary to establish the parameters or boundaries beyond which the source may decline sharply with respect to the accuracy of its forecasts.

4. The forecast concerns a dynamic reference system that is suspected of containing some components that can assume a substantial range of values which in turn may yield quite different outcomes.

We believe these conditions frequently confront the international relations scholar who evaluates the validity of forecasts.

Before proceeding further, it would be desirable to offer some definitions of the basic terms we have been using. A *deductive theory* is stipulated as a set of sentences closed under deduction; that is, the set contains any sentence that is logically implied by any other sentence in the set (see Thorson and Stever, 1974, pp. 15–32 for an explication of this definition). Further, the sentences in a theory are generally asserted to be true; that is, to provide an accurate description of some reference system.

A *forecast* is a statement made at one time about the state of some world or reference system at some other time. Thus, the theories to be considered for forecasting must be dynamic theories in the sense that the values (states) of some variables are related to values of other variables at other points in time.

More precisely, consider a theory about some reference system consisting of state variables (x_1, x_2, . . . , x_n). We want our theory to contain sentences relating at least some of these state variables to previous states of the system. In physics, for example, these sentences are often expressed in differential equations of the form:

$$\frac{dx}{dt} = f_i(x_1, x_2, \ldots, x_n).$$

The theory of arms races developed by Richardson illustrates a theory of this type in the international relations literature (1960a and 1960b). Richardson used differential equations to relate a nation's level of defense at one time to states of the system at previous times. Forrester's world dynamics simulation offers a second example (1971b). The sentences are in the DYNAMO language and levels of variables at one time are related to levels at previous times. This theory contains statements in the form of difference equations.

In principle, a theory need not be expressed in an artificial language (such as DYNAMO or differential equations) to be a deductive theory. Theories expressed in a natural language, such as English, may also satisfy the above conditions. It might be argued, for example, that Galtung's "rank theory" meets the criteria established above (1964, pp. 95–119). However, a person analyzing most natural language theories (including Galtung's) encounters a difficulty in attempting to unambiguously identify the objects and relations being discussed.

The analysis that follows excludes means of generating forecasts which are not dynamic theories of the kind identified above. Thus, we do not consider trend and cyclical analyses that simply project prior patterns without any antecedent explanations. Nor do we include forecasts generated from the development of speculative or plausible scenarios or Delphi techniques (Morgenstern, *et al.*, 1973). Each of these forecasting techniques lacks to a greater or lesser degree a bounded explanatory system whose component elements can assume different values. Forecasts that are extrapolated from observable trends and apparent cycles in world affairs involve no explanatory mechanism that can be adjusted if the projections fail to correspond to subsequent occurrences. Nor do they contain parameters that permit one to determine whether the conditions of the system at a given time parallel those from which the trend or cycle is derived. Sequential exchanges between panels of experts (as in the Delphi technique) may result in the gradual emergence of consensus around one or several forecasts. But the concurrence may be achieved by using multiple explanations for the same forecast. One explanation may convince some experts, while another persuades other experts to accept the same forecast. Or the explanation may be sufficiently ambiguous so that different authorities are able to attach quite different meanings to its key elements (or substitute their own when these elements are missing). Moreover, consensus may emerge from group influences processes that have little to do with the merit of the accepted explanations. Lest we be misunderstood, it should be emphatically stated that all these forecasting techniques may have a role in international relations. This chapter, however, concerns the validation of forecasts to improve theory. Evaluation of the validity of the forecasts from such sources as trends, cycles, scenarios, and Delphi techniques, has limited utility for their development.

Now that the class of theories to be discussed has been identified, it is appropriate to return to the concept of "validity" which was briefly defined at the beginning of this section. In discussing a concept such as validity it is important to distinguish between semantic questions of what it means to predicate validity of a forecast, and methodological questions of how it becomes known whether the assertions from a particular theory are, in fact, valid. Answers to the methodological question would seem to presume adequate answers to the semantic one. That is, it would be difficult to determine whether a theory is valid without first determining what is meant by validity. Therefore, the first task will be to explicate what will be meant in this chapter when validity is predicted of a theory. Roughly, a theory—a set of logically related sentences in some language—is valid if it does what it purports to do. Thus, as is noted by Forrester (1961) and Hermann (1967, pp. 216–231), the question of validity is inextricably intertwined with the purpose to which, in this case, a forecasting system will be put. A number of possible purposes and criteria of validity appropriate to these purposes will be treated subsequently. With this clarification, we stipulate that a theory, T, is valid with respect to purpose, P, to the extent T achieves P.

Relating validity to purpose is compatible with an extremely pragmatic view of theory evaluation. This compatibility, however, does not require that we adopt such a pragmatic view. One might argue, for example, that the purpose of a scientific theory is to generate (or be capable of generating) "true" sentences (Popper, 1965, pp. 223ff). Thus, the test of validity of a scientific theory is whether the sentences comprising the theory (as well as those logically implied by these sentences) accurately account for and describe features of some reference system. That is to say, for a scientist taking this position to assert that T is a valid theory is equiva-

lent to his asserting that the sentences comprising T accurately account for the operation of the reference system. Note again that this semantic definition of validity does not entail any particular methodological position as to how a particular theory is known to be valid (i.e., known to consist of true sentences). For example, although it might be argued that the goal of science is to construct true theories (i.e., theories whose sentences accurately represent the operations that control the relationship between components of a reference system), yet it could still be argued that it can never be known whether any particular sentence is in fact true.

It will therefore be useful to consider a variety of methodological positions which can be brought to bear on validity questions. Examples of such positions include rationalism, empiricism, and "positive theory." (Naylor and Finger, 1971). The rationalist perspective generally holds that a theory is simply a set of deductions from propositions of unquestioned truth. Thus, no empirical testing is necessary and instead efforts should be spent searching for the basic assumptions from which to generate the theory.

The empiricist response is to refuse to admit any assumptions that cannot be independently verified through controlled observations. The empiricist position—or at least a moderated version of it—is quite evident in the contemporary study of international politics. For instance, Singer (1972, p. 6) argues that the route to explanatory knowledge typically follows a progression: "Just as existential descriptions must precede correlational propositions, so the latter are an essential prerequisite to that explanatory knowledge which is the ultimate goal." Unfortunately, it is not clearly the case that correlational knowledge will lead to explanatory knowledge or that it must precede it. Regression coefficients are properly used to estimate population parameters only when the structure of the theory employed in forecasting is well specified. Data analysis strategies (such as regression analysis) cannot in general reveal the underlying structure of a referent system. This is generally the case whether the systems are analyzed cross-nationally at a point in time or individually as a time series. Thus, it would appear that prior empirical analysis is not a justification for validating a theoretical explanation or forecast of future events in and of itself. We must have a theoretical structure specified before any empirical analysis provides some sense of validity for our propositions. Popper has argued that simple extrapolations from past to future are not scientific forecasts: "Indeed, unless we have the theoretical explanation for why such an extrapolation should hold, we do not have theory which can forecast future events" (Popper, 1959).

A third perspective might be termed "positive theory" (Friedman, 1953; Riker and Ordeshook, 1973; and McGowan, 1974, pp. 25–44). The positive theorist argues that contrary to the rationalist and empiricist positions, the validity of assumptions ought not be a central question. Instead, the utility of a theory depends not upon the validity of its assumptions but rather upon the accuracy with which it predicts values of variables at other time points. Each of the three positions sketched here has been subjected to considerable criticism and the positions themselves are held in enough different forms to form more of a continuum than three distinct methodological perspectives.

There are, however, distinct differences in emphasis and these have led Naylor and Finger (1971) to suggest a multistage approach to validation in which "each of the above mentioned methodological positions is a necessary procedure for [validation] but that neither of them is a sufficient procedure for solving the problem of validation" (p. 156). Thus, in line with the rationalist position, some assumptions are seen as more "obvious" than others and preliminary empirical work should focus upon the less obvious ones first. To the extent possible we should subject our assumptions to empirical test. However, for a variety of reasons it will not be possible to test all assumptions and we must therefore examine the ability of the model to make accurate predictions about the referent system. Thus, the multistage approach attempts to incorporate a variety of methodological perspectives at various points of the ongoing process of validation.

III. SOME CONSIDERATIONS AFFECTING THE RELATIONSHIP BETWEEN THEORY AND FORECAST

Let us take a brief review. The theories of interest in this chapter must generate forecasts, that is, statements concerning changes in the values of objects at different points in time. We contend that the major question of forecast validity is actually one of using the forecast to assess the validity of the theory that generated the predictions. This does not mean that we can ignore the validity of the predictions themselves. The assertion that under certain conditions a particular pattern of events will occur during some future period of time suggests an obvious criterion for establishing validity of the theory. If the specified conditions transpired, did the projected pattern occur as predicted? The accuracy of forecasts is certainly an essential feature of the validation effort, but a number of issues must be taken into account in evaluating the relationship between a theory and its forecasts.

As we noted in the previous section, the user's purpose should determine whether inferences about the theory from confirmed forecasts are of major importance. Elsewhere some distinctive purposes of simulations (one type of theory) have been described together with their implications for validity (Hermann, 1967). Among the purposes mentioned were (1) the discovery of alternatives, (2) the evaluation of alternative outcomes, (3) prediction, (4) instruction, (5) construction of hypotheses and theory, and (6) exploration of nonexistent universes.

For the present, we need only establish that the user's purpose will make a difference. For example, if the user seeks explanation for why certain macro patterns seem to hold, then the confirmed forecast may be of minimal value in assessing a theory's explanatory adequacy. It is quite possible for a theory involving a number of stochastic processes to yield accurate forecasts about a closed system without providing much insight into why the particular pattern occurs as it does. With respect to the degree of accuracy in forecasting, numerous illustrations come to mind. In deciding whether to sell a particular weapons system to a Persian Gulf country, a United States policy maker may only be concerned with a forecast that qualitatively assesses whether the proposed sale would be stabilizing or destabilizing. No precise quantitative forecast would be required. On the other hand, a theory that estimated the number of ICBM launchers that could be built by the Soviet Union or the United States without detection by the other side would have to have a much higher predictive capacity if it were to be used as the basis for signing or, not signing, an arms limitation agreement. The users need must determine the precision.

In assessing the degree of precision necessary for the user's purpose, one criterion must be the alternatives available for forecasting. In statistical tests, forecast performance is often compared to change, but that may not be the relevant standard in a particular case.

Another issue we must address concerns the role of probability in the theory. Suppose we have a theory that leads to the following assertion: When nations of the world are ranked according to military and economic capability, the first-ranked nation will initiate war with the second-ranked nation if—and only if—the latter's rate of growth in both military and economic capability relative to the first-ranked nation will lead to a reversal of ranks within 5 years. Such a statement can be contrasted with one that concludes that the first-ranked nation is *more likely* to initiate war against the second if its projected economic and military growth rate will cause it to overtake the first-ranked nation within 5 years. The first statement claims to contain all the conditions that are necessary to produce the projected outcome. The first assertion is that the outcome will occur every time the conditions are met. The second assertion contends only that the specified conditions increase the likelihood of the outcome. Although the examples may seem a bit farfetched, some theories can generate forecasts that are held to be completely determined by the configuration of specified conditions; whereas others are probabilistic theories and provide only projections of the probability associated with various classes of events.[2] When the theory's specified prior conditions are not related in a deterministic fashion to the estimated outcome, a forecasting exercise can provide only limited insight into the theory's degree of validity without consideration of the impact of exogenous variables, such as random disturbances, that operate independently of the system to produce similar outcomes. Moreover, even in the case of the deterministic theory, the lack of congruity between forecast and outcome may lead no further than to recasting the relationship in probabilistic terms.

A deterministic theory yields a set of expected values in some future state but makes no provision for the outcome if the expected values do not occur. It is as if our theory projected the rate of descent of a ball of a certain mass down an inclined plane having an angle that is a certain number of degrees from horizontal, but taking no account of the surface of the plane and the ball, etc. Or, consider the example of theory that projects that a particular rate of economic development in a less developed country will begin, at a given point, to generate a certain amount of capital. These theories neglect what happens if the forecasts are not fulfilled—the amount of friction drastically slows the ball or internal revolution slows capital formation.

If the distribution of outcomes around the projected one involves only gradual deviations, we still might give the theory "high marks" even if slight errors occur. If the distribution of outcomes surrounding the one that is forecasted falls off sharply, then a deterministic theory poses severe problems—particularly if the forecasted outcome is regarded as desirable and those around it appear undesirable. Therefore, although forecasts of a deterministic theory may more readily be tested for their validity, inaccuracies may be more difficult to interpret (i.e., how far off is the actual outcome?) and pose serious difficulties for some purposes (e.g., policy analysis).

Actual international political systems have a counterpart problem to the deterministic-probabilistic characteristic of theories. We must consider the actual distribution of the forecasted events in international relations. Are the occurrences conceptualized as unique and noncurrent or are they defined so as to be repeated regularly? Examples of the former include the death of Mao or the acquisition of nuclear weapons by Japan. The frequency of changes in a country's political leadership, illustrations of recurrent phenomena, or the rate of diffusion of a technology are illustrations of the latter. If the phenomena that are the subject of the theory reoccur in the reference system, we need to take into account the frequency of their appearance. Are they frequent occurrences—such as diplomatic exchanges or trade negotiations—or relatively less frequent—such as interstate wars or global economic depressions? Suppose that a theory's forecast of the probability of the outbreak of war under certain conditions is .75 and in subsequent actuality the conditions are fulfilled but no war occurs. Over a series of such forecasts we could establish whether the forecasts correspond to events three-fourths of the time, provided that the class of predicted events occurred with sufficient regularity together with the set of conditions specified in the theory. Then we would have a situation comparable to that used in weather forecasts of precipitation: "The probability of rain in the next 24 hours is .80—or more precisely, the probability of precipitation is .80 under conditions such as those that are expected to prevail in this locality during the next 24 hours." Unfortunately, there are numerous events in international relations that do not occur with the frequency with which rain falls on many parts of the earth. Thus, we have a situation in which a theory can predict a pattern of occurrences that do not occur in the real world with sufficient regularity to assess with confidence.

One thoughtful critic has charged that the first author in his previous writing on the subject failed to consider that an error in forecasting (or other criteria for validating a model) can result from a misinterpretation of the reference system—or "real world"—rather than from an inadequate model (Powell, 1973). The charge highlights another problem in the inferential relationship between forecasts and theory. When an incongruity exists between forecasts and subsequent developments, one might ask whether it results from the theory—let us call it theory X—that generated the forecasts or another theory—designated theory Y—used to observe and interpret the reference system? When an astronomer calculates from deflections in the movement of other bodies in our solar system that a previously undetected planet should be observable at a certain point in space and none is found, is the astronomer's theory of the missing planet wrong or should we reexamine the theory of optics or the laws of physics used for locating other objects in space relative to the earth? If a simulation forecasts a certain pattern of national economic growth that is not substantiated in subsequent economic activity as measured by the GNP, do we reexamine the simulation or the indicator of actual economic performance?

Certainly, a committed scientist ought to consider all such avenues in cases of forecasts that appear to be at variance with occurrences in the relevant reference system. It ought to be possible for the investigator to develop a strategy for determining which explanation for the lack of a confirmed forecast he or she should pursue first. (Has the theory of optics been substantiated independently in other tests? Does the present test use GNP in ways the measure has not previously been used?) With respect to simulations, it is often concluded that inaccurate forecasts are indicative of inadequate theory as represented in the simulation. Perhaps such inferences are too easy. Our conceptualizations and observation techniques in international relations have seldom been confirmed in a systematic fashion. In a given area of international relations there may be no definition of the key concepts, no explicit statement of assumptions, and very unreliable measures of observation. Under such circumstances, the scholar must be acutely sensitive to the possibility that the means for verifying the forecasts require careful examination. This point will be considered further when measurement problems are discussed in the next section.

Another type of problem arises in instances having substantial goodness of fit between forecast and reference system events. How confidently can we infer from such verisimilitude in the forecasts to the theory assumed to have accounted for the observed developments? The possibility exists that the correspondence of events and forecasts results from spurious correlation, coincidence, or overdetermined events. The appearance of a substantial goodness of fit that actually resulted from fortuity should be eliminated by repeated forecasting attempts that would reveal the coincidence as random error. Repeated tests should also identify those situations that are overdetermined—that is, outcomes produced by any of several different factors and all of which happen to be present in a given instance. Across a variety of forecast occasions, some of the relevant conditions may not occur, and those accounted for in the theory will be responsible for the observed result. Somewhat more troublesome is the systematic error in the form of a spurious correlation. Although repeated forecast efforts may reveal the presence of this problem, one also can put the theory in an operational form—or simulation—and conduct sensitivity tests to determine the effects of individual components on the outcome when other elements are held constant.

The use of sensitivity testing to check for spurious correlations introduces a point applicable to all the issues discussed in this section. In order to clarify problems that can affect the assumed relationship between a forecast and the theory that generated it, we must examine the theory directly.

For spurious correlations we want to conduct sensitivity tests on the theory, perhaps, as represented in a simulation model. To determine the implications for forecasting of the user's purpose, we need to examine the theory for its correspondence with such purposes. If we have a deterministic theory, we need to identify with special care the variables not contained in the theory that could alter the forecast. Should the theory predict rare events in the reference system, we need to establish estimates of our confidence in the theory independently of its forecasts of those infrequent occurrences. (We will return to this point in the discussion of plausibility in the next section.) Again, in deciding between errors in theories that generate forecasts and errors in theories involved in assessing the actual occurrences in international politics, we must move outside the forecasts themselves.

In short, issues that can affect our inferences about theory which are made from confirmed forecasts require us to deal directly with the source. This observation is one reason why we contend that if validity concerns us more than the forecast itself, then the source of the forecast must be an explicit theory. Unless the source of the forecast reveals its components and their relationships, resolution of the issues discussed in this section often becomes impossible.

IV. VALIDATING THE FORECASTS

To say that a forecast is "valid" certainly involves making claims about the correspondence between the events asserted to obtain in the forecast and the events that do, "in fact," obtain in the referent system. However, forecast validity should not be viewed only in terms of the correspondence between forecasted events and observations made of the world. At the time a forecast is made, it describes future events.[3] Whether this description is "accurate" or not depends upon events that have not yet occurred. We still may want to make statements about the validity of the forecast. However, the precise empirical testing of forecasts is often quite expensive in time and money and we ought first to satisfy ourselves that such an effort is justified. Therefore, it will be useful first to consider several preliminary tests to which theories used in forecasting might be subjected, prior to explicitly confronting the forecast with observation-based data.

First, it seems reasonable to establish that the forecasts be plausible. By plausible we mean that the forecasted events do not grossly contradict present understanding of the way the referent system behaves. As an illustration consider the story— perhaps apocryphal—of the response of one of the developers of an American quarterly econometric model who was asked what he would do if his model forecast a 15 percent unemployment rate. He answered that he would ignore the model because no US government would permit unemployment to reach 15 percent. In other words, to him such a forecast would be highly implausible. One means of evaluating the plausibility of forecasts is to consult with people who deal with the particular domain about which the forecasts are made. Policy planners, for example, often are able to make informal judgments regarding the probable consequences of actions. The evaluation of these experts provides information useful in constraining the class of plausible forecasts.

Another method of testing plausibility is related to the point made earlier about sensitivity testing. Occasionally a theory that generates plausible forecasts when the values of variables are held to expected or previous levels yields absurd results if certain values exceed "normal" levels. For example, some education planners argued for a theory that forecast exponential enrollment growth in higher education. Predictions from the theory seemed to fit the data very well until about 1969. However, the model predicted exceedingly larger student enrollments for more extreme values of time. For the late twenty-first century, the number of US college students was forecast to exceed the total predicted population of the United States. Thus, we would want to be wary in using such a theory in making very long-range forecasts. Systems "stressing" of this kind is frequently ignored because the theory makes quite plausible predictions in shorter time frames or for more normal ranges of events. However, even very simple sensitivity tests such as that outlined above, may reveal that much of the process about which a theory forecasts is not yet understood.

In considering the empirical aspects of validation, one of the important questions concerns how observational data should be employed to accept or reject the propositions in the theory. Resolving such problems is one of the tasks of inferential statistics. The logic underlying the use of statistics in validating forecasts is fairly straightforward. Certain propositions in the theory state that variables are related in specific ways. These relations together with measures of observed values of these variables are used to forecast values of these variables at other times. More specifically, propositions $p_1, p_2, p_3, \ldots, p_n$ together imply forecasts f_1, $f_2, \ldots, f_m$. From logic we know that $\sim (f_1, f_2, \ldots, f_m) \rightarrow \sim (p_1, p_2, \ldots, p_n)$. Thus, if some of the forecast statements are false then so must be some of the theoretical propositions employed in generating these forecasts. Although the underlying logic of the procedure is relatively simple, problems in measurement and observation make implementation of the strategy difficult.

The problem is especially troublesome for the dynamic and complex referent systems of interest in international politics. For example, given that the referent system is parameterized by time and assuming we want to test the relative importance of particular independent variables using normal variance accounting techniques, ordinary least squares is not generally an appropriate technique. Hibbs (1973) demonstrates that if auto correlation occurs in the disturbance terms, ordinary least squares leads to a serious overestimation of the impact of independent variables. This impact can be subdivided into two particular classes. In the first case, when there are no lag variables in the analysis, the overestimation effects do not influence the prediction of the regression coefficient but they do affect the importance of the t test or the multiple R^2. In the second case where lag variables are included in the analysis, not only are the above effects noticed, but the actual level of the regression coefficients is influenced in such a way that usually the nonlagged variables' importance is decreased and the lag variables' importance is increased. These increases and decreases can be of a magnitude of 300 to 400 percent.

Although the problems sketched above stem largely from assumed dynamics, further problems arise when we consider the large number of variables and complex relations (e.g., nonlinear, nonstationary feedback, etc.) that probably occur in many interesting aspects of international politics. In such cases, a possible strategy is to decompose the theory into "subtheories" and evaluate each subtheory independently. However, in general, there is no guarantee that such an approach will work. For example, Ando, Fisher, and Simon

(1963) have demonstrated that only when dealing with linear relations and only when the variance to be accounted for is explainable by the variables in each decomposed subset will such a decomposition strategy work. They proceed to show that it is more frequently the case that the subsystems are only partially decomposable (most, but not all, variance is explainable by variables within the subset). In such cases the subsystem can be treated independently only over short periods of time. Over long periods of time, interactions between subsystems become dominant. Thus, in longer range forecasting it is generally an unwise strategy to attempt to break a theory into more manageable subsets having fewer variables. This conclusion is similar to that of George who suggests that, at least for policy making, theories with more variables may have greater utility (1971, p. xvi).

As was mentioned above, when confronting forecasts with observations to determine empirical validity, it is necessary to make assumptions regarding the procedure for measuring the referent system. These assumptions are necessary because employing any of the statistical strategies outlined previously requires that predicted values of the measures be compared to actual values of the measures. If the actual value is not interpretable in the same terms for both the referent system and the theory used to make the forecast, then any statistical comparisons will be suspect. In other words, it is important to establish the validity of the measures used to assess the accuracy of forecasts.

Not only must measures be valid, but as was mentioned earlier, they must also be accurate enough for the purposes to which they will be put. The accuracy of measures is especially important when doing forecasts that use present values of variables to project future values. As an example, consider a theory that proposes (Fucks, 1965, and Morgenstern, et al.) that the change in the power (M) of a nation at one time is some constant times its present power (M_t):

$$M = \rho M_t.$$

Letting M_o be the initial value, M_t for any t can be computed by:

$$M_t = M_o e^{\rho t}.$$

Suppose ρ is measured to an accuracy of ± 3 percent. Numerically, suppose the estimated value of ρ is 2.0. Then $\rho = 2.0 \pm .06$. By the time $t = 10$, the 3 percent error in ρ will have compounded to a more than 25 percent range in the predicted value of M_{10}.

Similar sorts of things happen when using the more standard one step linear model:

$$X_{t+1} = aX_t + \epsilon$$

where ϵ is a disturbance term with variance σ^2 and mean 0.

For example purposes, suppose $a = 1.01$, the expected value of $x_1 = 7$ and $\sigma^2 = 1$. At time 1 then the expected value of X is 1. If we set a tolerance region of three standard deviations, the observed value should be 1.0 ± 7.9. Using the linear model, the expected value of X_{25} is 1.3. However the variance of X_{25} is 41.75. Using the same three standard deviation tolerance region, the observed value should be 1.3 ± 19.38. Indeed, in general if the system being theorized about is not stable ($a < 1.0$), the farther out in time one projects, the greater will be the variance. In the example above, $\text{var}(t_{50}) = 100.7$. $E(X_{50})$ is 1.6. The three standard deviation tolerance region is 1.6 ± 30.1. Very small measurement errors are often greatly compounded in long range forecasts.

V. SUMMARY

This chapter has attempted to develop a series of observations about the validation of forecasts. They are summarized in the following numbered points.

1. Often our interest in confirming forecasts in international relations is to facilitate our judgment about the source of the forecast. For example, we may wish to evaluate the source in order to establish our confidence in its ability to make future forecasts.

2. A number of factors can affect the relationship between the forecast and the source that generated it, leading to incorrect inferences about the source. Among these problems are the effects of the user's purpose, whether the generating theory is deterministic or probabilistic, the frequency of occurrence of the forecasted events in international relations, the adequacy of the theories for measurement and interpretation of the reference system, and the confirmation of the forecast by observations other than those used in making the projection.

3. These obstructions to reasonable inference about the source can often be assessed if we can examine the source of the forecast in various ways. Such independent testing of the source is possible only if the components of the theory and their relationship are known and precisely defined. For this reason, we contend that the source of the forecast must be a deductive theory. Other sources of forecasts in international relations may produce valid forecasts and play a vital role. But problems will be encountered with them if we try to assess systematically their potential for subsequent forecasting efforts.

4. The task remains of determining the goodness of fit between the theory's projection of the future value of certain variables and the subsequent unfolding of actual occurrences. Before beginning empirical testing, some efforts should be made to determine if the forecast is within contextual constraints, that is, whether it is plausible. Empirical testing with statistical techniques can follow, but the investigator should be mindful of several factors—such as consistency in level of analysis—that can influence results.

NOTES

1. A major difficulty with much contemporary international relations forecasting is that the calculations, the conceptualizations, the mental images, the models in the mind—whatever we label the cognitive processes used to derive a forecast—often remain implicit and unarticulated. Kaplan has summarized the resulting problem in a delightful way. "Too often the hypotheses with which we work are at home only in the twilight regions of the mind, where their wavering outlines blend into a shadowy background . . . . Forced into the open, our ideas may flutter helplessly; but at least we can see what bloodless creatures they are" (Kaplan, 1964, pp. 268–269).

2. The distinction between the projected outcomes from probabilistic as compared to deterministic theories overlaps somewhat with Choucri's distinction between predictions and forecasts. We maintain, however, that a deterministic theory could still produce a forecast in Choucri's sense of the term. See her discussion in Chapter 1.

3. In the case of retrospective forecasting the events already have transpired but must be unknown to the forecaster. Hence for the purposes of this decision, they can be treated in the same manner as events that have not yet occurred.

CHAPTER SIX

SUCCESSFUL AND UNSUCCESSFUL FORECASTING IN INTERNATIONAL RELATIONS

Thomas W. Milburn

I. INTRODUCTION

Evidence still stands in England on the plains of Salisbury of an impressive and successful early attempt at prediction through extrapolation—the massive stone circles of Stonehenge that, about 4,000 years ago, were constructed to catch the first rays of the sun along the tops and through notches of stones at the time of the vernal equinox. Since ancient times that exploit stands out, although the Celts built many stone circles throughout the British Isles. Alongside Stonehenge the Egyptian achievement predicting the annual flooding of the Nile appears a lesser feat simply because astronomers so exceed meteorologists in terms of the accuracy of their predictions.

By contrast, a striking aspect of the modern age consists not merely of the ubiquity of predictions but of their validation. In a sense, every scheduled departure of an airline, train, or bus, every concert or college class schedule constitutes a series of predictions of events which mostly successfully validate the prediction within minutes. Of course, incentives exist to have such public commitments accurate ones, and reputations for failure to predict accurately can dearly cost their makers. In industry, safety, quality control, and planning departments all function to increase the accuracy of industrial predictions. We regard the regular validation of such announcements of intention quite highly; many consider them symbolic of the efficiency of contemporary literate civilization, a critical social indicator of the dependability of our institutions.

Yet, we do not equally successfully predict all classes of events, nor do all predictors, persons, or methods function equally well in assisting us to make forecasts. Lewis F. Terman, the American father of the intelligence test, which he used in part to identify a large sample of gifted individuals whom he and others have studied for many years, also studied factors in marital happiness. Extending statistical curves dealing with the premarital sexual behavior of women through the 1920's led him to predict in the early 1930's that no girl born after 1940 would enter marriage a virgin. Another famous psychologist, John Watson, a father of behaviorism, was quoted in 1927 as having said, on the basis of projections of rates of change, (that is, assuming no changes in rates of change) within 50 years the institution of marriage would no longer exist. With 1977 in the past, we now know that his prediction was unsuccessful.

Vannevar Bush made his famous and often cited statement of the infeasibility of intercontinental ballistic missiles in the late 1940's, about 15 years after some prominent physicists estimated the practical control of nuclear energy to be about 200 years away. Some of the technological and social significance of the high-speed computer was quickly recognized, and various persons made predictions about it. Peter Drucker has recounted some of the story as an example of less successful prediction.

> In the late nineteen-forties nobody predicted that the computer would be used by business and government. While the computer was a "major scientific revolution," everybody "knew" that its main use would be in science and in warfare.

> Indeed, the most extensive market research study undertaken at that time reached the conclusion that the world computer market would, at most, be able to absorb 1,000 computers by the year 2000. Now, only 25 years later, there are some 150,000 computers installed in the world, most of them doing the most mundane bookkeeping work.

> A few years later, however, when it became apparent that business was buying computers for payroll or billing, everybody predicted that the computer would revolutionize business.

> The "experts" predicted that the computer would displace middle management, so that there would be nobody left between the chief executive officer and the foreman.

> "Is middle management obsolete?" asked a widely quoted *Harvard Business Review* article of the early nineteen-fifties. And it answered this rhetorical question with a resounding "Yes." At that moment the tremendous expansion of middle management jobs began.

> In every developed country, over the last 20 years, middle management jobs, in business as well as in government, have grown about three times as fast as total employment. And that growth has been directly correlated with the growth of computer usage. (Drucker, 1973)

In the above examples, two kinds of limitations of past forecasts seem evident. (Both of these are mentioned by Nazli Choucri in Chapter 1.) The probability of inventions that lead to countervailing trends was not dealt with. The consequences of inventions were poorly evaluated; contingent predictions assuming consequences for such inventions would have been wrong.

Much effort has gone into making some predictions inaccurate, a particularly impressive example being Adolf Hitler's success in persuading Josef Stalin confidently to predict that the German army would not initiate a nonprovoked attack, at least not without an ultimatum, despite considerable evidence to the contrary. Hitler succeeded at that effort because of the careful injection at many levels of misinformation into many information channels. Though less spectacular, the Allies' deceiving Hitler to predict incorrectly the location of the D-Day assault on the European continent was analogous (Whaley, 1973). Deception pays off in warfare and other pure conflict situations about as well as honest accuracy pays off in more cooperative ventures. Moreover, parties to large- or small-scale conflicts rarely employ negative feedback loops; so, the signal-to-noise ratios of tactical aspects of conflicts tend to be quite low, and accurate predicting is difficult or impossible to achieve even for more understood and less multivariate processes. All of which suggests that humans will predict more accurately in cooperative than in conflict-rich environments, and more accurately in information-rich than in noisy settings.

To forecast an event accurately, to have assessed an event that does occur as highly probable, even a potential disaster such as an earthquake or a war, may or may not lead to handling it readily and effectively. We have foreseen the approach of several violent conflicts of the past few years, for example, the Arab-Israeli outbreak of violence of 1967, and the India-Pakistan war over Bangladesh, without dealing with them very successfully. One must note, however, that we can (and do) speak of the validity of prescriptions, by which we mean their applicability, workableness, and appropriateness as remedies for social, political, and other ills. Valid remedies cure or even prevent gross disturbances. Of course, valid forecasts and valid remedies are related, the latter depending on the former. Not to predict a serious event that does in fact occur means allowing no time to plan and prepare for it; thus the likelihood of disruption, chaos, and cost increases. To deal with unexpected costs may disrupt other processes from which resources are stolen, and steal time ordinarily spent organizing. One must balance the cost of planning for low-probability events with high costs should they occur. (I thus state the rationale for and against worst-case analyses as a planning tool.) We predict that valid remedies will work if applied to likely contingencies. Implicitly then, we predict good outcomes from situations to which we apply remedies we perceive as valid.

There is so far no close analogy in international forecasting to the medical model's interrelating such tools as diagnosis, prognosis, and related treatment of choice. Perhaps the nearest analogy would be Edward Azar's "early warning" monitoring of dangerous events that are about to happen. And psychologists who practice the experimental analysis of behavior deal with the experimental production of remedies but attend very little to matters such as diagnosis or prognosis.

II. ATTRIBUTES OF PREDICTABLE EVENTS

To forecast more accurately there are several routes:

1. It is easier to forecast some kinds of events.

2. Some forecasters function more effectively than others.

3. Not all methods of forecasting have proved equally efficacious.

4. Some classes of persons have shown more effective track records at forecasting than others.

Let me first suggest the attributes of processes that are easy to predict. The most obvious is stability, either in the sense of nonchange or of regularity of recurrence. I have been told that meteorologists often regard snidely the task of weather prediction in such places as Arizona or Southern California, where day-to-day variation is so small that one could establish a reputation for high accuracy by mostly repeating the same forecasts again and again. The ancient Celtic Druids who directed the building of Stonehenge benefited immeasurably in their quest for accuracy of prediction from the fantastic regularity of recurrence characteristic of so many astronomical events. It often takes many observations, distributed with care, to discover that invariance in aspects of phenomena of interest is likely to prove sufficient for accurate prediction. The choice of processes to be predicted is not trivial; to work with phenomena that one can predict accurately conveys status upon scientists. Those disciplines that predict more accurately aspects of the phenomena with which they deal receive more peer acclaim.

We forecast that habitual behavior or customary acts will continue and, indeed, their very regularity increases the ease with which we forecast them, at least over the short run; for they are highly probable events. We forecast such behavior more accurately and over longer time spans if we can predict that the structure of incentives or reinforcers that supported its existence will continue. Note that the long-run forecast can be made readily, given the structural contingency. The existence of stable economic growth should not surprise us to the extent that it results from a convergence of habits and customs support by technology.

We find that past grade-getting behavior or past job performance, each an amalgam of habits, skills, motives, and environmental support, predict similar future performance in similar tasks and settings better than any other predictors, given that environmental support remains as constant as the other factors. Similarly, job stability or residence stability both predict future stability, but then, as indicated above, we readily predict that stable patterns will continue.

The existence of multiple cues increases the accuracy of a wide range of predictions. Watch a driver approaching you from the opposite direction with his turn-light signaling a right turn. Does he slow down as he approaches an intersection? Does he move into the right lane? If he stops for a traffic light, does he turn his wheels to the right, even if ever so slightly? We trust, that is, believe in, or use the first information concerning his turn indicator with more confidence as a function of the various cues that support a prediction which itself forms the basis for our next action.

Or, assume that a major nation announces planned steps involving some unilateral disarmament. These announcements are more credible as a basis for our forecast that such events will indeed happen, given that the country is faced with other problems such as pollution, an unfavorable trade balance, or diminishing energy reserves, *and* if, despite a decreasing growth rate for GNP, more goods and services are being provided consumers.

Rather more neglected as an attribute of events to be forecast than their stability is the frequency of their occurrence within a population of events—or absolutely. It has largely proved infeasible to predict the personality attributes of those individuals within a population who will commit suicide, for example, sufficiently well to improve upon the base-line information available about the population as a whole (Meehl and Rosen, 1967). The suicide rate runs at about 20 per 100,000 per year in the United States. On the other hand, we can prove our predictions of suicide more readily among alcoholics or the severely depressed. The base line for suicide in the latter two categories of persons is far higher than in the case of the general population. We can predict more readily other events with higher base rates in the population under consideration. It becomes easier, as well as more worthwhile in a Pareto sense, to attempt to forecast which persons or classes of persons will die from heart attacks and related circulatory ailments than to predict who will die by suicide. We can predict more readily whatever occurs with regularity, that is, events with high autocorrelations. A wide variety of stimuli may elicit, provoke, legitimate, restrain, or inhibit some behaviors such as aggressive acts, so we may more readily and accurately predict their occurrence. By contrast, accident proneness, for example, as a concept has grown less interesting and useful because its unpatterned quality makes it too unreliable to predict. It is like predicting specific scientific inventions. It is easier to forecast what is already partially determined with respect to a general class or set of objects. If I wish to predict accurately that my car is about to run out of gasoline, it helps if I know that my gas gauge is an accurate one, and that I have looked at the dial carefully, and that perhaps someone else has looked at the dial, too, independently of me.

If I wish accurately to forecast that the "good will" between two nations has increased, that war between them now is less probable, it helps if we know that our set of cues for monitoring good will has in the past proved accurate in this and similar settings and that distinctly independent observers similarly read those signs.

One more readily makes accurate forecasts about the occurrence of an event or process if he has made any predictions before, even wrong ones, or if he has engineered the events predicted. However, a preferred method is to have a theory or a set of propositions that tell us why such a prediction as we make might be accurate in ways sufficient for us or another to say, "I understand." We trust theories more if they predict the nonoccurrence as well as the occurrence of events on the basis of some conceptual structure, say, why or how the errors occur.

Insight and understanding predict behavior. If a man understands himself, the processes of his behavior, and the effects of his actions, he will predict his own behavior and the consequences of his actions more readily, and we may predict that he may less often get other people angry at him and so may act with more political skill. Similarly, the existence of information to the leaders of an organization about processes of escalation in conflicts with others may lead us to predict that escalation is less likely than otherwise. To know and understand the nature of arms races in detail may make them less likely. But it is not sufficient to realize that wars may be very costly to reduce their likelihood.

If one knows what an organization reinforces or encourages as behavior, or what it elicits as behavior from its members, or what the world system reinforces or rewards, or in other ways pays off, then we are better equipped to predict these. What pays off is readily predicted. Dimensions of situations also predict, but the possibilities for prediction inherent in complex situations are only beginning to be widely understood.

Some events are notably difficult to predict accurately. These are ones where we are unacquainted with contingencies that increase causally the likelihood of the events. I know, for example, of no scholar who correctly predicted when, or the conditions governing when the ruling collective leadership in the Soviet Union would remove Nikita Khrushchev from office. Too many of the critical contingencies were simply unknown to Western scholars.

III. GOOD AND BAD FORECASTERS

Classes of events vary in terms of the accuracy with which they lead us to forecast various classes of future events. One such class of events concerns expressed preferences. What people prefer to do they will do more often than that which does not interest them, or toward which they have an aversion. Preference for an activity predicts choosing it over others, persisting at it, and finding it satisfying. Shared preferences of a group of people increases the likelihood that what they prefer will be done and done relatively well. There are two criterial dimensions: predicting an activity and predicting the level of performance. Students who prefer to study do actually study more and have more impressive grade-point averages.

The best single predictor of behavior is behavior; our acts predict our subsequent acts more readily than do our words. (See Chapter 15, by Edward Azar.) However, indicators of value preferences, whether verbal or nonverbal, test out a close second. A person's value preferences predict what he will do and enjoy (given that the choice is his and the structure of his opportunities is known), and do well (assuming that ability to perform and also instrumental motivation are held constant).

A nation's values similarly enable us to forecast its behavior more effectively. Psychologist David McClelland has found that nations that give strong indications of valuing achievement grow industrially at a more rapid rate (the correlations between need-achievement and future increases in kilowatt hours has been as high as .70; the correlation with growth of real income .50), given that the countries involved are industrial ones and that the sources for establishing the value placed on achieving include children's texts (McClelland, 1961).

Utility schedules are preferences also. It is widely recognized that one reason the United States did so poorly in Vietnam is that we did not appreciate our enemy's utility schedules. Therefore

we predicted their behavior poorly. Similarly, during World War II, we did not predict the general unifying or cohesion-generating effect of American bombing of German cities.

For reasons of conceptual clarity many scholars have preferred to make predictions on the basis of scales derived from factor analysis. However, factorially pure scales, ones with homogenous content (where items correlate with one another, or load statistically on the same factor) have not been astonishing in the accuracy of their predictions. Less pure, more empirically based scales (where all items survive because of their correlation with an outside criterion) have proved more effective and accurate in predicting behavior.

While value preferences predict reasonably well, values within contexts of situations predict more powerfully than do more general statements of preference—one of the reasons, I suppose, for the limited usefulness of the utiles concept designed to measure utility. Content analyses that have incorporated aspects of context have more successfully predicted behavior than ones that have omitted context. More globally based predictions have done somewhat better than less globally based ones (George, 1959).

Norms also predict. By norms I would include the oughts, the values of a group, as contrasted with values of individuals. These are also organizational values; these may come out of policies or as decision rules. Culturally, norms may appear as rules of etiquette, a subcategory of which might be table manners or forms of polite address. If we know the norms of a group, other things being equal, then it is clear that we can predict behavior in accord with those norms. Note that we can predict far more effectively if we know that norms are also preferences for the people involved.

Expressed intentions predict a good deal better than do inferred ones. Moreover, evidence of detailed plans and means to implement expressed intentions make intentions so accompanied a more accurate predictor than otherwise.

The norms or policies of an organization will to some degree predict what individuals within the organization will do. We would expect that such norms will predict more validly for persons (1) who are highly socialized (i.e., who have internalized many of society's rules and sanctions, and

(2) who have learned very well and perhaps internalized their organization's rules and sanctions. (If I criticize myself or my performance anytime I disregard or violate a company policy, even unintentionally, I have internalized that policy.) People who are highly socialized *vis-à-vis* aggression, who would not ordinarily strike or even loudly criticize another person, may even kill people or order killing carried out because to do so is "part of their job" (e.g., American airmen in Cambodia). Of course, not only norms but also incentives may be involved; one acts also because of career incentives such as chances for promotion.

Norms forecast behavior imperfectly; otherwise, even new laws or items of moral codes would forecast everyone's behavior with accuracy. Of course, norms (moral codes, laws) do predict behavior far better in small communities which socialize their offspring quite effectively and in some states, for example, Maine, Vermont, and Iowa, more than others. Social stressors such as crowding, anonymity, poverty, marked heterogeneity, and lack of socializing institutions all contribute to invalidate laws and other value norms as social forecasts. Incentives to behave in accord with norms increase the probability that norms can serve as effective bases for predicting behavior. Old laws forecast behavior better than new ones through the influences of habit, tradition (regularities of social functioning which take these into account), and successive waves of socializing influence. Norms predict more accurately for highly socialized individuals where individual preferences and organizational norms diverge. A psychopath or psychotic within an organization who may disregard many organizational rules may delight in carrying out organizational directives that call for violent behavior because they legitimate and protect what he has wanted to do anyway.

Value preferences are stable, the more so when they are supported by habits that are themselves satisfying ones. Normative values do not predict so well as do preferences. What one wants or prefers predicts his actions better than what even he sees he ought to do. Still, oughts, norms, or rules for action have often predicted well, especially in circumstances where they may have been internalized (Leites, 1953). Table manners may have come to be preferred by most who feel also that they ought to use their knives and forks in ways that enable them to eat rather satisfactorily. Negative sanctions—for example, dirty looks or critical comments in the case of table manners—for violating these norms increase the probability that they will be observed. Moreover, norms often are born of stress and conflict in groups (Thibaut and Faucheux, 1965) which said norms serve to diminish. In that case observance of norms is influenced by the satisfactions associated with the avoidance of those conditions that the norms were invented to avoid. Norms may, on occasion, predict behavior rather well, too, when norm violations are invariably punished. Note the famous "J" curve of conformity for arriving at a job on time (Allport, 1924) when penalties exist for arriving late. Fewer persons arrive late at musical performances or dramas when latecomers must suffer the loss of missing the first part of the performance.

Customs are not merely habits; some element of norm is associated with them, too. Customs provide bounds for permissible behavior. Customs predict well for groups and organizations, particularly if their observance serves to predict behavior more readily, and is intrinsically (some customs are simply satisfying to observe) or extrinsically (observance is paid in money or social currency) satisfying.

To forecast how well customs, contracts, or treaties will be observed, one needs to know what functions they serve—and how satisfying they are—as well as knowing the nature, strength, and certainty of sanctions for observance and nonobservance. Predicting observance of customs or treaties is a function of conditional probabilities. Predicting observance is an additive function of the probabilities of the occurrence of the various events that by their occurrence increase the likelihood of the observance of custom, rule, or treaty. Certainly, knowing that X benefits from some agreement (e.g., marriage), that he deems this agreement as helpful or instrumental to the achievement of other goals he has or advantages he would obtain, and that he operates with a fairly long-term perspective greatly increases the accuracy of predictions that he will adhere to a project.

Cultural values and beliefs even predict national behavior. People that value "honor" and violent response to insults engage more readily in violence, for example, Kaiser Wilhelm. In such cases violence is condoned or goes unpunished more often. In the United States, higher rates of homicide in the South have been accounted for in this way. Courage as a cultural value may predict courageous behavior; thus, many Mohawk Indians work on high-rise construction projects in New York City as ways to establish and maintain their masculine identities.

A group's style predicts itself, given that the conditions which maintain that style do not change. Most representatives of Japanese culture attempt to act politely in interpersonal relations. The Thai tend to act with indirection. Chinese national decision makers seem to handle crises essentially by talking about them a good deal before they act. That is, they reflect before they act so that our prediction of their future behavior would be that they would continue to act as they do now, in accord with the present style.

The presence of weapons, the capability to wage war, tend to predict war with greater frequency than their absence (Berkowitz and LePage, 1967). In general, the United States military has predicted the probable hostile behaviors of other nations on the basis of their resources. That is, they tend to assume that what a country they define as an enemy can do it will do, especially if the action involves something bad happening to the United States. Absurd as this basis for prediction may be under some circumstances, it should be noted that resources which provide a basis for capacity to achieve something may greatly increase the likelihood that it will be achieved. A person may want to go to medical school because his value within his family will increase, and thus he may feel that he ought to do so. However, if he lacks money, intelligence, or the capacity for persistent work through medical school, he simply will not make it.

Expressed intentions sometimes predict rather well, and the more public they are the better. But knowledge of a student's or a nation's capability to carry out expressed intentions is a necessary condition for us to predict that intentions will be carried out. If a mediocre or dull student announces that he is going to medical school, we are properly skeptical. If the Soviet Union announces that it will shortly become self-sufficient in wheat production, we may properly doubt its capability to do so. Investments of work or resources to implement expressed intentions increase the probability that predictions based on such publicly expressed intentions (plus investments) will prove accurate. However, our confidence in such expressed intentions may increase markedly if it appears that the actor's anticipated ratio of benefits to costs from acting as he says he will, will significantly exceed that for other apparent alternative lines of action.

Statements of intentions predict far more credibly for those who have shown consistent and strong relations between such statements and actual past behavior. We expect to discover that statements of intention will prove more valid as forecasts when social incentive and disincentive structures converge with, and support, statements of intentions. Thus, Abram Chayes, a professor of international law, has argued (1972) for the existence of bureaucratic forces within the Soviet Union that should serve to increase the probability that the Soviets will abide by the SALT (Strategic Arms Limitation Talks) I agreements. This agreement constitutes a public forecast by the Soviets and serves as a basis for our forecasts that they will (or will not) abide by their agreements. It is presumed that the Soviets make similar forecasts of the United States.

Assume that the United States wishes to predict the likelihood of observance of the SALT I Treaty. Several of the factors mentioned above seem relevant, but others are available. What, for example, is the Soviet record of observing treaties? Triska (1964) has found it useful to divide treaties into categories, A and B. A treaties (economic and technical) are almost always observed; B treaties (political) are violated more often. So the policy analyst involved in forecasting Soviet treaty-keeping behavior will want to discover more incentives for abiding by a new political treaty (e.g., SALT I) and fewer for breaching it than he would require for an economic agreement before he would recommend entering into such an agreement. What is the Soviet record for violating arms control treaties as a special subset? To what extent is such a treaty likely to prove self-reinforcing? Chayes addresses himself to this point and argues plausibly, though with less solid evidence than an arms controller might prefer, that Soviet nonviolation is strongly determined by many contextual factors such as bureaucratic politics.

Before signing an arms control treaty, we would like to know the probability of violation, the probability that violations will be detected, the cost to us, the nonviolating party, of violations by the other, and of minor violations compared to major ones. This would be predicted in part on the basis of Chayes' reasoning. For example, what satisfaction, increase in security, etc. does the USSR achieve from nonviolation? What satisfaction do they see the United States as having? What are their estimates of probability that we would violate and they would lose by our violation? Their probability of violation will be a function in part of their perception that we shall violate. Note that we could also seek to predict United States observance of such a treaty using similar reasoning.

One can predict choices and decisions better if he knows the nature of the opportunity structure that a person or group presents. That is, we may predict choices more effectively if we know a person's perceived set of alternatives. We may predict whom someone will marry more effectively if we know how real are other available options. This is in accord with Thibaut's and Kelley's concepts of comparison level and comparison level for alternatives (1959). Comparison level for alternatives essentially measures how much I like what I have compared to the other alternatives available. Other aspects of the environment may lead to and may offer eliciting stimuli which increase the likelihood of particular events or behaviors, or lead to none of these. Technology is a good example, since it presents opportunities as well as costs. With technology, we can do some things more rapidly or effectively than others; it may also mean a far more rapid depletion of available resources over a longer term because of the energy consumed by new technology. Technology also appears to increase the probability of war (North, 1962).

Growth rates and accelerations also permit us to forecast their continuation, although we need to know where we are on a growth rate curve to be able to predict with accuracy. Growth rates do have the special advantage of enabling us to predict negative and positive accelerations and changes in growth. It is easy to predict with confidence that the present population growth rates will not continue until 200 or 500 years from now. In less than 500 years, as anyone can figure out by using the law of geometric progressions, the earth would be so totally full of people, given current growth rates,

that there would not even be room to move around. That state of affairs is extraordinarily unlikely. Zero population growth appears likely well before then.

Important events are ones that influence the lives of many persons; they are often harder to forecast correctly than less important ones involving only a few or a single individual. There is more uncertainty associated with the contingencies involving the latter than the former. (But bureaucratic inertia can be a stable analog of habits.)

The presence of known habits predicts some unimportant events quite well. When President Nixon was in the White House, he reportedly often cooked his own cereal for breakfast and prepared cottage cheese for lunch. Unless one expected to interpose some special events, he would predict that the President would continue to have those same foods from one time to the next because such was his habit. He did not care much for cereal for breakfast and was reported to dislike cottage cheese at lunch sufficiently that he smothered it in catsup. But still he ate them out of habit and because his physician encouraged him to do so. Habits predict, of course, especially ones of some duration, but knowledge of regularities in certain stimulus situations that we conceptualize as instinctual preprograming in animals also predicts their behavior. The "dance" and "singing" of bees upon returning to the hive to announce the location and distance of new sources of honey constitute examples with near-poetic flavor.

To summarize concerning effective predictors: Value preferences permit us broadly to forecast a wide range of phenomena, and they show the most stability over time, given that the actors involved perceive substantial rewards and unsubstantial costs to be associated with them. Capabilities are a necessary condition for events, but are not a sufficient one. Value norms, while powerful, are yet a weaker predictor. Statements of intentions may predict behavior under some circumstances, but they are especially vulnerable to shifts in context or environment. Habits predict themselves reasonably well if they are suitably reinforced occasionally. Social exchange is a conceptual position with marked plausibility, stating that rewards and costs, including available alternatives, will strongly influence behavior; but rewards are only such when they are preferred and costs only such when negatively preferred. Preferences with other attributes, of course, predict behavior most effectively over long periods.

IV. EXPERTS

Experts may be defined as those who know more about a given phenomenon than do others. Currently our most substantial basis for judging who is an expert is the judgment of the person's peers. Typically some of the experts' knowledge is systematized in the form of theory. However, inherent in the use of experts is an adage of Polanyi, that "we always know more than we can prove." If we could prove readily, we would have less need for experts. However experts do better than others. In a series of experiments by Cline (1964), psychologists predicted the actual behavior of persons in filmed stress interviews more effectively than a group of engineers, although it should be noted that an intuitive housewife made the best predictions of all experts.

Dorothy Meier kept box scores of predictions of world events by three different groups of "experts" in order to be able to compare man-machine simulation with a base line (Guetzkow, 1966). Foreign Service officers did a better job of predicting political events than did journalists. And experts are sometimes wrong, often being too conservative, for example, Vannevar Bush's prediction that intercontinental ballistic missiles (ICBMs) were impossible, or the predictions during the early 1930's by physicists that atomic energy might be controlled in a few hundred years. But with superior knowledge bases we can expect experts to be right more often than people with less knowledge. Moreover, they can estimate the relative probable frequency of different events and add some rationale in connection with each. However, it should be noted that in one study (Milburn and Milburn, 1966), social and physical scientists forecast conflict events more optimistically and less accurately when dealing with the others' field than with their own. Social scientists were more willing to predict technological breakthroughs than were physical scientists. Physical scientists were more willing to predict certain forms of political and social change than were the social scientists. Lack of knowledge of an area seemed to lead to an increased willingness to forecast there, in a less discriminating way, and with less concern with hard-to-foresee contingencies.

Still, there was very considerable agreement between the two groups in areas where one group was clearly more qualified than the other. I organized this exercise in 1964, asking thirty social scientists and twenty physical scientists to answer a series of future-oriented, survey-like questions bearing on international relations. Some of these questions posed the task of forecasting likelihood of conflicts and conflict-related developments. Unlike Delphi surveys, the data collected were based on the independent judgments of members of the two groups of experts. There were no successive iterations and no efforts to influence the judges involved by telling them how the others perceived queries and possibilities. Independent judgments tend to distribute themselves so as to cancel random errors (and randomly distributed systematic errors) of a group of judges.

The survey does permit some test of its validity through the early 1970's. For this purpose the predictions made can be dichotomized; events then were treated as judged likely or unlikely. Under conditions of perfect accuracy, all events deemed relatively more probable would have occurred; and all events deemed relatively more improbable would not have happened. Some events deemed improbable that have not yet occurred may still happen before 1980. However, the situation provides an opportunity to test the validity of forecasts of two groups of experts, and to compare their accuracies with one another since they were not likely to serve equally well with regard to all predictions. Of course, it is not reasonable to generalize from these experts to all similar experts; these scholars were chosen because of their special knowledge. They did not constitute representative samples of similar experts; in fact, they exhausted certain conceptually defined populations, since potential sample sizes were rather small.

The predictions can be judged for accuracy by comparing what has actually happened. On the whole the experts did very well. Of the twenty-nine events deemed more likely than unlikely, all have now occurred. Of those events judged as more unlikely than likely, accuracy was far less. Nineteen of the twenty-nine predictions appear to have been made accurately, an equal number for social and physical scientist groups, although the groups differed slightly on some events. Social scientists predicted technological breakthroughs for both the United States and the USSR in the areas of antiballistic missile defense and antisubmarine warfare. The more conservative, and perhaps better informed, physical scientists did not so predict (Item 7, Table 6.1). Such events have not occurred and do not appear very likely to occur so far.

Some items are difficult to interpret. Neither group of experts predicted war within the communist bloc (Item 1, Table 6.2). There certainly was strife, and the Soviet takeover of Czechoslovakia could have meant warfare except that it was so swiftly and effectively carried out.

Physical scientists predicted at least one presently communist country becoming overtly noncommunist. The social scientists, relatively more conservative in dealing with political events, did not predict. The case of Indonesia is an ambiguous one. Under Sukarno the country was neutral but procommunist. Following a series of assassinations as part of a communist attempt to gain more com-

plete power, anticommunist leaders who escaped conducted their own massacre. Since then (1966) the country has been definitely and overtly noncommunist. Because Sukarno's regime was not officially a communist one and did, in fact, include the anticommunists who engineered the shift to the right, I scored that one as a hit for the social scientists and a miss for the physical scientists. In the series, the physical scientists were undecided as to whether a European country would go communist, with the social scientists predicting that such would prove quite unlikely. Both groups considered it likely that some Latin American country (not presently communist) would go communist. While Chile's Allende was an avowed Marxist, his regime appeared slightly more rightist than he and certainly was not close at any time to being a second officially communist nation in Latin America (Item 4, Table 6.2). African nations have moved farther away from communism than have Asian ones, although Cambodia and South Vietnam could prove to be exceptions to the trend by the end of the decade or before. Both groups agreed that major technological achievements by the United

Table 6.1 Box score of project Michelson predictions. I. Predicted threats.

			Predictive Accuracy	
Item	Prediction	Occurrence (as of 9/73)	Social Scientists	Physical Scientists
1. Small wars, that is, less than limited, largely of an intracountry sort	Yes	Yes	+	+
2. Wars between smaller powers	Yes	Yes	+	+
3. Various levels of economic, political, and ideological competition between major powers	Yes	Yes	+	+
4. Moderately large-scale limited strategic conflict between major powers	No	No	+	+
5. Moderately large-scale limited strategic conflict between major powers, including the use of nuclear weapons	No	No	+	+
6. World War III	No	No	+	+
7. Technological breakthroughs by the Soviet Union in the areas of antisubmarine warfare and/or antiballistic missile defense	Yes/No SS/PS	No	−	+
8. Technological breakthroughs by the United States in the areas of antisubmarine warfare and/or antiballistic missile defense	Yes/No	No	−	+

Table 6.2 Box score of project Michelson predictions. II. Likelihood of events in 1970's.

Item	Prediction	Occurrence (as of 9/73)	Predictive Accuracy	
			Social Scientists	Physical Scientists
1. Warfare within the communist world	No	No	+	+
2. Some (at least one) presently communist country becoming overtly noncommunist.	No/Yes SS/PS	No	+	−
3. Some European country going communist	?	No	−	−
4. Some Latin American country (not presently communist) going communist	Yes	No	−	−
5. Some Afro-Asian country going communist	Yes	No	−	−
6. Restoration of unity in the communist world	No	No	+	+
7. End of NATO, either *de jure* or *de facto*	No	No	+	+
8. Functioning MLF (Multilateral Force), that is, its effective functioning in deterring or controlling aggression	No	No	+	+
9. German neutralization	No	No	+	+
10. Substantial disarming of strategic weapons	No	No	+	+
11. Major technological accomplishments by the United States increasing the effectiveness of antiship or antiaircraft defenses	Yes	Yes	+	+
12. Major technological accomplishments by the USSR increasing the effectiveness of their antiship or antiaircraft defenses	Yes	Yes	+	+

States and the USSR were likely, which would increase the effectiveness of antiship or antiaircraft defenses. These have occurred.

It was on the third series of predictions (Table 6.3) that there was some disagreement between the social and physical scientists as to what the future would bring, and less accurate predictions. Social scientists predicted some likelihood of a substantial UN police force (which may have seemed reasonable until just before the 1967 Arab-Israeli hostilities). (Table 6.3) The social scientists predicted a partial disintegration of the Soviet bloc (Item 5, Table 6.3), and discounted the likelihood of increased cohesion of the Western Alliance (Item

4, Table 6.3). Certainly we have not yet seen increased cohesiveness of the West. Whether the relative independence of Romania and the continuing and often verbally intense conflict between the Chinese and the Soviets constitutes partial disintegration of the Soviet bloc is not altogether clear. Surely the Soviets feared liberalization of Czechoslovakian foreign policy and acted most vigorously and with much force to head it off. I counted the social scientists as having predicted more accurately on Items 4 (increased cohesion of the West) and 5 (partial disintegration of the Soviet bloc), although reflection leads me to feel that the "fence-sitting" of the physical scientists has proved more

Table 6.3 Box score of project Michelson predictions. III. Likelihood of events.

| | | | Predictive Accuracy | |
Item	Prediction	Occurrence (as of 9/73)	Social Scientists	Physical Scientists
1. A substantial UN police force	Yes/No SS/PS	No	−	+
2. A substantial agreement to inspection	Yes	No	−	−
3. Elimination of US overseas bases to a degree that makes them cease being major factor in US defense posture	Yes	No	−	−
4. Increased cohesiveness of the Western Alliance	No/? SS/PS	No	+	?
5. Partial disintegration of the Soviet Bloc	Yes/No SS/PS	Yes	+	−
6. Increased world conflict as a result of wider discrepancies in the rich-poor ratios between nations	Yes	No	−	−
7. A third power bloc (United States, USSR, and other nation or coalition)	Yes	No	−	−
8. "Internal wars" (not solely intra-country, but country) confined straining the international system	Yes	Yes	+	+
9. People's Republic of China seated in the UN	Yes	Yes	+	+

accurate on the latter item. Both groups so far have proved wrong concerning the likelihood that United States overseas bases would be eliminated "to a degree that makes them cease being a major factor in the US defense posture," and it was so counted in estimating their accuracy. Still, the next few years could permit events to prove that prediction a correct one. Both groups of experts correctly predicted the strain on the international system that resulted from the Southeast Asian wars and also the seating of the People's Republic of China in the UN. Both sets of experts saw as rather likely the development of a third power bloc—that is, besides those led by the United States and the USSR. New power centers may yet emerge, if slowly. Japan and Europe both gather economic power but are vulnerable in terms of their economic interdependence with the rest of the world. China has people, discipline, good morale, and may prove a major world power in the twenty-first century. Surely, she is not close to being one now.

What can be said of expert forecasting on the basis of the above? One is that either the ambiguity of the items or the difficulty of operationalizing the concepts involved in them to fit real world events decreased the utility of the exercise for a test of its validity. Another is that the two sets of experts answered the less specific, more general, queries with considerable more differentiation of response, with much more definiteness, and with more accuracy: compare the spread, intensity, and accuracy of responses to Query I with II and III. We might hypothesize on the basis of differences between the groups of experts that a tendency exists to estimate the future more conservatively as well as precisely in areas or domains of knowledge one knows best, although the data can not provide an adequate test of that hypothesis. It is difficult to judge what level of accuracy would be sufficient without a statement of purpose, but if chance alone would get fifteen predictions right, the results do not appear much better than chance. Possibly a better test would incorporate the frequency that the events predicted occurred—that is, eight out of twenty-nine. (How frequently would chance have obtained eight hits? The problem begins to look Bayesian.) Actually, all events that have happened were accurately predicted, at least by the social scientists (if one is willing to assume that partial disintegration of the Soviet bloc has taken place since 1964). So the problem of accuracy becomes one of false positives, events predicted to happen but that did not. There were no false negatives, that is, events predicted not to happen that did happen. Nature was more conservative than were the scientists or the author of the questionnaire.

This suggests a difficulty. If experts limit themselves to forecasting events that actually are very unlikely, or very likely, their forecasts will tend to be successful. If they predict where their evidential base is less substantial, their accuracy will approach chance—or below. Experts show a greater awareness of the causal implications of contingencies that may either increase or decrease the accuracy of their forecasts. If predictions are based strongly upon wishes, that is, upon social desirability or undesirability of the predictions, either positive or negative accuracy may well decline below chance; predictions could then correlate even negatively with events as they turn out. Moreover, the greatest accuracy throughout the survey questions—that is, events that occurred or did not, as predicted—was with items concerning which the scientists expressed the most definiteness—that is, items that were assigned the highest probability of occurrence or nonoccurrence—suggesting that, at least with these groups of experts, confidence in predictions correlates with accuracy. It is not difficult to show that box scores may vary as a function of the impressiveness and relevance of the credentials of the predictors to the predictions being made.

V. SUMMARY

Predictions and forecasts and their validation are an important and ubiquitous feature of contemporary life. The success rate even of experts has not proved strikingly high although some very accurate predictions were made in ancient times. Some increased leverage on improving the accuracy of predictions is possible. Some events and processes are more readily predicted accurately, especially stable recurrent ones, but also those that are not rare. Convergently produced ones, a function of any one of several forces that appear to occur in concert, are often predicted accurately with some ease. If we know how compelling are the forces involved in various contingencies, we can often forecast both contingencies and contingency-based events quite well.

Some classes of predictors have tended to prove far more effective than others. Some classes of value, particularly value preferences, enable us to forecast well—and rather better than value norms unless norms are supported by institutional incentives.

Predictors that include contexts which are not factorially pure have succeeded more often than more factorially pristine ones. Some methods predict more readily than others, but we expect that which methods show the most predictive validity will depend in part on the time spans over which we wish to predict.

Some persons forecast better than others. In general, those with more relevant knowledge concerning relations, processes, or events to be predicted do a more adequate job. We provided an example of partly successful prediction by experts in the area of international relations. Experts predict behavior more readily than do nonexperts, but expertise is a function of the mastery of particular content.

PART III

FORECASTING METHODOLOGIES: APPLICATIONS TO INTERNATIONAL RELATIONS

CHAPTER SEVEN

ANCHORING FUTURES IN PREFERENCES

A. Michael Washburn & Thomas E. Jones

I. DILEMMA CONFRONTING FORECASTERS

Contrast between Exploratory and Normative Forecasting

The primary aim of some forecasters is to project alternative futures of various degrees of likelihood; of other forecasters, to avoid undesirable futures and to actualize some desirable future. Appropriate to achieving the first aim is the general method of "exploratory forecasting";[1] to achieving the second, "normative forecasting" (also dubbed "normative planning"). The term "exploratory forecasting" is used here to embrace all methods that purport to avoid the evaluation of alternative futures, or at least to minimize the influence of such evaluation on forecasts. If an exploratory forecaster engages in intentional, explicit evaluation, he does so only as the final step of the forecasting process.

Early in the forecasting process, normative forecasting focuses on the preference-ordering of alter-native futures. If no plausible future among the recognized alternatives seems sufficiently desirable, the forecaster may attempt to construct such a future. Then he is obliged to make the selected future, or "target projection," more likely by devising scenarios that specify feasible paths to it. Since the target projection is usually quite unlikely apart from appropriate policy changes and an intelligently implemented program designed to achieve it, normative forecasting is unreliable unless it includes perspicacious planning.[2]

Though some forecasting methods involve intentional mixtures of normative and exploratory forecasting, the distinctions between the two processes and between the resulting forecasts are fundamental. Forecasts that are anchored in preference structures usually differ markedly from variously-anchored exploratory forecasts in their purpose and, consequently, in their initial design requirements, their selection of significant variables, and their validation (Choucri, Chapter 1, this volume).

Normative Forecasting: Important but Suspect

Kalman Silvert perceives that "the explanation of social causation requires consideration of the role played by human decision and the range of its play" (Silvert, 1970). Functioning as self-fulfilling prophecies, decisions by influential individuals to pursue new goals sometimes mark turning points in international relations. Examples are furnished by President Roosevelt's decision to inaugurate research aimed at inventing the atomic bomb and President Kennedy's decision to land American astronauts on the moon before the end of the decade. Normative forecasting of desired technological breakthroughs has proven to be quite successful, as evidenced by the Manhattan Project and the Apollo Project. The Marshall Plan's promotion of the rapid post-war recovery of decimated Europe is an instance of normative forecasting of the social genre. By opening to human choice a wide range of alternative futures, the revolution in science-based technology is enhancing the potential worth of reliable normative forecasting. Of special interest to international relations forecasters are the different futures that would probably result from policy choices between certain feasible new technologies for the production of energy. In view of the problems of disposal of radioactive waste and the possibilities of "nuclear blackmail" with plutonium bombs by frustrated less-industrialized nations, a normative forecaster might opt for a moratorium on breeder reactors and an expansion of American and Soviet programs for the research and development of controlled fusion.

Silvert cogently argues that policy planning should, whenever possible, involve rational choice among a wide range of options.[3] Many preferable goals that are discontinuous with present trends could not be achieved without normative forecasting. Several prominent forecasters[4] have maintained that a satisfactory resolution of such interrelated global problems as exponential population growth, depletion of nonrenewable natural resources, pollution, and food shortages would require the use of normative forecasting.

Nevertheless, several leading forecasters of international relations are suspicious of normative forecasting because of the procedures it employs.[5] The aim of these forecasters is to make forecasting as "scientific" (or at least as "value free" or "value neutral," "objective," and "rational") as possible.

Typically, they conceive of political science and of their own exploratory forecasting efforts as being relatively value free or value neutral; or normative forecasting, as being value laden, speculative, and unscientific. They are particularly bothered by the absence in many normative forecasts of a clear separation of normative from nonnormative elements, as well as by the problem of how to make rational transitions between the two kinds of elements. Thus, these forecasters shy away from normative forecasting because they perceive it as lacking a rationally justifiable conceptual framework. Consequently, they either ignore or dismiss as improbable an important range of preferable futures that are discontinuous with current trends.

Resulting Dilemma

Thus, these international relations forecasters are confronted by the following dilemma. To conform to "scientific" (or, at least, to "rational") requirements, it is often thought that forecasting must be as value free as possible. To make forecasting more useful by including within it normative techniques, social scientists must engage in what is deemed unscientific speculation. Hence, forecasting must either be of limited practical use or be blatantly unscientific.

This chapter points toward the resolution of the dilemma. First on the agenda is a brief examination of how exploratory forecasting, far from being value free, tends to be biased by concealed normative assumptions that need to be made explicit and evaluated objectively. Next is a clarification of normative forecasting, together with a specification of its weaknesses and suggestions concerning how if could be made sufficiently rigorous, rational, and reliable to justify its use by forecasters of international relations.

II. NORMATIVE ASSUMPTIONS UNDERLYING EXPLORATORY FORECASTING

Interdependence of Preferences and Expectations

Forecasters sometimes differ in their evaluations of the same alternative future. For instance, a future that involves a greatly increasing gap between less-industrialized and industrialized countries is deemed satisfactory by Herman Kahn as long as the less-industrialized countries are increasing their gross national products. Contrariwise, Dennis Meadows rejects such a future as undesirable, opting for an egalitarian future in which this gap would be eliminated, or at least reduced.[6] In some cases, one forecaster's utopia is another's dystopia.[7]

If such evaluations were made only as the last step of an exploratory forecasting process that was otherwise value free, they could still result in conflicting policy recommendations; but at least the conflict could be clearly traced to the divergent evaluations. However, forecasters manifest the human proclivity to evaluate implicitly if not explicitly. Of special interest among the various types of concealed preferences are those that are interrelated with expectations.

During the forecasting process, an exploratory forecaster's implicit preferences can combine with certain of his beliefs concerning causality to distort his estimates of the relative probabilities of alternative futures. For instance, a conservatively-oriented forecaster, recognizing the self-fulfilling tendency of exploratory forecasts[8] of a likely acceptable future, may (either consciously or subconsciously) excessively increase the likelihood that would otherwise be assigned to a continuous future that conforms to established values. Or, in a less complex instance, a forecaster's involvement with his favorite future may predispose him to exaggerate its likelihood.

Not only can exploratory forecasts be distorted by normative assumptions that masquerade in descriptive garb; questionable descriptive assumptions can bias both implicit normative assumptions made during the forecasting process and explicit normative conclusions derived at its end. The seeming improbability of preferable discontinuous futures may promote the upgrading in value of continuous futures. Continuous futures appear much more tolerable when perceived as inevitable and accepted as such. They may then be embraced as the only preferable ones that can be realistically hoped for. Suppose, for instance, Herman Kahn could show that any attempt during the next few decades to reduce the gap between less-industrialized and industrialized countries would be quite likely to backfire. Then his forecasted future—one in which the widening of this relative gap promotes the industrial development of practically all countries—would appear more desirable than before.

The conclusion that expectations and preferences are significantly interdependent during the forecasting process is particularly damaging to the claim that exploratory forecasting is value free. According to this claim, values are assigned to alternative futures, if assigned at all, only after probabilities have been independently estimated. However, a forecaster may consciously or subconsciously adjust his expectations to coincide with his preferences, or vice versa.

A Value-Laden Exploratory Forecast

Normative biases can be detected in many different forecasts of international relations.[9] For instance, in his review of *Things to Come*, Michael Marien convincingly argues that the forecasts and policy recommendations presented by Herman Kahn and B. Bruce-Briggs were affected by an implicit ideological bias toward conservatism (Marien, 1973). This bias emerges in such slanted labels as the "responsible center," with which Kahn and Bruce-Briggs identify, and the "humanist left," which by contrast is implicitly treated as irresponsible. The biases of established liberals are repeatedly attacked, whereas the biases of the center and the right are ignored. The "establishment" bias of the authors seems to have influenced their selections and interpretation of the elements that may comprise the future, thus enabling their supposedly descriptive forecasts to function subtly as normative forecasts (Marien, pp. 8, 12, 14–15; Kahn and Bruce-Briggs, pp. 82–85, 244–246).

The normative character of this bias becomes even clearer in the authors' support of a "counter reformation" against the threatening emergence of "late sensate culture." Contrariwise, Willis Harman interprets certain recent normative changes as appropriate for coping with the "world macroproblem" (Harman, 1970 and also the first section of this chapter). Thus, the countercultural challenge to established premises and value-priorities appears as a threat in Kahn's and Bruce-Briggs' forecast, but as a source of hope in Harman's forecast. Neither forecast is value free.

Pervasive Influence of Normative Assumptions

Such analysis reveals how prone exploratory forecasting is to subtle distortions by implicit normative assumptions cloaked in descriptive guises. This obfuscation of the fundamental distinction between genuinely descriptive and implicitly normative elements[10] undermines the reliability of many forecasts. An exploratory forecaster's hidden preferences can deceptively influence both the types of alternative futures that he projects and the inferences that he draws concerning how likely each is.

Furthermore, such preferences can lead him to embrace exploratory forecasting and to shun normative forecasting. The assumption that the directions in which trends are moving are desirable will not motivate him to formulate normative forecasts that advocate fundamental changes, as might the assumption that trends speeding toward disasters could be diverted by human intervention. Hence, a forecaster's preferences can, in conjunction with his beliefs, condition his purpose in forecasting, his consequent selection of method, and his forecast.

Despite definite methodological progress in exploratory forecasting during the last decade and a half, the goal of making such forecasting value free has proven to be more elusive than the proverbial ball of mercury. Thus, exploratory forecasting is implicitly subject to normative biases, the very kind of biases that cast special doubt on the reliability of normative forecasting.

Objective Treatment of Normative Assumptions

However, the conclusions that normative assumptions cannot be eliminated does not imply that forecasting is hopelessly mired in a morass of subjectivity. Science itself is not value free.[11] Rather, it comes closest to being value neutral when it is value explicit. *Values are so integral to policy-oriented forecasting that efforts to eliminate them produce more deceptive distortions than efforts to acknowledge them and treat them as objectively and rationally as possible.*

Therefore, to minimize such distortions, an exploratory forecaster needs to make his or her normative assumptions explicit as part of the forecasting process. The careful separation of normative from descriptive assumptions is a prerequisite for diminishing the implicit, misleading interdependence of these elements in estimates of the probabilities and desirabilities of alternative futures. Next, he should try to objectively estimate the effects of his preferences and expectations on each other. Then he may formulate forecasts that include clear identification of the consequences of

his various interrelated assumptions; or, better yet, he may first critically assess these assumptions to reduce any unjustifiable influence that they exert on his outlook.

Subsequently, it will be shown that normative forecasting, despite its value-explicit stance, is also susceptible to distortion by underlying normative and nonnormative assumptions. Hence, a normative forecaster is obliged to go through a similar process of clarifying and analyzing his assumptions.

As an aid to making their own assumptions explicit, forecasters could use comprehensive "check lists"[12] as integral components of the forecasting process. Such check lists would specify basic types of assumptions made by forecasters, and could cite examples of the most important implicit assumptions that frequently distort forecasts. Check lists must not be used thoughtlessly, as if they were final and exhaustive. Rather, their purpose is to help forecasters gain insight into their own assumptions.

A basic distinction is that between methodological assumptions and assumptions that are not inherent in the formal forecasting methodology that is employed. The latter type of assumptions can be divided into underlying beliefs (premises) and values (preferences). Beliefs can be individuated into further categories—e.g., beliefs about causality, time, human nature, society (including polity and economy), culture (including technology normative systems), and the environment—and subcategories, as can values.[13] Special categories pertinent to assumptions about international relations would be devised. By utilizing such a general framework together with the examples of particular assumptions, a forecaster could systematically explicate his own specific, often cross-categorical and interrelated assumptions.

After ferreting out his assumptions, a forecaster can clarify, interrelate, and evaluate them. To find whether his normative assumptions are justified, he must switch from describing his preferences to prescribing what they should or should not be. Furthermore, as the last step in an exploratory forecasting process, he may explicitly evaluate the alternative futures in his forecast. Someone must evaluate these futures if they are to be used in effective planning.

Since evaluation and prescription cannot be avoided in the forecasting/planning process, these normative activities had best be performed explicitly and objectively in ways that can be checked. A method that could help to bring about the impartial resolution of normative disagreements would remove an obstacle—the supposed subjectivity of all normative claims—that has made many exploratory forecasters wary of explicitly making such claims. Moreover, this method would be of crucial importance for improving normative forecasting, in connection with which it will be delineated.[14]

III. TOWARD RELIABLE NORMATIVE FORECASTING

Increasing Use of Normative Forecasting

Unsophisticated normative forecasting has been done for eons. During the 1960's, however, Hasan Ozbekhan, Erich Jantsch,[15] and others took significant steps toward systematizing the methodology for the normative forecasting/planning process. Harold G. Shane distinguishes the following phases in the development of American futures research:

> If linear projections are construed to be an early development in futures research—let us call it Phase I—then Phase II in the 1960's was concerned with a shift from predictions to exploring what organizations intend the future to be (implementation of desirable prophecies). Phase III, as of the early 1970's, seems to be an analytical and increasingly interventionist approach to the future. (Shane, p. 21)

If the procedures for using normative forecasting in the domain of international relations were to become reliable, such forecasting could prove to be extremely useful in promoting the achievement of mutually beneficial goals. Its present procedures as formulated by Ozbekhan must be understood as a reaction against the most established type of forecasting/planning process.

Movement Away From "Deterministic Planning"

Although Ozbekhan focuses on technological policies in "The Triumph of Technology: 'Can' Implies 'Ought'" (1968, pp. 204–233), he notes that his recommended planning methodology can be applied to international relations. He begins with a penetrating critique of the type of planning that lets technology, which often dictates what can be done, strongly suggest what ought to be done. The fundamental tool of this "deterministic planning" is extrapolation to a single future or to a limited range of alternative futures, each of which results from a different decisions and presupposes an unquestioned, unchanging value system. Ozbekhan argues that choices in such planning are primarily concerned not with ends, but with technological-economical feasibility. The key question is, "*Can it be done?*" It is often assumed that what can be done must be done. Technological feasibility has tended increasingly to become the chief criterion of decisions and actions, thus defining the ends that are sought. The tendency to envisage the future in relation to its feasibility has been strengthened by the positivistic attack on the objectivity of values and by the failure to revise traditional moral principles so as to make them applicable to problems engendered by new technologies.[16]

Since Ozbekhan wrote, technology assessment and an accompanying movement toward normative forecasting (Ozbekhan uses the term "normative planning") have begun to correct this tendency. Inherent in this movement is the recognition that mere feasibility is by no means a desirable end, for some feasible futures would be disastrous. Normative planning takes into account much broader considerations, encouraging choice among possible technologies, institutions, and actions in order to realize basic values.

Normative forecasting of international relations could expand the range of "oughts" (i.e., desirable goals), which has been circumscribed by the unnecessarily narrow range of *perceived* "cans" (i.e., what is judged to be feasible in the realm of international relations). One can plausibly argue that these "cans" are in turn restricted by certain outmoded imperatives of the nation-state system. Once the goal of making forecasting approximate a value-free science is abandoned and normative considerations are explicitly injected into the forecasting process near its inception, the range of perceived "cans" may be enlarged by the disciplined search for ways to achieve a variety of "oughts."

Stages of Normative Planning[17]

Ozbekhan distinguishes three stages or phases of normative planning. It is convenient to start from and build upon his formulation, since it both encapsulates what is usually thought of as the normative forecasting/planning process and is relatively easy to revise in response to criticisms that will subsequently be evaluated.

The first, least developed stage is that of policy-oriented choice. From among alternative future situations, goals are selected in order to realize intended values. Decisions are made concerning what *ought* to be done. The second stage consists of devising strategies that *can* achieve the selected goals. Unfeasible strategies are eliminated along with futures that can only be linked to the present by such strategies. In the third stage, decision makers determine how, when, and in what sequence the chosen strategies *will* be implemented. Thus, these stages proceed from the desirable to the feasible to the probable. The first stage formulates the "normative plan"; the second, the "strategic plan"; the third, the "operational plan." Being interactive as well as interrelated, they function as parts of a single integrative, iterative planning process (Ozbekhan, 1968, pp. 212–213).

Thus, goal evaluation is explicitly integrated into the planning process. Since imagined futures are taken as the starting point, policy-makers' options are increased. "A multiplicity of goals based on a multiplicity of norms enlarges the traditional boundaries of the practical and thereby lengthens the spectrum of alternative policies among which we could choose" (Ozbekhan, p. 214).

Whereas the process of normative planning initially expands opportunities, it subsequently eliminates the open-ended perspective that paralyzes action. A selected normative "image" indicates the kind of information required to achieve the desirable end that it represents, thereby reducing the uncertainties that confront current decisions (Ozbekhan, p. 214). To put it differently, the anchoring of a normative forecast in a particular preference ordering suggests the types of data and methodologies needed to fulfill the purpose of the forecasts. Once a normative forecast is anchored, the chief variables of interest are manipulables that can be controlled by a policy maker (Choucri, Chapter 1, this volume).

As Ozbekhan remarks, "Decisions made in the light of . . . future 'images' initiate that backward chain of calculable events which when they reach the present can be translated into it in the form of calculated 'change'" (Ozbekhan, p. 213). In this way, anticipating a future may become causative

of future-oriented action in the present. Hence, normative planning can overcome the tendency of planning to be mainly responsive to current events rather than "futures-creative."

Methods Used for Normative Forecasting

More specific than the general procedural framework laid down by Ozbekhan are a number of methods that are used for normative forecasting. These methods display various shades and grades of procedure. Some fit well into Ozbekhan's framework, whereas others do not go through all three stages or add other stages. To a certain extent this is beneficial, for different methods can be useful for different purposes. Nonetheless, improvements in methodology can provide common procedures that replace divergent ones. At the same time that specific methods are being improved, it might be worthwhile to work toward a paradigm that embraces commonalities in these methods and preserves justifiable differences.

Methods that are fundamentally exploratory are sometimes adapted to normative forecasting. Focusing on an emerging trend, a forecaster may regard policies supporting it as likely to exert a sufficiently powerful influence to attain his preferred future. Or he may alter the assumptions of his mathematical or nonmathematical model to coincide with the change in value-priorities necessary to achieve his preferred future. Alternatively, he may conduct a Delphi inquiry to seek consensus among experts regarding the most disastrous or the most preferable futures. Or he may employ scenario writing to ascertain feasible policies that might lead to his preferred future. Hence, all these methods have legitimate normative as well as exploratory uses.[18] As long as the exploratory and normative elements within and between forecasts are clearly distinguished, a method can be justifiably used to derive both exploratory and normative forecasts.

Three methods deserve special mention because of their relatively high ranking in degree of explicit theory employed, use of systematic procedures, and use of empirical data. All three integrate exploratory and normative forecasting. Two of these methods—relevance tree (or decision tree) techniques and feedback techniques[19]—are treated in detail by Thomas W. Robinson in Chapter 17. A third method is computer simulation utilized to explore paths to preferable futures and away from disastrous ones. Such simulation affords a potentially valuable technique for formulating forecasts that have both exploratory and normative components.[20]

Examples of Normative Forecasts

Most normative forecasts of long-range, comprehensive futures depend on prior exploratory forecasting and are cast in a "provisional-catastrophist" mold. After inferring the likelihood of discontinuous, disastrous futures from a continuation of interrelated trends and unresolved problems, forecasts typically use normative forecasting to show that radically different, preferable futures could be created by appropriate changes in value-priorities, institutions, policies, and/or technologies. Paradigmatic examples of such forecasts include those formulated by Lester Brown, Richard Falk, Dennis Pirages and Paul Ehrlich, Willis Harman and O. W. Markley, Robert Theobald, Dennis Meadows' team, and Jay Forrester.[21] (Though not all of them think of themselves as engaged in normative forecasting, some forecasts of each fit our description of it.) None of these forecasts specifies a complete operational plan, though they are intended to promote discussions that will eventually lead to such plans. Of these forecasts, five will now be described.

Dennis C. Pirages and Paul R. Ehrlich argue in *Ark II* that unlimited economic growth and unrestrained technological change are primarily responsible for such problems as depletion of natural resources, overpopulation, inflation, and political corruption. Pirages and Ehrlich identify a "tragedy of the commons" in the international system. Behavior in the international commons is uncontrolled by social conscience or even by "mutual coercion mutually agreed upon," as is evidenced in the exploitation and pollution of the oceanic commons and the atmospheric commons (Pirages and Ehrlich, 1974, pp. 216—254, especially p. 235).

Pirages and Ehrlich maintain that drastic political, social, and economic changes are urgently needed to come to terms with international and national problems. Somewhat provisionally, they present a normative plan together with suggestions for its implementation. Integral to the plan is the use of social policies to reduce consumption of nonrenewable resources and to dampen rapidly rising expectations. Unless the demand by "overdeveloped countries" for energy and for nonrenewable resources is stabilized or reduced, the authors claim, there is little hope that the industrialized world can maintain energy and resource flows sufficient to support itself (pp. 237–254).

Yet increases of living standards in developing countries are both possible and desirable. These increases could be fed by a massive transfer of development capital from overdeveloped to underdeveloped countries. Such aid to a fund for international development could come from a tax reflected in the pricing of energy-intensive items. In the United States, this tax could be imposed by an agency that would control resource purchases on the world market and would sell resources in a free market. Moreover, Pirages and Ehrlich opt for unilateral disarmament of the United States—perhaps reducing military expenditures 10 percent each year—accompanied by a challenge to the Soviet Union to do likewise (pp. 237–254).

According to the global computer models of Jay Forrester (*World Dynamics*) and the Meadows team (*The Limits to Growth*), five basic trends (i.e., state variables) determine, and by their interrelations ultimately limit, growth in the finite world system. (Forrester's sixth state variable, "crowding," is harder to handle and less important.) The exponential growth of industrialization and population generates similar growth in depletion of nonrenewable natural resources, pollution, and malnutrition. The assumptions modeled indicate that growth of the latter three trends will limit growth of the former two, and that delays in the effects of the latter three may cause counterintuitive overshoots of the sustainable carrying capacity of the global environment. A consequence could be catastrophic collapses of both industry and population within the next hundred years. The assumptions that Forrester and the Meadows team made about technological attempts to push back the limits to growth resulted in computer runs that suggest that these attempts would be unable to prevent such collapses.

Therefore, Forrester and the Meadows team recommend that the world's industrial and population growth be quickly brought to a halt by appropriate reductions in the capital investment and

fertility rates. Computer runs that tested consequences of these and certain other policies showed
no collapse of population or industry. Yet despite
similar exploratory runs of the two models, the
policies assumed for global equilibrium are markedly different. The differences are rooted in incompatible preferences.

Both Forrester and the Meadows team were
motivated to prevent disastrous collapses of the
world's industry and population. This common
purpose as well as their divergent value-priorities
seem to have exerted strong influences on the ways
in which they altered the assumptions of their two
respective models. To achieve global equilibrium,
Forrester's preferred computer run includes the
policy of cutting world food production by 20 percent, with the consequence of starvation and death
in the near future to prevent a much bigger subsequent dieback. His preferred future world would
involve continued inequalities between industrialized and less-industrialized countries, though
the latter would be allowed to raise their per capita
material standard of living by reducing their populations.

Contrariwise, the Meadows team placed top
priority upon preventing starvation and death at all
times and upon eliminating huge inequalities,
which were regarded as unjust. Judging from
Chapter V of *The Limits to Growth*, the team
seems to have sought changes in assumptions of
the World 3 model that would be compatible with
a specific kind of preferred future: a voluntarily-
achieved, egalitarian global equilibrium in which
the basic needs of each individual would be met.
An increase in current food production was advocated by the team, together with a redistribution of
available wealth. The United States, for instance,
would have to cut back to about half of its present
per capita material standard of living in order to
allow less-industrialized nations to reach this revised standard. These egalitarian recommendations
are compatible with, but are not strictly derived
from, the revised model and its runs.

Thus, the revision of the World 3 model seems
to have been goal-oriented from the beginning.
The goal, defined in accordance with the values
and beliefs of the Meadows team, was judged to be
the best possible sort of world permitted by natural
resource/pollution/arable land constraints. Therefore, the team was doing what we call "normative

forecasting," which in this instance involved a prior
exploratory phase and repeated interaction between Ozbekhan's first and second stages.

Using a morphological method of modeling as
well as a more intuitive method, forecasters at the
Educational Policy Research Center of Stanford
Research Institute concluded that transnational, interrelated problems constitute a "world macro-
problem." Three aspects of this macro-problem
are: problems of the ecosystem; an intrinsically expanding "have—have-not" gap; and technological
threats.

Willis Harman reports:

> Of the 40 feasible future histories, there are
> very few that manage to avoid some period of
> serious trouble between now and 2050. The few
> that do appear to require a dramatic shift of val-
> ues and perceptions with regard to . . . the
> "world macroproblem." (Harman, 1970, p. 6)

Hence, the normative plan for a "new society" in
the United States involves fundamental changes in
certain underlying cultural beliefs, in operative
values, and in institutions. During the 1970's and
early 1980's, a major national effort needs to be
mounted to reestablish a balanced ecology, to reduce pollution to acceptable levels, and to redistri-
bute wealth sufficiently to eliminate extreme
domestic poverty. Successful completion of this
program would result in a "new society" that is
both "open" (flexible, tolerant of diversity, able to
sustain decentralized decision making without
undue internal violence) and "adept" (both competent and motivated to control its destiny) (Harman,
pp. 7–8; Markley, 1971, p. 6ff).

In *World Without Borders* (Brown, 1972c), Lester R. Brown of the Overseas Development Council surveys world trends and problems, points to
dangerous consequences of some of them, and rec-
ommends basic planned changes as alternatives to
disaster. Many problems, such as the deterioration
of the world's environment, cannot be solved at the
national level. Solutions would require rather extensive international cooperation. In "Rich Countries and Poor," Brown observes:

> Birth rates do not usually voluntarily decline in
> the absence of a certain minimum level of
> living—an assured food supply, literacy (if not
> an elementary school education), at least
> rudimentary health services, and reduced infant

mortality. What we may witness is the emergence of a situation in which it will be in the interest of rich countries to launch a concerted attack on global poverty in order to reduce the threat to our future well-being posed by continuous population growth. (Brown, 1973, p. 163)

Brown's normative plan prescribes such a minimum living standard for all human beings. He argues that this plan could be implemented. Productivity could be increased and poverty eliminated in a matter of years if coupled with a concerted effort to reduce birth rates and a shift of a sizeable fraction of the global annual gain in productivity and wealth ($120 billion annual increase in GWP) from the rich countries to investment in the poor. A necessary condition for achieving this goal is a new societal ethic, the values of which define the more humanitarian society that Brown believes is beginning to emerge.[22] The problem, of course, is how in the real world of power politics, structural inequities, and truly conflicting interests, such an ethic can become politically potent.

In "Statist Imperatives in an Era of System Overload" (Falk, 1971), Richard A. Falk maintains that the interplay of pressures stemming from economic and demographic growth is responsible for a cumulative drift toward a deterioration of the quality of life. He contends that the international and national system is organized in such a way as to make catastrophe virtually inevitable. Appropriate ecological reforms run contrary to imperatives that govern the behavior of nation-states. The pattern of statist imperatives is constituted by maximization of growth, competition, national interest, and self-help, absence of empathy, family autonomy regarding reproduction, and short-range goals. Hence, Falk's exploratory forecast indicates that some mode of transition to ecological equilibrium will occur, and that this transition could follow the path of traumatic transition, of imperial transition, or of contractual transition. He believes that the survival of human civilization depends on some kind of contractual transition to "ecological equilibrium" (i.e., no growth in either aggregate population or industrialization) during the next few decades. An ecological model of world order seems to presuppose central guidance to define world interest, to manage planetary affairs on a unified basis, and to achieve equity as well as equilibrium. In

Falk's view, this contractual transition is not very likely, given the array and power of counter trends and interests. He sketches out the minimum requirements for such a transition process to succeed and suggests a schematic scenario of how it might develop, arguing that efforts in this direction of both an intellectual and activist sort are better than submission to more probable futures.[23]

Weaknesses and Suggested Improvements

What are some of the key weaknesses of normative forecasting? What kinds of improvements in the forecasting process could be made? A number of the following observations are based upon the findings of the World Order Models Project of the Institute for World Order. A series of books on the normative forecasts of the various regional groups started to become available in 1975.[24]

Premature Specificity. The Models Project assumed at its inception that a high degree of specificity, preferably in the form of a constitutional/institutional model, was required. However, in his Models Project book, *A Study of Future Worlds*, Richard Falk forcefully argues against "premature specificity" and suggests that only a broad normative, structural image is sensible. This revision seems conducive to creativity, for it does not inhibit or mislead one by presenting an overly concrete and structured model of the future.

Yet an intermediate approach that combines the virtues of the opposing approaches might be preferable. When a forecaster is assessing alternative preferred futures, much less specificity is required than when he is testing the workability of a goal. If implementation attempts are to begin soon, specificity—as well as flexibility—is appropriate.

Methodology for Working Backward. After beginning with a relatively detailed model of a preferred future, participants in the Models Project sought to construct a transition strategy through the identification of a series of necessary preconditions. This was done primarily by working back in time from this future. However, the lack of systematic methods for working backward made it necessary to use speculative and intuitive modes of thought, which are rather unreliable. It is difficult to link interesting ideals into a complete transition scenario, and easy to overestimate the feasibility and effectiveness of each isolated step.

A promising systematic method has been suggested by Robert North and others. Starting with a dynamic model, a forecaster could generate a series of possible futures by the systematic manipulation of assumptions and variables. Once a sequence leading to a preferred future is identified, it should then be possible to determine, for each manipulation of a variable or an assumption, what would have to have happened and how. Such determinations could provide the basis for a coherent long-term plan for sociocultural change.

To follow a related procedure, a forecaster begins with a model of a preferred future. He runs the model backward, manipulating until he arrives at a sequence leading to a model resembling the present. (This is one of the techniques used in Bayesian Analysis, see Chapter 10). This procedure might prove to be unusually valuable.

Overlooked Opportunities. The fundamental problem in the world order area is that the kinds of future that appear preferable seem either implausible in themselves or extremely difficult to achieve. Even a normative forecaster is obliged to regard such goals as excessively improbable unless he can use creative insight to make them plausible and to devise paths that are sufficiently likely to lead to them. Hence, realism in international relations forecasting needs to be supplemented by creative imagination in order to invent *preferable* alternative future histories. Being more imaginative does not imply being unrealistic. Science fiction writers, who have their imaginations unfettered by institutional constraints, have sometimes painted more accurate portraits of the future than have professional forecasters.[25]

Resort to imagination may seem to constitute regression from systematized, checkable methods to intuitive "genius forecasting." Indeed, the method of discovery differs from the method of proof. However, the results of the creative process would subsequently be subjected to scrupulous objective evaluation. Sufficient progress has been made in understanding the creative process to disclose certain techniques for removing blocks to creativity and for enhancing it. For instance, the method of brainstorming can be used for group creativity, as can "synectics."[26] Fritz Zwicky sets forth a mor-

phological approach to creativity, a way of seeing parts in terms of wholes (Zwicky, 1969). An attempt is made to visualize all interrelations in structural relationships, thus exploring all possible solutions to a problem. Zwicky's method could be used productively by forecasters of international relations, as discussed in the chapter on technological forecasting (Chapter 17).

Unforeseen Obstacles. Though a normative forecaster needs to be imaginatively open to opportunities, he also needs to be aware of unanticipated obstacles. International relations planning has often had unsatisfactory results (for example, see Chet Cooper's discussion in Chapter 23). Normative forecasting in international relations encounters formidable obstacles to the rapid, effective implementation of planned changes. Political events, such as key decisions and assassinations, are frequently unpredictable, yet influential. Unintended consequences (including second and *n*-order consequences) and other aspects of the counterintuitive behavior of social systems can easily upset the implementation of plans. Proposed changes in value-priorities and institutions can be resisted powerfully by vested interests. The difficulties involved in overcoming entrenched trends are often underestimated. In addition, exogenous factors may interfere.

The selection of utopian rather than realistic goals tends to breed failure. Even the relative successes of utopian schemes fall short of the ideal, thus shattering perfectionistic expectations. Such schemes contain the seeds of their own demise. Many a noble plan has backfired. Normative forecasting is unlikely to be effective if utilized without sufficient regard for the limitations of human ability to invent the future.

Thus, normative forecasting treads on dangerous ground when it shuns the guiding hand of exploratory forecasting. By not making exploratory forecasting an early stage of the forecasting process, Ozbekhan failed to assign sufficient importance to estimates of likelihood. This omission may well have arisen from the development of normative planning as a reaction—indeed, an overreaction—against deterministic planning. *Fundamental to the reliability of normative forecasting is the previous use of exploratory forecasting, preferably by a variety of methods, to derive relatively likely and less likely alternative futures.* This enables a fore-caster during the goal-selection stage to take into account explicit considerations of likelihood. Goals selected primarily for their desirability without adequate explicit attention to their likelihood may well turn out to be unattainable by normative fore-casting. Though such goals would sometimes be weeded out in Ozbekhan's subsequent stages, in-corporation of explicit considerations of likelihood into a preliminary stage should promote efficiency and wise goal selection.

This conclusion does not conflict with the need for creative imagination in forecasting. Goals must not be limited to those deemed most likely by an-tecedent exploratory forecasting, but must include preferable discontinuous goals as bona fide candi-dates for selection. The likelihood of achieving dis-continuous goals is typically difficult to ascertain without circumspect assessment in Ozbekhan's second and third stages. Hence, a desirable goal that seems quite unlikely, at least apart from ex-tensive planning, may be chosen pending estima-tion of its likelihood in the later stages. What is crucial is that all of this be done in the light of previous exploratory forecasting, and that a selected future be linked to the present by a work-able strategy.

Ozbekhan does correctly emphasize the impor-tance of increasing the likelihood of a chosen goal during the strategic and operational stages. From the process of relating the goal to particular situa-tions and strategies, feasible policy-oriented path-ways to it may emerge. If a forecaster is unable to sketch a plausible scenario connecting the goal to policies beginning in the present, he is obliged to make at least one of the following moves: keep searching for a feasible transition; reject the goal; or return to the first stage and redefine the goal to make it realistically achievable.

To implement a plan effectively, it is necessary during the operational stage to devise a set of prpriority-ordered, interrelated decisions. This task involves specification of a temporal continuity of actions capable of overcoming the disruptive ef-fects of systemic consequences of any of the actions taken to implement a plan (Ozbekhan, p. 216). In view of the possibility of unanticipated conse-quences and of disruptions caused by exogenous factors, contingency plans had best be formulated insofar as present knowledge allows.

Thus, in responsible normative forecasting, con-siderations of likelihood constitute one kind of criterion for choosing a goal. In some cases, a de-sirable goal will be regarded as too improbable to warrant the substantial risks involved in pursuing it. In other cases, the envisioned rewards of suc-cess will outweigh such risks.

Tendency to Overestimate Likelihood. In norma-tive forecasting, as well as in exploratory forecast-ing, estimates of the likelihood and desirability of a future can be deceptively interdependent. Conse-quently, it is easy for forecasters subconsciously to adjust their expectations to coincide with their de-sires (primarily in normative forecasting, though significantly in exploratory forecasting) or vice versa (especially in exploratory forecasting).

One might expect that distortion by implicit normative biases would not be a serious problem in normative forecasts, which profess to be value explicit. Yet in most normative forecasts, not all descriptive and normative elements are sufficiently distinguished. Underlying preferences are often not explicitly articulated. Moreover, the desire to actualize preferred futures can easily distort esti-mates of likelihood made either in a prior explorat-ory stage of normative forecasting or in later stages. Why do many normative forecasters—especially provisional catastrophists—tend to exaggerate the likelihoods of both desirable and undesirable fu-tures?

Inherent in attempts to attain explicit goals is the tendency to overestimate the probability of attain-ment. The need to achieve utopian or even non-utopian goals can make them seem more likely than they are. Yet biased estimates of probabilities are often much more subtle. Any adequate answer to the preceding question must take into account the relation of expectations, and of forecasts that can engender expectations, to action. A number of leading scholars in various fields[27] have called at-tention to the human tendency to fulfill expecta-tions and to the consequent impacts of positive and negative images of the future on individuals and societies.

The self-fulfilling propensity of normative fore-casts of desirable futures encourages exaggeration in estimates of likelihood, as does the self-negating propensity of warnings of disastrous futures. If a normative forecaster's favorite goal can be made to look attainable as well as preferable, it will tend to evoke policies directed toward actualizing it. Such policies increase the likelihood of its actualization. The less risky a commitment to this goal seems, the more likely (in most cases) that the normative forecast will become a basis for policy. Hence, a normative forecaster may consciously or subconsciously overestimate the likelihood of his preferred future's being actualized, thus making his recommendation seem more plausible and attractive. (He might, of course, also exaggerate its desirability.)[28]

A forecast of conditional future catastrophe may become self-negating when accompanied by a self-fulfilling forecast of a desirable alternative future. But unless a forecaster can make a conditional disaster seem quite probable, people are unlikely to take drastic steps to avoid it. Hence, in the exploratory part of his forecast, a provisional catastrophist may consciously or subconsciously exaggerate the threat of catastrophe in order to evoke adequate preventive measures.

Provisional catastrophism is structurally prone to misleading estimations of the likelihood and desirability of alternative futures. Its purpose is to mobilize people to work together for drastic change, in order to avoid catastrophe and to attain preferable futures. Believable exaggerations of both likelihood and desirability sometimes may be more suited to accomplishing this purpose than accurate estimates. Consequently, provisional catastrophists often pain oversimplified, exaggerated portraits of future options.

Nevertheless, provisional catastrophism sometimes contributes to the achievement of goals that might not be achieved—at least by the time desired—without it.[29] Furthermore, situations exist in which fundamental changes *are* necessary to avoid probable disaster and to achieve mutually beneficial goals. Hence, provisional catastrophism can be both "adequate" to accomplish its purpose and "reliable" in its estimates of likelihood and desirability.

Images of catastrophe also pose a special problem. Intended to be self-negating, they can become self-fulfilling. This is particularly true when a provisional catastrophist furnishes no genuinely positive alternative to impending disaster. In such cases, the only thing provisional about the forecast may be the degree of catastrophe.

Fortunately, quite a lot of normative forecasting can generate sufficient motivation to succeed without assuming the form of provisional catastrophism. Yet all normative forecasting has some propensity toward distorted estimates of likelihood, for all such forecasting faces the dilemma that the adequacy of some forecasts to fulfill their purpose might be enhanced by subtle exaggerations of likelihood and desirability that diminish reliability.

In summary, the following improvements in the normative forecasting process could appreciably diminish the biases that frequently distort estimates of likelihood. Assumptions, including underlying preferences, need to be explicated and evaluated as the first stage—another addition to Ozbekhan's stages—in normative forecasting. Check lists could be used to explicate assumptions. Descriptive and normative elements must be clearly separated. A forecaster should try to estimate likelihood and desirability as objectively as possible. This involves not only an examination of his own assumptions but also the use of exploratory forecasting. He had best take into account the self-fulfilling and self-negating effects of forecasting by making an intelligent guess concerning the impact that his forecast and feasible implementation might exert. Then he may design contingency plans to cope with possible obstacles to implementation.

By following this procedure, a forecaster would seek to make his forecast reliable as well as adequate. Even if adequacy must sometimes be sacrificed for reliability, realistic plans would be less prone to disruption and normative forecasting in general would become a more systematic, reliable method.

Undesirable Goals. Unfortunately, normative forecasting can be instrumental in the attainment of goals that, either in themselves or in their consequences, are contrary to the best interests of most people. Besides, the means employed may be productive of undesirable consequences that more than cancel out benefits derived from achievement of the goal. An extreme example would be provided by the creation of a totalitarian world government to solve global ecological problems. What could be done to improve the quality of goal selection?

Of crucial significance are the moral, immoral, and amoral criteria utilized for selecting goals. Too often these criteria are inadequately articulated and analyzed. Objective, efficacious techniques for making normative plans are urgently needed to replace the present tendency to make such plans on the basis of relatively intuitive judgments that depend little on explicit theory.

Why are goals that are undesirable for most people sometimes selected? One main reason is that they are conducive to the perceived self-interest of small groups of decision makers; another, that efforts to arrive at objective decisions on normative issues encounters formidable obstacles. Hence, two crucial normative problems in goal-and-path selection are expressed by the following questions: Who should select the goals and the paths, and for whose best interests? Are there any procedures for reaching objective, impartial decisions in normative disputes?

Who Selects Goals?

The first question springs from a series of important issues that can only be touched on here. An elitist approach would significantly restrict the domain of participatory decision making.[30] Might not entrenched elites further extend this restriction? In the absence of institutionalized public participation in the choice of goals and of appropriate means, normative forecasting might be dictatorially monopolized by manipulative elites that would control the communications media. On the other hand, lack of expert advice on complicated issues (e.g., interrelated ecological problems) could lead to kinds of normative planning—or the failure to engage in such planning—that would be to the detriment of all. What seems to be required is a blend of expertise and popular participation in the formulation of those goals which, if actualized by effective normative planning, would shape the destinies of all involved. To participate responsibly, the public would have to be willing to accept some plans that conflict with immediate self-interest.

Alvin Toffler has recommended the futurizing of educational institutions and broad public involvement in technology assessment. Gerald Feinberg has proposed the creation of institutions that would promote maximum participation of all human beings in choosing fundamental goals (Feinberg, 1968, pp. 222ff). Seeking to transcend ideological differences, these institutions would emphasize those aspects of the future that are of common interest to all people.

Acceptance of the "good reasons approach," which will now be discussed, involves a rejection of Gerald Feinberg's claim in *The Prometheus Project* that there is no such rational method of moral reasoning (pp. 52–53). From this, however, one need not infer that decisions concerning the comparative values of alternative futures must be left to moral experts. Extensive participation in selecting alternative futures as goals would still be feasible. Being relatively easy to understand and use, the goods reasons approach could improve both professional and public evaluation of alternative futures.[31]

The "Good Reasons Approach"

Next on the agenda is the second question: Are there any procedures for reaching objective, impartial decisions in normative disputes? Two kinds of methods can be used.

A Method for Resolving Disagreement in Belief. The first method can be applied whenever normative disagreements are a function of conflicting factual beliefs. The way to resolve these disagreements is to present evidence that induces agreement in belief. Disputes about which policies ought to be pursued are often rooted in divergent estimates of the likely consequences of the policies. An example is the controversy about the continued exponential growth of worldwide industrialization. When exploratory forecasting can be utilized to reach agreement on the consequences, such disputes can sometimes be resolved.

A Method for Resolving Disagreement in Attitude. Yet even when agreement is reached concerning probable consequences, forecasters can still disagree in their evaluations of these consequences (e.g., the distribution of wealth). Hence, in disputes about values, disagreement in attitude is not always a function of disagreement in belief about actual or likely occurrences. Therefore, normative issues cannot always be resolved by securing agreement on relevant descriptive issues. Answers to questions about which goals are better than others or about which actions ought (or ought not) to be performed are evaluations and imperatives that cannot be logically deduced from statements that describe empirical facts.[32]

Is it possible to answer such questions "rationally"? Consider two moral judgments: "Hitler acted wrongly in murdering the Jews"; "X acted wrongly in lying to the would-be assassin of Y, even though the lie saved Y's life." Such judgments purport to be true. The first judgment seems to be much more justifiable than the second. In daily life, some moral judgments are deemed to be nonarbitrary for deciding which actions ought (or ought not) to be performed; others, arbitrary. Typically, good reasons are supplied to legitimize the nonarbitrary judgments and to reject the arbitrary. For instance, Hitler's fanatical policy of racial extermination is rejected, for it was unjust and it unnecessarily caused enormous human misery. However, X's obligation to tell the truth was suspended by the higher conflicting obligation to prevent Y's being murdered; hence, the judgment that censors X is false.

Is there any method for making rationally justifiable normative claims that can help to resolve disagreements in attitude? Such a nonarbitrary method has already been formulated in philosophical ethics. Whether one speaks of a method or a group of similar overlapping methods is largely a semantic matter. Careful analysis of the methods advocated by such moral philosophers as Richard Brandt, John Rawls, Kurt Baier, and William Frankena discloses that these methods are refinements of the best procedures for answering ethical questions in everyday life, and diverge relatively little from each other.[33]

According to the "good reasons approach," which sets forth this method, moral judgments are not primarily "property-referring" (i.e., descriptive of natural properties like pleasure).[34] Therefore, they are not reducible to statements that can be tested by the scientific method. However, one cannot properly conclude that people use moral judgments merely to express their own arbitrary attitudes and to influence the attitudes of others. Rather, it is possible to formulate a rational method for guiding choices wisely and for impartially resolving cases of conflicting claims. This method can be used to reach objective decisions in many—though not all—moral disputes. Of course, a rational, impartial decision unaccompanied by sanctions will

prove efficacious in resolving a dispute only if the disputants are willing to accept it.[35]

Lucid expositions of this method are provided by Richard B. Brandt (1959)[36] and William K. Frankena (1963). An outstanding example of its application to ethical problems is John Rawl's *A Theory of Justice* (1971).

Upon analysis, the moral-point-of-view method expounded by Frankena turns out to be quite similar to Brandt's Qualified Attitude Method. Frankena favors a noncognitivist, multifunctional position that recognizes the claim of moral and value judgments to rational justifiably. Frankena states that normative discourse is:

> . . . a language in which we may express our sentiments—approvals, disapprovals, evaluations, recommendations, advice, instructions, prescriptions—and put them out into the public arena for rational scrutiny and discussion, claiming that they will hold up under such scrutiny and discussion and that all our audience will concur with us if they will also choose the same common point of view. (Frankena, 1963, p. 19)

Against "meta-ethical relativism" that claims that there is no objectively valid way to justify any basic moral and value judgments in cases where judgments conflict, Frankena observes that it is "extremely difficult to show that people's basic ethical and value judgments would still be different even if they were fully enlightened, conceptually clear, shared the same factual beliefs, and were taking the same point of view" (p. 92). Hence, one may retain the claim that certain ethical and value judgments are objectively justifiable in the sense that they will be upheld by all people who take the "moral point of view," the conditions of which are being free, impartial, willing to universalize, conceptually clear, and informed about all possible relevant facts (p. 95). Frankena applauds Baier's contention "that one is taking the moral point of view if one is not being egoistic, one is doing things on principle, one is willing to universalize one's principles, and in doing so considers the good of everyone alike" (p. 96). When different people meet the conditions of the moral point of view as best they can and moral disagreement remains, they can ascribe the disagreement to imperfect fulfillment of the conditions but must be tolerant and open-minded if they are to refrain from going outside the moral institution of life and utilizing nonmoral techniques of coercion (pp. 94–95). Frankena concedes that he may "have to admit a certain relativity, at least, in the ranking of things listed as intrinsically good" (p. 95).

Relevance to Normative Forecasting. In the goal-setting stage of normative forecasting, values and norms need to be defined and analyzed. A key issue not fully treated by Ozbekhan concerns the criteria that are utilized to choose goals. In normative forecasting, feasibility is a necessary but not a sufficient criterion for choice. Therefore, further criteria must be specified, together with priorities among them. As previously noted, the criterion of likelihood is of special importance. All of these criteria can be evaluated by the good reasons approach. By using this approach in conjunction with relevant data (e.g., from psychology and sociology), normative criteria could be derived from basic human needs and from the ideal values and norms of the society in question or (for broader issues) of the human race. Such criteria would embrace quality-of-life considerations as well as economic growth, and would encourage the research, development, and implementation of those technologies (e.g., controlled fusion and improved contraceptives) that would constitute constructive responses to world problems.

Hence, normative principles should serve as indispensable criteria for humane goal setting. To ascertain appropriate principles, a forecaster can either go through the worthwhile but complex and time-consuming process just mentioned, or he can consult various systems of normative ethics (e.g., the systems of Brandt and of Frankena) which have been derived by applying the good reasons approach. These systems are quite similar, though some differences exist.

Furthermore, the goal-setting stage requires the application of criteria of choice. Possible goals (e.g., landing astronauts on the moon, rebuilding city slums, creating an international agency for food distribution during famines) should be intelligently and exhaustively questioned by using the good reasons approach. Consequences of pursuing and achieving each goal must be estimated, particularly since actions that are often judged as desirable (e.g., extensive use of DDT, maximization of GNP) may produce undesirable consequences in the future. It is also necessary to ascertain the relevance of each goal to the realization of basic values in accordance with acceptable norms. These values (e.g., freedom, equality), that in certain instances can conflict with one another, may be given priority rankings in reference to the possible goals. A normative forecaster needs to ask why, and to what extent, these values would be valuable in new situations. By making such complicated determinations, he increases his chances of selecting as a goal a future situation that will realize the intended values. Finally, the goal is selected.

Since the good reasons approach can be used to decide normative disputes that arise in daily life and to evaluate alternative goals, it is applicable to practical as well as theoretical issues. Yet reaching justifiable decisions concerning practical issues requires the use of principles, the application of which is not always clear. Abstract principles, such as the injunction to maximize human well-being, must be operationalized to find whether, for instance, a plan to supply populous, less-industrialized countries with a certain amount of specific kinds of prophylactics would probably promote more well-being than carefully-defined alternative uses to which available funds could be put. To take another illustration: Unless those forecasters who favor increased equality determine what kinds of equality they want to achieve in what types of situations, their commitment to the abstract principle may have little positive impact on practical situations in their forecasted futures. General forecasts of preferable world order require lesser degrees of operationalization than do forecasts that call for immediate action to implement specific policies. Yet without the operationalization of principles and goals, normative forecasting would be an unreliable guide for bringing about desirable particular outcomes in the real world.

This process of operationalization continues into the strategic and operational stages. In the words of Ozbekhan, "objective action links" must be formulated "between the norm, namely, 'the ought' and the 'can'" (Ozbekhan, 1968, p. 216). What must be ascertained is the extent to which a particular goal is relevant to a particular situation and to a particular strategy. The earlier parts of the normative forecasting process must be translated into the probable realization of specific goals, thus making these parts consonant with practical considerations in the real world. Whatever is not consonant with reality must be eliminated.

Sometimes a desirable goal is attainable only through questionable strategies. Hence, it is advisable to return to the first stage for reevaluating the goal in view of proposed strategies. By being too costly, morally unacceptable, or generative of undesirable consequences elsewhere in the system, the means to an end can render that end unworthy of pursuit. In such a case, the good reasons approach prescribes that the goal itself should be abandoned. Thus, normative evaluation and prescription is not limited to the goal-selection stage, but continues throughout the rest of the process.

When computer simulation is employed, movement between Ozbekhan's first and second stages can occur repeatedly. Though the forecasting is goal-oriented from its beginning, goal definition and policy selection can be so intertwined that the first and second stages could even be regarded as two aspects of the same stage. The goal may be redefined to make it more compatible with feasible strategy in the interplay between the means and the end. Then more strategies are explored, further expanding the range of choice.

The good reasons approach could also be utilized to formulate a normative system that would furnish appropriate guidance for constructive international action in our technologically changed world. Then the abstract principles of the system would have to be justifiably applied to possible situations that planning could actualize. A social accounting system would prove helpful in facilitating this application. The good reasons approach could have been used (and to some extent, was used implicitly) as an integral part of the following forecasters' analyses of the extent to which the normative principles of current sociocultural systems need to be revised:

1. Richard A. Falk's treatment of the inappropriateness of certain directives of the nation-state system to global ecological problems (1971);

2. Jørgen Randers and Donella Meadows' critique of current disregard for the well-being of future generations and specification of the kind of orientation required to resolve global ecological problems (1973);

3. Lester Brown's recommendations for a new societal ethic (1972c);

4. Willis Harman's critique of present cultural beliefs and operative values as unable to resolve the world macroproblem (1970);

5. Kenneth Boulding's depiction of current economic systems as displaying "cowboy economics" (1972);

6. Garrett Hardin's claim that overuse of the global "commons" has rendered the doctrine of the "invisible hand" dangerously obsolete (1968);

7. Hasan Ozbekhan's evaluation of the technological imperative (1968);

Even though the good reasons approach requires much further development, it could in its present state furnish much aid to forecasters. The possibility of a fruitful relationship between the good reasons approach and Bayesian decision analysis (treated by Richard K. Ashley in Chapter 10) deserves investigation. The former could provide differential evaluation of future contingencies, and could be aided by the latter in integrating available information and calculating the implications of this information for action.

One condition for societal adoption of normative forecasting is a well-developed theory and methodology. Much effort needs to be focused on developing the goal-selection stage. Use of the good reasons approach would import explicit theory into this largely unformalized stage. Since this approach provides a systematic, nonarbitrary method for normative assessment of the strategic and operational plans as well as of the normative plan, its utilization could also make successive stages of the normative forecasting process more rigorous. Moreover, forecasters of international relations could employ this method to formalize evaluations and prescriptions at the end of the exploratory forecasting process. Furthermore, once the concealed normative biases that distort forecasts have been uncovered, this method can be used to evaluate them.

A Design for Normative Forecasting

The foregoing descriptions and suggested revisions of the normative forecasting/planning process can be integrated into the following design.[37] This tentative design emerges from a search for a common second-order methodology that, in addition to being useful for making forecasts, would improve the more specific methods by which normative forecasting is now performed.

Several general observations about this five-step design will help to clarify it.

1. Each step involves a series of explicit decisions about appropriate techniques and the standards they must meet, followed by the sequential application of these techniques.

2. Since each step establishes a basis for subsequent steps, the diverse choices made and methods used at each stage can easily issue in conflicting forecasts.

3. In this iterative process, a return to previous steps, a repeated interchange between steps, or a repetition of all steps is sometimes required.

4. To varying degrees, both normative and descriptive considerations enter into each step.

The design systematically proceeds through these steps:[38]

1. *Clarification and evaluation of assumptions.* Using a check list, a forecaster explicates his or her methodological and nonmethodological assumptions. He separates normative and descriptive assumptions so as to overcome the unclarity that tends to distort estimates of likelihood. As Marvin S. Soroos and the Institute for World Order maintain (Soroos, 1973, and footnote 24), a forecaster specifies the values (e.g., nonviolence, economic welfare, and social justice) that he would like to see realized in the future. He arranges these values in a priority hierarchy to cover conditions in which they could become competing goals. If he already has a particular normative plan in mind, he states it. He employs the good reasons approach to assess and, if necessary, to revise his normative assumptions. Insofar as the circumstances allow, he evaluates all of his assumptions. He estimates the impact his assumptions are likely to exert on his forecast.

2. *Exploratory forecasting.* Next, he analyzes present systems, problems, and trends, bringing into play relevant knowledge about the past. He then uses a combination of the most appropriate methods to formulate an exploratory forecast of relatively likely and less likely alternative futures. The scope and character of the alternative futures can be affected by the forecasting purpose (e.g., to design an international agency for the control of nuclear weapons or a world order that would resolve population/resources/environment problems),

but must be relatively broad and accurate. Previous exploratory forecasts made by various groups and individuals are also studied and appraised. Of particular importance is the extent to which the forecaster's preferences have already been achieved and would be achieved in each of the alternative futures.

3. *Selection of a preferable future as a goal.* He then fulfills the previously mentioned tasks in Ozbekhan's first stage. Both continuous and discontinuous futures must be *bona fide* candidates for selection. It is often advisable to select several desirable goals provisionally in order to check the feasibility of each subsequently and then reevaluate them. To evaluate and choose between alternative futures, he employs the good reasons approach. Thus, he uses a systematic method to anchor his forecast in an important, nonarbitrary preference ordering. Justifiable normative principles must constitute key criteria for choosing goals. Principles and goals must be operationalized from this step onward, so as to be applicable to relevant situations. Though the good reasons approach takes into account the likelihood of various consequences of actions, he may be able to inject more rigor into his analysis by also utilizing Bayesian decision analysis.

If his reassessed values could be realized in a relatively likely future that is basically continuous with the present, he selects this future. However, if all preferable futures are discontinuous with the present and quite unlikely apart from planned change, one (or more) is selected pending the results of the next two stages in the forecasting process.

3. *Use of creative imagination.* If none of the alternative futures seems to be both sufficiently preferable and feasible, a substage is called for in which the forecaster seeks to imaginatively construct an alternative future that meets these requirements. To broaden the range of options, this creative substage could be included in the forecasting process even when one of the alternative futures from the exploratory stage appears to meet the qualifications for being chosen as a goal.

4. *Detection of feasible strategies.* Next, the forecaster completes the tasks of Ozbekhan's second stage (pp. 215–216). He seeks to expand the opportunities for choice by devising a range of feasible scenarios. He may retain the goal only if he can link it to the present by at least one feasible path. For

instance, he may specify the chains of implementable policy decisions and technologies that, if applied at the proper pivotal points in the relevant systems at the correct times, could achieve the goal. Movement from the normative plan to the strategic plan and then to the operational plan can be facilitated by various techniques. Such methodologies as systems analysis, operations research, scenario writing, and computer simulation can be used productively in the formulation of strategic plans and operational plans. Moreover, a social accounting system and reliable assessment of the probabilities of alternative outcomes could be used in conjunction with the good reasons approach. These techniques would enhance calculation of which possible outcomes of planning would fulfill the requirements of the general normative principles that have been invoked in goal setting.

4a. *Return to the step of goal selection.* If no plausible scenario is found, the forecaster may search for more or return to step 3 to redefine the goal in such a way as to make it achievable. Alternatively, he may reject the goal and possibly select another.

5. *Selection of strategy for implementation.* The best strategy must be selected from the previous step. As Ozbekhan observes, the operational plan must set forth priority-ordered, interrelated decisions that specify a temporal continuity of actions capable of prevailing against disruptive side effects triggered by any of the actions (p. 216). Though final selection may be reserved for decision makers, a forecaster can make recommendations. One of the techniques he utilizes is the good reasons approach, for the goal must be reevaluated in terms of the desirability of the available strategies. The goal can even be rejected if all feasible strategies have decidedly undesirable consequences. Bayesian decision analysis can also be employed.

5a. *Revision of exploratory forecast on the basis of anticipated feedback.* An estimate is made concerning the impact of implementing the planned change on the system and hence on the original exploratory forecast. Any appropriate adjustments are made in the planning process.

5b. *Contingency plans.* Because of possible disruption, especially by exogenous factors, contingency plans are formulated. Planning becomes more flexible.

IV. SUMMARY

By now it is clear that both horns of the dilemma that occasioned this analysis can be effectively countered. Exploratory forecasting is by no means value free and normative forecasting of international relations can be done much more systematically and objectively than presumed. Thus, a choice between exploratory and normative forecasting is not reducible to a choice between science and arbitrary speculation. When these general methods are used to supplement each other, exploratory forecasting can make normative forecasting more reliable and normative forecasting can make exploratory forecasting more useful in the process of shaping the future wisely.

To make normative forecasting of international relations rigorous and reliable, much progress remains to be made. The improvements suggested in this chapter—especially employment of the checklist technique, of antecedent exploratory forecasting, and of the good reasons approach—could increase the degree of explicit theory employed, the use of systematic procedures, and the use of empirical data. Relevance trees and feedback techniques, discussed in Chapter 17, are prototypes of the kinds of formalized procedures by which the reliability of normative forecasting could be enhanced (see footnote 19).

NOTES

1. None of the names for this type of forecasting— "ontological," "exploratory," "conjectural," "primary," "descriptive"—is very enlightening. The term "descriptive" distinguishes it from normative (i.e., prescriptive) forecasting, but might incline one to make the mistaken assumption that there are at the present time future facts waiting to be described. Hence, we adopt the term that seems to be the most common in the literature, "exploratory forecasting," which is here used in a much broader sense than in Chapter 1 of this book.

2. If "normative forecasting" is defined merely as the specification of futures that should be sought, it is almost by definition bound to be unreliable as a systematic method. However, reliability becomes much more attainable when this method includes both planning that devises implementable paths to chosen goals and exploratory forecasting that likewise decreases uncertainty. "Normative forecasting" as used in this chapter is to be understood as an abbreviation for "normative forecasting and planning."

3. Silvert states that "the essential measure of political development is the relation between the range of choice open to a polity and the range it actually explores" (Silvert, 1970, p. xxiv).

4. The following works furnish examples of normative forecasting that are either concerned with, or relevant to, international relations. (The forecasts fit our characterization of "normative forecasting," though not all these forecasters use this term to refer to their methodology.): Pirages and Ehrlich (1974); Falk (1972); Brown (1972 and 1974); Hardin (1972); Harman (1970); Markley (1971); Forrester (1971b); Meadows, *et al.* (1972); Peccei (1969); Theobald (1968); Etzioni (1968); Boulding (1972); Wagar (1971).

5. We have constructed an ideal-type position that is reasonably accurate in characterizing the explicit or implicit orientations of a number of important international relations forecasters toward normative forecasting.

6. This normative disagreement is not merely a function of difference in belief concerning whether continued exponential growth of industrialization and population would lead to counterintuitive overshoots of sustainable levels of each and to the consequent collapse of both. Meadows also disagrees with Kahn as to whether increasing inequalities are unjust. This can be safely inferred from relevant statements in *The Limits to Growth* (Meadows, *et al.*, 1972) and *Things to Come* (Kahn and Bruce-Briggs, 1972).

7. To Herman Kahn, a certain kind of post-industrial age would be a laudatory achievement; to Jacques Ellul (*The Technological Society*, 1964), the same age might involve a dehumanizing domination by techniques; and to Alain Touraine (*The Post-Industrial Society*, 1971), a programed dictatorship by technocrats. Thus, forecasters sometimes differ in their preferences and in their consequent assignments of desirability and undesirability to the same alternative future.

8. Not only normative forecasts, but also exploratory forecasts can make their forecasted outcomes more probable. For instance, a forecast of an especially attractive, achievable alternative future tends to evoke policies aimed at achieving that future. Hence, an exploratory forecast can function as a self-fulfilling prophecy that helps to create a forecasted future.

9. In his review of Daniel Bell's *The Coming of Post-Industrial Society*. Michael Marien (1973a) detects an establishment bias. According to John McHale (1972), both "A Blueprint for Survival" (*The Ecologist*, England, January 13, 1972) and *The Limits to Growth* (Meadows, *et al.*, 1972) share "an intrinsically conservative set of implicit premises."

10. "Elements" here includes "procedures."

11. A plausible argument can be made for the claim that no descriptive statement is completely value free: All scientific observation statements appear to be theory laden, and theories are not value free. Hence, an assumption that is primarily descriptive can easily have normative overtones, and vice versa. An indistinct "twilight zone" may be resistant to separation. Despite this relativity, the separation of assumptions (or of components of assumptions) in terms of the descriptive-normative distinction is extremely important. At the same time, their interrelations must not be ignored, as they are part of a mechanical imposition of the descriptive-normative dichotomy on assumptions. Many implicitly normative assumptions have been regarded as value free by proponents of this dichotomy (e.g., by those forecasters who try to make forecasting as value free as possible.) In short, there is no substitute for painstaking analysis of the forecasting process, analysis by which descriptive and normative elements are distinguished *insofar as possible*.

12. In "A Paradigm for the Analysis of Time Perspectives and Images of the Future," Wendell Bell, James A. Mau, Bettina J. Huber, and Menno Boldt categorize the kinds of assumptions that forecasters make either explicitly or, more often, implicitly (Bell and Mau [eds.], 1971, pp. 45–55). Likewise, David C. Miller and Ronald L. Hunt compile lists of similar assumptions. Miller and Hunt attempt to categorize the basic decision tasks that forecasters need to complete (Miller and Hunt, 1973, pp. A 5–7, A 57–61, etc.). (See, for example, the tentative check lists presented in Michael Washburn, "Outline for a Normative/Planning Process," in Louis R. Beres (ed.) (1975).

13. In regard to values, a forecaster would seek to uncover such types of assumptions as: his needs and desires; his hierarchically arranged values and norms; the extent to which his normative orientation reflects his culture and socioeconomic class; and his purpose in forecasting. He would also assess: the current distribution of operational values; the ways in which this distribution could change and is likely to change; and the ways in which he would prefer it to change.

14. Much of today's exploratory forecasting is limited by its neglect or inadequate performance of three related tasks that concern values: (1) detection of deep-seated normative assumptions that distort forecasts; (2) prescriptions of which alternative futures should be sought; and (3) exploratory anticipation of likely and possible discontinuous changes in value-priorities.

15. Jantsch (1967), p. 44. Jantsch argues that trend extrapolation "can be expected to become less accurate the more developments over time are influenced by normative thinking . . ." (*ibid.*, p. 80).

16. Ozbekhan (1968), pp. 208–209, 212.

One weakness of the deterministic model of planning lies in its presupposition that the value system which serves as a frame of reference will remain unchanged and will be enforced by institutions. Another weakness is its inability to accept events that are exogenous to the single closed decision system. The most crucial weakness centers in the acceptance of feasibility as a sufficiently desirable end (*ibid.*, pp. 208–209).

Not only can normative planning correct weaknesses of deterministic planning; it can also incorporate its strengths (which Ozbekhan does not mention). A deterministic planner correctly perceives that it is generally easier to plan with a trend than to plan against it. The probability of successfully implementing relatively continuous goals is usually higher than that of discontinuous goals. Therefore, alternative goals need to be compared in terms of likelihood as well as desirability. Even though one goal is moderately less desirable than another, its selection may be warranted because it is decidedly more likely.

17. Inasmuch as the treatment in this section and the next draws quite extensively on Ozbekhan's article, his term "normative planning" will be temporarily used instead of "normative forecasting."

18. Jantsch mentions two other methods that tend to be normative in nature: systems analysis and morphological research (Jantsch, *op. cit.*, p. 45).

19. Feedback techniques begin with an exploratory forecast. On the basis of this forecast and a model of the present situation, a model of the future is constructed and then used to derive a set of alternative futures. This set can be used to revise current policy in order to increase the likelihood of achieving a desirable goal or of avoiding a threatening pitfall. Such revision necessitates reworking the model of the present situation and, therefore, the model of the future and the set of alternative futures. Feedback in this pattern of reciprocal influences continues (see Thomas W. Robinson, Chapter 17, this volume).

Relevance tree techniques, which include the Honeywell Corporation's "PATTERN" and US Department of Defense's "PPBS," have been used extensively by industry and government. Such techniques seek to ascertain which current decisions or other actions are relevant to fairly distant objectives (*ibid.*, p. 17; also pp. 15–16).

Relevance tree techniques provide a valuable aid for formulating operational plans. However, currently accepted goals could be more thoroughly questioned and alternative discontinuous goals more seriously considered than is the case in most uses of relevance trees today. On the other hand, relevance tree techniques hinder a drift into "provisional catastrophist" extremes when such extremes are unwarranted.

In principle, systematic priority-setting marks an important methodological contribution. Yet group assessment of expert intuitive judgment is a questionable method of moral evaluation. Use of the soon-to-be-examined "good reasons approach" would be helpful here, as would increased concern with the preferences of potentially affected publics.

20. See the subsection "Methodology of Working Backward" in this chapter.

21. See footnotes 4 and 22–24 for the relevant works of these forecasters. None of their forecasts of comprehensive changes completely fulfills (or was intended to fulfill) the requirements of Ozbekhan's third stage. The forecasts vary in the thoroughness

and plausibility of their strategic and operational plans. Certain other forecasts, notably those of Kenneth Boulding and Amatai Etzioni, display penetrating insight in sketching preferable futures in the first stage, but hardly even get to the second.

22. Brown, *op. cit.*, pp. 321–364. For a summary of Brown's *World Without Borders*, see his article "An Overview of World Trends (1972b). "How Global Forces Are Reshaping Human Life" is an unsigned review of Brown's book in the same issue of *The Futurist*, pp. 232–235.

Brown's proposed minimum standard of living for all human beings would include a minimum nutritional standard, at least rudimentary basic health services, and compulsory elementary educational and adult literacy programs. The new societal ethic enjoins a more harmonious relation between human beings and nature, recycling of raw materials, population stabilization, and a more equitable distribution of wealth.

Thus, Brown has set forth a normative plan and has sketched some features of a strategic plan. His forecast of the new societal ethic and of the new society resembles forecasts made by Harman and by Pirages and Ehrlich.

23. Falk (1971), especially pp. 19–23. Falk maintains that strategies must be designed for education, mobilization of support, and transformation of power structures. Though sometimes revolutionary members of a world political party will probably have to seize power from regressive forces, a contractual transition would not involve a reliance, especially in the latter stages of world transformation, on large-scale violence (*ibid.*, pp. 21–23).

For a fuller treatment of this transition strategy, see Falk (1975).

24. Falk (1975); Kothari (1975); Mendlovitz (1974); Mazrui (1975); and Galtung (1976).

25. Hampden-Turner (1970), p. 340; Livingston (1971); Sargent (1974).

26. The best introductions to synectics are contained in Gordon (1961) and Prine (1970).

27. In *The Image of the Future* (1961), Frederick Polak supplies many examples of the impact that positive and negative images of the future have had upon the development of societies. Experiments conducted by such psychologists as Elliot Aronson (1972) also reveal the human tendency to fulfill expectations. Harold Lasswell has called attention to the importance of "developmental constructs" that express expectations. He has analyzed both self-fulfilling and self-denying prophecies (Lasswell, 1966, pp. 157–166).

28. In an insightful article entitled "The New Copernical Revolution" (1969), Willis W. Harman seems to be overly confident about the emergence and likely consequences of a development that he supports, "the science of man's subjective experience (Harman, 1969, p. 7). Likewise, Wendell Bell and James A. Mau appear to overestimate the rate of likely prog-

ress toward the preferred goal of sociologists becoming future-oriented (Bell and Mau, *op. cit.*, pp. xii–xiii).

29. For instance, only because they feared that Hitler might first get the atomic bomb were many physicists motivated to work on the Manhattan Project.

30. See Ozbekhan, *op. cit.*, pp. 207, 218, 225. "Throughout all this discussion," Ozbekhan remarks, "I have tried to suggest that both our current institutions and the democratic process through which they and we operate in society might have become insufficient" (*ibid.*, p. 225). In regard to "the difficulty in determining *who* is going to plan," he states "I do not know whether the answer to this dilemma lies in pluralistic, or advocate, or elite planning, which we talked about" (*ibid.*, p. 218).

31. Even if wide public participation in goal-setting were achieved, what about future generations that will be affected by the planned changes implemented by the present generation? Certain policies (e.g., increased R&D expenditures) for controlled fusion would probably open up new options for our descendants, whereas consequences of others (e.g., depletion of certain nonrenewable natural resources) could foreclose options. The value-priorities that are currently judged to be proper for policy formation may not be the same as those of our descendants who are affected by the policies. To what extent is it possible to anticipate our descendants' priorities? To what extent should these priorities condition present policies? If likely changes in priorities cannot be anticipated, even normative forecasting would have a built-in conservative bias. Without proposing answers to these knotty questions, we suggest that the use of both the soon-to-be-examined "good reasons approach" and historical sociology would be conducive to anticipating to an appreciable extent the value-priorities of future generations.

32. In the parlance of moral philosophy, to deduce prescriptive conclusions from purely descriptive premises is to commit the "naturalistic fallacy." To make the deduction valid, a prescriptive premise must be supplied; but such an assumption of what is to be proved amounts to begging the question. Though the relation between purely descriptive premises and a prescriptive conclusion is not one of logical deduction, empirical facts are by no means irrelevant to prescriptive conclusions. The "good reasons approach" can be used to make justifiable inferences.

33. Among other moral philosophers who advocate the good reasons approach are Englishmen S. E. Toulmin, P. H. Nowell-Smith, R. M. Hare, and J. O. Urmson, and Americans Morton White and H. D. Aiken. Of special interest are the following works: Frankena (1963); Brandt (1959); Rawls (1951), pp. 177–197 and 1971; Baier (1958); Toulmin (1960); Nowell-Smith (1954); Hare (1952); White (1950).

34. The good reasons approach is best understood in the light of its origin in twentieth century moral philosophy. This approach was the outcome of the debate between "intuitionists" (e.g., G. E. Moore, Ross), "ethical naturalists" (John Dewey, R. B. Perry), and "emotivists" (A. J. Ayer, C. L. Stevenson). See Warnock (1960).

35. Careful examination of the good reasons approach could help to remove an obstacle that has caused many exploratory forecasters to shy away from making explicit value judgments. These forecasters have responded as if they were allergic to the supposed subjectivity of all normative claims. Once normative elements in forecasts are separated from elements that are descriptive, each can be handled objectively. Moreover, rationally-justifiable inferences can span the gulf between the "ought" and the "is."

36. Brandt, *op. cit.*, Chapter 10 (especially pp. 249–251). For an insightful critique of complete ethical relativism, see Chapter 11, pp. 271–294.

37. Remarks in this section parallel some of those made by Soroos (1973).

38. The explicit, systematic character of the design would be an aid both to forecasters during the forecasting process and to those who evaluate forecasts in terms of different decisions made at various stages of this process.

CHAPTER EIGHT

THE USE OF EXPERT OPINION IN INTERNATIONAL RELATIONS FORECASTING

Olaf Helmer

I. INTRODUCTION

The intent of this chapter is to acquaint the reader with the potentialities of two methods concerned with the use of expert opinion, the Delphi and the cross-impact techniques. To set the stage for a discussion of the application of these techniques to international relations forecasting, a few things should be stated for the record, although most have been said many times before.

First, forecasts are not predictions. While a prediction asserts the occurrence of some event with certainty ("the head of state of country A will abdicate next year"), a forecast is a probabilistic statement ("there is a 2-to-1 chance that the head of state of country A will abdicate next year"). A prediction may be viewed as a limiting case of a forecast, where the assigned probability is 1. In practice, forecasts very rarely take the form of predictions.

Second, forecasts are often cast in conditional form ("if the cost of living in country A continues to rise at the present rate, there is a 2-to-1 chance that its head of state will abdicate next year"). Although probabilistic, forecasts in this form often are of greater utility than predictions because they provide some insight into the causal connections between potential future developments.

Third, forecasts may refer either to events or to trends. A trend forecast frequently, but not necessarily, is phrased in terms of a probable deviation from a predicted trend. This may take the form of a fixed-probability statement ("there is a 0.9 probability that the GNP of country A during the next decade will rise at an annual rate of $5\% \pm 1\%$"); or be of an entire probability distribution around a central trend. For any particular point in time, a trend forecast degenerates into an event forecast.

Fourth, events and trend changes about which forecasts are being made must be verifiable, if forecasts are to be operationally meaningful. This puts a special strain on forecasts in the social science area as opposed to, say, technological forecasts, because the terminology we tend to use ("rising dissatisfaction," "detente," "nationalism") does not always have the crispness necessary to allow unambiguously verifiable assertions. As a consequence, forecasts, in order to be meaningful, sometimes have to be formulated in terms of certain indicators. If possible, these are social or political indicators whose values are objectively measurable. But there is also a place for indicators—I shall refer to them, for contrast, as "indices"—whose values are capable only of subjective estimation. Subjective indices will be reconsidered briefly in this chapter.

Fifth, forecasting is not an incidental but an essential feature of any science. The purpose of any scientific effort is to provide a better understanding of the world around us and, thereby, the ability to influence and, if possible, to control it. This purpose is achieved by forecasting the likely consequences of alternative courses of action and selecting that course which promises the most desirable outcome. Whether an activity qualifies as having scientific intent depends crucially on its capability of producing forecasts. (Historical analysis, in particular, qualifies as scientific under this criterion to the extent that it furnishes insights from which extrapolations can be made that aid in the assertion of forecasts.) The pragmatic utility of a scientific effort is determined by the reliability of the forecasts it is capable of generating.

Sixth, a formal theoretical structure, such as that on which forecasts in the natural sciences are based, does not exist in the social sciences. Admittedly, in sciences such as behavioral psychology or economics, which are conceptually contiguous to the natural sciences, sets of reasonably well established hypotheses are available that cover numerous but isolated aspects of these fields. But even there, the theoretical information generally is sufficient only to permit the derivation of forecasts concerning "pure" cases; that is, psychological experiments under controlled laboratory conditions or economic situations where the influence of exogenous factors (social, political, psychological) may be considered negligible. In a discipline such as international politics the situation in this regard is even worse, since there are very few generally

accepted hypotheses that might lend themselves to the systematic derivation of forecasts.

Finally, since social scientists surely do not wish to abdicate their right to make forecasts (as opposed to predictions, of course), despite the absence of a sound, formal theoretical foundation, they have to find alternative ways to utilize the enormous amount of expertise that has been accumulated. In the particular case of political science:

> Although it would indeed be gratifying to have political theories comparable in elegance, in logical persuasiveness, and in predictive reliability to physical theories, we cannot count on this to come about. In any case, the dangers that society faces are so great and the need for rapid progress so evident that we cannot afford to wait—perhaps for a generation or more—until satisfactory, well-tested theories of human relations are available. The time has come to emulate, not physical science, but physical technology. The potential reward from a reorientation of some of the effort in the social-science area toward social technology (or, in the special case at hand, toward political technology) is considerable; it may even equal or exceed in importance that of .the achievements credited to the technologies arising out of the physical sciences. (Helmer, 1966, p. 6)

To achieve this kind of reorientation, from general theory building to pragmatic political technology, requires the adoption of some of the methods of operations research, notably the construction of simulation models and the systematic use of expert judgment.

In what follows, I shall briefly discuss two of the techniques used for extracting and collating expert opinions and for simulation gaming, namely, the Delphi method and cross-impact gaming. Subsequently, I shall try to indicate how these techniques might be utilized in the specific context of the area of international relations.

II. THE DELPHI METHOD

Once the fact has been accepted that some reliance on judgmental information is essential for all planning processes, it is natural to want to make the procedures for obtaining such "soft" data as reliable and efficient as possible. The Delphi method was designed to deal with cases where several experts are available to contribute and pool their opinions on some particular issue. In recognition of the psychological drawbacks of an experts' roundtable discussion aimed at arriving at a group position on the issue in question, an attempt was made, in designing the Delphi method, to introduce some measure of anonymity into the individual contributions without, at the same time, forfeiting the stimulating give-and-take of a conventional debate. Anonymity in a debate can be achieved by having an intermediary question the participants individually and repeatedly by questionnaire or interview, while providing continual feedback on the opinions stated by others in previous phases of the questioning process without revealing the authorship of a particular opinion.

The method was first designed by the author in conjunction with Norman Dalkey for use in a military estimation problem that arose at the Rand Corporation in the early 1950's (Dalkey and Helmer, 1964), and since has been employed in several thousand cases all over the world, covering such widely divergent subjects as educational reform, long-range corporate planning, the future of medicine, assessments regarding the quality of life, and public-sector planning at the highest levels.

For example, in the case of a technological forecasting study, the procedure would be as follows: a suitable set of specialists is selected whose expert judgments are to be solicited. Depending on the complexity of the subject matter, ten to fifty are required. A questionnaire (or interview) is prepared asking for the probability of occurrence of certain events (say, technological breakthroughs) by a certain date (or, alternatively, for the date by which the occurrence is judged to have a given probability, or even for an entire probability distribution over time).

Round 1: A first set of estimated answers is solicited. (Sometimes the respondents are asked to select only the questions about which they consider themselves especially competent. Alternatively, answers to all questions may be requested, accompanied by a self-rating of relative competence for each question.)

Round 2: The participants are then provided with the Round 1 response distribution which is usually presented in terms of the median and the first and third quartiles, and new, possibly revised,

responses are solicited. In those cases where the new response is outside the interquartile range (i.e., the middle half of the first-round responses), the respondent is asked to provide a statement of the reason why he gave an answer that differed that much from the answers supplied by the majority.

Round 3: The resulting response distribution is fed back, together with a summary of the arguments defending relatively deviant responses. Again the participants are asked for reestimates. This time, if a response lies outside the new (second-round) interquartile range, a reason in the form of a counterargument is requested stating why the argument in favor of an answer at the opposite end of the spectrum was not persuasive.

Round 4: Again, the new response distribution and a summary of the counterarguments are fed back, and a final set of answers is requested, based on due consideration of all arguments and counterarguments that were presented.

The medians of the responses of this final round are then accepted as the group's position, representing the nearest thing to a consensus that is attainable. A report on the outcome usually also includes an indication of the residual spread of opinions as well as of minority arguments in defense of deviant opinions, particularly in case where a sizeable dissensus remains.

The first round as described above sometimes is preceded by an "open-ended" initial round intended to help delineate the subject matter of the inquiry. Thus, there might be an opening "Round 0" asking for entries to be considered in a subsequent round, for example:

Round 0: In a technological forecasting inquiry, the respondents may be requested to list (perhaps in descending order of estimated importance) the most important technological breakthroughs that have a nonnegligible chance of occurring during the period that is the subject of inquiry

Although the Delphi method has come to be used very widely during the last decade, it still has not been subjected to enough carefully conducted experiments to establish its relative reliability or to improve its performance. The experiments that have been carried out plus the experience gained in its practice suggest that, statistically speaking, the method is superior to face-to-face discussions but that the quality of the outcome depends not only on the selection of the participating experts (as, of course, does a non-anonymous debate, too), but also on the circumspection and integrity of the study conductor.[1]

III. CROSS-IMPACT GAMING

The cross-impact technique was developed with the intention of conceptually refining a certain aspect of the Delphi approach. When Delphi is used to forecast future developments, such potential developments tend to be examined in isolation from one another. In fact, of course, events are related by an intricate net of mutual causalities and influences, and the cross-impact concept represents an attempt to inject proper consideration of such interconnections into the process of estimating the probabilities of future occurrences.

To accomplish this purpose, it is convenient, when dealing with a number of prospective developments, $D_1, D_2, \ldots, D_n$, to create a "cross-impact matrix," obtained by constructing a two-entry table (see Figure 8.1), wherein information is entered in the ij-cell (that is, the intersection of the D_i-row and the D_j-column) as to how the occurrence of D_i is expected to affect the probability of occurrence of D_j.

More specifically, it may be assumed that some of the D_i are potential events that may occur at some point in time with an estimated probability, while others are trends whose anticipated future course may be estimated (perhaps by judicious extrapolation from past time series). If D_i is an event,

the ij-cell would contain judgmental information as to the impact of that event, if it were to occur, on either the probability of occurrence of D_j (if D_j is also an event) or on deviations of D_j from its anticipated course (if D_j is a trend). If D_i, on the other hand, is a trend, the judgmental information entered in the ij-cell could reflect the expected impact of a deviation of that trend from its anticipated value on the probability of occurrence of the event D_j or on changes in anticipated values of the trend D_j.

To obtain estimates of the probabilities of occurrence of the events in question as well as of the anticipated trends and, particularly, of the cross impacts among them can be an undertaking of formidable size. Since it inevitably has to be based largely on expert judgment, the use of the Delphi method (or some variant of it) may well be appropriate.

The process of constructing a cross-impact matrix, though cumbersome, is itself a useful task inasmuch as it forces the investigator to give systematic attention to possible causal interrelations among the relevant potential developments under consideration. Once the effort of putting together a cross-impact matrix has been completed, the matrix can be employed for a number of purposes, as discussed below.

The Identification of Indirect Impacts

The matrix can be utilized to find out what indirect impact a development may have via its direct impact on some other development. These "ricochet" effects—as these secondary and tertiary impacts have very aptly been called—often constitute unexpected repercussions that a more cursory examination would not reveal. They are, incidentally, a specific subject of inquiry in investigations conducted under the general heading of "technology assessment."

Sensitivity Analysis

The basic assumptions as to event probabilities and trend values are generally subject to considerable uncertainty since, at best, they represent merely the experts' best estimates. The cross-impact matrix can be used in examining how sensitively other developments depend on these assumptions made

	D_1	D_2	$\cdots$	D_j	$\cdots$	D_n
D_1						
D_2						
$\vdots$						
D_i						
$\vdots$						
D_n						

Figure 8.1   General form of a cross-impact matrix.

about a particular development. This is done by changing these assumptions by some amount (say, raising the probability of occurrence by 10 percent, if it is an event; or increasing the trend values by 10 percent, if indeed it is a trend), and observing the effect that these changes have on other developments by virtue of their cross impacts. Those developments to which others are thus found to be most sensitive are the ones that (1) may have to be subjected to particularly searching analysis in order to make the estimated inputs regarding them as precise as possible, and (2) represent the most likely target of interventions aimed at influencing other developments.

Gaming

The notion of sensitivity studies leads rather naturally to the idea of a planning game. Let us assume that we are interested in looking more closely at potential developments, say, during the next 10 years. Then we may, for convenience, divide this time span into ten intervals of 1 year each, and record the information in the cross-impact matrix in such a form that it shows how occurrences in one of the 10 years under consideration might affect occurrences in the following year.

Having structured the information in this form, we may, first of all, "play" a given matrix passively (i.e., without intervention) as follows: We begin by deciding which of the potential events included in the matrix occur during the first game year (using random numbers in standard Monte-Carlo fashion); depending on which events do or do not occur, certain cross-impact adjustments are carried out regarding the probabilities of the remaining events and the trend values during the second game year. Thereby a new initial position for the second year is created, and a new, similar move cycle can be executed. This procedure is continued through ten cycles, until the terminal year (10 years from the present, in the example) is reached. The result is a 10-year scenario, consisting of a succession of event occurrences and changes in the courses of the given trends. Since chance plays an important part in this scenario construction, the game should be played several (possibly many) times in order to ascertain the probability distribution of possible outcomes (and, with it, the probability distribution of scenarios leading to these outcomes).

Having thus established a benchmark, representing the expected outcome if no intervention is made, a planner can use the game format to test various alternative policies. A given policy will have the effect of changing some of the game's input assumptions (event probabilities and anticipated trend values). Playing the game with these changes having been carried out will produce a new outcome distribution. Comparison of such outcomes resulting from different policies will shed some light on the relative advantages of each.

This operation of the cross-impact model as a "one-person" game (i.e., as a one-sided planning game in which a single planning team tests alternative policies) can easily be extended into a two- or multiperson game, in which the interactions of independent interventions by several actors can be observed.

It should be noted that, while it will be very instructive to play such a game by hand a few times, the large number of plays required to obtain probability distributions of outcomes will necessitate computerization of the game-playing process (Helmer, 1972a and 1972b).

IV. APPLICATIONS TO INTERNATIONAL RELATIONS FORECASTING

There are several modes in which the methods described very briefly above can be applied to forecasting in subject areas within the international relations field. The range of possible forecasts extends all the way from direct, probabilistic assertions about specific potential events and the future course of specific trends to the building of "islands of theory" and the employment of such theoretical findings for long-range planning. Rather than confining myself to generalized statements about possible applications in these different modes, I shall attempt, as I go along, to offer some specific illustrations.

Direct Exploratory Forecasting

Future developments in the arena of foreign politics depend so much on individual unforeseeable events (an assassination, the outcome of a close election, the result of a negotiation, even the weather) that political scientists show an understandable disinclination to engage in prophecies.

To mitigate this reluctance in deference to the demands of foreign-policy planning, it is helpful, I think, to remind the would-be prognosticator of the following points:

No predictions but merely (probabilistic) forecasts are expected.

The stakes are so high that a substantial payoff can be expected from even a slight improvement in statistical reliability as compared with the average person's expectations.

Longer-range (say, 10- to 30-year) forecasts are less dependent than short-range (say, 1- to 5-year) ones on unexpected and unforeseeable occurrences.

No single prognosticator should be required to undertake the task of political forecasting alone, but the responsibility should be shared among experts.

A convenient tool for implementing this latter prescription is the Delphi method. While it could be applied to any specific topic, let me choose as an illustration the case of the future of Soviet-American relations during the next 25 years.

Imagine a well-selected panel of about ten specialists in Soviet-American relations, including some who are not just political experts in the narrow sense but well versed in closely related fields such as economics, cultural relations, military developments, and so on. Using the intellectual resource represented by such a panel, a Delphi inquiry might best be initiated by conducting an open-ended first round, using something like a "twenty-questions" approach:

Step 1: Ask each participant to list those twenty political developments (events or trend changes) that, in his opinion, have a reasonable chance of occurring during the next 25 years and that, were they to occur, would either have a profound impact on Soviet-American relations or be significant indicators of the status of those relations

Step 2: Collate the responses, weed out essential duplicates, eliminate others that are comparatively less relevant, and thus obtain a reduced list of trends and potential events that form the input into the forecasting inquiry proper. (If time and resources permit, this selection process could be carried out with the aid of the panelists, by interjecting another round, requesting a ranking of items by expected importance. Here, "expected importance" is defined as the product of the probability

of occurrence and the importance if occurring, where importance is measured on some intuitive scale, say, from 0 to 10.)

Step 3: For the events on the list, ask for probability distributions of their occurrence over time (most conveniently, in terms of the years by which each attains a probability of .1, .5, and .9 of having occurred). For the trends, ask for projections over the next 25 years, with some indication of the uncertainty of the estimate (possibly again in terms of not just the .5-curve but also the .1- and .9-curves).

Step 4, etc.: Continue through several rounds of inquiry, as prescribed in the general description of the Delphi procedure given earlier.

The result will be a set of forecasts, with indications of the uncertainties attached to them. Some of the forecasts will represent a narrow consensus, others merely the median of relatively widely dispersed responses accompanied, however, by indications of the reasons for such divergencies of opinion. Analysis of these reasons will reveal whether a lack of consensus is due to semantic causes (i.e., different interpretations of the questions that had been posed), to factual disagreements, or to the exercise of wishful thinking in the face of genuine uncertainty. To the political decision maker, who will have to base his plans on expert advice, the forecasts representing a narrow consensus will, of course, be most helpful. But he will profit, too, knowing about real uncertainties and, especially, about the reasons why different experts, in some cases, hold widely divergent views on some aspect of the future; for this will give him clues as to where he has to tread with particular caution and what areas are in need of further research.

Theory Building

The utility to the planner of a set of forecasts, such as might be obtained through a straightforward Delphi inquiry, may be far from negligible; yet it will be limited because such isolated forecasts, by themselves, shed no light, except incidentally (via the respondents' explanatory arguments), on the reasons for prospective happenings. If the planner wishes to proceed on a basis of more than just a blind trust in the forecasting reliability of a panel of experts and desires a better understanding of the causal relationships among potential developments, he needs, ideally, to be provided with a theory consisting of generalized propositions. That would put him in a position where statements regarding particular situations could be derived by him from the general case by specifying the appropriate parameters.

While such generalized propositions, as stated before, are as a rule unavailable, a modicum of an integrated overview, and therewith of quasi-theoretical insights into underlying causalities, can be attained by an application of the cross-impact technique.

In order to see how a cross-impact model might be looked upon as the next best thing to a theory, let us return to the illustrative case of Soviet-American relations. Suppose, for simplicity, that, among the developments about which forecasts were earlier assumed to have been obtained, the twenty most important events and, similarly, the twenty most important trends had been selected. These could be made the subject of a cross-impact inquiry (possibly using the same expert respondents who had provided the original individual forecasts); that is, a 40-by-40 cross-impact matrix could be constructed in which—as indicated in the earlier description of this method—the expected impact of the occurrence of any of the events or of the deviation of any of the trends from its anticipated values on any of the other developments would be recorded. This task, of course, is a difficult one, but it may be made somewhat easier by subdividing the estimation requirements for the 1560 matrix items (40x40, −40 for the diagonal) and distributing it among subpanels selected for their particular expertise with regard to the pairs of items whose cross impacts are to be estimated.

Also, it should be noted that many of the cells will remain blank, because for many pairs of developments the impact of the first on the second may be nil or negligibly small. With regard to many of the entries, even experts will be relatively uncertain as to what assessment of the impact to make; but at least each pair of developments will be given some reflection, and even an uncertain estimate by experts will be better than no estimate at all, which would be tantamount to totally neglecting the effect by default. For example, suppose that one of the trends is "the GNP of the United States" and one of the events is "a free-trade agreement between the United States and the Soviet Union." It may be hard to assess the effect,

all else being equal, of an unexpected rise of the former on the probability of the subsequent occurrence of the latter, or equally of the occurrence of the latter on a subsequent rise of the former; yet a planner will have some implicit conception of what these impacts may be, and it will be better if this matter is given explicit consideration not only by himself but by his panel of expert advisers.

It may be further argued that an examination of forecasts and cross impacts in their mutual context, rather than separately, will provide a check on systemic consistency. That is, if any counterintuitive implications seem to arise as a result of running the cross-impact model, either some of the forecasts or some of the cross impacts will be seen to require adjustment, and the input estimates may thus be improved.

Generally speaking though, the cross-impact approach, as a theory-building device, may leave much to be desired. For one thing, in its present form it permits examination of the influences among pairs of developments only, when in reality it is often the case that it is the joint effect of two or more developments that affects some other event. Moreover, at best, the approach is a causuistic one that attempts to build a theoretical system out of a mosaic of individual sparks of insight without necessarily producing an overall understanding of the causalities that characterize the subject domain in question. Actual trial applications will have to determine whether, on balance, the systems orientation of this method outweighs its simplistic features in importance.

It may be noted, in this context, that the systems-dynamics approach, such as it was applied by Donella Meadows, et al. (1972) to the world resources problem posed by the Club of Rome, can well be viewed as a cross-impact model of certain trends (population, food production, pollution, etc.). That model, suggestive though it is, suffers from the shortcoming of not including events in addition to trends. If the model were extended so as to incorporate events such as technological breakthroughs or governmental interventions, it would gain in realism, and its value as a forecasting and policy-testing tool might increase immensely.

There is one general point that should be made here that applies to any theory-building attempt in the social sciences but is particularly pertinent in the case of a cross-impact analysis. I am referring to the fact that there are circumstances under which subjective social indices or, in the case at hand, subjective political indices can have considerable utility. The social-indicator movement is replete with instances where an attempt is made to capture an intuitive concept in terms of a set of carefully defined objective indicators (e.g., "the quality of education" in terms of "teacher-to-pupil ratio," "number of college graduates," etc.), but we are often aware of the artificiality and inadequacy of such attempts. When using a cross-impact approach, since we are dealing with intuitive expertise in any case, we may as well forego the cumbersome process of translating subjective indices into corresponding sets of objective indicators and deal directly with the original, intuitive concepts. Examples of such concepts in the foreign relations field are "degree of belligerency (of a nation)," "level of technology," "degree of democracy," and so on, none of which lend themselves to direct, objective measurement but all of which are capable of intuitive estimation once some reasonable scale of measurement has been introduced. The use of such indices, it will be noted, is entirely in keeping with the epistemological style of the cross-impact approach, which after all seeks to establish a systematization of intuitive judgmental information.

Application to Planning

Foreign-policy planning, like planning in any other area, requires the following ingredients:

An inventory of the current situation, in terms of appropriate objective indicators and subjective indices, including past time series to indicate trend directions.

The identification of possible futures, in terms of scenarios of event sequences and trend changes, that may come about if no deliberate interventive action is undertaken. Since the number of such scenarios can literally be infinite, it may be convenient to select a relatively small set of "representative scenarios," in the sense that any actual scenario is sufficiently close, for planning purposes, to one of the representative ones so that policies and plans designed to cope with these representative contingencies can reasonably be expected to be adequate for any contingency that may arise.

A statement of policy, in terms of priorities among general goals to be achieved.

A statement of objectives in pursuit of these goals, formulated in terms of specific events to be brought about or of specific trend levels to be achieved.

The identification, including the invention, of actions that may be taken in pursuit of such objectives.

An assessment of the costs (monetary and other) of such contemplated actions, at various levels of intensity of enactment, including an estimate of "cost cross impacts" (i.e., of savings, if any, accruing from the joint implementation of several actions).

The selection, within given resource constraints, of alternative action programs.

The determination of an optimal program among those selected.

The planning process, as laid out here, can clearly benefit from the techniques described earlier.

Since judgment is involved at all stages, the Delphi technique can be invoked whenever it is felt that the judgment of more than one person should be utilized. This may apply particularly to the stating of objectives, the identifying of actions for pursuing the objectives, and the estimating of the costs of such actions. Even when it comes to inventing actions, and perhaps especially then, can the Delphi approach be helpful; for strategic moves suggested by individual planners can thus be conveniently submitted to their peers for evaluation in terms of feasibility, desirability, and cost.

A potential role for the cross-impact technique in the planning process may be seen in the development of noninterventive scenarios, leading to the identification of a set of representative scenarios that provide a planning benchmark; and in the testing of alternative action programs for the purpose of singling out an optimal one among them.

The techniques described here thus have considerable potential utility. It is still an open question whether their present quality, or the quality they may eventually acquire through continuing improvement, is high enough to justify their employment in the context of international relations forecasting and, by implication, in foreign-policy planning.

NOTE

1. For a recent evaluation of Delphi, see H. Sackman (1974).

CHAPTER NINE

ALTERNATIVE REGIME-TYPES: AN APPROACH TO INTERNATIONAL RELATIONS FORECASTING

Thomas W. Robinson

I. INTRODUCTION

In international relations forecasting, especially as concerns foreign policy, it is necessary to specify one's notions about the future political status of the nation-states and their environment. These include spelling out assumptions about the nature of the international system, the character of the states involved and their interrelationships, and presenting some statement about how the international and the various domestic political systems work and what the particular situation is likely to be during the time frame in the future with which we are concerned.

Two interrelated approaches seem possible for these tasks. One is to begin at the international systems level with general statements about its character, derive "rules" for its operation, work deductively down to the level of behavior of each

state, and arrive finally at a consideration of the relevant operating features of each domestic society. Forecasts are then made on the basis of the model thus worked out, whether that model is formal and (possibly) quantitative or less rigid and (usually) dependent upon the forecaster's subjective estimates. This tends to be the approach used in constructing "alternative future worlds"[1] and its success depends on the congruence between the real world and assumptions concerning the primacy of international systemic variables over domestic determinatives of foreign policy behavior. The other approach begins by specifying details of the domestic order of the several states and, through an interactive process, constructs first small and then ever larger international systems until the size required for the forecast is reached. This approach is grounded upon a somewhat different set of assumptions concerning the relationship between domestic and international determinants of politics. While it may be possible to work out a model that shares the best characteristics of the alternative worlds approach and the "alternative regime-type" approach[2] (as we shall term the latter mode of analysis), here we shall merely outline the steps necessary to work out the latter model and indicate the occasions when it is useful to adopt it as one of the bases for forecasting certain kinds of international political developments.

Thus, after indicating salient relationships between alternative future worlds and alternative regime-types, this chapter will discuss the comparative merits and assumptions of regime-type analysis, set forth the regime-type model (first in static and then in dynamic form), and build for illustrative purposes future two, three, and n-state worlds. Illustrations forecasting the domestic and foreign policy characteristics and behavior of major states will be presented, and the chapter will close with a listing of the benefits that can be expected from adapting the regime-type approach to international relations forecasting.

II. RELATIONSHIP BETWEEN ALTERNATIVE FUTURE WORLDS AND ALTERNATIVE REGIME-TYPES

The choice between the alternative future worlds approach to constructing future international political systems and the regime-type approach is neither absolute nor irreversible. The Hudson Institute rendition of alternative future worlds (Kahn, 1968), in fact, considers (at least initially) that what we term the regime-type approach is a subvariant of the alternative future worlds approach as a whole. Thus, three continua describe the form and the means for deriving alternative future worlds: synthetic-morphological; extrapolative-finalistic; and empirical/intuitive-abstract/analytic. Construction of a given alternative future world, in this view, can proceed by utilizing one, two, three, or even more of the six categories presented. Having noted this possibility, however, the decision was made to combine the morphological, extrapolative, and abstract/analytic categories into "approach" and term it "alternative future worlds."

The regime-type approach is not the direct opposite of this more restricted meaning of the term alternative future worlds. A process for constructing alternative future worlds directly opposite to that adopted by the Hudson Institute would be stress synthetic, finalistic, and empirical/intuitive categories. The regime-type approach, on the other hand, utilizes synthetic, *extrapolative*, and empirical/intuitive categories, thus sharing at least one common element with the Hudson Institute approach. Nonetheless, it is clear that the two approaches are, for the most part, quite different. The alternative future worlds approach from the outset emphasizes systemic variables, while the regime-type approach places its greatest weight on individual nation-states. The regime-type approach works from the state outward, conceiving that foreign policy is largely determined by the character of domestic institutions and policies (hence the term "regime-type," symbolizing the dominance of domestic variables). By contrast, the alternative future worlds approach tends to neglect domestic variables in favor of interstate relations at the regional, alliance, or world politics levels or to introduce domestic variables at the last moment to conform with conclusions (i.e., desired worlds, for whatever purpose) arrived at by other means.

Each approach has strengths and weaknesses and the strong points of one tend to be the weak spots of the other. Which approach one adopts depends upon the purpose of one's forecast. If, for instance, one is interested in testing theories of alliances or the effects of nuclear proliferation upon systemic stability, it is probably best to adopt the alternative future worlds variant. On the other hand, if one wishes to gain a better idea of the possibilities for Sino-Soviet-American relations today, given certain trends in the character of domestic politics and leadership structure of the three states, it may be better to adopt the regime-type approach. Generally, the alternative future worlds approach is preferable for forecasts of international politics as opposed to comparative foreign policy; for forecasts utilizing, testing, or merely depending upon a heavy dosage of theory; where a fairly large (say, more than five) number of states are involved; where policy questions are not heavily involved; where states are artificial constructs with little or no real world referents; and where the forecaster is neither a decision maker nor an area specialist. Nearly the opposite can be said of forecasts using alternative regime-types as their basis. They will be concerned mostly with foreign policy questions and relations among a relatively small number of states; will take less advantage of existing theory, preferring a more inductive approach; will test questions having a high empirical and policy content; will look to the real world of international politics for systemic configuration, state structure and policy, and characterization of decision makers and national style; and will likely be made by policy makers and/or area and foreign policy experts.

Being merely approaches, the two can end up at the same point. Thus, the alternative regime-type approach can consider questions dealing with the future of the international system merely by adding whatever propositions or projections one pleases concerning the character of relations between the states whose foreign policies one is considering. It may turn out that a given state's foreign policy, in the opinion of the country expert responsible for formulating its alternative regime typology and attendant future domestic and foreign policies, may be only residually dependent upon domestic regime change, varying instead almost uniquely with changes in the configuration of the international system itself.[3] In that case, systemic configuration questions are the very center of the process of figuring out regime-type variations. The difference between this situation and that which is produced by the alternative future worlds approach is still clear, however. In the regime-type approach, the international system is, by and large, the product of the foreign policies of the member states, while in the alternative future worlds approach it tends to be taken as given.

It is possible, and sometimes desirable, to combine the two approaches by including features of both, thus eliminating some of the shortcomings of each. Alternative regime-type formulations are likely to be rich in forecasting the details of a given state's domestic and foreign policy but will be progressively vague on systemic relationships as one moves toward ever larger international state systems. The opposite is true of the alternative future worlds approach. One way to effectuate a union would be to allow each approach to develop independently up to a point, then decide that the further evolution of one approach would be fed into progressive development of the other as a set of increasingly influential disturbing variables. Which approach would be taken as the base and which the storehouse of parameters to be intro-

duced in iterative fashion would depend on the purpose of the forecast.[4]

III. ASSUMPTIONS GROUNDING THE ALTERNATIVE REGIME-TYPE APPROACH

Five assumptions ground the alternative regime-type approach to forecasting international politics. The primary assumption is that it is possible to approach an understanding of the international political world *iteratively*, and from the perspective of the nation-state *outwards*. Moreover, it is presumed that it is *best* to take that path, for the product, it is thought, will turn out to be more realistic, have greater relevance, be more self-consistent and rich in detail, and be more theoretically interesting than other methods.

Second, it is postulated that the best means of expressing alternative future nation-state policy is by closely defining the major characteristics of a range of different types of governmental policies, attitudes, and political styles. This set of characteristics is called a "regime-type," and as many alternatives are produced as seem reasonably desirable for each nation-state in the international system under investigation. It is presumed that the process of defining such regime-types will subsume a number of salient elements not otherwise easily mixed. These include domestic needs, domestic policy alternatives, governmental characteristics, national interests, decision-maker personalities, bureaucratic political behavior, and other such qualities.

Third, there is an express assumption that, given the complex system of linkages between international politics at the system level, foreign policy at the nation-state level, and domestic politics within the nation, the best way (i.e., most parsimonious, easiest, and most highly reflective of international reality itself) to construct alternative future international political systems is to begin by defining several alternative regime-types for each nation-state, then combine the salient characteristics of each into ever larger subsystems, and arrive finally at a composite picture of future alternatives of the international system as a whole. Thus, from the very beginning there is a bias toward the structural characteristics and dynamics of the *internal* political system as determinative of the way international politics operates. This assumption is not necessarily true and can indeed be relaxed at a certain stage to allow for feedback between the internal and international systems.[5] Nonetheless, it is felt that to begin the process of constructing alternative future worlds in this manner is more productive than starting at the systems level and then trying to retrofit regime-type characteristics and their alternatives into a picture already largely drawn. Moreover, as we have already noted, there is no intrinsic reason why, in some nation-states, domestic regime-type variance cannot depend upon changes in critical international system variables or, more likely, in the foreign policies of important foreign states.

Fourth, it is presumed that a first approximation to future political variance is best obtained by defining gross future foreign policy alternatives and disregarding, for the time being, how one passes from those alternatives (expressed in regime-type terms) to variance in the international system. That is, during the process of defining each state's alternative regime typology, the influence of other states' foreign policies is assumed to be zero and the linkages between systemic levels are temporarily ignored. Also, passage of time is initially ignored, so that in the first approximation an entirely static model is set up. These assumptions can then gradually be relaxed, resulting in ever more dynamic models. Below, we discuss two end-point cases—the strictly static and the entirely dynamic —and point out how the transition between the two is made.

Fifth, given the initial bias in favor of domestic political variables, country experts or some combination of social science theorists[6] experienced in the general workings of domestic social systems are best suited to the task of actually constructing alternative regime-types. Which kind of expert one settles upon depends upon one's purpose. If some close approximation to real future worlds is deisred, then country experts are more appropriate. If one wishes to test international relations theory or to conduct controlled experiments, perhaps a team of social scientists is best.[7]

IV. THE REGIME-TYPE PROCESS MODEL

The Static Model

Constructing alternative future worlds by means of a regime-type process proceeds through several stages. A major division is between static, that is, non-time-dependent models, and dynamic models, where passage of time becomes an important determinant. Here we limit ourselves to the former, being simpler and, obviously, a special case of the dynamic process.

The first stage involves the definition of a series of alternative regime-types for each country under consideration. The regime-types will refer to given real-world countries or to abstract entities, depending upon one's forecasting purpose. The range of regime-types that the area expert or social scientist comes forth with will obviously be impossible to determine beforehand, and will depend upon who one chooses as his experts and scientists. Some general guidelines can be set, for example, the rough number of regime-types one would like at a maximum, but it would be a mistake to legislate conclusions in advance. It is important, on the other hand, to specify the time framework one is thinking of—2, 5, 10 years in the future—and the kinds of domestic and foreign policy groups, issues, areas, etc., one wishes to think about. The latter is particularly important, since these will to a large extent determine the specific qualities of each regime-type.

Each regime-type is defined by a short essay describing its critical characteristics. If possible, there should be congruence between these characteristics among alternative regime-types of a given state, although this is hardly likely to be the case between those of different states. Practical or theoretical reasons for adopting each regime-type should be presented and consistency among the spectrum of regime-types assured. If more than one person is assigned the task of working out alternative regime-types, some means of establishing agreement on a final set of defining essays must be found.[8]

A finished essay might read as follows:[9]

A *muddling-through* regime-type is characterized by a tendency to treat the problems of the day as sufficient unto themselves, with no attempt to set forth longer range national goals and procedures until more immediate tasks are dealt with. Concomitantly, there is a tendency to be carried along by events and not to deal with—indeed, not to notice—problems until they call out for immediate solution. In foreign policy, there would be a tendency to make friends with former enemies on all sides and to deal, as on the domestic scene, with issues as they arise. Domestically, there would be emphasis on experimentation, in more or less random and situationally-determined fashion, on compromise with various political groups, on production for its own sake, but no real plan or set of goals to be attained by a given date. Policy would be the resultant of bargaining between independently established groups and problems would be treated as they come up with little attempt to establish accord with overriding principles.

Once possessed of a set of essays defining the salient characteristics of alternative regime-types for a given country, and having gone through the same process for as many states as exist in the international system under consideration, the country expert or social scientist must decide what specific policies each alternative regime-type will adopt. A prior decision is to ascertain what kinds of policy issues and policy types are to be discussed, and which foreign states are to be considered in the analysis. The answer depends on the purpose of the forecast. For instance, in a five-state international system, each regime-type will have a specific policy toward each of the other four states in the system, based on its own vision of its interests as concerns each of the other states. It will also define policy according to issue-areas—nuclear proliferation, support of revolutionary groups abroad, foreign aid, etc.—and will approach its foreign re-

lations with a certain general policy type in mind. In each case, a range of choices is developed, closely defined, quantified if possible, and then related to each regime-type. The result is a series of two-by-two matrices with the independent variable—regime-type variation—ranged along the top and the dependent variable—policy according to foreign state, issue, and type—down the left side. The general form of the matrices is illustrated in Figures 9.1–9.3.

One object of producing more than one matrix table to represent the relationship between regime-type variation and a given state's foreign policy is increased sophistication of analysis—not all that the country expert or social scientist would like to say can be encompassed in one matrix. However, it may be that the forecasting purpose stresses one element of foreign policy—foreign policy toward specific states, for instance. The other matrices may then be dispensed with or used only to check the consistency of the statements made in the matrix concerned. Other matrices can, of course, be produced, depending again on one's purpose. Thus, for instance, a forecast may wish to deal only with the domestic politics of the given state or to compare domestic political change among several states as a function of regime-type variation. In that case, a range of salient domestic political issues or the status of various domestic political groups or institutions, can be considered.

Even at this stage important inputs to forecasting international relations can be made. Statements

Regime-type, state I / Foreign state	Regime-type A	Regime-type B	Regime-type C	. . .	. . .	Regime-type M
State 2						
State 3						
State 4						
:						
State n						

Figure 9.1 Foreign policy toward *n* states as a function of regime-type variation.

Regime-type, state 1 / Issue	Regime-type A	Regime-type B	Regime-type C	. . .	. . .	Regime-type M
Issue 1						
Issue 2						
Issue 3						
. . .						
Issue n						

Figure 9.2 Foreign policy issue as a function of regime-type variation.

can be made about the range of possible foreign policies that each state in the system might adopt, as well as ideas about why such policies may emerge. Domestic determinants of future foreign policies can be clarified and preliminary comparison made between the domestic and foreign policies of the several states, noting where interests could converge or conflict and where situations might develop leading to war, alliance, crisis, or reconciliation.

One object must be to reduce the number of combinations of regime-types and policies to the minimum, which otherwise tend to proliferate.[10] There are two ways of achieving such reduction. One is through inspection of the matrices. In all likelihood, two or more of the regime-types will be similar enough in the policies they would follow to warrant combination. It also may be that one matrix does a better job, in terms of the purposes of the forecast, of describing a given state's foreign policy alternatives. In that case, whole matrices can be eliminated. The other way of achieving reduction involves the next stage of constructing alternative future worlds through alternative regime-types—the step-by-step construction of two-state, three-state, and n-state worlds—and the opportunity to introduce further theoretical, methodological, or policy assumptions, according to the purpose of the forecast. Thus, one may wish to order regime-types according to the probability of their emergence in each state. Those that have low probabilities need not be considered until later, if at all, and the number of two-by-two combinations of foreign policies can be reduced by in-

Regime-type, state 1 / Foreign policy type	Regime-type A	Regime-type B	Regime-type C	. . .	. . .	Regime-type M
Type 1						
Type 2						
Type 3						
. . .						
Type n						

Figure 9.3 Foreign policy type as a function of regime-type variation.

cluding only those that have approximately equal probabilities of emergence.

One can also introduce the idea that a given state may in the future wish to order its foreign policies, either by devoting more attention to one foreign state, to one foreign policy issue, or to the probable adoption of one foreign policy type. Further, it is possible to stress domestic determination of foreign policy by allowing the series of domestic policies to be strongly linked with given foreign policies and then ordering the former according to some desired criteria. International systems determination can also be introduced at this stage, by stipulating that they determine the character of the alternative regime-types (and hence their domestic and foreign policies) or by asserting that systemic characteristics order foreign policies directly. Or, finally, one can introduce such notions as dependency politics, where the policies of one state depend upon those pursued by other states, or emerging state politics, where foreign policies are determined by such criteria as the relative stability of newly established political institutions, rates of economic growth, international appeal of ideological doctrine, or the personal magnetism of a charismatic leader.

In any case, criteria will have to establish *how* future two-state, three-state, and *n*-state foreign policy worlds are to be constructed. The generalized forms of two-state foreign policy worlds are illustrated in Figures 9.4–9.6.[11]

It is important to note that three independent variables jointly determine the character of the foreign policies of two states: regime-types for state I, regime-types for state II, and a set of policy issues common to both. (In some cases, it may be desirable to regard policy issue as different for each state, although we have not done so here. Then there would be four independent variables.) What the exact relationship among the three independent variables will be in a given forecast is not clear. Empirically, it may vary from case to case, and in any event is likely to be complex. Theoretically, it is possible to postulate some invariant relationship of the general form

$$P = KR_{\mathrm{I}}{}^{\alpha}R_{\mathrm{II}}{}^{\beta}I^{\gamma}$$

where P is policy, K an equation constant, R_{I} and R_{II} are regime-type variables for states I and II, I is policy issue, and α, β, and γ are exponential constants whose value must be determined either for each case or in general. Since our purpose is not the development of theory but the construction of instruments useful to international relations forecasting, we shall concentrate on ways of deriving policy variation empirically.

One empirical method is to dissolve the general equation into three parts, holding constant each variable in turn. One then decides by inspection to what extent each equation (i.e., matrix, as seen in Figures 9.4, 9.5, and 9.6) helps us to understand how policy varies. It may be that the forecaster will

Policy issue for state I, regime-type B / Policy issue for state II, regime-type C	Issue 1	Issue 2	Issue 3	. . .	. . .	Issue n
Issue 1						
Issue 2						
Issue 3						
⋮						
Issue n						

Figure 9.4 Policy of state II, regime-type C toward issues 1–*n* as a function of policy of state I, regime-type B toward the same issues.

Regime-type, state I / Policy issue for state II, regime-type C	Regime-type A	Regime-type B	Regime-type C	. . .	. . .	Regime-type Z
Issue 1						
Issue 2						
Issue 3						
Issue 4						
Issue 5						

Figure 9.5 Policy of state II, regime-type C toward issues $1-n$ as a function of regime-type variation of state I.

treat each equation (matrix) as contributing equally to policy variation, or that he will allow one to predominate to such an extent that the other two can be dispensed with. It should be noted, parenthetically, that our empirical approach, recorded in Figures 9.4–9.6, is equivalent to a two-dimensional matrix representation of three three-dimensional graphs (see Figure 9.7) or three simultaneous equations:

$$P_1 = k_1 R_{\mathrm{I}}{}^{\alpha_1} \; k_2 R_{\mathrm{II}}{}^{\beta_1}$$
$$P_2 = k_3 R_{\mathrm{I}}{}^{\alpha_1} \; k_4 I{}^{\gamma_1}$$
$$P_3 = k_5 R_{\mathrm{II}}{}^{\beta_2} \; k_6 I{}^{\gamma_2}.$$

If one were to decide upon quantitative measures of the four variables (three independent, one dependent), either through theoretical analysis or empirical representation (or, better, a combined theoretical and empirical exercise), such representation would increase one's confidence in the veracity of this procedure. If one were testing theory, of course, this would probably be the next, and all-important, stage. But for forecasting purposes, where theory is not clear and quantitative measures all but absent, this path is not generally open.

Regime-type, state I / Regime-type, state II	Regime-type A	Regime-type B	Regime-type C	. . .	. . .	Regime-type Z
Regime-type α						
Regime-type β						
Regime-type γ						
$\vdots$						
Regime-type ω						

Figure 9.6 Policy of state II, regime-types $\alpha-\omega$ toward issue 3, as a function of variation in regime-types of state I.

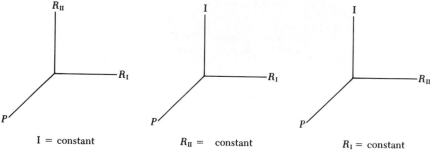

I = constant R_{II} = constant R_I = constant

Figure 9.7 Graphical representation of the general policy equation.

The Dynamic Model

Before exemplifying this approach by constructing two, three, and n-state worlds, it is useful to outline a dynamic version of the model. This merely adds time as an independent variable, that is, allows each of the three independent variables to change as a function of future time. Since any policy model claiming to represent future international relations must account for continuous changes in the value of its variables, and since most forecasts involve several time periods, it is imperative to set the regime-type analysis within a time-dependent framework. A time-related regime-type analysis is important for forecasting also because, with it, we can move from one regime-type and policy issue to another. Thus, for instance, in time frame 1, state I might be forecast as defining its policy through regime-type A, while state II works out its policy through regime-type α. In time frame 2, state II might be thought to switch from regime-type α to regime-type β, while in time frame 3, state I may begin a transition to regime-type C, completing it in time frame 4. These variations will obviously result in different future policy mixes for each state, and hence different forecasts of interstate relations. A similar mode of reasoning is used when allowing future policy issue to vary with time, regime-type being held constant.

There are two nonmathematical manners of representing the dynamic regime-type forecasting model: the normative, or matrix, form and the extensive, or decision-tree, form. The matrix form merely adds a third dimension to the matrices presented in Figures 9.1–9.6. For instance, Figure 9.2 depicts how future foreign policy issues might vary as a function not only of regime-type variation but now also of time, and would appear as in Figure 9.8. Figure 9.5, representing the forecaster's view of the foreign policy of a given regime-type of state II toward a series of issues as a function of variation in regime-type of state I, and now also a function of time, would appear as in Figure 9.9.

As with the static model, criteria must be brought forth. Three criteria come to mind. First, the future *regime-type* can vary with time, according to some criteria of domestic change. Thus, rates of economic growth may change, elites may age and new groups bid for power, the class composition of society may change, or a charismatic leader may die to be replaced with a group leadership. Drawing in these variables allows for the introduction of some of the ideas, for instance, of political developments, and allows quantitative indices to be utilized. *Issues* can also vary with future time, changing in their relative importance, disappearing from or being added to the list of items that decision makers might consider important for national security or defense of national interests. Such time-dependent variables as the emergence of new weapons systems, the solution of old disputes and the rise of new ones, and changing ideological orientation can be brought in.

A second criterion stems from the interaction through future time of the (regime-type dependent) policies of the two states. Thus, for instance, at time t_1, say 1 year in the future, state I might change its regime-type characterization or several aspects of its policy, while at time t_2, 6 months later, state II, in response might make certain changes in its own policy or in regime-type characterization. This would continue during as many time periods as the forecaster feels confident of his "data." Nothing would preclude, of course, both states making changes simultaneously or, for that

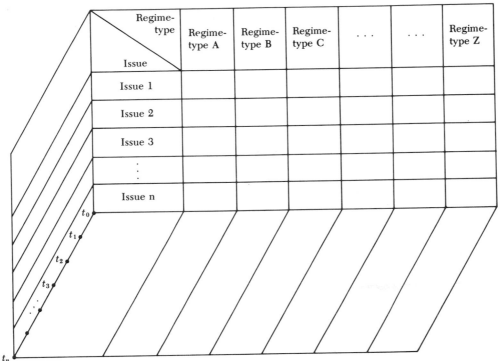

Figure 9.8 Foreign policy issue as a function of regime-type variation and time.

matter, making no change at all during a given time frame. This obviously opens the dynamic model to feedback-type interrelationships, and provides for further creative efforts on the parts of the country experts or social scientists, who would be asked how their respective states would act and react.

A third criterion concerns the reactions of states I and II to events external to their bilateral system. Thus, policies of third states, changes in alliance structures, or variations in the future state of the international system as a whole might be introduced at a given time frame and the country experts/social scientists allowed to consider how bilateral relations will vary as a result.

The second nonmathematical manner of representing the dynamic regime-type model is through the extensive, or decision-tree, form. The major advantage of this mode is that it enables the range of decisions available to a given regime-type at a given future time to be displayed in open fashion. Thus, for instance, if state I is considered to have three possible regime-types and a set of three

foreign policy issues, its decision behavior over time might appear as shown in Figure 9.10.

In Figure 9.10 the d's indicate alternative decision, the I's represent policy issues, and the t's signify successive time frames. Expressed verbally, at time t_0, state I is forecast to be governed by regime-type A and face policy decision on issues I_1, I_2, and I_3. It could (theoretically) adopt any one of five stances, that is, combinations of policy decisions: do nothing with regard to all three issues; change policy or take action on two of the three, leaving the third unchanged (three combinations present themselves); or change policy on all three. At future time t_1, decision option d_4 is forecast to be exercised and policy toward issues I_2 and I_3 modified (opinions on the precise form of such modification would be given by the country experts/social scientists). At time t_2, a further decision, d_7, is forecast to be adopted, modifying policy on issues I_1 and I_3. At this point, however, state I is thought, in all probability, to experience a change in regime-type, from A to B, which then proceeds, at time t_3, to adopt decision d_{15} and, at time t_4, d_{16}.

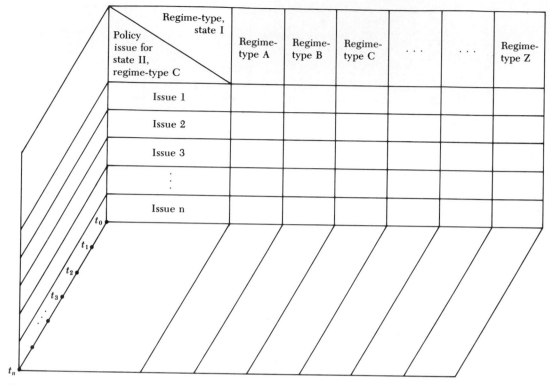

Figure 9.9   Foreign policy issue of state II, regime-type C, as a function of variation in regime-type, state I, and time.

The range of issues presented at any given time can, of course, also vary, although this is not depicted in Figure 9.10.

The forecaster can use one or more of the three decision criteria outlined above as means of giving estimates as to which policy option states might exercise. Thus, if, as with the second option concerning the time- and regime-type dependent interaction of states I and II, time t_1, t_3, t_5, . . . are reserved for state I's decisions and times t_2, t_4, t_6, . . . are reserved for state II's decisions, the decision-tree form gives a graphic display of the options open to both state as they interact.

V. TWO-BY-TWO CONFIGURATIONS, WITH ILLUSTRATIONS

In order to make explicit the general remarks comprising Section IV, let us illustrate the process by means of constructing a two-state world. In the next section, we will extend this to the three-state case, followed by the n-state case. Our choice for the two-state world is Sino-Soviet relations, as that bilateral instance with which the author is most familiar.

The first step is to decide on a series of salient alternative regime-types for both the Soviet Union and China during the 5-year period ahead. For the sake of parsimony, we limit ourselves to three alternative regime-types in each country.[12] For China, the three alternative regime-types are: Maoist, military, and pragmatic; while for the Soviet Union the three are evangelical, moderate, and liberal. Definitions follow.[13]

China

A *Maoist* regime radicalizes the domestic political situation whenever necessary and possible; puts ideological goals before economic and social de-

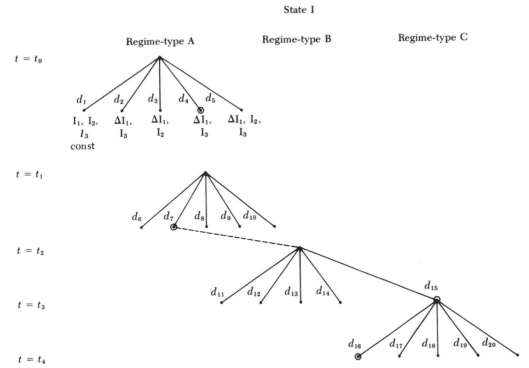

Figure 9.10 Decision-tree form of state I's choice behavior through time t_4.

velopment; opposes the tendency for society to settle down into a particular mold; assumes that age-old problems can be overcome overnight if only the correct attitude is adopted; emphasizes military security; and pursues a cautious but forward foreign policy based on China as the center of the modern Marxist-Leninist movement and the leaders of the developing world.

A *military* regime insists upon popular acceptance of the ideals of Mao but modified in those circumstances (increasingly numerous with time) when Maoist ideals do not accord with the militaristic virtues of order, obedience, division of function, and hierarchy of authority; a tendency to bring other institutions back into the political picture to perform those tasks of administration and development with which the military does not wish to involve itself on a daily basis; an inclination to place industrial development on a plane equal in importance to political stability, thus stressing high growth rates; a cautious foreign policy, with a less direct connection between domestic changes and

overt foreign policy moves; but a propensity to intervene abroad whenever it appears that state interests are involved; a stress on maximum military security, together with an emphasis on production and deployment of modern weapon systems.

A *pragmatic* regime thinks ahead, defines goals and methods closely, and manipulates events of the day and competing political groups to assert control; stresses ideology less than the other two; accentuates high rates of economic growth; tends to make foreign enemies into friends, but also utilizes one state as a foil against another; militarily, it would emphasize procuring a mixture of modern strategic and traditional conventional weapons and adopt a strategy of mixing nuclear deterrence, general purpose force mobilization potention, and guerrilla strategy.

Soviet Union

An *evangelical* regime, possibly headed by a rising charismatic leader, stresses high growth rates in heavy industry even if at the expense of consumer sentiment; articulates a high order of active commitment to revolutionary international changes, and is willing to incur costs and risks to achieve such aims; perceives a moderate threat from China but feels containment is possible; competes with the United States; sees the Third World as an arena of opportunity, pursues opportunistic policies there, and is prepared to support militarily communist insurgencies; and allocates defense budgets according to balanced force doctrines while seeking to emphasize modern rather than massive general purpose forces.

A *moderate* regime stresses collective leadership and bureaucratic compromise; stresses high growth rates, but emphasizes defense and consumption at the expense of investments; sees a relatively reduced threat from the United States and China; is moderately willing to support revolutionary movements, including undertaking costs and risks that are not escalatory; defends the *status quo* in East Europe; limits its degree of cooperation and negotiation with the United States on arms control issues; pursues a selectively forward strategy in the Third World, emphasizing Middle Eastern clients and penetration of South Asia; seeks balanced military forces and strategic equality with the United States; broadens its limited war doctrine to include "flexible response"; and dispatches visible military forces to distant spots.

A *liberal* regime, headed possibly by a charismatic leader, stresses bureaucratic compromise and semi-parliamentary procedures; liberalizes ideology and Party life; minimizes the Party's role in administration; depends on technological progress to assure high growth rates and increased consumption levels; perceives no immediate threats from abroad; supports revolutionary movements abroad verbally and by way of its own demonstrative example; cooperates with other states to assure strategic stability; projects its power abroad chiefly through naval power, and foreign and military aid; stresses strategic parity, chiefly through continual research and development and de-emphasizes the role of general purpose forces.

The second step is to decide which issues and policy types one wishes to address. In the present case, we choose four issues, all of which concern relations between the Soviet Union and China: the

Sino-Soviet border problem; the character and level of state relations; problems of differing interpretation of ideological questions; and comparative attitudes toward the Third World. The level of detail at which these questions are addressed is deliberately kept general, for illustrative purposes. In each case, it is necessary to define a range of policy response and initiative, as follows.

Border policy: sign a new treaty; continue negotiations; break off negotiations; renew military pressure.

State relations: improvement (more trade, exchanges, diplomatic contacts); status quo; decline (opposite of improvement); break diplomatic relations.

Third-World policy: active-interventionist (support of insurgencies); active-friendly (stress on good state relations); neutral; passive.

Ideology: major stress on ideological component of substantive issues; tendency to stress ideological component when substantive issues permit; proforma reference only to ideological component.

In addition, three foreign policy *types* will be considered: balance of power; assertive-interventionist; and passive-isolationist.

The third step is to construct two-by-two matrices for the various relationships that the above regime-types might hold for the several policy issues and policy types just defined. These are presented in Figures 9.11–9.15 and correspond to Figures 9.2–9.6.[14]

Figure 9.11 shows that, with few exceptions, our judgment is that the Chinese "pragmatic" regime-type would pursue an overall policy quite similar to the Soviet "liberal" regime, that a Chinese "military" regime would resemble the Soviet "moderate" regime, while a "Maoist" regime would, in foreign policy terms, be something of a mirror image of the Soviet "evangelical" regime. In terms of compatibility, the first-named combination would seem to tend toward peaceful resolution of tensions, the last-named would seem to be most likely to exacerbate tensions, with all other combinations less certain as to the outcome of their policies. An interesting question is what might happen when "nonsymmetrical" regimes (i.e., for instance, a Chinese "pragmatic" regime and an "evangelical" Soviet regime) face each other. Here might be a good arena for time-dependent

China / Soviet Union

Pragmatic	Military	Maoist	Regime-type Issue / Issue / Regime-type	Evangelical	Moderate	Liberal
Sign treaty	Continue negotiations	Break off negotiations	Border policy	Break off negotiations	Continue negotiations	Sign treaty
Improvement	*Status quo*	Decline	State relations	Decline	*Status quo*	Improvement
Active-friendly	Active-interventionist	Active-interventionist	Third-World policy	Active-interventionist	Active-friendly	Neutral
Pro-forma reference	Tendency to stress	Major stress	Ideology	Major stress	Tendency to stress	*Pro-forma* reference

Figure 9.11 Soviet and Chinese policies toward four issues as a function of regime-type variation.

"decision-tree" analysis, as per Figure 9.10, for in such situations there might be a tendency for one or even both regime-types to alter its characteristics in the face of disfunctional aspects of its foreign relations.

Figure 9.12 illustrates the relationship of regime-type characteristics to the three foreign policy types listed above. As in Figure 9.11, judgments are the author's own, but the symmetry previously evident is now lacking. Nonetheless, there is still a rough congruence between, say, the Chinese pragmatic and the Soviet liberal regime. Moreover, there is a progression among the policy types, with a balance of power policy most likely to be adopted, a policy of assertive interventionism somewhat less probable (but still one with better than even chances), and a passive -isolationist policy least likely to be chosen. This is characteristic of

our judgment of both Soviet and Chinese regime-types. The important question is whether casting judgments in this form is useful. In the context of two-state relations, it is probably not as useful a adhering to a set of matrices keyed only to policy issues. On the other hand, when three state or n-state worlds are considered, this orientation will prove more useful, for it provides indications as to how a given state will act in general and, in a "decision-tree" analysis, how one state might react to a policy change of another. For that reason, the rest of the matrices concerned with Sino-Soviet relations will treat issue-related matters only.

Figure 9.13 depicts the confluence of policies toward the four issues under consideration for one combination of regime-types—in this case, a "moderate" Soviet regime and a "military" Chinese government. This matrix provides additional in-

China / Soviet Union

Pragmatic	Military	Maoist	Regime-type / Policy type / Regime-type	Evangelical	Moderate	Liberal
Highly probable	Highly probable	Even probability	Balance of power	Improbable	Highly probable	Highly probable
Even probability	Probable	Probable	Assertive-interventionist	Highly probable	Even probability	Improbable
Highly improbable	Highly improbable	Improbable	Passive-isolationist	Highly improbable	Improbable	Improbable

Figure 9.12 Variation in policy type as a function of change in regime-type.

China

"Military" / "Moderate"	Border policy	State relations	Third-World policy	Ideology
Border policy: continue negotiations	Continue negotiations	Improvement	Active-friendly	Pro-forma reference
State relations: status quo	Continue negotiations	Status quo	Active-friendly	Pro-forma reference
Third-World policy: active-friendly	Continue negotiations	Decline	Active-interventionist	Pro-forma reference
Ideology: tendency to stress	Continue negotiations	Decline	Active-interventionist	Tendency to stress

(Soviet Union — row label at left)

Figure 9.13 Variation in policy toward four issues of a Chinese "military" regime as a function of variation in policy of a Soviet "moderate" regime.

formation compared with Figure 9.11, for now the policy of a given regime-type toward all four issues (*given prior knowledge* of the policy toward those same issues of a given regime-type of the other state) is provided. In Figure 9.13, the policy of a "moderate" Soviet regime is taken as given, and the policy in response of a "military" Chinese regime is then derived. That is, the question is asked: If Soviet policy toward issue X is stated and is known to the Chinese, what policy will China adopt toward that issue and all other issues? Thus, this matrix allows us to investigate the interrelationship among issues. The question posed in Figure 9.11 was different, where it was asked: What policy, in general, would a given regime-type adopt toward a given issue, irrespective of the regime-type variation (and, hence, policy variation)

of the other state? Once again, the author's judgment—the product of study of Soviet and Chinese political history—and the regime-type definitions provided the intellectual means of filling in the "boxes." This exercise can be conducted the other way around—that is, by assuming future Chinese policy toward a particular range of issues as given and asking what Soviet policy toward those same issues would be. In the present matrix, Chinese border policy under a "military" regime is thought to be insensitive to variation of issue under a Soviet "moderate" regime, while state relations and Third-World policy do show sensitivity to such variation and stress on ideology shows slight dependency.

Figure 9.14 shows another kind of exercise that flows from a two-by-two regime-type analysis. This

Soviet Union, "moderate" regime

Policy issue / Regime-type	Border policy	State relations	Third-World policy	Ideology
Maoist	Continue negotiations	Status quo	Active-friendly	Tendency to stress
Military	Continue negotiations	Status quo	Active-friendly	Tendency to stress
Pragmatic	Sign new treaty	Improvement	Active-friendly	Tendency to stress

(China — row label at left)

Figure 9.14 Variation in policy toward four issues of "moderate" Soviet regime, given variation of Chinese regime-types.

time, the regime-type of one state (here, China) is allowed to vary and the kinds of policies toward relevant issues that a given regime-type of the other state might adopt are described. The conclusion seems to be that future policy of a "moderate" Soviet regime-type is less influenced by variance between Chinese regime-types than might be thought.

Finally, one can inquire: How will future regime-type variance in one state influence the policy toward a given issue of the several regime-types of the other state? This is illustrated in Figure 9.15, forecasting the policies of Chinese regime-types toward the border question as a function of regime-type variance of the Soviet Union. As in Figure 9.13, the causal relationship should also be reversed for completeness. As is shown, our opinion is that the policy toward the border of the three named Chinese regime-types is surprisingly insensitive to variation in Soviet regime-type.

VI. THREE-STATE WORLDS

Bilateral international relations are of great consequence to the foreign policies of the states concerned and, in many cases, to the international system as a whole. It should be apparent from the above that two-state international relations are themselves quite complex and that, therefore, a systematic forecast of their policies, such as provided by the alternative regime-type approach, is desirable. However, interest often centers on forecasting interstate relations when the number of participants is three or more. Hence, it is desirable to illustrate how the alternative regime-type approach handles these more complex situations. In this section we consider three-state worlds, and in Section VII generalize to the n-state case.

Constructing a three-state world would involve grafting a regime-type analysis of the foreign policy of an additional state onto the already extant two-state analysis outlined above. As above, the first step is to define several alternative regime-types for the third state, then to decide upon the range of issues and policy types one wishes to discuss, and finally to link regime-types and policies to these same attributes of the first two governments. On the basis of step three, a discussion of some of the general aspects of this three-state world will be presented.

Using the alternative regime-type approach, forecasting three-state international relations can rapidly become quite complex unless criteria are utilized that will minimize the number of variables. In a three-state world, we have the following factors: regime-type—three states and several regime-types for each state (n usually ≤ 7); policy types for each state—that may or may not be shared among the three (n for policy type for each state usually ≤ 5); and policy issue for each state—that also may or may not be shared among the three (n for policy issue usually ≤ 7). If all variables were independent, the possible number of combinations would obviously be very large. While this is never the case in real future worlds, it is possible in a forecast to approach the point of unwieldiness rapidly, even when the number of variables is relatively small. Thus, for instance, three states, each with three regime-type alternatives, each with three choices of policy type and with a

Soviet regime-type \ Chinese regime-type	Pragmatic	Military	Maoist
Evangelical	Continue negotiations	Continue negotiations	Break off negotiations
Moderate	Sign new treaty	Continue negotiations	Break off negotiations
Liberal	Sign new treaty	Continue negotiations	Break off negotiations

Figure 9.15 Chinese policy toward the border issue as a function of Soviet regime-type variance.

shared set of four policy issues will produce eighty-one possible alternative future three-state worlds. Moreover, if the assumption of variable independence is relaxed (as would seem realistic), this number could increase by the number of dependencies (of, for instance, regime-type alternatives in state B on regime-type alternatives in state A) or policy types not shared among the three states.

It is therefore wise to possess a set of criteria for reducing the list of variables. Perhaps the easiest way is to relate the criteria to the purpose of the forecast, that is, policy or real-world relevance, theory testing, training students or sensitizing policy makers, or methodology development. In the illustrations below, we have adopted both policy-relevant, real-world, and theoretical criteria. One must also be sensitive to the fact that, with three or more states, additional assumptions as to variable primacy and dependency will have to be made. Thus, for instance, the regime-type likely to be met in state 3 may depend on that extant in state 1, or in 1 and 2, or neither, and the policy that state 3 may adopt toward issues a to c could depend upon the adoption of policies toward those same issues of states 1 and/or 2 (or neither) as well as the kind of regime-types each state is forecast to possess. Thus, even with a severely attenuated list of variables, assumptions stemming from the necessity of making judgments as to temporal and sequential importance must be made.

These generalities are illustrated as follows: In Figure 9.16, three of the possible variants of regime-type policy determination are shown. In the uppermost portion, Figure 9.16a, state 1 is forecast to have a series of regime-types independent of the regime-types of states 2 and 3 (that is, regime-type variations, and hence policy variation, in states 2 and 3 depend directly on regime-type variation in state 1). In the bottom portion, Figure 9.16c, future regime-types of state 1 are presumed to be independent of those of states 2 and 3, and those of state 2 independent of state 3 but dependent on state 1. Finally, in the middle portion, Figure 9.16b, regime-types in states 1 and 2 are assumed to be independent, and regime-types in state 3 dependent on those in 1 and 2. In this case, it is necessary to make the further assumption that regime-types in state 3 will depend first on emergence of a given regime-type in one of the other states (say, state 1) and only then on regime-types in the other (here, state 2). These are the three general kinds of variations in regime-type dependency in a three-state future world.

It is important to realize that these matrices forecast regime-type variation in a given state *as influenced by* variation in regime-type of one or more other states and not changes that might result from the influence of domestic variables. If variation is considered to be a function of internal changes only, then no matrices need be constructed at this point. If, as is likely, regime-type

State 1 \ State 2	Regime-type α	Regime-type β	Regime-type γ	State 1 \ State 3	Regime-type Δ	Regime-type E	Regime-type Z	Regime-type H
Regime-type A				Regime-type A				
Regime-type B				Regime-type B				
Regime-type C				Regime-type C				
Regime-type D				Regime-type D				

(a)

Figure 9.16a   Variation in regime-type of states 2 and 3 as a function of variation in regime-type of state 1.

State 1 \ State 3	Regime-type Δ	Regime-type E	Regime-type Z	Regime-type H
Regime-type A				
Regime-type B				
Regime-type C				
Regime-type D				

State 2 \ State 3	Regime-type Δ	Regime-type E	Regime-type Z	Regime-type H
Regime-type α				
Regime-type β				
Regime-type γ				

(b)

Figure 9.16b Variation in regime-type of state 3 as a function of variations in regime-types of states 1 and 2, assumed to be independent.

State 1 \ State 2	Regime-type α	Regime-type β	Regime-type γ
Regime-type A			
Regime-type B			
Regime-type C			
Regime-type D			

State 2 \ State 3	Regime-type Δ	Regime-type E	Regime-type Z	Regime-type H
Regime-type α				
Regime-type β				
Regime-type γ				

(c)

Figure 9.16c Variation in regime-type of state 3 as a function of variations in regime-types of states 1 and 2, assuming that variation in state 2 is dependent on variation in state 1.

variation is considered to depend upon internal *and* external influences, then some manner must be found to register them on the matrices. One way is to fill in the "boxes" with numbers (or words) representing the probabilistic forecasts of experts. Such forecasts would judge the emergence of a given regime-type from domestic or international factors alone or joint determination (i.e., the product of the judgments taken separately).

Figure 9.17 extends to the three-state case the relation between regime-type and issue-area, as illustrated for the two-state case in Figure 9.11, and now concerns policies of states 1, 2, and 3 toward four issues in common, as a function of regime-type. There are two differences between the diagrams beyond the addition of an extra state. One is that the relationships, of dependence or independence, between future regime-types must be specified beforehand and probabilistic forecasts to this end supplied. These judgments will obviously af-

fect forecasts concerning policies that a given regime-type will adopt toward a given issue. Another difference is that the list of issues in common will change. In a two-state world, all issues are common by definition. In a three-state world, some issues may be common to only two of the three states (and since there are three combinations of two states, a large number of issues might potentially not concern all three states) while others may indeed affect all three states. In Figure 9.17, all four issues are regarded as being of common future interest to all three states; issues in common to whatever combination of two states would result in increasing the number of rows by the number of new issues.

Figure 9.18 is the three-state equivalent of Figure 9.12, relating regime-type variation to policy type of states 1, 2, and 3. Since the two differences between two- and three-state worlds noted in connection with Figure 9.17 hold also for this matrix,

		State 1				State 2			State 3		
Regime-type / Issue	A	B	C	D	α	β	γ	Δ	E	Z	H
1											
2											
3											
4											

Figure 9.17   Policies of regime-types in states 1, 2, and 3 toward issues 1–4 (assumptions concerning inter-regime-type dependence to be made prior to completion of matrix).

the possible complexity of the real future world is not shown in the present matrix.

Figures 9.19, 9.20, and 9.21 are the three-state equivalent of Figures 9.13, 9.14, and 9.15, and show, respectively and for all three states variation forecast in policy toward issues of a given regime-type in a given state as a function of future change in policy of a given regime-type in another state; variation in future policy toward issues of a given regime-type in a given state as a function of change in regime-type of another state; and future policy of a given state toward a given issue depending on predicted variation in regime-type of another state. The results are expressed in a three-dimensional matrix, as shown. Once again, relations of regime-

type dependency or independence must be specified beforehand, as well as which issues are forecast to be held in common by what states. (In the figures, it is presumed that all issues are held in common.)

Several aspects of these figures might be noted. In Figure 9.19 various assumptions of regime-type primacy and dependency can be tested, by asking area specialists or social science theorists to fill in the matrix under different initial conditions. In Figure 9.20, the left hand "wall" is not filled in, since the matrix forecasts the policy of a given regime-type toward a given series of issues and not the relations between two sets of regime-types, which are considered as given. As in the two-state case, it is

		State 1				State 2			State 3		
Policy type / Regime-type	A	B	C	D	α	β	γ	Δ	E	Z	H
1											
2											
3											
4											

Figure 9.18   Policy types of different regimes in states 1, 2, and 3 (assumptions concerning inter-regime-type dependence to be made prior to completion of matrix).

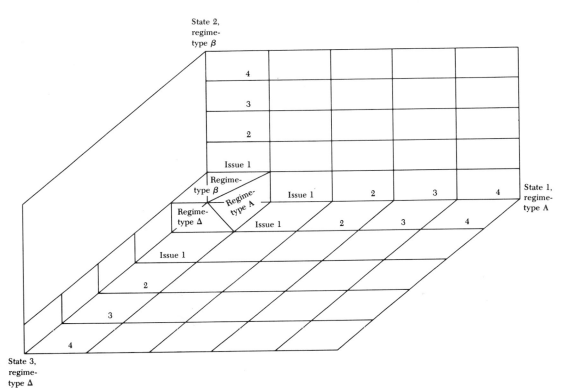

Figure 9.19 Variation in policy toward four common issues of regime-type A, state 1; regime-type β, state 2; and regime-type Δ, state 3.

possible to work out different versions of the matrix depending on what assumptions are made. For instance, regime-type A, state 1 can be regarded as given, and the question asked: What policies will alternative regime-types in states 2 and 3 adopt toward the four given issues? In Figure 9.21, assumptions concerning the relative primacy of regime-types can be varied to provide the basis for different final matrices. Thus, these three matrices open the way to inquire into a large variety of situations.

The dynamic (i.e., time-dependent) manifestation of three-state regime-type forecasting is easily illustrated by reference to Figures 9.8, 9.9, and 9.10. The normative form, corresponding to Figures 9.8 and 9.9, is presented in Figure 9.22, while the extensive form is shown in Figure 9.23. In the former case, extension of the matrix into the other three quadrants, represented by dotted lines, provides the added physical dimension

necessary for representation of time. This makes it possible for each future two-by-two combination (regime-type related to regime-type, regime-type related to issue, etc.) to be portrayed through passage of time. It does not lend itself, however, to simultaneous or time-dependent interaction between the variables as a group. For this, the extensive form is needed. This provides for simultaneity of decision among the three extant regime-types in the three states, or sequential decision as the case may be. It also makes possible a means of forecasting regime-type changes and relates such changes visually to subsequent changes in policy toward specific issues or in policy type. The number of decision choices possible will vary with the number of issues, as per the discussion accompanying Figure 9.10 above. (In Figure 9.23, for the sake of parsimony we have presumed that only three issues will be at stake and that they will be common to all three states.)

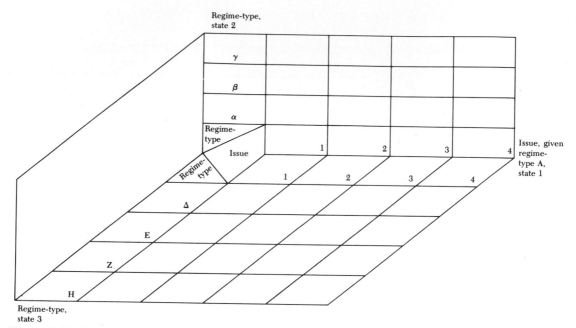

Figure 9.20 Variation in policy toward four issues of regime-type A, state 1, given variation of regime-types of states 2 and 3.

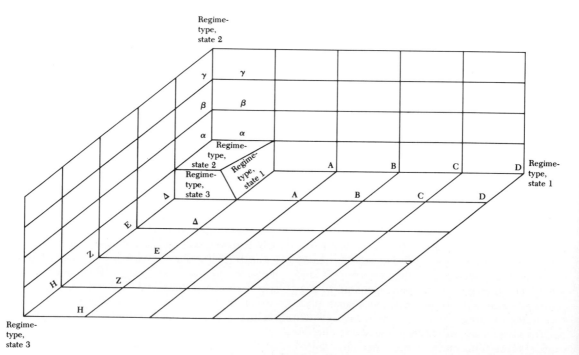

Figure 9.21 Policy of regime-types in states 2 and 3 toward a given issue, as a function of regime-type variation in state 1.

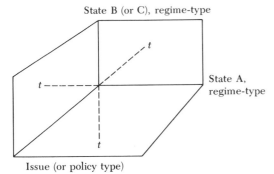

State B (or C), regime-type

State A, regime-type

Issue (or policy type)

Figure 9.22 Foreign policy issue (or policy type) as a function of regime-type variation and time.

In Figure 9.23, the eleven potential regime-types of the three states are shown at time $t = t_0$, with regime-types B (in state I), α (in state II), and Z (in state III) actually in power. As in Figure 9.10, there are seven possible decision choices for each regime-type, assuming, as we did there, that there are three (and not four, as we have in the more recent three-state exercise) issues in common. At time $t = t_1$, all three regimes make decisions on these issues, as shown, and at time $t = t_2$, each

makes another decision with regard to these same issues. At time $t = t_3$, however, only state I, regime-type B makes a policy decision, while the other two regime-types continue to adhere to their original policies. At time $t = t_4$, however, state II, regime-type α changes its policy in response to the change just made, while at time $t = t_5$, both α and Z carry out policy changes. This, along with other factors, causes a regime-type change in state I from regime-type B to C, a development that will, in subsequent time frames, influence α and Z to make changes in their policies in response.

VII. n-STATE WORLDS

Most real-world forecasting situations involve more than three nations, a fact that a regime-type analysis must deal with if it is to find successful practical application. The problem is three-fold. First, the number of variables will mount quite rapidly, as the three-state case demonstrated, and steps need to be taken to manage the situation. The obvious solutions are two. First, simplifying assumptions must be made and rigorously applied. Such assumptions may vary from state to state and from

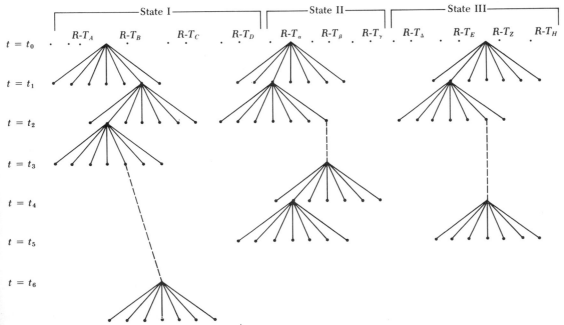

Figure 9.23 Decision-tree form of policy choices of regime-types in states I, II, and III through time t_6.

situation to situation, and will depend for criteria of relevance upon the purpose of the forecast. Second, the computer can be of enormous aid in generating the requisite combinations of two-, three-, and larger subsystems. While programs would undoubtedly have to be written to accommodate assumptions and propositions, and ways would have to provide for inputting expert judgment as to the kinds of future regime-types possible, their policies, and the issues at stake, there is little doubt that present equipment is adequate.

A second problem concerns how to represent $n > 3$ dimensions in three-dimensional space. It is impossible to make a graphical representation unless we wish to reduce all situations to some possibly artibrary combination of two- and three-dimensional matrices. Arbitrariness will be reduced, of course, if assumptions are spelled out in the beginning. The computer can help here, too, by being programmed to print matrices according to those assumptions and according to propositions that emerge during the forecast or that are taken from some theoretical approach. In the n-state case, moreover, it may not be necessary to project the relations between all n states. In that case, the international system may be divided into a number of smaller subsets, and if some of these are three-state or less in size, they may be graphically portrayed.

A third problem involves how to involve the area expert or social scientist, whom we have regarded as an essential element in the regime-type analysis. In n-state analysis, he does not have the advantage of visual representation. In this case, also, the solution would seem to be a combination of carefully spelled-out assumptions and propositions, use of the computer, and a breaking down of the larger system into its smaller components. It is particularly important, however, that forecasts of dependency between regime-types be noted, that dominance, at a given future time, of domestic politics, the international system, or the foreign policies of other states, be indicated, and that projected dependence of regime-type, policy type, or policy issue on time period be specified.

Although space limitations make it impossible to provide any more than general suggestions for applying the regime-type analysis to n-state forecasts, it may prove useful to outline the seven stages in constructing future worlds where the number of actors is more than three. First, and perhaps most important, it is necessary to have clearly in mind the purpose of the forecast—policy, teaching, theory-testing, sensitizing, or other goals. The purpose will dictate the "tone" of the entire forecast and assist in emphasizing some variables and alternatives while eliminating others.

Second, each alternative regime-type for each state must be defined, as exactly as possible, by means of a short essay. It is at this stage that one must choose between utilizing area experts or more general social scientists, according to the purposes of the forecast. It is necessary, moreover, to set an upper bound to the number of regime-types for each state, to specify the time frame, the issues, and types of policy to be considered, and to work out a means of arriving at agreed opinions among experts.

Third, the experts must decide what specific policies each regime-type would probably follow toward issues salient to the forecast. This involves making assumptions—for each regime-type—of the relative importance of, and the character of the relationship between, domestic politics and international politics in determining foreign policy. It also involves defining policies and issues, quantifying their values if possible, and specifying their range.

One can then move to the fourth stage, constructing two-by-two matrices. These usually compare, in different iterations, projected regime-types for the two states; regime-types and issues; and regime-types and foreign-policy types. As in most other stages, it is necessary to check for inter-expert consistency and to ask each to justify his reasoning. As we have said before, it is essential to reduce the number of combinations of regime-types and policies to a minimum. This constitutes the fifth stage. Reduction may be accomplished through inspection, by simplifying assumptions, or by rank ordering alternatives and then cutting off at some arbitrary level.

Sixth, a second set of two-by-two matrices are constructed, this time involving the relationship between policy issues of one regime-type in one state with those of another regime-type in another state. Here it is important to keep in mind what variables are independent and what dependent. While in a forecast any variable can be regarded as dependent or independent, these relationships must be clearly indicated, since the results will vary according to their character.

The way is then open to construct a dynamic model. This is done simply by adding future time as an independent variable. One can adopt either the normative (matrix) model or the extensive (game tree) form, although for forecasting it may be more convenient to utilize the latter. Additional decisions must also be made: what criteria to utilize for effectuating time-related changes or regime-types, issues, or policies; whether to employ area experts or social scientists; and what influence the character and rate of change of the future international system have on time-related changes or regime-types and policy issues. These seven stages constitute construction of static and dynamic forms of two-state worlds.

Three-state forecasts involve going through stages 1-3 for state three and then building three-sided matrices along the same lines as in the two-state case. However, there are two important differences. First, additional assumptions must be made as concerns the comparative primacy and dependency of regime-types, policy choices, and policy issues. Second, there is the complex problem of dealing with issues not in common among all regime-types. We have treated this difficulty in some detail above.

N-state forecasting involves adding, in an iterative fashion, the desired additional number of states by going through the above seven stages for each state. It is obvious that this process becomes more cumbersome with each additional state and that, at some point, an upper bound will be reached. However, increased computer utilization, reduction in the number of variables through simplifying assumptions, and dependence on the game-tree form will increase the probability of successful utilization of this method. And, as noted above, the forecasting purposes are determinative of its complexity: theory testing and teaching are not so demanding of detail as policy relevance and sensitization of policy makers.

NOTES

1. While this term is usually associated with the Hudson Institute project by that name, it should be noted that this approach is essentially common to all systematically determinative theories of international relations.
2. See Robinson (1971). A version was published in the *Journal of International Affairs* (1972), pp. 192–215.
3. This would be the case, for instance, with regard to India during the 1960's. See, in this regard, Wilcox (1970).
4. Although amalgamation of the two approaches may be desirable as an end product, no such attempt is made here. In this essay, instead, we concentrate on developing the alternative regime-type approach so as to be in position, in subsequent work, to combine the two.
5. This is done to some extent in Section VII, "n-State Worlds," in this chapter.
6. The numbers and types of country experts and social scientists will obviously depend upon the state being considered. In general, of course, smaller numbers of such people are more desirable than larger, as is a diversity of social science disciplinary orientations. Our emphasis, however, is on *combining* the detailed knowledge of country experts and the theoretical knowledge of other social scientists. One sometimes meets such a combination in one person (i.e., an economist knowledgeable about input-output analysis and also about the Soviet economy). But this would limit the inquiry at the most to one of the social sciences.
7. Neither the country expert nor the social science theorist is capable of doing the job without some sort of input from the other. In studying the foreign policy of a given country, just as international relations as a whole, there is no substitute for the combination of area expertise and social science theory. So far this combination is not often found, or even attempted.
8. There are a range of methods for arriving at agreement among experts. These include, among others, Delphi, cross-impact matrices, and decision analysis (Bayesian techniques). For Delphi techniques, see Gordon and Helmer (1964); for cross-impact matrices, see Gordon and Hayward (1968), pp. 100–116; for decision analysis, see Raiffa (1970).
9. Adapted from Robinson (1971).
10. As we shall note again below, the number of "boxes" tends to increase rapidly with the complexity of the initial analysis, the number of policy variables, and the number of states under consideration. It is all the more imperative, therefore, to be clear as to one's purposes and to constantly force one's self to choose that subset which satisfies those goals.
11. These figures are read as follows. Figure 9.4 states that if regime-type B of state I adopts a given set of future policies toward issues 1 through n, then regime-type C of state II will, in response, adopt its own series of policies toward those same issues. The upper right triangle contains information on the policies toward each issue of regime-type B, state I, and the lower left triangle describes the policies of regime-type C, state II. The policies that regime-type C, state II adopts toward issues 1 to n thus depend on the policies toward those same issues adopted by regime-type B, state I.

Figure 9.5 states that, as the future regime-type of state I varies, the policy of regime-type C, state II toward issues 1 to n changes accordingly. Figure 9.6

states that future variance in state C's policy toward issue 3 depends upon what sort of regime-type will be in power there, but that this in turn is dependent upon what regime-type is in power in state B.

12. In a full-fledged exercise of this sort, it would be desirable to enlist the advice of a number of country experts in the process of deciding what regime-types to discuss, their characteristics, and what policies they might well follow. Here, however, only the author's judgment is available.

13. These definitions follow from the author's (and from another former member of the Rand Corporation Social Science Department staff's) experience in studying the domestic politics and foreign policies of contemporary mainland China and Soviet Russia.

14. It should be noted that it is difficult for a given country expert to verbalize in a cogent manner exactly why he makes one choice as opposed to another in filling out the "boxes." At work is a combination of application of the definitions of the various regime-types and a "feel" that is the product of long-term study of the subject.

CHAPTER TEN

BAYESIAN DECISION ANALYSIS IN INTERNATIONAL RELATIONS FORECASTING: THE ANALYSIS OF SUBJECTIVE PROCESSES

Richard K. Ashley

Theory and research in the field of international relations have long suggested that *subjective factors*—particularly the value, beliefs, expectations, and perceptions of national leaders—play important roles in determining the international behaviors of states. This chapter introduces *Bayesian decision theory* as an appropriate and promising approach to the analysis of these factors.[1] More

I am particularly grateful to Nazli Choucri who originally suggested the relevance of the Bayesian approach to international relations forecasting and who provided valuable guidance and criticism throughout the development of this work. I would also like to express my thanks to Thomas W. Robinson whose systematic verbal analysis of the Sino-Soviet border dispute inspired the substantive application, and to Thomas Milburn who provided patient and helpful criticism at an early stage.

precisely, Bayesian decision analysis is here presented as the theoretical and methodological foundation for an analytic framework, a framework which stresses subjective factors and which, at the same time, is of sufficient generality to permit its application to a variety of dynamic, multiactor international situations.

Although other potential applications of the framework are envisioned, this chapter will emphasize the application of the framework in international relations forecasting. The framework can be used possibly for the descriptive analysis of policy decisions. And, largely because the roots of the framework are in an essentially normative body of "choice theory" (Bayesian decision analysis), the framework has potential policy prescriptive applications as well. This chapter, however, will treat the framework as an approach to forecasting in the *short-range,* as an approach to the systematic consideration of proximate future contingencies in international relations.

The first section of this chapter will briefly introduce the framework in broad terms, describing its theoretical orientation as well as its potential uses and limitations. In the second section, Bayesian decision analysis will be presented with emphasis on its relevance to international relations forecasting. The third section will present the framework in greater detail, will provide a short illustrative application, and will offer a critical appraisal of the framework as an approach to the analysis of the subjective in international relations forecasting.

I. INTRODUCTION

In that it addresses the subjective, the framework presented here focuses upon variables previously neglected by other forecasting methods that are similarly systematic. Systems theorists and econometricians engaged in forecasting have tended to adopt what Quincy Wright called a "deterministic point of view" (1965, p. 1236); that is, these analysts have tended to focus upon objective, environmental variables—technological resource, territorial, and demographic variables among others —and their direct, unmediated influences upon national behaviors. These analysts have not claimed a monopoly of predictive competence for the theoretical "islands" in which their efforts are grounded. Indeed, today's analyst of the objective consciously leaves a lot of "room for contingency and choice" (Wright, p. 1236) in his forecasts. However, analysts of the subjective have heretofore refrained from filling this void in forecasting approaches;[2] and the subjective has been left to the realm of the prophet.

The current framework is addressed to this void. It undertakes the analysis of subjective factors; and it requires that the analyst adopt what Quincy Wright called a "voluntaristic point of view," a perspective involving the analysis of choice, of decision-making processes. As Wright noted: "It is because governments know something but not everything that wars arise unpredictably. . . . Analysis of the process by which governments expand their knowledge and perfect their policies may provide a prognosis of war from a voluntaristic point of view" (p. 1237).

The theoretical framework presented here is in part one possible response to this implied challenge. It focuses upon the values, beliefs, expectations, and perceptions of national decision makers, and it ignores those variables associated with a "deterministic point of view."

Given its voluntaristic orientation, the current framework may lend greater time- and behavioral-specificity to previously wholly deterministic forecasting approaches by providing (in the subjective variables addressed by the framework) crucial links in the causal chain between objective, environmental variables on the one hand, and overt national behaviors on the other. When synthesized with approaches that address objective factors, the framework may be applied to the long- as well as the short-range future. But when used alone, as discussed here, the framework is best applied in the short-range, which can be defined as that period of the proximate future when the effects of objective factors may be analytically treated as constant and when the predictive power of a wholly deterministic point of view is therefore negligible.

The methodology presented here is akin to those recently developed approaches to international relations forecasting—like systems dynamics and simulation based upon econometric models— which stress logic, precision, and firm anchors in propositions emerging from available international relations theory. A computer-based structure has been developed that permits the analyst interested in specific international situations to define behaviors of salience and interest, to introduce data reflecting his assessments of the states of subjective variables, to manipulate parameters, to project the dynamics of an international-interactive model into the future, and to observe consequent behaviors. By undertaking several runs, the analyst may gain an appreciation of ranges of probable future behaviors given his assumptions. The methodology, in short, is very much in the tradition of simulation as an approach to forecasting.

At the same time, the methodology is necessarily flexible in order to accommodate the ambiguities still prevalent in that portion of international relations theory addressed to subjective processes. The forecasting structure cannot resolve these theoretical ambiguities. But it does provide the analyst with an opportunity for the systematic exploration of future contingencies by explicitly and formally manipulating what might be called "alternative conditionals"—the alternative subjective process assumptions upon which forecasts are based.

The framework reflects an attempt to merge "choice theories" and "process theories" of decision making, *with choice theories supplying the generalizable conceptual core*. Despite their origins in the fields of public administration, business administration, and economics, both sets of theory could potentially provide the theoretical foundation for an analytic framework addressing subjective factors in international relations: "Process theories aim at describing how persons with normal ability to collect and process information adjust to decision situations. . . . Choice theories prescribe how an (in some sense) optimal decision should be made in a given situation" (von Holstein, 1970, pp. 155–156).

Process theories are descriptive. Choice theories are prescriptive. Process theories—like those of Simon (1957), Lindblom (1959, pp. 79–88 and 1963), and Cyert and March (1963)—are familiar to participants in the field of international relations; at least we have found relevant insights in such concepts as "satisficing," "incrementalism," and "bureaucratic inertia." Similarly, choice theories—game theory in particular (Kaplan, 1957; Rapoport, 1960; Schelling, 1960; and *Journal of Conflict Resolution*)—have been extensively applied in the field. But the boundaries between the "is" and the "ought" have been carefully maintained. Process theories and choice theories usually have been treated separately.

Underlying the framework presented here is the presupposition that insights from each of these theoretical orientations can be meaningfully integrated in applications to specific cases. More precisely, propositions emanating from a subset of the choice theory literature—specifically, the *Bayesian decision analysis* literature—have been used in the construction of a generic subjective process structure, a structure intended to be useful in forecasting in (and the descriptive and prescriptive analysis of) a wide range of dynamic, multiactor international situations. This structure is developed such that, in specific applications, adjustments can be made in accordance with propositions emerging from a process perspective.

Although Bayesian decision analysis has been developed as a body of normative choice theory, it is here treated as a descriptive ideal type, as a potentially useful first approximation of the ways in which national decision makers, in general, actually do operate. According to R. A. Howard: "Decision analysis is a logical procedure for the balancing of the factors that influence a decision. The procedure incorporates uncertainties, values, and preferences in a basic structure that models the situation" (Howard, 1966; and von Holstein, p. 164).

As will be seen in the next section, Bayesian decision analytic procedures—while prescriptive, and while highly stylized—have been developed with an eye to the actual circumstances in which decision makers must operate. And, where decision analysis may appear overly stylized and unrepresentative of the processes by which decision makers in fact operate, the decomposability of decision analysis into its component procedures permits the analyst of the subjective to identify those points at which propositions emanating from a process perspective can be most appropriately asserted.

II. BAYESIAN DECISION ANALYSIS AND ITS POTENTIAL IN INTERNATIONAL RELATIONS FORECASTING

Definition

Bayesian decision analysis is a body of prescriptions concerning the optimal use of available information—both objective and subjective—in the making of decisions (1) when future contingencies are differentially valued, (2) when uncertainties about the realization of these contingencies exist, and (3) when it is expected that current choices among options can affect the probabilities that these contingencies will be realized and/or the values associated with these contingencies. Bayesian decision analysis is future oriented; it contains procedures (applying Bayes' theorem) for integrating information in determining and revising the probabilities of uncertain future events. But it is not, strictly speaking, a body of forecasting methodologies, for the ultimate concern of the Bayesian decision analyst is action, not disinterested contemplation. Bayesian decision analysts seek to answer the question: How should a decision maker, confronting an uncertain environment, proceed to choose among his available options?

In working toward this end, Bayesian decision analysts do not assume that decision makers are idealized, rational, economic, and superintelligent. Nor do they assert that decision makers applying Bayesian methods will magically acquire these qualities. Bayesian decision analysts simply want to provide the decision maker with the means to efficiently integrate information and systematically calculate the implications of information for action. The careful application of Bayesian methods guarantees only that these resulting implications will be reasonably consistent with expressed expectations and evaluations; it does not insure that the basic expectations and evaluations will be "rational" or will reflect the decision maker's meticulously scientific appraisal of patterned regularities in his environment. Thus, Bayesian decision analysis provides a model of logically consistent—but not necessarily rational—decision making.

Bayesian decision analysts are sometimes called "subjectivists" because they believe that subjective expectations ought to be incorporated into the decision maker's calculations. The subjectivist interpretation of probability differs markedly from the objectivist view (Raiffa, pp. 273–278). In the objectivist view, as first enunciated by Denis Poisson in 1837, probability is formally defined as a limit of a long-run relative frequency. The subjectivist (or personalist) interpretation, by contrast, takes probability to be a "degree of confidence" (or a "degree of belief") that an individual attaches to an uncertain event. Subjective probabilities can be based on hunch, intuition, rumor, or even ideology. The Bayesian decision analyst accepts both interpretations as relevant to decision making, he believes that the two forms can be integrated meaningfully, and he applies Bayes' theorem to accomplish this task—hence the label "Bayesian."

Bayesian decision analysts usually begin with the assumption that the decision maker is well acquainted with the options available to him and with the contingencies that he might encounter. They additionally assume that the decision maker operates in an uncertain environment, that the decision maker's expectations about the realization of future contingencies are at best probabilistic. Usually, the decision maker's probability assessments are assumed to be subjective in nature, although they need not be.

In order to assist decision makers in the choice of optimal (expected utility maximizing) options in such circumstances, Bayesian decision analysts have developed procedures that are roughly divisible into two stages. The first stage, the *informational stage*, includes procedures designed to permit the maximally efficient integration of available information in order to arrive at probability assessments more nearly reflecting "true" probabilities. These procedures involve the application of Bayes' theorem (defined later) to transform "prior" (usually subjective) probabilities into "posterior" probabilities in light of some new (usually experiential, often experimental) information. The second stage, which might be called the *decisional stage*, includes procedures designed to permit the selection of expected utility maximizing options at least in part on the basis of the "posterior" probabilities supplied by the first stage.[3]

Applications in International Relations Forecasting

The international relations forecaster may usefully draw upon the procedures in either or both stages of the Bayesian decision analytic approach. He may draw upon the informational stage procedures in two ways:

1. The forecaster may treat the Bayesian expectation revision procedures as models of maximally efficient information processing—as ideal typical *learning* models—and use these in simulate systems, the dynamics of which may be projected into the future. Treated in this way, the informational-stage procedures would be models of *national decision makers' learning processes*.

2. Alternatively, the forecaster may treat these procedures as *models for his own analysis*. That is, he may emulate the Bayesian informational prototype and apply Bayes' theorem to (1) develop a strategy for the continual updating of probability assessments assigned to future events as a series of theoretically and probabilistically interrelated events unfold; (2) introduce his or others' subjective expectations into his forecasts; and/or (3) integrate a diverse array of specific international relations forecasts and general forecasting approaches thereby permitting a cumulative use of expertise available in the field. Each of these applications has

been advocated and illustrated by others (Greenberg, 1969; Ben-Dak and Mihalka, 1972).

In drawing upon the decisional stage procedures, the forecaster may use his knowledge about the current values, beliefs, and expectations of national leaders to forecast probable future behaviors. He may accomplish this by mentally placing himself in the role of a decision maker; formulating a decision problem; considering options, consequences, and probabilistic relationships; identifying a preferred option on the basis of expected value calculations; and suggesting—or predicting—that national behavior will conform to the preferred option. This approach, which is very much in the game theoretical tradition, is simply an enforced systematization of a popular mode of purely verbal analysis. It assumes (at least as a first approximation) that national decision makers are logically consistent. It is, in effect, simulation as an approach to forecasting. But the approach is adequate only for the very near future, for, in and of themselves, the decisional components of Bayesian decision analysis cannot adequately account for decision making after the evolution of expectations.

The framework presented here draws upon both the informational and the decisional stages of Bayesian decision analysis. It uses the decisional approach outlined in the immediately preceding paragraph. But, in recognition of the dynamic nature of subjective processes and of the need to project these dynamics beyond tomorrow's decisions, the framework includes a "learning" component that is drawn from the informational stage procedures. The framework thus uses Bayesian decision analysis in toto, not as a model for the analyst to personally emulate, but as a model of national leaders' subjective processes to be used in simulate systems. This model is at the core of the framework. It assumes maximally efficient information processing and logical consistency in decision making. As such, the model is best understood as a first approximation: a model to be refined in light of process theoretical propositions relevant to particular international situations.

It is, of course, difficult to appreciate the framework, as well as the other applications outlined above, in the absence of a minimal familiarity with some of the specific procedures of Bayesian decision analysis. Thus, the following subsections on Informational Stage Procedures and Decisional Stage Procedures will offer a cursory introduction to these topics, stressing relevance to forecasting in international relations wherever appropriate.

Informational Stage Procedures

In 1763, the Reverend Thomas Bayes produced "An Essay Toward Solving a Problem in the Doctrine of Chances" (first published in the *Philosophical Transactions of the Royal Society*, Volume 53; edited version in *Biometrika* (1958) in which he advanced the proposition that subjective probabilities should be combined with frequentistic probabilities via what has come to be called Bayes' theorem, a very simple formula using conditional probabilities. According to the formula, the *prior* probability $P(H)$ of proposition H is revised to *posterior* probability $P(H|D)$ when the datum D is observed—and $P(D|H)$ and $P(D)$ are known—as follows:

$$P(H|D) = \frac{P(H) \cdot P(D|H)}{P(D)}.$$

In this formula, $P(D|H)$ is the *likelihood* of the sample information D given that proposition H is true.

Even in this simple form, Bayes' theorem has apparent applications in international relations forecasting. By way of example, let us assume that a panel of experts is interested in determining the probability of a Soviet-American agreement on the limitation of offensive strategic weapons in the *next* year:

Background

All members of the panel agree that—given the heavy costs of the arms race and other factors—the Soviets want an agreement within the next 3 years, but there is some debate as to the Soviets' intentions for the coming year. The Soviets have just initiated a costly new offensive weapons system that will not be operational for 2 years. Some of the experts believe that the Soviets are anxious for an agreement in the coming year, that the new system is simply a hedge against a failure to reach a quick agreement with the United States, and that the Soviets will readily give up the new program in an accord if the Administration's bargaining position approximates its public pronouncements. But others believe that the Soviets are serious about completing the weapons program, that their objective is to present the United States with a *fait accompli* prior to earnest bargaining, and that only major American concessions will permit a quick agreement.

All members of the panel agree that the attitude of the USSR is a major variable upon which the panel's forecasts for the coming year must be conditioned. As a preliminary exercise, the experts define two Soviet attitudinal hypotheses and, after much haggling, reach some consensus on the probabilities (degrees of belief) that each hypothesis is true (Table 10.1). These probabilities are "priors."

Revision of the Prior Assessment

Rather than introduce these "purely subjective" probability assessments directly into their calculations regarding an agreement in the coming year, the panel members decide to take fuller advantage of their available information. They take note of the fact that the United States has just sent a "feeler" to the Soviet Union on the subject at hand, and they conclude that the Soviet response in the coming week is potentially informative as to the Soviet attitude *(H)*.

The panel divides possible Soviet responses into three categories: "positive response" (D_1), "ignore" (D_2), and "rebuff" (D_3). And they decide that the probability of each of these responses is conditional on (i.e., is probabilistically dependent on) the Soviet attitude *(H)*. Applying their experiences, they construct Table 10.2. Then the experts wait for the Soviet response.

The response comes: the Soviets respond warmly to the American feeler (D_1). How do the panel members revise their prior expectations about Soviet attitudes in light of this new information:

The experts apply Bayes' theorem:

$$P(H_1|D_1) = \frac{P(H_1)P(D_1|H_1)}{P(D_1)}$$

where

$$P(D_1) = P(H_1)P(D_1|H_1) + P(H_2)P(D_1|H_2).$$

Thus the experts have:

$$P(H_1|D_1) = \frac{0.56 \times 0.61}{0.56 \times 0.61 + 0.44 \times 0.28}$$

$$= .734.$$

Similarly,

$$P(H_2|D_1) = \frac{P(H_2)P(D_1|H_2)}{P(D_1)}$$

$$= \frac{0.44 \times 0.28}{0.56 \times 0.61 + 0.44 \times 0.28}$$

$$= .266.$$

The panel members note the change in their probability assessments over the two hypotheses (see Table 10.3). These new values are "posterior" with respect to the information that the Soviets responded positively to the American feeler. But they may be considered "priors" with respect to some still newer information.

The panel members agree that these posterior assessments are more "informed"—and more in accordance with their current degrees of belief about the two hypothesized attitudes —than their earlier assessments. And they elect to use these posterior probability assessments as new "priors" to be revised in light of some new information about to surface: the diplomatic level at which the Soviets prefer to negotiate.

This fictional account is an illustration of an application of the Bayesian approach as a model *for* the forecaster's analysis.

At the same time, the account underscores three of the aspects of the Bayesian approach that make it particularly fitting as applied in the current framework. First, the Bayesian approach encourages the use of subjective probabilities, probabilities that reflect degrees of belief rather than relative frequencies. In the above account, the panel members were able to speak probabilistically

Table 10.1 Illustrations of Soviet attitudinal hypotheses and degrees of belief.

Hypothetical USSR Attitude	Label	Probability
USSR wants accord soon, sees new system as hedge	H_1	$P(H_1) = .56$
USSR wants accord after system is built	H_2	$P(H_2) = .44$

Table 10.2 Three categories of Soviet response and probabilities of each.

		USSR Response to Feeler		
Hypothetical USSR Attitude	"Prior" $P(H)$	Positive (D_1)	Ignore (D_2)	Rebuff (D_3)
Wants accord soon, sees system as hedge	$P(H_1) = .56$	$P(D_1H_1) = .61$	$P(D_2H_1) = .27$	$P(D_3H_1) = .12$
Wants accord after system is built	$P(H_2) = .44$	$P(D_1H_2) = .28$	$P(D_2H_2) = .43$	$P(D_3H_2) = .29$

about Soviet attitudes, not because they believed that these attitudes are random variables, but because the panel members viewed probability as roughly comparable to plausibility—a degree of personal confidence in a hypothesis or prediction. For purposes of simulating subjective processes in international relations, it is useful to think of subjective, as well as frequentistic, probabilities, for national decision makers can and do have expectations about contingencies that they have never experienced.

Second, the Bayesian approach to probability revision is really nothing more than a rigorous systematization of a quite natural way of thinking. Individuals, national leaders included, do integrate new information within the frameworks of their prior expectations as they revise and update these expectations.

As he prepares for bed on Tuesday evening, the foreign minister of the small Latin American country is very certain that the United States military assistance program will continue. The American ambassador, just that afternoon, had assured him that the President of the United States will resist mounting public and Congressional pressures to cut off aid. He decides that he can made a very optimistic report to the country's present ruler—an ex-colonel with strong ties to the military—in tomorrow's meeting.

Early Wednesday morning, the minister is awakened by a telephone call from an anxious assistant who reports that the American ambassador and military attaché have just left for Washington to attend an urgent meeting with the President and several Congressional leaders.

As he dresses for the morning conference, the minister revises his appraisal of the American aid situation: On the basis of yesterday's assurances from the American ambassador, the minister still expects that United States aid will continue. But the meeting in Washington *might be* a portent of change in US policy. The minister is less certain of a continuation of aid than he was the previous evening. He decides to temper his report to the ex-colonel with a few well-chosen words of caution.

The minister's report to the ex-colonel—the minister's posterior assessment—is a product of both his prior expectations and the new information. The Bayesian approach provides a systematic, logically consistent, and analytically tractable analogue of such expectation revision processes.

Third, as the "panel of experts" account illustrates, the Bayesian approach is useful in situations in which information arrives in a continuous flow—as it does for the national decision maker. The expectations that are posteriors with respect to one information "sample" may be treated as priors with respect to another "sample" yet to be "drawn." For the forecaster, this characteristic of

Table 10.3 Prior and posterior probabilities of hypothetical Soviet attitudes.

Hypothetical USSR Attitude	Hypothetical Label	"Prior" Probability	"Posterior" Probability
Wants accord soon, sees system as hedge	H_1	$P(H_1) = .56$	$P(H_1\|D_1) = .734$
Wants accord after system is built	H_2	$P(H_2) = .44$	$P(H_2\|D_1) = .266$

the Bayesian approach is of special significance: It permits the forecaster to apply the Bayesian approach in the simulation of continuing subjective processes in which a series of events have cumulative effects on expectations and consequent behaviors.

A fourth significant characteristic of the Bayesian approach is not reflected in the very simple application presented above. It is found in an extension of Bayes' theorem. In the formula

$$P(H\,|\,D) = \frac{P(H)P(D\,|\,H)}{P(D)}$$

the prior $P(H)$ need not be established with any degree of precision. It may instead represent a variable drawn from a distribution. Often this distribution is represented by a *judgmental density function* that reflects the assessor's strength of belief that the true probability of an event (or proportion in a population) falls within certain intervals on a probability scale. $P(H)$ might be the mean, mode, or median of such a distribution, although the mean is usually used.

As a result, just as it is possible to speak of prior and posterior subjective probabilities, it is possible to speak of prior and posterior subjective probability distributions. An extension of Bayes' theorem can be applied to revise the entire distribution in light of new information. And in such cases, a posterior $P(H$: new information) might be the mean of the posterior distribution (Raiffa, pp. 181–187).

The *shape* of a prior distribution has much to do with the *weight* it is given relative to the impact of new information in a Bayesian revision process. A *diffuse prior*—one with a large standard deviation—is more susceptible of major change in light of new information than is a prior that is sharply peaked around its mean. Thus it is possible for two or more prior distributions to have the same mean and still be differently weighted relative to the impact of new information.[4]

In the context of the present framework, this means that the Bayesian approach provides the forecaster with the ability to vary the strength (or certainty) of prior expectations while remaining free to establish the simulate actor's "best guess" as to the probability of an event anywhere on the scale from zero to one. The forecaster can thus use the Bayesian approach to represent conviction as well as confusion, cognitive rigidity as well as an open mind.

Regardless of the shape of one's prior distribution, however, the weight of new information always reflects the *size of the sample*: the larger the sample, the greater the impact on the posterior distribution. Sample size is yet another variable that the Bayesian approach permits the forecaster to manipulate. The forecaster might, for example, establish a common sample size for day-to-day events but use a greatly enlarged sample size to represent "shocking" events such as an explicit threat of war, a withdrawal of recognition, or an unexpected walkout during a negotiation session.

While these paragraphs have barely scratched the surface of the Bayesian informational stage procedures, they do suggest that these procedures provide a conceptually rich, analytically tractable model of maximally efficient information processing. In the framework presented here, such a model is used as a first approximation of national leaders' subjective "learning" processes.

Decisional Stage Procedures

Bayesian decisional stage procedures are addressed to a decision-making environment that is not unlike the environment confronted by national leaders. These procedures are addressed to situations of uncertainty. Uncertain situations are those in which at least one option available to a decision maker has at least two alternative outcomes, each of which may occur with a probability greater than zero. Thus, a characteristic of decision making under uncertainty is that the decision maker cannot exactly and absolutely identify each and all of his options with single, specific outcomes. For at least one of his competing options, the decision maker must admit that the outcome depends in part upon events and circumstances beyond his control. Such situations are frequently encountered by national leaders.

Uncertainty, however, does not mean ignorance. National leaders can and do have expectations about the occurrence or nonoccurrence of significant (outcome influencing) events and circumstances. They sometimes believe, for example, that one event is "much more likely" than another or that an event, "while improbable, ought to be considered."

Bayesian decision analysts—largely because they, more than others, favor including subjective expectations in the analysis of decisions—have addressed their procedures to these situations of "informed" uncertainty. In the case of *uninformed uncertainty*, the decision maker recognizes the uncertain nature of his situation but he is either unwilling or unable to assign probability assessments to significant events. By default, the assumption is that the true probabilities of significant events can with equal likelihood be found at any point on the probability scale between zero and one (i.e., a perfectly flat prior distribution). In the case of *informed uncertainty*, the decision maker is willing to assign probability assessments to significant events; even though his judgmental density function may be comparatively diffuse, it is not flat. Bayesian decisional stage procedures were developed with the latter case in mind, but they are generalizable to the former as well.

Central to the decisional stage procedures is the so-called *Bayesian decision principle*.[5] This principle adopts the position that an individual's prior hunches, convictions, or information about the "state of nature" (that is, significant events and circumstances) ought to be incorporated into his decision-making process in some systematic way. According to the principle, this is accomplished by weighting the possible "states of nature" in terms of expectations as to whether they will or will not occur. Thus, if an extremely large loss can occur for a given action when "nature" is in a state that the decision maker assumes to be extremely unlikely, the role of the extreme loss is minimized in the decision calculus by weighting only slightly the "state of nature" that would produce it.

This principle is often applied in the calculation of expected values associated with each option available to a decision maker. This expected value is sometimes called a *Bayes' loss* for an option.[6] It is usually computed as follows:

A decision maker has several available options x_i (where i can equal 1 through m, and m is the total number of options). He understands that the outcome ultimately realized will be determined by the combination of specific x_i and the state of nature s_j (where j can equal 1 through n, and n is the total number of mutually exclusive states of nature). He thus develops an m-by-n matrix—an outcome matrix—each cell of which defines a joint outcome o_{ij}.

The decision maker carefully considers each o_{ij} in the outcome matrix in terms of his value system and assigns consistent and transitive utility values

$U(o_{ij})$ to each o_{ij}. Next, on the basis of his prior convictions and hunches, he assigns a probability $P(s_j)$ to each s_j such that

$$\sum_{j=1}^{n} P(s_j) = 1.$$

The decision maker is then ready to compute his expected utility for each option x_j by weighting each $U(o_{ij})$ according to the corresponding $P(s_j)$. The expected utility for each x_i, denoted $EU(x_i)$, is computed:

$$EU(x_i) = \sum_{j=1}^{n} P(s_j) \cdot U(o_{ij}).$$

Using this formula, he computes an expected utility for each of his m options.

Once these expected values are calculated, the decision maker is able to select the option that minimizes his expected loss or maximizes his expected utility.

Given that situations of "informed uncertainty" are frequently encountered in international relations, and given that these are precisely the situations to which Bayesian choice theorists have addressed their procedures, the prescriptions of Bayesian decision theory might reasonably be borrowed by national decision makers as they confront their options. Bayesian decisional stage procedures have prescriptive potential in international relations.

Although they have emerged from a body of normative choice theory, these procedures also have promising predictive (as well as descriptive) applications in international relations. A forecaster with insights into the values and expectations of a nation's leaders can, as a first approximation, apply the Bayesian decisional stage procedures in order to identify behavioral options most consistent with those values and expectations.

The forecaster adopting this approach is not necessarily confined to the assumption that national leaders are always rational, economic decision makers, for Bayesian decisional stage procedures are of sufficient generality to permit the forecaster to incorporate mixed, even confused, motivational structures in his specifications of utility functions. The forecaster can, for example, develop utility functions that reflect a diverse array of attitudes toward risk.

The forecaster needs only to assume that national leaders are purposive and that their expectations about significant events and circumstances influence their choices among options in ways that are reasonably consistent with the weighting procedures prescribed by the Bayesian decision principle. While it is clear that national leaders do not assign consistent and transitive utility functions to possible outcomes, it does seem apparent that national leaders sometimes do weight events and associated outcomes in terms of their (often vague) expectations about them; this weighting process might take the form of the following (purely fictitious) monologues:

Oh, we can discount that contingency. Of course we'd be in some difficulty if it came to be; but, circumstances being what they are, I don't think there's much chance of that. Do you? We shouldn't be deterred from such a promising course of action by such an unlikely event. Let's go ahead. . . .

or

Sure, it would be great if they were to back down in the face of our reinforcements. We'd control all of that territory. But they just won't back down. They're pretty hard nosed, you know. And they're much more likely to raise their own troop levels or start trouble. Then what'll we do? Go to war? We want war with them a lot less than we want that territory. Now, we could negotiate instead and. . . .

That such probabilistic weighting does in some sense occur is evidenced by the fact that national behaviors do not always conform to the options that would be dictated by purely "worst case" or "best case" analyses.

In sum, the forecaster adopting this approach is accepting Bayesian decisional stage procedures as an ideal-typical model of subjective decision-making processes. He assumes that national decision makers are imperfect men who operate in uncertain environments. He also assumes that, despite their imperfections, national leaders are purposive and conscientious, that they police the consistency of their information, and that they systematically calculate the implications of their information for action. Taken together, these traits define a model of decision making that, while infrequently mirrored perfectly, is everywhere imitated by national leaders. In adopting a Bayesian model of decision making, the forecaster is thus using a model that is a universally appropriate first approximation.

III. THE BAYESIAN FORECASTING FRAMEWORK

Overview

The present framework draws upon both stages of the typical Bayesian decision analytic approach. It treats the decisional stage as a generic submodel of national leaders' learning processes. Taken together, these two submodels form a model of dynamic subjective processes that, when used in simulate systems, provides the forecaster with a new capability: By supplying his insights into the current states of subjective variables, and by manipulating these variables within reasonable limits, the forecaster can systematically explore future behavioral implications.

In applying the framework, the forecaster assumes the simple relationship between the two submodels that is depicted in Figure 10.1. Figure 10.1 is divided into two phases. The Bayesian phase governs the decision making—and the behavior—of the actor on whose behavior the analyst is concentrating. The environmental phase produces information (possibly in response to the behavioral output of the Bayesian phase) that is returned to the Bayesian phase. The analyst may use any reasonable device to generate the informational output of the environmental phase: he might personally play the roles of objective factors and of other actors in the system, he might use other relevant models to generate environmental data, and/or he might have the output of the environmental phase in part determined by other Bayesian processes representing other actors. The last is necessarily the case when the analyst wants to examine the implications of interaction among two or more national actors into whose subjective processes he has some insights.

In the decisional stage of the Bayesian phase, the simulate decision maker surveys his options and assesses each in terms of two sets of data: his utility (or loss) functions associated with various outcomes and his subjective probabilities with respect to the future states (as in "states of nature") that might occasion these outcomes. If the decision maker is

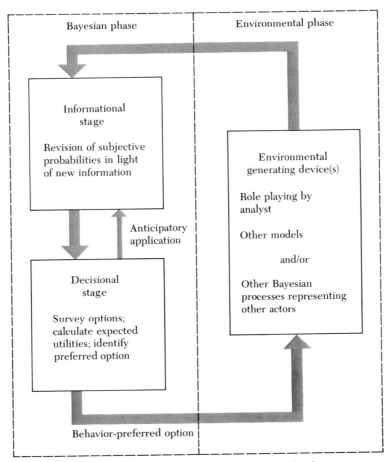

Figure 10.1 Overview of the framework; the flow of information.

assumed to foresee the possibility of change over time in his option selection—if, that is, his current behavior is at least partially experimental or tentative in nature—he applies informational stage procedures in order to anticipate possible future contingencies and avoid unnecessarily foreclosing potentially viable future options. The decision maker calculates expected utilities and identifies a preferred option: the option of the highest expected utility (or least expected loss). The actor's behavior conforms to the preferred option.

The behavior emerging from the decisional stage then enters the environmental phase where it interacts with other variables and perhaps influences the environmental output—the information returning to the informational stage of the Bayesian phase.

In the informational stage, the simulate decision maker looks upon the new information as a "sampling" from the environment. He applies Bayesian procedures to revise his prior (pre-"sampling") judgmental probabilities in light of this new information. He creates posterior judgmental probabilities. These posteriors are then introduced into the decisional stage where they are treated as new priors (with respect to the next choice and its consequences). And the process continues.

The general flow of information indicated by Figure 10.1 might be suggestive of a simple S-R model; but when one turns to what goes on within the submodels of the Bayesian phase, all resemblance to an S-R model ceases. The framework assumes that the subjective processes of national leaders are much more sophisticated than those suggested by a classical conditioning model. National leaders see subtle connections among apparently disparate events. They make generalizations. They draw inferences, albeit sometimes the wrong ones. They do not require immediate rewards and punishments in order to learn. The Bayesian framework permits the forecaster to put to work what knowledge he has about these complicated subjective processes.

An Illustrative Application

Precisely how this is accomplished will become clearer in an illustrative review of one possible application of the framework. This subsection will consider how an analyst might approach the Sino-Soviet border dispute. For the sake of brevity, and in order to keep the thrust of the review where it belongs—on the use of the framework and not on the intricacies of Sino-Soviet relations—this example will ignore many important substantive factors that would rightly and easily be included were this a seriously analytic rather than a purely suggestive exercise. For the same reasons, this subsection will review only a portion of a complete analysis. It will illustrate how an analyst might proceed, but it will not trace his every step.

Suppose that an analyst who is familiar with the contemporary history of Sino-Soviet relations decides to use the framework to generate forecasts of future Soviet behaviors toward China conditional on alternative Chinese behavior patterns. He believes that his insights into Soviet values, beliefs, and expectations with respect to Sino-Soviet relations will permit the useful application of the framework to Soviet subjective processes. But his insights into Chinese subjective processes are limited, so he decides to develop a number of plausible alternative Chinese behavior patterns, play these himself in a series of runs, and thereby develop projections of Soviet behavior conditioned on Chinese behavior (*inter alia*).

The analyst begins this effort by identifying seven behavioral options available to the Soviet Union. These are listed in Table 10.4. In the analyst's view, these are the options that the Soviets have available to influence the "outcome" of Sino-Soviet relations.

Next, the analyst determines that, although he is personally interested in short-range forecasting, Soviet leaders are taking a somewhat

Table 10.4 Soviet behavioral options.

X1	Appeasement	Withdraw troops and arms from border region; renounce use of force; propose, begin, or continue to negotiate formally; make major territorial, leadership, and ideological concessions
X2	Conciliation	Symbolic troop cuts; renounce use of force unless attacked; propose, begin, or continue to negotiate formally; make minor, symbolic concessions.
X3	Firmness	Maintain border military strength; no use of force; propose, begin, or continue to negotiate formally, stand firm on disputed issues
X4	Pressure	Build border capabilities slightly; threaten, but do not use, force; propose, begin, or continue to negotiate formally; state demands on disputed issues
X5	Coercion	Major increases in border military capabilities; initiate border skirmishes, minor incursions; make threats of escalation; urge negotiation or continue to negotiate; make demands on disputed issues
X6	Limited war	Large-scale mobilization and reinforcement of Eastern military forces; initiate large-scale, but restrained invasion (limited to border provinces with objective of securing defensive positions); counterforce nuclear strike; issue demands; threaten escalation
X7	All-out war	National mobilization; vast West-to-East redeployment of troops; full-scale invasion with objective of gaining control of CPR territory and population; counterforce and countervalue nuclear strikes; issue demands; urge surrender, capitulation of Mao regime

longer-range perspective on Sino-Soviet relations. A relatively complete picture of relevant Soviet interests, he decides, can be framed within the next 3 or so years. The worst possible outcome of which Soviet leaders can conceive contains these elements: a persistently hostile Chinese leadership plus an "unacceptable" level of Chinese military (primarily nuclear) capabilities. Given present trends, the Soviet leaders —according to the analyst—project such an outcome in about 3 years.

The analyst thus portrays a commanding issue underlying Soviet decision making: How best to avoid or prevent such an outcome. One response could be limited war or even all-out war. Although the leaders are reasonably confident that these options would now result in a Soviet victory—and would prevent the Chinese from obtaining an "unacceptable" level of military capabilities—these options do have immediate costs. Pursuit of these options would risk heavy losses of men and materiel; nuclear catastrophe could be risked; there are the intangible psychic costs associated with a decision to initiate war; attention and resources would be diverted from the West. Other, less violent options are presently available. These offer slimmer chances of insuring that Chinese capabilities do not reach "unacceptable" levels, but they are less likely to reinforce Chinese hostility and to produce the immediate costs associated with the violent options. If a nonviolent option (say "pressure" or "firmness") succeeds, then the costs of a violent option need never be incurred. On the other hand, if the nonviolent options are pursued and continue to fail, then the costs of the pursuit of a violent option later will be greater than they would be today (because Chinese strength continues to grow). This is the dilemma faced by Soviet leaders. It is a dynamic situation.

In judging the efficacy of each option—that is, whether each option tends to reduce or inhibit tendencies toward Chinese strength and hostility 3 years hence—the Soviet must look to clues in Chinese behavior, for future levels of hostility and strength cannot be observed directly today. According to the analyst, these clues are contained in three Chinese behavioral realms (see Table 10.5). By observing behaviors within each of these realms, the Soviets can gain some appreciation of, and revise their expectations about, the future levels of Chinese hostility and strength. China's deciding to negotiate formally, for example, might be viewed by the Soviets as an opportunity to settle disputed issues and thus lessen Chinese hostility. Similarly, a Chinese reduction in border military capabilities in the face of Soviet coercion might be viewed as an indication of Chinese weakness.

Having verbally portrayed the situation as viewed by Soviet leaders, the analyst attempts to reconstruct it in Bayesian decision analytic terms. He begins by developing a decision flow diagram that is as true as possible to Soviet perceptions of the situation. This tree diagram is illustrated in Figure 10.2. The initial branch point represents the current choice situation: the Soviets are free to select any one of the seven options.

The diagram indicates that in choosing an option, the Soviet leadership (hereafter SL) looks ahead one decision point (to the third set of branch points). They know that future decisions will be made in light of the new information contained in the clues following the current decision (the second set). They know also that following these clues they might find another option preferable to the one currently chosen. And they know that the continual growth of Chinese capabilities will affect their evaluation of future outcomes—making some options more costly with the passage of time. By looking one decision point ahead, SL, it is assumed, hopes to avoid choosing an option now that will foreclose—or make excessively costly—potentially viable future options.

Figure 10.2 departs from the typical decision flow diagram in two minor respects. First, it does not show all of the branch points throughout the three year period. There is no need to (given the assumption that the Soviets look ahead one decision point).[7] After the Soviets make a choice among options and witness con-

Table 10.5 Chinese behavioral realms.

Violence and Force		Negotiation		Border Military Capabilities	
V1	Do not use	N1	Negotiate formally	C1	Decrease
V2	Threaten but do not use	N2	Do not negotiate	C2	Maintain
V3	Skirmish and threaten			C3	Increase

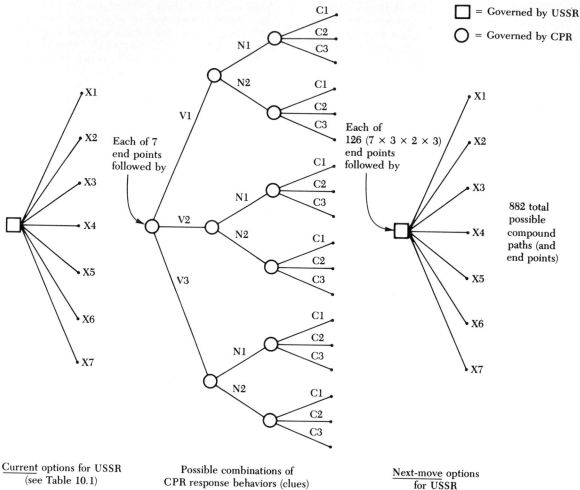

Figure 10.2 Decision flow diagram.

sequences, they advance to a new decision point that is exactly analogous (except for changes in probability entries) to the initial decision point. Second, there are no outcomes listed at the end of the branches that are shown. For most options, the Soviets are not immediately rewarded or penalized in any concrete way. Instead, they gradually become informed as to the rewards and penalties that they will eventually incur.

The analyst's next step is to assign probabilities to each of the branches governed by the CPR (indicated by 0 in Figure 10.2). He tries to assign the same probabilities that a Soviet decision maker would assign. The probabilities that he assigns now are initial prob-

abilities (priors) to be revised and revised again as interaction proceeds. These probabilities can differ from option to option. To gain an appreciation of how the analyst assigns and uses these probabilities, we will focus on the way he approaches one particular option, coercion (X5), and those branches that stem from it.

The first question that the analyst asks is this: If I (as a Soviet leader) were to continue pursuit of the coercion option throughout the next 3 years, what are my expectations regarding Chinese hostility and strength at the end of this period? He decides that coercion would probably exacerbate Chinese hostility while simultaneously encouraging the Chinese to step up

Table 10.6 Conditional relationships between Chinese behaviors and future strength.

State-component	Prior	a V1	V2	V3	b N1	N2	c C1	C2	C3
S1	.3	.109 (.033)	.399 (.120)	.491 (.147)	.730 (.219)	.270 (.081)	.280 (.084)	.560 (.168)	.160 (.048)
S2	.7	.096 (.067)	.400 (.280)	.504 (.353)	.544 (.381)	.456 (.319)	.023 (.016)	.474 (.332)	.503 (.352)
		.1	.4	.5	.6	.4	.1	.5	.4

the pace of counter-Soviet capability building. After careful thought, he assigns the following judgmental probabilities to the two state-components (hostility and strength):

H1: CPR hostility at acceptable level $P(H1) = .2$
H2: CPR hostility at unacceptable level $P(H2) = .8$
S1: CPR strength at acceptable level $P(S1) = .3$
S2: CPR strength at unacceptable level $P(S2) = .7$.

These probabilities, it must be emphasized, are conditional on the continued choice of the coercion option; quite different probabilities might be associated with these state-components given the Soviet pursuit of other options.

It is crucial for the analyst also to make some judgments about the conditional probabilities of future events (i.e., clues implicit in CPR behavior). These probabilities are conditional in the sense that they are believed to be reflections of trends in Chinese strength and hostility. The analyst constructs tables indicating his understanding of how the Soviets see these condi-

tional relationships. Table 10.6 shows conditional relationships between Chinese behaviors and future strength. Table 10.7 shows conditional relationships between these same Chinese behaviors and future hostility.

Each nonparenthesized figure in each table indicates the probability of imminent Chinese behavior in that column *given the tendency toward the future state-component indicated by the row.* The figures in parentheses indicate the unconditional probability of the concurrence of a row state-component and a column behavior. The marginals—which are the sums of the parenthesized entries of their respective columns—are the unconditional probabilities of their respective column behaviors. It should be noted that these marginals remain the same in both tables. All figures are conditioned on the assumption of continued Soviet coercive behavior.

How does one interpret these tables? As a rule, the more the nonparenthesized column entries deviate from their respective column marginals, the greater the conceived dependency relationship of behavior on state-component. In Section *b* of Table 10.6 this

Table 10.7 Conditional relationships between Chinese behaviors and future hostility.

State-component	Prior	a V1	V2	V3	b N1	N2	c C1	C2	C3
H1	.2	.211 (.042)	.460 (.092)	.330 (.066)	.880 (.176)	.120 (.024)	.240 (.048)	.480 (.096)	.280 (.056)
H2	.8	.073 (.058)	.385 (.308)	.542 (.434)	.530 (.424)	.470 (.376)	.065 (.052)	.505 (.404)	.430 (.344)
		.1	.4	.5	.6	.4	.1	.5	.4

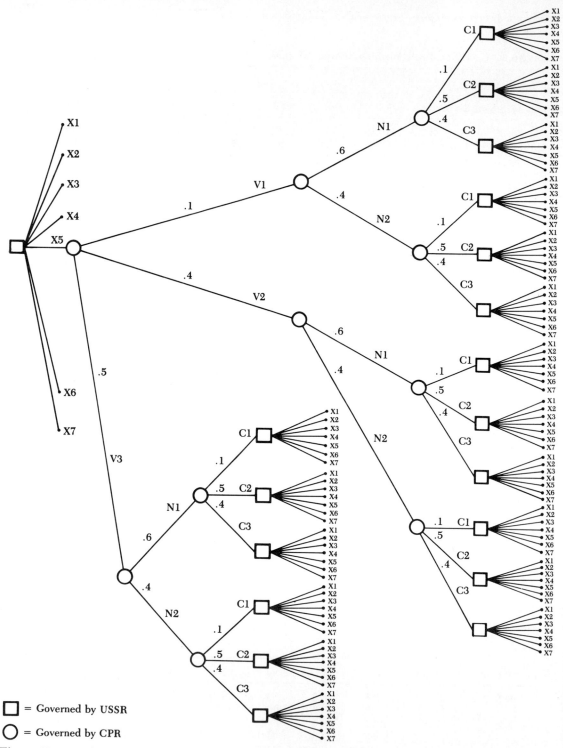

Figure 10.3 Probabilities of Chinese responses given Soviet coercion. Multiplying all probabilities on a compound path yields probability of response combination. (Probabilities are from the marginals of Tables 10.3 and 10.4.)

deviation is quite pronounced—suggesting a conception of a high degree of dependence of Chinese negotiation behavior on tendencies toward strength. In Section *a* of Table 10.6, by contrast, all column entries converge on their respective marginals—indicating a conception of immediate Chinese violent responses to Soviet coercive behavior as independent of tendencies toward strength.

Because the analyst assumes that SL does not know which of the future state components will obtain, he enters the column marginal probabilities on the appropriate branches of the decision tree—those stemming to the right of the coercion option (X5). See Figure 10.3.

The analyst now turns to the task of evaluating outcomes as SL is presumed to evaluate them. It should be recalled that outcomes are identified in terms of specific combinations of options and states. Utilities or losses cannot be attached to states alone unless the Soviet evaluation of a state is unaffected by the Soviet options pursued.

The analyst constructs an outcome matrix (see Figure 10.4). The rows of this matrix are defined by the seven Soviet behavioral options. The columns are defined by the four possible combinations of state-components. Each cell represents an outcome. The entry in each cell is the "loss" (i.e., negative utility) associated with each outcome by Soviet leaders (in the analyst's opinion). The value represents the currently perceived loss.

These values need not be assigned as if SL engages in systematic cost-benefit analyses, always gauging outcomes against a clearly defined set of concrete national interests. Instead, a loss value can reflect a variety of considerations that are taken into account, both explicitly and implicitly, by Soviet leaders. These considerations can range from the desire to resolve bureaucratic conflicts to the desire to avoid psychological stress, from the desire to improve economic conditions to the desire to maintain a position of strength with respect to the West.

The probabilistic theory of utility will not be detailed here except to emphasize one important characteristic. Utilities indicate more than a rank-ordering of preferences among outcomes. Both utilities and losses reflect an interval scale weighting of outcomes.

The matrix of Figure 10.4 is the current matrix in that the losses there displayed reflect the analyst's conception of the losses that the Soviets would associate with the various outcomes given that they were to immediately pursue the option of the corresponding row. Quite different losses might be associated with the later pursuit of an option not pursued now.

Since SL is presumed always to look ahead one move, and since SL's perceptions of the losses associated with outcomes can change from move to move, the analyst needs a way of producing losses to be associated with possible next move situations. The analyst believes that the losses that the Soviets will perceive at the next move will reflect Chinese behavior in the interim. In particular, he feels that an increase in Chinese border capabilities will suggest to the Soviets an increase in the costs of outcomes associated with violent options; other Chinese behaviors, he feels, will have little or no impact on Soviet perceptions of losses.

The analyst chooses one among many approaches to introducing this relationship into his analysis: For all compound paths of Chinese responses in which response C3 (capability increase) appears, he adds the matrix of currently perceived losses to a second matrix (see Figure 10.5); this produces next-move matrices in which the losses associated with violent options are increased (Figure 10.6). For all compound paths that do not include C3, he retains the original matrix.

Let us summarize what the analyst has done so far:

1. He has indicated options available to Soviet leaders.

States

	H1,S1	H2,S1	H1,S2	H2,S2
X1	.14	.28	.49	.63
X2	.09	.24	.45	.61
X3	.05	.21	.43	.59
X4	.07	.23	.44	.61
X5	.18	.27	.48	.66
X6	.29	.35	.59	.78
X7	.43	.58	.79	.92

(Options)

Figure 10.4 Losses associated with current Soviet options, given Chinese hostility (H) and strength (S) levels.

0	0	0	0
0	0	0	0
0	0	0	0
0	0	0	0
.01	.01	.01	.01
.02	.02	.02	.02
.03	.03	.03	.03

Figure 10.5 Additional losses associated with current Soviet options, given Figure 10.4 and a Chinese response of capability increases (C3).

		States			
		H1,S1	H2,S1	H1,S2	H2,S2
Options	X1	.14	.28	.49	.63
	X2	.09	.24	.45	.61
	X3	.05	.21	.43	.59
	X4	.07	.23	.44	.61
	X5	.19	.28	.49	.67
	X6	.31	.37	.61	.80
	X7	.46	.61	.82	.95

Figure 10.6 Losses associated with next Soviet option, summing Tables 10.4 and 10.5 and showing effect of projected violent Chinese behavior.

2. He has defined the future states—which include combinations of Chinese hostility components and strength components—with which Soviet leaders are presumably concerned.

3. He has identified Chinese behavioral signals—those forms of Chinese behavior that are suggestive to SL of the probabilities of future state-components.

4. He has constructed a tree diagram that displays all current options, all possible combinations of response signals, and all available options at the next move.

5. He has established prior Soviet judgmental probabilities for ·the possible state-components. These differ from option to option.

6. He has developed tables indicating the conditional dependence of possible Chinese behavioral signals on future state-components as presumably perceived by SL. These, too, may differ from option to option.

7. He has entered the marginals from these tables in his decision tree.

8. He has developed a current outcome matrix; and he has included loss functions which reflect his understanding of how SL would integrate a wide variety of considerations in the evaluation of outcomes.

9. He has devised a procedure for the updating of Soviet conceptions of losses in view of (and in anticipation of) changes in circumstances indicated by Chinese behaviors.

The analyst has now provided sufficient data for the continuing operation of simulate Soviet processes in light of and in response to Chinese behaviors. Having also determined a pattern of

Chinese behavior that he will personally "play," the analyst is now ready to systematically explore implications for Soviet behavior.

The process commences in the decisional stage with SL selecting an initial option. According to the Bayesian decision principle, SL will select the option of the least expected loss. Bayesian decision analysis provides a straightforward procedure for the determination of the expected loss of an option. Let us see how it is applied to the coercion option for which we have complete data (see Figure 10.3).

Because SL is always looking ahead one move, SL first focuses on the "next-move" decision points. Moving from decision point to decision point, SL in effect asks: If after selecting the current option I find myself at this point (i.e., if I witness the compound path of CPR responses leading to this point), what will my expected loss be? The answer, for each branch point, is that the expected loss would be the expected loss of the option that SL would select on the next move—given the changes in SL's judgmental probabilities and utilities that would be precipitated by the compound path leading to each point.

So, at each "next-move" branch point, SL takes the following steps:

1. Revise probabilities *as if* the associated compound path of Chinese responses was in fact observed (e.g., for the uppermost branch point, revise probabilities as if Chinese responses V1, N1, C1 were in fact observed).

2. Revise losses—using the appropriate transformation matrices—*as if* the corresponding compound path of Chinese responses was in fact observed.

3. With this new information (plus the information about the probabilities of state-components that is associated with each of the other six options), determine the expected loss of each option at this branch point.

4. Identify the option of the least expected loss. The expected loss of this option is the expected loss associated with this branch point.

In taking these steps, SL is not assumed to look ahead to the next, next move; SL calculates expected losses on the basis of next-move losses and next-move subjective probabilities. The following calculations correspond to steps 1, 2, and 3 for the coercion option at the next-move branch point following V1, N1, C1. The resulting expected loss for this option is .232. If this is the least expected loss among options at this

next-move branch point, then the expected loss for this branch point is .232.

SL takes these steps for all eighteen branch points. S1 identifies eighteen possible expected losses following the current selection of the coercion option; each is labeled $EL'(X5, Vi, Nj, Ck)$ according to the particular compound path that leads to it.[8]

SL can now calculate the expected loss associated with the selection of the coercion option at the current decision point. This expected loss, $EL(X5)$, is calculated by weighting each of the possible next-move expected losses by the probability of the compound CPR response path that would occasion it and summing across all compound paths. Thus:

$$EL(X5) = P(V1)P(N1)P(C1)EL'(X5,V1,N1,C1) \\ + P(V1)P(N1)P(C2)EL'(X5,V1,N1,C2) \\ + \ldots \\ + P(V3)P(N2)P(C3)EL'(X5,V3,N2,C3).$$

Step 1 Revise probabilities as if V1, N1, C1 was in fact observed. Bayes theorem is used:

$$P(S1|V1,N1,C1) = \frac{P(S1)P(V1|S1)P(N1|S1)P(C1|S1)}{P(S1)P(V1|S1)P(N1|S1)P(C1|S1) + P(S2)P(V1|S2)P(N1|S2)P(C1|S2)}$$
$$= \frac{(.3)(.109)(.730)(.280)}{(.3)(.109)(.730)(.280) + (.7)(.096)(.544)(.023)}$$
$$= .888.$$

Similar calculations give

$$P(S2|V1,N1,C1) = .112$$
$$P(H1|V1,N1,C1) = .816$$
$$P(H2|V1,N1,C1) = .184.$$

Step 2 Revise losses. Since C3 is not included in the path V1,N1,C1, the original matrix (Figure 10.4) is retained.

Step 3 Determine the expected loss of the coercion option at this branch point. First, determine the probabilities of the four states by taking the products of the probabilities of their respective state components:

$$P(H1,S1) = P(H1|V1,N1,C1) \cdot P(S1|V1,N1,C1)$$
$$= (.816) \cdot (.888) = .725$$
$$P(H2,S1) = (.184) \cdot (.888) = .163$$
$$P(H1,S2) = (.816) \cdot (.112) = .091$$
$$P(H2,S2) = (.184) \cdot (.112) = .021.$$

Second, weight each loss from the X5 row in the matrix of Figure 10.4 by the probability of the corresponding state; the expected loss of this option (X5) at this branch point is labeled $EL'(X5,V1,N1,C1,X5)$.

$$EL'(X5,V1,N1,C1,X5) = (.725)(.18) + (.163)(.27) + (.091)(.48) + (.021)(.66)$$
$$= .232.$$

SL similarly calculates expected losses for each of the other six of its current options. SL selects the current option of the least expected loss. This concludes the decisional stage.

Let us suppose, for the sake of convenience, that SL chose the coercion option. Let us also assume that the analyst's predetermined behavior pattern for China indicates a Chinese response to coercion that includes skirmishing and threatening, a refusal to negotiate formally, and an increase in border military capabilities (V3,N2,C3). How does SL revise its subjective probabilities?

The information of the preceding paragraph is returned to SL's informational stage where SL proceeds to revise its judgmental probabilities associated with the coercion option. The procedure has in fact been anticipated in the decisional stage (see the earlier calculations for such an example). SL applies Bayes' theorem to its conditional probability tables given the data V3, N2, C3. The application produces posterior probabilities for the state-components: $P(S1) = .073$), $P(S2) = .927$, $P(H1) = .025$, and $P(H2) = .975$. The judgmental probabilities of unacceptable levels of hostility and strength associated with the coercion option have increased markedly.

This concludes the informational stage. The revised probabilities are passed to the decisional stage preceding SL's second move. SL uses these revised probabilities to look one move ahead, to anticipate change, and to respond accordingly.

The analyst will continue the process through several iterations and systematically observe future behaviors given his assumptions and data, and given his predetermined Chinese behavior pattern. If the analyst is responsible, he will undertake several such runs, varying data and relationships, thereby gaining an understanding of the sensitivity of Soviet behaviors.

This example has necessarily been limited. It considers only a limited number of Soviet behavioral options. It assumes that the Soviets are concerned only with two state-components—future Chinese hostility and strength. It treats states as discrete variables when they could (and probably should) be treated as continuous dimensions. It neglects many Chinese behavioral signals that the Soviets would consider salient. It takes a rather rudimentary view of Bayesian probability revision procedures—addressing only firm probabilities and

totally ignoring applications to judgmental density functions—thereby forfeiting the capacity to capture some of the subtleties of Soviet prior expectations. It assumes that the Soviets see no probabilistic interdependencies among Chinese behavioral signals or among state-components. It analyzes only Soviet behaviors in Bayesian terms. And, most importantly, it adheres strictly to Bayesian choice theoretical prescriptions and makes no explicit adjustments in order to accommodate process theoretical propositions.

The particular virtue of the Bayesian approach, however, is that it is flexible enough to overcome all of these limitations. A Bayesian framework offers the analyst guidance; it provides the analyst with reasonably concrete directions as to the types of relationships to look for and the types of data to supply. At the same time, a Bayesian framework grants the analyst considerable latitude in the specification of utilities (or losses), probabilities, conditional relationships, behavioral variables, states, environmental characteristics, and the like. And because Bayesian decision analytic prescriptions are decomposable into "steps" and "subroutines," the forecaster interested in asserting process theoretical propositions will discover (1) that he can readily identify the logical points at which to assert and operationalize these propositions, and (2) that in the process he does not undermine other parts of the framework.

A Brief Appraisal of the Bayesian Approach

Theory. This chapter has presented Bayesian decision theory as an appropriate and promising approach to the analysis of subjective factors and processes in international relations. Bayesian decision analysis is a choice theory. It is prescriptive. And, with a little imagination, one can envision policy prescriptive applications for the framework presented here. But this chapter has suggested that the framework has descriptive potential; and it has emphasized a central role for the framework in forecasting.

A list of some of the more prominent propositions emerging from process theories of decision making might seem to indicate that Bayesian decision analysis is poorly cast in this forecasting role—that, while the Bayesian is right in prescribing behavior, he is probably wrong if he assumes that the behaviors of national leaders will conform to his prescriptions. As Braybrooke and Lindblom (1963) have argued, decision makers generally do not possess "synoptic conceptions" of their decision problems; that is, they generally do not carefully array all of their options and potential consequences, weigh each, and choose the one that stands up best. According to Simon (1969), selection among options more often takes the form of "satisficing"—pursuing the first option that is "good enough." Bureaucracies tend to make decisions "by branch" rather than "by root"—incrementalism prevails (Lindblom, 1959, pp. 79–88). Seldom do all members of a decision-making body share exactly the same values; individuals are sometimes motivated by considerations, often quite personal ones, that are totally extraneous to the group decision problem. Faulty perceptions, caused by a variety of factors, can lead to faulty conclusions, to poor analyses, and ultimately to nonproductive or counterproductive decisions.

While a review of these and other propositions does suggest that the Bayesian framework cannot be applied to specific cases without substantial modifications inspired by process theory, it also underscores the theoretical centrality of a decision-making ideal type. This ideal type is sometimes called the rational model of decision making. It is usually discussed on an abstract plane. Its use as an ideal type is often left implicit in process theoretical analyses. But, as the propositions of the preceding paragraph indicate, process theorists are generally oriented toward describing and explaining deviations from this model.

Bayesian decision theorists, too, have begun with this model. They have sought to devise means by which a decision maker can realize its ideals. But they have also understood that the decision maker is imperfect and that he operates in an uncertain environment. Consequently, Bayesian decision analysts have chosen to descend from the lofty abstractions of the rational model and to construct a model of logically consistent, systematic decision making. In the process, Bayesian decision analysts have developed a new ideal type—a new ideal type that could perhaps prove as serviceable for process theorists as for decision makers.

Bayesian decision analysis, then, is a likely candidate for the core of a forecasting framework designed for the analysis of subjective process simply because something quite similar to the Bayesian ideal is already a central, unifying conceptualization among descriptive process theories. In using Bayesian decision analysis as a generic first approximation, the analyst will in effect be defining a foundation on which otherwise disjointed process theoretical propositions can be structured.

The analyst might, for example, operationalize propositions suggesting incrementalism and satisficing by modifying the Bayesian option comparison procedures such that options most nearly approximating "what has been done in the past" are compared first and such that the comparison of options stops when an acceptable utility (or loss) level is reached. The analyst might also simulate perceptual phenomena by introducing a perceptual filter between environmental output and the Bayesian informational stage.[9]

This is not to say that Bayesian decision analysis can encompass and adequately simulate all aspects of subjective processes. Bayesian decision analysis does have limitations. One of the more serious of these is that Bayesian decision analytic prescriptions were designed to permit the decision maker to operate in environments governed by unintelligent factors about which he is uncertain—factors like the existence or nonexistence of a market for a product or the presence or absence of oil at a specific locus.

A national leader's environment is affected by the behaviors of other intelligent actors. He understands that other actors' decisions and consequent behaviors are governed by subjective processes much like his own. His decisions will not only reflect what he has learned—as the Bayesian structure indicates—but also will reflect attempts to teach, to influence the expectation revision processes of other actors.[10]

Such teaching/learning processes are the stuff of bargaining and negotiation theories. These processes are evident in the tacit communication that is to be found in deterrence relationships, arms races, and conflict spirals wherein each participant attempts to influence the others' expectations as to the consequences that they will incur in the pursuit of various options.

While the Bayesian framework adequately accounts for learning and adjustment (more correctly, adaptation), its facilities for dealing with attempts to teach or influence are insufficiently specified.

The analyst can imply the existence of national leaders' perceptions as to such influence relationships in his specification of prior judgmental probabilities. But there is no facility for handling such relationships explicitly, dynamically, and within the structure itself. This constitutes a major deficiency in the framework—one that can be at least partially overcome by borrowing from game theory, a close kin of Bayesian decision analysis.

Methodology. Data cannot be divorced from theory in the analysis of the subjective. The inferential distance between the analyst's concepts and their real-world counterparts is so great, the obstacles inhibiting the direct observation of variables are so difficult to overcome, that the analyst must ultimately rely upon his models in order to infer the qualities of current beliefs, expectations, and values. For the potential user of the framework, this situation presents two related sets of problems: problems in specification and problems in evaluation.

In specifying data (utilities and probabilities) and structural relationships, the analyst will encounter some rather severe ambiguities. He must rely upon models in order to infer the current characteristics of national leaders' values, beliefs, expectations, perceptions, and relationships among these variables; and he will find that there are at least as many possible ways to specify these as there are models. If the analyst is unable to satisfy himself that one model is uniquely valid, then he must include his specifications of data and parameters in his catalogue of "ifs" upon which his forecasts are based.

In such ambiguous circumstances, to rely upon only one set of specifications is to run the risk of basing forecasts upon so-called "counterfactual conditionals." The alternative—the only alternative when one examines such cloudy areas—is to exhaustively explore the implications of meaningful ranges of possible data and parameter specifications, to do sensitivity analyses.

In order to engage in sensitivity analysis, the analyst must be prepared to produce and manipulate large quantities of data. Unfortunately, although the current structure will rapidly process data, it provides no facilities for the generation, cataloguing, storage, and retrieval of data sets. It is left to the analyst to devise the means by which he can systematically produce and manipulate the ranges of data necessary to undertake a thorough analysis of specific subjective processes. And it is possible that the vast quantities of data required by the structure will simply overwhelm the analyst.

The second problem, one of evaluation, is closely related to the first. In general, if a model's predictions and postdictions are found—after repeated examination—to be always accurate, one may conclude that the model has "predictive validity." But it is more often the case that a model's predictions are only close or are sometimes on- and sometimes off-target. The responsible forecaster will then be concerned with reexamining and improving the model.

In this effort, the analyst of the subjective encounters particular difficulties in that his inferential distance from the operational variables of concern inhibits his ability to identify precisely his theoretical misspecifications. Because he cannot directly observe changes in expectations, beliefs, perceptions, and values—but can only infer them from observable behaviors that are related to these subjective variables in complex ways—the analyst of the subjective confronted with predictive failures is not immediately enlightened as to which components of his theory are misspecified.

NOTES

1. For an introduction to Bayesian decision analysis, it is useful to consult the following: Raiffa and Schlaifer (1961); Schlaifer (1967); Raiffa (1968). A helpful, short overview can also be found in Stael von Holstein, (1970), particularly Chapter 14.
2. This generalization is perhaps best restricted to highly systematic forecasting efforts. It is true that subjective variables have not been wholly ignored in the broad forecasting realm, but, in general, consideration of these variables has been confined to the less disciplined, more speculative forecasting approaches in which the relationships between current and future behaviors and circumstances are less than explicit. A noteworthy exception is the application of artificial intelligence models to forecasting, which, unfortunately, has so far been limited to institutional settings; see Alker and Christensen (1972.)
3. It should be noted that in practice these two stages are not nearly as neatly bounded as this paragraph might suggest. In practice, for example, one option often considered in the decisional stage is to seek more information (i.e., return to the informational stage) before acting; especially when decision makers

contemplate the value of additional information, the boundaries between the two stages are little more than nominal.

4. Considerable work has been done on the development of easily specified, easily manipulated prior distributions which represent relative ignorance (i.e., the state of being uninformed). See Jeffreys (1961) and Zellner (1971), pp. 41–53.

5. B. W. Lindgren compares and contrasts Bayesian and non-Bayesian decision principles in his *Elements of Decision Theory* (1971). The game theoretical minimax principle is a non-Bayesian principle because it assumes no information.

6. The term "Bayes' loss" is, of course, most appropriately applied to "losses" (which may be viewed as negatively valued utilities).

7. Moreover, it would be nearly impossible to display a decision tree covering 3 years. If a decision is made just once a month, such a tree would have 126^{36} final branches.

8. The prime notation is used to denote the fact that this is a second-order expectation, that the term refers to expectations at the "next-move."

9. Such a filter could be governed by a random number generator which in turn is cued by current values of subjective probabilities. A tendency to filter out—or distort—inconsistent or "dissonant" perceptions could thus be introduced.

10. I am grateful to Walter Isard for helping me to clarify this issue at the Northeast Peace Science Society section at Syracuse University, March, 1973.

CHAPTER ELEVEN

ELEMENTARY PROCESS MODELS: THEIR PLACE IN INTERNATIONAL RELATIONS FORECASTING

David Scott Ross

Forecasting projects in international relations often employ a simple trend extrapolation or large, complex models. Between these extremes, other mathematical forms are available. Elementary process models are one such group and appear suited to many forecasting problems. They emphasize process description or explanation, thus improving on naive trend extrapolation. But they retain simplicity and comprehensibility, which larger models often lack. Further, while many of the techniques described in this volume are new to the field, elementary process models employ more familiar approaches. These characteristics suggest a place for such models in international relations forecasting.

To examine their role, we consider model characteristics and structures. Further, forecasts and their evaluations and uses are explored. Finally, three forecasting exercises illustrate the arguments and a range of applications.

I. ELEMENTARY PROCESS MODELS

Any simple probabilistic or statistical model that describes or explains the process determining a phenomenon's characteristics over time will be classified as an elementary process model (EPM). The phenomenon may be either an event, such as mobilization; a class of events, such as riots; or a variable, such as the annual foreign aid commitment. Events may be frequent or infrequent; variables may be discrete or continuous. Therefore, any international phenomenon may be accommodated.

The characteristics of interest will often include an event's likelihood or a variable's value at some future time. Additionally, the certainty of these claims will require examination.

So far, trend extrapolation could have the same characteristics. However, the focus on descriptions or explanations of the generating process differentiates the EPM. Associated with each model is an interpretation specifying the analyst's conjectures or beliefs. These result from theoretical deduction, observational induction or speculation. Regardless of source, EPMs should be available to embody simple process descriptions or explanations.

Several kinds of elementary process models may be distinguished. They overlap considerably because of their diachronic concern and reliance on probability and statistics. But each implies particular process descriptions and has an associated literature. Therefore, we identify four classes of EPMs: stochastic processes, time series models, structural equation models, and probabilistic difference or differential equation models.

All EPMs take their metaphysics from the literature on stochastic processes. They assume that reality is a single realization of an underlying possibility space or probability distribution. In this sense, all EPMs are stochastic processes.[1] On the other hand, they also provide the simplest process models. For example, the underlying distribution may be fixed and constant. Or, it may depend straightforwardly on prior realizations. One exercise treats assassinations as drawings from a constant Poisson process. A second exercise uses Markov chains to describe guerrilla warfare. In this case, the probabilities depend on the presence or absence of warfare in the preceding year.

The theory of more general stochastic processes provides the foundation for time series models employed by Box and Jenkins.[2] Two basic forms are combined to produce the other time series models. The autoregressive (AR) model describes a variable's value as a linear function of its prior values and a random shock. A first order autoregressive process, depending only on the immediately preceding period's value, is therefore a particular form of Markov process. The other basic time series model is the moving average (MA) model that describes a variable's value as a linear function of the current and past random shocks. In combination, the autoregressive integrated moving average (ARIMA) model is capable of describing and forecasting many time series.[3] Further, they provide a particular specification for the generating process.

Time series models are also closely related to structural equation models (see Hibbs, Jr., 1974, for a comparison). However, the latter emphasize theoretically determined, causal relations between variables. As such, structural equation models supply explanations rather than descriptions. Particular interest focuses on econometric time series models with lagged endogenous variables, since the feedback structure influences process dynamics. The last exercise explains US and Soviet defense expenditures with a structural equation model.

Finally, probabilistic difference or differential equation models may be EPMs. Their connection to both time series and structural equation models with lagged endogenous variables is straightforward. But they have an independent literature focusing on rates of change and stability that sets them apart. Richardson's differential equations for action-reaction processes are a long-standing exemplar (Richardson, 1960a and 1960b).

Obviously, not all models from these four classes will be EPMs. As they expand to include more variables, more equations and more complex functions, they will depart from the EPM's goal of simplicity. To constrain the size and form of acceptable models, the following heuristics are offered.

EPMs should employ a limited number of endogenous, exogenous and/or random variables. The total number of variables should be less than 5 or 6, with only 2 or 3 endogenous. The functions or distributions employed should be simple. Simplicity implies that the form is well understood and commonly employed. Thus, linear functions and normal distributions are simple, while many nonlinear functions and multivariate distributions are not. Finally, additional constraints or flexibility may result with particular model types. For example, time series models may be employed for very complex phenomena by transforming or differencing the observed series, thus simplifying subsequent calculations. But estimation of ARIMA models where the order of the moving average process is greater than two or three proves difficult because of nonlinearities (see Box and Jenkins, 1970).

While a wide range of international relations phenomena may be described with this repetoire, EPMs are insufficient to account for all. Given the structural constraints, this is not surprising. Further, these constraints suggest the kinds of processes that may be described and forecast. In particular, such processes exhibit relatively stable patterns of variation. This may result from simple process mechanisms or stable interactions of multiple causes. Unfortunately, this description depends on perspective, since "stable variation" may appear from one point of view but not another.

The relativistic emphasis further reflects awareness that long-term, higher-order dynamics involving complex interactions, nonlinear feedbacks, or adaptive restructuring may be occurring. Since these are not captured, the models should be best suited to short-term forecasting. However, the short term varies with the process and the forecast's purpose. For defense expenditures, it may be 3 to 5 years; for a user in operations, it may be tomorrow to 6 weeks. With these limitations in mind, EPM forecasting projects may be considered.

II. FORECASTING WITH ELEMENTARY PROCESS MODELS

EPM forecasts generally seek to differentiate the probabilities of alternative futures, thus reducing uncertainty about the international environment.[4] Given this objective, the forecasting program may be elaborated.

Once a phenomenon is selected and EPMs are deemed appropriate, model construction begins. The choice of EPMs may result either from the process' behavior or a previously generated description or explanation. In the latter case, the problem is translation of the verbal model into a probabilistic or statistical one. If no description is available, then induction and speculation will serve to construct an initial process description and associated EPM.[5] Subsequently, cycles of observation, process description, model construction, and evaluation may be required to produce an acceptable model.[6] The final EPM will embody a description

or explanation, a set of mathematical assumptions and relations, and a set of parameter estimates.

Given an acceptable EPM, the next step is forecasting. The exact approach will vary with model type. But anchored in probabilities, EPM forecasts will usually be given as probability distributions contingent on the model structure, values of exogenous variables and the period to be forecast. Formally, the forecast is $f(Y{:}M,X,t)$, where f is the distribution, Y is the phenomenon forecast, M the model, X the exogenous or predetermined variables, and t the forecast period. This specification clarifies the conditional nature of all EPM forecasts.[7]

In particular, it recognizes that the forecast is no better than its model. Further, it demonstrates that the presence of exogenous variables implies a second forecasting problem that may compound errors. Finally, it hints at the increasing uncertainty of longer forecasts. In particular, the variance of point predictions and distributions may increase.

From the forecast distribution, point or interval predictions can be derived if desired. Discrete distributions allow precise specification of each event's probability. Similarly, continuous distributions provide probabilities for any given range of values. Thus, the forecast distribution contains all information that the EPM can supply about the process' future.

Before using an EPM forecast however, it should be tested and evaluated just as the model was.[8] Two kinds of criteria are identified: (1) criteria available when the forecast is made or at any later time prior to the forecast period; and (2) criteria applicable after a realization is obtained. Both kinds are problematic and important.

The analyst or policy maker wants to know how good the forecast is in order to make decisions or plan. However, he cannot compare the forecast to the actuality. To help surmount this difficulty several criteria are available.

First, the forecast should be logically valid. The forecast must be derivable from the model, exogenous variables, and forecast period. Further, it must be correctly derived. This ensures that the forecast is grounded and potentially reproducible.

Second, the forecast may be judged on its face validity. Plausibility is the criteria, but one that must be used cautiously. Overreliance implies a danger of ignoring unusual or unexpected forecasts that are otherwise valid and accurate. Therefore, this test must be weighed in conjunction with other evidence.

Third, the forecast should be statistically valid. Specifically, the forecast or predictions derived from it should have desirable statistical properties. In particular, they should represent some statistically best forecast. Fortunately, if the EPM is statistically valid, then valid forecasts can be produced.[9]

Fourth, the forecast should reduce uncertainty. Flat or uninformative distributions imply unsuccessful forecasts. By contrast, a peaked normal distribution with small variance would reflect greater uncertainty reduction.

Fifth, the forecast's reliability may prove helpful. Reliability, in this case, requires examination of successes and failures in past forecasting attempts. This record may serve to raise or lower our confidence in the current forecast.

Finally, when the forecast is made, the analyst should evaluate the forecast's utility.[10] A forecast has utility to the extent that it helps reach desired states or avoid undesired ones. Obviously, at this point the utility can be forecast. However, anticipation of the consequences could help avoid negative utilities. Geologists forecasting earthquakes are already concerned with this problem. Should they publish their expectations? The answer depends on the response that the public makes to them. They may prove helpful or harmful. Ethically involved political forecasters confront similar and perhaps equally dramatic utility questions.

After the flow of time supplies a realization, utility may again be evaluated. However, the assessment remains problematic. Being counterfactual, it requires evaluating the phenomenon's hypothetical future state assuming that no forecast had been made. Consideration of alternative actions that would have occurred in lieu of the forecast and a theoretically generated model can facilitate this test.

Finally, retrospection may allow evaluation of the forecast's accuracy. However remembering the contingent nature of an EPM forecast, accuracy may also be indeterminate.[11] The model's utility may lead to changes that invalidate either the model or the assumed values of the exogenous variables. Additionally, realizations are single values that must be compared with a probability distribution.

While the first problem can only be approached counterfactually, three tests are available when the conditions hold either approximately or precisely. First, point predictions may be compared with the realization. Expected values or other appropriate predictions may be employed. Mean square error criteria will measure such accuracy.

Second, the probability of the realization may be examined. If the forecast is a continuous distribution, then confidence intervals about the expected value can determine the likelihood. In the discrete case, the probability is immediately available. The occurrence of highly improbable situations may reduce confidence in the forecast. But, clear cut decisions are precluded by the possibility of unlikely events.

Repeated forecasts will help to overcome this problem. A series of realizations allows construction of another EPM that may be statistically compared to the original. If they are insignificantly different, then faith in the forecast's accuracy should increase.

This battery of criteria and others enables the user to better judge and evaluate forecasts before using them. Final judgment, however, depends on the project's goals and objectives. Only in this way can the forecast be guaranteed relevance.

Having prepared and evaluated the model and the forecast, several other uses may be considered beyond the immediate differentiation of probability and reduction of uncertainty. First, model analysis may benefit from forecasting exercises. The forecasts, by pushing the model beyond the range of its observations, may highlight implications embedded in the model's structure. This analysis aids in revising descriptions or theoretical explanations.

Second, if the model reflects theoretical, causal relations, then counterfactual forecasts are possible. The model's parameters or manipulable variables are systematically varied to test the forecast's sensitivity or to examine alternatives. While the same analysis may be employed with models only describing a process, much of the benefit derives from the clear interpretation of the manipulation with some activity in the real world. Thus, additional utility results when the parameters are theoretically interpretable, since meaningful parameters susceptible to influence more clearly suggest policy choices.

Third, the probability of events may be better estimated by combining an EPM estimate with expert evaluations. The expert may feel that the event is more or less likely than chance or normal conditions would indicate. This *a priori* judgment combines with the EPM estimate using a Bayesian approach to produce an *a posteriori* estimate. This approach may also facilitate the quantification of expert perceptions in a similar fashion.

Fourth, EPMs may serve as building blocks or components of larger models. For example, EPMs can generate values for otherwise exogenous variables, thus substituting for arbitrary choices or naive trend extrapolation. Examination of models elsewhere in this volume suggest the opportunities for such use.

Finally, elementary process models are a baseline against which more complicated efforts may be compared.[12] Given their simplicity, more complex forms must demonstrate other clear-cut advantages. Thus the larger model might provide significantly better forecasts, a more comprehensive, elegant or theoretically based explanation, or better facilities for policy analysis and counterfactual forecasting. This comparison sets the strengths and weaknesses of complex models in stark relief.

This survey has reviewed the structure and characteristics of EPMs, and the process of forecasting and evaluation employed in this kind of project. Besides meeting basic forecasting goals, a variety of other uses are possible. This strongly suggests that elementary process models should be employed in international relations forecasting. Three exercises follow to emphasize and illustrate the argument.

III. ASSASSINATIONS AS A POISSON PROCESS

Not surprisingly, assassinations are difficult to anticipate. They occur infrequently, and may or may not have obvious motivation. Still the prospect of governmental changes suggests a need to reduce uncertainty, in order to prepare for the low probability but possible event.

Examination of the data and familiarity with common discrete distributions allows generation of a possible process description. Assume that each day a government official faces a small but positive probability of assassination. Further, if assassinated, he will be replaced immediately. Then the number of officials in this position who would die during the year can be given by a binomial distribution. In particular, the probability of assassinating k officials from this position is

$$Pr(X = k)$$

$$= \begin{cases} \binom{N}{k} p^k (1 - p)^{N-k} & (k = 0, 1, \ldots, N) \\ 0 & (k > N) \end{cases}$$

where p is the probability of assassination each day and N is the number of days in a year, 365.

Besides this governmental position, others are possible targets. Using the same basic description, this implies that N increases rapidly, and that the chance of at least one assassination a year will rise.

If we assume that the number of opportunities is very large, then the above description will be well approximated by a Poisson process. The Poisson is the limit of a sequence of binomial distributions as the number of opportunities approaches infinity. The convergence is in fact quite rapid. The probability of k assassinations in a single year is then

$$Pr(X = k) = e^{-\theta} \theta^k / k! \quad (k = 0, 1, 2, \ldots; \theta > 0);$$

θ is the limit of Np, as N approaches infinity and p approaches zero. The Poisson is perhaps most famous for describing the number of deaths, per annum, from mule kicks in Prussian Army Corps (discussed in Johnson and Katz, 1969). Somewhat more seriously, a similar approach studying war alliances has employed one version of the Poisson (see Horvath and Foster, 1970).

Estimation of θ will complete model construction. The parameter is conveniently estimated by the mean of available observation, when the independence of each event is assumed. This estimate is both the maximum likelihood and minimum variance unbiased estimate of θ.

We choose to assume initially that the same distribution will hold cross-nationally. This parsimonious description allows the use of pooled cross section-time series data to estimate θ.[13] Using 1955 to 1960 data, the estimate is .2. Substituting this value in the equation above, maximum likelihood estimates of the probabilities can be obtained. Thus, the likelihood of no assassinations is .82; of one, .16; of two, .02, and so on.

Thus far, we have operated as if a Poisson description was correct. That assumption may be tested by comparing the theoretical and empirical distributions. It can be shown that

$$q = \sum_{i=1}^{k} (f_i - e_i)^2/e_i$$

is an appropriate test statistic (see Gibbons, 1971). f_i and e_i are the observed and expected frequencies in category i. e_i is the maximum likelihood estimate obtained by multiplying the theoretical probability by the sample size. k is the number of categories to test, where a rule of thumb suggests that there be at least five observations expected in each class. The test statistic is approximately chi-square with $k - 1 - s$ degrees of freedom, where s is the number of independent parameters. In this case, s equals one, θ.

Regardless of k's value, the Poisson assumption must be rejected in this case. The actual frequency of one assassination is sufficiently different from the expectation to require rejection. Thus our description is inadequate and would require revision for serious use. An obvious constraint to relax is the cross-national constancy assumption. A more complex description would also eliminate the assumption of independent events, allowing both conspiracy theories, organized guerrilla activity, or the influence of social conditions.

However, in the context of this exercise we may proceed. The forecast is clearly given by our theoretically determined distribution. It contains the model's best guess of future events.

If we assume model validity for the moment, then the forecast would evaluate well. It has both logical and statistical validity. Further, the description clearly differentiates probabilities and reduces uncertainty of the unexpected. Its face validity might be questioned when looking at a particular nation, but it is generally plausible. Lacking previous use, its reliability cannot be examined and employed. Finally, its utility and accuracy are left unevaluated in lieu of specific objectives and a valid model.

This kind of forecast and description would be useful in at least three situations beyond straight-forward forecasting. First, the Bayesian use of estimates and expert opinions would be possible. Second, this mechanism could be introduced in Monte Carlo simulations to create the chance of low probability but perhaps influential events. Third, such an EPM provides a serious challenge to other forecasting enterprises whose mission is in the same field.

This exercise illustrates the approach, potential problems, the forecast, evaluation, and possible uses of simple elementary process models.

IV. GUERRILLA WARFARE AS A MARKOV CHAIN

While assassinations were treated as totally random, the international relations literature recognizes that much conflict is not. Sophisticated explanations have been offered and tested. But here for the sake of illustration, many arguments are ignored and the focus is on two simple and obvious propositions.

Several writers have emphasized the importance of lead and lag relations in explaining foreign and domestic conflict.[14] A highly simplified version would suggest that the occurrence of an event this year will influence its future occurrence. Then, guerrilla warfare this year implies a different likelihood next year from what would otherwise have been expected.

Second, guerrilla warfare is often protracted, especially when a Maoist strategy is employed (see Boorman, 1969). Once begun, we would expect conflict to continue.

If we knew nothing else, these two trivial observations would be sufficient to improve our forecasts of guerrilla war. They suggest the use of a Markov chain to describe the phenomenon. The Markov is characterized by the fact that the best guess of a process' future state depends only on knowing the current one. Mathematically, the probability of being in a given state next time depends only on the current state of the process. Such a model obviously forecasts the probabilities of guerrilla war.

This information is recorded in a transition matrix, P, where $p(i,j)$ is the probability of going from state i at t to state j at $t + 1$. Simple contingency tables are sufficient to estimate the model, since the row percentages give maximum likelihood estimates for the transition probabilities (see Anderson and Goodman, 1957, pp. 89–110 and Billingsley, 1961). Further, a chi-square test with $s(s - 1)$ degrees of freedom examines the model's validity; s is the number of states for the process.

Again assuming that the model holds crossnationally, data from 1955 to 1960 were used to estimate the transition matrix. Denoting the absence of conflict as 0 and the presence of warfare as 1, the following matrix was produced.

		Guerrilla warfare at $t + 1$	
		0	1
Guerrilla warfare at t	0	.92	.08
	1	.28	.72

The corrected chi-square test indicates that this is a first-order Markov chain. More complicated forms may also fit the data implying choice on the basis of validity, parsimony, and the relation to theory and purpose. For our purposes, the above structure suffices.

To suggest the improvement in forecasting obtainable from such a structure, its projections may be compared to those from the simple frequency distribution. In the latter case, the mean supplies a best prediction of the probability and equals .16. Examination of the transitions suggest the errors resulting from the simpler approach. In particular, the frequency model significantly underestimates the probability when guerrilla warfare occurred in the previous year.

The one period forecast may be taken directly from the matrix, but higher order forecasts may also be calculated. The probabilities associated with being in a given state n periods in the future are given in the matrix P^n, obtained by repeated matrix multiplication. For example, P^2 contains the probabilities for transition from i at t to j at $t + 2$. These are given below.

		Guerrilla warfare at $t + 2$	
		0	1
Guerrilla warfare at t	0	.87	.13
	1	.46	.54

As the forecasts push further, the transition matrix converges to a matrix P^* with the property that each row is identical. In this example, P^5 equals P^*. The probability of no warfare is then constant at .78 and similarly the probability of conflict is .22. Any longer forecast will produce the same re-

sults. Thus, extended forecasts are independent of the Markov structure. This suggests the short-term applicability of such models, for otherwise they fail to differentiate the probabilities using the prior state as condition.

This model and forecast, though grossly simplified, meet all of the testable criteria established earlier. Its uses need not be repeated, since they resemble those of the first exercise. Let it suffice to point again to the possibility of use in Bayesian estimation and baseline comparisons. Though of limited utility, this exercise clearly shows the success possible with EPMs.

V. DEFENSE EXPENDITURES AND A STRUCTURAL MODEL

Rising defense expenditures have led to the creation of much interest in international relations. Two general schools of thought appear to dominate arguments surrounding the budget. One maintains that the defense budget is a reasonable construction based on estimated defense requirements. The other views the figures as excessive and the result not of rationality, but of bureaucratic politics and organizational routine.

While sophisticated explanations and, in some cases, models exist, this exercise views the argument in terms of a relatively complex EPM. Such a structure is still less involved than many other approaches. It combines prior expenditures from the United States and the Soviet Union with an indicator of economic strength to forecast future defense levels. For each nation, the response to the other's spending roughly indicates the importance of the first argument above. Response to their own spending reflects bureaucratic influences. Finally, the economic variable suggests the nation's ability to support its defense establishment and creates a changing constraint on spending. The structure strongly reflects the influence of Richardson's action-reaction models.

The estimated forecasting model is given at the top of the next page. [15] It is based on data from 1947 to 1972.

This first column of explanatory variables contains the nation's current spending level, its opposite's current expenditure, and the economic indicator. The second column contains the first difference for each. These equations appear to reproduce the

$$USDEF(t + 1) = 8760 + .7 \times USDEF(t) + .5 \times USDFD(t)$$
$$- .2 \times USSRDEF(t) + .0 \times USSRDFD(t)$$
$$+ 28 \times USGNP(t) + 82 \times USGNPD(t)$$
$$USSRDEF(t + 1) = 6940 + .6 \times USSRDEF(t) + .2 \times USSRDFD(t)$$
$$+ .0 \times USDEF(t) + .1 \times USDFD(t)$$
$$+ 55 \times USSRNMP(t) + 73 \times USSRNMPD(t).$$

series quite well, but would be inadequate for applied work.[16] Further, the limited number of observations makes inference suspect. However, these equations do suggest the importance of bureaucratic and economic influences, though additional analysis would be required to strengthen that conclusion.

Forecasts made with the structural equation model require values for the exogenous economic variables, illustrating the earlier argument on forecast contingency. In the presence of such data, the model may be simulated to produce point predictions. Normally, these forecasts will guaranteed statistical validity by the generating model. Calculation of the probability distribution is rendered difficult by the presence of lagged endogenous variables. While in simpler cases this may be derived analytically, this example could employ Monte Carlo simulation to achieve the same result.

To illustrate the approach and provide opportunities for evaluation, the model was simulated through 1974 assuming 4 percent growth in the economic variable. The point predictions are given below.[17]

Defense spending forecasts
(in millions of $US)

	United States	USSR
1972	—	59700
1973	90800	63700
1974	95800	67800

Evaluation of these forecasts must recognize the weaknesses in the model noted earlier. Further, comparison with prior observations suggests that the point predictions are high, resulting from overestimation of the bureaucratic effects. While these results impair the forecast's face validity and overall evaluation, they indicate the modeling analysis uses of forecasting.

Further, models of this type permit multiple other uses. Embodying theoretical and causal relations, counterfactual forecasts are possible. In this example, manipulation of US spending could be used to explore the sensitivity or insensitivity of Soviet expenditures. This model or one like it could also serve fruitfully as a baseline or component in larger forecasting projects.

This exercise has explored another type of EPM. It further illustrates the problems and possibilities of their use.

VI. SUMMARY

Elementary process models employ small numbers of variables with simple functional forms and/or probability distributions. Their forecasts take the form of probability distributions contingent on the model, values of exogenous variables, and the forecast period. Beyond normal forecasting uses, these models serve as good baselines for comparison, building blocks for larger projects, or as aids to quantification using Bayesian techniques. Several evaluation criteria exist such as logical validity, face validity, statistical validity, reduction of uncertainty, reliability, utility, and accuracy. Though none is sufficient to guarantee good forecasts, together they indicate appropriate levels of confidence. Three exercises involving assassinations, guerrilla warfare, and defense expenditures have illustrated the range of models and the forecasting process. While primarily illustrative, they should motivate the future use of EPMs, and help clarify the place of elementary process models in international relations.

NOTES

1. Doob (1953) is a classic and sophisticated treatment.
2. In particular, the theory of wide-sense or covariance stationary processes is employed. A comprehensive guide to these models is Box and Jenkins (1970).
3. Homogeneous nonstationary processes are the most general forms describable. These may be reduced to stationary by differencing.

4. See Choucri (Chapter 1, this volume) for elaboration on the purposes of forecasting.
5. Exposure to the properties and characteristics of particular EPMs should facilitate construction. For example, Poisson distributed events occur infrequently and independently, though many opportunities are available. Similarly, time series models employ correlational techniques for model identification.
6. See Hermann (1967), pp. 216–231, on validating and testing a model.
7. Difficulties in evaluation arise because of this contingency. When the preconditions no longer hold, the commonsense "truth" of the forecast may be indeterminate. See Pool (Chapter 2, this volume) for the argument.
8. Bobrow (Chapter 3); Hermann, Phillips, and Thorson (Chapter 5); and George (Chapter 21), all in this volume, are extremely suggestive in this regard.
9. Estimates that are unbiased, consistent, or robust, or have minimum variance, maximum likelihood, or minimum loss have desirable properties. Selection will depend on purpose and mathematical constraints.
10. This criterion was suggested in Theil's classic (1966) as well as by Bobrow (Chapter 3, this volume).
11. See Pool's argument (Chapter 2, this volume).
12. Mincer and Zarnowitz (1969) make a similar argument for trend extrapolation.
13. In particular, data collected by Rummel and Tanter for the period 1955 to 1960 were employed in both the first and second exercises.
14. See in particular Zinnes and Wilkenfeld (1971) for these arguments and a more elaborate study using Markov chains.
15. The equations were estimated using ordinary least squares that produces asymptotically correct estimates in the presence of lagged endogenous variables. Tests for correlated errors were negative. The data covers the period 1947 to 1972 and employs the *Economic Report of the President,* the *Stateman's Yearbook,* and the International Institute for Strategic Studies' *The Military Balance, 1971–1972* as sources. Data transformations were required for comparability. GNP figures were used for the United States and net material product values for the Soviets. The data are available on request.
16. In particular, the coefficient estimates must be assumed inconsistent due to the explosive nature of the time series. This can be seen by adding the estimates for the lagged endogenous variable and its difference. These both contain a first order lagged endogenous variable. For applied work, a logarithmic transformation and reestimation may suffice.
17. Data were available for the United States through 1972, but not for the Soviets. Estimates are rounded to the nearest 100.

CHAPTER TWELVE

APPLICATIONS OF ECONOMETRIC ANALYSIS TO FORECASTING IN INTERNATIONAL RELATIONS

Nazli Choucri

I. INTRODUCTION

This chapter examines some key issues and difficulties encountered in the course of applying econometric analysis to forecasting in international relations. We will note the problems involved and the solutions adopted, and indicate the consequences of faulty analysis, analytical bias, or mea-

surement error. In so doing, we shall draw upon our recent investigations into the long-range causes of international conflict. Our objective, during the past several years, has been to develop systematic procedures for isolating the determinants of international violence. The general approach we have employed is one common to any econometrician concerned with the analysis of time series data, or any statistician examining the properties of small samples.[1] But our applications of these methods are not common to political analysis. Economists, for example, appear to know much more about the nature of market systems, business cycles, inflation, and so forth, than political analysts know about conflict and warfare, arms races, lateral pressure, or international alignments.[2]

In the course of our inquiries we have developed a partial theory of the dynamics in question, translated this theory into a model from which structural equations were developed, and then estimated the unknown parameters. The purpose of

I am particularly grateful to Hayward Alker for critical comments and suggestions at every stage of these investigations; to Douglas Hibbs, Michael Leavitt, Amy Leiss, Michael Mihalka, Thomas Robinson, and Scott Ross for helpful comments and suggestions on an earlier version of this paper. For assistance in computer analysis I am most grateful to Jonathan Shane, Alexis Sarris, and Walt Malling of the TROLL Project and to Raisa Deber for research assistance. This chapter draws upon Chapters 2, 10, and 17 of Nazli Choucri and Robert C. North, *Nations in Conflict: National Growth and International Violence* (1975). An earlier version of this chapter appeared in the *Papers* of the *Peace Science Society (International)*, Volume 21, 1973, pp. 15–39.

this enterprise was to investigate the implications of alternative parameter estimates upon the behavior of the system as a whole. Experimenting with "high" and "low" coefficients, and comparing these with baseline parameters and system outputs provided us with a reliable means of looking into alternative outcomes and alternative futures.

It is not our objective here to question the nature of causality, or to dispute the assumptions underlying the social and behavioral sciences. Others have done this elsewhere.[3] Nor is it our intent to deliver an introductory lecture on the algorithms upon which elementary statistical methods are based. Rather, our purpose is to make explicit the critical problems inherent in econometric analysis and the ways we have sought to resolve them.[4] Toward this end we discuss: (1) the structure of our model of international conflict as an extension of the general linear model in regression; (2) methodological implications of alternative perspectives upon causality; (3) some key statistics and common problems in causal inference; (4) simultaneous estimation and the problem of identifiability; (5) serial correlation and time dependent corrections; (6) the use of instrumental variables and generalized least squares; (7) system change and breakpoint analysis; and finally (8) procedures employed for simulation, forecasting, and policy analysis and some practical illustrations.

II. A MODEL OF INTERNATIONAL CONFLICT: EXTENSIONS OF THE GENERAL LINEAR MODEL

In a recent study of international politics, we have argued that the roots of conflict and warfare can be found in the basic attributes and characteristics of nations and that the most critical variables in this regard are population, resources, and technology. We have then attempted to specify the intervening sequences between these three sets of variables on the one hand and conflict and warfare on the other. On the basis of empirical and historical analysis, we suggest that the chain of developments relating population, resources, and technology to violence appears to be the following:

A combination of *population* and developing *technology* places rapidly increasing demands upon *resources,* often resulting in internally generated pressures. The greater this pressure, the higher

will be the likelihood of extending national activities outside territorial boundaries. We have termed this tendency to extend behavior outside national boundaries *lateral pressure.* To the extent that two or more countries with high capability and high pressure tendency (and high lateral pressure) extend their interests and psycho-political borders outward, there is a strong probability that eventually the two opposing spheres of interest will intersect. The more intense the intersection, the greater will be the likelihood that *competition* will assume *military* proportions. When this happens, we may expect competition to be transformed into *conflict* and perhaps an *arms race* or cold *war.* At a more general level of abstraction, *provocation* will be the final act that can be viewed as the stimulus for large-scale conflict or violence. But an act will be considered provocation only in a situation that has already been characterized by high lateral pressure, intersections among spheres of influence, armament tensions and competitions, and an increasing level of prevailing conflict.

Major wars, we have argued, often emerge through a two-step process: in terms of internally generated pressure (which can be traced to population dynamics, resource needs and constraints, and technological development) and in terms of reciprocal comparison, rivalry, and conflict, on a number of salient capability and behavior dimensions. Each process tends to be closely related to the other, and each, to a surprising degree, can be accounted for by relatively nonmanipulable variables (or variables that are controllable only at high costs). And it is these variables, we hypothesize, that provide the long-range roots of conflict and warfare.

The first step in the transition from a general theoretical statement to a model capable of sustaining the empirical test is to identify the variables to be explained. These will eventually serve as the outputs of the model. The second is to specify those effects that contribute to outcome variables by developing equations designed to explain the behavior of each of the dependent variables.

Those explanatory variables that are thought to contribute to our understanding of the outcomes in question can be other dependent variables (lagged or unlagged) or they may be exogenous variables and not to be explained by the model. For policy purposes it is important to select at least some explanatory variables that are manipulable by the policy maker. For obvious reasons, it would not be useful to select only variables that are all "givens" or variables that are manipulable at very high costs, unless, of course, one's objectives were to test for the extent to which nonmanipulables dominated system behavior.

Our theoretical statement can thus be transformed into graphic relationships, as noted in Figure 12.1. These relationships can then be translated into structural equations, the parameters of which could then be estimated in the context of the general linear model. This particular model pertains to the pre-World War I period, 1870–1914.

The general linear model in econometrics and causal modeling is a conceptual mechanism to determine the values of variables when quantitative data are supplied.[5] This mechanism includes a set of equations, their functional form, and an accompanying set of specifications and restrictions. We combine observed data, specifications of a model, and the laws of probability to obtain estimates of unknown parameters.[6]

This basic linear model is of the following form:

$$Y = X\beta + U$$

where Y represents a vector of observations of the dependent or endogenous variable over time;

X represents the matrix of independent variables (explanatory, predetermined, and exogenous);

β is the vector of coefficients to be estimated from empirical data;

U represents the vector of error or disturbance term, which has three error components: (1) error due to a linear approximation of the "true" functional form, (2) error resulting from erroneously included or left out variables, and (3) random noise.

The general linear form can be extended to the case of m independent variables and n equations, with the assumption that each dependent variable can be expressed as a linear function of the independent or exogenous variables (linear in the parameters only; the variables can be nonlinear

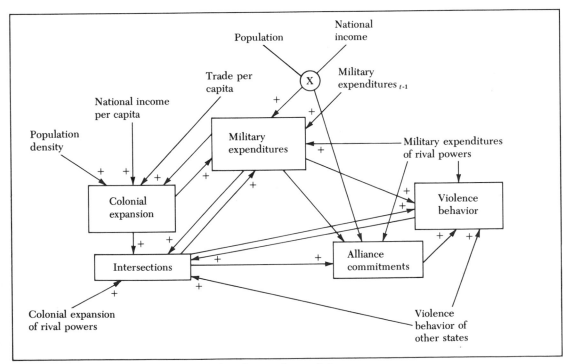

Figure 12.1 Dynamics of international violence: the model.

functions of other variables). It is also assumed that empirical observations are generated by a stochastic mechanism. In the case of the general model, ordinary least squares (OLS) provides the best linear unbiased estimates of the parameters only if the following assumptions or *a priori* constraints are not seriously violated: (1) that the disturbance terms (U) are random variables, with zero mean and homogenous variance; (2) that the disturbances are uncorrelated over time; and (3) that the exogenous variables are not correlated with the disturbances.

The model we have developed is more complex than the general linear case. Some of the complexity is due to the nature of the processes being modeled, the procedures we have employed to correct for significant departures from the assumptions underlying an ordinary least squares solution of the general linear model, and the use of simultaneous equation estimators to obtain unbiased coefficients of feedback systems. The resultant system of equations is presented in Table 12.1.

The entire analysis was undertaken on TROLL/1, an interactive computer system developed at the

Table 12.1   Systems of simultaneous equations used to represent the dynamics of international violence (italics indicate variables endogenous to the system).

colonial area $= \alpha_1 + \beta_1$ (population density) $+ \beta_2$ (national income per capita) $+ \beta_3$ (trade per capita) $+ \beta_4$ *(military expenditures)* $+ \mu_1$.

intensity-of-intersections $= \alpha_2 + \beta_5$ *(colonial area)* $+ \beta_6$ *(military expenditures)* $+ \beta_7$ (colonial-area-of-nonallies) $+ \beta_8$ *(violence-behavior)* $+ \beta_9$ (violence-of-others) $+ \mu_2$.

military expenditures $= \alpha_3 + \beta_{10}$ *(military expenditures$_{t-1}$)* $+ \beta_{11}$ (military-expenditures-of-nonallies) $+ \beta_{12}$ *(intensity-of-intersections)* $+ \beta_{13}$ *(colonial area)* $+ \beta_{14}$ (population-times-national-income) $+ \mu_3$.

alliances $= \alpha_4 + \beta_{15}$ *(military expenditures)* $+ \beta_{16}$ *(intensity-of-intersections)* $+ \beta_{17}$ (military-expenditures-of-nonallies) $+ \beta_{18}$ (population-times-national-income) $+ \mu_4$.

violence-behavior $= \alpha_5 + \beta_{19}$ *(intensity-of-intersections)* $+ \beta_{20}$ *(military expenditures)* $+ \beta_{21}$ (military-expenditures-of-nonallies) $+ \beta_{22}$ *(alliances)* $+ \beta_{23}$ (violence-of-others) $+ \mu_5$.

colonial area = in thousand square miles
population = home population, in thousands
population density = home population divided by home area (in thousand square miles)
national income = in thousand US dollars standardized to 1901–1910 = 100
trade = imports plus exports, in thousand US dollars standardized to 1901–1910 = 100
military expenditures = army plus navy allocations, in thousand US dollars standardized to 1901–1910 = 100
nonallies = dummy variable representing dyadic relationship: 1 if two states are not formally allied, 0 if they are
alliances = number of formal alliances
violence-behavior = metricized variable (from 1 to 30) representing the highest intensity of violence of the behavior of the *actor state toward all other states*
violence-of-others = metricized variable (from 1 to 30) representing the highest intensity of violence of the behavior of *all other states toward the actor state*
intensity-of-intersections = metricized variable (from 1 to 30) representing the highest intensity of violence in *specifically colonial conflicts between the actor state and other major powers*
population-times-national-income = multiplicative variable representing the interactive effect of home population and national income
$\alpha_1 \ldots \alpha_5$ = constant (or intercept) term
$\mu_1 \ldots \mu_5$ = error (or disturbance) term

Instrument list: iron and steel production, pig iron production, government expenditures, merchant marine tonnage, military expenditures of nonallies, colonial area of nonallies, population density, population times national income, national income per capita, trade per capita, intensity-of-intersections$_{t-1}$, violence behavior$_{t-1}$, violence of others, alliances$_{t-1}$, wheat production, coal production.

Massachusetts Institute of Technology for the analysis of econometric models and complex systems.[7] We have used generalized least squares, transforming the independent variables according to the structure of the serial correlation in the disturbances, in conjunction with two stage least squares (a limited information maximum likelihood estimator), so as to incorporate a time-dependent correction as well as simultaneous effects in the final estimates of the parameters.[8]

It is important to appreciate that the parameters of an equation cannot be estimated purely on the basis of empirical data, no matter how complete, reliable, or extensive these may be.[9] The role of data is as follows: Information is useful for identification purposes only if it can serve to distinguish among structural equations. Observational data alone *cannot* perform this necessary step in model building, although analysis of one set of data can provide clues for specification of the next set. Nonetheless, only in conjunction with *a priori* restrictions and specifications can empirical data be put to good usage.[10] But the most basic issue of all in making the transition from a theoretical statement to a formal model is specification of causal ordering.

III. DIRECTIONAL RELATIONS AND CAUSAL INFERENCE

In the most general sense, "causation" refers to hierarchies of influences or effects, most readily characterized by asymmetrical relations within a specified system. Causation, however, is not necessarily implied by a particular time sequence—a consideration that is commonly neglected in systematic social and political inquiry. Because of this simple but almost self-evident point, it is important to adopt alternative criteria for the specification of causal relations. In a persuasive argument, Herbert Simon suggests that causal orderings are determined by the appearance of non-zero coefficients in a system of equations (Ando, *et al.*, 1963). The *a priori* specification of zero coefficients thus raises the issue of identifiability.[11] "For complete identifiability of a structure those restraints must preclude the existence in the same model of a different equivalent structure, that is (in linear models), a different set of equations whose members are linear combinations of the original equations" (Ando, *et al.*, 1963). Causation

is, therefore, closely related to identifiability, while the requirements of identifiability, by necessity, impose certain constraints on the process of model building.

The question of causation gives rise to a related set of philosophical and empirical problems (Ando, *et al.*, 1963, p. 23; see also Orcutt, 1952, pp. 305–311). The long-standing debate among social scientists regarding causal perspectives upon the "real world"—whether it be essentially hierarchical or recursive, or whether it be essentially nonrecursive or simultaneous—can be resolved through a combination of these two positions, namely that the overall framework or system of relations (or equations) in the structure under consideration may basically be recursive (thus negating simultaneous relations at a macro level), but that small components (or blocks) thereof may be nonrecursive (thus allowing for feedback relations within a localized context). For applied analysis, the approach one takes has one important effect: How one perceives the phenomena one seeks to model (whether they are considered basically recursive or nonrecursive) will dictate the kind of estimation procedure employed, and the ways in which the phenomena are represented in a system of equations. We have adopted the nonrecursive view of causality while recognizing that in the long run greater understanding of the dynamics in question may be obtained through the expansion of our model and the use of a block-recursive approach. The general linear model provides the intellectual tools to structure reality and to think about directional influences. Our analysis goes far beyond, to causal modeling, simultaneous estimation, simulation, and policy analysis.

IV. CAUSAL INFERENCE: SOME KEY STATISTICS[12] AND COMMON PROBLEMS

Two of the more common criteria for evaluating the performance of a model are (1) how well the specified equations can predict known data, and (2) where and why findings differ from known data. Examining the patterns of errors (or residuals), therefore, becomes an important aspect of model building.

The variance of the coefficient (or standard error) indicates the precision of the coefficient as derived from empirical data. The statistical significance of a parameter is inferred from the magnitude of the t statistic, and the significance of several parameters is inferred from the F ratio. In a regression equation, the value of F measures the joint significance of the parameter estimates. The summary statistic, R^2, refers to the amount of variance in the dependent variable explained by the independent variables (and the associated stochastic mechanism). A very high R^2 may imply an identity or a trivial regression equation, while a low R^2 does not necessarily indicate an invalid equation.[13] Other summary statistics are needed before an educated judgment is drawn, such as the standard errors around the parameters. In practical applications, however, these statistics are often subject to bias in the parameters.[14] When the disturbances are serially correlated, the variances and standard errors will be deflated, producing inflated t, F, and R^2 statistics, leading to possible erroneous inferences. Correcting for serial correlation is a crucial aspect of causal modeling, highlighting the importance of the Durbin-Watson statistic.

The Durbin-Watson statistic, otherwise known as the d statistic, is a test of the significance of serial correlation in the autocorrelation parameter.[15] The statistic is not applicable in cases with lagged endogenous variables—since the test was developed for nonstochastic vectors of explanatory variables. The Durbin-Watson statistic is no longer valid when there is a coincidence of lagged endogenous variables and autocorrelated disturbances. In that case, the statistic is asymptotically biased upward and no longer tests for autocorrelation. Thus, a nonsignificant d statistic does not preclude the possibility that OLS estimates are inconsistent when there are lagged endogenous variables in the equation. In the case of simultaneous systems, the same problem exists for the system endogenous variables. The endogenous (including lagged endogenous) variables must be replaced by instrumental variables (see Section VII below).

A common difficulty in statistical analysis is high collinearity among the explanatory variables. But we cannot rule out the use of a particular variable or the estimation of a particular equation simply because of multicollinearity. Other problems might arise (see Rao and Miller, 1971, p. 48). High intercorrelations result in the loss of precision, but the exclusion of a theoretically relevant variable on those grounds might exacerbate serial correlation

in the disturbances.[16] Further, multicollinearity affects the precision of coefficient estimates rather than their values.

By far the most serious problem in data analysis and parameter estimation involves measurement error. It is customary to equate measurement error with faulty data or erroneous quantitative measures. While such problems are undoubtedly the source of much distortion in both analysis and results, it is important to broaden the conventional definition in at least two ways. First, specific estimates of the error in quantitative measures may be obtained from the measures themselves and incorporated as confidence intervals around the basic data for purposes of modifying the results according to the degree, magnitude, and direction of cumulated error.[17] The second extension of measurement error thinking lies in the structure of the underlying equation itself. Measurement error may be attributed to cases where the magnitude of the disturbance of the error term raises serious questions concerning the validity of the equation and the viability of the resulting specification. Ideally, the most desirable situation is one in which (1) errors in the quantitative measures are known to be negligible and (2) the disturbance term is small and exhibits no discernible trend of either positive or negative serial correlation. In practice, however, neither of these conditions hold: The extent of fault in the data is often not known, and the disturbance term exhibits significant serial correlation, especially in trend analysis of time series data.[18] The methods employed to minimize the effects of serial correlation will be discussed below.

V. SIMULTANEOUS INFERENCE AND THE PROBLEM OF IDENTIFIABILITY

When there is mutual dependence among the endogenous variables, simultaneous estimation of the parameters is called for (see Christ, 1960, pp. 838–871). This set of procedures is more complex than standard regression analysis. Estimation in the classical regression mode involves one dependent variable and several independent ones. In the simultaneous case there are several jointly dependent variables. This situation generates an identification problem. This means that even if infinite data were available from which the reduced form of the parameters could be derived exactly, the values of the coefficients cannot be estimated without some *a priori* theoretical restriction upon the number of exogenous and endogenous variables in each equation.[19]

The addition of *a priori* restrictions to identify an equation is useful only if the same restrictions are not employed to identify other equations as well. However, such additional restrictions generally occur in the form of linear inequalities for the coefficients to be estimated. Inequalities of this nature add to the efficiency of the estimates but do not assist in the identification of a particular equation. Furthermore, if a model is not identifiable, manipulating the equations or the order of constituent variables will not assure identification — either a model is identifiable or it is not.

The problem of identifiability is thus closely related to theory and method, and is central to any model building effort. An equation is identifiable when a combination of *a priori* assumptions and empirical observations allows for a distinction between the parameters of the equation and those of other equations. By extension, a model is identifiable if each equation represents a distinct set of relationships. The problem is one of having sufficient *a priori* information to distinguish among equations. A certain minimum is necessary. Beyond that, any added information may be put to use. In *just-identified* equations there is exactly one way to obtain the "true" equation from the reduced form. In over-identified cases there is more than one way. In *under-identified* situations, where *a priori* information is insufficient to provide a discriminating service, there is no way in which the "true" equation may be recovered or distinguished from others in the same functional form. The model we have developed through experimentation and alternative specification is an *over-identified* set of equations: There is more than one way to retrieve the reduced form of each original equation. In practical terms, the problem is generally one of choosing among the various alternatives for an over-identified equation or model.

Standard statistical theorems, developed for the case in which the explanatory variables are treated as if they were fixed in repeated sampling, cannot be used when there are lagged endogenous variables. Furthermore, the coincidence of lagged endogenous variables *and* autocorrelated disturbances inflates the *t* statistic and may signal erro-

neous inferences. Marked departures from the assumptions underlying the general linear model produce biased parameter estimates, often necessitating equally marked departures from standard regression procedures. The practical implications of serial correlation in simultaneous systems for parameter estimation are sometimes overwhelming.

VI. SERIAL CORRELATION AND TIME DEPENDENT CORRECTION[20]

Because the nature of the serial correlation in the disturbances is often unclear—if it were known, the solution to the problem would be simply to adjust the parameter estimates accordingly—we are confronted with the necessity of estimating the nature of the autocorrelation parameter empirically and identifying the underlying stochastic process. This involves (1) isolating the systematic component of the disturbances, and (2) adjusting the independent variables so as to develop consistent estimates of the parameters.

Aitken has demonstrated that the generalized least squares estimator produces an unbiased estimate of the error variance when disturbances are autocorrelated (Aitken, 1935, pp. 42–48). But the estimate is not the "true" autocorrelation parameter ρ. However, it does have a known statistical distribution and in small samples it is consistent.[21] Our objective is to identify the theoretical structure of the time dependent parameter, and to determine its statistical properties.

Four disturbance structures have properties that are tractable and well known: (1) first order autoregressive process, where each error term (u_t) depends only upon its previous value (u_{t-1}) plus a random component (ϵ_t); (2) second order autoregressive structures where u_t depends upon u_{t-2} and u_{t-1}, plus a random component (ϵ_t); (3) first order moving averages, where the disturbances depend only upon a series of temporally adjacent, independently disturbed, random variables, and hence all the disturbances prior to u_{t-1} do not contribute to generating u_t; and (4) second order moving averages, where, for the same reason, the autocorrelation of u_t is effectively zero with all terms beyond u_{t-2}. In the "real world," higher order structures are probably operative, but their statistical tractability amounts to a major computational problem, and it is not always clear that the benefits accrued by computational complexity are greater than the costs incurred.[22]

We seek to identify the structure of serial correlation parameters so as to obtain unbiased general least squares (GLS) estimates of the parameter values and their statistical variance and other attributes. A critical aspect of GLS involves a careful analysis of the residuals. There are at least two ways in which this can be done. The first, a correlogram analysis, involves retrieving the residuals from regression analysis and then correlating the first $t/5$ terms with the initial value of the residual, generating empirical values. These empirical values are then compared to the "theoretical" values that would be expected from a particular autoregressive structure. The second way, applicable only for autoregressive processes, involves regressing the residuals (u_t) upon their previous values (u_{t-1} for AUTO1 and u_{t-1}, u_{t-2}, for AUTO2,) and observing the statistical significance of the two equations and the value of the Durbin-Watson statistics. In applied analysis, however, it is often difficult to distinguish moving average processes from autoregressive processes that dampen off sharply (see Hibbs, 1972, p. 51 and Hanna, 1960). There are also difficulties in determining whether the discrepancy between the theoretical autocorrelation parameter and its empirical counterpart is significant rather than attributable to noise. Identifying the structure of serial correlation and making appropriate adjustments amount to an important aspect of any such investigations.

VII. INSTRUMENTAL VARIABLES AND GENERALIZED LEAST SQUARES

As noted earlier, OLS yields inconsistent parameter estimates in dynamic models with lagged endogenous variables and serial correlation in the error term. The OLS residuals are no longer the "true" underlying disturbances, in that Y_{t-1} has a tendency to co-opt the systematic component of the disturbances.[23] This results in an upward bias for the coefficient of the lagged endogenous variable and a downward bias for the other exogenous or explanatory variables, frequently leading to erroneous inferences. This was a particularly serious problem in our investigations since determining the effects of the previous year's military alloca-

tions upon next year's budget amounted to an important aspect of our research. For this reason we must find ways of compensating for expected distortions.

One important assumption of least squares is that the errors are uncorrelated with the co-terms and uncorrelated with each other.[24] To meet this assumption, instrumental variables—which are assumed to be uncorrelated with the error but highly correlated with the original co-terms—are created. The constructed variables are linear combinations of the original terms and, therefore, assumed to be uncorrelated with the disturbances. They can thus be used to estimate the coefficient of the original equations. The *original* data, and not the constructed terms, are used to calculate the residuals (Eisner and Pindyck, 1972). Good instruments must have the following properties: (1) they must be truly exogenous and, in theory, uncorrelated with the disturbances, as a lagged endogenous variable usually is not;[25] (2) there must be no simultaneous feedback loops connecting the equations to be estimated with the equations explaining the potential instrument; (3) the disturbances in the equation to be estimated must not be correlated with the explanatory variable.

One question remains: Should the time dependent correction be made before or after the instrumental variable substitution?[26] In the analysis reported below we have followed the algorithms implemented in TROLL by undertaking generalized least squares first, then the instrumental variable substitution. But we have tested empirically for the differences that are yielded when the reverse procedure is employed; that is, first the instrumental variable substitution and then generalized least squares, and have found no significant differences for the model in Table 12.1. Several rounds of generalized least squares rarely produce theoretically meaningful results. For this reason, if an initial use of GLS does not appear to correct for serial correlation adequately, respecification is definitely called for.

In sum, the correction for the coincidence of lagged endogenous variables and serial correlation involves a two-stage instrumental variable substitution and the use of generalized least squares. If we treat lagged endogenous variables as endogenous, then a consistent estimate of the equation can be obtained using an instrumental variable estimator with current and lagged exogenous variables as instruments, provided the system has a sufficient number of exogenous variables. This estimator is robust against all forms of autocorrelation in the disturbances, but not against serial correlation in the explanatory variables. In this case, it becomes necessary to estimate the structure of the disturbance and then confront the problem of sequencing with respect to generalized least squares and two stage least squares, as noted above.

VIII. SYSTEM CHANGE AND BREAKPOINT ANALYSIS

The occurrence of breakpoints and problems relating to the estimation of system change and prediction beyond the break are central issues in model building and forecasting. Sharp shifts in dynamics may signify discontinuities in some underlying empirical realities (but they may well be quite natural regularities of other empirical realities). Often breakpoints indicate incompleteness of theoretical specification.

We can think of breakpoints either as sharp changes in slope, or as nonlinearities. Some shifts may signify discontinuities which may be directly included in the equation as dummy variables (as we have done when defining changes in rivaling powers).[27] The incorporation of a break directly in the analysis increases the fit between historical and estimated data and between historical and simulated dynamics.

In some instances the break results from quantitative changes. In others it results from qualitative changes. There are as yet no known methods whereby the particular points at which a significant shift has occurred may be identified precisely (other than costly and complicated iterative procedures). For this reason, the best alternative is to plot the data, then to hypothesize the occurrence of a break based on empirical observation and to test for its statistical significance. The Chow test is still the most appropriate significance test for breakpoints. Quasi-experimental techniques for coping with such problems provide additional perspectives upon these issues, but they are cumbersome and complicated.[28]

The Chow test, modified recently by Fisher, involves the comparison of a set of coefficients with those of another array of which it is a subset.[29] We

have inquired into the statistical significance of differences among two sets of regressions, one yielding coefficients for the period as a whole, the other for a particular subperiod. Cases where a significant difference emerged provided important clues into system change or transformation. Phase shifts can be identified with systemic breaks. But breaks that are more in the nature of nonlinearities may not always be identified as such. The result is simply a "bad" fit that cannot be attributed to an underlying break, but rather to nonlinearities that are not specified in the functional form of the equation. A search for breakpoints also assists in identifying poor specification or areas of misspecification.

In sum, the analysis of residuals and identification of breakpoints becomes, much like sensitivity analysis, a critical aspect of the research enterprise.[30]

IX. SIMULATION, FORECASTING, AND POLICY ANALYSIS

The next step in this analysis is to develop variable simulations of the system as a whole and to observe its behavior under various conditions. This is done in two stages: The five equations are simulated equation by equation (by employing historical values at each iteration in place of calculated endogenous variables), and then the entire system is simulated in simultaneous mode (by employing calculated values for all endogenous variables). A successful (single equation) forecast increases the probability of a valid simulation: a successful simulation almost certainly implies a successful forecast.[31] A forecast (of a single equation) is conducted independently of the other equations and its solution depends primarily upon the existence of historical values for the endogenous variable, period by period. A simulation involves the entire system of equations, solving for the jointly dependent variables without recourse to their historical observations. A completely self-contained structure is operative in a simulation, allowing a fairly controlled method of varying parameters and observing the implications for the system as a whole.[32]

The TROLL/1 facilities, upon which our simulation of the system of simultaneous equations was undertaken, calculate values of the jointly endogenous variables in the model over a period of time for which exogenous data are available, or for any subperiod therein. For simulation, four types of information are required: the structure of the model itself, initial historical (or known) values for the endogenous variables, data for the exogenous variables, and constant files (coefficients and parameters that have been estimated earlier).[33]

A dynamic simulation proceeds as follows: For a given model in which Y and Z are endogenous variables, and A, B, X are exogenous variables:

$$Y_t = a_1 + b_{11}A_t + b_{12}Z_{t\text{-}1} + u_1.$$
$$Z_t = a_2 + b_{21}X_t + b_{22}B_t + u_2.$$

In the first period, Y and Z are calculated using exogenous values for A_t, B_t, and X_t, and an exogenous starting value for the endogenous variable Z_{t-1}. In the second period, $(t + 1)$, Y_{t+1} and Z_{t+1} are computed using exogenous values for A_{t+1}, B_{t+1}, and X_{t+1} and the simulated endogenous value for Z_t from the previous period. Historical values for the endogenous variables are no longer employed. This procedure then continues, calculating the endogenous variables from their simulated values during the previous period and the current value of the exogenous variables. It must be noted that at each step subsequent to the initial t, historical values for the exogenous variables must be provided.

The solution for a variable at any given period is a function of a series of iterations in which all the equations in the block are solved and iteration values of the endogenous variables produced. Convergence criteria identify the point at which the iteration has reached a solution. Sometimes it is necessary to relax the convergence criteria in order to obtain a solution. A common procedure for checking the performance of the simulation when convergence is attained, is to examine the summary statistics, particularly percent error, and compare the simulated values of the endogenous variables with the actual, or known historical values.[34]

There are several sources of error in a simulation: First, the disturbance in period t may not be accurately forecasted; second, there may be errors when estimating the parameters from observed samples (errors arising during the sampling period or measurement error), and third, there may be errors in forecasting the exogenous and lagged endogenous variables for period t.[35]

The basic procedure for undertaking simulation experiments is to resimulate the model with different inputs (or sets of information) from those used in the base simulation. Changes in parameters/values, in estimated coefficients, in endogenous variables, or in exogenous files may be made. To compare the results, we note the discrepancies between historical data output for the initial simulation and that for the modified simulation. For policy purposes it is necessary to modify the *coefficients* of key variables and then observe the effects upon the simulated output. This is done by changing coefficients one by one and obtaining the simulated output after *each* modification. Only in this way is it possible to identify the effects of policy changes upon the entire simulation.[36]

X. SIMULATION, FORECASTING, AND POLICY ANALYSIS: THE BRITISH CASE

By way of providing some empirical reference to the above discussion, we draw upon recent investigations of the British case, 1871–1914. Table 12.2 presents summary statistics of the mean values for historical data, simulation values, and forecasts for each of the dependent variables in the system of simultaneous equations depicted earlier in Table 12.1 and, in diagram form, in Figure 12.1. These summary statistics (and the plots noted below) provide useful insights into the structure of the dynamic system modeled. Space limitations prevent an extensive commentary upon the political significance of these results. Some brief observations may be in order concerning the quantitative findings and their "real-world" implications.

In terms of colonial expansion, the simulation of British territorial acquisitions began slightly below the real-world level, but the two remained fairly close until 1880, when the simulation (and the single equation bootstrap projection) continued an upward trend and failed to replicate a slight drop in the real-world level. Between 1885 and 1889 the simulation and the real-world data were again close, but in 1890 and 1891 the simulation failed to replicate two sharp increases in the real-world level largely accounted for by British territorial gains in Africa. The two plots (and also the single equation bootstrap projection) were close from 1896 until 1899 and 1900, when the real-world level, reflecting additional British gains in Africa and elsewhere, underwent further sharp increases. In 1909 the simulation moved on above the real-world level.

In general, the simulations of military expenditures in the Great Power systems were quite successful. The British simulation ran slightly lower than the real-world expenditure levels during the 1870's. In the earlier years of this period, Britain fought the Ashanti Wars and was involved in other colonial conflicts, but in many respects the period was characterized by an 1874 declaration from the throne of friendly relations with all powers. Military expenditures remained fairly stable into the early 1880's. At this point, the simulation overtook the real-world levels of expenditure and became consistently a trifle higher. Between 1895 and 1900 the simulation overshot the actual levels consistently. By the outbreak of the Boer War in 1899 the simulation was registering well above real-world expenditures. A year later the two were close. Then the real-world data rose to a sharp peak in 1903, leaving the simulation behind but above its 1900 level. At this peak point, the single equation bootstrap projection was closer to the real-world data than was the simulation. After the 1903 peak, the simulation and the real-world data both dropped back and then rose more slowly to substantially the same 1914 level (see Figures 12.2 and 12.3).

Although the mean values for the simulations and forecasts of intersecting spheres of influence were close to the mean historical values, the percentage errors—calculated over the entire period—were considerable. Percentage errors take into account each deviation from the mean in a calculation of the overall percentage. Since the metrics involved were of small magnitudes—covering the range of the interaction scale from 1 to 30—any increment of deviation makes a greater impact on the percentage error calculations than similar increments in the cases where the metric itself involves large numbers—such as military expenditures in monetary values or colonial area in thousands of square miles.

The actual discrepancy or error between the historical alliance commitments and the simulated or forecasted commitments was small. But, because of the nature of the metric involved—low values and variance in the alliance commitment series—these minor discrepancies in absolute terms become

Table 12.2 Some comparative statistics: Historical data, simulation, and forecasting. The British case, 1871–1914.

Variable	Historical Mean	Simulated Mean	Mean of % Error: Simulation	RMS of % Error: Simulation	Forecasted Mean	Mean of % Error: Forecast	RMS of % Error: Forecast
Lateral pressure (Colonial area: sq. mi.)	10,968,400	10,919,900	-0.206	3.354	10,920,400	-0.204	3.308
Intersections (level: scale 1–30)	12.989	12.896	73.917	211.261	12.988	72.705	264.524
Military expenditures (1906 US $)	212,392,000	211,742,000	1.563	24.396	211,856,000	0.934	27.762
Alliance commitments (number)	1.568	1.578	-15.627	27.270	1.581	-11.645	34.829
Violence behavior (level: scale 1–30)	20.364	20.419	67.101	276.158	20.364	70.664	307.747

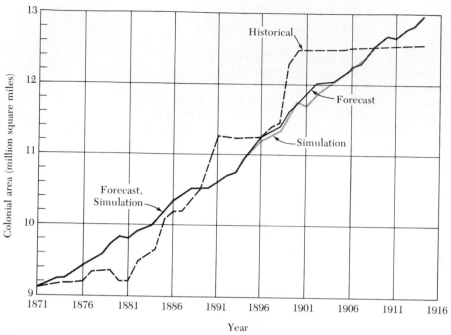

Figure 12.2 Simulating lateral pressure: British colonial areas.

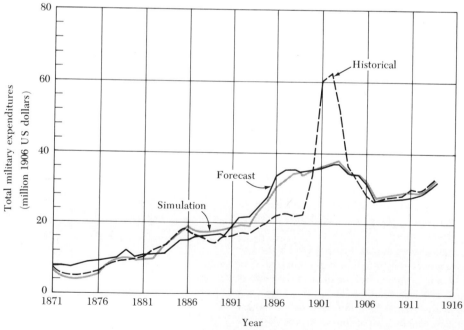

Figure 12.3 Simulating British military expenditures.

major ones in percentage terms. In such cases, we can only observe these two sets of statistics and draw the appropriate inferences. Since the actual error between historical and simulated alliance commitments was very small, we find it reasonable to conclude that our simulation of these dynamics captured much of the underlying processes. Such an inference is reinforced by the high congruence between the actual or historical changes in alliance commitments and our simulation of these changes. The correspondence between the two is almost perfect. As much cannot be claimed with respect to percentage change over time, however. But although the correspondence between actual and simulated percentage changes in alliance commitments is not as good as in the case of actual changes, the degree of fit is still within bounds that define a fairly successful simulation.

A similar assessment may be made with respect to the results of the simulation of prevailing levels of international violence: There was a high level of congruence between the actual level of violence — as measured by scaled interaction data — and the simulation and forecast of these levels. The actual error between simulation and forecast, on the one hand, and real-world data, on the other, was negligible, but the percentage errors were considerable. Again, much as in the cases of the intersection and alliance variables, this outcome is due to the nature of the metrics involved. Changes in the violence behavior of the powers were also extremely well replicated, both in terms of simulating the violence variables within the five equation systems and in terms of simulating violence as a single equation forecast. In each case the artificial replication coincided closely with the real-world data. But the year-to-year percentage changes were not reproduced as satisfactorily as the actual changes.

A successful simulation model should do more than enhance our understanding of the dynamics of a system and the interdependence among its components. Once such a model is developed and its parameters estimated from empirical data — the values being robust and the coefficients statistically significant — we must still address ourselves to the

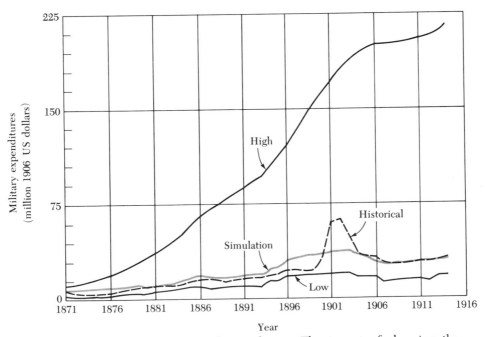

Figure 12.4 Policy experiment: Explosive change. The impact of changing the coefficient for military expenditures t-1 (in the military expenditure equation) upon British military expenditures.

"so what?" query. By allowing us to raise questions of a "what if" or "if . . . then . . . " nature, a viable simulation should identify critical intervention points where policy changes (alterations in coefficients) will yield specific future outcomes.

By modifying the parameters in each equation and observing the changes in the behavior of the dependent variables, it is possible to draw inferences concerning real-world equivalences and expected behaviors. Although even a summary discussion of our policy analysis for the British case cannot be presented here, suffice it to add that the entire system was much more sensitive to *upward* swings in the dynamics under consideration than to downward swings. In other words, the dynamics in question were imbedded, seemingly, in explosive tendencies that surfaced with any slight upward changes in key parameters, whereas the system did not respond as dramatically to counterbalancing downward changes in the same parameters (see Figure 12.4).[37]

Such findings bear witness to the complexities of decision making and indicate the counterintuitive tendencies and behavioral characteristics of many large social systems. This type of experimental application of econometric analysis to political inquiry provides a methodology for assessing both theory and the outcomes of conventional regression analysis (including departures therefrom) and also a basis for experimenting with various alternative policy formulations. Overall, these partial and, in some instances, nonobvious outcomes of an "if . . . then . . ." nature serve as further tests of a model and accompanying equations. Political scientists must now investigate the full range of political problems to which econometric analysis and forecasting might be put to use. Unless the issues raised in the earlier sections of this paper are given sufficient attention, it is unlikely that the exercise described in the last sections will be undertaken with any degree of validity. And, at this stage in the development of quantitative methodology, the issues of theory, method, and procedure assume paramount importance.

NOTES

1. See, for example, Deusenberry, *et al.* (eds.) (1965 and 1969).
2. Dynamic modeling, which is current in econometric

analysis, can be used for political inquiry to provide (1) an aid to understanding political dynamics, (2) a tool for simulation, and forecasting political behavior and outcomes, and (3) a guide to the choice of public policy. The crucial test of a model lies in its internal and statistical validity. Its prime usefulness is to make forecasts and compare the forecasts with actual historical values as a means of understanding how systems behave. For a survey of the development of econometrics as a field of inquiry, see Klein (1971), pp. 415–421. For an instructive application of econometric analysis to political inquiry, see Kramer (1971).
3. See, for example, Blalock and Blalock (1968) and Ando, *et al.* (1963).
4. Although the broad lines of our investigations are common in econometric analysis, we have found that applied econometrics is not always consonant with econometric theory. In many cases we have also found that the problems confronting us—such as the coincidence of lagged endogenous variables and serial correlation in the disturbances—are raised in econometric texts as critical problems, but rarely are sufficient guidelines or practical direction provided to assist in resolving such issues. For this reason, our approach has been highly exploratory, and the solutions we have adopted amounted to practical applications of theoretical arguments. Since there are, as yet, no clear cut solutions to problems such as these, much of what we have done is both controversial and experimental.
5. See, for example, Johnston (1972), especially pp. 1–8 and 121–176; Christ (1966), especially pp. 1–15, 243–298.
6. For related considerations, see Fennessey (1968), pp. 1–27, and Rao and Miller (1971).
7. See TROLL/1 *User's Guide*, Computer Research Center for Economics and Management Science, National Bureau of Economic Research, Inc., June, 1972.
8. The dynamic elements in a model are usually generated by lagged relationships, by first (or higher order) derivatives, by employing endogenous variables as explanatory, and by introducing random shock variables. These considerations are important in drawing inferences about the structure of the system of equations in question and about the ability of the system to predict both the behavior of the model and the behavior of outcome variables. In the course of our investigations we have employed each of these procedures for approximating dynamic systems. Here we note only the most effective approaches. See, for example, Franklin M. Fisher, "Dynamic Structure and Estimation in Economy-Wide Econometric Models," in Deusenberry, *et al.* (eds.) (1965), pp. 590–635. Dynamic models can be constructed by employing explicit functions of time, linear approximations, exponential functions, quadratic trends, first and higher order differences, distributed lags and spectral analysis. The result is a system of equations in the correct form, whose parameters are subject to probability error associated with the inference procedure

used. We solve the estimated equation of the model in order to obtain an estimate of the reduced form. An earlier version of this analysis was undertaken with the use of rates of change variables on both sides of the equations. In that case, we have found that the resulting parameter estimates were surprisingly fragile throughout.

9. The necessity of *a priori* specifications, endemic to the question of causality, is predicted on two considerations. First, these specifications must allow the investigator to develop a particular system of equations, and to identify the dependent and independent variables, and the nature of the inequalities. This initial specification in itself constitutes an operational statement of theory, however vague, inarticulated, or implicit it may be. Second, *a priori* information is necessary for the distinction of one equation from another. Information of this nature generally constitutes restrictions on the coefficients of the variables (where some are set at zero) and on the nature of the random or disturbance term. Without the specification of zero coefficients for *some* variables in *each* equation, there is no way to distinguish one equation from another. See Fisher (1966), Chapters 1 and 2.

10. For a theoretical treatment of data, see Coombs (1964).

11. For conditions of identifiability, see Fisher (1966).

12. The formulae for the statistics discussed below can be found in any standard econometric text. Here we are concerned primarily with the problem of inference. See, for example, Johnston (1972); Christ (1966); and Rao and Miller (1971).

13. The smaller the variance of a parameter estimate, the less sensitive the estimate will be to errors in the dependent variable. Furthermore, the smaller the correlation among the independent variables, the higher the precision of the regression estimates. However, computation precision does not necessarily guarantee that the most theoretically precise estimation procedure has been used. See Rao and Miller (1971), p. 24.

14. The "bias" of a parameter estimate is the difference between the mean value of the distribution of the estimate and its "true" parameter value. Bias may also result from the omission of relevant variables in the equation. But this will not increase the variance of the estimates of the coefficients, nor does the introduction of superfluous variables severely impede the precision of the estimate. Although no statistical tool is a substitute for good theory, some errors are likely to have greater consequences for robust inferences than others. For example, regression coefficients with the wrong sign indicate most likely that some misspecification has taken place, or that the variables are not appropriately defined, or that we are mistaken about the "right" sign, or that there is an interactive effect that has not been taken into account. It is often difficult to identify the "real" reason for a "wrong" sign. See Rao and Miller (1971), pp. 27–35. "Precision" seeks the minimum variance estimate, regardless of bias. As a summary statistic,

the mean square error provides importance to bias and to precision:

$$MSE = Var(\hat{\beta}) + [Bias(\hat{\beta})]^2.$$

When the estimated equation is the "true" equation, ordinary least squares provides the minimum variance unbiased estimate. See, also for example, Kendall (1954), pp. 403–404.

15. Durbin and Watson (1950 and 1951); also see Johnston (1972), pp. 250–254. See also Section VI of this chapter.

16. The precision of the parameter estimate depends upon the serial correlation parameter as well as upon the process generating the independent variables. Ordinary least squares is still unbiased in the presence of serial correlation, but it does not have minimum variance. If we can identify the structure and value of the autocorrelation parameter, then by an appropriate transformation of the variables we can use ordinary least squares to provide minimum variance estimates. This is appropriate only in the single equation case where simultaneous effects are not thought to operate. When the dependent variables in the equation are also serially correlated, then the bias depends also on the parameters that generated their serial correlation. And when the variance in the error term is not constant, ordinary least squares does not produce the best linear unbiased estimates. See also Schink and Chiu (1966), pp. 36–67. We have attempted to attain high precision (by seeking sharp and robust parameter estimates) and minimize bias (by respecifying each equation to account explicitly for the effects of separate independent variables.)

17. The conventional use of measurement error may thus be viewed in the context of confidence intervals, the problem being defined in terms of the absence of vital information rather than the presence of known error in the quantitative measures.

18. For related considerations, see Blalock (1965), pp. 37–47.

19. The two necessary conditions for identifiability are the order and rank conditions. For the order condition to hold, there must be at least M-1 independent restrictions in an equation where M is the number of endogenous variables. This is clearly an exclusion restriction. The rank condition stipulates that at least one nonvanishing determinant of the order M-1 can be formed from the ordinary least square structure of an equation, corresponding to the variables excluded by *a priori* specification from that equation. See Fisher (1966), pp. 39–42 and 60–62; and Fisher (1959), pp. 431–447. For an excellent exposition of the identification problem in multiequation systems, see Hibbs (1973b), Appendix III.

20. This section discusses the nonsimultaneous, nonlagged endogenous case. See below for the simultaneous and/or lagged endogenous case.

21. See Hibbs, Jr. (1972) for a derivation of the residuals in the generalized model, and Goldberger (1965), Chapter 5, for a derivation of the disturbance vari-

ance. See also Fisher (1970a) and Rao and Miller (1971), especially pp. 70–74. For a comprehensive treatment of issues in time series analysis, see Hannan (1960) and Anderson (1942), pp. 1–13.

22. Econometricians have focused primarily upon first order autoregressive structure (due to the case of computation) and, as a result, a general tendency to assume that the world is of a first order autoregression pervades much of the econometric literature. In our investigations, however, we have rarely encountered an AUTO1 structure. An AUTO2 usually appears to be a suitable trade-off between complexity and accuracy. For empirical analyses, see Rao and Griliches (1969), pp. 253–272, and Orcutt and Winokur, Jr. (1969), pp. 1–14.

23. See Rao and Miller (1971), Chapter 7. The true error does not depend on the value of the independent variables, but the residuals do. Residuals, therefore, reflect the properties of the independent variables as well as the errors and the effects of left out variables. If errors are homoscedastic and random, the residual corresponding to a particular value of the independent variables (X_n) has a statistical distribution with zero mean and small variance. See Christ (1966), pp. 394–395; Goldberger (1964), pp. 232–235; and Johnston (1972), pp. 208–242.

24. In cases where collinearity among the instrumental variables is high, principal component transformation produces a new set of variables that are orthogonal linear combinations of the original variables. The new variables are so ordered so that each variable explains as much of the remaining variance of the original variables as possible. In such cases, it is possible to use a smaller number of variables while still accounting for the major fraction of the variance explained by the original equation. We employed a principal components solution only when it was not possible to create instruments in any other way due to excessive collinearity among the instruments.

25. The choice of instruments is theoretically intuitive. A predetermined list can be refined in two ways: (1) through the use of principal components. This method reduces multicollinearity since the components are mutually orthogonal, and principal components summarize the information in the list of instruments; and (2) through structurally ordering instrumental variables by first establishing a list of preference ordering of instruments relative to a particular explanatory term; then regressing the endogenous variable on the instruments in differing combinations to determine whether an instrument further down the list has an effect or whether its contribution is simply using up a degree of freedom; the constructed elements of Y_t, together with the elements of T_t, are then employed as instrumental variables in constructing Y. See Rao and Miller (1971); and Eisner and Pindyck (1972).

26. There are differences of views concerning this ordering, and hence, the residuals to be employed when undertaking an instrumental variable substitution. When combining time dependent corrections,

generalized least squares, instrumental variables, and two stage least squares, it is not intuitively obvious which residuals, and at which stage, should be used in calculating the relevant statistics for evaluating the parameters at the final stage. On the one hand, it is argued that when generalized least squares and instrumental variables are combined, the transformed residuals should be calculated without the substitution. On the other, it is maintained that substitution should first take place, and then the time dependent corrections performed. In the latter case, the proper asymptotic variance-covariance matrix must contain the instrumental variable substitution. In the former, it does not. See Hibbs (1972) and Wallis (1967), for the single equation case, and Eisner and Pindyck (1972). For other ways of dealing with this problem, see Fair (1970).

27. For other illustrations, see Theil (1970), pp. 103–154.

28. Chow (1960), pp. 591–605; and Campbell and Stanley (eds.) (1966).

29. In our analysis, we have compared the residuals generated by the regression of the n observations with those of the m observations (given k number of variables) and it becomes clear that in instances where the deviations are great, the F test picks these and registers them as statistically significant, thereby rejecting the null hypothesis. See Fisher (1970a), pp. 361–366; and Johnston (1972), p. 206–207.

30. For purposes of experimentation and increasing our understanding of the model we have developed, we found it desirable to identify and test for breakpoints (using the Chow test) in cases where the coefficients were estimated with and without the uses of instrumental variables. We found, generally, that there were no significant differences in terms of the results obtained with and without the use of instrumental variable substitution.

31. Econometricians generally talk of forecasting when the endogenous variable in each equation is replaced by historical values at each point, and of simulation when the coefficients, the exogenous variables, and the error terms together with the jointly dependent variables are employed to generate an artificial replication of the entire system. This replication is commonly referred to as simulation. In looser parlance, we often talk of forecasting as simulation beyond the existing data that was used to estimate the coefficients initially. Clearly, that is not the usage intended in this paper.

32. See Naylor, et al. (1968), pp. 184–200 for an informative study.

33. The following observations are based on Chapter 8 of the *TROLL/1 User's Guide,* June, 1962.

34. If the object is short-term forecasts, multicollinearity need not be a necessary drawback. If some of the explanatory variables are multicollinear, the prediction interval obtained will be large. By eliminating some collinear variables, one can reduce prediction interval for a given value of the included independent variables. But the actual outcome will change

very little. Pragmatic forecasts and simulation would be indifferent to the extent of collinearity while sophisticated ones will not. Both will make similar forecasts and the errors will be very similar. See Kuh and Meyer (1957), pp. 380–393.

35. The root mean square of the error (RMS) is the most important summary statistic in indicating how well the simulated model tracks empirical observations. Other important summary statistics include the mean of the forecast and the mean of the simulation, the percentage error for each, their mean errors, the mean of their first differences, and the mean of their percentage first differences. These statistics, presented further along, are compared with counterpart statistics for the historical data, and the discrepancy indicates the extent of fit between actual observations and simulated values. *TROLL/1 User's Guide*, 1972, pp. 8–28.

36. This procedure assumes that changes in one coefficient will not lead to counterbalancing changes in others.

37. See Chapter 17 of Choucri and North (1975) for a detailed discussion of the experimental analysis.

CHAPTER THIRTEEN

SYSTEM DYNAMICS FORECASTING IN INTERNATIONAL RELATIONS

Nazli Choucri

With the assistance of Brian Pollins

I. INTRODUCTION

System dynamics represents a theory of system structure and is a set of tools for identifying, depicting, and analyzing multiloop, nonlinear feedback relationships. It is a relatively new method of analyzing the structure and behavior of social systems, although its theoretical foundations were set several years ago by control theory and systems engineering. In its present form, system dynamics draws upon the intellectual world view now associated with general systems theory, systems analysis, and cybernetics. As a method of analyzing social systems, it was initially developed at MIT two decades ago and was first employed as a means of analyzing the management problems associated with production schedules and product distribution in industrial firms. More recently, a wider range of social and political problems have been examined through the use of this methodology, and only in the past 4 to 5 years have scholars of international relations drawn upon the underlying analytical tools for investigating global problems.

The objectives of a system dynamics study are as follows:

1. To understand the *structure* of the system under consideration;

2. To identify *policies* that might propel a system toward the desired objectives, or assist in avoiding negative outcomes;

3. To clarify prevailing *theories* regarding the system in question and provide the basis for the comparison of alternative theories;

4. To identify and resolve differences in *assump-*

tions, perspectives, and views regarding the structure or processes under consideration; and

5. To isolate *sensitive parameters* in a model whose modification would affect overall system behavior.

Given the complexities of international interactions, the frequent nonlinearities, and the difficulties of identifying, measuring, and predicting the future behavior of key variables, system dynamics as a methodology has important potential uses for the analysis of international behavior. Many of the problems confronting national leaders involve a host of factors over which they do not have direct control and whose interactions they do not fully understand. Different assumptions are made and policies identified accordingly. Yet there is little provision within conventional modes in inquiry—in either academic or policy-making circles—for systematic investigation of the consequences of alternative assumptions or of the ways in which one's analysis of a situation is shaped by the assumptions one employs. The system dynamics paradigm is extremely well suited for the organization of information, theories, and expectations regarding the problem at hand; and the accompanying algorithms allow for ready investigation of the implications or consequences of enacting alternative policies. Thus, a decision maker can define the boundaries of his problem, specify in even loose fashion the relationships among key variables, and articulate his expectations regarding their future behavior. With this information, it is then possible for an analyst to develop a formal specification of the problem at hand, isolate major interactions and feedback relations, and observe the consequences for system behavior of the adoption of alternative policies.[1]

By way of illustrating the applications of system dynamics to international relations forecasting, this chapter outlines the basic research method and underlying methodology, specifies the assumptions, biases, and perspectives, and compares these with econometric analysis, a more frequently used mode of inquiry among quantitative political scientists. Since scholars and analysts of international relations have, as yet, not been fully exposed to system dynamics, one purpose of this chapter is to provide some specific examples of the uses of this methodology for forecasting purposes, and to indicate the attendant gains and losses.

II. THE APPROACH

The most fundamental tenet of system dynamics relates to the nature of systems and to the limitations on the capacity of the human mind to anticipate the behavior of higher-order complex systems. It is assumed, first, that in all nontrivial systems, cause and effect are often widely separate in time and space. This results primarily from the fact that *delays* are present in the system structure that tend to widen the link between an action and its effect. Such delays involve information gathering, policy implementation, and policy effects. Thus, actions intended to produce one kind of outcome at one point in the system all too often result in an adverse or unintended outcome at that same point, or at some other point in the system. The inability of the human mind to trace the higher-order effects of even a singular action underscores this problem. In addition, human comprehension is thwarted by the fact that many critical relationships in systems are *nonlinear,* discontinuous, or have no adequate linear approximation. It is difficult for the human mind to incorporate nonlinear relationships into "thought experiments" or mental models, or in any kind of nonformal analysis. Finally, since the sheer number of relationships within the complex systems is overwhelming, it is extremely difficult to comprehend system behavior without recourse to formal modeling. Thus, system dynamicists argue that because delays, nonlinearities, and complexities are inherent to social systems, it is necessary to employ a computer-based simulation for understanding their behavior and for identifying the higher order and long-term effects of individual decisions or policy interventions.

The second important aspect of this approach is derived from the first. Since any formal model is superior to its verbal counterpart, our understanding of the system under study is better served if we begin formalization at an early stage, rather than wait for total conceptual closure. Therefore, the value of a model lies in its utility more than in its validity. Questions of model validity are less important than model *utility* for system dynamicists, and the usefulness of a model for pol-icy purposes is the most important criterion for model evaluation. However, there is nothing in the accompanying algorithms that would prevent an analyst from employing rigorous validation criteria or from constructing a fully specified and deduc-tively complete model, conformable to standards of formal validation. However, since a system dynamics model is generally formulated in terms of the search for solutions to a specific problem, its purpose is always articulated as a basic input into the model, and the level of technical detail and specification is determined by the objectives of the investigator. Thus, if his purposes were to deter-mine and apply standards of formal rigor to his in-quiry, then the algorithms would accommodate such an effort.

Third, this approach assumes that an investi-gator's purpose is to search for policies that would increase the probability of desirable outcomes and decrease the probability of negative ones. This leads to a research strategy of *satisficing*, rather than optimizing as is more conventionally the case with other formal modeling approaches. A key philosophical contention in this regard is that op-timizing is not a legitimate activity for social mod-elers, in view of the complexities of interactions among components of a system and the limitations of existing analytical tools.

Fourth, it is assumed that complex systems are dominated by feedback relations. A feedback sys-tem is influenced primarily by its own internal structure involving elements related through nega-tive and positive feedback. The behavioral tenden-cies of a system depend on the balance of positive and negative loops. The obvious bias is upon en-dogenous explanations of system behavior: A model that resorts to exogenous factors for producing sys-tem behavior is, by definition, a poor model. Thus, a system dynamics model is exclusively a *closed system*. Defining the boundaries of the problem amounts to the single most important prerequisite for developing the structure of the model, and boundary definition is predicated on an explicit statement of problem and purpose. The implica-tions of the foregoing for simulation are fairly straightforward. Since the basic structure of a feedback loop is "a closed path connecting in se-quence a decision that controls action, and the level of the system, and information about the

level of the system, the latter returning to the decision-making point" (Forrester, 1968, pp. 1–7, and 1971), the model is first approximated by spe-cifying the loop structure.

Fifth, as an outcome of the above assumptions, system dynamics is predicated on the analysis of *functional relationships* in a feedback system and not, as is common in social sciences, on the analy-sis of stochastic relationships. The difference in emphasis is one of interlocking feedback with non-linear relations in a system of differential equa-tions, versus (1) best fit criteria; (2) simultaneous solutions of algebraic equations; or (3) optimization of key parameters. But there are, again, no methodological reasons why stochastic analysis cannot be undertaken within a system dynamics paradigm or, alternatively, why the parameters of a system dynamics model cannot be derived from empirical data. In some cases, both approaches may, in fact, be complementary. However, no one has, as yet, employed both methodologies to ana-lyze the same problem and determine the gains and losses accompanying each approach. This emphasis on functional rather than stochastic relations is pred-icated on the utility assumption noted above and on the desire to use a model for policy purposes. It emerges from the general policy orientation of sys-tem dynamics investigations and is a necessary consequence of the modeling approach. System dynamicists would argue that the emphasis on statistical relationships constitutes misplaced effort for modelers concerned with analyzing the implica-tions of policy interventions in complex systems, since such systems can more readily be understood in terms of their constituent parts interacting through feedback loop structures. Efforts to de-velop statistical specifications of these functional re-lationships would deprive the investigator of the analytical flexibility brought to bear on his under-standing of the system structure. This issue re-mains much debated among supporters and oppo-nents of system dynamics. In the last analysis, its resolution depends on an accurate specification of the gains to be attained by focusing on stochastic relationships, in contrast to the losses of analytical flexibility incurred in efforts to meet assumptions underlying statistical analysis.

Sixth, the operational directive is for *conditional* analysis, not point prediction. Within this para-digm, accurate point prediction is not possible, although a system dynamics forecast can provide a better understanding of international behavior than a purely probabilistic model or models based on linear-additive assumptions. This is a particularly powerful perspective for analysts concerned with modalities of behavior rather than specific predictions at a particular point in time. System dynamics is thus concerned primarily with the overall behavior of a system over time; in policy testing, it is interested in finding out how policies will change system behavior, not in predicting the specific point at which the change will occur or where a system will be at any given moment.

In sum, the approach of this forecasting technique is basically defined by the following suppositions:

Formal models are necessary for understanding the behavior of complex systems.

The behavior of a system can be best understood if it is modeled as a set of *endogenous* processes.

Endogenously determined behavior is generated by *functional* relations.

Forecasting is specified in *conditional* terms.

III. THE RESEARCH PARADIGM

System Dynamics and Systems Analysis[2]

System dynamics is actually a specialized method for performing systems analysis. As such, it professes a systems-analytic ontological view as well as a systems-analytic form of problem representation. As in all systems analysis, a system dynamics study will focus its observation and analysis upon (1) those elements or variables relevant to the question at hand, (2) the arrangement of those elements and their patterns of interaction, and (3) the way in which the system transforms inputs into outputs over time; that is, the dynamic behavior of the system.[3]

In systems analysis, the elements of the system under study and their arrangement is generally referred to as the *structure* of the system, and the "rules" by which inputs are transformed by the structure into dynamic behavior define the system's *function*.[4] To avoid any confusion, it should be restated that the inputs are generated endogenously: The system is closed. In a dynamic study,

the outputs (behavior) of one period become the inputs of the next period. The structure and function of the system are assumed invariant, at least over the time horizon of the study. Since both structure and function are time invariant, and system inputs result from feedback relations, the behavior of the system is said to be "state-determined." In system dynamics, structure and function are also treated as time invariant. However, the possibility of structural transformation is recognized, although not accommodated by the attendant algorithm.

Some system-analytic algorithms, such as linear programming, are structured to maximize or optimize certain values. This is not the case with system dynamics; it is not an optimizing strategy and carries no specific optimizing techniques. As noted earlier, system dynamicists are interested in the behavior mode of the entire system over time, so that long-term direct effects of various policies may be examined and unanticipated consequences may be identified anywhere in the system. The investigator's goal is to increase (rather than maximize) the probability of desirable outcomes and decrease (rather than minimize) undesirable outcomes. This, in Herbert Simon's words, is a satisficing rather than an optimizing approach.

The Structure of the Forecasting Language

The modeling language is DYNAMO, a formal representation of the system dynamics worldview, as well as a computer language to represent the system mathematically. The attendant graphical representations of the functional relations and of the computer program are key aspects of the modeling procedure, since they are designed to assist the investigator in understanding the basic assumptions built into the model.

The major elements of the modeling language are: (1) *levels*, which are the state variables in the system, the major structural determinants; (2) *rates*, which control the fluctuations in the state variables; and (3) *auxiliaries*, which help define the rates. The basic mathematical tool is integration, through which we are able to relate a quantity (level) at any given moment to the rate of change of that quantity over time. So, for example, if we think of rates as representing "decisions," then levels are the accumulation of all past decisions. In reality, rates are action streams that *may* be determined by conscious human intervention (e.g., all policies enter the system as rate changes), but may also be determined unconsciously by structural factors in the system. Auxiliary variables are actually expansions of the rate equations, and they are included as distinct entities in the system simply to assist human understanding of the relationship between levels and rates. Auxiliaries and rates may change rapidly, in comparison with levels, which change more slowly.

There are three additional elements in the modeling language: delays, table functions, and constants. Delays, essentially, represent lags in the system. They are of two kinds: material delays, representing the lags of material flows, or information delays, referring to information flows. These delays usually account for the separation in time between cause and effect. At times, delays will enhance system stability since they may dampen the effect of a "shock" in the system. More often, delays thwart system stability in that unanticipated consequences are usually caused by delays in problem recognition and policy implementation. In fact, the "overshoot and collapse" behavior mode exhibited by many systems could not occur without the presence of delays. The specification of delay structure is necessary for the investigator to formalize the temporal influence throughout the model. This consideration iş crucial in forecasting, where the importance of delays in shaping behavioral responses is infrequently recognized.[5] To a very large extent, the structure of delays shapes the response of the system to alternative policy specifications.

Table functions represent functional relationships between two variables, and they are the primary means by which the system dynamicist is able to incorporate nonlinear relationships into the system. They are graphical representations of bivariate relations, and the shape of the graph provides the program with the information necessary for specifying the value of a system variable at any given moment. Like a bivariate regression, the computer will assign a value to a specified variable that is dependent upon the value of another variable (time may be used as the independent variable as well as any other variable in the system). The important feature, of course, is that this func-

tion need not be linear. Table functions can also be used to incorporate information that is not easily quantified (so-called soft variables) or to include qualitative relationships in the same manner that an econometrician would include dummy variables. Finally, constants may act as coefficients, or they may be employed as multipliers influencing other variables.

The first formal representation of the relationships is a model of the causal loop diagram; but it does not distinguish among levels, rates, auxiliaries, or delays. These distinctions are made in the DYNAMO flow diagram and become the necessary precondition for writing the equations. It is always better to have as simple a representation of the processes modeled as possible. The more complex the model, the more difficult it is to understand its behavior or to gain a grasp of the dynamic processes. Generally, complexity is proportional to the number of state variables in the system, so the more levels that a model includes, the more difficult it is to understand its behavior. This emphasis on understanding is predicated on the concern with evaluating policy alternatives, for unless one understands the structure and behavior of a model, it is not possible to assess the relative implications of alternative policies.

Procedure

A typical system dynamics study is composed of ten stages with interactions back and forth:

1. Become familiar with the issues to be modeled and obtain an understanding of the system in question, delineating the issues and problems;

2. Provide a verbal description of the general question or problem to be addressed, specifying the endogenous, exogenous, and excluded issues;

3. Identify the reference mode of the system, that is, the dynamic behavior one would wish to model and reproduce initially as the first formal representation of the issues of concern;

4. Specify the system boundary, delineating endogenous, exogenous, and excluded variables and relationships;

5. Formulate the causal loop diagram representing the structure of the system, and the basic mechanisms believed to cause the reference mode specified in the previous stage;

6. Formulate the DYNAMO flow diagram as an unambiguous graphical specification of the system structure;

7. Write the DYNAMO equations, that is, the program input into the computer;

8. Examine the computer output, noting the model behavior for changes in the structure or in the parameters and undertaking systematic experiments with alternative policy runs to understand the behavior of the system in cases of different policy interventions;

9. Provide additional detail in the structure of the model until it is sufficiently realistic to meet the needs of the user; and

10. Make policy recommendations based on the results of the sensitivity runs.

The construction of a causal loop diagram (stage 5) is the first step in transforming a verbal and intuitive understanding of system structure into a formal representation. It specifies how the elements of a system fit together and the direction of the influences. It is the initial formal representation of the positive and negative feedback loops. The DYNAMO flow diagram (stage 6) then specifies the model in terms of its constituent elements: levels, rates, auxiliaries, and delays. And the development of computer (model) equations follow formally from the detailed DYNAMO flow diagram. These equations enable the investigator to undertake stages 8 and 9 in the development of a system dynamics model.

So far we have described the research paradigm underlying system dynamics, the basic assumptions, methods, and procedures, and structure of the computer language. At this point, we compare the key assumptions of system dynamics with those of econometrics. Our purpose is to identify the convergences and divergences between these two modeling traditions, by way of evaluating the gains and losses of each.

IV. A PARTIAL COMPARISON OF ASSUMPTIONS: ECONOMETRICS AND SYSTEM DYNAMICS[6]

Our comparison revolves around several generic issues at the base of all computer modeling techniques:

System Boundary

Econometric models are *open* systems, including many factors that are, relative to the time horizon under consideration, not determined by the system modeled. Furthermore, econometric models make necessary use of exogenous variables in order to estimate the parameters of the model. But there are specific assumptions about the nature of these exogenous variables, and restrictions on their use. By contrast, a system dynamics model seeks to represent a *closed* system. Its objective is to generate reasonable system behavior without recourse to exogenous variables. It is assumed that if all the key relationships have been included within the feedback loops, the phenomenon modeled will be adequately explained.

The Role of Stochastic Factors

Econometric models assume that a forecast is not meaningful unless accompanied by a statement regarding level of uncertainty, and that the error around the parameters estimated from empirical data provides information regarding the reliability of the forecast. Again, by contrast, a system dynamics model does not take account of random factors, but it assumes that these are not strong enough to determine system behavior. Since the purpose of a system dynamics model is to isolate the impact of key policies, delineating the effects of stochastic factors is not considered important. An econometric model, however, makes use of the information contained in the level of uncertainty and in the disturbances or residuals.

Validation

Econometric assumptions adopt a statistical perspective on validation, where conventional statistical criteria are employed to determine the significance of individual equations and their correspondence to empirical observations. The criteria are external to the model and do not depend on the purposes of the investigator. By contrast, validation in a system dynamics perspective is almost exclusively determined by the extent to which the model replicates historical behavior, even on face value, and assists in understanding a specific situation, or is useful in making decisions about a real problem. Validation is relative and there are no external criteria by which to judge the validity of a model other than its usefulness for policy analysis. (There are other ways in which validation is regarded, but they are not critical here.)

The Uses of Data

Econometric models require data to estimate the parameters and to evaluate the validity of the model. Without data, the model cannot be tested. Access to data is critical for any econometric model. There are conventional data requirements and constraints and established procedures for evaluating their characteristics and the extent to which they can be used for estimation purposes. On the other hand, in a system dynamics model data does not assume the paramount role that it does in an econometric one. It is believed that there are too many nonmeasurable factors of importance, that data cannot represent the dynamic attributes or a system; that the length of time for which a model is run is usually too short to rely profitably on the information contained in data; and that specifying functional relations among variables is more important than seeking to identify their statistical relationship. Data are often inadequate for identifying functional relations. This is to suggest, not that a system dynamics model does not make use of empirical information, but that the observations employed are not required to meet the strict requirements posed by econometric and statistical models.

Reference Mode

The reference mode is the historical behavior of the system under study, or the future behavior mode of the system that the researcher would like to duplicate. By replicating historical behavior, we validate the model. By replicating the desired future behavior mode, we find the correct policies. For pragmatic purposes, it is useful to specify the desired future behavior in terms of an equilibrium condition. The policy exercises, therefore, identify the options that would contribute to this outcome or to any specified alternative. An econometric model does not rely on comparing alternative policy runs with the standard run. While this is often

done in practice, it does not assume the same importance in the research design.

Time Frame

Most uses of system dynamics adopt a long-range perspective on the problem modeled; it is generally assumed that only a long-run perspective will yield full evidence and insight into the behavior of the system and its characteristics. In an econometrics model, by contrast, it is customary to focus on the shorter range, largely on the assumption that the parameters estimated from empirical data are valid only over a short time period, and that changes in the system result in parameter changes that may invalidate the initial models used for economic planning require a short time horizon to be maximally useful. The difference in perspective results from the practices of the modelers, and not from any built-in requirement or attribute of the methodology. The algorithms of system dynamics can adapt to any time perspective with any time interval. The same is generally true for analysis.

Feedback

The system dynamics model is, most centrally, based on interlocking positive and negative feedback. Dynamic processes are built into the model—by assumption, algorithm, and functional specification. Econometric models are generally less dynamic and less prone to feedback specifications. This is due in part to the nature of the algorithms, and in part to established practices in the field.

V. APPLICATIONS TO INTERNATIONAL RELATIONS

Few scholars of international relations have, as yet, drawn upon system dynamics for either modeling or forecasting purposes. At this point, we summarize some recent efforts in this direction, by way of illustrating the general uses of this methodology, and attendant problems and prospects.

Two examples will be employed, both drawn from recent investigations on the international implications of resource problems undertaken at the Massachusetts Institute of Technology. A third example will be reported on more extensively in

Chapter 21 (p. 308). Suffice it here to illustrate the general approach and the attendant gains and losses. The three studies represent different stages of a research program in international relations forecasting, the empirical investigations of which were supported by a grant from the National Science Foundation. The basic purpose of this research is to understand how a nation's resource endowments shape its foreign policy behavior, and to test the implications of different policies pursued to assure access to resources. A second objective is to determine the conditions under which various policies might be conducive to international violence, and to determine the responses that would decrease propensities for conflict among nations.

The first study represents a general statement of the relationship between resource endowments and foreign policy and presents some initial policy runs. The second study is an examination of the policies and interactions of petroleum exporters and importers in their attempts to develop means of meeting their respective foreign policy objectives. The third study is a more detailed analysis of the domestic sources of external behavior and of the role of resource scarcity in the calculus of determinant variables, with the United States as a specific case study.

The following sections of this chapter describe each effort briefly as a means of illustrating the ways in which system dynamics has been, and continues to be, a useful tool for international relations forecasting.

Resource Scarcity and Foreign Policy: A Simulation Model of International Conflict[7]

This model represents the first application of system dynamics to international relations. Its purposes are to formulate a generic structure of interactions among the various determinants of foreign policy behavior, to isolate the factors that shape a nation's resource needs, and to identify the policies that could assist in meeting these needs. A basic concern is to determine how different policies could be conducive to international conflict. The basic theory adopted for modeling purposes is predicated on the proposition that major wars often emerge by way of a two-step process: In terms of internally-generated pressures toward expansion of interests and in terms of the reciprocal compari-

sons, rivalries, and conflict for control over resources or valued goods, territory, or spheres of influence. Each process tends to be closely related to the other and each, to a surprising degree, can be accounted for in terms of more aggregate considerations or variables that are relatively state determined or nonmanipulable in the short run.[8] For this reason, it is important to find out what variables policy makers can, in fact, manipulate and what effects such manipulations might have on the behavior of a system.

The model is composed of a set of feedback relationships representing the demands for resources generated by a growing population with military and economic capabilities to pursue these demands through various modes of international behavior. The more pressing the demands, the greater will be the pursuit of external sources, particularly if resources are not available domestically, or if they can be obtained more cheaply elsewhere. Conflict is modeled as occurring when two or more countries with high capabilities and unsatisfied demands extend their activities outward and increase their allocations to the military in pursuit of such activities. The problem, thus, is to find policies that would ensure access to needed resources, while at the same time decrease external violence.

The forecasting model is composed of several distinct but interrelated sectors, each composed of one or more feedback loops, and connected through a series of loops. These sectors are: (1) population, determining the demands on resources, and demands for productive capital to assist in pursuing resource needs; (2) productive capital and technology, to yield the relationships generating capabilities to pursue resource demands; (3) domestic pressures, representing the outcome of the interaction between population, resource needs, and productive capital; (4) military expansion, representing the effects of allocations to the military; and (5) resource usages and allocations, representing the acquisition of external resources and the extent to which such acquisitions detract from the exploitation of internal sources.

The types of policy options investigated included behavioral alternatives available to a nation as it seeks to attain its foreign policy goals, as well as inputs into the decision system of a nation occasioned by the actions of other states. Thus, we looked at the impact of the decision to refrain from exploiting domestic resources and to rely exclusively on external sources, and observed the implications for the behavior of the system. Our analysis suggests that such a policy would result in increased foreign costs, as well as increased allocations to the military, both of which would necessitate drawing excessively upon available productive capital, and channeling it to resource acquisition activities rather than to economic growth. The long-term impact would be to reduce the availability of productive capital. Alternatively, we investigated the consequences of a policy of refraining from employing external sources and focusing specifically on domestic resources, and observed that the net effects depended largely on the initial level at which the domestic resources of a nation were specified. In the prototypical US model specified as having a relatively high resource base, such an option would not have negative effects economically, and would avoid accelerated investments in the military, and, by extension, detract from diverting productive capital to nonproductive uses. In still another set of policy runs, we set up the forecasting problem so as to reflect a situation in which the United States would be faced with low internal and external usable resources and high foreign costs of acquiring these resources. Any policies designed to increase the availability of resources in such a context would result in the initial increases in consumption per capita (reflecting a situation before the full impact of foreign costs were incurred), but then consumption would fall off (indicating the constraints encountered). In the longer run, however, declines in consumption per capita will have positive effects, enabling increases in subsequent investments available for expansion. With a persisting shortage of resources, the overall behavior of the system exhibits a gradual decrease in expansionist propensities and in foreign policy activities.

These broad observations are designed to indicate how a problem in international politics can be defined in system dynamics terms, and the kinds of issues that can be fruitfully investigated. This first study has led to a clearer specification of the foreign policy problems associated with the desire to gain access over scarce resources. The second study, referred to above, represents a continuation of this effort. Its purpose is to be of assistance to foreign policy analysts concerned with United States policies toward the exporters of its raw materials.

Energy Demand and International Politics: Imports, Price, and Costs[9]

The extension of the forecasting work described above focuses on the problems to be encountered by the United States in the next 30 years in its attempt to meet its petroleum needs. We begin with the fact that the United States is the world's largest producer of energy, but also its largest consumer, and, being a net energy importer, its economy is increasingly vulnerable to disruption by international factors. Even with the stipulations and policy directives of Project Independence, and its favorable resource/consumption position in relation to other advanced industrial societies, the United States will not become self-sufficient by 1980 or even 1990. Policies designed for self-sufficiency, if implemented today, will not reduce the United States' dependence upon external imports in the immediate future. The country will continue to face the same problems confronting other consuming states.

The complexities of interdependencies between petroleum exporters, the importing countries, and the multinational oil companies who manage petroleum exchanges require a model that takes into account the international determinants of economic and political costs of meeting resource demands with attendant sources of conflict; enables analysis of the consequences of potential policies of and for both producers and consumers; assumes a global perspective by taking into account constraints upon the physical process of resource production; and assists in identifying potential long-range impacts of immediate decisions.

As presently structured, the model is strongly influenced by the difference between domestic production and consumption. The demand for petroleum affects the consumer's trade balance and overall balance of payments; this balance is also influenced by the extent to which the producers pursue policies of increasing repatriation of overseas investment profits. The greater the repatriation, the more positive the effects on the country's balance of payments, but the lower will be investments in expanding the availability of overseas resources. Thus, there are clear trade-offs identified from the consumer country's perspective. For the producer countries (whose policies and decisions inevitably affect the consumers), investments, tax rates, patterns of resource consumption, and imports of commodity goods from the consumer countries are all determined by development priorities and by accumulation of capital stock. The producer's long-term capital investments in the consumer countries will offset the latter's capital account. Thus, to the extent that the producers choose to repatriate investment income, they directly influence the consumer's balance of payments.

This series of interactions provides the structure of the model and enables us to examine the consequences for the consumer countries of various investment and tax policies enacted by the producers, and vice versa. The application of system dynamics to this kind of behavioral problem in international relations is very useful in assisting foreign analysts to identify potential outcomes of alternative policies. It is also of assistance to identify the types of policy experiments and forecasting runs that would be helpful for thinking about the future implications of alternative US postures in interactions with the producers of crude petroleum.

This forecasting project was completed in the winter of 1975. The modeling activity is structured to take account of the flows and interactions among producers, consumers, and the investment activity of the multinational oil corporations. It incorporates the international financial consequences and the flow of revenues across national boundaries as consumer countries seek to find means of meeting their oil import payments; it takes into account the decision processes within the producer and consumer governments, and the decisions governing investments in exploration and development of petroleum sources. The first forecasting goal is to reproduce the historical behavior of interactions between producers and consumers; the second is to determine the effects on each of the policies adopted by the other.

A third forecasting study employing system dynamics to examine an international relations problem is described in great detail in Chapter 21 of the present volume, where we present specific forecasts and analyze their implications. This study is a systematic attempt to examine the implications of alternative US government priorities upon the disposition to extend national behavior outside territorial boundaries. As such, it represents a partial theory of the sources of foreign policy, specifies the functional relationships among constituent elements in the theory, and examines the implications in terms of alternative futures for the United States.

NOTES

1. Further along in this chapter, we shall present specific examples of the foregoing.
2. The material under the heading "System Dynamics and Systems Analysis," Section III, was written by Brian Pollins. The purpose of this section is simply to acquaint the reader with the relationship of system dynamics to systems analysis, a more widely known research paradigm. It is not an exhaustive discussion of the issues involved.
3. The observations on systems analysis in this section of the chapter are drawn largely from Cortes, et al. (1974), p. 336. This book is an excellent introduction to systems analysis as a research paradigm, and is written for the nontechnical reader.
4. Despite the terminology, this method is not similar to the "structural-functional" analysis that pervaded the early literature in the field of political development.
5. Witness the fact that the impact of delays are not examined in other chapters.
6. I am grateful to Peter Senge for long discussions on this issue and for describing the results of his experiments. This section is based on a table prepared by Senge, designed to juxtapose the assumptions underlying these two approaches to modeling complex systems. See Chapter 12 for some key elements of econometric analysis.
7. Choucri, et al. (1972), p. 81.
8. A detailed theoretical statement with accompanying empirical referents and analysis is presented in Choucri and North (1975). See Part II for an historical analysis and Part III for quantitative investigations.
9. Choucri and Ross (1975).

CHAPTER FOURTEEN

GAMING: PROSPECTIVE FOR FORECASTING

Garry D. Brewer

I. INTRODUCTION

The ever-present desire to anticipate and manage the future intelligently has so far been directly thwarted by the complexity of most social systems (LaPorte, 1974; Brunner and Brewer, 1971; and Weaver, 1948, pp. 536–544). For instance, the by now classic method of extrapolating trends may be an effective forecasting technique only so long as a complex system is largely inert, the number of fac-

This chapter was originally prepared and delivered as remarks to a Conference on Forecasting in International Relations held at the American Academy of Arts and Sciences, Brookline, Mass., October 3–5, 1973. Support for that conference and encouragement for the overall project came from Saul Mendlovitz and the World Law Fund. Special thanks are due Thomas Robinson of the National Defense University and Nazli Choucri of the Massachusetts Institute of Technology, both of whom conceived and have shephereded the project throughout. Robinson's careful and tactful editorial hand helped to shape an earlier draft, although he is absolved of responsibility for the final result.

tors considered is relatively small, the interconnections between factors are few and basically understood, and no unexpected exogenous or structural changes occur. If these conditions do not hold, as they usually do not, forecasting by extrapolation may be impossible or may generate erroneous and misleading information (Brunner and Brewer, 1974). A revised conception of projection and alternative methods then may be required, in which case, simulations, games, process models, scenarios, group judgment techniques, planning, utopia writing, and developmental constructs must be utilized.

Moreover, up to now, forecasting specialists have limited themselves to a few of these techniques. Ideally, the techniques could be combined in the following fashion:

One technique is to extrapolate quantified trends and distributions to locate zones of probable contradiction or conflict, and to utilize available knowledge of the interdependencies among conditioning factors to make an estimate of the probable outcomes. The hypotheses thus developed can be evaluated in the light of non-quantified information provided by competent observers. (Lasswell, 1968, pp. 3–18)

The raw ingredients for useful forecasting are thus clear: quality data on important trends, some understanding of data relationships, a reasonably clear understanding and statement of individual and collective goals, and finally systematic methods and procedures by which a full and appropriate range of information may be brought to bear on what is indicated by the projected trends. It is the last—or methodological prerequisite—on which we shall focus attention, particularly gaming.

The gaming art exists in an unsettled condition, one indication of which is that there are no generally acknowledged and useful definitions to characterize it. In a recently completed survey of modeling, simulating, and gaming activities (Shubik and Brewer, 1972), the authors were forced to adopt the acronym "MSG" to designate "model, simulation, or game" so that particular usages of these terms could be accommodated. Lack of agreement about the meanings of these three primitive terms is the norm, and serious, unresolved definitional problems continue. It is hoped that the following terminological exercise establishes meanings that are sufficiently clear for the purposes of this exposition (Shubik and Brewer, pp. 80–82 [abstracted]).

Gaming: A gaming exercise employs human beings acting as themselves or playing simulated roles in an environment that is either actual or simulated. The players may be experimental subjects or participants in an exercise being run for teaching, operational, training, planning, or other purposes.

A major application of the basic technique is international relations gaming in which activities involving two or more interacting nation-actors are depicted using rules, data, and procedures designed to replicate the essential features of an actual or assumed real-life situation. Games can be accomplished manually, can be computer-assisted, or can be wholly computerized.

Simulation: Simulation involves the representation of a system or organism by another system or model, which is designed to have a relevant behavioral similarity with the original system. Games utilize a simulated environment or simu-

lated roles for the players or both. In general, all games are simulations. However, not all simulations are usefully regarded as games.

Computer simulation is an analytical technique that involves the use of mathematical and logical models to represent the study and behavior of real-world or hypothetical events, processes, or systems over extended periods of time.

Model: Conducting a computer or computer-assisted game or related simulation requires the use of a computerized model. As used in this context, a model is a document or program containing all rules, methodology, techniques, procedures, and logic required to simulate or approximate reality. A computerized model is a computer program or series of programs, designed to simulate the logic of actions or interactions of an environment or context and provide the results to player personnel for subsequent analysis.

Contained in these definitions are two important ways in which the gaming field may be conceptualized: according to the *types* of games that exist or according to the *purposes* for which games are played.

II. TYPES OF GAMES[1]

While many individuals label themselves "gamers," it is useful to distinguish four general types of games: analytic models, machine simulations, man-machine games, and free-form games. Examples of each type may be found in fields as far removed as educating pre-schoolers and calculating assured destruction in a nuclear exchange; however, these four typical categories are capable of encompassing most activities.[2]

Analytic models are usually quite abstract, poor in the number of variables explicitly considered, but rich in ease of manipulation and clarity of insight (Schelling, 1958, pp. 203–264 and Dresher, 1961). For many questions, the analytic model may give a single number for an answer, as contrasted with multiple, interrelated indicators of system behavior that may result from the use of other techniques.

Game theory has had certain applicability in analytic modeling, although applications of the theory have resulted in highly variable degrees of success, an outcome frequently related more to the sophistication and ingenuity of the analyst than to simple technical virtuosity (Shubik, 1972, pp. 37–49).

An analytic model may help in sorting out basic problem elements in a real setting that, once recognized, usually can be resolved or at least better understood. Analytic models are usually too circumscribed to solve actual problems directly. However, because normally they are simply and clearly posed, they may shed light on potential difficulties, indicate where additional measurements are most needed, and identify and order critical omissions. Such is the case, for example, in the well-known "prisoner's dilemma" game, where the barest essentials of a complex decision process are reduced to simple matrix form.

While analytic models have important uses, those using them often act as if there were no limitations; there are.

> Methodology *per se* is less crucial in determining the worth of the product produced than the skill and judgment of the analyst who applies it. A highly simplistic and objectively inadequate model may produce valuable and insightful conclusions in the hands of a skilled and thoughtful analyst who is substantively knowledgeable in his subject. The same model may produce faulty, erroneous, or misleading conclusions in the hands of a less thoughtful analyst, even when its application is technically correct. (Strauch, 1974)

In harsh contrast with analytic models, machine simulations frequently involve many variables; many seem to make a fetish of "realism."[3] Rationales for simulations by machine are many and varied. One common and frequently valid reason is that mathematics is a relatively impoverished language, whereas the computer allows one to capture the richness of a real system. Often left unsaid is the enormous price one is likely to pay to approximate that reality, as measured in the quantities of data needed and in the difficulty anyone has in understanding the logical processing of the large simulations.

Man-machine exercises usually involve a digital computer and people playing some of the roles in the modeled system. People may be used because they are cheaper than the software needed to reproduce some required behavior, or people may be used because human factors (particularly judgment)

are important in the situation being analyzed. The Rand Corporation's Logistic Simulation Laboratory provided an example of a man-machine simulation in which people were used more as an integral part of the machinery than as subjects for human factor analysis (Geisler and Ginsberg, 1965).[4] John L. Kennedy's pioneering work, on the other hand, is an example of human factor analysis (Chapman and Kennedy, 1955). UCLA's Center for the Computer Based Studies of Behavioral Sciences has in more recent years carried on that tradition.[5]

Free-form gaming involves teams and a referee group operating within the framework of a scenario. If computational equipment is used at all, it is often relegated to a simple bookkeeping role. Of the four types, this is the least amenable to tight technical control; however, it is the most likely to produce an impressive array of new insights into complex problems as a result of the "playful" and often open-ended course that the free-form game is capable of taking. Free-form gaming is also the least expensive, receives far and away the most publicity, and is often done at the highest policy levels. (Goldhamer and Speier, 1959, pp. 712–83). It is a form of activity that could be exploited to a far greater extent than it has been in the past, a point to which we return below.[6]

III. PURPOSES OF GAMES

The need to define the purpose of a game carefully cannot be stressed enough. For instance, criteria for assessment or validation are related directly to the explicit purposes of a game, although the connection is rarely made in practice. One does not judge teaching games, where the intention is to impart a skill or to motivate students, as harshly or in the same way as an experimental game, where the intention is to generate scientific insights or to test theory.

Martin Shubik (1972, pp. 20–36) has differentiated six basic gaming purposes with examples of applications arrayed under each. His basic list includes teaching, experimentation, entertainment, therapy and diagnosis, training, and operations. In this thorough exercise, "forecasting" occurs only as one of eight possible applications under the general purposive heading of gaming for operations. Generally, operational games are used almost exclusively by adults in military, governmental, or corporate organizations; their largest use, by far, is in the military and diplomatic-military communities. It is for this reason, among others, that many of the examples occurring throughout this chapter are drawn from these experiences. Relative to military and military-diplomatic uses, corporate operational gaming is insignificant, and the use of operational gaming for social planning is infantile.[7]

Operational games have been used to *cross-check other techniques,* an application suited to the full exploration of a problem rather than reliance on a single, dominant method. Games may serve the unstated but important purposes of *extra-organizational communication* and mutual assessment. Busy decision makers may be as much interested in the personal styles of their bureaucratic and political colleagues and competitors in a game setting as they are in the topic, play, and manifest outcomes of the game itself. The tendency of the highest level American federal officials to participate in political-military games soon after a new administration comes to power—a tendency that soon and significantly attenuates—is an example.

Planning, exploration, and testing represent a third operational use of games. Such games are characterized by elaborate, detailed preparatory activities, deliberate play where interesting questions raised are often set aside for detailed post-game analysis and reflection, and painstaking debriefing of all participants.[8] To be productive, planning games should use the real people involved in the fine detail of the operations and contexts being scrutinized.

Eliciting group opinion and judgment is a fourth operational application, especially where decisions are not replicable. For example, in discussing strategic arms limitation, there is no way of testing the comparative advantage of complementary weapons systems to determine which of them are relatively more effective, liable to be launched successfully, or subject to a more positive command and control. The role of expert opinion in such situations is clear, and various group judgment techniques (among other methods) have been created in recent years that at least confront the issue. Such techniques may easily and correctly be viewed as a specialized form of gaming activity[9] in which present and forecast planning factors are elicited in a formal, game-like structure.

"Brainstorming" has been developed and used for forecasting and other operational applications with mixed degrees of success over the years.

Advocacy uses are often discernible in operational gaming activities. One need only recall the advocacy use of games in Japan's Total War Research Institute prior to Pearl Harbor to show how games could be used to bolster institutional or personal preferences.[10]

The *forecasting* use of operational games is slight as compared with these other possibilities. A key point is that a forecaster is likely to use a variety of methods to aid him in arriving at a *best* estimate of the future; however, the distinction between contingency planning and forecasting helps to explain why a variety of methods in addition to gaming should be used to make specific estimates.

> A good operational game may make use of good forecasting procedures but it is not in itself aimed at providing forecasts. This should not be confused with its use in discovering new alternatives and in helping to evaluate future possibilities. *Forecasting and contingency planning are related but extremely different activities.* In particular, a good forecaster may not be in the slightest interested in the importance or worth of his forecast. Accuracy may be a goal for the forecaster in and of itself, not because of its relevancy to the planning process.
>
> A game may be a useful device for stressing the need for coordination of forecasting activities with planning and decision-making processes. In this sense the involvement of forecasters in the design and play of operational games may be of considerable use. (Shubik, 1972a, pp. 11–12)

This means that if one wants to make a point estimate of some future event, gaming is probably not the sole method of choice, although it may be a valuable supplement to alternative techniques. A game may tell one a great deal about the relative importance of events in some setting, their possible interactions, and a range of feasible and probable outcomes—and for all of these reasons, and more, it is important. However, the hard specification of a single, most *likely* outcome—including its extract time and magnitude—is generally beyond the capacity of the method.

To exploit gaming's relative strengths and to minimize its actual weaknesses, we must reconsider our usual way of thinking about forecasting and projection.

IV. AN EXPANDED CONCEPTION OF PROJECTION

The general concept of projection commonly employed is ill-developed, and the following discussion raises several issues in an attempt to improve the current state of affairs.

Contextuality, Operations, and Creativity

If higher level analytic details cannot be deduced from statements about constituent parts, point prediction is not always possible. However, this strictly logical constraint ought not limit our impulses to anticipate and manage the future.

Contextuality. Emerging phenomena are unpredictable only in the strictly logical sense. Such phenomena can be anticipated using a consistent frame of reference or context.[11] Historians remind us that contexts are usually unique in specific details and hence making a point prediction can be a hazardous business. Key elements in a given context may never exactly reappear, thus creating great uncertainty that a given phenomenon will likewise reappear. Seeking relief from this uncertainty, one is led to reply on different approaches, to use a variety of methodologies, and to draw his conclusions from several distinct (but related) levels of analytic detail. It also means that all approaches, levels, and methods should be set in as rich a context as possible.[12]

Basically one attempts to concentrate on the "zones of probable contradiction or conflict," recalling an earlier comment from Lasswell, and to examine the factors underlying the zones of tension so that some understanding and estimation of likely outcomes follows. These are all context-dependent activities, and one should not expect to have much projective success without first having a great deal of detailed understanding about a specific setting.

Operations. The probability of an anticipated event actually occurring is relative to the state of theoretical knowledge, historical developments, and the purposes of those participating at each level of analytic resolution. Projections are subject to modification, deflection, or reinforcement in accordance with purposeful, manipulative steps, commonly referred to as policies. To be concerned about operational matters—as one presumes the gamer-forecaster is—is to be concerned about several related aspects of any specified context, for example, operating goals, past trends, structural relationships, and implemented policies. Projecting the future then is equivalent to figuring out what might happen in such a context if nothing is done to intervene, if ranges of plausible interventions are adopted, and if a single option is in fact taken.

Creativity. Resolving the problem of relating actual future events to the range of possible and plausible interventions concerns one's creative orientation to the subject, and anything that stimulates this orientation is to be encouraged. Given this broadened conception of projection, the analyst moves between thinking deeply about the narrow details of a context and synthesizing its fullest, most information laden, and complex forms. This process and its results are more an act of creativity than they are one of automatic forecasting. It is not an idle argument, but one prompted by several observable pathologies that plague current applications of gaming and closely related techniques.

Some Current Pathologies

Sometimes extraordinary emphasis is placed on specific outcomes of gaming exercises as *the* point of interest. The term "outcome" suggests a single, well-defined event to be compared, *ex post facto*, with a prior point prediction.[13] Shooting craps and betting on horses are activities amenable to this type of thinking about projection; forecasting complex behavior such as that encountered over long periods of time in an international setting is not.

Methodological Deformations. Noticeable success with a given method, regardless of the purpose at hand, tends to produce an urge to apply it in all subsequent situations, appropriate or not. In the end the method often becomes an obsession. Faithful technicians set up schools to propagate the method among true believers, and throughout the separation of the method from its original success-ful application is lost. The extension of some in-teresting methodological ideas developed in an in-dustrial setting to encompass the world is one clear case. One finds little to quibble with in Jay Forres-ter's early probings of the Sprague Electric Com-pany with a method that has since come to be known as "system dynamics"; however, his and others' later efforts to capture the world with the same method have drawn fire from many quarters (Forrester, 1961 and 1971; Meadows, *et al.*, 1972; Cole, 1973). Science is sometimes perverted to the propagation of means, and the original end, the de-sired objective, is quickly forgotten. A single-minded concern for the technical mechanisms of a given game or model is one unhappy manifestation of this tendency.[14]

If one is willing to accept our expanded concep-tion of projection, then a harsh demand for strict empirical validation of one's projective efforts seems somewhat out of place. We engage in pro-jection primarily to explore contingencies; we do not, accepting the creative premise and purpose, strive to make hard, point estimates—which are probably out of reach anyhow. Particularly in in-ternational relations forecasting the distinction is not subtle, but fundamental.

Even the predictive excellence of physical theories, the model from which we take many of our professional cues, and the relationship of em-pirical investigation to insightful and creative breakthroughs in the "harder" disciplines are not always as great or as direct as natural scientists would lead others to believe. Thomas Kuhn's work on scientific paradigms is directed exactly to these points; others could be mentioned (Kuhn, 1964 and Rostand, 1960). Furthermore, in those cases where a direct connection between one's rigorous method, empirical findings, and conclusions seem to have been made, this often proves illusory. Re-cent efforts of "decision theorists" to predict indi-vidual level behavior using advanced applications of Bayesian statistical techniques have evoked a great deal of attention within both research and policy communities. However, the connections made between the decision theoretical corpus and the findings generated uniformly concern highly selected aspects of the empirical settings, and the implications following from such selections are sel-dom acknowledged.[15]

It is sometimes argued that such assumptions [a general reference to the problem considered here] are made for "analytical convenience," and the results must, of course, be interpreted in a larger context. This argument would be valid if, in fact, the problems of interpretation in a larger context were regularly considered and addressed; but they seldom are. (Strauch, 1972, pp. 32–44, at pp. 38ff)

This is not to deprecate the efforts of decision theorists to advance viable and reliable predictions; it is to stress the fundamental problem that arises when one demands hard, point estimates in an en-vironment where such estimates are not likely to be forthcoming.[16] It further stresses the impor-tance of taking an expanded view of projection and the need for a more creative and open approach to the basic problem: understanding and projecting a variety of likely and plausible contingencies for specified contexts.

Deformation of the Level of Analysis. A related point is suggested by efforts to forecast system level outcomes based primarily on individual level information. Naively mixing levels of analytic detail deforms this task—a deformation that is at least addressed in contextual efforts to game.

One must make distinctions between the differ-ent levels of analytic detail that may be operating in a given setting. For instance, categories such as the following have been used to do this: *individual level detail*, including studies of elite behavior, in-depth psychological studies of key individuals, and psychological profiles containing extensive background information about the socialization of ruling and key decision makers;[17] *group or institu-tional interactions*, including crisis behavior, com-parative studies of relevant decision-making bodies, and interorganizational studies;[18] *national level analyses*, including (disreputable) "national character" studies, and macroprocess studies;[19] and finally, *international relations*, comprising much of the literature so identified.[20] Alternative and com-plementary dimensions exist with which to struc-ture the level of resolution or detail and include the following: *temporal*,[21] *spatial*,[22] and *military-operational*—in which spatial and temporal con-cepts are related to specific activities, e.g., en-gagements, battles, wars, campaigns—(Shubik and

Brewer, 1972; and Livermore, 1898). Various dimensions and associated level are consistently and erroneously mixed in practical application, and we must be continually aware of differences in structure, process, and behavior of each conceptual dimension and between each of the representative levels of analysis.

This is a serious problem having grave consequences for those who must make estimates and decide policy involving vast resources.[23] To oversimplify, the problem appears partly to be a misapplication to the institutional level of methods, theories, and techniques of analysis that are more appropriately used to study individual level details.[24] As is patently obvious upon examination of the various examples presented in conjunction with different levels of analysis, each level requires different kinds of data, different analytic methods, and different research "styles." While we need to be conscious not to mix them indiscriminately in making forecasts or projections, the demand for systematic methods and techniques to integrate these analytic perspectives is acute. Carefully and conscientiously employed, gaming may have a distinct role to play in this regard.[25]

Deformations of Simplification. Three simplifications commonly occur in efforts to conduct operational gaming for forecasting and related applications: (1) treating a simply structured gaming device as if it were reality itself rather than only a substitute for, or perspective of, reality (Flook, 1970, pp. 181–184); (2) assuming symmetrical configurations of opposing teams or forces;[26] and (3) selecting rather narrowly from among the set of candidate topics for inclusion in one's games and models.

Games by definition are abstract simplifications. This fact is routinely overlooked in the course of game design, play, and use, and the results have been detrimental for projective applications.[28]

Resources are often employed in game settings far better than in the real world, leading to inflated expectations about future levels of performance and efficiency. Institutional structures, introduced into the game setting as a given, are frequently eliminated or severely modified in the interests of game play, leading one to presume that moribund, inert, and intractable institutions could be simply

managed in the real world.[29] Again, expectations about future performance far outstrip the maximum feasible levels of effort expected by the most optimistic of reasonable people. Time rates of change of gamed or modeled elements are accelerated unrealistically in the game setting, creating false perceptions of the actual rates of change attainable in the operational setting.[30]

There will always be discontinuities between the gamed or modeled setting and its reference system; however, being common and persistent, they generally impede improved applications of operational games. The difficulties presented by these factors in any given application are primarily a function of the skill and experience of the analyst-gamer responsible for the work.

The concept of symmetry is well known enough in gaming circles; at its simplest, it means that opposing teams are equivalently structured and endowed. However, less well known are the simplifications that flow directly from careless reliance on the concept, particularly in the areas of forecasting military force postures and structures (Isaacs, 1965). With respect to current discussions of mutual and balanced force reduction, for example, symmetry assumptions could very easily lead one to the conclusion that equivalent reductions in forces would have approximately equivalent effects on either side; of course, this overlooks the fact that a Soviet division removed from Poland only travels across a border, while an American division removed from West Germany ends up some 4000 miles from the scene. The impact of symmetry assumptions in Strategic Arms Limitation Talks (SALT) is reflected in the fact that a Soviet missile or weapon system is not equivalent to an American one, and crude "numbers games" matching absolute amounts of missiles and warheads tells one very little about either the weapons or their relative effectiveness.

The problem is easily seen in the gaming context where, given an imagined or predetermined number and configuration of the opposing force, maintenance of symmetry compels one to have a proportionate or equivalent number and configuration (Dresher, 1959). The most obvious result of such simplification in the real world has been a rather unimaginative tendency to progress in lockstep fashion with one's imagined foe of the moment; innovations, as achieved in research and development initiatives, tend to focus on "keeping up" or "staying ahead" by making marginal adjustments to the current hardware and forces and resisting basic changes in extant procedures, tactics, strategy, or doctrine. At base is the simplifying (and distorting) concept of symmetry.[31]

The selection of topics for inclusion in one's games or analyses is a third source of simplifying distortion. The act of selection implies that the topics chosen are relatively more important and that items omitted are of less value. The problem of selection is not an abstract or simply "academic" one. In our survey of the active inventory of 132 operational models, simulations, and games in the United States Department of Defense inventory at the end of 1971, we found only one listed as having a political-diplomatic-military/international relations primary purpose. Given present-day concern over SALT, the Middle East, and the expansion and clarification of Sino- and Soviet-American relations, this is a startling finding (Shubik and Brewer, 1972, pp. 16–17). By far the bulk of MSG activity is devoted to all-computer technical evaluations and force structure analyses. Technical evaluations turn out to be weapon system evaluation, most accurately characterized as value-free engineering work, where the selection process has operated vengefully to exclude many important but hard-to-quantify components.

V. SOME FUNDAMENTAL QUESTIONS

Several even more fundamental questions and issues related to gaming have received little or no attention by responsible professionals. This is not only surprising, but inhibits the development and productive utilization of the various types of gaming and closely related methodologies for serious operational and research purposes.[32] It is through careful attention to the fundamentals that progress toward improved forecasting with games may one day be realized to a greater extent than at present. For this reason, primarily, a few of the fundamentals are spelled out in the following section.

There is nothing approximating a distinct theory of gaming, as distinguished from game theory, decision theory, small-group theory, or any one of a number of theoretical paradigms. There is also no

serious scholarship devoted to the exploration of the limits and validity of the knowledge—or the epistemology—generated by modeling, simulating, or gaming. For instance, how might one go about identifying and then comparing the underlying, implicit theories involved in models, simulations, and games? Everyone works with simplified representations of contexts as those found in the international relations sphere; the question focuses on the need for systematic ways to expose and then compare the simplifications that are actually being used to make forecasts. At the current state of knowledge, games are more likely to yield insights than to solve a problem directly; however, no one is certain about what game players and builders actually are "getting out" of the play or construction activity. It is an empirical problem, the resolution of which would improve game construction and play for many purposes, forecasting included.

A common feature of nearly all gaming activities is the scenario.[33] Scenarios range in style and complexity from the elaborate, fully articulated version often used in free-form games to implicit scenarios embedded deeply within hard, all-machine models. Little is known about the differences a scenario makes for game play and outcomes. Even less is known about what constitutes a "good" versus a "bad" scenario. However, these matters may be investigated, although very little effort has been expended to date. For example, what differences are caused in game play and outcomes when teams play a common scenario, scenarios based on inferred perceptions of one another, or scenarios with excessive "noise" or other diversionary elements embedded in them? (Jarvis, 1970 and Iklé, 1964) The problems of perception and signaling are fundamental in the international context, but we have not yet undertaken enough systematic investigation of these topics to know with certainty just how much or how little impact different versions of the same situation will have on game and realistic outcomes. The critical importance of these matters for forecasting decisions in an international bargaining or negotiation setting is clear, but apparently little appreciated.

Given the extraordinary time and resources devoted to all-machine, "engineering-like" MSGs, one should be able to expose the implicit scenarios built into these representations to understand them and to begin to assess whether and in which ways the scenarios have distorted the models. Not only is this seldom done, but because of a number of technical and management problems related to documentation and secrecy, it is usually not possible to recreate the images and assumptions that underlie most quantitative MSGs. The user, as a result is frequently faced with a "take it or leave it" situation that makes questioning the forecasted results of many operational MSGs problematic at best.

Confusion of purposes has intruded on scenario construction and stimulated subsequent abuse. For example, in Herman Kahn and Anthony Weiner's *The Year 2000* (1967), an exercise in speculation with basic research purposes, Japan's role in future international relations was noted as becoming third only to the United States and the Soviet Union; however, the scenario upon which this forecast was based made some important assumptions, e.g., with respect to world stability and the likely growth of natural resources, which many Japanese operators either did not appreciate or chose to ignore in leaping to the questionable conclusion that Japan would *in fact* become the third most powerful nation in the world by 2000. This example calls attention to an important, unresolved, and fundamental question: How does one safeguard against eager users taking a scenario originally intended for a narrow research question and promoting it to support some point of view or choice already taken by other means? No one knows, and the question is ripe.

A basic point is that we know almost nothing about the effects of a scenario, but we do know that as long as scenarios are regarded merely as aids to research and operational problem solving and not as valued entities in themselves, we are not likely to make much progress in developing using the scenario methodology.

Citing some of the fundamental problems associated with scenarios calls attention to the more general deficiency of institutions and procedures to control, monitor, and evaluate the construction, developing and use of models, simulations and games. It is an unhealthy situation and deserves consideration as to who should be responsible, what institutions need to be created or changed to ensure faithful and valid operation and use, and

what sorts of incentives should be structured into the present system to alleviate many current abuses. This is a major message contained in the results reported for the Shubik and Brewer survey of operational MSGs in the Department of Defense, and hence it encompasses many devices being used for forecasting purposes.

Another fundamental question, or more correctly a collection of questions, concerns the uses or applications made of MSGs. It appears that many operational MSGs are built after decisions are made, that is, the devices are used to justify choices made for other reasons by other means. Applications of games and related techniques to policy problems have received inadequate professional attention. The over-enthusiastic use of methodologies (particularly where quantification is involved) has been caused, to a certain extent at least, by inattention to limitations of the methodologies and to difficulties of interpreting results of the analysis of problems whose quantifiability is itself subject to question (Strauch, 1974).

IV. GAMING PROSPECTIVE: SPECIFIC DIRECTIONS FOR RESEARCH

As the foregoing partial recitation of fundamental, unresolved questions indicates, the determination of a list of research topics easily becomes an open-ended task, and the list's overall utility correspondingly decreases. What follows is a brief characterization of a few topics that appear especially susceptible to research probings and and where the interconnection of gaming, forecasting, and international relations is pronounced.

Size

There is generally only the slightest appreciation for the effects of game size on the construction and operation of models, simulations, and games, and there is even less understanding of the effects of size on applications.[34] Is it better, for instance, to build small, simple, and easily understood MSGs (such as those currently referred to as "elementary process models" by Ithiel Pool and his associates), knowing full well that they are not "realistic," or should one opt for large, highly detailed, complicated devices that purport to capture reality?

Those electing the former point of view have implicitly adopted the old modeler's dictum to "model simple and think complex". It is difficult to identify the philosophy of those building and using the larger devices, much beyond saying that reality is not easily or cheaply captured in a black box.

Data Bases: Validity and Control

Very little attention has been given to data validation. All too frequently a set of data is used commonly by a large number of diverse operators without their giving adequate thought to whether the data are suitable to a specific application (Shubik and Brewer, 1972, pp. 35–37). Validation has become an article of faith justified by such familiar expedients as saying that a data source is the only one known to exist, others use it in "similar" activities, collecting data is too time consuming and expensive, or the data, it is claimed, have become "standards" for the generation of planning factors or estimates.

The control of data bases has also not received adequate attention. In international relations, the best known data base management system is probably the US State Department's CASCON (Bloomfield and Beattie, 1971, pp. 33–53; and Tanter, 1972, pp. 7–39), but it is still in the development or earliest implementation stages. We do not know yet, in straightforward terms, whether the system works for State Department decision makers or not.

Ex Post Facto Reconstructions

One productive way to answer the question, "How good have games been in forecasting international relations?" is to conduct *ex post facto* analyses of the game play and outcomes and make comparisons with realized events. Better information about appropriate game use will certainly result; more importantly, such reconstructions might clarify erroneous assumptions made in the *a priori* setting, sort out good from bad forecasters and forecasts, and improve the future use of games and related projective methodologies.

Many of the observations reported in the above section, "Some Current Pathologies," were derived from a rather unsystematic *ex post facto* summary of a large number of games. There is no reason

why this kind of work could not be done routinely. If assumptions about a supposed opponent's decision-making processes yield consistently incorrect results in a number of gamed and modeled situations, there is an obvious need to reexamine those assumptions. If past exercises produced incorrect results because of the embedded assumptions, there is good reason to believe that prospective analyses and exercises will continue to do so.

Terrorism

Several common structural features of the act of terrorism might lend themselves to game or game-like treatment. The "players" in the terror "game" may include any or all of the following: audience, terrorist, victim, media, spectator, authorities, allies, and sanctuaries. The separate phases of the terrorist act, that is, the "play" of the game, include the following: preparation, execution, climax, and dénouement. Such a structural framework could serve the very useful purposes of organizing much of the existing, fragmented case study literature on terrorism and of understanding terrorism's many forms and processes so that preventive and ameliorative policies might be developed.[35]

Deception Games

Deception has been a normal matter in the practical conduct of international affairs; surprisingly, scholars have not directed their full attention to this topic in recent times.[36]

Deception might be tackled with gaming techniques by first beginning to build up a contextual base of information of those instances in international affairs where deception has been employed. There is some literature on this, particularly Barton Whaley's almost single-handed efforts of the 5-year period 1969–1973 (1969 and 1973). One could move from these beginnings to the creative tasks of figuring out ways to practice deception better, more effectively, and more efficiently, and hence, figuring out what might be done to counter the typical forms discerned in history.[37] Because the creative aspect of gaming combines systematic with more speculative purposes and procedures, it seems to be one excellent methodological vehicle for this sort of activity.

Crisis Games

Extraordinary actions may become plausible in a crisis, but this does not mean that more, more interesting, or better actions present themselves. On the contrary, one of the major consistent findings of crisis analyses is that the number and variety of options rapidly diminish in the short- to no-lead time, high-stakes situation (Buchan, 1966 and La Porte, 1974). In fact, one of the prime objectives of crisis analyses is to figure out ways to expand the set of feasible and plausible options available to decision makers (Averch and Lavin, 1965 and Holsti, 1971, pp. 53–67).

One might also view Graham Allison's study of the Cuban missile crisis as a gaming exercise (1971). The construction of his three explanatory models was a creative and successful attempt to develop alternative decision-making scenarios. One of the major findings of the work was that there were too few options available to the relevant decision-making participants, e.g., bombing the Cuban missile sites had far less to recommend it when the chips were down than when it was considered in military contingency plans. In short, creativity inherent in the use of gaming as an option-generating device had largely been ignored in the pre-crisis period with the result that decision-makers had to "play it by ear" far more than they should have when the crisis actually unfolded. Gaming techniques, for example, the specification of assumptions, the structuring the flow of likely and consequent events from those assumptions, and the examination of alternative assumptions, structures, and so forth, have something to offer to improve these matters.

Termination Games

It has been argued that insufficient thought is ordinarily given to the different ways in which hostilities might end. The process of war is seldom considered from its initiation to its eventual and likely conclusions.[38] Several distinct topics shed light on this most overlooked of the phases of war. The first relates to understanding the characteristic decision-making styles of those thought most likely to be involved in war termination. The second concerns systematic comprehension of the negotiation strategies and tactics used by politico-military authorities. The third focuses on the kinds of communication, command, and control apparatus that would be depended upon to wage and then terminate a war. The fourth, and perhaps the most important, task is figuring out ways to end a war before it begins, and failing that, to end the war at something less than total destruction of the hostile parties.

Each of these topics may be discussed with respect to gaming's potential contributory role. This is done below to stress the importance to forecasting of termination games, to indicate the kind of thinking that should be applied to each of the foregoing research tasks—but which has been omitted from this overview—and to summarize the main themes and arguments of the chapter through examples of a gaming-based, prospective research outline.

While credible work exists that attempts to discern the decision-making styles of powerful individual and institutional actors in the world arena (see Leites, 1959), little has been directed to answering the critical question, "How will a given individual or institution likely behave when it comes time to end hostilities?"

For decision makers close at hand, it may be useful to question them directly to discern the operating images and assumptions shaping particular ways they perceive the world.[39] What are the key individuals' identifications, expectations, and demands, particularly as they relate to war termination potentialities? This exceedingly difficult research problem could be left unexplored if war were not so terrible; fortunately, there are research and evidentiary procedures that might be used. For instance, the in-depth interview, careful biographic construction, and cross-examination all should be brought to bear with an end in view of establishing the parameters, or operational constraints, of those involved in a war termination game. Lacking such basic information, forecasting the likely outcomes of a conflict situation will continue to be more guesswork than science.

For those to whom accessibility is restricted, research is naturally more problematic, although not impossible. Psychoanalytic profiles can be used to build up the stock of contextual materials for the termination game. The skill of the analyst is, as always, a primary ingredient required to do the job well, and the power of the technique has been admirably demonstrated by an especially capable researcher in his dissection of *The Mind of Adolph Hitler*.[40] Similar, equally skillful, and detailed investigations are needed of the key decision makers who would likely play in future termination games.

Negotiation is widely regarded as an art, but as with other art forms, it yields to systematic scrutiny (Iklé, 1964). To this end, gaming has a distinct, but unexploited role. Several questions illustrate a few possibilities:

What is the characteristic scope of bargains struck with those most likely to be participants in a termination situation? Is it usually narrow and concerned with very specific details or is it general and vague?

How much worth is attached to human life?

How is the future generally perceived? Are there characteristic discount rates associated with bargains struck in the past? If so, how might this affect future bargaining situations?

How is the concept of "sincerity" operationalized? What is required to signal the fact that one's position is preliminary and negotiable as contrasted with a final and nonnegotiable one?

What kinds of bargaining strategies and tactics have been successful and unsuccessful, and why?

What can be said about the chemistry of successful and unsuccessful bargains? For instance, if there is some latitude in the selection of individuals to do the actual negotiating, then what are the likely combinations of personalities and circumstances that will enhance, retard, or abort proposed discussions? (This of course depends upon one's hopes and expectations about eventual outcomes.)

Once again, we are confronted with difficult and complex questions. Rather than despairing, we should begin to figure out ways of overcoming some of them. As a start, too little was done to carefully observe the proceedings at the Strategic Arms Limitations Talks (SALT II). Better observation and analysis here could provide an up-date on the Soviet bargaining style and decision processes to complement the knowledge assembled from past dealings. Are the processes the same, détente notwithstanding, or are there important, probably subtle, differences operating? What are the likely consequences of such changes? And so forth. Another source of information is private businessmen who increasingly, from multinational bases of power, bargain with bureaucrats quite like those who would conduct aspects of termination.

To assume that a Chinese general views the world in the same ways that a Russian or American general does could be quite unfortunate in some future negotiations, for example in trying to minimize the consequences of overt hostilities. Some work has been done to sort out the images and styles of potential antagonists, but given the requirement to know a great deal about a few specific individuals who would be involved in a termination negotiation, one has the impression that more and better quality efforts should be expended to this end.

Communication, command, and control together constitute a third area worthy of concerted investigation if one's overriding objective is to determine whether and if a future war could be brought to conclusion short of total devastation.[41] Are there natural "stopping points" that might be established ahead of the outbreak of war that would not exist if serious thought had not been expended beforehand? If one's objective is to end a war with minimum damage to all parties concerned, presuming that all efforts have failed to prevent it in the first place or that it has started accidentally, what can we say about the configuration of communication systems, weapon systems, or prearranged actions on the part of any or all parties? If, for example, the maintenance of Washington, DC as a command center is judged to be critical to the retention of a termination-before-total-destruction-is-realized capability, how might this information be made known to one's likely opponents in a nuclear war?[42] That is to say, if American command and control of a strategic war transfers by default to the military leadership resident inside a distant mountain in the Rockies, what happens to the likelihood that war can be terminated short of total devastation? How might the configurations of current and planned weapons systems be altered if one adopts a termination attitude? Instead of arguing over the merits of specific defensive weapons in the B-1 strategic bomber, could at least a small part of the discussion and attention be turned to the need to equip one of these aircraft as a weapon of negotiation instead of as a weapon of destruction?[43] There may exist an option to end a future war short of devastation that depends upon equipping at least one aircraft with appropriate communications equipment and upon the existence of some prearranged location where end-of-war discussions could take place. This option would not logically occur unless the termination perspective were explicitly adopted. One final example helps to make the basic point. The disarmament of specific submarines or missiles may be a critical element in any terminal negotiations. How might procedures for voluntary disarmament be agreed upon in advance to avoid the less desirable contingency of having to say, "If you do not disarm, we will do it for you"?

There are extraordinary difficulties involved in terminating a war, and many of these—although far from all—[44] are based on communication with, command over, and control of the war-making machinery. Imperative is contingent planning based on a microscopic scrutiny of the likely operations of the three deadly "Cs." The use of variable levels of analysis, distinct observational perspectives, and detailed scenarios—all strengths of gaming or game-like endeavors—is obvious, even though it has not yet been undertaken with a fraction of the resources that we expend to study war initiation and implementation.

NOTES

1. Shubik and Brewer, 1971, pp. 15–33.
2. A more thorough review of the general gaming literature is contained in Subik, *et al.* (1972). This document is organized around some thirteen separate, coded categories including game type, purpose, mathematical sophistication, game name, year published, and so forth.
3. TEMPER, a very large international relations machine simulation, appears to have suffered particularly from this problem. For a short summary of the model, see Abt (1964), pp. 29–37. A thorough critique is contained in Balinski, *et al.* (1966).
4. The Rand Corporation's leadership role in many of the activities discussed is considerable, and will be reflected in the references and examples cited throughout.
5. Others could also be noted. For instance, the Management Science Laboratory at the University of California at Berkeley; NEWS, the Naval Electronic Warfare Simulator, at Newport, R.I., the POLIS Laboratory at the University of California at Santa Barbara. See Shubik, *et al.* (1972a), pp. 24–26, for a more complete listing.

6. The fact that free-form games have slighted several important scientific requisites has been presented as one basic reason for inattention; the matter is resolvable, however. See Shubik and Brewer (1972), pp. 329–348.
7. Many of gaming's operational possibilities, including forecasting, have been discussed over the years. The works of Clayton J. Thomas, Walter L. Deemer, Milton Weiner, and Edwin Paxson are recommended particularly: Thomas and Deemer (1957), pp. 1–27; Weiner (1968), Chapter 14; and Paxson (1963). Each of these individuals is a gaming professional of long and rich experience, and each has in his career made significant and creative contributions to the craft. As a crude indicator of the fragmentation of the field, however, the odds are that few educational, experimental, or academic gamers have even heard of them, read any of their work, or know about their many contributions.
8. Many examples are known among professionals, and Edwin Paxson's X-RAY series of games is a clear case in point. Paxson (1972), Chapter 3.
9. Norman Dalkey and Olaf Helmer are readily identified with the creation and development of Delphi techniques. A recent summary of the status of Delphi is contained in Dalkey, *et al.* (1972).
10. Wohlstetter (1962) contains an account. The highly revealing debate before the US Senate conducted by Albert Wohlstetter and George Rathjens on the Safeguard ABM system illustrates the point in more contemporary terms. The entire issue of *Operations Research* (1971) was devoted to this.
11. This is precisely the message contained in Harold Lasswell's formulation and use of the "developmental construct," where the primacy of *contextual detail* is stressed to good effect. See Lasswell (1938), pp. 704–716 and the classic statement of the idea in his *The Garrison State*, (1941), pp. 455–468.
12. This is the issue considered in DeWeerd (1974). "A contextual framework helps one to exclude irrelevant materials and permits a concentration on the central problem under analysis. Unless one is dealing with present-day problems and can be assured that all members of a game or research team know precisely what the present situation is—and can agree on it—one needs a context to avoid wasting time in reaching a common approach to the subject. When dealing with future problems, it is even more desirable to have a context to provide a common understanding of what the particular future under consideration is like. Otherwise, each man will form his own ideas about the future and these ideas can vary widely, making group research or game efforts difficult." From the manuscript, same title (1973, p. 1).
13. Hitchcock (1958) treats this concept in making comparisons between games for operational, demonstration, research, and training purposes.
14. Bull (1966), pp. 361–377, states the case well in arguing that technique-intensive efforts to understand international contexts have "succeeded in providing

figures only to be blinded by the illumination they cast" (p. 374). What he objects to most is the simplification inherent in any MSG and the failure of the methods-oriented theorist to occasionally make connections with the real world. His point is often valid.

15. Harold W. Kuhn stresses this matter in the context of negotiations and points out that game theoretic efforts abstract out essential aspects of an empirical context and assumptions made in the interests of theoretical tractability produce results that are insufficiently detailed. The blame, in Kuhn's view, is shared by game theorist and behavioralist alike. (Kuhn, 1962, pp. 1–4). An excellent general source is Raiffa (1968); a detailed technical statement is contained in Slovic and Lichtehnstein (1971), pp. 649–744.

16. The literature here is burgeoning, but one early and well-presented man-machine example is Miller, *et al.* (1967). In this case, one gets a sense of one area where decision theorists have been relatively successful. The question—and it is moot—is whether international relations contexts are sufficiently congruent with that exemplified by JUDGE to allow easy transferral of the theories and methods. Insufficient results exist to make the judgment.

17. A durable example of this kind of work is contained in Lasswell and Lerner (1965), especially the substantive chapters on the Politburo, the Fascists, the Nazi elite, and the two Chinese elites—the Kuomingtang and the Communists. George and George (1965) is an example of a detailed personality assessment that could conceivably be developed as a complementary activity to the actual play of a game in which the actions of key figures dominate. To the author's knowledge, such has not been done, although the possibilities are fascinating to speculate on.

18. Graham T. Allison's well-known *Essence of Decision* (1971) has many of the requisite characteristics for this level of analysis; and Leites (1951), is another excellent case in point.
    In the gaming setting, this level of detail has been studied experimentally. One example is Binder (1966), pp. 129–139, and another is the so-called "risky shift" phenomenon reported in Wallich and Kogan (1965), pp. 1–19. The connections between these experimental games and operational-forecasting efforts are tenuous.

19. Mead (1951); Cantril (1961); and Lipset and Lowenthal (1961), all exemplify attempts to work with this style and level of analysis. The idea of "national character" has gained common coinage; however, it is for the most part meaningless, even mythical, derived from the most casual of observations.

20. G. Modelski (1970), pp. 111–134, takes as a point of departure some of the limitations of the Inter-National Simulation (INS) with respect to monolithic assumptions made about the analytic unit "nation" and develops some alternative and supplementary model-building strategies. L. P. Bloomfield (1970) discusses the possibilities of predicting policy behav-

ior using free-form gaming techniques with specific attention to multilateral and great power relations as well as arms control issues.

21. S. A. Boorman (1969) presents a fascinating account in gaming terms of the Chinese Communists' rise to power. The timing and general conceptions of play contained in the board game *Wei-ch'i* (Japanese *Go*) are relied on as the descriptive and explanatory analogy, and done so with impact. A more technical discussion of the importance of time in model building and use is Nance (1971), pp. 59–73, in which the basic ideas of timing moves by "fixed" and "event" clocks are carefully laid out.

22. Board and map maneuver games typify an emphasis on this level of analysis. McHugh (1966) is one of the most comprehensive summaries of the type.

23. One policy maker has summed the matter up in the following terms with respect to forecasting bureaucratic behavior: "Until it is possible to understand, much more completely than we do now, the decision-making process within typical military bureaucracies, it is doubtful that we can do an effective job of forecasting likely future military postures beyond those relatively few years into the future, during which the inertia and commitment implied in current posture and current program decisions decisively determine the future posture. In other words, forecasts for planning purposes and estimates which involve implicit estimates of military power beyond about four to five years in the future require an understanding of the decision-making behavior of military organizations that we do not have. To continue to rely to any extent on the notion that such organizations have a well-defined consistent set of objectives which they seek to attain with fairly optimal expenditure of resources given them by their government is seriously in error" (Marshall, 1966, pp. 21–22).

24. In my opinion, this is one of the nagging problems of several of the more popular free-form gaming activities. In a game setting where individual level activities are undertaken and observed, there is little reason to make the considerable inferential leap to speculate on aggregate institutional behavior not actually observed in game play. In Crow (1963), pp. 580–589, one is given a very good example of this problem; and in Bloomfield (1971), pp. 9–13, major institutional problems are discussed whose solution, it is suggested, could be worked out by playing games that have typically stressed the individual level of detail.

25. The difficult matter of selecting an appropriate method to forecast international relations settings is addressed in Davis (1963), pp. 590–602. Davis suggests that small, well-defined aspects of the arms control issue might be studied under laboratory or experimental conditions, but the broader, more inclusive topic will most likely defy conventional or single-purpose analytic treatment. His argument follows closely one developed earlier in this chapter: for complex settings, one will probably have to rely on a number of methods and techniques to begin to un-

derstand the context sufficiently well that informed judgments about the future may begin to be made. Shubik and the author deal with this explicitly (1972).

26. One example of the mischief that this assumption can cause is presented in Hatry, *et al.* (1962). The difficulty is more commonly seen in verbal rationalizations presented to the Congress in support of generally increased expenditures or in support of a specific weapons system.

27. There is an understandable, but unfortunate, tendency in many military games to stress quantifiable elements to the virtual exclusion of nonquantifiable but important ones. Hence in the Shubik and Brewer survey of activity in the Department of Defense in 1971, less than 1 percent of all models surveyed dealt with international relations and/or political-diplomatic-military purposes.

28. W. J. Crow and R. C. Noel (1965) have considered this situation in terms of players' psychological attributes, the social context of game play, and the nature of the simulated situation confronted. At base were concerns for a game's purpose and the kind of players used in a free-form situation. Both concerns have been ill-appreciated for the most part by advocates and users of free-form, international relations games for forecasting and policy purposes.

29. Both TEMPER and World Dynamics illustrate this contention. For the former, Balinski, *et al.* (1966), and for the latter Cole, *et al.* (1973), make the appropriate comments.

30. In his critical, annotated bibliography, M. Patchen (1970), pp. 389–407, touches on this problem, especially in the two sections labeled "Models Predicting Influence Behaviors," and "Reaction Process Models." The issue is treated well and somewhat differently in Dalkey (1966), where the concepts of *payoff, criterion,* and *complexity of the representation* are all discussed. It should also be noted that these problems are seldom handled in a forthright manner in typical game representation and play, with harmful consequences for forecasting and other purposes.

31. Andrew Marshall (1966) is one rare example where the concept has been appreciated, both in gaming and operational terms.

32. R. C. Snyder (1962), pp. 103–171, conducted a parallel exercise and noted with respect to many "fundamental" questions, "Hopefully we stand at the threshold of a period of further efforts to give greater depth and breadth to the configuration of hypotheses and applications of conceptual schemes" (p. 118). I fear Snyder was too optimistic, for, a decade and a half later, the work has scarcely begun.

33. DeWeerd (1967 and 1968) represents a variety of work that has been done in the areas of scenario construction and applications. The first is a survey of the state of the art by one of the trade's master scenarists, and the second is a 5-year forecast of Middle East events (1968–1973) which is striking for its plausibility and the extent of its accuracy in "calling the shots." Other examples of scenarios include Bloomfield (1968); Hawkes (1968), pp. 14–16; Kahn

(1964 and 1965); Ogden (1932); and DeLeon (1973).

34. Besides TEMPER, where the problem has already been noted, consider the "Air Battle Model," a major activity that evolved into a specialized supporting institution within the Air Force command structure in the 1960's. See Adams and Jenkins (1960), pp. 600–615. The basic problem, that of constructing huge, impossible to understand, MSGs continues, although the paucity of available documentation masks the practice. One exception is CODE 50, which was still operational in 1971. See Bick and Everett (1967) (unclassified).

35. This section on terrorism was suggested in conversation with Abraham Kaplan in August, 1973. He is carrying out some of the initial investigations implied in the formulation.

36. Roberta Wohlstetter's excellent work (1962) failed to stimulate very much activity in the area, despite the many research leads she created.

37. The second task has been undertaken with some interesting preliminary results in Harris (1974). Besides coining the label "sprignals"—meaning "spurious signals"—another interesting feature of both the Whaley and Harris works is that they have been developed entirely with open, published sources, that is, deception is not necessarily an ethereal topic whose development and clarification need be hamstrung by classification restrictions.

38. Iklé (1971) must rank as one of the most important and underrated books of the past few years.

39. One of the key lessons Richard Neustadt presents in his *Alliance Politics* (1970) is the importance of different perspectives of the same situation, different expectations about likely and desirable outcomes of some shared event, and different scenarios that are operating to guide the decision making processes of *players who share a common tongue.* Left unsaid is the additional complicating influence of language on the matter.

40. Termination possibilities were daringly spelled out in broad terms in this remarkable work. Langer (1972), pp. 209–213.

41. The military has extensive experience with what is known as C³ analysis. However, the prevalent question investigated is whether a command, control, and communication system can function and/or function under attack or with varying degradations. The question posed here is fundamentally different; furthermore, it has not been as well considered.

42. The "decapitation" problem known to strategic analysts.

43. This idea was generated by Thomas Schelling in conversation.

44. Termination may be adjudged "treasonous" by those who are determined to press on to secure retribution for losses already incurred. The dissension and fragmentation of command inherent in this possibility may make internation communication extremely treacherous for those involved. Kecskemeti (1958) has dealt with this matter somewhat, although considerably more reflection is called for.

CHAPTER FIFTEEN

AN EARLY WARNING MODEL OF INTERNATIONAL HOSTILITIES

Edward E. Azar

I. INTRODUCTION

In the last 20 years, some progress has been made toward the building of forecasting strategies in international relations. Methods, data bases, and models have proliferated (e.g., Alcock, 1972; Brody, 1963; McClelland, 1968 and 1969; Newcombe and Wert, 1972; North, 1967; Richardson, 1960; Rummel, 1972; Wright, 1965). Recent developments have been aided by the following: (1) the growth in the quality and quantity of longitudinal data sets about the attributes and behavior of

We wish to thank the Department of Political Science, the Institute for Research in Social Science, the University Research Council of the University of North Carolina at Chapel Hill, and the National Science Foundation (#GS-366689) for their support. Our thanks go also to Anne Cooper, Carol Glaser, Thomas Havener, Lynn Igoe, Gernot Koehler, Robin Layland, and Thomas Sloan, who helped in preparing this chapter.

international actors, primarily nation-states; (2) the continuous improvements and sophistication of research methods in social science; and (3) high-speed computers, where many variables and large amounts of data can be processed.

Taking this body of literature as our starting point, in this chapter we (1) discuss the need for forecasting future inter-nation activities or events; (2) present an early warning model for forecasting inter-nation hostilities; (3) explain one way for gathering and analyzing internation events data; (4) use the model to forecast future profiles of international hostile activities between the United States, USSR, Israel, and Egypt and compare the projected profiles with the data we have gathered from public documents; and finally (5) discuss some of the problems, prospects, and needs of forecasting international hostilities.

For the purposes of this discussion, *social forecasting* is the science of projection into the future, comprising a set of research strategies applicable to a wide variety of human activity. *An early warning model of inter-nation hostilities is a social forecast that allows the observer to project into the immediate future and construct a profile of the likely hostile behavior of one nation-state toward another, based on monitoring and recording inter-nation activities and selecting appropriate strategies and tools for making these short-term projections about dyadic politico-military relations.* Early warning models are, therefore, empirical and quantitative; and they assume that international hostilities such as crises, wars, violent escalation, and even verbal conflict are projectable. Early warning research aims at being useful for governmental and nongovernmental consumers of scientific findings (see Section V for a discussion of potential users).

Most consumers of early warning research knowledge are interested in directly relevant knowledge, especially when it is derived from the analysis of good data and provides reasonable answers to their questions. They want, in other words, *valid* forecasts—ones that are sound, cogent, to the point, and convincing.

Given that many methods for forecasting exist, how can one distinguish between forecasts that are valid and those that are not? The classical argument suggests that validity equals accuracy—or, technically, statistical significance. In other words, when a finding can be obtained, not by chance, but because certain data fit reasonably well into a structure defined by a model and arrived at through the use of appropriate statistical tools, then the forecast is valid. Or if one can forecast into some future time such that one's computations more or less duplicate real-world data, then the forecast is accurate or valid. Conversely, a forecast that does not duplicate real-world data is said to be inaccurate or invalid.

We suggest an alternative to this constraining rule. We view the six criteria established by Davis Bobrow (Chapter 3 of this volume) regarding valid forecasting as extremely useful and very enlightening. Bobrow argues that accuracy (in the sense suggested above) does not constitute a valid forecast, for inaccurate forecasts may still have served a good purpose for individuals or groups, whether within or outside the governmental structure. Bobrow's general criteria for valid forecasts (discussed

at length elsewhere in this volume) include: importance, utility, timeliness, reduction of uncertainty, relevance, and durability. To Bobrow's list, we would add two more criteria:

Accessibility: the knowledge must be present, readily usable, and intersubjectively transferable —with minimal understanding—to the concrete situation within which the consumer is acting. Different situations and roles (educator, administrator, official) call for different types of scientific findings which emphasize different aspects of the total set of knowledge.

Cumulativeness: new knowledge ought to take into account and build upon previous findings.

It may also be important to stress that Bobrow's criterion of "relevance" is directly related to the researcher's ability to raise the difficult questions that foreign policy makers and the concerned citizen must consider, although the answers may not be available. It is important to stress that not *all* aspects of a scientific research project are so new or so useful that its entire product will be directly useful for earning warnings. In some instances, the data base generated by the researcher may be found partially useful. Or the method used by a researcher may be partially useful, if for nothing else than training persons engaged in policy making in how to use new and helpful methods. In other instances, findings may have some direct use. Likewise, models and theories may be useful, if not *in toto,* then in their ability to pose questions, present unorthodox ideas, and probably affect the structure of models or theories and the manner they explore reality.

The above criteria cut across the lines that divide one kind of basic research from another and one research technique or data base from another. For the consumer if often matters little whether a finding about, for example, hostile behavior of small states is based on aggregate data, events data, diplomatic history, or something else. What matters is whether a finding from research can help in diagnosing what small nation A will do, or in suggesting or reinforcing certain courses of action. Unfortunately there is at present a lack of "marketing" procedures, that is, the consumer cannot readily obtain early warning research findings or confirm their policy relevance or practical reliability. In this chapter we hope to show how events research can be used to reliably forecast hostile behavior. First, however, we will explore some general theories on forecasting and dyadic behavior, which will serve as background for our technique.

II. ACADEMIC FORECASTING: ITS PURPOSES, NATURE, AND UTILITY

Forecasting as a technology for social science research has had its opponents as well as its proponents and practitioners. Some have argued that this trend in international relations research, for example, is neither feasible nor even desirable, at least at the present. Some regard it as a potential threat to human liberty, and others feel it may be a self-defeating venture. A roundtable discussion on "The Nature and Limitations of Forecasting" held in 1966 by the American Academy of Arts and Sciences' Commission on the Year 2000 (and reprinted in the summer, 1967, issue of *Daedalus*, pp. 936–947) spotlights other somewhat pessimistic views. One participant, Lawrence Frank (p. 946), doubted the validity of assuming causal relationships and "deterministic linear formulations." Others held a rather pessimistic view of forecasting for different reasons. Harvey Perloff noted (p. 945) that a governmental decision or edict can upset the most meticulous forecast. Wilbert Moore felt that we lack the skills for creating genuine models from trend data and that "the best we can hope to do is predict the probability of a class of events" (p. 942). Herman Kahn (p. 945) doubted the feasibility of computer simulations.

Donald Schon holds a more pragmatically optimistic view. He reasons that decision makers will continue to make plans that may be based at worst on mere assumptions or at best on the most careful and reasonable forecasts that can be made (1967, pp. 768–769). "All forecasts," he contends, "are used principally for planning" (p. 764). In general, those who feel that researchers in various disciplines should give first priority to forecasting probably outnumber the pessimists. Indeed, Igor Bestuzhev-lada (1969, pp. 532–533) calls for—in fact, expects—the emergence of a new, separate science of forecasting, which he would call "prognostics." As he has pointed out (p. 533), the country whose scientists can formulate a usable theory of forecasting will reap a tremendous payoff—a

very effective weapon for scientific, economic, ideological, and political purposes.

But the fact is, arguments for and against forecasting have become largely academic. As we have noted, quantitative research in international relations and peace research has grown in such a way as to increase our capacity to forecast hostile behavior. The need for forecasting, however, preceded all these developments: it is probably as old as interpersonal and intergroup interactions themselves. This need stems from the individual and collective desire to reduce anxiety about the future, to plan for or anticipate the future, and to control the future. A forecast is thought to be capable of providing the actors involved with sufficient time to think out their alternatives and work toward reducing future human and material costs.

Of course, the precise nature of each case that could benefit from a forecast varies, and thus the reasons for a forecast vary in their particulars. Davis Bobrow has isolated seven purposes for forecasts: social mobilization, system replacement, warning, adaptive planning, group perquisites, efficient resource allocation, and administrative control (see Chapter 3).

Nazli Choucri (1974) has evolved a somewhat different, more general typology. She identifies four types of forecasting goals: (1) understanding the unknown; (2) planning for the immediate future; (3) anticipating long-range futures; and (4) controlling future outcomes. We concern ourselves with goal (2) and feel that the achievement of this goal is contingent upon developing forecasting methodologies for short periods of time and within relatively limited ranges of contingencies. Although control and prevention of future outcomes that tend to increase inequalities among individuals, groups, and societies remain the ultimate goal of many social scientists, we would add that "creating futures" is a most rewarding research activity.

The literature on social forecasting suggests that there exist over 100 methodologies for manipulating variables and projecting into the future (Bestuzhev-lada, 1969, p. 532). However, the major methodologies, according to Choucri (1974) may be grouped under four headings (ranging from least to most systematic): (1) *normative projections*, such as the group-opinion Delphi survey method; (2) exploratory or *trend-projections*, useful only for unchanging or slowly changing conditions; (3) *mod-*

els, either statistical or functional, Bayesian or Markovian; (4) *simulations* ranging from man-machine to all-computer simulations, such as artificial intelligence.

In terms of the time span covered by a projection, Rudoph Rummel (1969, p. 2) defines two types of forecasts: the specific or point forecast and the trend forecast ("predictions about what the international system will be like in 5, 10, or 25 years"). Long-range or "trend" forecasts tend to be made in the socio-economic and politico-military areas. They require sophisticated models of social change that include numerous variables.

We will limit our discussion here to short-range forecasts (profiles of the behavior of A toward B for a period of one month). In very pressing and highly tense conflict situations, such as border conflicts or crisis escalation, short-range forecasts are important because of their immediacy and potential cumulative effect on future developments, and nations have been shown to rely heavily on them (see Hermann, 1969; Holsti, *et al.*, 1969; McClelland, 1961; Zinnes, 1968). On the whole, these short-range predictions employ models that include only a few critical variables, such as costs, goals, and violence behavior. It is our assumption that as short-range forecasting grows to overcome these obstacles, long-range projections will benefit substantially. Thus the forecasts in the latter part of this chapter have been made on a short-range (monthly) basis.

Of the purposes enumerated by Bobrow, we shall specifically stress *warning*, and of the four approaches enumerated by Choucri, we shall use the *model*. Thus, we will emphasize in this chapter the forecasting of future hostile acts between a pair of nations (a dyad), because hostile acts (which tend to be costly in human and material terms) are easier for us to isolate and project. Our previous research on crisis escalation and reduction (Azar, 1970 and 1972) has made this task much simpler to deal with, and there is a larger body of knowledge regarding conflict behavior than on any other inter-nation activity. This knowledge has increased our confidence in the theoretical base used in forecasting. There are also sufficient conceptual schema for the description and explanation of foreign policy actions of nations, thus making our task of forecasting much easier. Discovering how a system of relationships is established and how a

system functions in the future (i.e., knowing something about the mechanisms of change) is one of the forecaster's most difficult problems. The fact that some of these problems have been resolved by others, as we shall see in the following section, makes our task much simpler.

As the reader will observe, the models we present in the following section tend to be descriptive and explanatory and at times predictive, although prediction must be inferred in some cases. To carry out useful forecasts, the models we use have to specify their predictive capability. Prescription is one criterion we shall examine scientifically. Although early warning forecasting is loaded with prescriptive overtones, we maintain that the findings generated from such research can serve as data for potential users.

III. AN EARLY WARNING MODEL OF INTER-NATION HOSTILITIES

The Signal Assessment/Response Process

In formulating responses to perceived signals from other nations,[1] international actors go through a process of assessment. As the final outcome of the process, they may select strategies of many different kinds—trading or not trading, breaking off diplomatic relations or not, even a "no response" response. Most likely, the choice will reflect goals that they hope to achieve. The process as we see it includes the following steps:

1. locating the signal within the normal relations range;

2. projecting behavior of the target nation;

3. selecting and implementing a strategy; and

4. monitoring the target's response.

Let us examine these stages in detail, concentrating especially on the concepts underlying them and the implications they present.

Locating the Signal within the Normal Relations Range. We feel that a helpful approach to understanding inter-nation behavior is through focusing on the smallest truly meaningful interaction unit in international politics—the dyad. Over a period of time any two nations establish between themselves an interaction range that they perceive as "normal." This *normal relations range* (NRR) of any pair of nations is an interaction range that tends to incorporate most of the verbal and physical actions, reactions, and interactions exchanged by the two nations. The NRR is bounded by two critical parameters—an *upper* and a *lower*. Interactions within those boundaries include those types of events that a pair of nations expect to exchange with each other. The concept of the NRR thus implies a conceptualization of inter-nation relations as an aggregate of acts or events.

We contend that nations too are subjectively very much aware of the NRR boundaries (assuming, of course, that they have established an NRR through previous interactions). When they receive a signal, they locate it in relation to the boundaries; obviously, signals that fall outside have more important implications, the degree of import depending upon the degree to which the signal deviates from the parameters and whether a series of such signals lasts for a relatively long period of time. Also, a researcher can empirically establish the NRR of a pair of nations by quantifying historical events which have occurred between a pair of nations and, therefore, can substantially increase projection capabilities. Since some events are likely to be located outside the NRR, we posit that signals which fall above the upper critical limit can produce a crisis; if responded to in kind, an escalation process sets in—one likely to exact high human and material costs. Behavior below the lower limit, if responded to in kind (and providing the signal does not invoke a suspicious, hostile reaction), could presage conflict reduction and greater cooperation (Azar, 1972).

Obviously, the level and width of the NRR of a pair of nations does change over time, but the process is a long one. Changes are usually due to significant shifts in a nation's economy, technological capacities, political system, or military capabilities. Over short periods of time, such as one to two years, very little change occurs. Our examination of the behavior of 105 dyads has shown us that dyadic relations between nations tend to be stable over periods of 5 or fewer years. In some instances, dyadic NRRs remain stable over 25-year periods.[2]

Assuming that friendly-to-hostile interactions can be differentiated and aggregated, the NRR therefore can be used to delineate at least three types of interaction clusters: (1) the normal interaction layer containing most of the actions of that dyad (the NRR proper); (2) the layer of exceptionally hostile activities (the crises and wars between that dyad); and (3) the layer of nonroutine cooperative events (the necessary prerequisite to rewarding integrative experiences). Using the NRR concept increases our theoretical capability in studying the whole array of normal, usual, and probably unexciting day-to-day international behavior, as well as extraordinary behavior.

Projecting the Behavior of a Target Nation. Having assessed where within the NRR signal falls, an actor (nation A) must then formulate a number of behavior options and estimate how its opponent (nation B) will likely respond to each. In doing so, A relies heavily on its memories of how B has responded to similar signals in the past.

The nature, content, and role of memory in relation to other mental processes is a very complex area of investigation, even more comprehensive than the area of learning (Krech, Crutchfield, and Livson, 1969).[3] In this chapter, we will not be able to overcome the Alker paradox; and, therefore, we define memory as simply that part of the information that actor A retrieves, as though there were no discontinuities, in order for that actor to assess and project the performance of actor B and in order to formulate its own response towards B. We will call this information "relevant memory." Duration of relevant memory refers to the length of time during which actors keep a set of issues alive, public, and well covered by the media.

The content, range, and influence of what an *individual* remembers during a lifetime is hard enough to ascertain, much less how memory operates in what Karl Deutsch (1966, p. 135) calls a "social mind," and how that memory affects decisions and initiates responses. Nevertheless, these are questions we must confront in order to forecast future behavior. How much of the past can an actor remember efficiently? Is the memory of last month's performance more important than that of the preceding month? When does memory die, atrophy, or become relegated to the subconscious? Obviously, the answers all vary either slightly or substantially, depending upon the dyad, the issue-area (national security, for example, is likely to induce different memory retrieval mechanisms than a minor border clash), the level of capability (memories might compensate for lack of actual capabilities in past situations), and so on.

According to Deutsch (1966), the concept of memory has a time dimension, with "deep memory" referring to recollections held over long periods of time in the subconscious and "current memory" referring to those recollections held for a short time uppermost in the conscious. The memory facilities of a group entity include the minds of its members as well as its libraries, files, reference staffs, and so on (p. 137). The effectiveness of how an entity functions (i.e., makes and carries out decisions) depends a great deal on how these facilities operate. They must (1) have adequate storage capacity; (2) be able to recall and recombine data; and (3) be able to screen out and identify the most relevant of the many possible data combinations. Requirement (2) is illustrated in Figure 15.1 by arrows, or information flows; Deutsch believes (p. 137) that mind is a "single run pattern of information flow." Requirement (3) is represented by the

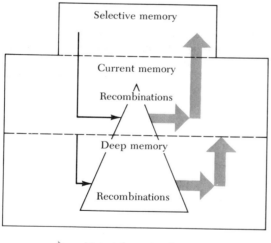

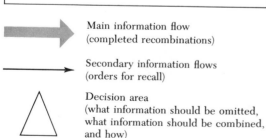

Main information flow
(completed recombinations)

Secondary information flows
(orders for recall)

Decision area
(what information should be omitted, what information should be combined, and how)

Figure 15.1 The relation of the various types of memory. (Based on Deutsch, 1966, p. 258.)

box labeled "Selective memory." Deutsch emphasizes (p. 206) that data from the past processed by a well-functioning memory system must be balanced by full observations and accurate judgment of data from the present (in the case of international actors, nation A might estimate B's capabilities and priorities and costs incurred or likely to be incurred by B).

Selecting and Implementing a Strategy. Having projected B's probable behaviors, nation A then assesses various strategies to direct toward nation B and selects an appropriate course of action for implementation. Nation A will select the strategy and method of operationalization that he feels presents the best chance for achieving his own objectives effectively and at low strategic, political, and economic cost. A critical assumption is made at this point. We assume that the output of nation A is a direct isomorphic actualization of the assessment, projection, and selection processes just described, and for the purposes of scientific theory may be analyzed as such. There is no doubt that the value of this assumption is very low in light of the powerful bureaucratic politics models.

Monitoring the Target's Response. Finally, nation A monitors B's response (or possibly the lack of it). Then nation B, now a sender of signals, makes his response by going through the stages described above.

Characteristics of Early Warnings

Introduction. As we have noted above, an early warning of inter-nation hostilities is a profile of the range and type of behavior that two actors exhibit toward one another. It yields a set of quantitative findings regarding one actor's behavior toward another during a short-term period in the immediate future. Early warnings findings can be (1) *relatively specific* in terms of type and time dimensions (e.g., nations A and B will fight over their border dispute without awaiting arbitration and within the next two weeks—in the absence of any external intervention) or (2) *somewhat general* (e.g., nations A and B are likely to engage in relatively more hostile or more friendly activity during the next two weeks or so). Early warnings that can yield relatively specific event-mixes and time and place projections are more desirable than those that do not explicitly spell out the substantive and quantitative properties of their projections. We have tried to make the forecasts presented later in this chapter relatively specific in terms of intensity and quantity for inter-nation hostile signals from one month to the next.

Our main question now is, how does a researcher obtain quantitative findings about an actor's future behavior? Some researchers argue that this is an empirical question that can be answered by examining one's data (e.g., Bean, 1969), but others suggest that one needs some conceptual framework prior to examining one's data. We accept the latter position that certain concepts are needed in order to build sufficient confidence in the findings of an early warning of international hostilities. (The general topic of confidence in forecasting models is well discussed by Bobrow elsewhere in this volume.)

Some theorists would have us construct models that must account for such master variables as national capabilities (the source of national power), elite and mass perceptions, available alternatives, and national overt behavior (events). It seems to us that the variables taken into account depend upon the longevity of the forecast (how far ahead it projects) and the kind of questions it asks. For the purposes of short-term forecasts, highly complex models are cumbersome and have very limited advantages over simple but useful models; further, over short periods of time (1 month or even 1 year), changes in national capabilities and international strategic situations are small enough to be considered as parameters rather than variables.[4]

Clearly, when two nations interact, they may exchange various kinds of signals and respond in various ways. Theoretically, each and every combination of variables might be thought of as an early warning. However, operationally, we believe that three variables are most crucial for an early warning profile: A's behavior in the present, B's behavior in the present, and A's "current" memory, to use Deutsch's term, of its interactions with B in the past. Further, of all possible descriptors of behavior, the following two are sufficient for telling us whether an important warning is being signaled and yield enough data for developing a short-range profile: (1) changes in the maximum hostile signal and (2) changes in relative hostility-to-friendliness.

In the section below, we will discuss our reasons for choosing these descriptors.

Maximum Hostile Signals. We assume that, on the whole, nations usually have a definite purpose in directing behavior toward each other. They communicate with one another and engage in a variety of activities in order to accomplish certain objectives or pursue certain desires. These preferences may differ from one dyad to the other and from one member of a dyad to the other. For example, in the United States–Iran dyad, the United States probably wants, among other things, to (1) secure the purchase of Irani oil; (2) maintain good, stable relations with Iran; and (3) insure that in the military bipolar subsystem (the poles being the United States and the USSR), Iran is on the side of the United States. On the other hand, Iran wants, among other things, to (1) strengthen its military posture by securing US military aid; (2) have a most-favored-nation status *vis-à-vis* the United States; and (3) continue to acquire US technological skills in order to develop itself further economically. These desires require that this dyad develop a fairly cooperative NRR to insure the flow of goods, services, and privileges. In trying to achieve these desires, the two countries' signals must remain fairly cooperative and capable of continuously reinforcing good will and mutual benefit.

If, on the other hand, two hostile nations get "locked into" an escalatory trend, they will probably act to clarify their goals and articulate those conditions that are perceived as capable of removing existing incompatibilities. Thus, in the case of the Egyptian-Israeli dyad (whose NRR is very hostile), each party tries to achieve its desires by marshaling its domestic and international resources, increasing its armaments capacity, and exchanging hostile signals.

Although it is important to know the preference schedule of a party to an interaction situation, we believe that over short periods of time, changes in preferences are not so easy to detect, but changes in behavior are. The degree of seriousness with which parties pursue certain objectives can be monitored, however, and can indicate their priorities at any given moment; their seriousness will be reflected in the signals they communicate toward one another. For example, if Israel most desires to guarantee its border's security *vis-à-vis* Egypt (such as in 1956), then Israel is likely to warn Egypt verbally (publicly or through diplomatic channels), take the issue to the world community, or threaten Egypt by mobilizing her (Israel's) armed forces to redress any Egyptian actions. Should Israel fail in altering Egypt's perceived or actual threat with respect to the issue of border security, then Israel will most likely try other means, for example, bombarding strategic Egyptian sites. Thus, whereas the goal of border security remained constant during this sequence. Israel has probably emitted a number of signals with varying degrees of hostility for the purpose of demonstrating her seriousness and concern about border security.

The degree of seriousness accorded a preference depends on a number of conditions and shifts within each of the parties to the conflict or within the external environment(s); it is indicated by the most hostile signal that an actor is willing and capable of directing toward its opponent. Changes in the intensity level of the most hostile signal indicate quite well the changes in one party's willingness to interact with another, not necessarily its preferences. In most cases, the most hostile signal represents a consideration for its domestic and international resources and costs.

The Relative Amount of Hostile and Friendly Interactions.

Whereas the maximum hostile signals indicate the seriousness of the interactions profile, the relative amount of friendliness to hostility conveys to us information about the intensity and density of activities and informs us whether there has been a change in the quantities of frequency and intensity of the dyadic relationship from one time period to another. The amount of interactions, for example, can change in their relative hostility or cooperation even though no change has occurred in the maximum or even minimum hostile actions. Such a change, whether in the direction of more friendliness or more hostility, if occurring from month to month, and even in the absence of any change in the highest hostile signals, is important information for a student of early warning research.

In the following discussion, we present a method of gathering and measuring events data. This section is followed by a discussion of how one obtains maximum hostile signals, as well as how to compute the relative amount of friendly or hostile interactions between two nation-states.

IV. DATA AND METHOD

Events

Monitoring and Coding Events Data. Conceptually, an event is any overt input and/or output answering the question, "Who does what to whom and/or with whom and when?" and having possible ramifications for the behavior of an international actor or actors (Azar, 1970). Some events may be considered relevant to a given international situation, and others irrelevant. Relevant events are actions that a nation-state takes in order to influence the behavior of its target and to convey its own intentions, interests, and policies. The event outputs of a nation-state are assumed in this chapter to be the operational indicators of that nation's foreign policies.

Operationally, an event is defined as any overt input and/or output recorded at least once in any of the reputable and publicly available sources that we use at the Conflict and Peace Data Bank at the University of North Carolina at Chapel Hill (COPDAB).[5] At COPDAB, we code the text of inter- and intranation events in a form that retains the maximum informational content of the event. This information is scaled and computer-stored in the following manner: (1) time, (2) actor, (3) target, (4) source, (5) activity (action-word), and (6) issue area.[6]

Our experience with events data gathering and analysis has taught us a number of things. We have learned, for example, to expect the event text to vary from one source to another or even within the same source. This variation is manifold; some sources contain sufficient and specific information, whereas the wording in others creates problems for systematic coding. Of course, sources tend to be biased and, therefore, report different events (Azar, 1970; Burrowes, *et al.*, 1972). Because this is a serious problem, at COPDAB we have decided to inventory many sources.

We have also learned that one tends to typologize events as either "international" or "domestic" without paying much attention to the intricacies of inter-nation signaling. We argue that certain strategic events, such as mobilization of forces, maneuvers, coups, demonstrations, and large-scale protests, cannot be thought of simply as domestic events. They are as important to the analysis of inter-nation behavior as other events that have clear and obvious external targets and have been treated as such in this chapter.

Measuring Events with a 13-Point Scale. In the last 30 years, a number of researchers (e.g., Klingberg, 1961; Holsti, 1963; Moses, *et al.*, 1967), have attempted to measure changes of inter-nation behavior with the aid of some yardstick. In the absence of an absolute yardstick in international relations, their specific techniques were designed to measure the particular inter-nation behavioral properties that interested them. With such advances in mind, we inquired into the similarity and redundancy in scaling instruments and developed the 13-point interval scale (Azar, 1970, and Azar, *et al.*, 1972).

We presently use the scale to measure the amount of violence contained in each of the events included in COPDAB. The scale contains thirteen behaviors, ranging from most to least cooperative:

1. nations A and B merge to form a new nation-state

2. nations A and B establish their own regional organization

3. nation A extends economic aid to nation B

4. nation A and B establish a friendship agreement

5. nation A receives support for its internal and/or external policies

6. nations A and B communicate regarding issues of mutual concern

7. nation A experiences limited internal political difficulties

8. nation A makes a protest directed against nation B

9. nation A increases its military capabilities

10. nation A encounters domestic politico-military violence

11. nation A initiates subversion in nation B

12. nations A and B engage in limited war activities

13. nation A engages in an all-out war against nation B

While the 13-point scale can differentiate events into classes, we determined the interval widths between these 13 points through the technique of paired comparisons (Torgerson, 1958).[7] All possible distinct pairs of the 13 markers (totaling 78 pairs) were submitted in random order to 52 students. The resulting scale values are shown in Table 15.1.

Furthermore, we tested the adequacy of the internal scale by correlating the scale widths resulting from the paired comparisons technique with results from the rank-ordering task. The Pearson product-moment correlations between the 13-point ordering and the paired-comparison scores equaled .98.

Computing Relative Hostility to Cooperation

The most hostile actions of A to B were taken to be those monthly events from A to B having the highest value based on the above 13-point scale. The relative hostility is measured in a more complicated manner according to the following procedure, which allows us to compare the relative amounts of hostility contained in the data and the changes in those amounts over time:

1. Divide the 13-point scale into two regions:

Region I, the less hostile end of the scale (points 1–6)

Table 15.1 Paired comparison scale values.

13-Point Ordering	Paired Comparison Values
1	.000
2	.405
3	.957
4	1.321
5	1.623
6	2.331
7	2.774
8	3.011
9	3.247
10	3.741
11	4.203
12	4.828
13	5.536

Region II, the more hostile end of the scale (points 8–13)

Scale point 7 becomes the midpoint between the two regions.

2. Convert the scale points in each region as follows:

Region I		Region II	
13-Point Scale	*Converted Value*	*13-Point Scale*	*Converted Value*
1	= +6	8	= −1
2	= +5	9	= −2
3	= +4	10	= −3
4	= +3	11	= −4
5	= +2	12	= −5
6	= +1	13	= −6
7	= 0		

3. Develop a measure of the amount of interaction between a dyad by multiplying the intensity level (converted value above) times the quantity of events at that level (i.e., frequency) and then adding these values for each of the two regions.

The results generated from step 3 are called *DI's* (dimensions of interaction). Thus

$$DI_{\text{Region I}} = \sum_{+1}^{+6} f_j \cdot i_j$$

and

$$DI_{\text{Region II}} = \sum_{-1}^{-6} f_j \cdot i_j.$$

The time interval can vary according to the researcher's interest. In this chapter, 1 month is our unit of time, and our *DI's* were computed using events data from COPDAB.

The *DI* from Region II are the more hostile quantities of dyadic interactions, and the *DI* from Region I are the more friendly quantities of dyadic interactions. To compare *DI's* from both regions by computing ratios of $\dfrac{DI\ (\text{Region I})}{DI\ (\text{Region II})}$ would allow us to characterize the type of dyadic interaction during that period of time (e.g., a month). Thus, a more friendly interaction would yield friendly *DI* (from Region I) in excess of hostile *DI* (from Region II). The lack of interactions would be characterized by the value zero. Thus, for a *relatively friendly interaction period*,

$$R_f = \frac{DI\ (\text{R I})}{DI\ (\text{R II})} > 1;$$

for a *relatively hostile interaction period*,

$$0 < R_h = \frac{DI\ (\text{R I})}{DI\ (\text{R II})} < 1;$$

and for a *lack of interaction (indifference) period*, $R_i = 0$.

The Linear Regression Model

In attempting to determine profiles, we employ a linear regression model that we think is only useful under certain conditions; it applies (1) to states that have symmetrical politico-military capabilities; are important to each other, and compete with each other for politico-military influence; (2) during a period of an unchanging or fairly stable normal relations range, or NRR (discussed above); and (3) over a short-term period (i.e., 1 month). Thus, when we have an asymmetrical dyad or an unstable NRR (even for a symmetrical dyad) or a long period of time, we believe that this model may not work.[8] Figure 15.2 gives examples of dyadic interactions for which the model does apply (upper left block) and may or may not apply (all other blocks).

The following are the variables in the regression:

1. A's and B's most hostile acts at a specified month, t

2. A's and B's most hostile acts at $t + 1$, that is, the average for A and B of the most hostile acts from $t − 6$ to $t − 1$ (or at $t − 1$)

3. A's and B's cooperation *DI* (R I)/hostile *DI*(R II) at t

4. A's and B's cooperation *DI*(R I)/hostile *DI*(R II) at $t + 1$

5. A's and B's average of cooperation *DI*(R I)/hostile *DI*(R II) from $t − 6$ to $t − 1$ (or memory of *DI(F)*/*DI(H)* at $t − 1$)

Variable (2) accounts for the fact that, as discussed in Section III, Nation A tends to employ memories of past interactions with B in determining its own best response to a signal from B. We have operationalized "current" memory as $t − 1$ to $t − 6$ because, in our surveys of the actions of certain dyads, we have found that a period of 6 months constitutes the relevant memory span that the nations we investigate in this chapter employed in determining their future behavior toward salient target nations over short periods of time (i.e., 1 month). This was done by surveying the time span covered by actions of these nations. We found that

CAPABILITIES

	Symmetrical	Nonsymmetrical
NRR STABLE	United States⟷USSR 1960 to 1970 Israel⟷Egypt 1967 to 1971	United States⟷PRC 1962 to 1968
NRR UNSTABLE	Israel⟷Egypt 1948 to 1957	Great Britain⟷UAR 1963 to 1968

Figure 15.2 The applicability of linear regression model capabilities.

most cases related to *specific* interaction concerns tended to receive attention in the media for from 3 to 9 months. The specific issues we refer to may very well be part of or related to much larger and older questions. Most specific issues that required immediate action or response had, according to our data, an average life span of 6 months. Thus, we assume that between mutually salient actors, many specific issues do exist, and immediate past behavior (i.e., behavior over the previous 6 months) tends to partly influence the intensity and scope of immediate future action. In this chapter, the memory variable of A's behavior toward B at t is computed by averaging A's behavior toward B from $t - 6$ to $t - 1$. The 6-month figure is a kind of smoothing operation, such as are used in economic time-series analyses to adjust data on a seasonal basis (i.e., to remove variance due to seasons), thus highlighting other kinds of variance. Memory at $t - 1$ is a moving average which decays as time increases (see Caspary, 1968).

The basic equations are:

$$A_{t+1} \begin{bmatrix} Max \\ DI(F) \\ DI(H) \end{bmatrix} = xA_t + yA \text{ mem}_{at\ t-1} + zB_t + \epsilon$$

and

$$B_{t+1} \begin{bmatrix} Max \\ DI(F) \\ DI(H) \end{bmatrix} = x'B_t + y'B \text{ mem}_{at\ t-1} + z'A_t + \epsilon',$$

where $x, y, z, x', z', \epsilon$, and ϵ' are constraints that we assume do not change for a period of 1 year. They are computed from regressions done on data from a 12-month period preceding the 12-month period we are concerned with; $x, y,$ and z, are the weights that A places on the behavior of itself and its target; $x', y',$ and z' are weights that B places on its own behavior as well as on the behavior of its targets.

Results and Discussion

In order to test the adequacy of the model, we decided to start with data for US⟷USSR and Egypt⟷Israeli relations in 1969, generate forecasts based on the model for the entire year of 1970, and then compare these 1970 forecasts with real-world (in this case, COPDAB) 1970 data. We started with a data base of 12 months for 1969, with interactions from COPDAB data, and, using the model, made a forecast into month 13 (i.e., January, 1970). Then, using these model-generated data for month 13, we made a forecast into month 14 (i.e., February, 1970). We repeated the procedure until month 24 (i.e., December, 1970). This means that we made twelve forecasts based substantially on relationships described in the model. The results are set forth in Tables 15.2 through 15.6.

The high degree of closeness between the means of the monthly observed maximum hostile signals based on COPDAB's set and those projected from the model (based upon an actor's own behavior and memory of that behavior and the target's behavior) is very rewarding. The overall agreement between the observed and projected interactions for the entire year is rewarding as well. The major weakness of these results is that of poorly predicted changes. But because this is a first attempt, we are satisfied

Table 15.2 United States → USSR, 1970.

| Month | Maximum Hostile Signal | | Friendliness/Hostility Ratio | |
	Observed	Projected*	Observed	Projected
01	8	7	+	+
02	8	7	+	+
03	6	7	+	+
04	8	7	+	+
05	8	8	+	+
06	8	8	+	+
07	8	8	+	+
08	8	8	+	+
09	8	8	−	+
10	8	8	+	+
11	9	8	+	+
12	8	8	+	+
	Mean = 7.9	7.7	92% agreement	

*Rounded off.

that dyads that are symmetrical to each other on the diplomatic-military dimensions and that seem to be preoccupied with one another tend to behave symmetrically toward one another and that is an important thing to know. Our findings support those of many other scholars in international relations and foreign policy (e.g., Hermann, 1969; McClelland, 1968; Holsti, *et al.*, 1968). While these results look quite satisfying, we feel that to use our simple model for projections on more than 12 months would not be useful. We have tried

employing the model to project into months 36 and 48 and found the results only moderately satisfying, compared to those obtained in profiling 12 months on a month-to-month basis. Our model does seem most satisfactory for 6-month interval projections.

We are not at this point prepared to make very sweeping generalizations about asymmetrical dyads. Furthermore, we must emphasize that our effort represents an attempt at making short-term projections of future behavior profiles and not an

Table 15.3 USSR → United States, 1970.

| Month | Maximum Hostile Signal | | Friendliness/Hostility Ratio | |
	Observed	Projected	Observed	Projected
01	8	6	+	+
02	8	8	+	+
03	8	8	+	+
04	6	8	+	+
05	8	8	−	+
06	8	8	−	+
07	6	8	+	+
08	8	8	+	+
09	8	8	+	+
10	8	8	+	+
11	8	8	+	+
12	8	8	+	+
	Mean = 7.7	7.8	83% agreement	

Table 15.4   Egypt → Israel, 1970.

Month	Maximum Hostile Signal		Friendliness/Hostility Ratio	
	Observed	Projected	Observed	Projected
01	12	12	−	−
02	12	12	−	−
03	12	12	−	−
04	11	12	−	−
05	12	12	−	−
06	12	12	−	−
07	12	12	−	−
08	11	12	−	−
09	8	12	−	−
10	8	12	+	−
11	8	12	+	−
12	8	12	−	−
	Mean = 10.5	12	83% agreement	

attempt at explaining why these projections are as good as we found them to be. Although we have suggested some explanatory variables such as symmetry of capabilities and mutual salience between dyad members, we feel that more powerful explanations are necessary.

Given a certain level of satisfaction with the results obtained, we suggest that one can make early warning projections from month to month. The potential application of these early warnings is that they can suggest possible trends, costs, and consequences. They can highlight the need for nations to behave within those ranges that reduce the opportunity for miscalculations.

V. THE FUTURE OF FORECASTING

Despite the pessimism of some scholars, we maintain that the potentially important role of forecasts of international hostilities impels us to give this new "science of projection" a first research priority. Thus, the problems that forecasters will en-

Table 15.5   Israel → Egypt, 1970.

Month	Maximum Hostile Signal		Friendliness/Hostility Ratio	
	Observed	Projected	Observed	Projected
01	12	11	−	−
02	12	12	−	−
03	12	12	−	−
04	12	12	−	−
05	12	11	−	−
06	12	12	−	−
07	12	12	−	−
08	9	11	−	−
09	11	11	+	−
10	8	12	−	−
11	8	12	+	−
12	11	11	−	−
	Mean = 10.9	11.4	83% agreement	

Table 15.6   Summary results of Tables 15.2 through 15.5.

	United States ⟷ USSR 1970	United States ⟷ USSR 1970	Egypt ⟷ Israel 1970	Israel ⟷ Egypt 1970
Means of maximum (observed) Monthly signals (most hostile	7.9	7.7	10.5	10.9
events, projected)	7.7	7.8	12	11.4
Agreement between observed and projected ratios of hostile monthly interactions vs. friendly monthly interactions	92%	83%	83%	83%

counter and are encountering must be recognized because of their effect on validity. Therefore, we will first review the obstacles to valid forecasts; we will then discuss what can be done to improve the science of early warning forecasting and survey the prospects—both positive and negative—that valid forecasts will probably present.

Problems

Obtaining and Assessing Data.   How can the researcher be sure of identifying a satisfactory number of quality data sources that account for sufficient frequencies of inter-nation actions/reactions/interactions, include all institutional spheres, and transcend the narrow political definition of "political events"? Adequate source coverage, an important tenet of a theory of events data, requires reducing the quantity and quality of biased documentary data. It calls for delineating a typology of event errors and suggesting solutions to *reduce* these errors.

We believe that the magnitude of the problem of source coverage is only in a *limited* sense a matter of missing data. Bad coding or lack of documentary evidence for this or that day, month, or year may be resolved statistically by applying interpolations of one sort or another. Most complications of source coverage (e.g., reporting of conflictive events only, lack of attention to certain international actors, absence of documentary material) do not lend themselves to statistical solutions in the same manner as "missing data." The *severity* of the problem can be reduced on the basis of one's knowledge of the political system or region, past experience in the area of events research, sufficient

theoretical competence in the area of international behavior, and the reliance on multiple sources.

Inadequate source coverage affects our ability to make valid assessments. Another major obstacle is the attitude of the predictor. Lloyd Jensen (1972) suggests that data selectivity, assumptions of "rationality," conservative estimate making, overly optimistic estimates, and the dulling effect of forecasting within a dangerous (but static) international climate can severely constrain the researcher and reduce the usefulness of his findings.

Still another problem is that of "noise," or the mixing in of relevant signals with nonrelevant ones. The problem usually stems from three types of data that forecasters often tend to overweight: messages designed for domestic populations only; actions and statements by low-level officials; and "innocent" actions that are not meant to convey "signals" (Jervis, 1970). Another form of noise can be deliberately caused (Jensen, 1972, p. 19); an adversary can intentionally distort relevant signals and/or feed in erroneous ones.

Making Inferences.   Early warning of inter-nation hostile activities, like all forms of forecasting, involves making inferences from one medium of symbols to another and from one time-space to another. That is, we infer substantive conclusions from quantified data by carrying out rigorous mathematical manipulations of the data within the framework of a theory of international behavior. The difficulties of making inferences from quantified indicators of behaviors—identification of assumptions, choice among statistical tools, specification of "permissible" interpolations and projections, etc.—are well known to researchers. Beyond technical problems such as multicollinearity and autocorrelations, there are conceptual problems such as accounting for the dimension of time and defining the science of observing social aggregates. Galtung (1970) has suggested that one of the major difficulties in social research stems from forgetting *time* as a research variable. He has argued that in causal models, attempts at manipulating time-free data (i.e., data gathered at the same point in time) have been successful, but that interpretations and findings are often *not* time free. Although we do not know how to resolve the problem of time, we suggest that researchers might learn from the French sociologist Georges Gurvitch's (1953) work on "social time" and from Simon Kuznets' (1951) research on the use of statistical data for the analysis of long-term economic changes.

Identifying Users and Communicating Findings.
We suggest that the early warning researcher should generate a product and create the mechanisms to distribute it to potential users in such a way that the individual needs of the various users are matched. Although this author is ill-prepared to resolve the producer-consumer relationship, here is a typology that might serve the present purposes:

	Product			
Consumers	*Theory*	*Data*	*Method*	*Findings*
Government			x	x
Professional persons and academic centers	x	x	x	x
Peace groups			x	x
Media				x
International organizations			x	x
Community and group leaders				x

Those who suggest that governments are unlikely to use the product of academic early warning research do not clarify whether they refer to the methodology, theory, data, or findings component of the product. We have a feeling that their case is better made with respect to the *findings* part of the product than for the *methodology* of early warnings.

The major obstacle to communicating the product of academic early warning is organizational. Even if the product were useful to policy makers, it may never reach them or may not be acted upon. Even if an in-house forecast were made by a lower-level bureaucrat, the bureaucratic organization may prevent such a forecast from reaching policy makers. Bureaucratic structure tends to isolate agencies, because of the "need" for secrecy and the reduction (i.e., loss) of information as it moves through various echelons. In addition, policy makers tend to see information as a rationale for existing policies. not as a tool for shaping or changing policies (Jensen, 1972). Thus one of the most pressing needs in the field of forecasting is for researchers to concentrate on the practical applications of their work.

Needs

Better Theories. Earlier in this chapter we alluded to the need for developing better theories of international behavior, social change, and events data. We maintain that a *theory of events data* would be a very important step in the development of international relations science. A theory of data would allow us to state assumptions, specify units, and determine parameters—necessary prerequisites for serious intellectual activities. Obviously, a theory of events data can only help us accomplish other goals—namely, developing one or more general theories of international behavior and one or more theories of transformation or change in the international system.

What do events researchers know about technologies (they prefer the term "theories") of behavior? The answer may be surprisingly encouraging, for these researchers have accumulated a body of knowledge about a considerable variety of international interaction situations (e.g., arms and international conflict, cooperation and international stability, political and cultural transactions, and economic and social cost/benefits).

Such theory will undoubtedly necessitate a general "systemic" theory of history. The latter might be advanced by establishing a classification of types of behavior and then transforming these types into explanatory types; by distinguishing between *genotypic* and *phenotypic* dimensions of historical social systems; by developing propositional inventories of mechanical and statistical experimental models; and by establishing data-banks of historical social events which allow researchers to make "explanatory sketches" where possible (Nowotny, 1971; Levi-Strauss, 1953).

Significant steps toward a theory of behavior can be accomplished when convergence occurs between researchers who stress the need for design models (e.g., Burgess) and those who stress the need for establishing and influencing patterns of inter-nation behavior (e.g., McClelland). We maintain that these steps are preconditions of successful attempts at time-free and space-free (though *not* value-free) inference. In sum, we must agree with Beardsley (1973) that the basic problem with respect to theories of behavior and of data is not that international relations researchers do not possess any theories of these sorts, but rather that their theories often contain significant elements that are implicit and arbitrary and are not tested by the explicit manipulations they guide.

Better Methods. Basically all methodologies attempt to identify basic trends, modify the trends by quantitative or qualitative means, and extrapolate them to some future time in the form of models (Schon, 1967, p. 765). According to Wilbert Moore (1967, p. 942), the first step toward a better method for creating valid models of the future lies in breaking the whole into parts to derive the rubrics for a matrix. But model building must be preceded by improved methods of data handling.

We suggest that better methods for forecasting will probably develop through the coordination of interdisciplinary effort. The presently fragmented efforts at forecasting by economists, sociologists, philosophers, and political scientists ought to be consolidated in some way (Schon, p. 766). The logical extension of such a consolidation would be the development of better measurement tools and more systematic knowledge of testing and confirming findings.

NOTES

1. See Holsti, *et al.* (1968) and Zinnes (1968) for a discussion of perception of signals.
2. According to preliminary assessments made by Thomas Sloan and Gernot Koehler of Studies of Conflict and Peace, University of North Carolina at Chapel Hill.

3. Obviously, one of the major limitations of this line of reasoning stems from Alker's work on serial actions where he shows that there are discontinuous kinds of remembering models (personal note).
4. We have discussed national goals, interests, capabilities, and roots of power elsewhere (Azar, 1973). We should add that without sufficient economic or military capabilities, a supply of resources, or certain basic powers, a nation can hardly achieve even minimal objectives; indeed, it may not even consciously set goals. A great power or a nation with great military or economic capabilities can afford to conduct much more extensive foreign policy than a small power, which cannot even satisfy its domestic needs. But knowing a nation's capabilities and goals and the sources of each only partially explains what motivates a nation to behave.
5. Sources for COPDAB data include: *New York Times; Middle East Journal; New Times—A Weekly Journal of World Affairs; Swiss Review of World Affairs; Middle Eastern Affairs; Deadline Data; Facts on File; World Almanac and Book of Facts; Keesing's Contemporary Archives; London Times Index; Annual Register of World Events; Asian Recorder; Al-Ahram* (Egypt); *Jerusalem Post; Al-Nahar* (Lebanon); *Arab Political Documents; Arab States and Arab League; China Mainland Review; Peking Review; Hsinhua News Agency Release; China Quarterly; Current Scene; China Report; Mizan; Mideast Mirror; Washington Post; Christian Science Monitor; Asian Almanac; Far Eastern Survey; Far Eastern Economic Review; Chronology of Events; Arab World* (Mansoor); *Diario las Americas; El Mercurio; El Nacional; Excelsior; Granma; La Nacion; La Prensa; Le Monde; O Estado de Sao Paulo; Manchester Guardian,* and *Times of the Americas.*
6. These components do not account for outcome or effect of actions. Alker, in a personal communication, has pointed out that effect categories tie into the learning precedent logics that he has been working on. He argued convincingly that coding for the precedent rationales cited by actors at the time of an action would add much to the theoretical utility of the data. He did recognize, however, that these rationales data are hard to get—in fact, harder than goals and intentions. We believe that one way to reconstruct an approximation to these learning precedents logics would be to conduct an in-depth assessment of the descriptive events that precede or follow an actor's needs or words.
7. It would probably be useful to construct this scale by using diplomats as judges.
8. Since this paper is a part of a larger project, we try only to deal with a simple and very limited aspect of our forecasting efforts. For example, while other models (e.g., Azar, *et al.,* 1974) focus on mixed autoregressive forecasting and its many problems, this paper reports and discusses much simpler (and to some, not very interesting) quantitative results. In future research reports, we will focus on forecasting *changing* situations and we will most definitely employ Alker's "precedent logics" in order to get at this crucial problem.

CHAPTER SIXTEEN

COMPUTER SIMULATION IN
INTERNATIONAL RELATIONS FORECASTING

M. R. Leavitt

The purpose of this chapter is to discuss the use of computer simulations for forecasting in international relations. The chapter begins by defining a computer simulation and a computer simulation experiment. It then considers various forms of simulations, and the kinds of forecasts appropriate to each form. After the two primary forms—continuous and discrete simulations—are compared, discrete simulation is described by means of an example of its use. The final section reviews the classes of forecasts most appropriate for discrete simulation.

An earlier version of this chapter was presented at the International Studies Association Annual Meeting, March, 1973, New York City. The author wishes to thank Nazli Choucri, G. Robert Franco, Herman Weil, Robert Escavich, Larry German, Douglas Hartwick, and Aaron Greenberg for their substantive comments; Carol Franco for very substantial editing; and Sharon O'Rourke and Kathy Watkins for technical preparation. Conclusions contained in this paper are those of the author and do not necessarily reflect the views of the United States Government or any of its agencies.

I. INTRODUCTION

Forecasting in international relations, as Choucri has noted, accounts for the following considerations at a minimum: "the direction of the activity modeled; the direction of sharp breaks or reversals; the extent of change; the period over which change is likely to persist; the points in the system most amenable to manipulation; and the costs of manipulation" (Chapter 1, this volume).

International relations, in particular among the fields in the social sciences, has many "breaks or reversals," great amounts of change over both the long and the short term, substantial capability for manipulation, and, of course, very great potential costs of manipulation. When the number of interesting variables and the lack of reasonably "hard" theory in the field are added to the characteristics of the system, it becomes clear that the forecasting will be difficult, risky, costly, but nonetheless crucial. Computer simulation (a generic classification for a group of techniques) is capable, perhaps uniquely so, of capturing the complexity of international behavior in order for that behavior to be forecast over a relatively wide range of time spans.

Computer simulations are a broad class of techniques that have certain common characteristics and that, as a group, can be distinguished from other problem-solving uses of computers. The general definition of simulation given below is followed by a more precise scheme for distinguishing among different kinds of simulation for use in forecasting.

Definition

Naylor, *et al.*, have defined simulations as "a technique that involves setting up a model of a real situation and then performing experiments on the model" (1966, p. 2). The model is described in a computer programming language (the model *is* the set of computer instructions) and is then simulated (experimented upon) by executing the program using different sets of values of input variables.

The meaning of "experiment" in this context needs elaboration. The primary purpose of any experiment is to relate alternative inputs to corresponding outputs, or to forecast or predict the results when the inputs are varied. Yet the term "experiment" has various meanings. In the strict sense, an experiment is a procedure performed to validate rather than to make a forecast. Predictions or forecasts are generated by theory—verbal, mathematical, or otherwise. The experiment is performed to determine whether *reality* conforms to the expectations (the prediction) of the theory.

A much broader definition of experimentation includes any procedure that is conducted simply to examine results. The term "experiment" in the context of computer simulations lies somewhere between these two definitions. When experimenting with a simulation, the environment of the experiment is a *model* of reality rather than reality itself. The amount of confidence the experimenter has in the model determines the extent to which the strict definition can be applied.[1] Such formulations of the experiment assume that a valid model exists; the process of creating such a model is not considered.

According to the strict definition, a simulation must undergo the same experimental procedure against some other preexisting model in order to attain the status of a "referent model." In this process, the simulation may be considered the theory that, when executed, deduces its own consequences. The outcomes become the predictions of the theory that in turn need validation by comparison to a referent. Such validation may be accomplished by a traditional experiment or, in international relations, by a comparison of referent data with the simulation outputs. Appropriate (defined by context) ranges of similarity and difference must be specified to permit acceptance or rejection of the theory (the simulation).

The validation of a theory generally ends the interest of the "pure" scientist while the applied scientist is just becoming aroused. Each uses simulations and experiments in significantly different ways. The applied scientist usually directs basic research findings to real-world problems and uses theory (which is valid by implication) to predict or forecast real-world outcomes. These predictions are not intended to validate theory. The simulation run may be called an "experiment," but it will not determine the acceptance or rejection of theory. Rather, it will influence decisions based on the results of the experiment: whether or not to build a bridge; to build it a certain way or not; whether to double or halve a sales force; or whether or not to reduce arms levels. Thus, although the terminology is identical, the applied scientist and the pure scientist have substantially different uses for simulations and experiments.

The variations in meaning of the same terms may have confusing consequences. Simulations can be created explicitly to develop new theory (or reformulate old, untested theory) and thus require (in the eyes of the theorist) validation according to available criteria. Yet, if the validation procedures are not explicit and forecasts are nevertheless made, the value of the forecasts is difficult to determine. Is the theory to be tested by a comparison with referent data that will be collected in the future? Or is the forecast to be accepted and decisions made on the basis of its outputs? Unless the purpose of the simulation enterprise is explicit and the appropriate future or past validity criteria clearly stated, the reader (both the scientific community and the user of the forecast) will be unable to judge the value of the results.

It should be noted that many forms of experimenting via computer simulation combine both the "scientific" and the "applied" phases of analysis. For example, econometric simulation (see below) first estimates the parameters of a model (determines the "fit" of the model to prior data), and then applies the estimated parameters to future data. The first step is scientific because it attempts to validate the model (equation structure); the second is applied because it uses the model to forecast future values.

Forecasting via computer simulation is subject to the same kinds of problems encountered by other forecasting techniques. Naylor's definition, however, does help distinguish forecasting by simulation from forecasting by other means, and the use of computers for simulation from the use of computers for other purposes. The definition suggests that the simulation forecasting model must be more specific than models that underlie other kinds of forecasts. To enable a computer to execute a program, the full details of the program (set of instructions) must be complete and unambiguous. Of course, completeness and clarity are merely necessary, but by no means sufficient conditions for successful execution of any computer program (not just simulations). However, these are not necessary conditions for other more qualitative forecasting techniques. But where these conditions seem desirable, computer simulations[2] may be of use.

Typology: Continuous and Discrete Simulations

It is customary to recategorize types of computer simulations for each new purpose, or at least for every purpose discovered anew by a particular author. However, one of the best known typologies is applicable to categorizing simulations for forecasting purposes. The distinction between *continuous* and *discrete* computer simulation techniques is based on their treatment of time. In discussing "time flow mechanisms," Naylor, *et al.* (1966, p. 126), state:

> Two general types of methods have emerged for moving a model of a system through time on a computer—fixed time increment methods, and variable time increment methods. With *fixed time increment methods*, a "clock" is simulated by the computer which records the instant of real time that has been reached in the system in

order to maintain the correct time sequence of events. The time indicated by the "clock" is referred to as "clock time." The clock is updated in uniform discrete intervals of time; for example, minutes, hours, etc., and the system is scanned or examined every unit of the clock time to determine whether there are any events due to occur at that particular clock time. With *variable time increment models,* clock time is advanced by the amount necessary to cause the next most imminent event to take place. Events can occur at any desired point in clock time because time is advanced by variable increments rather than being divided into a sequence of uniform increments. When a particular event has been executed, clock time is advanced to the time at which the next significant event is to occur (according to past calculations), whether it be minutes, seconds, or hours away. . . .

In fixed time increments, time flows "smoothly." In simulations of economic systems, for example, national accounts are updated every quarter, or census data are modified every year. Although the system (real world) that underlies these observation systems may change irregularly, the effects are not observable (in the scientific sense) until the data are collected. Some complex systems have different cycles that operate at different time periods. If the "clock unit" is set to the smallest real-world cycle, and if multiples of the clock unit are equal to other real-world cycles, then the simulation can be run with fixed time increment methods.

Another version of fixed time increment methods is the continuously running system. Many physical systems are of this form. Changes in the system occur at infinitesimal time points and the values vary by very small amounts. Yet it is impossible to produce measurements at precise time points, particularly of social systems. Thus, if the time interval is very small relative to the amount of time over which change is expected to take place, such systems can be successfully modeled to approximate an infinite number of infinitesimal changes. Thus the approximation also uses fixed time increments.

Both of these techniques are similar in many ways and have been grouped together as "continuous" simulation techniques. In these terms, econometric simulations are continuous models of the first type (although it could be argued that the changes are "really" of the infinitesimal variety), and the system dynamics models are of the second type.[3] *Continuous simulations are thus defined as simulations that utilize fixed time increment methods in their portrayal of the passage of time.*

Similarly, discrete event simulation is the label for these techniques that utilize variable time increment methods. Discrete event simulation, then, requires no fixed cycles in the real-world situation being modeled. Events can occur sporadically or even randomly, since the clock advances to take account of the next event, whenever that event is scheduled to occur. The "cycle time" is not predetermined and, for conceptual purposes, does not exist. Programming discrete event simulation requires a "scheduler," a mechanism for determining which "kind" of "event" is to take place "next." This will be further elaborated below.

Although important consequences may result from the choice of the computer simulation category, "continuous" models can ultimately be represented in the "language" of "discrete" models and vice versa. For example, a continuous process might be identified as a discrete simulation since the "next event" is always one clock unit from the "present." Similarly, a discrete process could be considered in a continuous simulation framework if the possibility of "no action" is taken for those "clock units" where nothing should happen.

In international relations, the choice of the proper set of simulation techniques depends on the nature of the subject matter being simulated. Aggregate economic and social-change forecasts usually require continuous methods since the data, if collected cross-nationally or for the system as a whole, are usually available only in an annual aggregate form. Brunner and Brewer (1971) used this approach in their econometric model of Philippine and Turkish development, where variables such as population, national income, government expenditures, etc., were used. Their cycle time was 1 year, and they ran their model for the 16-year period 1950–1966. Although they did not attempt to forecast with it (they stopped at the "scientific" stage), such forecasting is certainly possible. In one of the few examples where forecasting using continuous methods was actually attempted, Choucri, Laird, and Meadows (1972) used annual cycles for predicting aggregate levels of national "lateral pressure," or tendencies toward war. They selected this technique because of the nature of their variables as well: population, military expenditures, etc., which are available on annual bases.

When the unit of analysis in international relations is the "event," and the purpose of the forecast is to generate sequences of future events, discrete simulation is required. In Leavitt's study of alliances (1971), the basic event was the "message" between nations, which was generated according to a probabilistic distribution based on past activity. In such situations, the continuous model would be inappropriate. Zinnes, Van Houweling, and Van Atta (1969) developed a similar model, although not for forecasting, in which national behavior occurred at irregular intervals.

Since there are various possible techniques for forecasting via simulation within each of the two basic methods, discussion of particular applications will be postponed until the specific varieties have been discussed.

II. VARIETIES OF CONTINUOUS AND DISCRETE SIMULATIONS

It would be most convenient to be able to state that definite distinctions can be made between the classes of forecasting situations which would indicate the use of either continuous simulation or discrete-event simulation. Although some forecasting problems imply a particular simulation technique (e.g., short-term data-based prediction requires econometrics simulation), this is rarely the case in forecasting using discrete or continuous simulation. In most situations, the specific problem will determine whether continuous or discrete simulations are appropriate, as well as which specific variety of the two basic techniques should be used.

Continuous Simulation Techniques

As previously stated, continuous modeling techniques are those in which time advances by fixed increments, whether or not events or processes actually "occur" each time period. This is not to imply that other variables move in such a regular fashion. The response of variables to either changes in time or to changes in other variables may be uneven and irregular. In system dynamics, for example, the unit of cycle time (DT) does not change during a single experiment. Yet the other variables may occasionally oscillate wildly. In econometrics, the unit of time is fixed in the estimation process. While short-term, simple econometric models rarely experience nonlinear change, the more creative econometric efforts can experience substantial nonlinearities where appropriate. Since system dynamics and econometrics are effective continuous methods in simulation forecasting, they will be examined briefly in this chapter.

Econometrics as a Computer Simulation for Forecasting. (See Chapter 12, this volume, for a general discussion of econometrics for forecasting.) Econometrics methods involve the development of theory about processes in the form of equations that contain measurable variables. Subsequently, the theory is examined to determine how well it "fits" reality by considering the values of the coefficients in the equations that maximize that fit. If the maximum fit is "acceptably" high, the theory gives an adequate description of the system's past behavior. Consequently, when applied to future situations, the theory may be a useful forecaster.

Computer simulation using econometrically derived equations is perhaps one of the simplest forms of simulation. Econometric models advance by fixed time intervals, thus obviating any complexity resulting from a "scheduling" program. Although the estimation process is heavily based upon stochastic ideas, once the equations are developed, the forecasts are invariably deterministic. That is, for a given set of variable values at one time point, a unique set of variable values at a future time point will be generated. This is thoroughly appropriate to its methodology since econometrics deals with maximum likelihoods and expected values in the estimation process, rather than in the forecasting process. It would be appropriate to classify econometric simulation as a "trivial" or "degenerate" case of computer simulation generally (where those words are to be understood in their technical, nonconnotative sense); but since time is progressing and the computer is performing fairly large numbers of calculations, the generation of forecasts from econometrically derived equations is a perfectly legitimate form of continuous computer simulation.

System Dynamics as Computer Simulation. Whereas econometrics has its roots in the process of estimating coefficients, system dynamics is concerned with model building. System dynamics is associated with its own computer simulation forecasting language—DYNAMO—and uses concepts derived from cybernetics and feedback-control theory to model social processes. As described elsewhere in this volume (a more complete discussion can be found in Chapter 13), the basic units of system dynamics models are rates and levels. Information about levels will feed back upon rates, which in turn determine future values of levels.

System dynamics is an appropriate forecasting methodology if (1) the model can be formulated in terms of rates and levels,[4] (2) the system is controlled by feedbacks, (3) expertise on the behavior of the components of the system is present, and (4) time flows in fixed time increments.

It is theoretically possible to combine econometrics and system dynamics approaches. The procedure would be to formulate the model using the "power" of the system dynamics "world view" to estimate those portions of the model amenable to estimation by econometrics techniques, and to reformulate the results in system dynamics equation form. The model would utilize expertise to formulate the model as well as to estimate the parameters, and would provide forecasts as accurate as the underlying data.

Discrete Simulation Techniques

As useful as the techniques may be, there are a number of situations in which continuous techniques are awkward for modeling. If, for example, one wished to forecast the pattern of communications between nations, one would need to aggregate communications to create the kinds of levels (for system dynamics) or interval variables (for econometrics) required by continuous techniques. Yet an analyst may wish to forecast a system characterized by irregular communications. For example, the analyst may know that a particular country desk officer receives approximately one urgent cable per week. The disposition of the communication may differ according to *when* the cable is received (in the morning or just before lunch), *what* the officer is doing when it arrives (reading *The Washington Post* or consulting with his Assistant Secretary), or how many such cables he has received in the past week. The focus here is on the individual item rather than on an aggregate. It is possible to formulate probabilistic distributions and expectations for each situation and analyze aggregates of all combinations. But the issue is not whether it is *possible* to use alternate techniques but rather to determine which is the most appropriate technique.

Because discrete simulation techniques rely on variable time increments, individual events can be examined to determine how they affect the behavior and attributes of entities within a system. An entity is any unit within a system. In the above example, the country desk officer and the message are entities. The officer is a *permanent entity* in the model since he continues to exist; the message is a *temporary entity* since it is "processed" and then "disappears" from the system (although its effects on the events it causes or influences may be prolonged).

Attributes of entites are simply their characteristics. An attribute may be the degree of urgency in a message, the time it was sent, its origin, and its destination. The officer's age, weight, height, and marital status are a number of his attributes. Other attributes that might affect his processing of the message include his length of service, the person with whom he most recently conversed, and even the quality of his sex life. The system as a whole has attributes, time being the most important. The time of day may determine whether or not the officer receives the communication immediately (it may arrive during lunch). Other attributes of the system may include the number of desk officers who receive messages; whether the system is in a precrisis, crisis, or postcrisis stage; or even the number of messages that may accumulate before the "permanent" desk officer is fired.

In the discrete world view, events cause changes in systems. The system can change its state, the entities can alter their attributes; temporary entities can be "created" and "destroyed" only as a result of an event.[5] In discrete simulations, an event occurs instantaneously, beginning and ending in a split second. Thus a process that occurred over time is characterized by two events—its beginning and end.

In the above example, the receipt of a message is an event. Events can initiate other events, for example, an important event may prompt the desk officer to forward the message to his superior. Thus the dynamics of discrete simulation are revealed. By forwarding the message, the desk officer reschedules the event—"receipt of message"—to a

different recipient. Events cause other events[6] in the sense that entities take certain actions as the result of events; the notion of "taking action" implies scheduling future events.

Discrete modeling, then, is most appropriate for forecasting a system when (1) the system is composed of entities with attributes and events, (2) the focus of the modeling process is on individual units, and (3) time progresses in variable time increments.

III. DISCRETE COMPUTER SIMULATIONS

To understand forecasting with discrete simulation, it is necessary first to discuss the details of computer simulations that use discrete techniques. An example of such a simulation is first presented, followed by a discussion of some varieties of discrete simulations.

Discrete Simulation: An Example

Discrete simulation can be used to model and analyze many systems in international relations. One such system is the international communications network where various kinds of messages are sent from government to government. The following paragraphs outline a simulation that traces causal linkages from message flows to large scale "important" events such as alliance formation and conflict (the model described here is presented in more detail in Leavitt, 1971).

Entities. *Permanent entities* in a simulation are those that remain for the length of the simulation experiment. Nations and dyads are permanent for this simulation, since we are not considering lengths of time over which any nation is likely to lose its "independent status," and a dyad is simply a pair of nations. Messages and offers of alliance, however, are *temporary entities* that carry information from one nation to another. They are "created" by their sender, and "destroyed" by the recipient. Alliances are also temporary (for the purpose of this model) since they are "created" when two or more nations decide to form one, and "destroyed" when all but one of the members decide to leave.

The attributes of the entities relate to traditional concerns in international relations. National attributes include population, economic capacity (GNP), military budget, domestic stability, and a measure of international activity. Dyadic attributes are properties of nation pairs, such as geographical distance, history of past messages, and the number of common alliances. The primary attribute of a message, the information it carries, is a measure of the degree of hostility or friendship expressed by one state toward another. A nation determines the degree of hostility or friendship it wishes to express toward another nation; this, with some distortion, becomes the attribute of the message. Attributes of offers of alliance are simply the identity of the sender and the recipient of the offer. The attributes of an alliance, however, include the number of member nations, the actual identification of those nations, and an identification of the "leader" of the alliance. Finally, an alliance conference's attributes include the identity of the nation whose threat precipitated the conference.

As stated earlier, events drive discrete simulations. In this example there are three primary events: receipt of a message, receipt of an offer of alliance, and the beginning of a conference within an alliance. These events can "cause" each other and create substantial activity in the simulated system.

All of the simulation events are generated by previous events. Thus the simulation must begin with "initial events."[7] For a message to be received, it must first be sent. This usually follows the receipt of another message. The circularity is broken in one of two ways. The first is to start with a bank of messages that are scheduled to be received at particular times at the beginning of the experiment. The system can then "react" to those messages and generate its own activity. The other alternative is to use a method similar to the "sinks" and "sources" of system dynamics.[8] Messages are also generated within the system for reasons external to the causal relations expressed within the simulation. Thus, one can create a self-regenerating event that randomly selects dyads between which communication is to take place. This pseudo event then sends the message that is received at a later time by the intended recipient. Either of these two techniques can be used to initiate events.

When a message is received, it is evaluated according to whether it is more hostile, more friendly, or nearly the same as previous messages. If it is nearly the same, a nation may or may not respond. A number of stochastic (probabilistic) processes occur in the simulation. First, whether or not a nation responds to a neutral message results from sampling a distribution based on the "international activity" of the recipient; the more active a nation, the more likely it is to respond. In addition, although a nation "intends" a message to carry specific information back to the sender, distortion applied to it is likely to change the content. The *actual* hostility or friendship is determined by a sample from a normal distribution with the "intention" as the expected value, and a measure of the dispersion of previous messages as the variance. Finally, the message is "scheduled" to arrive by yet another sample from an Erland distribution such that the expected time of transit is determined by the activity of a nation (the more active the nation, the faster the message arrives).

Once a response is "scheduled" (or not scheduled), the event is over; the simulation proceeds to the next scheduled event and resets the system time for the scheduled event. If the message is friendlier, one of two mutually exclusive responses follows: either a still friendlier message is returned, or an offer of alliance is submitted to the sender. If the message is more hostile, four responses are possible: a still more hostile message may be sent; the recipient may offer an alliance to another nation in the system; if no other allies are available, the recipient may "call a conference" (an "alliance conference"); or, if the recipient has no allies and none are available, the nation may schedule a conflict action. The process by which these alternatives are selected involves a combination of logical rules (if . . . then . . . decisions), and arithmetic calculation.

If an offer of alliance is received, a recipient may respond in one of three ways. (The recipient may or may not have sent the original message that "caused" the offer.) First, the offer can be rejected. If this occurs, the recipient will send a message more hostile than the average message sent in the dyad's history. Second, the recipient can accept the offer and form a bilateral alliance with the sender. This action "creates" a new alliance. Its attributes are its number of members (two), the identification of the two members, and the identity of the "stronger" of the two nations. Third, if the recipient is already the leader of another alliance, it can offer the sender membership within that alliance. This will modify the attributes of the alliance accordingly. One way in which alliances can be broken occurs during the receipt of a message. If one nation sends a hostile message to another allied nation, the recipient can break some or all of the alliance ties by leaving the alliance. An alliance may also be broken during an alliance conference.

When a nation is threatened and unable to find additional allies, it calls (schedules) a conference, during which at least four distinct outcomes are possible. If more than one ally is threatened by the same nation, they may schedule a conflict action with the threatener. If all but the leader are threatened, a "deadlock" occurs and the conference is rescheduled for a later date. If all are threatened except a nonleader, that nation withdraws from the alliance and the alliance proceeds as if all were threatened. If only the sender (who is not the leader) was threatened, the sender withdraws from the alliance and the conference ends. Any time a nation withdraws from an alliance and leaves only one other nation in the alliance (i.e., it had been a bilateral alliance), the alliance (a temporary entity) is "destroyed."

In all events, decisions are made by combinations of logical and arithmetic rules. Some of the rules are *deterministic* since, given a set of conditions, only one result is possible; some are *stochastic* since probability distributions are used to help make the decision. This example, like many discrete simulations, mixes various modes of analysis to obtain outcomes. The modes of analysis are at the unit level—the individual country, message, and alliance—and sequences of outcomes are the result. In this example, the outcomes might be the number of conflict events that occurred during the course of the experiment (which might last from 1 to 3 simulated years), the number of conflict events divided by the number of alliances, or the number of messages divided by the number of alliances.

At the conclusion of each simulation experiment, the system has produced some simulated data or outputs. If the experiment is run several times with the same initial conditions (varying only the random numbers used in the stochastic processes), one can obtain distributions of the outputs of interest and perform standard statistical analyses on them. Further, one can systematically modify certain input conditions to determine whether there is a corresponding difference in the outputs. In the above example, two input conditions were systematically modified to examine their relationship to certain outputs. The size of the system (number of nations) and the initial alliance structure (bipolar versus multipolar) were each set at two different levels and run four times. The result was that the size of the system did not affect the level of conflict, but the initial polarity had a substantial effect; bipolar systems experienced more conflict.[9]

Discrete Simulation: Species of the Genus

The above example could have been modeled with relative ease by using any one of a large number of different discrete event techniques. One writer (much of this section is a summary of I. Kay, 1972) has isolated thirty-four different computer languages, not including general purpose programming languages such as FORTRAN and ALGOL, nor the languages written for discrete simulations in such fields as electrical engineering or civil engineering. (International relations has not developed such a language.) There is substantial overlap in purpose and "world view" among the languages. Kay has suggested two categories of discrete simulation languages: those that use the "event" approach described above, and those that use a "process" approach.

> First, those that are "activity" or "process" oriented view the world as a collection of facilities capable of processing the transactions or tasks which come their way. As an illustration, a garage will repair cars which drive in for service. The second orientation is that of the "event." In this world view, an event occurs at some scheduled time, and searches for a facility to process it. In effect, it is a car requiring repair and it looks for a garage which can accomplish it. For those reasonably acquainted with the best known simulation languages, GPSS and SIMULA are "process" oriented, while SIMSCRIPT and GASP are "event" oriented. (Kay, 1972, pp. 119–120)

This distinction is much less important than the continuous/discrete typology.

The choice of techniques is usually based on relatively minor factors rather than on the extent to which any particular language "fits" a particular problem. The familiarity of the computer programmer with a particular language, for example, may be more important than whether one or another language is optimally suited to the particular problem. The basic reason for this indifference is that *any* substantive system will usually need translation from a conceptual model to a computer language. And it is very difficult to determine *a priori* whether one world view is better than another, particularly if they are complementary, as is the case with process and event languages.

The choice of languages is sometimes limited by the inability of some computers to use particular languages. GPSS and SIMSCRIPT (in particular the SIMSCRIPT I.5 dialect) are the most popular and most available languages.[10] Less common languages are often found only on the particular brand of computer for which they were written (the BOSS simulation language for Burroughs machines) or at a particular institution (the SPURT language at Northwestern University). But where they are available,[11] SIMSCRIPT and GPSS are preferable to their alternatives.

The relative lack of difference among discrete simulation language does not hold for the choice between simulation languages and general purpose languages. If retraining and language availability were no problem for a particular research project, a simulation language should be chosen. A primary reason for this choice is that simulation languages permit a great deal of flexibility in the construction and revision of models and experimentation on them. One of the key advantages of simulation languages is that they provide the researcher with a mechanism that takes advantage of the variable time increments that characterize such models. Each language contains a "clock" mechanism that permits easy scheduling, descheduling, and rescheduling of events according to the requirements of the model, rather than the convenience of the programmer. There are other advantages such as built-in statistical accumulation routines, output report, and display routines, and with some languages, notably SIMSCRIPT, list-processing capabilities.[12]

The availability of a simulation language may present substantial problems. If a particular research site has no simulation languages, one of the "simulation subroutine packages" currently available could be adopted. The most widely used package is called GASP II.[13] Although referred to as a "language," GASP II is actually a set of preprogrammed instructions (subroutines) that permit the modeler to concentrate on the model itself rather than on the mechanics of the model. The subroutines are written in FORTRAN, and the model is written as a FORTRAN program that uses the GASP subroutines as necessary. GASP is very similar to SIMSCRIPT in its event-oriented world view, and the subroutines enable the modeler to more easily accomplish a number of detailed tasks. However, the use of GASP (or SPURT, a similar package written for the Control Data Corporation 6000 series computer) should be used only where the exigencies of the situation so dictate.[14]

IV. FORECASTING WITH DISCRETE SIMULATION

Discrete simulation is a set of techniques that permits the direct forecasting of individual events, as well as the performance of systems characterized by the occurrence of irregular events. Performance includes any quantitative or qualitative measure of the system's operation (what events are occurring) at a particular point in time or over a time period.

Forecasting is distinguished from prediction by the former's relative vagueness. Prediction implies point estimation rather than range estimation and requires deterministic rather than probabilistic modes of expression. Where prediction may state that "event X will occur at time point T," a forecast would state that "event X will occur at time point $T \pm t$ with a probability of p." A prediction for the year Z might yield variable X with a value of Y. However, a forecast might give X a value of $Y \pm u$ between the years W and Z with a probability of p. Reliable predictions are difficult to make and may be obtained only for systems with appropriate deterministic characteristics. Forecasts, on the other hand, can be made with varying degrees of precision by trading off exactness of outcome for reliability (Franco, 1973, pp. 383–391). By producing distributions of outcomes, discrete simulation can provide forecasts to the extent that the model has been validated. If the simulated outcomes represent a random sample from a universe of future possibilities, strict statistical inference procedures can be brought to bear on the forecast. The language of forecasting, then, is essentially the same, whether one is describing the individual event or the aggregate level of performance.

As other chapters have indicated, reliable, precise forecasting is not required for all forecasts. For example, in the case of speculative forecasting, the experimenter attempts to determine what might happen, rather than what is *likely* to happen. Both precise and speculative forecasting may be important to the policy analyst at different stages of his investigation, although the former is generally considered to be the more important of the two. This section will discuss the use of discrete simulation in both precise (variance-reduction) and speculative (variance-increasing) forecasting.

Variance-Reduction Forecasting

The term "variance-reduction" is derived from the set of techniques used in this more predictive, reliability/validity-oriented style of forecasting, which is undertaken to discover the most likely set of future outcomes or variable values. Such experiments usually examine no more than one or two "dependent" variables, and the validity of the examination is determined by statistical means (two works of substantial value for the evaluation of simulation experiments are Naylor 1969 and 1971). As discussed in the first section of this chapter, the purpose of such an exercise is to manipulate the input variables to produce different values for the output variables. When this is done experimentally, one has the controls needed to correlate changes in the outputs with changes in the inputs.

However, certain problems arise. In a complex system like the example in the previous section, one might have a theory that associates a particular change in an output variable with a set of interacting inputs. Thus, each possible combination of input values must be run at least once (more if the simulation is stochastic); for example, a simulation with three input variables and three different values for each variable requires 3^3 or 27 separate runs. Increasing the number of variables or discrete levels increases drastically the number of required combinations. This situation appears to be particularly important for international relations whose theories and frameworks are composed of many causal factors interrelated in complex ways with many effects. Therefore, it is necessary to de-

velop techniques to sample "important" combinations of the inputs. These techniques, generally known as "variance-reduction" techniques, produce samples of the population of possible experimental situations that are more efficient than strict random sampling (Moy, 1971, pp. 269–289). The object of efficient samples is, in the statistical sense, to make the rejection of null hypotheses[15] more definite. There is still a basic question about the validity of the model.

Fishman and Kiviat have distinguished between model verification and validation (1971, pp. 595–609) for both the data in the model and the structure of the model. For their purposes, data verification is concerned with ensuring that the sequence of random numbers is truly random. Verifying the structure of the model is more crucial. "Verifying the structure of simulation models means examining substructure outputs and determining whether they behave acceptably. One value of this exercise is that it identifies unwanted system behavior" (Fishman and Kiviat, 1971, p. 601). This does not mean that at this stage the simulation *must* behave precisely like the real world, but rather that its behavior is not radically different from some image of that world. Fishman and Kiviat demonstrate that one value of the exercise is the ability to determine where simplifying assumptions make a difference in behavior, and where they do not (1971, p. 603).

Validating a model, on the other hand, "means establishing that it resembles its actual system reasonably well" (Fishman and Kiviat, 1971, p. 604 and Herman, this volume). For data validation purposes, this implies that one cannot validate a hypothetical system, nor can one validate a system for which quantitative data cannot be collected. Fishman and Kiviat suggest various time-series techniques, particularly spectrum analysis, for "long" time-series of both the referent data and simulated outcomes. Spectrum analysis can also be used to validate the *structure* of the model, but with substantially less confidence.

It is generally accepted that validation of complex models of complex systems is, at best, an unsolved methodological problem, and, at worst, insoluble. (The degree of solubility, of course, refers to models in general and not to a specific model of a particular real system). However, the difficulty is of crucial importance to forecasting and is not restricted to discrete simulations or to computer simulations. Unless the applied researcher and the user of the forecast have confidence in the simulation's validity, it will not be a wholly satisfactory vehicle.

It may well be that discrete simulation is less amenable to these kinds of validity checks than are other techniques, especially econometric forecasting. It is the structure of the model that is being validated by the estimation process. With discrete simulations it is possible to make structural changes; but the consequences of those changes is much less clear than the consequence of modifying the structure of an econometric model. Where a theory contains logical (if . . . then . . .) as well as numerical statements, the uncertainty of the consequence of change is substantial.

However, if the model can be validated according to the above techniques, forecasts can be made from it. Validation of the model implies that the variance in the outputs is low enough to have permitted rejection of some kind of hypothesis. Thus, the variance in the outputs of the forecasts will be low enough to permit the determination of future ranges of those variables, and the forecast can be made with some precision. The variance itself will then provide an estimate of the reliability.

The importance of discrete modeling can now be clarified. In continuous, equation-based systems, there are manipulable variables—variables that are assumed to be manipulable by the policy maker or some other political actor. However, they are manipulable only in the sense that a policy maker can change the value of a referent variable. Although this may be true in some economic models (for example, changing a discount rate), changing values of variables in real systems is not an easy practical matter: for example, changing the price of gold sold by the United States requires an act of Congress; lowering the price of oil requires agreement between oil companies and regulatory agencies, even in the country in which the oil is drilled as well as in the country in which it is sold. In such situations, the political actor is not often told what to do to manipulate the variable.

If a discrete simulation model is built properly, it will be an *event* that is manipulable, generally an exogenous event; and a political actor who is advised to *do* something rather than *change* something will consider the former piece of advice more useful. Forecasts with a valid discrete model would enable the experimenter to insert exogenous events at the times of his own choosing.[16] Again, the experimenter is not simply changing values of variables; he is initiating the action that may or may not effect those changes.

Variance-Increasing Forecasting

If variance-reduction techniques for forecasting increase the precision of forecasting, then variance-increasing techniques reduce the precision in order to gain variety. For many planning purposes, knowing what is likely to happen is of some interest; but of greater import is knowing what low-probability (but high-cost or high-benefit) situations might be possible. Models that are developed to fit the former criteria will be hard pressed to perform the latter. If an international relations model is developed that has forecast real-world events at some point in the past (postdicted them), its precision will necessarily exclude most events that did not occur. But in international relations, with relatively few actors and poor descriptive theory, can the experimenter be confident enough to make the deterministic assumption that the other events could not have happened? (This point is further developed in Leavitt, 1974.) The point is that forecasting in international relations should perhaps take the form of "systematic speculation" rather than strict range-prediction.

Here, too, discrete simulation can be of substantial value. A simulation such as the one mentioned in the previous section can be replicated until a pattern in the outputs emerges. If no pattern does emerge, then the investigator knows that the simulation is probably not of great interest. (Note that validity is not an issue, at least not validity in the strict sense.) If a pattern of outputs does emerge, this can be investigated with techniques similar to those used for the "strict" verification studies; their time series can be examined, distributions of events can be discovered, conditonal probabilities calculated, etc. And perhaps the patterns can be identified: a bipolar conflict situation emerges 25 percent of the time, a multipolar small-power conflict system 45 percent of the time, a strict hierarchical system 15 percent of the time, and a peace system 10 percent of the time. If this were the distribution of identifiable patterns, one might begin to investigate those factors that were operating in the particular system preferred by the experimenter. The experiments then would be attempts to manipulate starting data, exogenous events, and internal relationships to modify the distribution.

Such efforts would undoubtedly be criticized on the same grounds as are some current efforts in systematic speculation, most notably the "Limits to Growth" debate (the debate revolves around the publication of the book by Meadows, *et al.*, 1972). *The Limits to Growth* does not predict the future, nor does it intend to provide a forecast whose precision and reliability can be effectively determined. Rather, it identifies the likely causes of certain characteristic system behaviors, and, given that, determines the requirements for changes in those behaviors. This is the general purpose of "speculative" forecasting.

V. SUMMARY

It would be fair to say that, barring a "secret society" as portrayed by Isaac Asimov in *Foundation*, long-range forecasting of social systems will be effectively limited to systematic speculation. Without a model that can predict the consequences of changes it brings about (through its publication), a kind of macro-Heisenberg effect takes place in social systems. The closer the focus on a particular aspect of a society, the more likely it is that the society will modify its position or rate of changing its position. The primary consequence of this effect is the great difficulty in obtaining valid forecasting tools, and, therefore, valid forecasts. The effect becomes progressively less pronounced as the time focus moves toward the present. Presumably some of the medium-term's potential variance has been "explained" by current events. In such situations, systematic forecasting can take a more effective stance, and, given validity, discrete simulation can be of use in particular systems. In the short run, however, there may be substantial question as to the utility of discrete simulation. Whereas econometric techniques are best at predicting one or two cycles ahead, the very irregularity of events in discrete simulation models makes short-run forecasts risky.

The conclusion then is that discrete simulation—computer simulations that attempt to model systems characterized by irregular but substantively important events—may be of substantial utility in medium-range, "strict" forecasting efforts in international relations. They may also be of substantial value in the systematic speculation about the long term, but they cannot be used extensively in predicting the short term.

NOTES

1. Since all observations of reality are filtered through some model—for example, a measurement model, a perceptual model, an image—the experimenter does not validate theory against reality itself, but rather against a well-established and believed model of reality. Thus simulation can conceivably represent such a "referent model" of reality, against which other theoretical formulations can be tested. See also Charles Hermann's chapter in this volume for a general discussion of validity in forecasting, and his previous study (1967, pp. 216–231) for a simulation-oriented study of validity.
2. Not all computer programs are "simulations." A practical corollary should be added to the definition: The model and its operation should be sufficiently complex to require the use of computers. In this way a trivial exercise such as the addition of three sets of numbers five times would not be labeled a "simulation" even though the model is otherwise sufficiently complete and unambiguous.
3. The closeness of these two important computer simulation methods may "explain" the occasional hostility generated between proponents of the techniques. They are competitive in some contexts, although the relative utility of the two should not produce such problems since they are distinct in important areas discussed below and elsewhere in this book.
4. Partisans of system dynamics informally proclaim that *all* systems worth modeling can be so formulated.
5. This "world view" is notably similar to the "world view" of individuals who utilize "event data" in international relations. The implicit assumption is usually that the occurrence of events and situations cause changes in the international system.
6. See Choucri (Chapters 1 and 12, this volume) for a further discussion of the issue of causality. As is evident, a very Aristotelian philosophy underlies discrete simulation.
7. This corresponds directly to initial values in "number-driven" simulation techniques such as system dynamics.
8. System dynamics applied to population models answers the two age-old questions: "Where do little boys and girls come from?" and "Where do we go when we die?" The answers: sources and sinks respectively! In system dynamics there is an infinite external source of materials to supply the levels; the amount that enters the system is controlled by the

appropriate generation rate. Similarly, there exist repositories (sinks) for those levels whose values are reduced again by rates. Such conceptualizations may sometimes appear forced but they are usually necessary in closed systems.

9. The primary problem with this study is the ambiguous nature of the test itself. A simulation experiment can be tested against the results of a referent model in order to validate the simulation. In this case, the referent model was a verbal theory concerning polarity and conflict (Deutsch and Singer, 1964, pp. 390–406) that suggested a negative relationship between conflict and size. Forecasting was not possible since, for control purposes, the simulation was run with "imaginary" nations. Given the ambiguous nature of both the referent model and the results, it is difficult to determine the usefulness of the model for forecasting.

10. Each is available on all modern IBM computers usually found at a university or available to a research office. Both are also available on most other large "scientific" computers.

11. "Availability" refers both to the ability to program in the language, and the presence of human resources required for the effort. The neophyte, as well as the relatively experienced modeler, needs accessibility to the "expert" in a particular language. One potential drawback concerns the competence of the programmer who develops the model. A programmer may be competent in standard scientific programming in a language like FORTRAN. If a new language is introduced, however, the researcher must either pay for the reeducation of the programmer (or find a new programmer) or allow the programmer to develop the model in the language of his or her competence. That this trade-off is a real one is shown by the large number of simulation models that have been written in FORTRAN rather than in either SIMSCRIPT or GPSS. This is particularly true when the programmer is also the researcher. Yet very few researchers have both substantive expertise and enough training in computer languages to choose among different languages.

12. SIMSCRIPT II, an advanced but not widely available language, is described by Kay (p. 131) and others as a "programming language which can also be used for simulation." SIMSCRIPT II permits highly flexible programming as well as complex discrete computer simulations. See Kiviat, et al. (1968). SIMSCRIPT II.5 provides the most complete version of SIMSCRIPT II to date. See Russell (ed.) (1973).

13. Documentation for this language is contained in Kiviat and Pritsker (1969). An expanded version of GASP is now available, entitled GASP IV.

14. The international communications model described above was originally programmed in GASP II for two reasons. First, there was no working version of SIMSCRIPT or GPSS on the computer available for model development (a Digital Equipment Corporation PDP-10 computer). Second, there was a set of GASP subroutines. Had SIMSCRIPT been available, it would have been the original language of the model.

15. Null hypotheses compare the simulation outputs to referent data.

16. In *interactive* forecasting, the experimenter does not need to decide on all such insertions in advance. If the experimenter is observing the output as it "happens," then changes can be made—exogenous events submitted—on-line. There are potential disadvantages to this approach, in that systematic examination of policy alternatives may become difficult; but the possibilities for running planning exercises and "games" with the future can, for some purposes, outweigh the need for "system."

CHAPTER SEVENTEEN

SEEING INTO THE FUTURE: ON USING SEVERAL METHODS OF TECHNOLOGICAL FORECASTING IN INTERNATIONAL RELATIONS

Thomas W. Robinson

I. INTRODUCTION

This chapter inquires into the desirability and feasibility of adapting some of the well-known methods utilized in technological forecasting to forecasting in international relations. It sets forth, tentatively, several ideas as to how much methods might augment the storehouse of techniques presently utilized in international relations predictions. It does not, however, illustrate the intervention and influence of technological developments *per se* in international relations, important as that may be. Rather, the emphasis is upon the utility of

An oral version of this chapter was presented to the panel "Peace Research That Makes a Difference," American Association for the Advancement of Science, Annual Meeting, Washington, DC, December 15, 1972.

converting the most promising methods from the one field to the other, making suggestions as to how they might be used to improve the sophistication of international relations forecasts, and indicating what pitfalls may arise during the conversion process.

Several reasons may be advanced why looking at methods of technological forecasting may be useful for international relations futures. First, technological forecasting provides a storehouse of methods—over 100 such methods are described in Jantsch's *Technological Forecasting in Perspective* (1967)—and many have been widely applied during the past decade with a modest degree of success. Given the mere number of these methods, international relations forecasters would be remiss not to consider what of value to their field lies beyond its boundaries but not out of reach. Second, most of the thinking about forecasting in general has been in the area of technological forecasting. It would therefore be foolish not to consider what usefulness this body of knowledge has for international relations. Third, as international relations forecasting is at present relatively underdeveloped, it can well use the input of ideas, if only for testing them out, from whatever source. The interest and the need are obviously present. Lacking is sophistication and experience in assessing and applying a broad range of techniques to fit an equally large spread of projected developments. Finally, in the last 10 to 15 years, there has been a great deal of theorizing and gathering of data in international relations proper. Some of it has been "good," in the sense of finding general acceptance and broad application, but a great deal of it has not. Since a new phase, emphasizing evaluation and consolidation rather than the production of new ideas at random, appears now to be upon us, it seems sensible to view the field as a whole, draw it together, and set forth conclusions as to what is needed next. International relations forecasting, and particularly the adaptation of certain technological methods, seem a useful integrating device for this purpose.

Thus, our present task is to illustrate how several of the methods of technological forecasting might be utilized in producing more accurate and/or sophisticated forecasts. Technological forecasting methods as a whole are divided into exploratory and normative techniques, according to whether they purport not to discuss preferred futures and how to obtain them, or whether they explicitly do so. A number of forecasting methods have already found application in international realtions as well as in the technological realm. These include: extrapolation of time series, use of experts, scenario writing, historical analogy, probabilistic forecasting, econometric methods, gaming, modeling, operations research methods, sytems analysis, and cross-impact matrices. Accordingly, they will not be discussed here.[1] Of those that remain, four seem most useful as illustrations. They are envelope curves and the morphological approach, under the heading of exploratory forecasting techniques; and relevance trees and feedback techniques, two examples of normative forecasting methods. Others could have been utilized. These four, however, have not yet seen application to in-

ternational relations, or at least not the sort discussed in this chapter. They also point up some of the potentialities of technological methods if properly modified for use in international relations forecasting, and illustrate some of the difficulties often met in forecasting in general.

II. ENVELOPE CURVES

Envelope curve forecasting (see Ayres, 1966 and 1968) is a branch of trend analysis that attempts to fit a curve to the general trend of events tangent to individual performances. As such, it is useful for forecasting trends that go beyond, or sum up, the state of a system as a whole, as various specific influences succeed each other in turn. If the past history of a system is shown to be made up of successive trends and if they display some recognizable pattern, an envelope curve may be extrapolated, even though it is not known what particular events will occur in the future and even though the history of the system is not linear.

An example from technological forecasting illustrates this idea. Empirically, it has been found that the rate of increase of operating energy in particle accelerators used in high-energy physics exhibits a rather smooth overall pattern, even though the rate of increase for a given type of accelerator "tops out" after all possible improvements in design and performance are made. If the separate curves for each type of device are drawn on the same graph, one can draw another line, an envelope, tangent to the series of particular curves themselves, which represents the general trend. This curve can then itself be extrapolated in time to provide some indication of what the future will probably hold. This is illustrated in Figure 17.1.

There are certain initial conditions that must be present for envelope curve forecasting to be feasible. First, one must possess firm data on or reasonable estimates of past trends. Second, a recurrent pattern must have been established such that extrapolation, whether linear or curvilinear, is possible. Third, sound reasons must be present for why the system as a whole in the future will behave much as it had in the past—that is, it must be reasonably shown that the system will not experience any major intervention of extrinsic factors sufficient to break the pattern already established. Fourth, one must inquire what absolute limits exist that

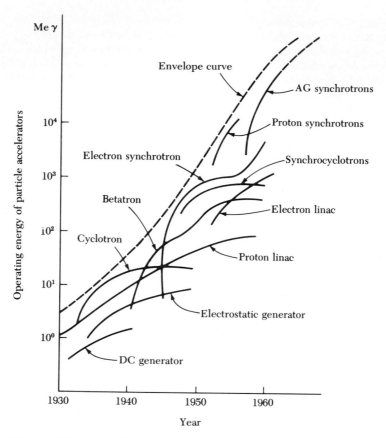

Figure 17.1 Rate of increase of operating energy in particle accelerators. (From M. Stanley Livingston, Introduction to *The Development of High Energy Accelerators*, Dover, 1966, as reproduced in Ayres, 1968.)

might cause the system to move asymptotically toward some final upper bound.

Ayres (1968, pp. 79ff) sets down four "rules" that are really steps, for proceeding through an envelope curve analysis. First, one or more macrovariables are selected that seem to encompass a relatively large number of operational variables. Such macrovariables should be chosen with an eye to their intensive or extensive nature, the former being one that has a natural limit, the latter being one that has no such discernible limit. In envelope curve analysis, it is very important to establish the existence or nonexistence of such limits, as they will (or will not) constrain the system as a whole in the long run. The determination of the existence of such limits, and their values, is the second step. The subvariables that make up the macrovariable

may themselves exhibit tendencies to change from extensive to intensive (from limited to unlimited value) during the course of their lives, because of changes in their nature (in technological forecasting, for instance, there might be a breakthrough in technology or a new invention), and these must be noted. Investigating possible changes in the upper bound of one or more of the primary operating variables, which obviously influence the shape of the envelope curve, constitutes the third step. The fourth and final step, which is complementary to the third, is to determine the sensitivity of the macrovariable to changes external to the system (and not internal to it, as in step three).[2]

Perhaps the best manner of illustrating the possible uses of envelope curve analysis in international relations is by way of illustration. One exam-

SEEING INTO THE FUTURE

ple concerns the degree of future complexity of the international system. Complexity is a macrovariable of importance to international relations since it not only sums up, and is therefore sensitive to, many variables and trends but also because it in turn is a determinant of the behavior of the foreign policies of states. While complexity is the joint product of several variables, not all of the latter are present at any given time. Thus, from 1945 to 1965, the degree of systemic complexity was largely the product of the rather swift rise in the number of independent national entities as a result of World War II and decolonization. Several other influences were coming to be felt, however, including the number and influence of international organizations, the number and importance of nongovernmental actors (including multinational corporations), the steep increase in international trade and other economic transactions, the number of independent nuclear actors, and the role of greatly eased and rapid international communications and transportation. While some variables do not possess clear upper limits (or if they do, what those limits are likely to be is unclear), others have strict bounds.

For instance, while the number of nation-states seemed by 1970 nearly to have reached an upper limit, the increase in systemic complexity due to the operations of multinational corporations, international trade, and communications and transportation was being felt more and more, and at least in the last named instance, an upper bound was not yet in sight. In the two other instances, the impact has not yet been felt: even though the number of independent nuclear actors has not risen since 1964, it may do so in the future, and the influence of governmental international organizations, having reached a plateau soon after the onset of the Cold War, seems likely to expand again when the complexity of the system demands it, which seems probable.

These notions need to be given much closer definition and, where possible, empirical and quantitative content. Since in this chapter we are primarily interested in illustration, we are unfortunately not able to pause to achieve as high a degree of precision as possible. Rather, we shall presume that a forecast of the joint product of the variables mentioned above might look like Figure 17.2.

There are four variables intrinsic to the system,

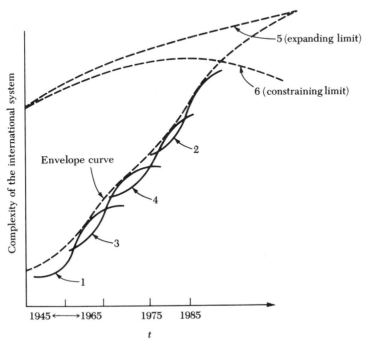

Figure 17.2 Complexity of the international system.

that is, that directly affect the degree of complexity of the international system: (1) the number of independent nation-state actors (indicating the importance of political and military factors); (2) the number and importance of international organizations; (3) the number and importance of non-governmental actors (multinational corporations and the like, reflecting the role of international trade and other economic factors); and (4) the number of independent nuclear actors. Their projected influence is as shown on the graph, with (1) dominating systemic complexity from 1945 to 1965; (3) coming into increasing prominence from about 1960 and continuing to influence the shape of the curve to perhaps 1975, when a combination of international regulation and diseconomies of size is forecast to set in; (4) beginning to change the system from the early 1970's, when first Israel and then India "go nuclear"; and, finally, (2) increasing its influence during the late 1970's and 1980's as the system attempts to control the otherwise dysfunctional effects of the previous factors. In all four instances, it is assumed that an S-shaped curve generally reflects the time-differentiated weight of the named variables. Thus, while at first the variable is of little consequence, it gains momentum, until naturally limiting factors intervene to set an upper limit to its potency.

The graph portrays two other factors that should be regarded as external bounds to the system. These are: (5) the role of greatly eased communication and transportation, which is shown analogous to the impact of a new "breakthrough" invention—it transforms the bounds of the system as a whole; and (6) the constraints imposed by ever larger levels of population and ever more difficult accessibility to natural resources. Factors (5) and (6) "compete" in influencing the system, inasmuch as (5)—which can be viewed as a general variable measuring the weight of technology—tends to free the system from otherwise natural limits of complexity, while (6) tends to constrain the degree of systemic complexity within increasingly severe limits. The two curves are drawn as shown to reflect these notions. Once forecasts concerning the comparative influence of the six variables are recorded, an envelope curve can be drawn to produce an idea of the general degree of complexity of the international system in the next two to three decades. The envelope curve is shown as a dotted

line tangent to curves (1), (3), (4), and (2)—in that order—and bending toward the horizontal as the differential effects of variables (5) and (6) are felt. It is also drawn as an S-shaped curve, in conformity with the experience generally found in utilizing envelope curves in technological forecasting (Jantsch, 1967, p. 162).

A second illustration concerns the degree of foreign policy involvement of a given state, Figure 17.3. China and the United States are taken as examples, since they show quite disparate short-term variation and rather similar long-term trends. China, whose foreign policy since 1949, if not before, has depended on the state of her domestic politics, shows a cyclic pattern, as the number of states with which she maintained active diplomatic relations grew, leveled off, dipped, and then grew again. In the case of the United States, this has not been true at all, since the intensity of her foreign relations tends to reflect her status as a post-World War II superpower. With a few exceptions, the United States maintained active diplomatic relations with nearly all other independent nation-states. In both the Chinese and the American cases, however, there is a trend toward approaching the absolute upper limit represented by the total number of available states with which to establish diplomatic relations.

III. THE MORPHOLOGICAL APPROACH

The morphological approach, as the name implies, attempts to forecast the future by investigating "all of the solutions of a given definite problem" (Zwicky, 1957 and 1962). Developed by Fritz Zwicky in 1942, this method challenges us to include all relevant variables of importance to the problem with which we are seized; it forces us to explicate what is of importance and why; it makes us spell out models in the utmost detail; it imposes order on thought; and it excludes the normative element until it is proper to introduce it. Its weakness is that it is really not a forecasting method. Instead, it merely sets the stage for a forecast based on other methods. What it needs as a supplement is a model or a theory of how the international system or the foreign policy of a given state works, which a morphology—being essentially a taxonomy—cannot provide. Also, because intuitive or expert judgment is an important feature of the

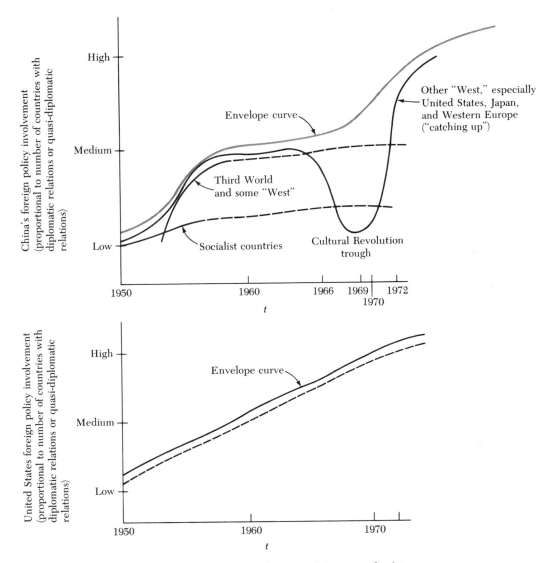

Figure 17.3 Foreign policy involvement of the United States and China.

morphological approach, it shares all of the weaknesses of that element.

As in the case of envelope curve forecasting, several stages must be completed. First, the problem must be stated with great exactitude, complete with precise definitions of each element. Second, and as a result, the exact statement "will reveal automatically the important characteristic parameters on which solution of the problem depends." Third, "each parameter will be bound to possess a

number of k_i different independent irreducible values $P_1, P_2, \ldots P_k$." (Jantsch, p. 176, quoting Zwicky). One then writes out a matrix of all such parameters and their values, circles one element of each row, and joins these circles together in a chain. The result represents one solution to the problem posed. It should be stressed that, up to this point, no question is asked concerning the value of one or another of the possible solutions, the object being to find all possible solutions before asking which one might suit the investigator's purposes. The fourth step, which may not always be possible in international relations analysis, is to ascertain the operational characteristics (where obtainable and relevant) for each of the systems described in step three. Finally, in step five, one applies normative criteria to decide which values of each parameter are most desirable. It is apparent that the morphological approach is not much more than an orderly approach to what forms and changes in operation of the international system or its components are possible in the future. Likelihood estimates and normative evaluations are delayed until the very last, however, and this, plus the emphasis upon achieving "a systematic perspective over all the possible solutions" (Jantsch, p. 177, quoting Zwicky) of the problem at hand, constitutes the strength of the system.

In international relations forecasting, the morphological approach would be useful when posing such questions as: What are all the possible forms of the international system? What are the possible foreign policy orientations of a given state? What are all the national interests held in common among three states? What is the totality of means of policy in support of a certain policy goal? To illustrate this method, we address the first of these questions.

Having posed the question as stage one of our inquiry, stage two sets forth all the relevant parameters, while stage three concentrates on their specific range of values. These are shown in Table

17.1. Fourth, we can describe the present international system by indicating which of the values best describes the contemporary arrangement (Table 17.2). Finally, we can, through evaluation, forecast where there is likely to be change in the international system (Table 17.3).

Conclusions can be drawn from this exercise. The degree of violence in the system, p_8, is perhaps the most important variable, depending on the values and their changes, of all of the other parameters. On the basis of the morphological approach, however, it is not possible to forecast with certainty how this aspect of the system is likely to change. What is needed is a theory more highly developed than a taxonomic structure. The morphological approach, however, is useful for signaling those elements that must be considered in any theory, as well as indicating where, in a forecast, one might expect change and where further thinking must be done. A second conclusion concerns answers to the question: Which of the systemic parameters are controllable in the future and which are, in all probability, not? In our illustration, it would seem that p_5 (degree of economic concentration), p_6 (intensity of communication), and p_7 (ease of transportation) are not likely to be controllable in the foreseeable future, since decisions as to their values are taken at the subsystem level—in the inventor's laboratory, in the multinational corporation office, and at the engineer's drafting table—and not at the level of national government or international organization. On the other hand,

Table 17.1 Morphology of the international state system.

p_1^1	p_1^2	p_1^3	*State-centered* or *system-centered* (i.e., dominated) or *region-dominated*
p_2^1	p_2^2	p_2^3	*Nuclear weapons* widely distributed, held by 5 or fewer states, or by 2 or 1 states
p_3^1	p_3^2	p_3^3	*Conventional military power* concentrated in 5 or fewer states, 20 or fewer, or dispersed among many states
p_4^1	p_4^2	p_4^3	All states *participatory*, 20 or fewer, or just a few
p_5^1	p_5^2	p_5^3	High, medium, or low degree of international *economic integration*
p_6^1	p_6^2	p_6^3	High, medium, or low intensity of *communications*
p_7^1	p_7^2	p_7^3	High, medium, or low ease of *transportation*
p_8^1	p_8^2	p_8^3	High, medium, or low incidence of *interstate violence*
p_9^1	p_9^2	p_9^3	Total *wealth* concentrated in 10 or fewer states, in the 30 or so (out of, say 150) technically advanced states (have vs. have not), or dispersed relatively evenly among all states
p_{10}^1	p_{10}^2	p_{10}^3	*Population* concentrated in 10 or fewer states, in 30 (out of, say, 150), or relatively evenly dispersed across total habitable land surface
p_{11}^1	p_{11}^2	p_{11}^3	*Kind of government* of states: largely democratic, largely authoritarian, mixed
p_{12}^1	p_{12}^2	p_{12}^3	*Number* of states in the system: c. 50, c. 100, c. 150

Table 17.2 Characteristics of the present international state system.

p_1^1	State-centered
p_2^2	Nuclear weapons held by 5 or fewer states
p_3^2	Conventional military power concentrated in 20 or fewer states
p_4^1	All states participatory
p_5^2	Medium degree of international economic integration
p_6^2	Medium degree of communication
p_7^2	Medium degree of ease of transport
p_8^2	Medium degree of interstate violence
p_9^2	Most wealth concentrated in $\leq$ 30 states
p_{10}^2	Population concentrated in $\leq$ 30 states
p_{11}^2	Mostly authoritative governments
p_{12}^3	c. 150 states

parameters p_2 (degree of dispersion of nuclear weapons), p_9 (concentration of wealth among the various nation-states), and p_{10} (concentration of population) *are* controllable, to a comparatively greater degree, at the state or international level. Hence, if one wishes to attain a certain change in the character of the system—in our example, a reduction in the probability of violence—one should perhaps concentrate on ways to induce desirable changes in the values of these parameters in the hope that other benefits would follow.

IV. RELEVANCE TREES

Whereas envelope curves and the morphological approach eschew from the inclusion of normative aspects, at least until the very end of their respective processes, the relevance tree approach[3] introduces goal-oriented questions from the outset. Relevance trees (sometimes termed reliance trees or decision trees when the purpose is to aid decision

Table 17.3 Possible changes in morphology of the international state system.

From	To	
p_2^2	p_2^1	Widely distributed nuclear weapons
p_5^2	p_5^1	High degree of economic integration
p_6^2	p_6^1	High degree of communications
p_7^2	p_7^1	High degree of ease of transportation
p_8^2	?	Depends on p_2, p_9, and p_{10}

makers) have already had extensive application in industry and government, the most well-known example being the Planning-Programing-Budgeting System (PPBS) of the United States Department of Defense and the PATTERN (Planning Assistance Through Technical Evaluation of Relevance Numbers) scheme of the Honeywell Corporation. The relevance tree approach is a broadly based technique that fuses several other forecasting techniques, including scenario writing, trend extrapolation, matrices, and envelope curve forecasting. As the name implies, it seeks to determine what decisions and other actions taken today are relevant to objectives realizable only in the fairly distant future.

As with the two previous approaches, one must proceed through several steps in constructing a relevance tree. In the first, a scenario is worked out that attempts to assess the objectives, activities, missions, and tasks of the system that one is attempting to forecast. Second, on the basis of the scenario, and with the addition of the other forecasting methods mentioned above, one identifies and relates the relevant primary, secondary, and functional systems and subsystems. These are put together by ordering them according to level of generality, as in Figure 17.4. Third, normative criteria are adduced for each of the levels indicated and a matrix is set up matching criteria with level of generality. Fourth, each criteria is weighted according to the degree of emphasis one wishes to give to each, significance numbers assigned to each item of each level. Both criteria and significance numbers can be assigned through quantitative work when numerical indices and computational methods are available and appropriate, or qualitative assessment (expert judgment, group assessment) when use of such methods are desirable. Both sets of numbers sum to unity to assure logical homogeneity. A relevance number for each item is then computed according to the formula

$$r_i^j = \sum_{x=d}^{\gamma} q_x s_j^x,$$

where r_i^j is the relevance number of item j on level i, q_x is the weight of the criterion applied to level x, and s_j^x is the significance number of issue j to criterion x. The general form of the matrix and the relation of criteria, weights, significance numbers,

Level number and nature of items

- National objectives

A 3 national activities

B 13 forms of activity

C 64 missions

D 204 tasks

E 697 primary systems
    (approx. 400 different ones)

F 2,368 secondary systems
    (approx. 790 to 800 different ones)

G Several thousand functional subsystems

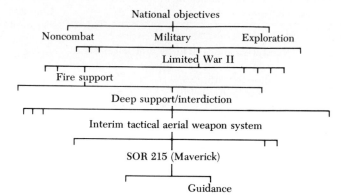

Figure 17.4 A typical relevance tree in technological forecasting. (Organization for Economic Cooperation and Development.)

and relevance numbers are shown in Figure 17.5. Table 17.4 shows a relevance tree matrix filled out for the relevance tree of Figure 17.4.

It can be seen that, once the relevance numbers are computed, one has a measure, however crude, for deciding how to apportion one's energy, decision time, budget, material, etc., among the rele-

vant items at each level. In this manner, a start can be made at getting hold of the future in the sense that present decisions, made on the basis of a combination of normative goals and perceived trends, will vitally affect the future in presumably desirable ways.

An example in international relations of rele-

Criteria	Weights of criteria	Items on level 1						
		a	b	c	$\cdots$	j	$\cdots$	n
α	q_α	s^α_a	s^α_b	s^α_c		s^α_j		s^α_n
β	q_β	s^β_a	s^β_b	s^β_c		s^β_j		s^β_n
γ	q_γ	s^γ_a	s^γ_b	s^γ_c		s^γ_j		s^γ_n
$\vdots$	$\vdots$							
x	q_x	s^x_a	s^x_b	s^x_c		s^x_j		s^x_n
$\vdots$	$\vdots$							
v	q_v	s^v_a	s^v_b	s^v_b		s^v_j		s^v_n
		r^a_i	r^b_i	r^c_i	$\cdots$	r^j_i	$\cdots$	r^n_i

s^x_j = Significance (how significant is the contribution of issue j to criterion x?).
r^i_y = Relevance number of item y on level i.

Figure 17.5 Generalized relevance tree matrix.

Table 17.4 A relevance tree with numerical values for level A. (Organization for Economic Cooperation and Development.)

| Criteria | Weights | Items on Level A | | |
		Noncombat	Military	Exploration (Earth and Space)
Insuring national survival	0.6	0.3	0.6	0.1
Demonstrating credible posture	0.3	0.1	0.6	0.3
Creating favorable world opinion	0.1	0.1	0.4	0.5
		0.22	0.58	0.20

vance trees concerns deciding how much effort should go into promoting which set of foreign policy objectives for a given state. Our example will be the United States during the next 10 to 15 years. Carrying the relevance tree down to the fourth level—from national objectives to activity form to mission to task, and considering for purposes of illustration that the author is a one-man scenario writer/expert assessment board, a relevance tree might appear as in Figure 17.6. This shows a relevance tree for survival as a national *objective*, diplomatic activity as an *activity form*, negotiations as a *mission*, and five *tasks* useful as a means of negotiation. Criteria, weights, significance numbers, and relevance numbers are then assigned according to the procedure outlined

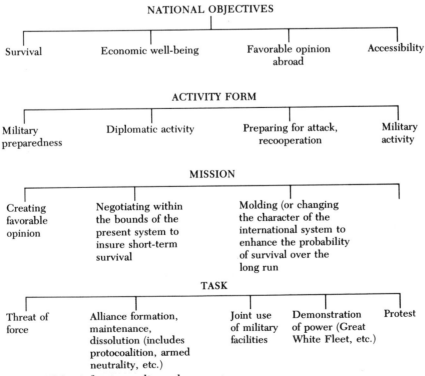

Figure 17.6 A foreign policy relevance tree.

above. The product is displayed in Table 17.5, which is a relevance tree matrix for the national objectives level for the United States. The weights shown give highest prominence to absence of war, second to a decline in domestic disharmonies due to past and current foreign policies, and only then consider increasingly good relations with adversaries and a rise in national wealth due to foreign economic activity as goals to be pursued. The significance numbers and relevance numbers shown give some indication of the degree of effort that national policy makers should put into each effort if they wish the results to be consonant with the criteria noted. Thus, this method provides a means of translating forecasting into planning, when one is concerned with promoting the national objectives of one's own state. If analysts in one state evaluate the objectives, activities, etc., of another state, however, then forecasting remains forecasting.

Three additional points may be noted. First, the criteria and their assigned weights change for each level and thus the relevance tree matrix exercise must be worked through each time. Second, normative evaluations are introduced almost at the outset, but because the method also depends upon a rather large degree of exploratory forecasting and utilizes a variety of forecasting methods, it could become a powerful means of integrating the various approaches to forecasting in international relations. Finally, although this forecasting method is not specifically time related, it can be made so by conducting the relevance tree exercise in an iterative fashion with different future time periods in minds.

V. FEEDBACK TECHNIQUES

Feedback techniques are already in use in international relations forecasting, but several additional suggestions can be made by reference to the literature of technological forecasting. Feedback techniques belong under the heading of normative approaches in that, in addition to forecasting possible futures, they help to show how to construct preferred worlds or how to avoid undesirable developments. As with the other methods we have discussed, it is impossible to utilize this approach without linking it to some theory or model of that aspect of international relations one wishes to forecast. Moreover, feedback techniques are seldom applicable without some mixture of other forecasting methods, particularly scenario writing and the use of expert opinion. One strength of feedback techniques is that they bring together forecasts of changes in the functioning of a system (new stages of development, step-level changes in the values of systemic determinants, etc.) and forecasts of when events are likely to happen. This may be represented schematically as in Figure 17.7 (Jantsch, p. 243).

A forecast is built up out of the application of forecasting techniques to the data provided by the present situation, as is shown in the left-hand column. A model of the future is then constructed on the basis of that forecast, and also by means of working out and adjusting a model of the present situation by utilizing the original data base and the forecasting techniques at hand. This is the center column. Finally, in the right-hand column, alternative future worlds are constructed. The process

Table 17.5 Relevance tree matrix for national objectives level, United States.

Criteria	Weight	Item			
		Survival	Economic Well-Being	Favorable Opinion	Accessibility
Absence of war	0.4	0.7	0.1	0.1	0.1
Increasingly good relations with adversaries	0.2	0.3	0.1	0.3	0.3
Rise in national wealth due to foreign trade investment (etc.)	0.1	0.1	0.5	0.1	0.3
Decline in domestic disharmony due to foreign policy	0.3	0.3	0.2	0.3	0.2
	1.0	.44	.17	.20	.19

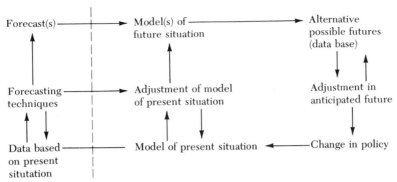

Figure 17.7 A generalized feedback model for forecasting.

does not cease here. The set of alternative futures itself can be regarded as a data base that can be utilized to argue for, and make changes in, current policy in order to increase the probability of attaining a desired goal or avoiding some anticipated pitfall. This necessitates reworking the model of the present situation, as shown, and hence the model of the future and the series of alternative possible futures. Thus, a feedback situation is set into motion such that forecasting technique, model building and adjustment, policy goals, and policy itself can be interwoven into a complex pattern of reciprocal influences.

As an illustration of this process, consider the future of the Sino-Soviet-American tripolar system.[5] From the onset of the Chinese Cultural Revolution, the three states went through eleven stages of development of their three-sided relationship, as is represented in Figure 17.8.

These series of diagrams symbolize the development of Sino-Soviet-American relations from times t_1 through t_{13}, roughly from the beginning of the Cultural Revolution in China in 1965 through 1975. As is shown, a fundamental realignment occurred as a result of the Sino-Soviet military conflict in 1969, which in turn can be traced to Soviet worries about the external effect of the Cultural Revolution. Although Soviet-American relations lived a somewhat autonomous life in the early stages of triangular developments, after the American warning against further Soviet military intervention in China, even the SALT talks were linked to the dangerous decline in Sino-Soviet relations and the comparative thaw in Sino-American ties.

The degree of feedback among the policies of the three states was great, as the stability extant in 1965 was upset and the system "sought" a new point of equilibrium. This is found by mid-1972, symbolized by the Nixon visit to Peking and the signing of the Soviet-American strategic arms limitation agreements in Moscow. By then, however, the United States and China had constructed a proto-coalition to balance the Soviet military threat to the latter and the comparative weakness that Washington felt after Vietnam.

On the basis of this data, together with estimates of Soviet, Chinese, and American strategy, tactics, and capabilities, and by utilizing various forecasting methods, it is possible to outline at least three alternative futures for this system. These are labeled (a), (b), and (c) in Figure 17.8 showing, respectively, outcomes some years hence of developments strongly inimical to American interests (i.e., restoration of the Sino-Soviet alliance), trends detrimental but tolerable (deterioration of relations with the Soviet Union as the result of acute Sino-Soviet military conflict), and a favorable outcome (relatively good relations all around on the basis of settlement of outstanding disputes and increased trade ties). Again, feedback relations are shown to play a critical role in these anticipated developments. Having reached the point of alternative future construction, and having been satisfied that each of them stands a chance of coming to pass, the policy maker would then wish to modify current policy in order to maximize the probabilities for alternative (c) coming to pass, followed by (b), and taking steps to avoid alternative (a) as

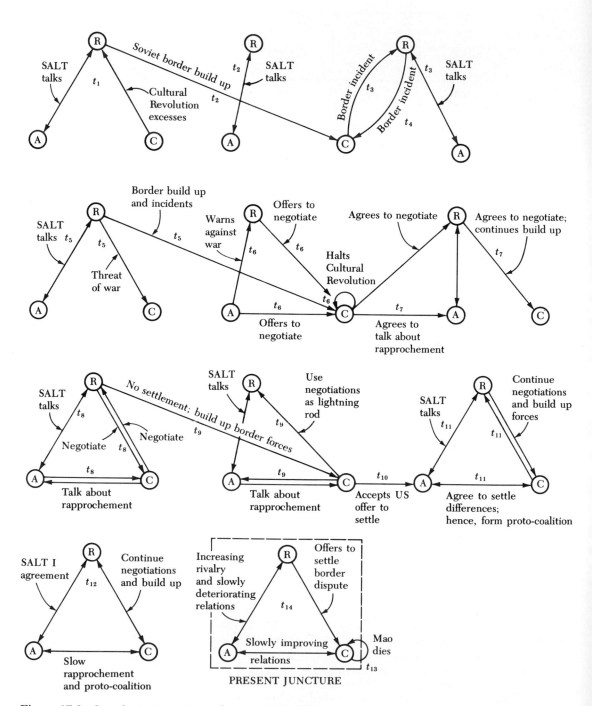

Figure 17.8 Sino-Soviet-American relations, 1965–197x.

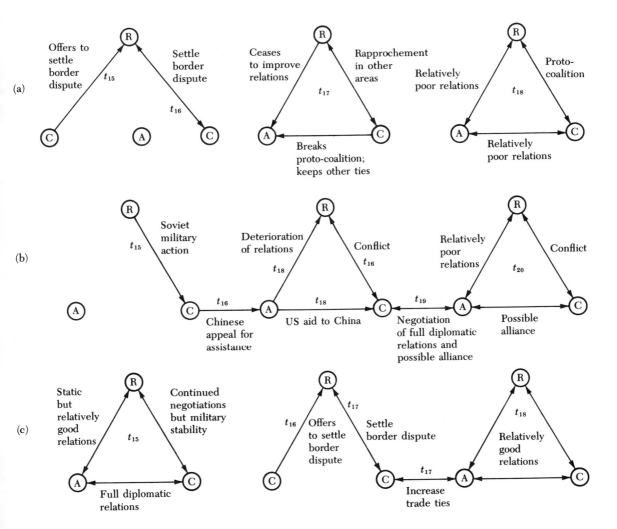

much as possible. Accordingly, policy would be altered, new models of the future constructed, and new alternative futures worked out. Several iterations of this process are possible, since forecasts, alternative futures, and policies interact through time. Thus, the feedback model for forecasting in Figure 17.7 links the real world, explorative forecasts, and normative (goal-directed and policy-changing) recommendations.

VI. SUMMARY

This foray into the world of technological forecasting methods leads to five conclusions. First, inspection of the corpus of such technique and experimental adaptation of some of them for use in international relations forecasting demonstrates that some of them may prove helpful. Not only are several techniques presently unknown to international relations futures research, but a smaller number would seem to be candidates for intensive application. Second, technological forecasting methods make clear once again the need to link data gathering to the kinds of techniques one wishes to adopt. A symbiotic relationship exists between the two, and one cannot merely take data from whatever source and expect that the proper forecasting technique will be available later. While one does not always have a choice as to the kind or the quality of data available, the use to which it is to be put should be kept in mind from the outset. This is especially the case if one wishes to adapt technological forecasting techniques, since their data demands are often strict. It is better to seek the "right kind" of data from the outset than not to be able to use certain methods later because the data gathering effort did not take their requirements into account.

Third, technological forecasting methods are no different from other methods in that they cannot be separated from the theories and models specific to the field being forecast. It is desirable to bring methods of technological forecasting into the storehouse of international relations forecasting techniques, but they must be connected with existing approaches to and assumptions about the international system before they can be put to work. This is, incidentally, perhaps the most efficient manner of evaluating their use to the field. Fourth, values are an integral part of international relations forecasting, even when dealing with methods supposedly value free. Experience with technological forecasting demonstrates that several techniques are usually applied at once and that at least one of them will require an expression of normative assumptions or goals. On the other hand, it is probably best to separate, to the extent possible, norma-tive questions from explorative and expository topics and couple the two only at what seems to be the most appropriate moment. While in some cases this may be relatively early in the forecasting process, it is perhaps better to delay the normative intervention until at least the construction of empirically derived alternative futures is past.

Finally, because it is impossible and undesirable to hermetically seal one method from another, the quality of the forecast depends upon the quality of *all* the methods (and theories and models) being used. Because the product will be no better than the worst of the techniques, a successful forecast will strive to minimize the range of techniques chosen for application.

NOTES

1. All of them are discussed in the present volume. See Chapters 8, 10, 11, 12, 13, 14, 17, and 19.
2. We have compressed Ayres' original five steps into four.
3. See, among others, Churchman, *et al.* (1957) and Jestice (1964).
4. Reproduced from Jantsch (1967), p. 220, who in turn has taken it from Jestice (1964). Figures 17.5 and Table 17.4 are also from these sources.
5. See Robinson, "China in a Tripolar World," in his *Chinese Foreign Policy* (forthcoming).

PART IV

THE TIME PERSPECTIVE IN INTERNATIONAL RELATIONS FORECASTING

CHAPTER EIGHTEEN

SOME OBSERVATIONS ON FORECASTING BASED ON LESSONS FROM RETROSPECTIVE ANALYSIS

Robert C. North

Many criticisms of prediction and forecasting techniques arise from the conclusion that claims are being made for a kind of crystal ball capability. This is unfortunate, since some of the more practical possibilities for social science prediction and forecasting are thus obscured. There should be no intention, at this stage at least, to aspire for anything like the prediction of detailed events of the future, such as an outbreak of war at some particular time, or the date of a coup d'etat. A reasonable expectation is to forecast broad trends, at best, or more probably, to identify two or several different possible trends. But the greater usefulness of simulation and forecasting techniques is likely to involve the planning function, the generation and comparison of alternative courses of action, and "mind-stretching" as a means for encouraging creativity and policy innovation. Within the foreseeable future "the step-by-step mapping of the costs and consequences of different paths of social change" may emerge as "one of the main con-tributions of 'prophecy' or 'futurology' to large-scale human affairs" (Platt, 1971, p. 39). For these purposes, the aim of the forecaster "is not to eliminate uncertainty but to understand and work with it" (Linstone, 1974, p. 48).

Traditionally, "predictions" of the future have been apocalyptic, based upon a fundamental assumption that the human race is somehow doomed. Or they have been messianic, deriving from the assumed possibility of a future of redemption and glory. Or they have assumed that human affairs are random or cyclical or determined by economic, technological, or biological imperatives. In addition to these predispositions, however, there is the possible assumption that human affairs are conditional, that we are involved in an "'if . . . then . . .' process, with the future shaped by what we choose and do" (Platt, 1971, p. 33). The purpose of this chapter is to suggest some ways in which an "if this, then probably that" approach to forecasting may improve our understanding of how large and complex systems work, widen our perception of policy alternatives and possibly lead to improvements in old institutions or the invention of new ones. The emphasis will be upon problems of the nation-state within the world environment, but the discussion will touch upon other levels of organization as well.

Although the development of computers and computer simulations has stimulated a new awareness of "prediction" as an element in policy formation and planning, the fact remains that policy decisions have always implied some degree of "prediction," some "if this, then probably that" assessment of outcome—whether consciously or unconsciously arrived at. The Marshall Plan was based upon the prediction that systematic aid to European nations would bring about certain consequences. Viewed in retrospect, this prediction seems to have been generally sound. The basic prediction inherent in Khrushchev's decision to establish long-range missiles in Cuba was much less accurate. Obviously, there is nothing magic in this kind of prediction. Even the weatherman is correct only a part of the time, and international politics, being human, is considerably more perverse than the weather. Yet, predictive skills can be improved. Computers and computer simulations, for example, can provide the investigator or planner with a new ability "to 'play' with complex systems, to get the 'feel' or experience he relies on to comprehend such systems" (Linstone, 1974, p. 46).

A major focus in the study of foreign policy has been on the governmental institutions that are mainly responsible for formulating and administering the activities of states and empires in the international environment. A large part of the effort has involved the identification of more efficient and effective ways of organizing the machinery of policy making in order to serve the interests or purposes of the statesman in terms of economy of action, speed of decision, singularity of authority, or coherence in execution. Growing attention has also been paid to the planning function on the assumption that unless institutional responsibilities for thinking about the future are clearly and appropriately assigned, no one will find the time to think in advance about emerging problems and how they can be avoided or solved (Cohen, 1968, p. 531).

Until recently, the disposition has been to assume that trends of the recent past will continue into the near future, to obtain on this basis a pre-

diction of what is "likely to happen," and thus to proceed with a kind of linear planning "along given tracks and within a given framework" (Jantsch, 1972, p. 2). But increasingly, now, a new concern for worldwide problems involving population, technology transfers, issues of food, oil and other resources, pollution, inflation and the like has broadened the planning function to include "the search for a new cultural basis, new sets of values to be brought into play, and new and flexible responses to a rapidly changing world" (Jantsch, 1972, p. 3). From this perspective, as suggested by John Platt, "Social processes should no longer be compared to a railroad train running on fixed tracks to an inevitable destination, but rather to a wagon train of settlers moving across the country towards the frontier, in an on-going collective search for a better place to live" (Jantsch, 1972, p. 33).

There are at least three common responses to requests for "courses of action aimed at changing existing situations into preferred ones" (Simon, 1969, p. 55). The first, which has been referred to as descriptive utopianism, consists of statements of the form "The desired world will have properties $X_1 \ldots X_n$." Such statements may deal with economic distributions, world government, schemes for taxing the rich to aid the poor, and so on (Bobrow, pp. 1–2).

A second common response involves negative prescription: "To attain the desired world one must eliminate attributes $X_1 \ldots X_n$ of the world as it is and appears to be developing" (Bobrow, p. 2). But such statements fail to specify how such unwanted attributes can be eliminated or, if they are eliminated, how to go on to secure the properties that we think the world ought to have.

A third response tries to identify causal connections through some type of macro-modeling. This approach typically begins with a formal model linking "the values of highly aggregated attributes of the international system (and its component elements) to outcome variables represented in the criteria used to judge alternate world futures" (Bobrow, p. 3). The difficulty with this response is that it must deal with a considerable array of intensely interactive variables that seem to behave in ways that are not intuitively obvious or superficially plausible.

For a forecast to be meaningful, it is vital that the exploratory and normative—the extrapolative and the goal-setting—approaches be linked in a cybernetic feedback fashion. This means that, while the past is recognized as important in establishing the initial directions for the future, new futures are considered as a basis for changing the trend. (Linstone, p. 47)

In presenting this "wagon-train" concept as a model for guiding efforts toward coping with the national and worldwide problems that are emerging, Platt has compared the process of change to the driving of a vehicle. At any given moment, a society, like a vehicle, is "at a particular place with a particular direction of motion determined by its previous history" (Platt, 1971, p. 33). The problem is, how far down the road can the driver see and how much control over his vehicle does the driver have. From this perspective, the road of the future can be divided into three sectors or periods of time. For a short time ahead, however well the driver can see, there is little he can do to change course. "We hit the dog on the road, or our society gets into war, regardless of the most heroic efforts to swerve away" (Platt, 1971, p. 33).

During this first period of time when the course immediately ahead seems to be set and substantial change is difficult, social science tends to be deterministic in the sense that—to the extent that the causal chains in society are understood—noninterfering predictions or extrapolations are feasible. But even during this brief perspective, we may expect some oscillations, extra-societal intrusions, and exponential explosions and decays that may confound all efforts to predict (Platt, 1971, p. 34).

During a second period of time, the choice period, the possibility exists for present steering, policy planning, or decision making to be increasingly effective in avoiding danger and following an intended path or pursuing a goal. During this second period the whole nature of prediction changes. Thus, in driving a vehicle, the momentum physics of the next half-second is steadily replaced, in anticipating future seconds, by the cybernetics of goal-directed steering. The 'weak interactions' of the natural sciences, where the observers or his prediction does not change the phenomenon, become replaced by the "strong interactions" of organism-environment feedbacks, where prediction changes to a range of alternatives with cybernetic choice. It ceases to be prediction and becomes an "if . . . then . . ." prophecy, "which

does not tell us what will happen, but rather what is the range of directions we can go in, and where we will go if we turn the wheel of initiating action by a particular amount one way or another." Under such conditions, "'predictions' cease to be predictions and become something more like 'advice' or 'warnings' so that the alert society, or the alert driver, can avoid the foreseen dangers or choose the desirable directions that have just become apparent. For this period, the problem is not to predict the future but to change it" (Platt, 1971, p. 34).

A third time period extends into the more distant future, a span of uncertainty "which is too far off and too dependent on intervening hazards and our intervening responses for present planning or steering to be relevant except in terms of very general directions" (Platt, 1971, p. 33). This third period of the future, the ultimate period of uncertainty, is comparable to the period "after the next bend in the road" (Platt, 1971, p. 35). This is a period for which only general goals, or preparation for general goals, can be set. The details for how to get there have to be worked out as we move along and are able to see better. During this period we can be guided only by some very general values, heuristics, or moral guidelines "that have worked in the past, or by some kind of Sitzgefühl as in chess" (Platt, 1971, p. 35).

For a long-range time frame, it is only the short-range end of planning that has to be "frozen in" for immediate realization. "For the more distant future *alternative options* are brought into view and kept open as long as possible." Thus, strategic planning is less concerned with one inescapable future than with a multitude of possible futures (or "futuribles," as Bertrand de Jouvenel calls them) (Jantsch, 1972, p. 1). In terms of a long-range future, the outcomes of consciously and rationally orienting thinking, policy formation, and action cannot yet be fully measured. Yet such thought, policy, and action may revolutionize the ways in which human beings deal with each other from the family and the community to the nation and the world as a whole (Jantsch, 1972, p. 1). But is it realistic to assume that human beings "now possess the technological power to make the world a Garden of Eden, a Garden of Abundance?" (Platt, 1971, p. 32). A great many serious difficulties will have to be overcome first. One of the most illusive of these involves what has been referred to as the counterintuitive behavior of social systems —a bundle of social, economic, and political considerations that have powerful implications for technological applications.

Among many social scientists there is a growing consensus that very little is understood about how large and complex social systems—including states and empires—really work. All too often, the intuitively obvious outcome of a policy or action does not occur. And all too often, the program that is undertaken to solve a problem—whether to alleviate highway crowding, fight crime, reduce the number of people on welfare, regenerate a ghetto, deter an enemy, or reduce armaments—has a reverse effect or, in solving one difficulty, creates another.

It appears, therefore, that many social systems are

> inherently insensitive to most policy changes that people select in an effort to alter the behavior of the system. In fact, a social system tends to draw our attention to the very points at which an attempt to intervene will fail. Our experience, which has been developed from contact with simple systems, leads us to look close to the symptoms of trouble for a cause. When we look, we discover that the social system presents us with an apparent cause that is plausible according to what we have learned from simple systems. But this apparent cause is usually a coincident occurrence that, like the trouble system itself, is being produced by the feedback-loop dynamics of a larger system. (Forrester, 1971a)

There are real and specific reasons why politicians, planners, managers, and statesmen, as well as scholars and the public at large, tend to misjudge the behavior of large and complex social systems. A part of the difficulty is that theoreticians and practitioners alike tend to focus too exclusively on certain aspects of the system at the expense of other aspects. Jay W. Forrester wrote a number of years back:

> It is my basic theme that the human mind is not adapted to interpreting how social systems behave. Our social systems belong to the class called multi-loop non-linear feedback systems. In the long history of evolution it has not been necessary for man to understand these systems until very recent historical times. Evolutionary processes have not given us the mental skill needed to properly interpret the dynamic behavior of the systems of which we have now become a part. (Forrester, 1971a)

As a consequence, a society may suffer "a growing sense of futility" as it repeatedly attacks deficiencies which the "symptoms continue to worsen" (Forrester, 1971a).

Social systems are characterized by equifinality, that is, similar "paths" of behavior often lead to different outcomes, and similar outcomes are often reached by different "paths." Across systems, the large number of variables, the high degree of interdependence among them, and the nonlinearity of relations may all lead to fundamentally dissimilar behavior. System structure, as a consequence, is far more important than system state. This means that "the nature of interrelationships among elements is much more critical than the precision of the input data." Yet the common predisposition among analysts and practitioners alike is to focus upon "input" rather than upon "structure." This difficulty is often obscured by the further fact that many complex systems tend to be "stable in response to most changes in input, yet exhibit catastrophic changes in the face of a few gradual alterations in input." Also, there may be very long time lags in the tendency of systems to accommodate to change. The consequence is that their behavior often appears all the more unexpected or counterintuitive (Linstone, 1974, p. 44).

Most social systems seem to have relatively few sensitive influence points through which the behavior of the system can be changed. Often, such influence points are not in the location where either decision makers or analysts expect them to be. Furthermore, if someone has identified a sensitive point where influence can be exerted, the chances are still that such a person "guided by intuition and judgment will alter the system in the wrong direction" (Forrester, 1971a). The situation is further complicated by the fact that, in any hierarchy of systems, there is likely to be a conflict between the goals of a subsystem and the interests of the broader system. Thus, "Rational micro-decisions all too frequently lead to irrational macro-decisions" (Linstone, 1974, p. 44). The interests of any single group or sector in a society are likely to be at odds with the welfare of the society as a whole, national interests will tend to conflict with worldwide human interests, and so forth.

These tendencies are exacerbated by the conflicts that normally exist between short-term interests and long-term interests. From the individual, the family and the community to the state and the world as a whole, decision making is often plagued by this paradox. And all too frequently, in groups and societies, the prevailing pressures for the short-run advantage lead to a discounting of the longer-term cost. Possible occurrences that appear to be far removed from the present are heavily discounted. "The forecaster points to distant threats and opportunities only to find a frustrating and maddening unresponsiveness. He is a victim of the law: short-term problems drive out long-range planning." Most of us tend to shrug off the more distant future. "In the long run we are all dead anyway, or *après moi, le déluge*" (Linstone, pp. 43–44).

There are other paradoxes—or decision-making dilemmas—in the affairs of large social systems, including nation-states. Among these is the growth paradox. A certain amount of growth is considered desirable, even necessary for a vigorous society. Unless a country's production increases year by year, the economy may be depressed and large numbers of people may suffer. Historically, those societies that have ceased to grow economically and technologically have often begun to decline. On the other hand, unlimited growth over an extended period of time may contribute to resource scarcities, pollution, urban stagnation, trade imbalances and a range of other difficulties.

Strong growth in a country's economy and production capacity may increase competition with other countries for resources, markets, and the strategic advantages considered necessary for securing trade routes. This consideration often leads to a further paradox. In seeking to strengthen its own position, each country tends to validate the competitive anxieties of its rivals. As resources are depleted or markets flooded, each of the countries is likely to redouble its efforts, thus exacerbating demands and competitive anxieties.

In recent years this paradox has assumed new and complicated dimensions. Until World War I, and to some extent thereafter, the industrialized countries of the world were able to secure protected access to resources and markets through colonial expansion. This is no longer the case. The world is still characterized by powerful industrialized countries, but new sovereignties in Asia, Africa, and elsewhere have replaced the former colonies, and physical possession of colonial territory is no longer as feasible. Penetration of these so-called underdeveloped countries has accordingly become both more complex (modern techniques, institutions, and organizations for the conduct of foreign affairs) and more crucial, with the realization, by strong and weak societies alike, of the need for secure access to energy and other resources in a world of scarcities.

During recent decades, rival powers have developed ingenious new mechanisms for pursuing their interests in foreign countries, all of which can be viewed as manifestations of expansionism. This is true whether we are concerned with Soviet assistance to the People's Republic of China in the 1950s, and to Middle Eastern, African, Latin American, and Southeast Asian countries; or with American or Western European economic, technical, and military aid and "peace corps" operations throughout much of the Third World. Under some conditions, these programs have undoubtedly served the donor power well and at the same time contributed to peace, economic advancement, and political stability within the recipient country (and perhaps in the world at large). But there have also been some grossly unanticipated consequences, as the United States discovered in Vietnam, and the Soviet Union in China, which policy makers would prefer to have avoided.

Perceptual problems complicate growth-competition situations among countries and contribute to an even more subtle, but very powerful type of paradox. No human being, including a head of state, can ever know for certain how his own actions will be responded to or interpreted by another human being. And, in turn, he has no way of ascertaining beyond any doubt what the other intends by his actions. He can only infer such predispositions and intentions by what the other does (or has characteristically done in the past). In psychological terms, this paradox of uncertainty lies at the source of the classic Richardsonian spiral: The leader of country A, fearing that country B may increase its military budget, increases his own. Meanwhile, the leader of country B, anxious lest country A increase its military budget, increases *his* own. The underlying predisposition for the increases in each of the budgets may be generated largely by domestic, technological, and economic growth and by bureaucratic and other internal ambitions and rivalries, which may nonetheless elicit violent responses from rival powers. In any case, each country validates the fears of the other—to the point where the pursuit of security may generate a pervasive sense of insecurity and even contribute to conflict and war.

Obviously, there is no single, best way of getting at such paradoxes or of understanding better some of the counterintuitive aspects of nation-states and other large and complex social systems. But to some extent, these problems can be attacked through computer modeling, simulation, and forecasting along lines suggested in the previous chapter. Several such techniques have been put forward in the last few years as tools for achieving a better understanding of how social, political, and economic systems work. In general, such methods are still in the early stages of development. And far too little work has been done so far toward integrating social, political, economic, demographic, technological, and other variables within unified, interactive models. But in spite of their limitations, some of these attempts have already provided early steps in the analysis of complex systems.

The analysis of the behavior of nation-states in the international system involves three main types of empirical data: attribute data; cognitive, affective and decision data; and action, interaction, or event data.

Attribute data may be divided into two subcategories: those data pertaining to a country's basic dimensions and characteristics, such as area, population, natural resources, and general level of technology (knowledge and skills); and data such as yearly investments in various sectors of the economy, annual expenditures for health, education, welfare, military affairs, and the like, production figures for specific industries, men-under-arms, and so forth.

Cognitive, affective, and decision data include statements of the perceptions, feelings, values, intentions, expectations, goals, and policies of national leaders or of their agents or advisors. Such data are usually acquired through some form of content analysis from archival papers, including diplomatic reports and position papers, speeches, diaries, and the like.

Action, interaction, or event data also tend to fall into two main categories. Included in the first of these are trade and aid statistics, the number of troops dispatched or returned from overseas, and any other activity in the international environment that can be reported in cardinal numbers. The second category of action, interaction, or event data involves metricized or scaled data that have been rank-ordered on some dimension such as conflict, cooperative, or level of violence.

The causal analysis, simulations, retrospective forecasts and predictions, and the sensitivity analyses described in the previous chapter involved the use of attribute data and action, interaction, or event data. Other studies have used cognitive, affective, and decision data in combination with action, interaction, or event data. A major difficulty associated with cognitive, affective, and decision data is that content analysis procedures still tend to involve complex, time-consuming, and expensive procedures wherein high levels of reliability are often difficult to achieve. But each of the three types of data has its uses, its advantages, and its vulnerability. In the future, especially with the further development of optical scanning devices for purposes of content analysis, all three types of data may be used in the same modeling enterprise. In the meantime, there are other ways in which values, for example, can be handled on a systematic basis in causal modeling, simulation, prediction and forecasting, and sensitivity analysis.

Only a moment's reflection is needed in order to realize that every attribute statistic is, in a sense, a trace left by some human decision. Each increase in a country's population is the result of a "decision," conscious or unconscious, on the part of two people to have a baby. Each invention and each application of knowledge and skills is also the result of human decision, as is each movement of goods, each budgetary allocation, each investment, and so forth. And to the extent that each datum represents the outcome or trace of a decision, some value or set of values is also implicit. In this sense, a country's annual budgetary allocations are an accurate quantitative measure of the society's *operational* as distinguished from its *professed* values. This does not mean that all the citizens of a country necessarily approved the allocations that were made or shared in the values that were invoked. On the contrary, large numbers of people may have preferred that less be spent on defense, and more on health, education, and welfare—or the reverse. But the statistical data do tell us, beyond any doubt, what values were in fact acted upon by whatever executive authorities and/or legislators drafted and approved that country's budget.

In the past there has often been a considerable amount of confusion with respect to professed as opposed to operational values. Speeches, proclamations, the preambles of treaties, and other state documents yield professed values in great abundance, and all too frequently they are accepted at face value. In fact, from an analytic perspective, such data may indicate a great deal about what a head of state, legislator, or other national leader wants the public or the leaders of another country to *think* he believes in, but very little about what he is intending or likely to do. In general, the record of the decisions made in the past (and the values thus operationalized) are likely to be much more accurate predictors of what he will do in the future. This consideration opens the possibility of using attribute data in order to introduce value concepts into the modeling, simulation, forecasting, and sensitivity analysis of nation-state behavior.

Through causal modeling, simulation, and retrospective forecasting it is possible to infer with a high degree of confidence what values a given country has acted upon with some consistency over a period of 40 or 50 years in the past. Suppose such an investigation were made into the behaviors of four interacting states—A, B, C. and D—for the years from 1946 until the present. And suppose, then, that a base-line forecast was made to the year 2000 on the assumption that each of the four countries would continue acting upon the same set of values over the same future span. This exercise would provide a rough indication of what might be expected of countries A, B, C, and D by the year 2000 if trends of the last three decades or so were to continue on into the future.

Having achieved this base-line forecast, or projection, on the basis of very explicit—though perhaps unrealistic—assumptions, it would be entirely feasible, using sensitivity analysis, to introduce alternate values. This could be done, as it was done retrospectively in the British case put forward

in the previous chapter, by modifying the parameters in each equation, or by altering the empirical data, one independent variable at a time, and observing the consequences. The levels or the rates of population growth could be increased or lowered; zero population growth could be instituted (in one, two, three, or all four of the countries); new technical breakthroughs could be postulated; new sources of energy could be introduced; military budgets could be cut by 10 percent, 50 percent, abolished, or doubled; education on various levels could be improved or expanded; domestic growth could be speeded or curtailed; countries could be provided with more (or less) relative access to resources; domestic products could be more (or less) evenly divided among the populace of one country, or two or all the countries, and so forth. In this way, not one or a few, but literally thousands of alternative futures could be generated with all assumptions and each introduction of a new value recorded and made explicit. It would be possible not only to introduce a new value in country A's decision making and watch the outcome for A, but also to trace the consequences further in terms of B, C, and D.

All such procedures would be subject to the most rigorous statistical controls available. But there would also be a further, ultimate check. The previous chapter has described how retrospective forecasting made it possible to introduce data for the early years of a 44-year period; to allow the forecast to "track" the real-world data through to the end of the period, and to measure the difference, or the forecast error. Once multiple forecasts were made into the *real future*, it would be possible to monitor events for countries A, B, C, and D as they unfolded, year by year, and compare the reality with the various alternate forecasts.

The prospects, of course, are not as promising as the discussion so far might suggest. The previous chapter dealt with the problem of break points, and it became evident from the discussion that such discontinuities create serious problems for retrospective analysis and forecasting, let alone efforts to project into the real future. Possibilities for attacking the problem are implicit in the procedures discussed so far, however. Essentially, break points are the result of the operationalizing of new values, or the result of a new technological development, or the acquisition of new resources, or a major change in a rival or closely allied country, and so forth. Hence, the sensitivity analysis procedures suggested in this chapter allow for the systematic creation of breakpoints through the insertion of new values into the simulation and observation of the consequences.

So far in the discussion we have set aside content analysis and related techniques for analyzing perceptions, professed values, expectations, intentions, goals, and the like. With improvements in the techniques of content analysis it should be possible to compare professed values and operational values retrospectively over considerable periods of time. Under what conditions do professed and operational values tend to converge or diverge? It should also be feasible, in applying sensitivity analysis to the future, to introduce and operationalize values that have been professed in the past, but not operationalized on a sustained basis, and to observe the results. Are the professed values practical; can they be invoked profitably; do they yield the outcomes that one might expect or that seem to be intended? For retrospective studies content analysis can be of great value, too, for measuring differences between perceived capabiltiies and operational capabilities, the function of threat, fear, hostility and other "soft" variables in international dynamics, and so forth.

The future has always been difficult for human beings to deal with. There seem to be no easy answers to the dilemmas of our ever more complex affairs.

> . . . in the past, with warring nations and uncertain catastrophies, we had to leave it to God or chance to determine the large-scale future. Random surprises, or statistical stabilization, or the feedback stabilization of the Invisible Hand of the market-place, or self-stabilizing attitudes or organizational structures, were likely to thwart any deliberate plan. (Platt, 1971, p. 33)

If society is to avoid serious dislocations, disruptions, wars, or other thoroughgoing upheavals, the gathering, transmission, and accurate evaluation of information—as well as the capacity for acting on it (sometimes in new, unprecedented ways)—will need to be built into the day-to-day operation of human systems worldwide. Such a continuing process requires a methodology of some sort for ongoing cost/benefit analyses of alternatives—not just in

monetary terms but, more importantly, in environmental and societal terms, and not just in terms of individual societies, but for humankind as a whole. The challenge will be to modify or replace old institutions *before* their malfunctioning or other inadequacy does too much damage, to try out new methods and institutions on a tentative, carefully monitored basis, to assess the benefits against the costs, and to effect the appropriate adjustments. This amounts to an individual and social " . . . learning capacity, not merely in terms of limited operational reserves, but also in terms of the capacity for deep rearrangements of inner structure and thus for the development of radically new functions" (Deutsch, 1967, p. 297).

Today, modeling, simulation, and forecasting techniques can be used to generate large ranges of alternatives with probable benefits and costs made explicit. Numbers of difficult questions can be addressed in a disciplined fashion. For what purposes and within what limitations should growth be encouraged? How is it to be furthered? What are the expected benefits? What are the possible damaging side effects? Who will reap the rewards and who will bear the costs? Under what conditions do benign activities such as trade, economic aid, and transfers of technology contribute to conflict, violence, or other undesirable outcomes? In what ways does domestic development affect foreign relations, and how do international transactions affect domestic programs? What is the relationship between the interests of a nation and the interests of humankind as a whole? Within the limits of this information, value choices concerning future policy can be made more rationally, in that policies can be chosen that are likely to achieve the desired ends. In terms of such tools as these, explicitly normative strategic planning becomes feasible on a controlled and systematic basis while remaining inherently "open" to inventiveness and receptive to innovations (Jantsch, 1972, p. 65).

In presenting his "wagon-train" model, John Platt has envisaged the pioneers of today and tomorrow using a contour map, rather than a "flat" map showing completed roads. Such a contour map should help us to "make our own road as we go." On this map the heights and depths are "fairly exact metaphors for the social costs and consequences of any given path of travel" (Platt, 1971, p. 39). In moving ahead into the future, the wagon train of humankind will have to avoid the regions with high social costs "because society generally tends to 'go downhill' or in the direction of least resistance except when it is carried into a high-cost region, so to speak, by its own momentum" (Platt, 1971, p. 39)—the momentum, presumably, of excessive or unbalanced growth on certain dimensions, or other run-away "positive feedbacks."

Refinements in prediction, forecasting, and sensitivity techniques should help in the plotting of such contour maps as societies move into the future. Such refinements should open the possibility of assessing the costs and benefits of alternative policies and ascertaining how unavoidable costs are likely to be—or *should* be—distributed among different system levels or among different classes, occupations, or interest groups within a society. It might be possible—if communications are kept sufficiently open—for virtually everyone in the world to ascertain beforehand what some of the difficult trade-offs may be.

This latter consideration may be the most important one of all. For the control of information and communication—like the control of any other vital resource—is a potent reservoir of power. A monopoly in the hands of government or any other special interest group of the concepts, the methodologies and the information touched upon in this discussion could become a fearful instrument of domination and oppression. The only feasible alternative seems to lie in pluralism—the possession of such capabilities by many different groups all around the world.

CHAPTER NINETEEN

SHORT-ORDER FUTURES:
SHORT-RANGE FORECASTING IN FOREIGN AFFAIRS

Lincoln P. Bloomfield

It is quite true that time is limited and governments work in terms of decisions that have to be made. . . . Now even very harried men do not fail to use their minds, but it is true that you end up deciding what you have to do right now. That can limit the amount of time you can give to the questions that lie down the road further.

MCGEORGE BUNDY, after leaving the White House

That's the trouble with Americans, isn't it, really? All that emphasis on the future. So dangerous.

A British character in JOHN LE CARRÉ's novel, *A Small Town in Germany*

To predict is difficult, especially with regard to the future.

Ancient Chinese proverb

I. DEFINITIONS

Futurology, usually speaking of long-term prospects, typically distinguishes between *predictions,* which specify particular events that are "going to happen," *anticipation,* which expects certain classes of events, and *forecasting,* which assigns probabilities to classes of future events. But in the short run, the futurologist's usual distinctions become blurred. If the short run means "from tomorrow to about 6 months from tomorrow," all is prediction. In that condensed time frame one cannot dodge the detailed event by withdrawing into generalizations. What happens next week is not generic; it is specific. If the short-term prognostica-

tor wants to say something useful, he must address himself to the likelihood of concrete events happening or not happening, and to the probability of each. What for the sake of uniformity I call "forecasting" in this chapter thus has a special meaning here.

Short-term forecasting differs from long-range forecasting in another way. In the long run, the differences are notorious between theoretical analysis—including theories of forecasting—and the day-to-day lifestyle and optique of the working bureaucrat. But in the close-in time range one finds far less of a gulf between theoretical analysis and the realities of bureaucratic life. Theories about forecasting in the near term must be close to day-to-day operating problems and operating styles. In fact—and this is one of my chief points—in the short run many bureaucrats find themselves in the forecasting business, for better or worse.

The State Department country director, the chief of the political section in an embassy, the intelligence analyst, and the National Security Council (NSC) staffer make forecasts every time they draft a cable or prepare a memorandum to their superiors concerning an upcoming foreign election, a developing conflict situation, or the probable effects of an aid program. The question is thus not whether operators forecast; it is how well they do it.

But my second chief point is that this close relationship between operations and short-term forecasting does not preclude the social scientist's attempt to build a greater amount of rigor and system into operational forecasting. The fact that operators forecast does not have to mean that we must be limited to short-term forecasting that derives solely from the traditional political art forms such as seat-of-the-pants hunch-playing, not to mention tea-leaf reading or rheumatic pains. Nor should we be constrained in this analysis by the bureaucratic frame of mind at its worst, so fixed on today's constraints that it cannot or will not apply the imagination necessary to glimpse a different future.

I happen to believe that at their best, intuitive policy skills are likely to produce astonishingly accurate forecasts of political events. It is my argument here that the addition of intellectual aids such as serious policy planning, better systematic techniques of analysis, and such potentially useful tools as properly designed simulations will improve that record still further. At the same time, such tools should help compensate for some of the artful bureaucratic intuition that is not so wise nor so prescient—in fact, intuition that sometimes is disastrous in its failure to make successful short-term projections.

The bulk of this chapter attempts to subject short-term foreign policy forecasting to analysis in order to try to surface some of those possible correctives. Before doing so, however, I wish to elaborate on the earlier point—the relationship of short-term forecasting to the bureaucratic situation in government, specifically of the United States.

II. THE BUREAUCRATIC SITUATION

The most distinctive feature of short-range as contrasted with long-range forecasting is that it is by definition both a direct extension of the continuous, ongoing process of decision making and, as I have suggested, an integral part of the staff work leading up to decision making. The point is made sharper by contrasting this close relationship with the gulf between *long-range* planning and forecasting, and day-to-day operations. One of the unresolved dilemmas of foreign policy planning is the chronic sense of remoteness from what is "relevant," and the consequent degrading of the planning process in order to reduce the hostility of the operators. The reasons for this disparity are many, but at root are: (1) the necessity for the planner to have the freedom to reexamine first-order assumptions underlying policy; and (2) the resistance of the harassed policy official who is struggling to carry out the very policy that he sees the planner mischievously undermining with his questioning.[1]

On the other hand, rather than something apart from and even hostile to day-to-day operations, *short-range* forecasting resembles what the foreign policy operator does in his job, and thus is spared the tension involved in the tasks that the long-range planner performs (or should perform).

I have suggested that an experienced professional analyst or diplomat is at his best when, on the basis of his knowledge and his analytical skills, he successfully predicts, for example, the outcome of an election that is about to take place, identifies the probable winners and losers in a struggle for political power, or correctly estimates the outcome of a vote in the General Assembly. There are few real surprises for the experienced and sensitive mind at work on these matters—but when a major error in short-term prediction is made, it can be monumental. For example, a September 19, 1962 National Intelligence Estimate, approved by the United States Intelligence Board, deemed emplacement of offensive missiles in Cuba as highly unlikely. The missiles were, of course, first spotted by a U-2 overflight October 14 (Hilsman, 1967, pp. 172–173). Another example is the failure of US and Israeli intelligence to anticipate adequately the Egyptian-Syrian attack on Israel on October 6, 1973.

The most explicit short-term forecasting regularly done in the foreign policy community is by the intelligence analyst. In his normal line of work in the Central Intelligence Agency (CIA), the Defense Intelligence Agency (DIA), or the State Department's Bureau of Intelligence and Research (INR), the estimator is expected to conclude his appraisal with predictions of impending events, stated usually as nonmathematical probabilities. But as I have said, he is not the only prognosticator of short-run events and effects. To the extent that foreign policy making in its essence entails the making of estimates or guesses about events that have not yet happened, to that extent all operators forecast and are thus *ex officio* planners (which is another reason why there is such an intractable problem in sustaining a genuine policy planning operation in the State Department or the National Security Council staff.)

Thus one is entitled to expect operators to make forecasts about the consequences of the policies they recommend or the events they study. The first head of policy planning on the NSC staff under Henry Kissinger tellingly described his own private conception of the planning task as "adding a paragraph of implications to foreign policy memoranda before they get to the President." But that is—or should be—the job of the drafters of the memoranda, since good operators are *expected* to do short-term forecasting. If they do not, the staff head argued, the planners have to do it for them. The fact that the State Department was "not doing its job," thus defined, gave the NSC staff much of its *raison d'être* since 1961.

But that was only one kind of "role-substitution" between operators and planners. Because of the inherent weakness of the policy planner's status, the people paid to do policy planning often *deliberately* limited themselves to analysis and forecasts *within a short time frame* rather than the longer periods that the operators are not likely to probe. The reason was that the planners, acutely aware of skepticism and impatience in the foreign-policy operators' culture about "dreamy," "theoretical," "speculative" forms of time wasting such as long-range planning, sought in self-defense to relate to that which the operators seemed to value and said they needed.

The results of having operators and planners both confine their thinking to the short-term have

been, I believe, very serious. The planners, instead of elevating the decision-makers' sights, often lowered their own to win acceptance by the more powerful operators' subculture. At its worst, that subculture lives by the forgettable aphorism of Lord Halifax (on, as it happened, the eve of World War II) to the effect that "I distrust anyone who foresees consequences and advocates remedies to avert them" (Quoted in Simpson, 1962, p. 311). The matter was well put by Robert Rothstein:

> . . . everything in the universe that the practitioner inhabits—the political system he participates in, the bureaucracy he works in, the beliefs he learns to take seriously—is preoccupied with the problems on today's agenda. The long run is left to shift for itself, and thus prediction is ignored or transformed into another effort to get a piece of the action. (1972, p. 165)

This created the problem that to the extent policy planning and forecasting tried to be responsive to what the operators believed their own needs to be, to that extent the planners sacrificed their capacity to do the very thing the operators could not do, and in the process made themselves even more redundant. For in working from the operators' agenda rather than from their own, they deprived the policy apparatus of precisely that which was not normally done by even first-rate bureaucrats—*challenging basic assumptions and projecting into time periods that did not look reassuringly like the present.*

The attempt to become more relevant by making short- rather than middle- or long-term analyses and forecasts thus has had another substantial intellectual cost. The shorter the time fuse and the more the planner felt he should be on the same wavelength as the operator, the less likely he was to challenge accepted premises and assumptions. At best he limited his challenge to second-, third-, or fourth-order, rather than first-order, assumptions (more about this later).

Another characteristic of the forecasting of events or consequences in a framework of days, weeks, or months is to shrink the catalog of available options for action to those *that are imaginable to adopt or implement within the fixed, visible constraints of today's politics.*

The wide divergence of forecasting roles between the foreign policy planner and the foreign policy operator has an instructive analogy in meteorology. Long-range forecasts both about the weather and about world trends tend to be intellectually more satisfactory than short-term forecasts. The short term is always subject to small uncertainties, idiosyncrasies, or momentary tactical perturbations that are significant on a day-to-day basis but not in the longer term. Similarly in foreign policy analysis it is easier to forecast the shape of the energy demand supply curve for the 1990's than it is to say how much oil the Gulf states are likely to pump over the next 3 months.

Unfortunately, most of the customers in both fields prefer short-range estimates. We don't care what the weather will be 5 years from now, but we are interested in the weather forecast for the immediate future when we plan a trip or project when to harvest the crop. Six years is a lifetime to a President with 2 more years to serve; 4 years is a lifetime to a foreign service officer posted to an embassy for 3 years; 3 years is a lifetime to a congressman elected for 2 years; 2 years is a lifetime to a delegate to the UN General Assembly whose appointment is for 1 year.

Of course numerous external events have a fuse of 6 months or less. A prime example was the series of threats issued by Soviet Premier Nikita Khrushchev commencing in 1958 and repeated at approximately 6-month intervals until 1961, demanding that the West sign a peace treaty with the German Democratic Republic within 6 months or face a situation in which the sovereignty of the GDR would be recognized by the Soviet Union, and any efforts to assert Western rights of access to Berlin thus considered a *casus belli.*

About that time some members of the Policy Planning Staff of the State Department asked this author to organize political games simulating hypothetical situations arising from the implementation of the Soviet threats. In requesting this, the members of the staff made a more general query as to whether we at the MIT Center for International Studies could put ourselves in a position to respond through simulation to an agenda of other problems likely to reach a critical point within 6 months. (For various reasons related to our own bureaucratic and intellectual situation we declined, but shortly thereafter we assisted in the creation of the political-military branch of the then Joint War

Games Agency (JWGA) for the express purpose of dealing with such problems in-house.) The point illustrates both the importance of 6-month forecasting *and* the questionable tendency of planners to work in that time frame in order to seem relevant.

The time cycle of institutional clocks always seems short to governments. The NATO foreign ministers or defense ministers meeting has to be prepared for every 6 months; the UN General Assembly demands the preparation of 100 or more position papers during the spring and summer; the House Appropriations Committee hearings take place in the early winter; the State of the Union message goes to press then too. In foreign policy the alarm clock always seems more relevant than the calendar.

The Policy Analysis and Resource Allocation (PARA) and "net assessment" procedures experimented with in the State Department were designed to improve the capacity of the Department to anticipate effects of probable policies, actions, and reactions. The techniques involved matching specific policy goals with obstacles in order to generate priority rank ordering and estimates of probable success. The specified time span for a cycle of the net assessment process was 3 to 6 months. The PARA system on the other hand sought to impose a slightly "longer term" view of events, that is, 1 to 2 years; it also encouraged the bureau or country team to explore "what if" questions about that future. Unfortunately, both innovations failed to take hold.

The point can be summed up by saying that most situational factors in United States foreign policy making conspire to ensure that the bulk of current official forecasting, whether done by the desk officer or by the policy planner, will in fact fall into the "tomorrow-to-6-month" time period. Both empirically and theoretically, this is entirely normal for the foreign affairs bureaucracy. But the effect is to reinforce an "uncertainty avoidance" rule that invariably favors solving pressing "now" problems rather than developing long-run strategies.[2] The basic agenda for the forecaster is thus already prescribed. *The future is what he already knows is coming up,* and his focus will invariably be on the trees rather than the forest. For in this time frame, foreign policy is what realistically can be done within the sweep of those short-term clocks, with minimal change in the rest of the system.

I have to note here that the estimator's reward for accurate prediction may not be much better than that of the messenger of an earlier era who was beheaded for bringing bad news. The classic instance may well be the extraordinarily accurate forecasts made by members of the political section of the American embassy in Kunming in the latter part of World War II. For their pains the reporting officers were professionally destroyed when their forecasts came true about likely political evolutions in China. A lesser case of rejecting pessimistic estimates was the decades-long Indochina policy that ended in ruins.

To sum up, close-in forecasting is precisely what the foreign service establishment is best at, most comfortable with, and most successful over time in doing. The bureaucracy and planners in recent years were both predisposed in favor of short-term activity; the demand they found was for judgments about the probable events everyone else perceived as most salient to foreign policy, even if this shortchanged that which was scarcest and most needed. It is inevitable that the short-run dominates politics and diplomacy (and weather), and that the market for short-term forecasts is always brisk. It is also sad that policy planners feel they will be listened to only if they fulfill someone else's definition of what is relevant, because their chief value is in transcending the evanescent present. But the pressures to stay "relevant" are immense and persistent. In the same interview cited in the beginning of this chapter, McGeorge Bundy when on to say:

> . . . I think it's generally a tendentious argument to assume that somebody else hasn't thought about the future. Everyone was charged with that duty, and everyone did it to some degree. To try to charge one man or institution with the task of long-range planning is to lock the door having had the horse already escape. The government today cannot bind the government tomorrow. (Interview with Boorman, et al., n.d.)

And in the same collection of interviews former Director of Defense Research and Engineering Herbert York said of the Secretary of Defense:

> If he has got another guy who is working on long-range problems that man may call on the intercom and ask to see the Secretary, and the Secretary will reply, "Yes, but not today," and

he will never get around to it. The problems that take up most of the time are economic ones, and on the use of funds today, not hazy problems five years in the future. (Boorman, et al., p. III–32)

The bureaucratic situation is unequivocal and seems never to change. Let us turn then to a more analytical approach to see how short-range forecasting can become more of a planner's science even while reflecting, as it does and must, the operator's art.

III. THE ANALYTICAL COMPONENTS OF SHORT-RANGE FORECASTING

Trend Analysis

The limitation of foreign policy or international relations forecasting to a short-term period such as 6 months tends to eliminate the effect of secular trends such as population growth and dynamics, business cycles, cyclical climatic phenomena that may influence good and bad harvests, recurrent plagues, natural resources depletion, generational changes, crossing of GNP curves, gross changes in per capita income, and so forth. These do not change much in a period of less than 6 months, and thus in the short term tend to be treated as constants, merely noted as marginally relevant background conditions, or simply ignored, sometimes with profound consequences such as the "newly discovered" energy crisis of the 1970's.

Some quantitatively measurable trends do get accounted for in short-term forecasting when there are likely to be wide fluctuations in a relatively short time. Examples are GNP, employment, crop yields, sales, exports and imports, the flow of armaments, and arms balances. (The latter is a good example of short-term fluctuations as a result of arms transfers, major new weapons systems coming into the inventory of a country, the start of indigenous arms production, and so on.)

Reliable short-term forecasting can of course also use known scientifically accurate projection, such as those that astronomers and navigators refer to as "ephemera." Examples are phases of the moon, times of sunrise and sunset, tides, average mean temperature, sunspot cycles, and monsoon seasons. These have obvious relevance for such political-military purposes as invasion, defense, infiltration, and reconnaissance, as well as for such economic purposes as planting, harvesting, and control of borders for health purposes.

But the great secular trends and cycles may simply be missed if forecasting is habitually restricted to a relatively short focus on trees rather than forests. A provocative metaphor may be found in the fear expressed when the early Mariner space probe was designed to unreel a sticky string intended to pick up unicellular life, which would then be reeled back in and scanned electronically. One biologist suggested the possibility that, while the sticky string with its microscopic cells was being reeled in, an unobserved pink elephant might be stepping over the string. The danger of missing the main trend is frequently driven home when society confronts a "new" technology that in fact has been gestating for up to a decade. Whether new weapons systems, polluting industrial plants, or diplomatically unsettling national capabilities, all have in common the passage through a process that *could* have been foreseen, and perhaps channeled into cooperative or socially desirable forms.

Figure 19.1 is the author's crude process model of interaction between the evolution of technologi-

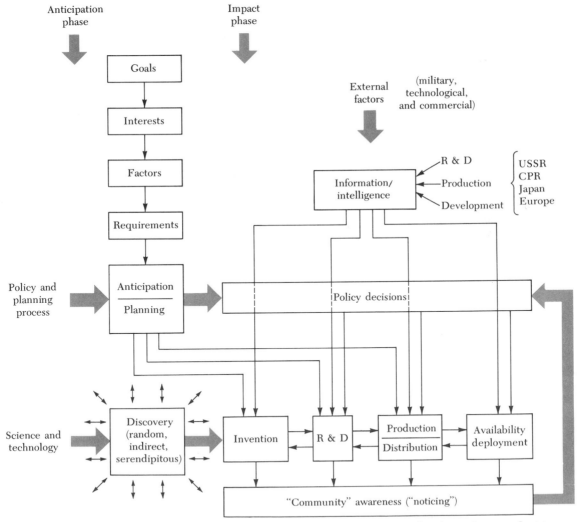

Figure 19.1 Process model of interaction between science–technology and policy planning–decision making. (Modified May, 1971, with the assistance of Conor Reilly.)

cal developments on the one hand, and policy planning, forecasting, and decision making on the other. It breaks down the technology development process (lower level) to four relatively distinct phases: invention, research and development, production-distribution, and availability (or, in the case of weaponry, space, or oceans systems, etc. —deployment). Policy decisions by political authorities can affect any phase. But obviously if they are not arrived at until the "production phase," they could not affect the prior stage of R&D, let alone the earliest phase when the genie, so to speak, was let out of the bottle. The ideal would be for the "Policy decisions" factor to impinge on the process early rather than late, after undergoing its own rational activity of defining national goals and planning with the aid of anticipation, that is, forecasting.

Unfortunately, the policy-decisions process is often not galvanized until the parallel process (lowest level) of what I call "Community awareness or Noticing." Three glaring examples might be the protracted failure to plan alternative energy sources to fossil fuels; the unchecked creation of an ecologically destructive industrial plant; and the US deployment of MIRV'd warheads just prior to the SALT-I talks.

As can be seen from this process model, forecasts of less than 6 months would be clearly incapable of leading to effective action other than in a single phase of the process. A 6-month forecast could catch a single segment of process—for example, where decisions were being made to go to R&D from technical invention, or to production from R&D, or to deployment from production. What can *not* be done within a short time frame is to anticipate and act upon longer-term consequences to be found within the much longer time span of a technological revolution or the creation of a new industrial power (at least 20 years), the lead time for a new major weapons system or space system (8–10 years), or the lead time for completion of facilities to provide major new sources of energy in the United States and Europe (8 years or so).[3]

There is one other element that longer trend forecasts tend to wash out, but which is often dominant in short-run prediction—that is the role of the individual. Perhaps this is as it should be because (*pace* Thomas Carlyle and his theory of the great man in history) the relevance of political personalities would seem to be far more salient in the

short run than in the long run. It is admittedly a debatable point.

In forecasting events in a period of under 6 months, one normally makes basic assumptions concerning the system that do not deviate from those being made by politicians in office or officials in the bureaucracy. The consequence is that a *series* of forecasts made at 6-month intervals would each be incremental, and never explicitly take account of trends whose "period" exceeds 6 months. Of course such a "rolling" series would in the end produce circumstantial evidence of the larger trends. But to take my earlier examples, there could be a high cost for arms control, the environment, or world order in the lag that such a process creates.

The remedy lies not in expecting the normal behavior of humans—or their institutions—to change radically, especially in a society where the state has no monopoly on planning and decision making. The remedy lies in building into a relatively unplanned economy more adequate long-term planning, which means of course better long-term forecasting.

Contingency Planning and Gaming

Long-term forecasting is capable of specifying an almost infinite variety of possible situations and outcomes (which is why it is sometimes hard to take seriously). This is because the number of crucial variables and their interrelationship increases roughly in proportion to the distance from the present. As the short-term yields to the longer future, the number of combinations and permutations approaches infinity. The standard argument against contingency planning for political or diplomatic events on the part of the policy planning staff is that when concrete crisis situations arise they are rarely, if ever, in the exact form specified in the contingency plan, and the latter is thus deemed unusable or even dangerous. (Whether this is a persuasive argument against contingency planning is open to question. Often the reason a previously drawn up plan is not used is that people forget that it exists. Moreover, the argument understates the high value of "structured open-mindedness" about the future.)

But if one confines planning to the *shorter run*, the range of contingencies that can be expected with reasonable probability is significantly narrowed, and *most longer-term variables can be held as constants* while manipulating only one or two. Thus some forms of contingency planning are eminently justifiable for the relatively short-term.

For this reason there is far greater obvious utility in the short term for such techniques as simulation and gaming, if they are done properly,[4] for pretesting strategies and anticipating outcomes. Despite my unwillingness in the late 1950's and early 1960's to set up a gaming service function at MIT responsive to a less-than-6-month crisis agenda for State Department planners, I think now that perhaps they were right in their judgment that political games could have been profitably focused on their close-in critical list. For only in problems likely to reach a head within months can one legitimately control for most of the elements in the system, manipulating only one key variable in order to analyze likely alternative outcomes by projecting present trends. This enables the short-term political exercise to pass the first acid test in the bureaucracy, that of relevance.

From the standpoint of gaming methodology, the role playing in short-term games is also easier to manage. The players can move directly from today's newspapers and cables to a world essentially unchanged except for one feature, thus requiring a minimum suspension of disbelief. Ironically, the Joint War Games Agency—now Studies, Analyses and Gaming Agency (SAGA)—has been unable, for various administrative, bureaucratic, and methodological reasons to do regularly the kind of very short-term gaming this would have entailed.

There is a danger of overselling political games, and sometimes they do fail to optimize their own value. For example, in a game run at MIT in the spring of 1958 a move by the "French" team to bring General DeGaulle into office was ruled out by the umpires as implausible—which at the time it was—but of course DeGaulle did come into office within 2 months. And in a game that I directed in Moscow in 1970, I severely criticized the behavior of the "US" team for what seemed to be excessively provocative behavior, including the flight over the Sinai Peninsula by jets from the US 6th Fleet. Three days after I left Moscow, jets from the 6th Fleet did precisely that.

In 1969 at one of our MIT professional senior games (CONEX IV) focusing on Indian and Pakistan relations, some of the best governmental and nongovernmental specialists on the subcontinent focused intensively on the problem of West Bengal, but no one raised any queries whatsoever concerning probabilities of unrest in *East* Bengal (East Pakistan, now Bangladesh). One can see over the longer run certain possibilities beginning to look like high-order probabilities. But that is only because, as I pointed out earlier, *in longer-term forecasting one does not accept all the first-order assumptions within which operational agendas are constrained.* On the contrary, longer-term forecasting has the responsibility to look under rocks, examine the woodwork, and play with heterodox premises in order to see what other contingencies are thinkable, possible, likely—or perhaps inevitable.

To sum up the point, political gaming is best used as an adjunct to short-term planning and forecasting. Even here one remains trapped to some extent by the inherent limits of short-term perspectives.

The difference in perspectives between short and longer range forecasting is well illustrated by the contrasting outcomes that are plausible under varying time frames. In 1968 I tried to look ahead to alternative futures for Western Europe, dependent on the way one varied a number of critical parameters. The time frame was approximately 7 years (Bloomfield, 1968). I have tried in Table 19.1 to update its skeletal structure to include two additional time frames, to illustrate the above point. The question it addresses is "How do your predictions differ given different time frames of 6 months, 5 years, or 10 years?" Although the answers are impressionistic, they may be instructive. It can be seen that those of the five scenarios that are plausible on the basis of a 10-year prediction are *not predictable on a 6-month basis* (and only partially so on a 5-year basis). Clearly, forecasts are highly sensitive to the time frame employed. The point is not that short-term planning and forecasting is futile—far from it. It is rather that the fullest range of options and outcomes can only be derived by exploiting techniques appropriate to *both* time frames, and being self-conscious and explicit about the differences between them.

Rank-Ordering Probabilities

Despite the built-in limitations of very short-range forecasting, systematic analysis can be applied, I

Table 19.1 Three forecasts for Europe in the context of five alternative scenarios.

Five Scenarios for Western Europe	6-Month Forecast	5-Year Forecast	10-Year Forecast
a. Status quo (i.e., no significant change from 1978)	a. Seems far more probable and believable than any other.	a. Unlikely but more probable than at 10 years.	a. Hardly believable, given the secular trends.
b. European unity	b. Seems unbelievable, particularly as recession continues, although some fragmentary positive evidence in the resources and monetary field, plus directly elected Assembly.	b. Can not legitimately be expected, but some trends are visible toward diplomatic and defense planning along with greater economic unity, monetary unification, etc.	b. Very possible, particularly given pledge contained in 1972 and subsequent summits.
c. Atlantic/NATO*	c. Diminishing under foreseeable conditions; NATO still declining, although perhaps stabilizing temporarily.	c. Seems most improbable because of detente and unlikelihood of Sino-Soviet rapprochement or general hardening of the Soviet line.	c. Possible because it is legitimate to assume fundamental alteration in Soviet policy, replacement of present leadership, Sino-Soviet rapprochement, etc.
d. US withdrawal	d. Occasionally trendy but not serious.	d. Continued detente, plus unsuccessful trade negotiations, plus some Eurocommunism increases probability.	d. Equally possible to assume reversal of detente, with renewed US involvement.
e. European nationalism/ Finlandization/ Eurocommunization	e. Currently feared, given trends and clues.	e. Some trends becoming more visible but still only fragmentary.	e. Still problematical.

*The 6-month forecast, made in 1977, was already dubious in mid-1978! I have left it as written to demonstrate the point.

believe, with useful results. In fact, the raw materials for systematic analysis are always at hand. More than this, an often hidden process of analysis is usually underway, which can be made more explicit. I believe that what diplomats and foreign policy operators and analysts in fact do in their workaday routine involves a "meta-systematic" but nevertheless logical and complex process of assessing situations, forecasting probable outcomes, and recommending appropriate policy action, all within the context of specified national interests and identified goals and objectives. Much of this process is tacit, though not as fecklessly so as academic critics believe. Certainly the intelligence community is expected to account in its written estimates for specific aspects of the external environment in which policy must be made.

Because there is no accepted theory within which systematic analysis is normally made, the approaches and methods vary widely. But in general there is an underlying typical structure to official policy analysis. The key question official analysts invariably have to ask in preparing short-range estimates of the situation or appreciations of possible events (and which competent policy officials implicitly take into account) is "*What transforming events are likely to happen within, say, 6 months, and in what order of probability?*" Or, put differently, "What things that *could* happen within a 6-month period would significantly change the situation under examination?" Posed this way, a structured response is called for even if it is never explicitly surfaced.

Assume for the moment that such a question is posed authoritatively. Our hypothetical example might be the Middle East situation in 1973. The answer may emerge illustratively as follows, in no particular order at first:[5]

1. Egyptian attack. (Would result in defeat of the Arabs and doubtless enlarge the territories occupied by Israel. It *might* involve Soviet help, thus escalating to the super-power level. Though intended to force a settlement, it *might* make Israel even more intransigent.)

2. Israeli attack. (The same results are likely. It would probably involve Soviet help—and US response.)

3. All-out war between the Lebanese army and Palestine guerrillas in Lebanon. (The Lebanese army would probably defeat the guerrillas currently in Lebanon, but Syria would probably furnish aid that would in turn probably trigger Israeli retaliation. This *might* reopen the Egyptian front, and in turn possibly involve the Soviet Union.)

4. Revolutionary change in one or more of the Arab monarchies or feudal societies—for example, Jordan, Saudi Arabia, Kuwait, United Arab Emirates, Yemen. (If protracted, this could confront the two Arab camps, thus reducing pressure on Israel to make concessions. If brief in time, it probably would not change the basic Middle East lineup, but *could* exacerbate the oil supply problem.)

5. An oil crisis arising from blackmail, curtailed supplies, sabotaged pipelines, refusal to increase quotas, etc.

Assigning an admittedly subjective probability in summer, 1973, produced this result:

1. .4 probability
2. .1 probability
3. .6 probability
4. .2 probability
5. .3 probability

Rank ordered, the events would fall this way:

3 .6 probability
1 .4 probability
5 .3 probability
4 .2 probability
2 .1 probability

(A version of event 3 took place, 1 and 5 did, 2 and 4 did not.)

If policy makers took seriously the results of such an analysis and decided to allocate their efforts in accordance with this rank ordering, US 1973 policy in the Middle East would have focused on containing the anticipated Lebanese blow-up, while accelerating efforts to bring Egypt (and Israel) to the conference table. If necessary, special task forces or watch committees would be set up (or continued) on both these situations. What was not likely, however, was a comparable effort with regard to the potentially more serious event 5—an oil shortage—either because it was not acute at the time the analysis was made, or because we have no adequate *long-term* forecasting and planning process to "game out" the possible consequences of various options or courses of action. A good *planning* process would of course add a third column of what, if anything, the United States might do, with or without other states, to alter the probabilities and thus the rank ordering. It is in this sense that short-term action—or inaction—can shape the longer term; alternatively, short-term action or inaction can preempt a desirable longer term plan or goal.

Once again, then, we can observe that, even at its best, the short-term planning process is inadequate unless the perspective is simultaneously broadened to encompass longer range trends and probabilities. Holding the rest of the world constant and playing with only one variable (which short-run forecasting does) carries the danger that over a longer period not visible within the field of vision and depth of focus assigned to the short-term forecast, *the seeming constants are themselves variables.* What I cited earlier as an advantage in favor of relative simplicity for short-run planning is clearly full of hazards unless this dynamic overview is maintained.

For example, the preceding analysis suggests that "radicalization" of the Gulf states oil suppliers is unlikely in the short run, enabling the Western planner to assume a degree of political and social stability in the region. But, even apart from the proven dubiety of "stability" as the dominant US policy goal, as a prediction this may be equally flawed. We may thus conclude that a simple extrapolation of the *status quo* may turn out in the longer run to be, not the most conservative, but *the most radical forecast of all.* Other examples that come to mind are short-term predictions in the Cuban situation in 1958 or 1959, the Libyan situation in 1970, the post-Mao situation in China in 1975–1978, and the Soviet leadership situation prior to each change. Each was severely handicapped by being unable to take account of the dynamics of historic change or even the gerontological inevitabilities given the ages of some political leaders.

Official forecasts made by American analysts with respect to the Vietnam War represent egregious examples of this phenomenon. Such forecasts were invariably short range, particularly since the prime consumer was that master of the short term, the President of the United States. It was the President who wanted advice as to what he should do;

that advice was based on what was likely to happen if he changed one variable, such as bombing the North or increasing the number of ground troops. The responses he was given by the bureaucracy were responsively optimistic in the short run, but realistically pessimistic in the long run. Acting in 6-month increments made it possible to make incremental bad judgments and decisions, even in the face of dubious longer term success. Moreover, when the administration wanted to be determinedly optimistic, long-range considerations could be dismissed as "theoretical" or "speculative." The key reality to the leadership was that which would take place during the present session of Congress, dry season, Saigon junta, or whatever. Thus, one could always afford to finesse the more devastating questions. Short-term 6-month forecasting enabled the President to be shown lights at the end of subtunnels, as it were, but with each inside the longer and darker tunnel of an endless 20-year war.[6] As pointed out by Rothstein in his valuable work on planning, "The most significant effect of an incremental policy process is that predictions will mentally be foreshortened, parochial, and conservative" (Rothstein, 1972, p. 181).

But, of course, that is simply a description of the normal life style of governments, at least in political democracies. We will continue to live with a governmental apparatus dominated by short-term, tactical, incremental slicing of the larger corpus of policy and history. This is the reality, and this is the realism its devotees practice (see Cooper, this volume). The difference between living successfully and unsuccessfully in that world of reality lies not in altering the system, but in protecting it from its own defects. It is not that short-term forecasting should yield to the longer term variety; such advice is not only unreal but substantively specious. It is that only with the additive of independent and courageous middle- and long-term planning and forecasting can the short-run realities of the system be converted from a chronic liability to an asset.

NOTES

1. For elaboration, see Bloomfield (1974, 1977, 1978). On other theoretical underpinnings, see Smoke and George (1973). See also Friedlander (1966).
2. Allison (1971), p. 77. The principle is from Cyert and

March (1963) which has profoundly influenced the "foreign policy process" theorists.

3. According to Richard T. Gonzales of the Advisory Committee on Energy to the Secretary of the Interior, letter to *Foreign Policy* (1973), p. 128. It should be added, however, that particularly in forecasting resource problems such as energy, it may be that the longest term—that is 20 years and more—is as unpredictable as the next 5 years, with predictable trends only clearly visible in the middle range of 5 to 10 years. On technological forecasting and related assessment procedures, see two comprehensive OECD publications—Jantsch (1967) and Hetman (1973).

4. An explanation of desirable methodological directions may be found in Bloomfield and Gearin (1973).

5. I first sketched this illustration in summer, 1973. Despite the October, 1973 Arab-Israeli war and the oil crisis that followed, as well as the "Sadatsmanship" of 1977–1978, I have kept my original formulation to illuminate both the potential and the flaws in thus trying to tap systematically one's unsystematic assessment of a complex foreign policy situation.

6. As David Halberstam put it, ". . . it was one of the marks of the breakdown in the entire decision-making process that because the bombing was going to be an instrument to prevent the use of combat troops, to win the war cheaply . . . the decision was a procedural one" (1972), p. 507.

CHAPTER TWENTY

LONG-RANGE FORECASTING IN INTERNATIONAL RELATIONS

Robert A. Young & G. Robert Franco

Long-range forecasting has received relatively little attention to date. There are a number of reasons for this state of affairs. Chief among them are its inherent difficulty, the lack of useful feedback, and the low priority it has been given by both social scientists and government decision makers. This situation, however, has changed significantly in recent years; many social scientists are now beginning to realize that the current state-of-the-art in

long-range forecasting is relatively underdeveloped.[1]

This chapter will have four major sections: (1) definitional considerations; (2) an assessment of the current state-of-the-art; (3) presentation of an analytic framework; and (4) use of the framework in a policy-oriented long-range forecast.

I. SOME DEFINITIONAL CONSIDERATIONS

Few would argue with a definition of short-term forecasting that specifies a time frame of 0–5 years in the future or with a definition of long-range forecasting that sets the time dimensions at 15–100 years out. However, to leave one's definitional chore at this point is to leave it unfinished, since, as Professor Choucri states in her introduction to this volume, ". . . different forecasting methods are applicable to different time frames and differ-

This chapter was written when the authors were associated with the Policy Sciences Department of CACI, Inc. Dr. Robert A. Young is presently with the Defense Advanced Research Projects Agency and Dr. G. Robert Franco is an economist with the International Monetary Fund. Portions of this research were supported by the Defense Advanced Research Projects Agency under Contract Number DAHC15-71-C-0201.

ent purposes." Two major goals of this chapter will be to delineate a framework for making long-range forecasts of international relations phenomena and to discuss the most appropriate forecasting methods to be used under varying circumstances. However, a definition of long-range forecasting must include not only a time dimension but a degree of uncertainty dimension as well. As will be seen, it is not enough to simply state that all long-range forecasts can best be approached with system dynamics or econometric analysis, since the choice of an appropriate method will depend more on the degree of uncertainty in the forecast than on the time frame of the forecast.

While it is true that we normally assume a high positive correlation between time and uncertainty, this is by no means always the case. One can easily think of many examples of 20-year forecasts that contain significantly different degrees of uncertainty and call for the use of different analytic methods and the inclusion of different variables. For example, one may be able to forecast with accuracy the British form of government in 1990; yet a similar forecast for Chile is very difficult to undertake. The difference in difficulty encountered in making accurate forecasts for these nations arises because there is less minimizing of uncertainty necessary in the British case then in the Chilean case. Yet, both forecasts would be termed "long-run," that is, more than 10-year forecasts under the usual classification.

Another way to view this issue is to differentiate the long run from the short run by distinguishing between parameters and variables. A "variable" is defined here as a value that probably will change during the time frame of a forecast. A "parameter," on the other hand, is a variable that can assume many fixed values but is expected to be stable for a particular time period. For example, the wealth of a nation is usually assumed to be fixed in the very short run. However, as the time horizon of the forecast expands, many of the parameters in international affairs become variables. By using this approach, the short run and the long run are defined in terms of the parameter and variable intensity of the concept forecast rather than just in terms of time frame. The long run would be characterized by many variables and few parameters, while the opposite would hold true for the short run. Con-

sider a forecast of Yugoslavia's alignment with the United States over the next 6 months. In this short run forecast, little uncertainty characterizes the system and many of the important factors are parameters. We can assume that Yugoslavia will maintain its Marxist form of government and that Tito will continue to be the head of state and hence influence Yugoslavia's alignment posture. On the basis of these parameters, a forecast of Yugoslavia's alignment can be generated. If the time frame of the forecast is extended to 10 years, however, uncertainty is injected into the system and many of the factors will become variables. It is questionable, for example, whether Tito will still be in public service in 10 years, let alone chief of state. Furthermore, over the next 10 years, Yugoslavia might adopt a more or less authoritarian form of Marxist rule.

This parameter and variable intensity classification of forecasts should complement the usual (arbitrary) time frame classification because it enables forecasts to be grouped according to their level of uncertainty. The level of uncertainty present in a forecast then is a function of the ratio of the number of variables to the number of parameters that characterize the forecasting model. If the ratio is close to zero, then the forecast is characterized by very little uncertainty. The previously mentioned British forecast that possesses less uncertainty than the Chilean forecast is parameter intensive, while the latter is variable intensive. Both forecasts refer to the same time frame (1995). Yet the British forecast could probably be undertaken more efficiently by employing techniques that are more appropriate to short-range forecasting, such as, for example, Markovian processes or a Bayesian approach. The Chilean forecast, on the other hand, is probably more suited to forecasting techniques such as system dynamics.

Another approach to the parameter and variable intensity classification of forecasts is to consider the degree of linearity in the functional relationships. For short-range forecasts where the forecast is parameter intensive, relationships (functional forms) between variables can reasonably be assumed to be linear since the parameters are constants. Over the longer run, however, parameters become variables, that is, the slope of the functional forms becomes a variable and hence nonlinear. Thus, situations with high uncertainty usually are characterized by nonlinear systems while situations with high certainty can be characterized by linear systems.[2]

II. THE STATE-OF-THE-ART IN LONG-RANGE FORECASTING

In discussing the state-of-the-art in long-range forecasting of international affairs, we will first narrow the focus of our review and then discuss the literature according to two major components. First, we will consider the "conceptual" literature that has attempted to provide definitions, organize ideas, and suggest approaches to the subject. After briefly reviewing the literature on techniques,[3] we will discuss those studies of a more substantive nature, that is, those in which actual long-range forecasts of international relations have been attempted. Finally, we will draw some conclusions regarding the state-of-the-art and its implications for near-term research on long-range forecasting.

In narrowing the focus of the brief review, major emphasis is placed on long-range forecasting in international affairs, as opposed to technological, economic, social, or demographic forecasting. We, of course, realize that these and other areas are necessary components of and must be included in a long-range international relations forecast. Nevertheless, space precludes a more extensive survey. Instead, we will concentrate on long-range forecasting in international relations *per se*.

In terms of conceptual research in this area, most work has been a part of or associated with two major projects. The first, headed by Bertrand de Jouvenel, is based in Paris, and is known as the Society for Economics, Industrial Social Study, and Documentation (SEDEIS); it also is known as the Futuribles Project. The second project is the Carnegie Corporation supported Commission on the Year 2000, chaired by the Harvard sociologist, Daniel Bell. In both cases, the concerns of these groups go far beyond international relations, but they have produced virtually all of the conceptual work done recently in long-range forecasting— work that has been heavily drawn upon by those few international relations scholars and analysts engaged in long-range forecasting research.

The purpose of de Jouvenel's SEDEIS group was originally to "stimulate speculation about likely social and political changes" (de Jouvenel, 1964). Members of the society have published their research in various books and journals, particularly *Futuribles*, the society's professional journal. Of the various published works, a book by de Jouvenel entitled *The Art of Conjecture* is the most famous (1967). In the book, de Jouvenel treats mainly logical and philosophical issues in an attempt to lay the basic groundwork for his general argument that social and especially political scientists should be much more concerned with the future than heretofore has been the case. He discusses, for example, nonhistorical and historical predictions in the context of primary forecasts (challenges), secondary forecasts (contingencies), and tertiary forecasts (most likely futures based on primary and secondary forecasts). According to de Jouvenel's argument, only a tertiary forecast is historical (1967, p. 55). He also develops a distinction between scientific and historical prediction and devotes an entire section of the book to quantitative predictions in the context of primary forecasts (challenges), secondary forecasts (contingencies), (1967, p. 1962). He goes on to assert that quantitative forecasting has two functions: "It can contribute to the solution of specified problems, and it can make us catch sight of new problems."[4]

A second important work to come from the Futuribles Project is an article by Saul Friedlander entitled "Forecasting in International Relations" (1965). In this article, Friedlander distinguishes between the impact of various explanatory variables on the time frame of a forecast. For short-run forecasts, Friedlander feels that the decison of the actors in the international system (viz., politicians, nations, international organizations, etc.) and the interaction of these decisions are the important predictor variables to be considered. Over the longer run, however, "the processes which operate independently of the actors" must be considered. Examples of these processes may include the impact of demographic social and economic variables on the international system. Yet these processes seldom are independent of the decision of the actors. The socio-economic demographic variables are largely determined by the decisions of the actors. This has repeatedly been demonstrated, especially by development economists in their attempts to discover the sources of economic development. Note should also be made of the fact that Daniel Bell's famous article "Twelve Modes of Prediction" was originally written for the Futuribles Project.

The purpose of the work of the Commission on the Year 2000 is well summarized by its chairman:

> It is an effort to indicate now the future consequences of present public-policy decisions, to anticipate future problems, and to begin the design of alternative solutions so that our society has more options and can make a moral choice, rather than be constrained as is so often the case when problems descend upon us unnoticed and demand an immediate reponse. (Bell, 1967, p. 639)

In 1965, the Commission on the Year 2000 listed the various themes that were to be studied by the Commission. They included, among many others, population and the age balance, biological control, and the state of the international system. Since its inception, the commission has produced a massive amount of material. Best known in international relations is the *Daedalus* publication in 1967 of a series of articles entitled "Toward the Year 2000: Work in Progress." Included in that issue was an article by Ithiel de Sola Pool on "The International System in the Next Half Century." In the article, Pool suggests that "Those of us whose profession is the search for understanding . . . must learn to live with self-exposure. Just as understanding is gained by unrelenting exposure of one's unconscious, so also can understanding be aided by exposure of one's conscious assumptions" (Pool, 1967, p. 930). In other words, produce explicit forecasts. While we would suggest that producing explicit forecasts on the basis of more public and replicable methods would constitute a greater contribution to the building of a science, we nevertheless strongly support the statement.

Much of the work authorized by the Commission on the Year 2000 has been done by Herman Kahn and his associates at the Hudson Institute. They have produced at least five books containing long-range forecasts of international affairs in the past decade.[5] Kahn's principal technique for long-range forecasting is scenario building. Scenarios are defined by him as hypothetical sequences of events constructed for the purpose of focusing attention on causal processes and decision points. This technique is based on several interrelated devices such

as standard econometric projections of key variables (such as population, literacy percentages, GNP, energy sources, military strength). Long-term manifold trends, on the other hand, are basic trends (many of which are sociological) that have characterized Western societies for many centuries. An example is the accumulation of scientific and technological knowledge. Using the scenario approach, Kahn develops "surprise-free" projections of the international system, that is, projections that are not surprising to its originator. These are reached by keeping certain aspects of the situation forecast constant while others are allowed to change. A second approach used by Kahn involves the use of "alternative futures," the formulation of scenarios that generate a range of alternate plausible futures that can be evaluated against one another. It is not our intention to discuss in great detail Kahn's work,[6] but rather to point out that many of his forecasts meet the imperatives suggested above by Pool. And although many criticize the work, we nevertheless are hard-pressed to point out a large number of other examples of effort in this difficult area.

The work of the Futuribles Project, the Commission on the Year 2000, Herman Kahn, Ithiel de Sola Pool, Raymond Tanter,[7] and others has served to focus our attention on forecasting problems and imperatives and to provide a basis for significant new work in the field. This basic and necessary research, in combination with the available techniques, provide the necessary ingredients for the production of substantive forecasts that will be reviewed subsequently.

Virtually all the tools and techniques available for use in long-range forecasting in international relations have been drawn from other fields of endeavor, reflecting the true interdisciplinary nature of the discipline. Application of statistical techniques has come from psychology, sociology, and economics; computer simulation has been adapted from operations research; probability theory from engineering, and so on.[8] The variety available is wide both from the point of view of explanatory power and the ability to handle differing levels of measurement and data. The efforts of technological forecasters certainly have been important in providing guidance for long-range international relations forecasters. Several excellent compendia are available, including J. P. Martino's *Technological*

Forecasting for Decision-Making (1972) and Erich Jantsch's *Technological Forecasting in Perspective* (1967). One relatively new technique, however, borrowed from industrial operations research, stands out in terms of both its potential utility for long-range forecasting and its current notoriety. That technique is system dynamics. The method was developed by Jay Forrester as a means for modeling sets of differential equations, and was implemented by Donella Meadows and her associates in a long-term forecast of five variables to the year 2100 (Meadows, *et al.*, 1972). The variables were population, capital investment, natural resources, fraction of capital devoted to agriculture, and pollution.

A crucial distinction between system dynamics and many other forecasting techniques involves the manner by which the parameters of the rate and level equations are established. Although it is highly desirable to have "hard" data to establish parameters, it is not necessary for some applications of this technique. For example, econometrics requires fairly strict assumptions about the nature of the data before estimation of equation parameters can meaningfully take place. System dynamics, because it is usually used for different purposes than econometrics, has far less rigorous requirements about assumptions. For complex models that cannot be expressed mathematically, the system dynamics approach becomes particularly useful since it can be used to evaluate model characteristics without having to estimate the model's parameters. The technique, as implemented and described in *The Limits to Growth* has been the subject of widespread criticism, most of it based on the actual rates and levels used in that study.[9] Much less attention, however, has been paid to the technique itself and the possibility it offers for a useful new approach to the difficult problem of long-range forecasting in international relations.[10] Despite these criticisms, there is no doubt that the research using the technique has served to focus attention on the real need for much additional research in this area.

Most of the research reviewed to this point has been concerned largely with either conceptual or methodological considerations. We must now turn to consideration of what we will call substantive long-range forecasts, that is, those in which the re-

sults are in the form of actual forecasts and in which the intent of the investigators is primarily to produce such forecasts rather than to advance the state-of-the-art. When viewed from this perspective, one gets a somewhat different impression of progress. In international relations *per se*, we can point to the aforementioned long-range forecasts produced by Pool, and by Meadows, *et al.*, and we can cite the work of North and Choucri (1972, pp. 80–122)[11] and the study by Phillips (1975). Beyond that, substantive work in the field has been accomplished almost exclusively in the "think tank" community in response to fairly specific policy needs. Under this rubric comes some of the work done by Kahn and his associates, and studies completed at Syracuse Research Corporation, General Electric-TEMPO, Holloman Air Force Base, McDonnell-Douglas, and Battelle Memorial Institute.[12] In most of these reports, the specified need was for either a "threat" forecast (what are the potential military threats to the United States 15–20 years in the future?) or an "environmental" forecast (what political, economic, social, technological environment will we be facing in 15–20 years?). In many of these efforts, the analysts have attempted to be explicit in their methodology and to use data where possible, but they have purposely not attempted to advance the state-of-the-art. Rather, their intent was to take maximum advantage of it to produce the best possible forecasts. Often the results have been justifiably criticized on a number of grounds by those few who have seen the work. Nevertheless, the major demand for such substantive research to date has come from the national security community, and the vast majority of the long-range forecasts in international relations are of this type.[13] If we judge them to be of poor or mediocre quality, then political scientists outside the think tank community must either begin to produce such substantive forecasts or enter that community and do them from within.

Our major point, then, is that a good segment of the necessary foundations for doing long-range forecasting are in place. Many of the difficult philosophical and conceptual issues have been taken up, and if not resolved, at least exposed so that individual investigators can make reasonable choices. A comparatively large arsenal of techniques and approaches to measurement are at our disposal that make possible attempts at forecasting that would have been difficult at best a decade ago. We have computer programs for storage/retrieval and statistical analysis available that are oriented toward social science research so that those with little knowledge of computer science can nevertheless employ the computer as a tool. Even the problem of the availability of long time-series data has begun to ease. Projects begun in the mid-sixties have come to fruition; others are continuing. Many governments and international organizations are finally beginning to make large data files available at modest cost.

The conceptual and methodological state-of-the-art is more than adequate. Much data are available. What now remains is the task of bringing the substantive segment at least up to the level of the others. That is, we must make many multiple attempts to produce explicit long-range forecasts for a wide variety of specific topics using a diversity of techniques and approaches. Otherwise, the state-of-the-art, from the point of view of available forecasts, will remain at its present underdeveloped stage.

III. AN ANALYTIC FRAMEWORK FOR LONG-RANGE FORECASTING

In presenting an analytic framework for long-range forecasting, we will initially concern ourselves only with the process of moving from stated purpose through predictor selection. Subsequently, we will suggest a framework within which one can consider alternative forecasting techniques.

The analytic framework is shown diagrammatically in Figure 20.1. At the most general level, the purpose of the forecast (problem, goal, etc.) drives many of the selections necessary to formulate one's approach. For ease of discussion, we will limit our treatment of purpose to two areas: policy *or* science. While it is clear that the purpose of a forecast will influence the choice of time frame, its impact is somewhat less obvious for the other elements of the process and will be discussed as we proceed.

The second step, *concept selection*, is probably the least understood and consequently most frequently incorrect step in the process. A fundamental property of long-range forecasting is the trade-off between precision and reliability. As uncertainty rises (in many cases as the time horizon extends outward), one must sacrifice precision for reliability. Thus, for a long-range forecast, if one adopts a narrow definition of the concept to be forecast—that is, one that requires near perfect precision—the reliability will be very low, rendering the results virtually useless. There is a direct (but not linear) relationship between the degree of reliability and the precision with which a concept should be defined.[14]

An example may help to clarify and illustrate this point. A subject of general interest to many forecasters and planners is that of the stability of foreign governments. In the short-run, the appropriate concept probably would be "irregular change in government," for example, a coup, while in the long run, it would be meaningless to to forecast such a precise concept. To do so would yield a highly unreliable forecast. What we are doing, then, is admitting that any attempt to forecast that there will be a coup d'etat in a given nation in a given year is doomed to failure. There are simply too many unique factors involved in such an event to permit any acceptable degree of reliability to be associated with such a forecast. Perhaps, instead of a coup, there might be a series of riots, a revolution, or major governmental change through peaceful resignation. It would be much more appropriate to forecast the probable "level of government instability," a more general concept that sacrifices precision, but should gain in reliability. Instead of forecasting a coup then, one might forecast "high" instability or even a level of 0.9 on a scale of 0. to 1.0. While many planners would like to develop forecasts of the more precise concept of "coup d'etat," they must be willing to accept less precision in order to achieve an acceptable level of reliability.

Moving to the *indicator selection* step in Figure 20.1, it should be apparent that we are using the term "indicator" as an operational measure of the selected concept(s) rather than as a pointer or predictor of some future event, as the term is sometimes used. Here again, theory and available analytic approaches will hopefully provide significant inputs and guidelines and we must guard against the use of indicators that are too precise in nature. Use of event data, for example, probably would be an

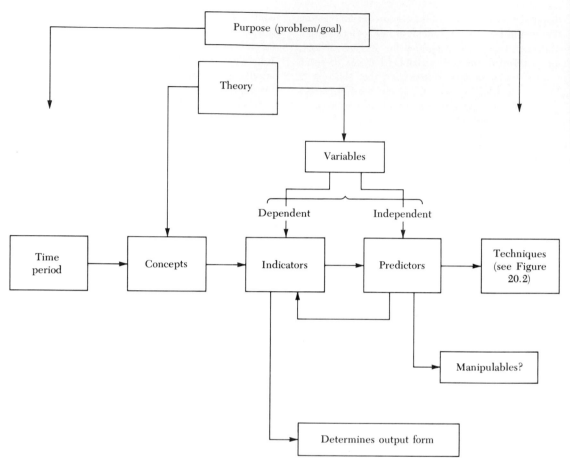

Figure 20.1   A long-range forecasting analytic framework.

inappropriate indicator of conflict or hostility in the long run since it is both too precise and subject to high rates of change. A more appropriate measure of conflict in this case might be war-years between dyads.

Note, however, that the selection of indicators then becomes an absolute constraint on the form of the forecast output. In this context, war-years might be an excellent indicator for scientific purposes, but a poor one for policy purposes. Decision makers or planners would be hard-pressed to utilize such a forecast even if they were convinced of its accuracy. Rather, they need a statement of the probability of conflict between a given pair of nations. This suggests that a more policy-oriented operational measure of the dependent variable

would be presence or absence of war or, perhaps, a more continuous variable such as "war-proneness." The principal point, then, is that we must not only consider the level of generality of the indicator and the guidance provided by theory, but that we must also pay close attention to the constraints in utility imposed by our selection.

Still referring to Figure 20.1, one can see that the next step in the analytic framework is the choice of *predictors* or independent variables. Here again, many of the same points just made can be repeated, but some additional factors must also be taken into consideration. The degree of variability in the short run should be low and any theoretical clues available should be seized upon. Furthermore, the consideration of forecast purpose in relation to selection of predictor variables high-lights three important factors, the first relating to policy use and the last two to scientific efficiency. In the former case, the exclusion of manipulables as predictor variables, of course, will sharply curtail, if not altogether eliminate, the policy relevance of the forecast. In the latter case, the first point relates to the small amount of attention paid to lagged relationships in long-range forecasting, although this if fairly common in short-range forecasting. While it is more difficult to identify variables that lag 15 or 20 years, it is by no means impossible and should be more thoroughly considered. Second, it is not uncommon to find long-range forecasts in which the predictor variables are as difficult, if not more difficult, to forecast than the dependent variable. Thus, analysts sometimes discover a strong positive relationship between GNP (predictor variable) and education expenditures/capita (dependent variable), and then project GNP in order to forecast educational expenditures (or vice versa). In this case, as in many others, direct estimation is both easier and more accurate than indirect estimation. Note also that there is often a feedback loop between predictors and indicators since predictors might be either endogenous or exogenous, depending upon the type or stage of the analysis.

Having completed our discussion of an analytic framework, we can now turn to a brief presentation of available forecasting techniques categorized as either basically quantitative or qualitative in nature. We will not elaborate on any of these techniques here since most readers are familiar with them and most of these methods are discussed in some detail in other chapters of this volume.[15] Rather, we will attempt to make two brief points regarding the use of these techniques for short- versus long-range forecasting and then will discuss a framework within which the techniques listed may be considered.

The first point relates to the traditional thinking of the techniques "best" suited to either short- or long-term forecasting. For example, system dynamics and econometric techniques are usually thought to be more appropriate to long-term than to short-term forecasting. Yet there is nothing inherent in the techniques themselves to suggest such a distinction. Rather, it probably has arisen as a result of the usual application of the techniques.

However, both methods can deal with linear and nonlinear relationships, a common distinction between the short run and long run. The selection of variables and, more importantly, the unit of analysis will actually determine the short- or long-range aspects of the analysis, not the technique itself. Thus, instead of using years or decades as units of time measurement in a system dynamics analysis, why not use days, or weeks, or months? By the same token, one can easily define state in a Markovian process model that would make it long range in nature. Given the state-of-the-art in long-range forecasting, it seems imperative that we make maximum use of those tools available to us without regard for previous or "accepted" utility.

The equally common dichotomy between "qualitative" and "quantitative" also hampers our progress in long-range forecasting. For scientific purposes—theory building, hypothesis testing, measurement development—the use of one or the other (particularly in the context of the development of a given technique) is in many cases desirable. For policy purposes, however, such a rigid approach is dysfunctional at best. Instead, one should use the most powerful and systematic techniques available for any set of given requirements, taking into account cost-effectivensss considerations. And the choice of techniques should not be made on the basis of their quantitative or qualitative nature, but rather on the basis of the best we can do with the total state-of-art. Such an "integrated" approach—integrated from the point of view of the techniques used in all phases of the analysis—is required if we hope to produce credible, useful, and relevant long-range forecasts.

In order to illustrate this point, consider a forecast wherein we wish to consider "power blocs" in the decade of the 1990's. Assume that it has been decided on the basis of available theory that there are two major components of such a forecast: political and economic. Assume further that we have been able to obtain acceptable data on promising variables for the economic component of the forecast and for parts of the political component, for example, UN voting data. However, in addition, we are convinced that in order to produce a reasonable forecast, we must take into account the probability that certain of the nations will possess nuclear weapons in the time frame of concern. We could either leave the variable out of the analysis altogether or use a very indirect (and perhaps inappropriate) measure such as defense expenditures, or convene a Delphi panel of experts. In many cases, it is better to integrate the Delphi forecast of the variable into what is otherwise a quantitative analysis than to leave the variable out altogether or to use an inappropriate surrogate measure.

Having made these two points, we will now briefly discuss several well-known forecasting techniques in the context of two dimensions: amount of knowledge and level of measurement.[16] By amount of knowledge, we are referring to the goodness of our theoretical and empirical knowledge about relationships of interest. Do we feel we have sufficient reasons to think we understand the phenomena with which we are dealing? Have there been a number of studies with converging results? Level of measurement, of course, refers to the type of data we are dealing with for our indicators and predictors (nominal, ordinal, interval, or ratio). Figure 20.2 attempts to place each of the techniques in the context of these two dimensions in order to

demonstrate the requirements for the appropriate use of each in long-range forecasting.[17] For example, econometric methods are the most demanding, usually (but not always) requiring at least interval level data and very precise knowledge of the form of the relationship among one's variables. Cross-impact matrices and system dynamics models, on the other hand, can be used with substantially lower levels of both dimensions. Our point here is principally that there are various available methods for making long-range forecasts, relatively few of which have been used extensively in international affairs and even fewer of which have been used in combination with one another, even though many of the long-range forecasts completed to date have had to deal with widely differing levels of knowledge and measurement.

IV. A POLICY-ORIENTED LONG-RANGE FORECASTING MODEL[18]

Having specified an analytical framework, it is now possible to discuss a long-range forecasting model

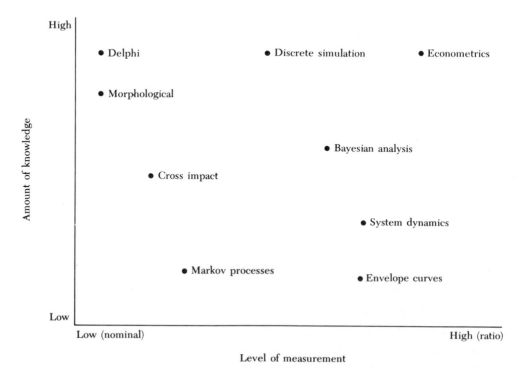

Figure 20.2 Requirements for the use of forecasting techniques. (See the text for a definition of "requirements.")

that has been developed within this frame-work. In this case, the clear purpose of the effort is policy related. Alexander George distinguishes between two types of forecasts: exploratory and problem-oriented. The former are not closely tied to policy making, but are technique-oriented. The latter, on the other hand, "define the purpose of the forecast in order to relate it to specific policy decisions that are (or ought to be) under consideration."[19] Every four years, the Joint Chiefs of Staff (JCS) produce a document called the Joint Long-Range Strategic Study, or the JLRSS. Figure 20.3 illustrates the relationship between the JLRSS and the many other planning documents produced by the Army, the Office of the Secretary of Defense (OSD), and the JCS.[20] The purpose of the JLRSS is to provide guidance to the defense community regarding the international environment 15–20 years from now. Historically, the results have lacked credibility and consequently the study has been used infrequently.

The purpose of the CACI effort reported upon herein is two-fold. First, the task was to assist the responsible JCS analysts to produce the best (most accurate) forecast possible by making available to them the most appropriate techniques and data

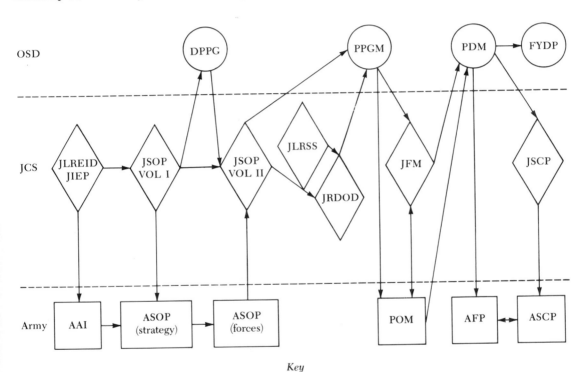

Key

OSD	Office of the Secretary of Defense
DPPG	Draft Defense Planning and Programming Guide
PPGM	Program Planning and Guidance Memorandum
PDM	Program Decision Memorandum
FYDP	Five-Year Defense Plan
JCS	Joint Chiefs of Staff
JLREID	Joint Long-Range Estimative Intelligence Document
JIEP	Joint Intelligence Estimative Plan
JSOP	Joint Strategic Operations Plan
JLRSS	Joint Long-Range Strategic Study
JRDOD	Joint Research and Development Objectives Document
JFM	Joint Forces Memorandum
JSCP	Joint Strategic Capabilities Plan
AAI	Army Acquisition Instruction
ASOP	Army Strategic Operations Plan
POM	Program Objective Memorandum
AFP	Army Forces Plan
ASCP	Army Strategic Capabilities Plan

Figure 20.3 Relationship of Army, JCS, and OSD plans. (Excerpted from Cameron, 1973, p. 2.)

files extant. Second, experimental forecasts for selected regions of the world were produced to be tested against forecasts of the JLRSS. In this section, we will discuss a model that was developed to forecast the European environment 20 years hence. Referring back to Figure 20.1, the time frame of the forecast is 1985–1994, which corresponds to the interest of the user—in this case, the Joint Chiefs of Staff, J-5 (Long-Range Branch). The concept selection process involved identifying those concepts of special interest to the user. Furthermore, only those concepts that could be forecast meaningfully (i.e., with the proper mix of precision and reliability) over the long range were considered. These concepts were labeled "central environmental descriptors" for purposes of ease of communication. The five descriptors are international alignment, international conflict, national power base, international instability, and economic interdependence (bilateral trade). The forecasting model developed depends on three sets of theoretical frameworks: substantive social science theory, statistical theory, and cybernetic theory. The assumptions of the model were expressed in the form of relationships between variables and were subjected to validation against each of the three sets of theoretical frameworks. The results of this validation led to the formulation of a system to twelve equations that constitute the structure of the forecasting model. A characteristic of the structure is the interaction between the central environmental descriptors. The linkages between the variables or coefficients were estimated from 1950–1970 data using multiple regression techniques. Application of the equations to a set of initial data (1970) produced a forecast for the long-range European environment of 1985–1994. Equations were developed to produce forecasts for population, energy consumption, gross national product, trade, distribution of major power alignment, extent of major power alignment, turmoil, defense expenditures, military manpower, monadic conflict, revolt, and dyadic conflict. These variables represent components of the five central environmental descriptors. Each of the descriptors is now examined individually.

International Alignment

Two aspects of alignment were explicitly described in the study: the extent of major power alignment and the manner in which nations distribute their major power alignment between the United States and the Soviet Union. The modified bipolar alignment scheme was represented on a two-dimensional plane. The extent and distribution of major power alignment were derived by considering the characteristics of a two-tuple vector that originates at the point (0, 0; 0, 0) and ends at a given nation's coordinates. The length of this vector (designated R) served as a measure of the extent of alignment; the angle of the vector (designated θ) represented the distribution of that alignment between the United States and the Soviet Union. Thus, a nation whose coordinates lay quite close to the point (0, 0; 0, 0) has a very short vector and is relatively nonaligned with the major powers. A nation whose vector has an angle of 0° from the horizontal axis is completely aligned with the Soviet Union, while a nation whose vector has an angle of 90° from the horizontal axis distributes its major power alignment totally with the United States. A vector angle of 45° indicates alignment is distributed equally with both major powers. These two aspects of major power alignment, although distinct, are explicitly related. Together they enable the research team to describe and forecast clusters of nations aligned with the United States or with the Soviet Union, as well as clusters of nonaligned and multialigned nations.

Tables 20.1 and 20.2 present forecast alignment blocks for 1985 and 1994. It is not at all surprising that the membership of these groups remained fairly constant during the forecast period; international alignment was conceptualized as a rather stable and persistent aspect of politics in the international system. The tables rank the European nations within each of these groups according to the extent of their alignment with the respective major power or, in the case of the nonaligned and multialigned group, with the two major powers. Thus, of the Soviet-bloc countries, Bulgaria was consistently the strongest ally of the Soviet Union, followed by Poland, Romania, and Hungary. Czechoslovakia remained the least aligned with the Soviet Union of this group. Similarly, the relative extent of major power alignment of the nonaligned and multialigned group was constant during the forecast period. Turkey and Spain were clearly aligned with both major powers, although they do lean slightly toward the United States. Portugal was also multialigned, but distributed its major power alignment

Table 20.1 Rankings of the 26 European nations within alignment groups, 1985.

Aligned with Soviet Union	Nonaligned/ Multialigned	Aligned with United States
Bulgaria	Turkey	Italy
Poland	Spain	France
Romania	Portugal	United Kingdom
Hungary	Greece	West Germany
East Germany	Austria	Yugoslavia
Czechoslovakia	Finland	Netherlands
		BLEU*
		Iceland
		Ireland
		Switzerland
		Norway
		Denmark
		Sweden

*Belgium/Luxembourg.

more or less equally between the United States and the Soviet Union. Greece, Austria, and Finland were substantially less aligned with each major power. These nations occupy the borderline between nonalignment and multialignment throughout the 1985 to 1994 period. None of these six nations was unambiguously nonaligned; yet Greece, Austria, and Finland were far less tied to the major powers, as indicated by their substantially lower ALIGNR scores. Within the group of Western European nations that were forecast to be

Table 20.2 Rankings of the 26 European nations within alignment groups, 1994.

Aligned with Soviet Union	Nonaligned/ Multialigned	Aligned with United States
Bulgaria	Turkey	Italy
Poland	Spain	United Kingdom
Romania	Portugal	Yugoslavia
Hungary	Greece	France
East Germany	Austria	West Germany
Czechoslovakia	Finland	Netherlands
		BLEU
		Ireland
		Iceland
		Norway
		Denmark
		Switzerland
		Sweden

aligned with the United States, there was some fluctuation in relative levels of alignment throughout the forecast period. While the two most aligned nations, Italy and the United Kingdom, maintain their relative positions from 1985 to 1994, Yugoslavia increased its alignment with the United States rather substantially during that period. Yugoslavia begins the forecast period as the fifth most aligned European nation with the United States; by 1994 it overtakes both West Germany and France and is ranked third. The other important rank change in alignment with the United States involves Switzerland. That nation shows a two-rank decrease in alignment with the United States between 1985 and 1994.

International Conflicts

Security analysts generally agree that war is the least probable form of conflict in contemporary Europe. Thus, a definition of conflict was chosen to encompass acts of verbal hostility as well as more severe actions involving physical violence. Verbal conflict includes common· diplomatic maneuvers such as threats, warnings, and criticisms whereas physical violence ranges from border skirmishes to military engagements. Conflictive actions included in the study are nonroutine, newsworthy activities reported by the *New York Times*.[21] They were divided into three general categories: physical violence, coercion, and pressure. The categories were weighted according to their relative severity, and the weighted conflict acts were summed to obtain measures of conflict for nations and dyads. These measures were not intended to correspond to particular combinations of observable events, but rather to indicate relative levels of conflict for the European nations. A two-stage process that employs two closely related indicators of international behavior was used to generate a measure of international conflict. The first monadic conflict measures the total amount of conflict that a single European nation experiences with the other twenty-five nations in the region. Dyadic conflict provides more specific information about which pairs of nations are likely to conflict. As a supplement to the monadic forecasts, dyadic conflict measures locate potential sources of conflict for those countries that are expected to have relatively high levels of conflict within the region as a whole. Monadic conflict is a good predictor of dyadic conflict. Thus, the European nations' general propensity to conflict was forecast first and then used to predict the likelihood that conflict will occur between particular pairs or groups of countries. The objective was to develop two distinct forecasting equations, one for monadic and one for dyadic conflict.

Table 20.3 ranks the European nations according to their forecast levels of monadic conflict in 1985 and 1994. Two points were of special interest with respect to these results. First, the distribution of nations on measures of monadic conflict reflected to a large extent their relative levels of national power base. This is because conflict is best understood as a component of nations' general patterns of behavior in the international system and large, wealthy, and powerful nations are typically those countries that interact extensively with others. Smaller and poorer nations seldom take part in international interactions since they have neither the

Table 20.3 Rankings of the 26 European nations on monadic conflict.

1985	1994
Soviet Union	Soviet Union
West Germany	West Germany
France	United Kingdom
United Kingdom	France
East Germany	East Germany
Czechoslovakia	Czechoslovakia
Sweden	Sweden
Italy	Italy
Poland	Poland
BLEU	BLEU
Netherlands	Netherlands
Denmark	Denmark
Switzerland	Switzerland
Norway	Norway
Romania	Romania
Hungary	Hungary
Austria	Austria
Spain	Bulgaria
Bulgaria	Finland
Yugoslavia	Spain
Finland	Yugoslavia
Greece	Greece
Ireland	Ireland
Portugal	Portugal
Turkey	Turkey
Iceland	Iceland

resources nor the motivation to become major actors in the international system. Thus, the Soviet Union, West Germany, France, the United Kingdom, and East Germany led the list of nations in terms of monadic conflict, a situation that is quite consistent with the patterns of conflict observed during the 1960's. Sweden, which has traditionally been a low conflictor, was forecast to experience rather extensive conflict during the forecast period because it is expected to show considerable growth in both economic and military power bases. The second major point to be made here concerns the stability of these rankings throughout the forecast period. Between 1985 and 1994, only two nations, Finland and Spain, show any significant change in rank or monadic conflict forecasts. The increase in Finland's conflict during the period was due to its shared border with the Soviet Union. Since Finland is not aligned solely with the Soviet Union, the potential for conflict between these nations is high, particularly in the absence of restraint in the interactions between these two countries. Spain, on the other hand, evidenced a decline in total conflict throughout the forecast period. As will be noted later, Spanish economic and military power showed a decline relative to other European countries between 1985 and 1994. Concomitantly, Spain's level of conflict within the European region decreased relative to other nation's conflict experiences.

Dyadic conflict forecasts were used to identify the patterns of conflict expected between the European nations during the 1985–1994 time period. Table 20.4 shows mean dyadic conflict scores within and between the three forecast alignment groups previously identified. The Soviet Union was excluded from this analysis because its levels of conflict tended to overshadow all other conflict patterns. Suffice it to say that the Soviet Union experienced extensive conflict with nations in all three alignment blocs during the entire forecasting period. As Table 20.4 suggests, the patterns of conflict among the European nations remain rather stable from 1985 to 1994. Excluding the Soviet Union from these figures, the Western European allies of the United States consistently experienced the highest levels of conflict during the forecast period. Interestingly enough, the levels of conflict among these nations were higher than levels of conflict between this group of nations

Table 20.4 Mean interbloc/intrabloc conflict scores (excluding Soviet Union).

	Aligned with United States	Aligned with Soviet Union	Nonaligned/ Multialigned
	1985		
Aligned with United States	.28		
Aligned with Soviet Union	.25	.00	
Nonaligned/Multialigned	.20	.14	.10
	1994		
Aligned with United States	.40		
Aligned with Soviet Union	.33	.20	
Nonaligned/Multialigned	.30	.23	.10

and either the Soviet bloc countries or the non-aligned and multialigned nations. In addition, those nonaligned and multialigned nations tended to experience more conflict with the US allies than they did with Soviet bloc countries. Conflict among Soviet bloc nations remained at a relatively low level throughout the forecast period.

National Power Base

"Power base" was defined as the material and human resources a nation can bring to bear to influence the behavior of other nations. However, while power base was thought of as a national attribute, the primary concern in the model was to forecast the power position of nations relative to other nations in the European region. Therefore, the major criterion for evaluation rested on the ability of the models to rank nations relative to other nations on the power base descriptor. National power base was a vital central environmental descriptor for the long-range forecasting mode. In its interaction with other central environmental descriptors, it served as an important predictor variable. For example, power base was linked to do-domestic instability as an indicator of the resources available to nations to suppress instability. Furthermore, the dimensions of national power base were used as predictor variables in the international conflict, international alignment, and international trade forecasting models. Power base was divided into two dimensions: economic power base and military power base. The economic dimension

was constructed from four indicators: population, gross national product, energy consumption, and gross national product per capita. The military power base dimension was composed of: military manpower, defense expenditures, and defense expenditures per man in the Armed Forces. Table 20.5 shows the rankings of the twenty-six countries considered in the forecast on the economic dimension of national power base. Two time periods are given—1985 and 1994. In Table 20.6 the forecasts for the military power base are presented. These forecasts suggested that the large, wealthy nations will continue to have the bulk of economic power in the long-range future. The only significant change in relative power during the forecast period occurred in Sweden. Examination of two important components of economic power base, GNP and GNP per capita, revealed that Sweden led the European countries during the forecast period in per capita GNP, while GNP, which reflects country size as well as relative wealth, was dominated by the larger, more traditional powers of Europe. Yet Swedish GNP per capita grew so much faster than the GNP of other countries during the forecast period that, size notwithstanding, its relative economic power increased rather dramatically. Military power base rankings for the 1985 and 1994 forecast period showed the same kind, and nearly the same degree, of stability as did the economic power base rankings. As Table 20.6 shows, the Soviet Union, West Germany, France, the United Kingdom, and Italy retained the top five positions in military power for the entire 10-year period.

Table 20.5 Rankings of the 26 European nations on economic power base.

1985	1994
Soviet Union	Soviet Union
West Germany	West Germany
France	France
United Kingdom	United Kingdom
Italy	Sweden
East Germany	East Germany
Czechoslovakia	Italy
Sweden	Czechoslovakia
Poland	Poland
Netherlands	Netherlands
BLEU	BLEU
Switzerland	Switzerland
Romania	Denmark
Denmark	Romania
Norway	Norway
Spain	Hungary
Hungary	Spain
Yugoslavia	Yugoslavia
Austria	Austria
Bulgaria	Bulgaria
Finland	Finland
Greece	Greece
Turkey	Portugal
Portugal	Turkey
Ireland	Ireland
Iceland	Iceland

Sweden, in fact, was the only nation evidencing dramatic shifts in its military power base ranking from 1985 to 1994, moving from ninth rank in 1985 to sixth rank in 1994. The Swedish increase was due to increasing levels of defense spending relative to manpower levels; the level of training and equipment available to the Swedish armed forces, always high, is expected to increase rather dramatically, partly because of the increased level of wealth in that nation during the long-range future.

Internal Instability

Consistent with previous theoretical and empirical work, stability was divided into two distinct dimensions: turmoil and revolt.[22] "Turmoil" was defined as those destabilizing activities aimed at altering governmental policies or practices, and "revolt" was explained as destabilizing actions aimed at replacing governmental policy makers or altering the

structure of the policy making process itself. Turmoil was operationalized with measures of antigovernment demonstrations and antigovernment riots, whereas revolt was measured by occurrences of assassinations, coups d'etat, and armed attacks against public and quasi-public institutions. The two components of turmoil were summed to form a composite measure. Unfortunately, these event counts only indicate the number of times turmoil activities occurred; they suggest nothing about their scope or severity. In order to weight the event counts by their relative severity, the number of deaths resulting from domestic conflict was used as a weighting factor. Thus, levels of both turmoil and revolt were computed by multiplying transformed event data for each category by transformed death tolls. Since the transformations in both cases adjusted for the expected directions, combining the two measures in a multiplicative manner further offset the effects of these biases.

Table 20.6 Rankings of the 26 European nations on military power base.

1985	1994
Soviet Union	Soviet Union
West Germany	West Germany
France	France
United Kingdom	United Kingdom
Italy	Italy
East Germany	Sweden
Poland	East Germany
Czechoslovakia	Czechoslovakia
Sweden	Poland
Netherlands	Netherland
BLEU	BLEU
Spain	Romania
Romania	Spain
Switzerland	Switzerland
Yugoslavia	Yugoslavia
Hungary	Hungary
Denmark	Denmark
Austria	Austria
Norway	Bulgaria
Bulgaria	Norway
Greece	Finland
Finland	Greece
Turkey	Turkey
Portugal	Portugal
Ireland	Ireland
Iceland	Iceland

The composite measures of the levels of turmoil and revolt, then, were intended to tap the number and severity of those actions.

Table 20.7 presents rankings of the twenty-six European countries on domestic strife scores for 1985 and 1994. Of particular interest is the fact that four large European powers—the Soviet Union, the United Kingdom, France, and West Germany—have rather high levels of internal instability at the outset of the forecast period, 1985. This is because these are large countries with histories of extensive domestic unrest. Between 1985 and 1994, however, the military power bases of these four nations increased substantially, in part as a response to external conflict pressures. As military capabilities rise, internal strife in these four countries decreases accordingly. Thus, by 1994, the Soviet Union ranks sixth or internal strife scores, while France, West Germany, and the United Kingdom are among those European na-

tions with the least domestic unrest. Two smaller European countries, Iceland and Bulgaria, have rather low levels of internal strife at the beginning of the forecast period primarily because they are small and typically peaceful nations. Relative to other European nations, however, their military power bases stagnate between 1985 and 1994. As a result, they evidence substantially higher relative levels of domestic unrest in 1994 than they did previously. By 1994, both countries have average, as opposed to low, levels of domestic unrest.

International Trade

"Economic interdependence" or "trade" was defined as the quantity of goods and services exchanged between two countries per time period. The term does not include capital flows between countries, investment flows, and unilateral transfer payments such as aid and gifts. The model used to generate forecasts of international trade was based on the concept of income elasticities of imports.[23] These elasticities measure the responsiveness of the percentage change in imports to percentage changes in GNP, and can be formulated as follows: percent change in imports = elasticity (percent change in GNP). The elasticity of imports can therefore be used to forecast imports, provided future GNP has been forecast.

Since the goal of the model was to forecast bilateral or dyadic trade, bilateral elasticities had to be estimated. These elasticities reveal by how much the imports of country I from country J will rise when the GNP of I rises by 1 percent. These imports are also the exports of J to I by definition. By estimating bilateral elasticities for all the European dyads, total intra-European trade was forecast the desired period. Twenty-six European countries were considered in the international trade analysis. When taken two at a time, 325 dyads were obtained. The elasticity values, however, are not symmetrical for a given pair of countries. This asymmetry means that a total of 650 elasticities, or twice the number of dyads, had to be estimated.

Table 20.8 ranks the twenty-six European nations according to their expected levels of total trade in 1985 and 1994. The temporal stability of relative levels of trade for the European countries reflected the stability observed in forecasts of the GNP component of economic power base. Substantial changes in relative trade for two nations, how-

Table 20.7 Rankings of the 26 European nations on domestic strife.

1985	1994
Soviet Union	Turkey
Italy	Spain
Turkey	Italy
Spain	Poland
United Kingdom	Greece
Poland	Soviet Union
Greece	Romania
Yugoslavia	Portugal
West Germany	East Germany
France	Hungary
Portugal	Iceland
Romania	Yugoslavia
East Germany	Bulgaria
Hungary	Norway
Czechoslovakia	Austria
Switzerland	Czechoslovakia
Austria	Finland
Netherlands	Denmark
Ireland	Ireland
Iceland	Switzerland
Norway	United Kingdom
Denmark	BLEU
Finland	France
Bulgaria	West Germany
BLEU	Netherlands
Sweden	Sweden

Table 20.8 Rankings of the 26 European nations on trade.

1985	1994
United Kingdom	United Kingdom
France	BLEU
West Germany	France
BLEU	Sweden
Netherlands	West Germany
Sweden	Netherlands
Italy	Yugoslavia
Switzerland	Italy
Yugoslavia	Switzerland
Soviet Union	Spain
Spain	Ireland
Denmark	Denmark
East Germany	Finland
Czechoslovakia	Austria
Austria	Soviet Union
Norway	East Germany
Finland	Norway
Ireland	Czechoslovakia
Portugal	Portugal
Poland	Hungary
Hungary	Bulgaria
Bulgaria	Poland
Romania	Turkey
Greece	Romania
Turkey	Greece
Iceland	Iceland

ever, did appear in these forecasts. Between 1985 and 1994, the Soviet Union's trade decreased substantially relative to other European nations. Although Soviet GNP remains the largest of the European countries during this period, the rate of growth of the Soviet economy is expected to decrease considerably. The decline in relative quantity of trade observed for the nation reflects this economic stagnation. Ireland, on the other hand, shows marked increases in relative trade from 1985 to 1994. This results from the high propensity to trade exhibited by the Irish relative to their level of economic wealth. Thus, moderate increases in Irish GNP result in substantial increases in that nation's trade with other European countries. Nations that typically trade very heavily and have large economic power bases are usually those countries with high levels of relative trade. The United Kingdom, of course, remains the most extensive trader of the European countries since it depends on imports for most raw materials and on exports for balance of trade. Other large members of the European community—France, West Germany, and BLEU—are also large traders. Not unexpectedly, the smaller and poorer nations are forecast to engage in the least amount of international trade. Bulgaria, Romania, Greece, and Turkey have among the lowest levels of international transactions, while Iceland, the smallest and poorest of the twenty-six European nations, consistently ranks last in international trade.

V. SUMMARY

In this chapter on long-range forecasting, we have attempted to make several major points. First, it was argued that the technical definition of long-range forecasting should include not only consideration of time frame, but of degree of uncertainty in the forecast as well. This trade-off between precision and reliability, it was asserted, is particularly important in the designation of appropriate techniques to be used for any given long-range forecast. Next, the state-of-the-art in the field was reviewed with an emphasis on the Futuribles Project under de Jouvenel and the Commission on the Year 2000 under Bell. The recent system dynamics work at MIT was also briefly discussed. After pointing out that a large proportion of the *substantive* long-range forecasting work had been done in the "think tank" community, we concluded that the conceptual and methodological state-of-the-art was far ahead of the accomplishments in the substantive applications. That is, many of the necessary conceptual foundations have been laid, and techniques and measurement approaches developed so that now it is necessary to take advantage of this knowledge and expertise to produce a variety of explicit long-range forecasts.

The analytic framework presented in the fourth section of the chapter is a reasonably straightforward set of sequential steps, beginning with consideration of purpose and specification of time frame. Next, the selection of forecasting concepts was discussed, with an emphasis on the trade-off between precision and reliability in the selection process. Thus, it was pointed out that in many long-range cases, it is necessary to choose broader concepts and sacrifice precision in order to attain an acceptable level of reliability.

After pointing out that the choice of operational

measures of these concepts will dictate the form of the forecast output, we went on to consider the choice of predictor variables. There, it was suggested first that if the forecast was intended to have a policy input, at least some of these variables must be manipulable by policy makers. Next, we pointed out that, from a scientific point of view, more emphasis should be placed on the selection of variables with 15 or 20-year lags whenever possible and direct rather than indirect estimation should be done more frequently. We then presented an argument for using an integrated approach to long-range forecasting, in this case "integrated" referring to the use of a variety of techniques and approaches. Finally, a framework based on levels of knowledge and measurement within which appropriate techniques can be chosen was provided.

In the final section of the chapter, we presented the major components of a policy-oriented long-range forecasting model. The model is concerned with forecasting values of five key variables for the European environment of 1985–1994. These variables, or central environmental descriptors (national power base, international alignment, international conflict, internal instability, and bilateral trade), were chosen for their significance to the national security community and their feasibility, and were operationalized in a manner that permitted the generation of credible forecasts. Parameter estimation of the various selected forecasts for each of the central environmental descriptors were presented.

NOTES

1. See Section II of this chapter for further discussion of this point.
2. A word of caution at this point. It is quite possible that certain variables in a short-range model are related in a nonlinear fashion. This is particularly true in physical systems. In international relations, however, long-range forecasts are usually characterized by nonlinearity. This property has important implications for the choice of appropriate estimation techniques.
3. Specific techniques *per se* will not be treated in any detail in this chapter since this has been accomplished elsewhere in this volume (see footnote 8). Rather, we will restrict discussion here to methodological and technical work to particular importance to international relations.

4. De Jouvenel (1967), p. 1963. It is interesting to note that de Jouvenel implicitly assumes that only economic or demographic factors are quantifiable.
5. Kahn (1964 and 1965); Weiner (1967 and 1970); and Bruce-Briggs (1972).
6. See Kahn, "On Studying the Future" (1974), and his "The Alternative World Futures Approach," in Kaplan (ed.) (1968), pp. 83–136; or Marien (1973).
7. For an excellent discussion of basic epistemological with philosophical considerations in forecasting, see Tanter, "Explanation, Prediction, and Forecasting in International Politics," in Rosenau, *et al.* (eds.) (1972).
8. For a more complete listing of available techniques, see Section IV of this chapter. Most of the techniques are discussed in detail in other chapters of this volume. See, for example, the following authors: Helmer, Ashley, Ross, Leavitt, Choucri (Chapters 12 and 13), and Robinson (Chapter 17).
9. For a detailed discussion of the technique, see Choucri (Chapter 13 of this volume).
10. Exceptions to this statement are Choucri, Laird, and Meadows (1972) and Weil and McIlroy (1975).
11. See also Choucri, Laird, and Meadows (1972) and Chapter 13 of this volume.
12. Syracuse University Research Corporation (1964); Rubin (1970); Holloman Air Force Base, Office of Research Analysis (1968); Ivanoff, *et al.* (1967); Battelle Memorial Institute (1971).
13. See Section IV below for discussion of the several different forecasts of this kind produced by the national security community.
14. For a mathematical treatment of precision and reliability, see Franco (1973), pp. 383–391.
15. See footnote 8 for a full citation of these chapters.
16. Special acknowledgment to Michael Leavitt for suggesting this framework.
17. We have not attempted to be precise in the placement of each technique, but merely to give one an idea of the usual requirements for its use.
18. This section of the chapter is based on the work that the Policy Sciences Division of CACI, Inc. has performed under ARPA Contract Number DAHC15-71-C-0201. Besides the authors of this chapter, the research team consisted of Drs. Herman M. Weill and Michael R. Leavitt, and Aaron Greenberg, Larry German, and Douglas Hartwick.
19. See Chapter 22, A. L. George, "Problem-Oriented Forecasting."
20. Note that none of the other services (e.g., Navy, Air Force) or intelligence agencies are included in the figure.
21. This is the WEIS data or World Event Interaction Survey initially developed and collected by Professor Charles McClelland of the University of Southern California.
22. See Rummel (1966), pp. 65–73, and (1963), pp. 1–50; Tanter (1966), pp. 41–46; Gurr (1968), pp. 1104–1124; Gurr (1970).
23. The technique used to estimate import elasticities is based on the work of H. S. Houthakker and S. P. Magee (1969), pp. 111–124.

CHAPTER TWENTY-ONE

ALTERNATIVE FUTURES: AN EXERCISE IN FORECASTING

Nazli Choucri & Marie Bousfield

With the assistance of Brian M. Pollins

I. INTRODUCTION

It is somewhat ironic that in this volume on fore-casting in international relations, few of the contributors have engaged in actual forecasts. So far, we have only talked about the problems attending forecasting and reviewed these from different perspectives, noting alternative methods and procedures. This irony is due partly to the shared lack of experience with actual forecasting in international relations, partly to the complexities of international realities, and partly to the difficulties involved in disciplined speculation—let alone systematic inquiry—into the structure of alternative futures. Even more salient are inhibitions resulting from the high probabilities of being in error: "wrong" forecasts are invariably more frequent than "right" ones. And, while the criteria for evaluating the validity of forecasts are still being debated—with dif-ferent criteria relevant for different purposes—considerable uncertainty remains regarding optimal means of validation. It is, thus, with appropriate caveats and qualifications and with pleas for tolerance from friends and colleagues, that the authors of this chapter summarize their efforts in forecasting alternative futures for the United States, focusing specifically on sources of foreign expansion.[1] In so doing, we shall draw upon the theoretical directives presented in Chapter 1, on the substantive issues described in Chapter 12, and on the research procedure and methodology discussed in Chapter 13. In this limited fashion, we present specific forecasts to illustrate the application of an integrated approach to forecasting in international relations and the research program that has guided this work.[2]

The forecasting exercise is presented in five major sections. The first presents a brief description of the process of expansion and isolates the important elements of the underlying theory; the second describes the essential components of a forecasting model of lateral pressure; the third describes the interrelationships among the determinants of national growth and foreign expansion, presenting a simplified causal loop diagram and noting the major linkages throughout; the fourth compares the performance of the model against historical data; and the fifth section describes the use of the model for forecasting and presents some specific forecasts. The chapter concludes with a summary of the overall forecasting endeavor.

Our procedure is to operationalize recent thinking about domestic sources of foreign policy, develop a feedback model of these determinants of expansion, obtain key parameters from empirical data, employ the historical record as an initial validator and, on this basis, to undertake systematic forecasts into the future, observing the consequences of alternative policies or decisions. The validation method is to compare retrospective forecasts against the historical record from 1930–1970. The ensuing forecasts to the year 2000 are derived from a series of experimental analyses of the implications of national growth for international behavior. These investigations illustrate some aspects of the research program in international relations forecasting at MIT.

II. SOURCES OF EXPANSION AND THE THEORY OF LATERAL PRESSURE

Despite impressive theoretical advances in the study of international relations, many uncertainties remain regarding the sources of foreign policy. Some theorists argue that international behavior can be accounted for primarily by variables like power, capability, force, or coercion; others maintain that bureaucratic factors, public opinion, and administrative capabilities are more relevant; others emphasize ideology, preferences, and values; still others argue for the preponderance of aggregate societal factors like the level of technology. Our own contributions to ongoing debates focused on the processes that shape national dispositions toward foreign activity and the ways in which structural variables in society determine propensities for external expansion. This chapter develops a model of the process of expansion and makes

some forecasts regarding alternative futures for the United States.

Perhaps one of the most important developments in recent years is an emerging recognition that the behavior of nations is as much shaped as it is constrained by their resource endowments, by their level of technology, and by the size and composition of their population, and that these factors provide the parameters of permissible behavior, and assist in determining their priorities and aspirations. The phenomenon of national growth, then, is an important underlying determinant of foreign policy behavior since the growth process directly affects the demographic and technological characteristics of a society as well as its resource needs. As a nation seeks to satisfy its domestic needs by interacting in the international arena, it is likely to exhibit a wide range of behaviors including trade, foreign investment, diplomacy, and military activity. Certainly, different modes of international behavior have varying implications and not every expansionistic activity will necessarily lead to international violence. But it is important to note that this propensity for expansion is a necessary precondition for conflict and, as such, its underlying dynamics become a critical concern. The importance of this process is amplified when we note the fact that these dynamics are common to all nations and, therefore, as their interests expand, it is increasingly probable that opposing interests will collide. So while the propensity for expansion does not inevitably entail conflict and violence, its consequences are potentially disruptive. We use the term "lateral pressure" to refer to this propensity for foreign expansion.

The *substantive* question, therefore, is whether nation-states—particularly the advanced industrial societies—can continue to grow without expanding outside their territorial boundaries and generating potential conflicts of interests. The *theoretical* question involves defining the interrelationships among the constituent determinants of growth and expansion. The *policy* question involves the identification of decisions and instrumentalities that would affect the nature and extent of a society's lateral pressure. The *structural* question is the extent to which policies designed to affect population, resources, or technology result in an increase or decrease of a society's lateral pressure. And the *methodological* question is the specification of the appropriate functional form of these relationships, including their dynamic feedback linkages.[3]

The idea of lateral pressure and of the underlying dynamics it seeks to represent is not new. Its origins lie in classical theories of imperialism[4] and in modern economic theory.[5] From the former has emerged a clarification of the expansionist process and the factors that predispose nations to establish spheres of control or influence. From the latter has come an attempt to formalize both the economic factors that underlie such behavior and the governmental efforts to cope with and manipulate a society's productive capabilities. The synthesis of these two approaches has been provided by the first attempt to specify the dynamics underlying expansion in ways so as to accommodate the determinants that go beyond simple economic factors, on the one hand, and purely structural ones, on the other.

There are five aspects to the process of extending national activities outside territorial boundaries that must be distinguished:

1. the societal *demands* engendered by processes of national growth;

2. the *capability* to engage in behavior beyond national borders;

3. the *disposition* to extend behavior beyond territorial boundaries;

4. the particular *activities* that result from this disposition;

5. the *impact* these activities have on the external environment.

Lateral pressure refers to the disposition to extend behavior beyond territorial boundaries. It is the product of the interaction of societal demands and capability. Societal demands are determined by the society's demographic and resource characteristics, its surplus economic capacity, and the influence of the military on the determination of national priorities.

A country has capabilities on many different levels of organization, purpose, and activity. The *national capability* of a society refers to a country's overall operational potential in terms of its general level of knowledge and skills, the capital and other resources that are available to it, the size and broad characteristics of its labor force, and so forth. A country's national capability is roughly synonymous with its technological and economic base and the

ability to employ this base productively. National capability defines the limits of what a country can do in the short to intermediate run if it chooses.

The *type* of external activity undertaken by a society depends upon the nature of the demands being generated domestically and the characteristics of a nation's capability. A nation will likely respond to its resource needs in a different manner than it would respond to pressures generated by excess economic capacity; similarly, the nature of this response will depend upon the specialized capabilities that a nation has at its disposal. These differences will generate different modes of lateral pressure, that is, different forms and types of foreign behaviors.

The term *specialized capability* refers to any major instrumentality that is available for the carrying out of a society's public and/or private goals. Agriculture, light industry, heavy industry, banking, shipping, armed forces, educational establishment, health facilities as well as the military are examples of specialized capabilities. Specialized capabilities define the limits of what a country can do *right now*. The array of a country's specialized capabilities at any given time, together with their respective levels, determine the range and scope of possible activity that a nation may undertake to satisfy societal demands. A country cannot exert lateral pressure on a mode in which the appropriate specialized capabilities and demands are not present.[6]

Still another way of explaining the issues at hand is by viewing lateral pressure as the outcome of the interactive effects of structural, behavioral, and value attributes. The *structural* characteristics of a society are conceived primarily in terms of the levels of population, resources, and technology; the *behavioral* attributes in terms of patterns of economic production and consumption, national investments in economic activities, and the size of the military; and *value* attributes in terms of national priorities such as supporting continued economic growth as opposed to constraining growth, and the proportional allocation of resources and expenditures to the military and civilian sectors.

Some sources of demands and capabilities can be manipulated at relatively low cost, others are basically nonmanipulatable, or manipulatable only at high cost. For example, the proportional expenditures to the military or to the civilian sectors might be altered more readily than any changes in the general knowledge and skills throughout the country. The proportional effects upon lateral pressure might differ considerably. But it is not entirely clear what the precise nature of the difference is, or how changes in individual components of lateral pressure would shape the nature of the resulting pressure and, by extension, the foreign activities undertaken.

The theoretical specification of lateral pressure is summarized in Table 21.1.

III. A FORECASTING MODEL OF LATERAL PRESSURE

The United States provides an excellent example of the processes of expansion discussed thus far: The country's continued growth, in conjunction with an increasing burden upon indigenous resources, is becoming an issue of national concern. Identifying policies that might lead to the reduction of lateral pressure, possibly by decreasing resource consumption and placing lesser loads upon the environment, emerges as an important corollary of this concern. And specifying the determinants of expansion is a necessary prerequisite for such an effort.

The dynamics of lateral pressure—as the interactive outcome of societal demands and capability—are modeled as five separate sectors, representing the demographic, economic, resource, military, and technological factors influencing the propensity for expansion. As presently specified, each sector is in fact a model in its own right, and their interaction contributes to overall system behavior, which generates the resultant lateral pressure. A sixth sector seeks to combine the interactive effects provided by the other five in order to calculate the disposition for expansion.

In computing lateral pressure, we have employed the gross national product as the index of national capability. However, we have not modeled individual indices of specialized capability. Since the measure of capability presently employed is undifferentiated, we have also used an aggregated measure of demand. Demand is modeled as a multiplier on lateral pressure.[7] This aggregate multiplier is determined by individual multipliers from the five separate sectors of the model. In this way, it is possible to monitor the

Table 21.1 Theoretical specification of the process of expansion.

The theoretical dependencies representing the process of expansion can be distinguished as follows:

1. the *demands* engendered by the processes of national growth;
2. the *capability* to undertake activities outside national boundaries to meet demands;
3. the *disposition* to extend behavior beyond territorial boundaries;
4. the *activities* that result from this disposition;
5. the *impact* of these activities on the external environment.

Processes represented in 1–3 refer to the antecedents of actual behavior. Processes specified in 4–5 represent such behaviors and their consequences. In each case we are dealing with dynamic processes that are characteristically interactive. The constraints of verbal specification preclude an adequate description of this interaction: Feedback effects are always at work and are of fundamental importance in the determination of behavior. For this reason, even an approximate representation of this process requires formal analytical specifications. Toward this end, we have employed system dynamics.

This chapter is concerned with the determinants of behavior, defined as the product of demands and capabilities that generates the disposition for foreign activity. We term this disposition "lateral pressure," specified as follows:

Lateral pressure = (Demands) · (Capability)

Demands = A combination of four component multipliers on lateral pressure.

Multipliers = The sectoral influences of the individual demands generated by growing population, resource constraints, surplus economic capacity, and the military.

The model of the determinants of national behavior represents the processes generating individual sectoral demands, their interaction with national capability, and the resulting lateral pressure.

contribution of the individual demand multipliers to the aggregate *demand* variable. The lateral pressure variable, computed by the sixth sector, is a generalized measure of a society's overall propensity for expansion. This means that we can (1) forecast future trends in the level of external activity; and (2) examine both short- and long-term effects of various policies upon the general propensity for expansion as well as any fluctuations in the individual demand multipliers. This feature will gain added importance when the model is developed further to forecast specific modes of lateral pressure. The model is thus composed of:

1. A *population sector,* which represents the interaction between birth and death rates and total immigration. Together they determine population size. The larger the population, the more extensive its basic demands are likely to be; and the more technologically advanced the society, the greater will be the impact of population size in terms of the burdens placed upon available resources.

2. A *resource sector,* which models the impact both of resource needs and of resource availability upon lateral pressure. For our modeling purposes, resources are conceived primarily in terms of energy and, more specifically, petroleum. Thus, the resource sector generates a dual impact on lateral pressure. On the one hand, the need for resources serves as a multiplier, increasing propensities for expansion. On the other, resource scarcities and constraints create a dampening effect upon a nation's base capability and thereby reduce lateral pressure. Moreover, resource scarcities can introduce a second-order effect on societal demands by reducing potential economic output, hence decreasing the level of investments available for expansion.

3. Two *economic sectors* designed to represent a society's productive activity (GNP), as well as its potential output (potential GNP). The gap between the two produces an excess multiplier upon lateral pressure; the greater the excess, the greater will be the impact on lateral pressure. These sectors also embody technological growth and specify its impact upon national productivity.

4. A *military sector,* which generates the level of military expenditures and derives a measure of the influence held by the military in the society. It is hypothesized that the propensity for expansion is positively associated with the size of the military establishment. This sector calculates only a military demand multiplier, and does not incorporate the military as a specialized capability since the model considers only undifferentiated national capability. In future work, we will incorporate specialized capabilities in the model, and the influence of the military will certainly be included.

Each of these sectors generates a separate multiplier upon lateral pressure. The combined effects of these multipliers are observed in the behavior of the lateral pressure sector which constitutes the integrative module, pulling together the impacts of demographic, resource, economic, technological, and military factors to calculate lateral pressure. Thus, the sixth sector of the model is lateral pressure.

5. The *lateral pressure sector,* seeking to model the interactive effects of these four sets of determinants, taking into account countervailing trends, nonlinearities, and feedback effects. The linkages of the preceding sectors to lateral pressure are provided by the four separate multipliers, whose combined effects represented by the aggregated demand multiplier, when considered in tandem with national capability, determine the resulting pressure.

An extremely simplified diagram of the design of the model is presented in Figure 21.1. It is to be viewed as a guide to the following discussion only, and is not an adequate representation of all the interrelationships modeled. These are specified, still in an oversimplified manner, but more accurately, in Figure 21.2. They represent the disaggregated specifications of the propensity to extend activity outside the national domain. These processes constitute a more complex theoretical specification in dynamic nonlinear terms of the relationships presented in the first equation of Table 12.1. Figure 21.2 thus presents greater theoretical sophistication than the expansion process specified in Chapter 11 of *Nations in Conflict* (1975).

IV. THE MULTIPLIERS ON LATERAL PRESSURE: DYNAMIC FEEDBACK RELATIONS

The functional relationships among variables in the model, the numerical values of key parameters, and the data employed are all based on empirical

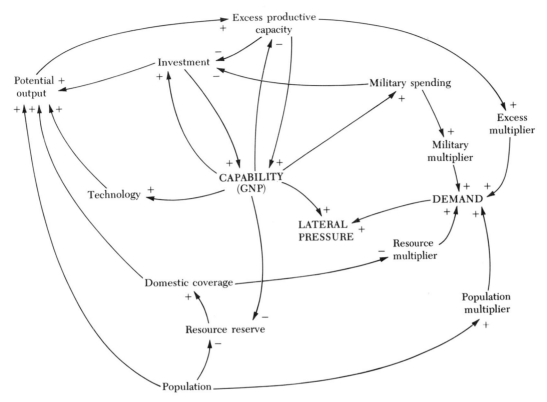

Figure 21.1   Processes generating lateral pressure: major causal relations.

observations for the United States from 1930–1970. Our procedure has been to employ the historical record as a validator of functional relationships, testing our results against known values. Thus, the period between 1930–1970 constitutes the reference mode for this model. The estimated values provide an input into simulation for comparison with historical data. In view of the complexities at hand, a brief description of the model, sector by sector, is presented here for illustrative purposes. Constraints on space make it difficult to present as detailed and technical a description of the model as would be desirable. (A listing of the computer program can be obtained from the authors.)

Population

The population sector seeks to model only population size and performs two functions. First, it delineates the impact of population size on national productivity and resource utilization; second, it

generates a demographic multiplier on lateral pressure, representing the impact of numbers on propensities for expansion. *Size* is determined by the net effect of birth rate, death rate, and immigration. Birth rate is defined as births per 1000 population and determined, in turn, by per capita gross national product. The functional relationship is derived from cross-national empirical data. As per capita output increases, the *birth rate* has been observed to decline. The quantitative values of the relationship between output and birth rate are based on empirical data. *Death rate* is specified as a function of average lifetime. Average lifetime is modeled to increase slowly over the period modeled. The quantitative value of average lifetime is taken to be just over 60 years in 1930 (based on empirical data), and it is specified to increase steadily to 76 years by 2000. While birth rate and death rate are linked endogenously, immigration is provided as an exogenous input, being purely a function of time. The values for the period 1930–1970

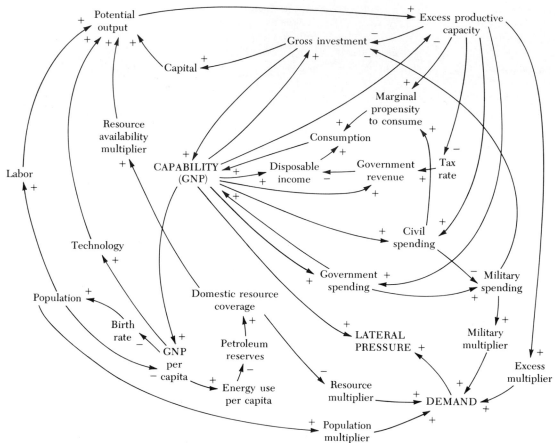

Figure 21.2 Lateral pressure specification.

are based on empirical data; subsequent values are predicated upon recent demographic estimates. It must be stressed that our purpose is not to model the causes of population growth, but the consequences. However, the latter can be represented accurately only if the interrelationship among the variables that determine population size are well specified.

Resources

The focus of this sector is primarily upon petroleum, taken as a fraction of total energy usage in the United States. The demand for energy is derived by multiplying population size and the per capita energy usage variable. Per capita energy usage is specified as a function of per capita GNP.

Like the birth rate, above, the quantitative values for the relationship between output and energy usage is derived from historical data (controlling for exogenous influences like major wars that distort time trends for short periods). Once the yearly value for petroleum demand is computed, it is then subtracted from the level of resource reserves. By comparing petroleum demand to the reserve level, we derive *domestic coverage*. Domestic coverage is a key variable in the model since it determines the resource multiplier on lateral pressure. The value of the coverage variable in any given year represents the number of years that reserves could last, given the petroleum demand for that same year. Domestic coverage may change quite dramatically. When petroleum demand increases through time and reserves are initially fixed, domestic coverage will decline exponentially rather than linearly. Changes in either demand or reserve or both will effect domestic coverage. It is presently hypothesized that when domestic coverage is greater than 20 years, the resource multiplier on lateral pressure will be zero. When coverage drops below 20 years, the multiplier gradually increases until it reaches a maximum of 1.0 (and coverage equals 0 years).

Technology and Potential Gross National Product

The surplus productive capacity of a society—that which is producible over and above that which is required for domestic consumption—provides another factor contributing to lateral pressure. In those periods where the actual economic output is less than the economy's potential, surplus investment capital is generated. It is this surplus that is critical as an indication of *excess* capability. "Potential GNP" (PGNP) refers to the society's potential for economic output; it is conceptually independent of its actual economic production. Potential GNP is derived primarily by employing the Cobb-Douglas production function. PGNP is thus dependent upon the levels of industrial capital and labor in the system (labor being a fraction of total population size). Drawing upon Robert Solow's work on technology (1957, pp. 312–320), we conceptualize technology as a multiplier on the efficiency of labor and capital and, as such, is included explicitly in the production function computing PGNP. It is fairly well established empirically that technology is positively related to per capita GNP; the rate of technological growth is also related to the rate of growth of GNP. We have provided an implicit constraint in this sector, preventing technology from declining absolutely, allowing only for possibilities of stagnation. This is important because while GNP may decline, technology—which refers to a whole array of factors related to efficiency, knowledge, and skills—rarely declines. In reality, the effects may stagnate or lessen; but an absolute decline seldom occurs. In the case of the United States all empirical indications point to increasing rather than declining technology. The output of this sector is one side of the calculation yielding the gap between potential GNP and actual GNP. This sector, then, includes the impact of technology on a society's production potential, and that potential will be subsequently compared to the actual productivity. To the extent that potential GNP is greater than actual GNP, the excess multiplier on lateral pressure will rise.

Gross National Product

The actual economic production sector of this model is derived entirely from modern economic theory.[8] The modeled representation of GNP is quite standard, in that GNP is specified as the sum of consumption, investment, and government spending. (Net exports are not taken into account in this simplified version of the model). "Consumption" is calculated by multiplying disposable income and the marginal propensity to consume. At any point, disposable income is determined by subtracting government revenue from the value of national income during the previous period; the marginal propensity to consume varies slightly as a function of general welfare. The variable representing welfare is defined as the percentage of GNP allocated to civilian spending. "Gross investment" is calculated as a fraction of GNP in the previous period. This variable constitutes the "normal" investments of a society. From this value, two variables are subsequently substracted. One is the fraction of the expansion investment derived from excess production capacity (if any); the other is military spending. These two variables provide a drain on gross investment. "Government spending" is derived in a similar fashion. It is specified as a fraction of national income during the previous period. This "normal" fraction increases over time. In addition, it will also rise in times of war (World War II, Korea, and Vietnam) and when actual GNP is below potential. The latter specification amounts to an endogenous policy assumption that stipulates that in slack economic periods the government will increase spending in the effort to stimulate demand.

The purpose of incorporating GNP specifically in the model is to compare actual output (GNP) against potential output (PGNP) in order to derive a measure of excess capacity for the *excess multiplier* on lateral pressure. In addition, GNP is the structural variable that is multiplied by the demand multiplier to yield the amount of lateral pressure generated by a society, in this case the United States. Thus, actual production (GNP) fulfills two tasks in this model: (1) it assists in generating the excess multiplier on lateral pressure; and (2) it constitutes a basic capability indicator that, in combination with the demand multiplier, influences propensities for expansion.

Military Expenditures

This model takes account only of the internal determinants of military expenditures. The effects of arms race, external rivalries, competitions, or tensions are not taken explicitly into account, although these influences are accounted for in times of war. Thus, World War II, the Korean War, and the Vietnam War are included as exogenous specifications and expenditures increase accordingly. In non-war years, exogenous influences such as threat perception or arms-race effects (which we have considered elsewhere as determinants of military spending) are not included in the model. The primary reason for their exclusion is that this model expressly seeks to represent the internal determinants of lateral pressure. This assumption is justified not only by the fit with historical data (as will be observed below), but by the success which other studies have had in explaining levels of military expenditures using expressly internal, domestic determinants (see Choucri and North, 1975, Chapter 13). Generally, the amount allocated to the military is a fraction of national income. The actual fraction is based on empirical observation. It is stipulated to increase during war and, at other times, to remain as a fairly constant fraction of national income. However, in any recessionary period we assume that the government will attempt to stimulate demand by increasing dollar allocations to the military as well as to civilian sectors. This sector yields the *military multiplier* on lateral pressure and is equal to the fraction of per capita government spending allocated to the military.

Lateral Pressure

Lateral pressure is a function of a society's productive capabilities and the propensity multiplier. It is derived by multiplying demand and capability, represented here by the gross national product. Demand, in turn, is composed of four variables: the *population* multiplier, the *resource* multiplier, the *excess* multiplier, and the *military* multiplier. Each

of these multipliers is scaled from 0 to 1. This scaling convention is necessary for standardizing differences in units. The population multiplier is derived by dividing the level of the United States population by total world population. It will be recalled that population size is modeled as the outcome of the interrelationship among birth, death, and immigration. The resource multiplier is a function of domestic coverage; if coverage is greater than 20 years, it will assume a value of zero. The excess multiplier is specified as the difference between total production and total demand, or between actual production (GNP) and potential production (PGNP). However, if demand is greater than full-employment output (termed "negative" excess), this multiplier will not go below zero. The military multiplier is a function of per capita government expenditures to the military.

Thus, the sectors of the model are integrated in the lateral pressure sector by the following specification:

$$\text{Lateral pressure} = D \times \text{Capability},$$

where D is the demand multiplier representing sectoral influences on lateral pressure (LP) specified as:

$$D = (1 + C1 \times \text{POPMLP}) (1 + C2 \times \text{URRMLP})$$
$$\times (1 + C3 \times \text{XSMLP}) (1 + C4 \times \text{MILMLP})$$

where POPM = population multiplier
URRM = usable resource multiplier
XSM = excess multiplier
MILM = military multiplier.

The coefficients C1, C2, C3, and C4 are scale factors to weight the effects of these multipliers. These are determined largely in an experimental manner, through trial and error, according to theoretical stipulation that the greatest effects come from population, followed by excess productivity, resource needs, and the influence of the military. We recognize the tentativeness of this specification. Unfortunately, little empirical evidence exists regarding the specific (or even relative) magnitudes of the expected individual effects. Furthermore, attendant theoretical specifications are not as precise as would be desirable. Thus, there are few alternatives other than experimentation with different weights.

A simplified causal loop diagram of the entire model is presented in Figure 21.2. Its purpose is to indicate the major linkages throughout, rather than to present a detailed statement of all modeled relationships. These are presented elsewhere, with detailed discussion and attendant rationale for the choices made. Here we note only the more general linkages.

V. RETROSPECTIVE FORECASTING AND THE HISTORICAL RECORD

An important indication of the validity of the model is the extent to which it tracks historical data. While replicating known values is only one criterion for validation, in the case of complex models it is generally a rigorous test of model structure and robustness. Figure 21.3 presents the estimated

values and historical data for United States population, again 1930–1970. The fit between the model output and known values is excellent. In view of the importance of the population variable in the overall structure of the model—having a direct impact on the lateral pressure multiplier, potential GNP, and resource usage—the close fit with historical data improves the performance of the model and increases our confidence in its forecasting capabilities.

Figure 21.4 presents historical values and retrospective forecasts for United States GNP and for total consumption, 1930–1970. It will be noted that forecasted GNP tracks historical values quite well. The same is true for forecasted consumption: The replicated series tracks historical values well. Since

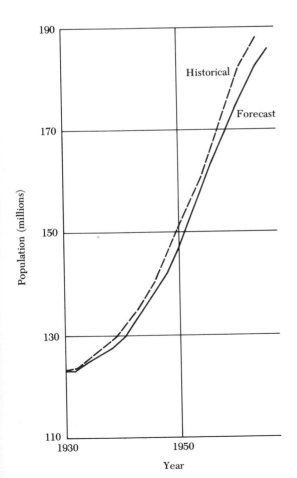

Figure 21.3   United States population: retrospective forecast.

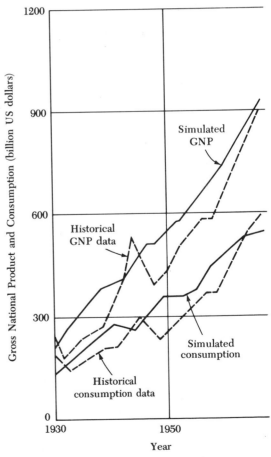

Figure 21.4   US gross national product and consumption: retrospective forecast.

the purpose of the validation check is to forecast general tendencies, the numerical discrepancies between forecasted and historical values do not shed doubt on the performance of the model. However, it is possible that with added experimentation, more precise "fits" could be obtained. Accurate point prediction, however, is not the purpose of this analysis.

Figure 21.5 presents estimated and historical values for U.S. military expenditures throughout the same 40 years. Again, the fit is good, particularly since critical breakpoints are well tracked. The war years are clearly reflected in the retrospective forecasts and their behavior corresponds closely to the known record. This goodness of fit is accounted for partly by the exogenous introduction of a "war" expenditure influence, and partly by an accurate specification of the dependence of military expenditures on national income.

Historical and retrospective forecasts for energy usage and for petroleum consumption are presented in Figure 21.6. The forecasts appear to

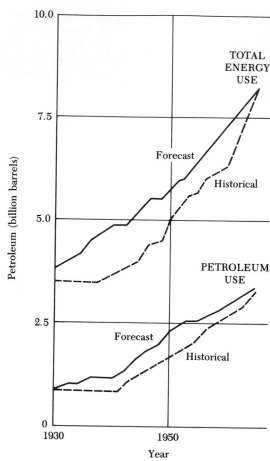

Figure 21.6   US total energy and petroleum consumption: historical forecast.

consistently overestimate resource utilization. However, the overshoot is not dramatic, and the general behavior of the retrospective forecasts is consistent with historical observations.

Considering the overall fit of the simulation output to the historical data, the model effectively represents the processes of national growth underlying expansion. Having no ready empirical counterpart against which to plot the lateral pressure variable, definitive validation of the model as a tool for forecasting modes of external expansion must await further specification. At this stage, we can explore alternative futures for the general propensity for expansion in light of our confidence in the model's ability to represent the underlying processes.

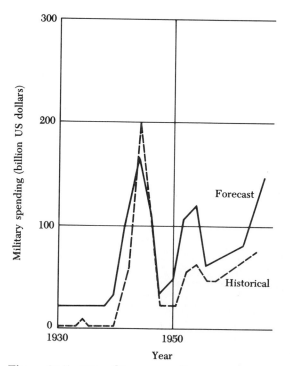

Figure 21.5   US military expenditures: retrospective forecast.

VI. ALTERNATIVE FUTURES

One purpose of this forecasting study is to examine the effects of different policy interventions on United States lateral pressure and identify some of the ways in which changes in governmental allocations, or in demands generated by growth, may influence the disposition for external expansion.

We noted in Chapter 13 that historically based assessments are often used as the standard to evaluate the consequences of different initial conditions and different policy interventions. Policy runs represent the result of alternative decisions postulated by the investigator to identify future impacts. For our model, the standard run to the year 2000 is a "least surprise" forecast based on a past shaped entirely by 40 years of resource abundance. This is certainly an unrealistic situation, in light of the petroleum price increases of October 1973 and the resultant energy crisis; but such forecasts would provide important clues regarding what is likely to happen if trends between 1930 and 1970 were to have persisted. It is a useful standard against which to evaluate alternative, more "realistic" possibilities. We are familiar with the past, and this familiarity is an important asset in helping us think about alternative futures. We know that past trends will not continue; but history may often be an important source of insights into the future.

Abundance and Scarcity

Forecasts of United States lateral pressure based entirely on past trends in demands and capability thus assume continued and unlimited access to energy resources. In such a situation, the future would have the following characteristics: (1) the country's capabilities would continue to grow, GNP will not encounter any significant constraints and potential production will also increase; and (2) pressures from population will remain constant, if not decline slightly, thereby generating little pressure for expansion. On balance, the demand for expansion will decline slightly, but since capabilities continue to grow, the general predisposition will be toward expansion. The interactive effect of growing capability and virtually constant demand will, in fact, result in *increasing* lateral pressure. Thus, a resource-optimistic future is one in which United States disposition for external expansion will con-

tinue to grow over time, but the sources of expansion will come from increasing capability rather than from demand. In such a situation we would expect *more*, rather than less, foreign involvement and expansionist activities.

What would happen if, or when, the United States encounters significant resource shortages? How would the disposition for expansion be affected, and in what ways?

When we introduce a sharp resource constraint in 1970, we observe a dramatic rise in the demand multiplier, solely because of strong pressures from the resource sector. However, pressures from the military remain fairly constant, and population continues to have little impact. Even significant changes in population have no substantial effect on demand; a higher level of population increases the size of the labor force and, by extension, its contribution to productive capacity, but only marginally; and population decreases have only a slight effect on reducing demand. Resource constraints offset any contribution from the labor force and the general effect is to reduce the country's economic capability; a decline sets in over time. Despite the strong pressures for expansion from the resource sector, the disposition toward external expansion will decline because of declining capability. The change is observed most clearly around 1950, when lateral pressure in a "resource-constraint" situation decreases in comparison with the forecast for the "resource-optimistic" case. Thus, confronted with a situation of sharp resource constraints—and no other changes in the model—we would expect the United States to become involved in *less*, rather than more, foreign activity in the future. These constraints may, in effect, seriously limit the country's disposition for external expansion.

Figure 21.7 presents the model forecasts for United States lateral pressure in both situations.[9] It must be emphasized that the disposition for expansion is the outcome of the *multiplicative* relationship of demand and capability. In any situation, the impact of resource constraints on demand may be different from that on capability. Lateral pressure reflects the *combined* pressures from demand and capability. Figure 21.7 represents the initial runs—one stipulating the continuation of past trends and the other indicating future impacts in a situation of significant resource shortages. For experimental purposes, the critical intervention

320

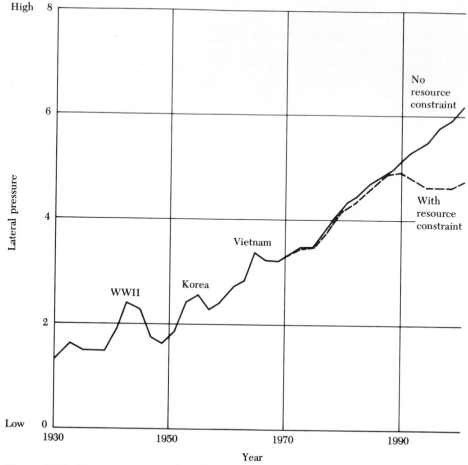

Figure 21.7 Lateral pressure: abundance versus scarcity of resources.

was made in 1970. Thus, the two cases are identical from 1930–1970. These initial runs will be employed to evaluate the effect of (1) technological change and (2) changes in governmental allocations to the civilian sector and to the military—in a situation of resource abundance versus one of resource scarcity.

The Impact of Technological Change

Technology is a critical factor in shaping the capabilities of nations and conditioning their modes of international behavior. Any changes in the level of technology are likely to influence a country's propensities for external behavior. We have ex-

perimented with two interventions—one where rapid increases in technology are postulated; the other where a reduction in the rate of technological growth is hypothesized. In each case, we observe the impact of these interventions in a situation of resource abundance and in one of resource constraints.

If rapid *increases* in technology occur, in a "resource-optimistic" future the demands of the United States will increase, but the country's capabilities will grow at a much faster rate than its demands. In fact, the growth in national capability is likely to be quite dramatic, and the interactive effect of this dual growth will result in a tremendous increase in the country's disposition for external expansion. In such a case, *we would expect more external involvements and greater extension of activities beyond national boundaries.* If the rate of technological growth were to *decrease* substantially, but by the same margin, we would observe the impact of pressures generated by demand; although such pressures will be lower than in the previous situation, their effects on capability will be comparatively much greater. Slower technological growth will have the substantial influence of generating marked reductions in national capability. In large part, however, these impacts will be in the nature of "band effects" as noted in Figure 21.8. Thus, in the absence of other changes, the disposition toward external expansion will be strongly influenced by the rate of technological change; increases or decreases in the growth of technology will have a substantial impact on lateral pressure.

In a "resource-pessimistic" situation with constraints, any changes in technology will also have only a marginal effect on the disposition for expansion, in that lateral pressure will be shaped by the resource shortages and technological changes will do little to offset such constraints. Thus, higher rates of technological growth will increase pressures generated by demand and influence capabilities somewhat; the net effect will be a slightly higher level of lateral pressure than in a "resource-pessimistic" situation with normal technological

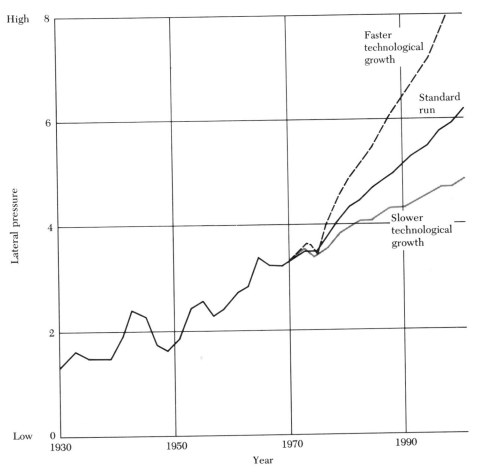

Figure 21.8 Lateral pressure: technological change in a resource-optimistic situation.

increases. Similarly, slower technological growth will result in a reduction of lateral pressure, since both demand and capability will decline appreciably. The important point, however, is that *the impact of technological change on lateral pressure is mediated by the effect of resource shortages.* Indeed, the shortages interjected in 1970 provide an important constraint on lateral pressure, while technological change—in the absence of other changes—is not likely to have an effect. Figure 21.9 presents the forecasts for the impact of technological change in a situation of resource constraints. It will be noted that similar "band effects" are generated; however, the width of the band is considerably narrower than in the "resource-optimistic" case. Technological change may well have an ac-

celerated impact on lateral pressure when there are no significant resource constraints; but when shortages occur, this impact will be overshadowed by what happens in the resource sector. We do not address ourselves here to the impact of technology in reducing resource constraints, but we make some inferences about the impact of technology on lateral pressure in a situation of resource constraint versus one of resource abundance. Figures 21.8 and 21.9 present the resulting forecasts to 2000.

Changing Priorities in Government Expenditures

Changes in governmental priorities provide perhaps the most counterintuitive impacts on lat-

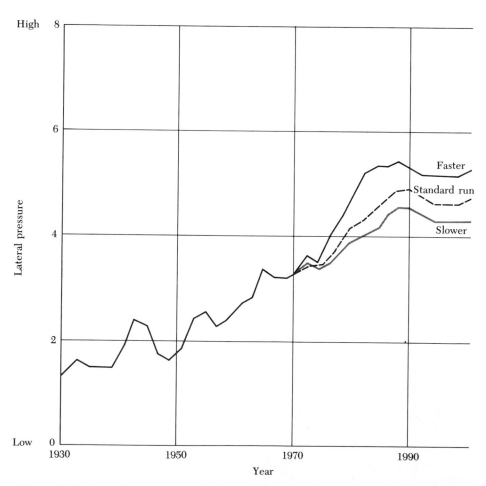

Figure 21.9   Lateral pressure: technological change in a resource-scarcity situation.

eral pressure. It is not so much the magnitude of the effects that are unexpected, but their nature. The net result is to raise substantial questions about the implications of "peaceful" versus more "warlike" governmental priorities. Increasing the government's spending on civil programs at the expense of the military will not necessarily reduce a country's disposition for external expansion.

In the absence of significant resource shortages, a sharp increase in governmental allocations for civilian spending (thus lower expenditures to the military) will result in somewhat lower demands but markedly higher pressures generated by increasing capabilities. An increased governmental concern for welfare will lead to higher consumption, therefore also greater investments and, by extension, a higher level of productive capability. Combined with increased demands, growing national capability will generate greater dispositions for external expansion. In the absence of severe resource constraints, greater concern for national welfare (expressed as a larger fraction of the budget allocations to the civilian than to the military sector) will result in marked growth in lateral pressure. The pressures for expansion generated by the military appear to be less influential than those generated by growth in national capability. Greater allocations to national welfare will allow greater consumption, higher investments, and more productive capacity. The disposition for external expansion will increase accordingly.

If the decision is made to increase the share of the budget allocated to the military (thereby reversing a welfare orientation), the pressures generated by the four multipliers on demand will result in greater demand (by the year 2000 about twice as high as the demands generated in the standard run with no resource constraints noted in Figure 21.7). By contrast, increasing allocations to the military will reduce consumption, detract from investments, and result in generally lower productive capacity than when the government adopts a welfare priority. In the case of increased allocations to the military, by the year 2000 lateral pressure will be *lower* than when the civilian sector is given greater priority. The point is that increasing allocations to the military will result in greater pressures from the demand multiplier, but lower productive capability; the net result is indeed an increase in lateral pressure—quite dramatic—but toward the end of the century appears to taper off because of the constraints on productive capacity. However, it is when the government makes a greater commitment to national welfare—by increasing the proportion of expenditures allocation to the civilian sector versus the military—that productive capacity increases most dramatically, with the net outcome of an exponential growth in lateral pressure. By the year 2000, *the disposition for expansion is no higher in a situation of greater emphasis on military spending than in one in which welfare is given the higher priority.* Figure 21.10 presents these forecasts.

The effects of changing government priorities will be markedly different in a "resource-pessimistic" future. In the event of significant resource constraints, any decision to increase welfare allocations (at the expense of military expenditures) will result in lower lateral pressure than would be the case if priorities were in favor of the military. It is revealing to observe that increasing military expenditures in a situation of marked resource constraints is likely to give rise to greater pressures from the four multipliers on demand; however, the effects on capability are such that constraints on consumption and investments result in declining production. However, since the pressures from the demand multipliers are increasing, the outcome is higher lateral pressure than in the standard resource-pessimistic situation. Over time, when the full impact of such shortages become realized, the result is a sharp decline in the country's propensity for external expansion. By the year 1985, a significant decline in lateral pressure sets in, occasioned by the combined effect of resource constraints and declining productive capacity. The first is occasioned by an exogenous intervention; the second by the impact of increasing military expenditures. In the long run, that is, toward the last decade of this century, in a situation of resource constraints, *any changes in governmental priorities will result in a decline in lateral pressure,* relative to the standard resource shortage run presented in Figure 21.7.

In sum, greater allocations to the military will generate more pressure from the demand multipliers, but there will be marked constraints on productive capacity. Therefore, dispositions for external expansion will eventually decline. And any increases in allocations to the civilian sector will reduce demands comparatively, but allow for more rapid growth in productive capacity. In the ab-

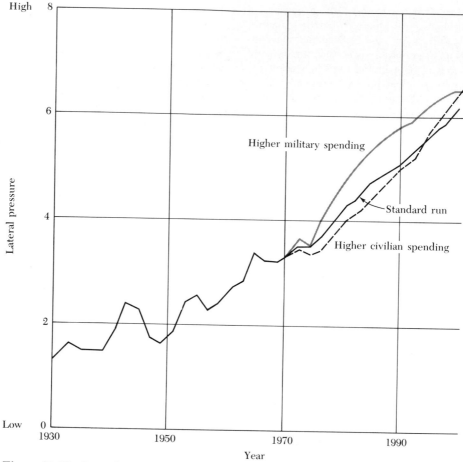

Figure 21.10 Lateral pressure: government priorities—military versus civilian in a resource-optimistic situation.

sence of sufficiently strong pressures from the demand multipliers, lateral pressure will decline eventually. In each case, however, this decline sets in following an initial rise that continued until the mid-1980's. In each case, the model behavior is similar, but the magnitude of increases and declines differs substantially. Thus, it well appears that, given no other changes, a relative stabilization of the disposition for external expansion toward the end of the century would occur in a situation of high resource constraints (interjected in 1970) *and* a government commitment of greater allocations to the civilian sector. In the absence of resource shortages, such a commitment will result in *greater* lateral pressure; but with a strong structural constraint imposed by the resource sector, in-

creasing expenditures to the civilian sector may well stabilize the country's propensities for expansion (see Figure 21.11).

VII. SUMMARY

This chapter is in the nature of a progress report and illustrates an integrated approach to forecasting in international relations. In Chapter 1 of this volume, we have identified some of the key issues at the basis of any systematic forecasting exercise. In Chapters 12 and 13 we have described different approaches to forecasting—one statistical and the other functional—and we have compared the advantages and disadvantages of each. We have also tried to employ these different forecasting methodologies for the analysis of the same international problem—namely, forecasting the processes of expansion and the extension of national activity outside territorial boundaries. This process is an important determinant of conflict among nations, and to the extent that we develop some reliable theoretical specifications of the determinants of international behavior, our forecasts of future outcomes will be enhanced accordingly.[10] In the present chapter, we have presented a theoretical specification of the dynamics of expansion in significantly greater detail than the representation of the same processes in Chapter 12. There, the process of expansion was formulated as one equation, the parameters of which were estimated on the basis of empirical data. The same process is presented in this

chapter as a nonlinear feedback model of the disposition for external expansion. Figure 21.2 represents a more complex formulation of only the *first* equation of Table 12.1 in Chapter 12. Through trial and error and through the comparison of the advantages and disadvantages associated with alternative forecasting methodologies, with an accumulation of attendant experience, we hope to develop more reliable means of bounding our uncertainties regarding future outcomes.

This chapter is a progress report in yet another sense. It remains for us to undertake considerably more experimentation with contingency analysis and with alternative policy interventions. More work remains to be done regarding the potential implications of alternative population policies, dif-

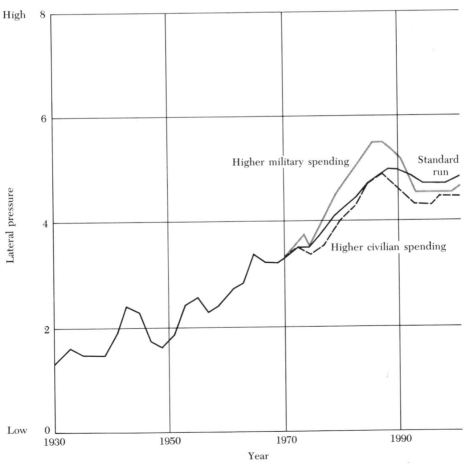

Figure 21.11 Lateral pressure: government priorities—military versus civilian expenditures in a resource-scarcity situation.

ferent policies regarding investments in research and development of alternative energy sources, alternative governmental spending strategies, different labor policies and their impact on national productivity, and so forth. But, most important of all, it still remains for us to model and forecast foreign policy *behavior*. As modeled here, lateral pressure refers to the *disposition* for external expansion; its behavioral manifestations must now be developed into an adequate specification for forecasting purposes. In Chapter 12, we have undertaken some retrospective forecasts of actual behavior generated by lateral pressure and of its implications for conflict and violence among nations. These forecasts (based on the equation specifications of Table 12.1 in Chapter 12) were tested only against the historical record. Such specifications must now be formulated in dynamic, nonlinear terms, and employed for forecasting into the "real" future and observing the implications of alternative decisions and policy interventions. This is the next step.

NOTES

1. For theoretical and substantive background, see Choucri and North (1975). Part I presents a theoretical statement of the determinants of international behavior.
2. Choucri (1976).
3. See Chapter 13 of this volume for a comparison of statistical (econometrics) and functional (system dynamics) modeling procedures.
4. See, for example, Hobson (1938) and Lenin (1939).
5. A useful synthesis is presented in Pen (1969).
6. Conceivably, a country of higher capability could turn inward. It may not require great amounts of resources from the external environment. It might choose to apply its technological capabilities to exploiting indigenous sources of supplies—if they are available—or to make use of old ones (if the resources in question are renewable). But, empirically, one has difficulty identifying countries with high capabilities that are not manifesting lateral pressure. Inward-turning countries have generally been low capability countries. Advanced societies—particularly the industrialized countries of the West—have turned outward and often this tendency has been accompanied by conflict and violence.
7. Economists would be uncomfortable with our notion of "demands." Their concept of demand is tied to purchasing power and willingness to exercise that power. Ours is a broader analytical concept pertaining to all individual claims on society and government.
8. Samuelson (1970). A simplified statement appears in ment appears in Pen (1969).
9. On all lateral pressure plots, the units have no specific meaning since lateral pressure is the product of two variables that are measured in different units (GNP in dollars and demand measured by the four component multipliers). However, the placement of the zero-value is nonarbitrary and the intervals do have meaning. Therefore, it is a ratio scale.
10. A related forecasting effort modeling relationships in the global petroleum system is described in Choucri and Ross (1975) and presented in an expanded and validated version in Choucri with Ross (in preparation).

PART V

POLICY ANALYSIS AND INTERNATIONAL RELATIONS FORECASTING

CHAPTER TWENTY-TWO

PROBLEM-ORIENTED FORECASTING

Alexander L. George

I. FORECASTING IN THE CONTEXT OF VALUES, KNOWLEDGE, AND ACTION

In pursuing the development of scientific knowledge and valid theory, academic specialists in the study of international relations have been reluctant for the most part to come to grips with the complex relationship between values, knowledge, and action. The complex interactions embodied in this triangular relationship are suggested schematically in Figure 22.1.

We shall not attempt to discuss all of the intricate processes implied by this schema. Rather, the present paper will limit itself to suggesting some of the ways in which values, knowledge, and action can be brought closer together not only in forecasting and in policy planning but also in the study of international affairs. I will argue that "design theory" and "design exercises" provide a unique framework for dealing analytically and prescriptively with interactions between values, knowledge, and action.

The term "design theory" is perhaps insufficiently familiar. It can be clarified by distinguishing between the sciences and the professions. Thus, whereas the job of the scientist is to create new knowledge, professionals specialize in *translating knowledge into action within a set of socially*

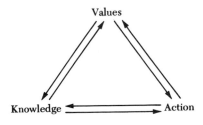

Figure 22.1

This chapter draws in part on two addresses given by the author while President of the International Studies Association during 1973–1974.

defined norms. Design theory refers to the activity of professionals, so defined.

Several years ago Herbert Simon published a book with the somewhat catchy title, *The Sciences of the Artificial.* Simon noted that what many professions such as engineering, medicine, and architecture have in common is that they are "concerned not with the necessary but with the contingent—not with how things are but how they might be—in short with design." (p. xi)[1]

Far from distracting attention from the task of improving forecasting capabilities, design exercises are likely to facilitate progress in this direction precisely because they require particularly well-focused kinds of forecasting. Similarly, far from diverting attention from the fundamental task of developing firmer scientific knowledge of international affairs, design exercises are likely to help investigators to define better the requirements for theory and also to assess better the gaps and deficiencies in the scientific knowledge they are accumulating.

Academic specialists engaged in the development of scientific knowledge and theories of international relations are often wary of participating in, or even encouraging design exercises. They are only too keenly aware of the limits of available knowledge and current theories for purposes of policy making. Insofar as academic specialists do attempt to conceptualize the relationship between knowledge and action and to offer prescriptive frameworks for dealing with the decision maker's dilemma in situations characterized by inadequate knowledge and information, they generally work with models of rational choice under conditions of uncertainty. This perspective is valuable to be sure, but while it recognizes that values constrain choice under conditions of uncertainty, it defines rationality in terms of the criterion of "efficiency," which is then used to evaluate alternative means for furthering the decision maker's stated goals and objectives.

This approach to "instrumental rationality" is clearly more useful in circumstances in which the decision maker's stated goals and objectives adequately reflect the values at stake than when stated goals and objectives obscure important value conflicts that have not been adequately identified and assessed. We shall return to this problem shortly. First, however, it should be noted that value conflicts can be dealt with by means other than efforts to apply—and misapply—the criterion of "efficiency" in selecting the best means. Instead, *decision rules* may be formulated to serve as guides to action. Such decision rules explicitly take into account those value conflicts that are imbedded in a particular kind of choice dilemma; and, further, they serve to safeguard the value priorities that have been authoritatively established for that issue area.

Instructive in this respect are the ways in which the established professions deal with situations of choice that are constrained by multiple, conflicting values and by inadequate knowledge. In law and medicine, for example, it has been decided that certain *moral and ethical values* are to be given priority over other social values in the decision rules to be applied in important situations characterized by inadequate information and knowledge. Thus, in criminal trials the decision rule is "when in doubt, acquit." This decision rule stems from fundamental political values that lead us to hold that a person should be considered innocent until proven guilty. We are willing to accept as a cost for this decision rule that guilty persons may often remain unpunished for their crimes.

In the practice of medicine, too, value priorities dictate how doctors are to resolve certain decisional dilemmas. Thus, in considering the hypothesis whether a patient has an illness, the decision rule in medicine generally has been "when in doubt, continue to suspect illness." The norms of the medical profession hold it to be a far more serious error to dismiss a possibly sick patient than to retain and treat one who may not be ill. Once again, certain costs and risks are accepted in return for adhering to this value priority (cf., e.g., Scheff, 1963).

In the sphere of foreign policy, however, society has not found a way to effectively linking moral-ethical considerations to decision rules. Rather, both the formulation of decision rules and their application is left to those responsible for conducting foreign policy, subject to the weak constraints of public opinion, the political process, and international law. I mention this familiar problem not in order to offer solutions, but to suggest that it is an appropriate and necessary one to take up in connection with design theory and in specific design exercises.

II. FRAGMENTATION OF FORECASTING ACTIVITIES

An interest in forecasting does not necessarily lead specialists in international affairs to confront the task of interrelating values, knowledge, and action in more intimate ways. Rather, it would seem that most of those who have contributed to the upsurge of forecasting activity in recent years have oriented their interests in one specialized direction or another. Unless this tendency is counter balanced by forecasting within more comprehensive frameworks such as design exercises, the net result of the burgeoning interest in forecasting may well be to reinforce, rather than to narrow, the gap between values, knowledge, and action in the study of international relations.

Three types of specialized forecasting interests can be readily detected. Thus, some international relations specialists are interested in using forecasting largely to arouse more serious consideration of important individual and social values that are affected by perceived trends in international and national affairs. They have a didactic purpose and their forecasts often assume an apocalyptic character. Other specialists employ forecasting and prediction largely as a means of testing and improving the theories of international relations they have been developing, usually in the academic setting. And still others focus more on sharpening the tools and techniques of forecasting for application in concrete policy contexts in the hope of improving the efficiency and effectiveness of governmental policy making and decisions.

While all of these forecasting enthusiasts work within a very general framework of values, knowledge, and action, they gravitate pretty strongly toward one or another of these three poles. As a result, certain cleavages (perhaps that is too strong a word for these rather sharp differences in emphasis and purpose) can be seen among specialists who are active in international affairs forecasting. This was very noticeable in the conference on forecasting that preceded the publication of this volume. Difficult problems of communication arose between the value-oriented, the theory-oriented, and the action-oriented forecasters at the conference.

My purpose is not to discourage the emergence of specialized interests and different approaches to forecasting. But I do feel some concern lest the tendency toward fragmentation that accompanies the burgeoning interest in forecasting result in failure to make greater use of more comprehensive frameworks for forecasting that would bring these three foci of interest—values, knowledge, and action—closer together rather than drive them further apart.

Problem-oriented forecasting can contribute to such a synthesis—to a closer meshing of values, knowledge, and action—more effectively than it has generally done in the past. But merely to focus on policy problems will not ensure progress in this direction. In the remainder of this chapter I would like to make several suggestions for improving the quality of problem-oriented forecasting from this standpoint.

Limitations of the "Efficiency" Criterion in Policy Analysis

Basic to everything else is the need to define good policy analysis in terms broader than the familiar criterion of "efficiency." Policy analysis based upon this criterion takes the stated values and objectives of the policy maker as given, and defines the task of the policy analyst in terms of evaluating the relative "efficiency" of available options for furthering those stated values and objectives.

"Efficiency," so conceived, suits cost-benefit analysis extremely well. It facilitates the use of more easily quantified rational choice models. It simplifies greatly the task of employing policy analysis and forecasting on behalf of decision making. And it encourages us to believe that good—that is, "efficient"—decisions are more likely to be achieved through a formal procedure for orderly, systematic consideration of alternatives. And, related to this, it encourages us to believe that a highly centralized, depoliticized policy-making system in which "objective" analysis is provided by professional technicians is far preferable to the more disorderly process of multiple advocacy and competitive analysis by participants with somewhat different interests and perspectives on the policy issue in question. I will not restate here the case for multiple advocacy in making foreign policy (George, 1972).

It does seem unfortunate that the heretofore illustrious goal of "rationality" in policy analysis has come to be identified with "efficiency" and the narrowly circumscribed type of cost-benefit analysis that goes with it. If policy analysis and forecasting are squeezed into this narrow framework, they cannot make their full contribution to policy making. It is obvious that criteria broader than that of efficiency are necessary for policy analysis. It is well known that policy makers often fail to perceive the full range of their own values that are actually engaged in current or future situations. Under these circumstances, the initially stated goals and objectives of the policy maker should not be regarded as a given. The search for efficient means for realizing these goals is premature and should take second place to efforts to clarify the full range of values and interests at stake. It is far more important to ensure that the problem posed for decision by policy makers has been adequately understood by them in terms of the various interests and values actually at stake. This, in turn, requires that latent value conflicts be identified so that the difficult question of value priorities can be dealt with in a more informed and reasonable manner.

My first suggestion, therefore, is to free analysis for policy making from the narrow criterion of efficiency and to give *value-oriented forecasting* greater scope in policy analysis (see also Tribe, 1972).

Coordination of Problem-Oriented Forecasting with Decision Strategy

Values, knowledge, and action are likely to be brought into more intimate interaction in policy analysis if forecasting is coordinated closely with decision strategy and policy planning. It is generally agreed that policy-oriented forecasting should be concerned not only with identifying trends and determining to what extent they can be projected into the future, but also more generally with clarifying those uncertainties in the future that have relevance for today's policy choices. There is also substantial consensus on the related proposition that forecasters should try to "bound" and "bracket" these uncertainties in ways that will clarify their implications for the invention and assessment of policy options.

Not so well understood, on the other hand, is that effective implementation of these tasks requires close coordination of the forecasting effort with decision analysis and decision strategy. This is

so because policy often evolves in stages. It grows out of a series of interrelated decisions over a period of time rather than from a simultaneous determination of all of the components of a complex policy.

It is often the better part of wisdom to break up a big policy decision into a series of related smaller-step decisions over time. This is what is meant by "decision strategy." Decision strategy is valuable insofar as it brings *incremental decision-making into the framework of sophisticated policy planning*, thereby giving policy makers an opportunity to avoid or curb the worst consequences associated with the practice of "muddling through."

To argue, as I do here, on behalf of a purposeful use of the strategy of serial decision making is not to ignore the fact that there are important limits and costs attached to a management strategy that seeks to create a variety of options and to retain as much flexibility as possible. The policy maker who wishes to create options and to postpone the decision to employ them sometimes finds that these planning options create or attract support and achieve a momentum that forces the decision maker's hand. As in the ABM decision of 1967, the decision maker may end up losing the very freedom of action he had hoped to preserve. But while the management strategy of "flexible options" may have been oversold or misapplied in the past, and while the lessons of experience need to be absorbed into a better understanding of the uses and limitations of this strategy, the desirability of maintaining forecasting in a close relationship with decision strategy must surely continue to engage our attention.

In developing an appropriate decision strategy for dealing with a complex policy problem it is important to determine what has to be decided now and what can be or should be left for decision later. Making the component decisions seriatim often enables the forecaster to provide better inputs to policy making. Not only do the informational, analytical, and forecasting requirements differ for different parts of an evolving policy, time is often an important resource in that it provides an opportunity to improve the quality of some of these inputs to decision making.

Thus the question becomes: *How good* a forecast of *what aspects* of the relevant future is needed for *what has to be decided now?* At the same time that he attempts to answer this question, the forecaster also considers a related, but different question: How good a forecast of what other aspects of the relevant future will be needed for what will have to be decided later on? And with respect to this, the additional question is posed: What can the investigator do in the meantime to improve the quality of the forecast that will be needed later?

But for the investigator to deal intelligently with uncertainties that affect his forecast it is necessary, as systems analysts have stressed, to differentiate and decompose the various kinds of uncertainties imbedded in a forecasting problem. In addition to statistical uncertainty, there are technological and economic uncertainties, and uncertainties with regard to human behavior and the future state of the world (environments or "strategic context"). Stratagems appropriate for dealing with certain types of uncertainty are not at all appropriate for coping with other types of uncertainty (see, for example, Quade and Boucher, 1968, pp. 39–40, 312, 355–357, 371–372, 384–385; see also, Quade, 1964, pp. 136, 170–172, 228ff, 232, 235).

III. THE "LEVEL-OF-CONFIDENCE" PROBLEM IN FORECASTING

Greater synthesis of values, knowledge, and action is likely to emerge in policy-oriented forecasting—and in the study of international relations more generally—if investigators pay more attention to and grasp the implications of the "level-of-confidence" problem when attempting to link available knowledge and forecasts to the requirements of action.

My position on this issue can be summarized rather succinctly. The search for knowledge and theory in the field of international relations should not be guided exclusively by a desire to achieve the high levels of validity associated with the goals of science. In addition, we have to ask "knowledge for what purposes?" And we have to consider that even knowledge and forecasts that do not achieve high levels of validity can still be useful and useable. The assumption that policy makers invariably need high-confidence forecasts can easily inflate and distort the requirements we levy on forecasting.

While it is always desirable to have forecasts to which high probability and/or a high level of confidence can be attached, this is, as we know,

often simply not possible. Fortunately, it is also not essential for many policy-making purposes.

I would suggest that the problem of the level of confidence required of forecasts is often virtually inseparable from the problem of deciding what policy actions to take. The confidence required of forecasts cannot be fixed arbitrarily at the same level for all policy-making purposes. Rather, forecasting should be geared to the assumption that the nature of the policy decision being made determines the required minimal level of confidence.

It should also be clear that different levels of confidence attached to a forecast often have different action implications. For many purposes policy makers do *not* need high-confidence forecasts of developments that pose threats or offer opportunities in order to take at least *some* sensible measures to protect or to promote the values engaged by those possible developments. Of the many historical and hypothetical examples that might be cited to illustrate this general point, I will elaborate one mentioned during the conference by Daniel Bell. Following the Soviet invasion of Czechoslovakia in 1968 and the enunciation at that time of the Brezhnev Doctrine, policy makers in Washington (as well as other observers) speculated that these events may have heightened Peking's anxiety regarding a future Soviet move into China. Was Peking's anxiety sufficient to make it interested in a detente with the United States? The point to be emphasized here is that it did not require a forecast that confidently predicted Peking's readiness for a detente to make it worthwhile for United States policy to discreetly explore this possibility. Sensible steps could be taken to reinforce and activate any latent disposition for a detente on Peking's part. From the standpoint of United States policy, the matter of a possible detente was actionable even in the face of considerable uncertainty as to Peking's readiness and conditional willingness to reorient its policy toward the United States.

Let me take this general argument about the level-of-confidence problem in forecasting a step further. We are all familiar with preprogramed "warning-and-response" systems such as those that military forces employ to reduce their vulnerability to surprise attack and to enhance readiness for possible action. In such systems response options are graduated and calibrated to different degrees of warning. Similar preprogrammed, calibrated warning-and-response systems exist also for smog control in urban areas.

Such preprogrammed systems are possible in part because the relationship between values, knowledge, and action in such problem areas is perceived to be fairly straightforward and predictably stable over time. But such is *not* the case for many other policy issues; and, so, sensible policy makers do well to avoid efforts to preprogram response options in advance to different types or degrees of warning. Rather, they will prefer to *improvise* an appropriate response to the kind of warning that becomes available. And, as a result, the requirements for forecasting are more fluid than when working with preprogramed warning-and-response systems, and forecasting must be continuously coordinated and integrated with policy making.

There are other reasons why preprogramed warning-and-response systems may be highly undesirable as a way of dealing with more complex policy issues. The examples of military alerts and smog control systems cited above illustrate the principle of selective, *graduated* responses to reduce the expected damage from undesirable events that are being forecast. That is, there is a *continuity* in both the objective of policy and the direction of the graduated response options. In other policy situations, however, the relationship between forecasting and policy responses should not be constrained by the same principle of graduated response; rather, it may be much more rational for policy makers to be prepared to make *discontinuous* responses.

Thus, when foreign policy makers are confronted with warning indicators that an opponent may be about to attack an ally, they may respond in a variety of ways. One, but only one, of the response options in a situation of this kind is to attempt to reinforce deterrence of the opponent by issuing threats. But it may be more rational in these circumstances for the policy maker to respond in several other ways.

He may act on the basis of the low-grade warning to acquire more information in order to clarify the equivocal warning.

He may take advantage of even low-grade warning to reevaluate the earlier "commitment" he had made to the ally.

He may respond to the warning by employing diplomatic conciliation and/or positive inducements of one kind or another to dissuade the opponent from attacking the ally.

He may utilize the warning to take time to consider whether options other than military intervention are available for reducing the expected damage to his national interests that an attack on the ally would entail.[2]

These remarks about warning and response only scratch the surface, but perhaps they suffice to emphasize the main point: namely, that both forecasters and policy makers need to consider the level-of-confidence problem from the standpoint of the action implications of forecasts having different probabilities attached to them.

Before leaving this topic, we should also distinguish explicitly between the *probability* of a forecast and its *significance*. The latter refers to the consequences that a future event would have for the interests and values of the policy maker, should that event occur. Forecasts of high significance are likely to demand the attention and resources of the policy maker even though a relatively low probability is assigned to them. Thus, the probability required of a forecast in order for it to become an "actionable" matter in policy making is a variable; whether a forecast is actionable is a function of its probability and its significance. Significance, in other words, can often dominate probability from an action standpoint. At the same time, of course, the various actions that can be taken on the basis of low-confidence (or uncertain) forecasts often differ strikingly in the costs and risks they may entail. This complicates the problem of decision but, as our discussion of the possibility of calibrating action to levels of warning suggests, reasonable solutions to the problem may still be found.

IV. ANALYTICAL FORECASTING IN DESIGN EXERCISES AND DEVELOPMENTAL MODELS

Finally, it is time to clarify the kind of forecasting that is associated with more comprehensive policy-planning frameworks—such as those employed in design exercises—in which an attempt is made to bring values, knowledge, and action into a close relationship with each other.

Forecasting that is part of a specific design exercise often starts with some hypothetical future state of affairs—for example, a system of world order—that is considered desirable by policy makers or by citizens who would like to see it adopted as a policy objective. The object of forecasting is not merely to assess the likelihood that the desired state of affairs will materialize. In addition, the forecaster undertakes the more ambitious and difficult task of identifying the conditions, variables, and causal processes on which the occurrence of that designated event will depend. What is wanted from the investigator, in other words, is not merely his single best guess regarding the probability of its occurrence but an *analytical forecast* of what its occurrence depends upon. The investigator is expected to identify and assess the conditions, variables, and dynamic interactions that together in some combination would markedly increase or decrease the probability that the future state of affairs of interest will occur. What conditions and developments would "favor" the emergence of the designated future? Alternatively, what conditions and developments would prevent its occurrence or make it very unlikely? One can imagine that analytical forecasts of this kind were produced within the government in 1968 when possibility of a detente with Peking emerged, and that they were updated periodically thereafter.

As already suggested, this type of problem-oriented forecasting is similar in important respects to what has been referred to by Harold Lasswell, Ernst Haas, and others as the construction of developmental models.[3] It is also very similar to what other writers such as Herbert Simon, Davis Bobrow, and George Kent refer to as "design exercises" or as the "engineering" approach (Simon, 1969; Bobrow, 1972; Kent, 1972).

Whatever term is used to refer to this type of problem-oriented forecasting, analytical forecasting encounters many intellectual difficulties and its requirements are difficult to satisfy. It should be noted that a full blown analytical forecast attempts to specify the *necessary and sufficient conditions* for the occurrence of the designated future event, and also to indicate the *transitional strategies* and *scenarios* by means of which to bring about that historical outcome. Obviously, most analytical forecasts can only approximate this; many of them will fall well short of this objective. Not only is the product likely to be incomplete when compared to

these ideal requirements of a full-blown analytical forecast, the causal developmental analysis provided by the investigator may also be uncertain or of questionable validity and, therefore, it will have to be used selectively and cautiously in policy planning.

There is a tendency to disparage or dismiss studies that fall short of providing a full-blown analytical forecast to which high confidence can be attached. Instead of disparaging them, however, both the forecaster and the policy maker would do better to regard them as exercises that help to clarify the uncertainties imbedded in the policy problem at hand. Precisely insofar as a forecast does identify these relevant uncertainties, it will provide useful inputs for the policy planner whose task it is to devise plans and decision strategies for dealing in a reasonable way with those uncertainties.

In this connection the role of the "expert" in analytical forecasting needs to be considered. In the first place, the concept of "expert" as well as the practice of endowing those who engage in forecasting with the status of "expert" needs careful, critical attention in each case. It has been wisely noted that a policy problem is one for which there are no experts *per se* but for which the specialized knowledge of various experts may be relevant and indeed of critical importance. That is to say, when a policy problem is broad and complex, forecasting requires several different kinds of expertise. Each expert, however, is an expert on only part of the problem. Somehow a synthesis of the relevant expertise must be obtained within the framework of a problem-solving approach.[4] Since there is no adequate overall theory to serve as a forecasting model for policy problems of this kind, analytical interaction among the relevant experts is necessary in order to construct an *ad hoc* theory for the purpose at hand.

The need for analytical interaction in these circumstances cannot be replaced by treating each specialized expert as if he were an expert on the problem as a whole. And yet this is often done by asking experts (and pseudo-experts) to provide their "single best guess" with regard to the forecasting problem, and by the additional practice of polling and averaging-out in some way the best guesses provided by a larger number of "experts." Instead of using experts in this dubious manner, policy makers would do well to encourage and to insist upon more analytical forecasting. This is much more likely to identify and clarify the uncertainties and conditional probabilities embedded in the problem than the practice of soliciting the expert's "single best guess." In other words, the expert should be expected not merely to offer his judgment of what is most likely to happen but also to identify the critical conditions under which a different outcome to which he presently assigns a lower probability would become much more likely in the future. Analytical forecasting of this kind has the considerable virtue of forcing experts to articulate and improve the analytical basis for their intuitive best guesses.

Analytical forecasting also stimulates multidisciplinary work. Typically, design exercises and developmental model construction require a difficult intellectual synthesis that can be achieved, if at all, only by combining different analytic frameworks and different bodies of specialized knowledge, and by blending general theory with specific historical models and simulations. Participation in a design exercise or in the construction of a developmental model forces experts on different components of the problem to interact in a focused manner in

order to produce a theoretical model for the purpose at hand. Therefore, forecasting for the purpose of design can be useful not only for the policy planner; it can also have considerable heuristic value for the further development of international relations theory. And it can also help to clarify the different kinds of theory—empirical, normative, and policy science—needed for the conduct of international relations.[5]

NOTES

1. I would like to express appreciation to Davis Bobrow and Robert Holt for their assistance in introducing me to some of the literature on design theory.
2. For a fuller analysis of the problem of responding to warning indicators that deterrence may be failing, see George and Smoke (1974).
3. Developmental models are discussed by Haas (1968), pp. 6–8. Harold Lasswell's concept of "developmental construct" and his cursory references to it are the subject of Eulau's article (1958).
4. See the discussion of the "collegial" mode of policy making in George (1972), pp. 763–765.
5. For a detailed discussion of the latter point, see Smoke and George (1973).

CHAPTER TWENTY-THREE

MICAWBER VERSUS DE JOUVENEL: PLANNING AND FORECASTING IN THE REAL WORLD OF WASHINGTON

Chester L. Cooper

I have no doubt I shall, please Heaven, begin to be beforehand with the World, and to live in a perfectly new manner, if—in short, if anything turns up.

MR. MICAWBER, *David Copperfield*

If it seems likely the future will differ from the past, we think it is desirable that this future should be a foreknown of which we are warned, rather than an unknown "something or other."

B. DE JOUVENEL, *The Art of Conjecture*

I. POLICY MAKING IN THEORY AND PRACTICE

The burden of most of the chapters in this volume is that the quality of international relations forecasting and planning in the field of international relations could be significantly improved by application of methodologies that social scientists, particularly political scientists, have developed over the past two decades. This essay focuses on how forecasting and planning is *actually* performed in the international affairs community of the United States government; it does not address the issue of how it *could* be done, if only these functions were to be undertaken in Cambridge rather than Washington, or if, in any case, bureaucrats were as able or as right-minded as professors. It will probe into why it is that forecasting and planning is done the way it is—to the extent it is done at all (at least in the

sense that these terms are used elsewhere in this book). And finally, it will suggest how the policy process might be improved within the limitations of the real world of Washington. In a word, then, this is a pragmatic rather than a methodological approach to the issue. This chapter may thus turn out to be an ugly duckling among a flock of swans. But old Washington-watchers will observe that the ugly duckling, at least, is floundering downstream —which is a value judgment on Washington's hazardous currents rather than on the cleverness of the swans.

Despite lofty rhetoric on the part of Secretaries of State or Defense, by Assistants to Presidents, or, on occasion, by Presidents themselves, long-range planning (and, thus, long-range forecasting) is rarely done in Washington and, if done, is usually ignored. Indeed, even mid-term (say from 2–5 years) planning is a rare and sometime phenomenon. Washington's top-level foreign policy makers, many of whom have come from university backgrounds, many of whom would describe themselves as "political scientists," operate pragmatically on a day-to-day, week-to-week basis. And on the next level down the process is dominated by experts in one or another aspect of international affairs rather than specialists in futurology, by pragmatists rather than by social science theorists. And so it is that for the decades since World War II, American foreign policy makers have been largely preoccupied with crisis management and damage limitation rather than systematic, rational policy planning. Even if they had chosen to do otherwise, events and personalities touching upon important American interests are fluid and are beyond the influence of American policy. Reaction rather than initiative must often by the policy maker's posture. It should come as no surprise, then, that forecasting and planning have remained the thankless and frequently the bootless tasks of the "boys in the back room."

This lugubrious description of planning and forecasting in international relations may produce anguished hand-wringing or knowing shrugs in study groups at the Council on Foreign Relations or in seminars at Berkeley. But, except for occasional golden moments, and with some minor differences of tone and nuances of style, this is how the foreign policy-making process has worked in Washington since the end of World War II. And, one must hasten to add, how it has worked in most world capitals.

The effectiveness of forecasting and planning depends, in the last analysis, on whether these functions are taken seriously by key officials in the policy hierarchy. This, in turn, depends not only on how well forecasters forecast and planners plan, but at least as much on factors beyond their control, sometimes even beyond their ken. In a rationally ordered process of policy making, the higher the quality of forecasts and plans, the more seriously the efforts will be regarded. But this is not necessarily the case in a system where day-to-day events and demands take precedence over the orderly consideration of long-term objectives and long-term strategy.

Forecasters and planners, no matter how sophisticated their techniques or methodologies, no matter how soundly conceived their conclusions must

operate with "The System." And The System in Washington makes for heavy going. Not only the working style of any given President, but his personal and professional relations with the Secretary of State, or Secretary of Defense, or Director of Central Intelligence must be reckoned with. And then, of course, there are the working styles of these Great Men as well as their relations with the Chief Policy Planner, or the Assistant Secretary of Defense for International Security Affairs, or the Director of the Office of National Estimates. And finally and perhaps, most importantly, planners and forecasters must recognize that despite the pejorative that Washington is a "paper factory," Washington is an *oral* rather than a written-driven community. In the last analysis, the telephone and the small meeting are the operative instruments—and these effectively exclude both the planner and the forecaster.

It will be worth a moment or two to examine The System as it has evolved over the past two decades.

Secretary George Marshall established the Policy Planning Council, with George Kennan as its first Director in the spring of 1947. From this point and for a decade or so after, the Cold War was at its most intense; the issues engaging American policy makers seemed sharply defined. At this time, too, under the strong leadership of Marshall, then Dean Acheson, and later John Foster Dulles, the Department of State's leadership on international policy making was generally acknowledged. Moreover, the National Security Act of 1947, especially as it was subsequently implemented during President Eisenhower's tenure, provided a sense of order to the process of international affairs forecasting, planning, decision making, and follow-up.

By 1960 the world had become more complex and fluid. The questions at issue—if indeed they ever were as clearly defined as they had earlier seemed—appeared much less so with the now apparent strains in the Moscow-Peking relationship, the strident claims for attention and the uncertain political orientation of new countries, and the emerging power of Germany and Japan. Hitherto ignored and virtually unknown little countries were presenting an ill-prepared Washington with thorny problems, even major crises—Cuba, Laos, Vietnam, the Congo, Yemen—countries that the Policy Planning Staff, preoccupied as it was, with the towering issues of the Cold War, found unfamiliar and intellectually uncongenial. It was just about this time, too, that President John Kennedy took office.

One of the first acts of the Kennedy administration was to demolish the elaborate structure that had been built in and around Eisenhower's National Security Council. The Planning Board and the Operations Coordination Board, as well as a myriad of *ad hoc* committees serving the council were dismantled with quick dispatch and little ceremony. The National Security Council, itself a statutory body, could not be disposed of without congressional action, but it remained dormant during the Kennedy years. The Assistant to the President for National Security Affairs, together with a few of his assistants and members of the NSC staff, would provide the day-to-day links with those departments and agencies carrying a wide range of foreign affairs/national security responsibilities from disarmament to war making, from economic assistance to economic warfare, from political analysis to intelligence collection.

John Foster Dulles was the last "strong" Secretary of State until the advent, almost 15 years later, of Henry Kissinger. At the outset of the Kennedy administration the management of international relations moved from the Department of State to the White House. On any matter in which the President was—or should have been, or could have been, or might become—involved, staff work, which had earlier been performed through the Planning Board system, was now performed by the White House/NSC staff. The staff was headed by a Special Assistant to the President who wielded more bureaucratic clout than any of his predecessors. Follow-up on Presidential decisions, previously the task of the Operations Coordination Board was now, also, the responsibility of those in the basement of the White House's West Wing and the adjoining Executive Office Building (although there were occasions, too, when the President's brother Robert moved into action). When problems reached a point where the Great Men had to convene, they met in the Oval Office or the small second floor dining room rather than in the cabinet room of the White House or the Secretary of State's conference room. Instead of the large, cumbersome and sometimes uninformed NSC membership with their coterie of aides, only a handful of carefully selected people was now

involved—the President, his Special Assistant, the Secretaries of Defense and State (frequently in that order), the Attorney General and, on occasion, the Chairman of the Joint Chiefs, and Director of Central Intelligence.

During the Johnson administration, the approach was pretty much the same—reliance on individuals rather than institutions, the old-boy net rather than tidy bureaucratic processes. Although the National Security Council was convened somewhat more frequently in the late 1960's than in Kennedy's time, the sessions were designed primarily as ornaments to be displayed every month or so to press photographers. Johnson's chief policy-making forum was the small group that comprised the "Tuesday lunch." Its lack of a formal agenda and detailed minutes reflected the tightly controlled White House management of international affairs. More often than not, emergency, sensitive decisions would be made over the secure telephone, saving key officials a trip to Pennsylvania Avenue—and circumventing, too, the speculation that inevitably accompanied hastily called White House meetings. This may have been how President Johnson would have preferred to conduct business in any case, but the pressure and hostility surrounding the all-consuming issue of Vietnam exaggerated his perceived need for an ever narrowing perimeter of trusted advisers and confidants.

The Nixon approach to international relations, with its announced emphasis on the National Security Council structure, stirred memories of the structured and systematic practices of the Eisenhower administration, but the similarities are superficial. While Eisenhower had a passion for tidy staff work, as all good generals do, he gave the leading oar to the Department of State, particularly to Secretary Dulles. Until the late summer of 1973, however, the Department continued to play the role it had been relegated to for many years; it was but one of several contributors to the policy process. The President's Special Assistant, Dr. Henry Kissinger, rather than the Secretary of State, was the chief architect, with the President his principal client ("A bit more elbow-room in the Indochina area, if you please, Henry."). To pursue this analogy, the large NSC staff—larger, by far, than any of its predecessor staffs—provided detailed drawings and wiring diagrams and the Department of

State together with other elements of the foreign affairs community acted as subcontractors.

The appointment of Dr. Kissinger as both Secretary of State *and* Special Assistant to the President was greeted by many, including frustrated State Department officials, as a new Renaissance. The action would now move from Pennsylvania Avenue to "C" Street. In a sense, that is what happened; Henry Kissinger picked up his bulging briefcase, collected a few members of his staff, and set up shop a few blocks uptown. His early months in office were marked by international crises, personal diplomacy, and constant peregrination—a pattern that was very much part of Kissinger's style. And so, while the seventh floor, or at least the secretary's corridor in the Department of State was bustling with activity, much of the rest of the Department continued to watch and wait.

The National Security Council itself had become a somewhat more visible institution than it was during the Kennedy and Johnson administrations, but it was probably not much more effective. Like his predecessors Presidents Kennedy and Johnson, President Nixon regarded the NSC as a body to be informed of decisions already made, rather than one to be consulted about decisions in the making. The advisory/consulting function, as in the two earlier administrations, was performed in other, smaller and more privileged forums.

In a system where the gut issues are addressed by a tight circle of busy, top-level advisors and where the Department of State below the level of the Secretary and his immediate staff is pretty much excluded from the decision-making process, forecasters and planners have an up-hill struggle. Why must this be so? These are questions we will come back to later, but first let us examine the planning and forecasting functions and the various elements within the structure where these arts are pursued.

II. THE PLANNING FUNCTION

Planning is obviously not an end in itself. Nor should planners properly ply their art in isolation from other aspects of the elaborate process that characterizes the shaping and molding of American foreign policy. Indeed, the difference between an international affairs planner and an international affairs essayist is that the former is an integral part of a larger foreign policy process; he is linked substantively and organizationally with information collectors, analysts, and forecasters, on the one hand, and decision makers, on the other.

Only the hopelessly naive would maintain that planners' plans should always be adopted by high-level policy makers. But if the foreign policy process is to be a rational and thoughtful one, planners' plans must be seriously regarded as important contributions. Thus, a planning paper becomes an effective policy instrument only if policy makers take cognizance of it as they come to their decision. Unfortunately, this does not happen very often. Not because the Secretary of State or the Special Assistant to the President, or, indeed, even an Assistant Secretary chooses consciously to ignore the planning function. Rather, because the pace of events, actual or perceived, is such that "policy" (i.e., a *decision*) tends to be postponed until it is forced on the top level of government. (The euphemism for this is "keeping the options open.") The very atmosphere that surrounds the making of consequential decisions—tension, secrecy, the pressure of time—tends to shut policy planners out of the process.[1] This does not mean, obviously, that decisions are reached mindlessly or without plan; it does mean that the decision maker relies on his own and his close colleagues' viscerae and on his accumulated reservoir of wisdom to determine what is apparently the best of perceived available alternative courses of action. What typically happens under these circumstances is that "planning" becomes part of the intellectual process the policy maker employs to reach his decision. It is informal, unstructured, and frequently divorced from the work of the nominal planning staffs. In such a system the role of the planners and their elaborate planning papers get short shrift.

Ideally, communication between planners and policy makers should flow in both directions. Planners, for their part, should share with others the fruits of their unhurried study; decision makers should, in turn, keep planners and forecasters in touch with their current concerns. But all processes are less perfect in their implementation than they are on flow charts. The foreign policy process breaks down at several critical points, and in terms of planning, at the most critical point of all: decision makers, by design or oversight, rarely inform planners of their current or likely future interests.

Thus, planning staffs tend to be insulated from the real world. Much planning effort is consequently self-generated, based on what planners in their innocence assume the decision makers want or based on what they think they ought to have.

This is not good enough—by a long shot. If the planning function is to serve a useful purpose, and if advances in planning methodology are to contribute to a more rational American foreign policy, planners must be given a more active and direct role. It is one thing to write essays outside the government for a wide audience that might include (as it would in the case of such journals as *Foreign Affairs* or *Foreign Policy*) influential government officials. It is another to write "essays" within the government and have them ignored—especially by those same officials.[2] When George Kennan wrote his famous article on containment under the pseudonym "X" (1947), he had an audience among government officials that would not have been possible if his views were in the form of a memorandum forwarded through channels to the Secretary of State. Kennan's article was based on an informal memorandum previously sent to Secretary of the Navy Forrestal for his personal use (Kennan, 1967, p. 355), but without exposure in *Foreign Affairs*, the containment thesis would have stirred few ripples in official Washington.

And so it is that Policy Planning, even on a short time scale, has not been distinguished by stunning successes, for reasons that have little to do with the validity of the planning process itself. Long-range international policy planning and, by extension, international relations forecasting as conceived of by most contributors to this volume, is, for all practical purposes, nonexistent in Washington. (I am excluding here, of course, military planning and the weapons systems planning done by the Joint Chiefs of Staff and by the Office of Secretary of Defense.) This is not to say that every government official from the President to a Deputy Assistant Secretary doesn't profess the importance of long-term planning. It is to say that despite all the good intentions and an innate sympathy for the process, events tend to take over. Faced with a decision, even one having a long-term effect, the policy maker will rarely think to retrieve the relevant long-term planning paper—even if he was aware that there was one—and even if, indeed, there was one.

The budget cycle presents the planners with an almost insuperable obstacle. It has led to a concentration on annual programs rather than longer range plans. Although this is especially true for such operations-oriented institutions as AID and USIA, preoccupation with the next fiscal year's program pervades every agency in Washington's foreign affairs community. To the extent that forward thinking goes beyond this, it is constrained by the period remaining in any given presidential term—which obviously tends to put a maximum of 4 years on any planning effort. Thus, if the time scale we have in mind when we think of long-range planning is in terms of at least 5 years, it is fair to say there is no such planning being done within the United States government—or at least no *effective* planning.

Something called "planning" is performed in Washington, of course, and there is a veritable regiment of people in the foreign affairs establishment who would answer to the occupational title "planner." But this function in the field of foreign affairs (and indeed in most areas of *domestic* policy) has been a stepchild that has been abandoned in the haram-scaram of day-to-day, week-to-week imperatives of routine decision making. It is no secret that the most expeditious road to career advancement is through the operating rather than the planning elements of any agency; few ambassadors or assistant secretaries are plucked from the ranks of those who have spent much of their prior careers on planning staffs. This is not the stuff of inspiration and encouragement. And it should surprise no one that Washington planners are typically a disillusioned and frustrated lot. When all is said and done, planners write planning papers, but decision makers "plan."

So much for the general state of international affairs planning as it is practiced, rather than preached. It is time to examine some of the key elements in the process.

The Planners

The Department of State—or the Voice of the Turtle. The Policy Planning Staff of the Department of State was the product of a realization by Secretary George Marshall that the problems of Western Europe and the difficulties of dealing with Moscow required more systematic thought and more sustained attention than busy operating officials in Washington could bring to bear. And so in the spring of 1947, a staff was organized under George Kennan to undertake the following missions: (Kennan, 1967, pp. 325–327)

1. Formulating and developing, for the consideration and approval of appropriate officials of the department, long-term programs for the achievement of US foreign policy objectives.

2. Anticipating problems that the department may encounter in the discharge of its mission.

3. Undertaking studies and preparing reports on broad politico-military problems.

4. Examining problems and developments affecting US foreign policy in order to evaluate the adequacy of current policy and making advisory recommendations on them.

5. Coordinating planning activities within the Department of State.

Note the operative words: "long term," "anticipating," "broad politico-military," "evaluate," "coordinating." A large order.

In the 25 years since the Policy Planning Staff was established, it has had only a few periods of success—if by "success" one means having significant influence on policy formulation and if by "significant influence on policy formulation," one means that views of policy planning, whether conveyed in oral or written form, were sought and taken seriously by the top layer of policy-making officials.

First-rate thinking, a credible methodology, and elegant presentation are necessary but not sufficient conditions for success. If, for example, a Secretary of State regards the planning staff as just another element, like the motor pool, of his inherited bureaucracy, there is little chance that even the most brilliant ideas or persuasive arguments will penetrate the wall of indifference. Much depends therefore, on the relationship between the chief planner and the Secretary. Indeed, that most precious of bureaucratic advantages—*access*—hangs on the quality and intimacy of this relationship. But, the secretary-planner alliance must not be one in which the planner is regarded as simply a special advisor or speech writer on current issues. Otherwise, the planner will find himself divorced from his staff and, even worse, will have to default

on his "long term," "broad," "evaluating" responsibilities.

The Marshall-Kennan Planning Staff relationship was a "success"; the staff was Marshall's creation and Kennan was Marshall's choice. The Acheson-Nitze Planning Staff relationship was also a "success"; the relations between the two men were close and Nitze was a skilled director of an able staff. The Dulles-Bowie Planning Staff relationship was a qualified "success"; although Robert Bowie was one of Dulles' closest advisors, it was Bowie *qua* Bowie, rather than Bowie, Director of Policy Planning, who played a key role. (It should be noted here, however, that during this period the Policy Planning Staff had direct, formal responsibilities in the policy process through its membership on the National Security Council Planning Board. We shall address this arrangement in more detail below.) The Rusk-Rostow Planning Staff (or rather planning "Council"—a name change that reflected a cosmetic rather than a real change in status) was not a "success"; Rusk and Rostow had a guarded relationship and the planning staff, with only a miniscule number of exceptions, had little influence on foreign policy during this period.

The Rogers-Cargo Planning and Coordination Staff (a name change that reflected an attempt to bring the planners closer to operations) cannot be regarded as a "success" either; when planners become too closely caught up in day-to-day issues, what emerges is not planning, but operations analysis. Indeed, with this change, long-range planning in the Department of State suffered a virtual *coup de grace*.

The positioning of a planning staff within the Department's bureaucratic structure and the relationships of the planners to their brethren in other elements of the structure are subtle but critical factors in determining the effectiveness of planners. For planners must be protected, but not isolated. They must be aware of current problems, but not be caught up in them. They must be privy to the short-term objectives of the President and his chief advisors, but be ready to remind their more politically minded superiors and colleagues when short-term considerations prejudice attainment of long-term goals. This neat balance between keeping aloof and getting involved is easier to prescribe than to put into effect. But if the planners are to avoid the cruelest of experiences—producing work that is "interesting, but not relevant"—the balance must be achieved and maintained.

Since the demise of the NSC Planning Board in 1961, State Department planners have found that many of their papers have been "interesting, but not relevant"—that their ideas have rarely been sought, let alone seriously considered. All too often, over the past decade or more, the Policy Planning Staff has been regarded as a manpower pool, rest and recuperation area, or a convenient personnel assignment for foreign service officers with modest prospects, but with an inclination to read and write.

If this seems a harsh judgment, consider the decade when Indochina preoccupied virtually every high-level policy maker in Washington. During this period the State Department's planners, except for preparing some early contingency bombing policy studies, had no significant role to play. For several years during this time, the staff was instead almost exclusively engaged in the preparation of elaborate, expensive, and universally ignored Country Policy Studies. These studies, which presumably were to provide policy Bibles for a score of countries, began to gather dust almost immediately upon completion. Some members of the staff, to be sure, were active in 1963 and 1964 in the planning of the Multilateral force, but they lost much of their credibility when they became passionate advocates of this ill-starred scheme. Since 1969, with the focus of foreign affairs policy moving to the White House, State Department planners lost even more ground.

Although forecasting can be done without planning, the obverse is not true; implicitly if not explicitly, planning must incorporate some predictions or assumptions with respect to the future. It is fair to say, then, that no systematic forecasting has been performed in the Department of State for at least a decade.[3]

To say that little, if any systematic long-range policy planning is done within the Department of State is not to say that the Department muddles its way through the years without some effort to rationalize policy or anticipate events. Thus, every geographical and most functional bureaus have file cabinets bursting with plans—but these are, whether they are formally dubbed so or not, *contingency* plans—"what happens if . . . ?" Washington is chock-a-block full of plans to deal with remote and unlikely contingencies. The irony is that if, by some improbable roll of the dice, one of these contingencies did rise in a form that was anticipated, the odds are against anyone remembering that there was a contingency plan filed away. And if one could be found, it would be surprising if it were taken seriously. If the contingency is important, *really* important, of course, the issues become too immediate, too sensitive, and too momentous to involve planners.

The National Security Council System—"The President needs. . . ." In President Nixon's first State of the World Message, he emphasized the need for "new methods of planning and a more rigorous and systematic process of policy making . . . We do not want to exhaust ourselves managing crises; our basic goal is to shape the future." And then, in a fuller description of the planning process he had in mind:

> American foreign policy must not be merely the result of a series of piecemeal tactical decisions forced by the pressures of events. If our policy is to embody a coherent vision of the world and a rational conception of America's interests, our specific actions must be the products of rational and deliberate choice. We need a system which forces consideration of problems before they become emergencies, which enables us to make our basic determinations of purpose before being pressed by events, and to mesh policies. (US Foreign Policy for the 1970's, 1970)

Henry Kissinger originally structured his National Security Council Staff to reflect this early emphasis on long-range planning. Some of the most senior members of the staff were assigned this function. There were high hopes that they together with Kissinger, who was himself no stranger to the process, would introduce at the highest level, the kind of perspective on policy making that had previously been lacking. The new apparent interest in planning at the NSC level proved to be the death knell for policy planners in the Department of State (they were already in *rigor mortis*). But as is the case with many lofty enterprises in Washington, the NSC's long-range planners turned out to have a brief half-life; within a year they began to wither away. This should have come as no surprise to old Washington hands: the White House and the staffs within its perimeter quickly

and inevitably become enmeshed in operational issues, whether by conscious choice or by force of
circumstance. The very atmosphere of 1600
Pennsylvania Avenue puts a premium on the quick
fix as opposed to the long-range plan. The "big
man on campus" is not likely to be the government
official or civil servant who has ample time to read
or to contemplate. However congenial such enterprises may have been in earlier incarnations, the
way to the top in the White House structure, the
key to admission to high councils, is to be part of
the action. And thus it was (and if there be any left
in forgotten corner, thus it *is*) that NSC "planners"
find themselves lonely, forlorn, frustrated. Which
is not to say, of course, that there are not some
activists, Kissinger chiefly among them, who, because of past training and innate capacity, do not
bring some perspective to their daily tasks.

And so, cautionary, qualifying observations are
again in order. The President "plans"; his Special
Assistant "plans"; some of *his* assistants "plan"; the
actual decision to open contacts with Peking did
not emerge as an idle thought while shaving. But
neither—and this is the fundamental point—did it
emerge from the elaborate system of review groups
or planning staffs. Indeed, it is a safe assumption
that no one whose occupational title is "planner,"
either in the White House complex or the Department of State, was even privy to the extended
exchange of written and oral views between Richard Nixon and Henry Kissinger ("plans," if you
will) precedent to a shift in American policy toward
China. Negotiations precedent to the Vietnam
cease fire, steps toward a detente with the USSR,
and, almost certainly, the Middle East settlement,
were prepared with little or no reliance on
"planners"—or for that matter even on the appropriate desk officers.

The "rigorous and systematic process of policy
making" Richard Nixon referred to in his first Report has engaged a thousand analysts, estimators,
planners and researchers throughout the international affairs/national security community. During
the early years of the new system, a swollen river
of paper flowed into the White House West Wing
and the Executive Office Building—churned up by
scores of NSC staff members initiating their requests with the heady phrase, "The President
needs. . . ." Thus, in 1969 alone, there emerged

eighty-five National Security Study Memoranda,
based on a vast number of background substantive
memoranda, research papers, statistical analyses,
planning documents, and staff critiques. Their
scope ranged from "Turkey" to "Toxins," from
"SALT" to "South Asia." The flow of paper to and
from the NSC has since diminished somewhat, but
it is still accurate to say that no consequential official has had either the time or the inclination to
read, or even scan, much of the written wisdom
the new system has generated.

*The Department of Defense—Loud and Clear
(Sometimes).* In terms of real, direct influence on
the shaping of American policy toward the world
outside, the role of the Assistant Secretary of Defense for International Security Affairs (ISA) at
times has been second only to the President's Special Assistant and such key cabinet members as the
Secretaries of State, Defense, and—in the days of
international economic crises—Treasury. ISA is
the Pentagon's "State Department," providing guidance to the Secretary of Defense on those issues
and in those circumstances where political developments have military implications or call for an
actual military response. As we hardly need remind ourselves, these have been abundant over
the decades since World War II.

The history of ISA has been a spotty one over
most of its institutional life. During the Kennedy
and Johnson administrations some of the most consequential figures in the international relations
community have served at its head or on its staff.
During those 8 years ISA was distinguished by
imaginative and energetic leadership and contributed much to the formulation of American foreign
policy. In more recent years ISA has fallen on lean
and sterile times with little or no influence outside
the Department of Defense and probably within
the Pentagon itself.

The Assistant Secretary, ISA, can play an important role in major policy forums at and just below
the White House level. The issues that engage the
Assistant Secretary, touching as they do on a mix of
foreign policy and international security considerations, tend to be of more than routine significance.
It should come as no surprise, then, that some Assistant Secretaries, even in their advisory and
planning functions, have wielded more influence in

the policy process than the typical Assistant Secretary of State, to say nothing of the State Department's chief planner.

One of the key aides to the Assistant Secretary is the Deputy Assistant Secretary for Plans and Policy. But he undertakes no "planning" in the sense we have been discussing it. For him, too, short-term, crisis considerations make long-term planning a residual claimant for time and attention. Critiques of State Department or JCS papers, quick-response memoranda prepared for the NSC, briefing papers for the Secretary characterize the ISA workday.

The only offices in the Pentagon, indeed, perhaps the only places in the entire international affairs community, where long-range planning is taken seriously are within the Joint Staff of the Joint Chiefs of Staff, the Military Service Staffs, and the Research and Development elements within the Office of the Secretary and the Services. Here 5-, 10-, and even 20-year plans (and implicitly, if not explicitly, 5-, 10-, and even 20-year forecasts) comprise a principal mission. We noted earlier that the military and technical planning functions are beyond the scope of our present concern, since, strictly speaking, they lie outside a discussion of "international affairs." A few gnawing questions come to mind, nonetheless, and they should be aired, if not answered. How realistic, or at least, how relevant, are the long-range plans for the structure, deployment, and use of American military forces? And to what extent are these long-range plans for military forces and military technology likely to constrict or unduly influence the kind of political/military options we might at some future time wish to exercise? And what are the forecasts on which long-range military and technological plans are based? Are they consistent with the key assumptions (forecasts) that implicitly, at least, drive American political, diplomatic, and economic views of the world? In brief, do we really know what we are doing? Or wish to do?

III. THE FORECASTING FUNCTION

Policy planning in international relations, by definition, deals with the future and proceeds from some implicit or explicit anticipation (i.e., forecasting) of events or trends. Anticipation may extend over a period of many years ("our dependence on Middle East oil will reach a peak during the mid-1980's") or over a period of weeks ("Egypt will attack Israel before the summer"). It may deal with broad trends ("Sino-Soviet relations are likely to deteriorate over the remainder of the decade") or with specific contingencies ("if the United States resumes the bombing of North Vietnam, Ambassador Bruce may become *persona non grata* in Peking"). It may reflect an elaborate prior process of coordinated interagency "estimating," or it may simply reflect personal assumptions by the author of a particular planning paper.

Bertrand de Jouvenel defines forecasting as the "intellectual activity of forming opinions about the future (serious and considered ones, but with an uncertain verification)" (1967, p. 16). In this sense, "forecasting" *does* take place in the Washington foreign affairs community. What does *not* occur is the systematic application of the increasingly sophisticated forecasting methodology that has been developed over the past decade or so. Indeed, it is fair to say that in more cases than not, there is not even an awareness of the new methodological advances in the art of forecasting.

And so it is that international affairs "forecasting" as practiced in Washington is far removed from the kind of forecasting discussed elsewhere in this volume. To be sure, there is weather "forecasting" and crop "forecasting" and even, God help us, political "forecasting." But there is no international affairs "forecasting."

The plight of forecasting as related to public actions, is eloquently portrayed by Bertrand de Jouvenel:

> No problem is put on the agenda until it is a "burning" issue, when things are at such a pass that our hand is forced. No longer is any choice possible between different determining acts designed to shape a still-flexible situation. There is only one possible response, only one way out of the problem hemming us in. The powers that happen to be, submit to this necessity, and will justify themselves after the event by saying they had no choice to decide otherwise. What is actually true is that they *no longer* had any choice, which is something quite different: for if they cannot be blamed for a decision that was in fact inevitable, they can hardly escape censure for

letting the situation go until they had no freedom to choose. The proof of improvidence lies
in falling under the empire of necessity. The
means of avoiding this lies in acquainting oneself with emerging situations while they can still
be molded, before they have become impera-
tively compelling. In other words, without forecasting there is effectively no freedom of decision. (1967, p. 276)

Note that de Jouvenel is addressing the problem
of governmental forecasting generally. He is not
pointing an accusing finger at international forecasting only. Nor is he scolding American officials
in particular. There is an important point here:
Washington is not unique in its insouciant approach to planning and forecasting. Some governments (France and The Netherlands, for example)
seem to have had some success in working out
long-term domestic planning arrangements at the
national level while avoiding the heavy hand of the
"central planners" that dominate the economies
and individual lives in China and the USSR. But
even these cannot claim to be very successful at
forecasting in the terms that de Jouvenel has in
mind.

There is much to be said for Peter Drucker's
view—at least in the mind of this skeptic:

> All we can ever predict is continuity that ex-
> tends yesterday's trends into tomorrow. What
> has already happened is the only thing we can
> project and the only thing that can be quan-
> tified. But these continuing trends, however
> important, are only one dimension of the fu-
> ture, only one aspect of reality. The most accu-
> rate quantitative projection never predicts the
> truly important: the meaning of the facts and
> figures in the context of a different tomorrow.
> (Drucker, 1968, p. xii)

The Forecasters

*The CIA's Office of National Estimates—"On bal-
ance, we believe. . . ."*   If by forecasting in international affairs we mean an attempt to obtain a feel
for future trends or events with a view to permitting more effective planning and ultimately more
rational decisions, the closest Washington comes to
this is an activity known as "estimating." While
both forecasting and estimating concern them-

selves with the future, the similarity pretty much
ends there. Forecasting involves some measure of
quantitative analysis, the application of a developed or at least an evolving methodology and,
by implication, at least, a certain degree of precision. Estimating, even in the minds of its practitioners, is a visceral matter—a "gut" feeling. "We
believe . . . ," "We feel. . . ."

When the CIA was reorganized in 1950 to provide more effective substantive and operational
support for the National Security Council, one of
the new elements created was the Office of National Estimates (ONE). It consisted of a small
group of wise, older men and bright, younger
ones, most of them with previous intelligence experience, some fresh from the academic world. Its
first director was the brilliant and demanding Professor William Langer, on leave from Harvard University, who established standards of craftsmanship
and integrity that endured long after his own brief
tenure.

Although President Truman's description of the
role of the new CIA group implies a more perfect
process than actually existed at the time, it
nonetheless captures at least one of the major functions of ONE: "Each time the National Security
Council is about to consider a certain policy . . . it
immediately calls upon the CIA to present an estimate of the effects such a policy is likely to have
. . ." (Truman, 1955). Several National Intelligence
Estimates a year have focused on "The consequences to the United States" of a given set of
contemplated policy options. Another type of estimate was more general in scope, but still predictive in thrust. It addressed "probable developments" in country X over 3 to 5 years. (For a
time there was even an effort to project probable
developments in the "world situation" over a
5-year future). Many others dealt with the "capabilities and intentions" of one or another country that
could threaten American interests. Some of the estimates produced each year were, as President
Truman suggests, intimately tied to matters under
current discussion at the National Security Council; some were initiated by ONE, by other elements within the intelligence community, or by a
senior official in the White House or Departments
of State or Defense.

National Intelligence Estimates have four distinguishing characteristics: they deal with the future

(occasionally measured in weeks, more likely encompassing 2 years or more); they are "coordinated" in the sense that they incorporate data and views contributed by all important intelligence elements within the government; they make a conscious attempt to be objective and apolitical; and they stay clear of specific policy recommendations. The National Intelligence Estimate has been the only systematic, comprehensive "forecasting" effort undertaken in Washington's international affairs/ national security affairs community. It is an elaborate, analytical process involving direct or indirect participation by a vast array of American collectors, researchers, and analysts both in the United States and abroad. It is a matter of some concern, then, that the vast majority of National Intelligence Estimates have, for the past many years, been ignored by senior policy-making officials. Indeed, it is doubtful whether most of the officials ever see an Estimate from one year to another. Why?

With few exceptions involving economic or military projections, the subject matter of the Estimates leans heavily on qualitative information and judgments—political, diplomatic, propaganda, personalities. This is hardly the stuff of precise, confident "forecasts," and it is not surprising that most of the estimates are liberally seasoned with such phrases as "we believe," "the odds are," "possibly," "probably," "on balance." Critics argue that this represents an excess of caution on the part of the estimators. A more friendly view would be that the implicit admission of uncertainty properly evokes the humility that should accompany attempts to assess consequential future developments on the basis of incomplete information and crude forecasting techniques. But, whatever the explanation, National Intelligence Estimates apparently have not possessed the kind of sharpness and pungency that produces good notices or attracts important audiences among the upper levels of Washington officialdom.

Credibility has always been a problem that the Office of National Estimates has had to live with. Since, in most cases, the clinching statement—"we believe that X will probably not attack," "we conclude that the odds are better than even that the present government of Y will remain in power over the remainder of this year"—is a judgment containing a high visceral quotient, there is a not unnatural tendency on the part of a policy maker to

regard his own hunch as being at least as sound as that of a group of anonymous analysts holed up in Langley, Virginia. This is especially true, of course, if the NIE serves up an incongenial judgment. (However, when an Estimate confirms a policy maker's predispositions or buttresses his policy position, he tends to be less loathe to cite its findings.)

Yet another problem has more to do with the policy process than the estimates themselves. Busy policy officials have too little time or think they do (which is the same thing) to wade through or wallow around in long, overintellectualized expositions. Nuances of probability, while meaningful to the estimators, must seem overly precious to harried operating officials (what is the difference, for example, between "this will probably occur", and "the odds are better than even that this will occur", and "we believe that this will occur"?). Although seven administrations, each with its own policy-making style, and hundreds of key policy officials have passed through Washington since ONE was established, the format, approach, and presentation of National Intelligence Estimates has remained pretty standard for two decades. Even the most rudimentary methodological advances in forecasting techniques discussed earlier in this volume have been largely ignored. For the past few years the Office of National Estimates seemed to have been living on borrowed time and in the summer of 1973 its lease expired. The National Intelligence Board and Staff have been replaced by a group of senior specialists, "national intelligence officers," each of whom produces the estimates in his area of responsibility on the basis of information available throughout the community. It is still too early to judge whether the new arrangement will be an improvement or a retrogression. Indeed, it is still unclear whether, in the zeal of reorganization, the objectivity and intellectual quality of the Estimates have been thrown out with the Office.[4]

Before we leave the late Office of National Estimates, we should take note of Professor Ernest May's plea that the proper use of history has much to contribute to forecasting in international affairs "if used properly" (1973). The eminent historian William Langer was succeeded as Director of ONE by the eminent historian Sherman Kent who, in due course, was succeeded by two other Directors with strong backgrounds in history. Whether this made the National Intelligence Estimates any more sound, it is hard to say.

The Military Estimators—"If they can . . . they will. . . ."

The military intelligence staffs have had their own stable of estimators for a generation or more. They have concentrated, primarily but not exclusively, on "The Threat." Typically, the approach has hung on assessments of enemy capabilities and on the proposition that "if the enemy *can* do it, they *will* do it." Indeed, much of the tension and controversy that has characterized the relations between the military estimators and ONE centers on the issue of how much weight to give to the difficult and subtle matter of judging enemy intentions. For many years there has been a well-founded suspicion that the Defense Intelligence Agency's assessments of enemy capabilities were prepared with one eye on the United States defense budget. We are now told (Graham, 1973) that DIA's approach has become more balanced and sophisticated. Let us hope so.

And the Others.

The Bureau of Intelligence and Research of the Department of State, the Nuclear Regulatory Agency, and even the Federal Bureau of Investigation, all contribute, as appropriate, to the estimating process and all provide their respective principals with their own judgments on more parochial issues. None of them, it is probably fair to say, employs the kind of forecasting techniques discussed elsewhere in this book.

The Think Tanks: Have Scenario, Will Travel

The network of policy research outside of, but related to, Washington's decision-making system represents a consequential government commitment to the innovative, thoughtful, scholarly pursuit of knowledge bearing on American foreign policy. It is a commentary on bureaucratic practice in the realm of international relations and national security that a government as large as ours must turn to outside experts for research and analysis and even for the development of policy options. The Department of Defense, which is by far the best heeled of the various members of this community, contracts for the vast majority of studies.

There are scores, perhaps hundreds, of think tanks and research groups and thousands of individual consultants operating close to or on the outer edges of policy formulation. Much of their work is security or hardware-oriented; some of it, especially that done on behalf of the Assistant Secretary of Defense for International Security Affairs, addresses the critical area where national security and international politics merge. The research and analysis performed for those parts of the government dealing with foreign aid programs, arms control, intelligence, political, and diplomatic issues, together with that done for ISA, covers a wide range of short- and long-term policy questions.

If there is any place within the international relations structure where forecasting and planning are pursued with some regard for recent methodological advances in the social sciences, it is here, on the periphery of the policy process. Contract research organizations and consultants are well in advance of the government itself in developing and applying quantitative (or at least more systematic) analytical techniques. It is in the think tanks, too—or at least in some of the think tanks, at least some of the time—where "forecasting" and "planning" are married, as opposed to the situation in the government where the two functions tend to go their separate, chaste, frequently sterile ways.

Some groups—RAND and the Hudson Institute come to mind—have taken the lead in developing innovative approaches to national decision making. The danger, of course, is that many analysts can become so captivated by new methodological approaches that their substantive contributions turn out to be naive or nonsensical. Of late, both the think tanks and their government sponsors are beginning to recognize that techniques appropriate for the analysis of alternative hardware systems are not directly transferable to the problem of developing foreign policy options.

A key question, of course, is the extent to which the product of this large network of outside research has significant influence on policy formulation. As one who, when in the government, contracted with or was generally exposed to studies produced by outside research organizations, and as one who, when in another incarnation, directed the social science division of a large think tank, my hunch is probably as good as the next man's. From the height of Delphi, my answer would be: "Not much. But it all depends."

"Not much," because the questions put to outside researchers (especially in the less precise areas of political, social, and general strategic analysis, but often, also, in the more technical areas) tend to be poorly or inadequately framed by government counterparts. More often than not, the sponsor's questions are answered, but they turn out to be the wrong questions because the one whose task it is to monitor contract research is too low in the departmental hierarchy or too removed from its center to know the right questions. Those who *do* know are much too busy to deal with outside researchers—even though they pay substantial sums (in the order of $80,000 per man-year) for think tank assistance.[5]

"It all depends," because some studies do, in fact, play an important role in influencing the judgments and decisions of key policy makers. It is fair to say, however, that to the extent this occurs, it is more likely in the case of quantitative rather than qualitative analyses. After all, every policy maker in the international affairs area is, or thinks he is, a social scientist; there is an inclination to feel that there is little that any think-tanker can tell him that he may not already know, or thinks he does.

It is one of the many ironies of our sytem of decision making that although think tanks flourish because the government evidently recognizes that it is unable to do long-range thinking for itself,[6] the product, however good (and expensive) it may be, rarely finds its way into the mainstream of the foreign policy process.[7]

IV. WHERE TO GO? WHAT TO DO?

It is by now commonplace that institutional refurbishing, bureaucratic reshuffling, and legislative overhauling have only marginal, temporary influences on the actual process of decision making. In the last analysis, one has to find the most effective way to work within the existing system—a system dominated by the personalities of the moment and the chronic syndrome of crisis management and damage limitation. Well-conceived innovations in techniques of forecasting and planning would obviously be useful. But let us not be de-

ceived: Even if they were adopted, it would be merely fiddling around the edges of the principal problem.

The original concept of policy planning in the Department of State must somehow be reconstituted with a small group of innovative thinkers close to the policy process but protected from the demands of day-to-day pressures. The group must have the confidence of and ready access to the Secretary of State. Its senior members must be *persona grata* in meetings at the White House and National Security Council levels. Moreover, the planning staff must establish close associations (perhaps through representatives seconded to it) with other components of the international relations community—the estimators in the Central Intelligence Agency, program planners in the Agency for International Development, and appropriate officials in the Department of Defense, the Joint Chiefs of Staff, the Arms Control and Disarmament Agency, and the United States Information Agency. In particular, an intimate working partnership must be developed between the forecasters and the planners wherever they may be.

Forecasting is obviously not solely the prerogative of those engaged in producing National Estimates. Virtually every participant in the policy process makes judgments about the future, if not explicitly in orally or written form, implicitly in his thought process. But this is not the point here; we are concerned with the formal and systematic process of planning and the formal and systematic process of forecasting. Here, National Estimates could play a key role. The process can bring together all available, relevant information and experts from all concerned elements of the government. What is needed is not necessarily an Office of National Estimates, *per se*, but a group of individuals who can approach a critical, complex issue free from passion and past policy preconceptions and with expertise in political, economic, and military affairs. One can only hope that the decision to eliminate the Office of National Estimates was made not solely on the basis that the format and personnel may have become incongenial to current policy makers, but rather that a new organizational approach would be more effective and that such an approach would attract the most able and wisest experts available to serve this function.

To give the Washington policy establishment its due, there has been, especially over the past decade or so, a fair degree of receptivity to new methodologies and more vigorous analytical techniques. Operations analysis, systems analysis, computer adaptations, and policy budget and programming systems, even in the qualitatively oriented world of the Department of State, have made their appearance. Scenario writing has developed into a fine art within the government. This should not be altogether surprising since many key analytical and even policy-making jobs in the government are filled from time to time by experts in these new techniques.

Washington is a hard-sell town, but it is also a gullible one. Rational policy making is inhibited not only by the prevalence of hide-bound intellectual Neanderthals but by eager, shiny men riding their hobbyhorses. (Incidentally, whatever happened to PPBS?)

But once again, we come back to the crisis mentality. While our current energy plight is not quite the same as (but neither altogether different from) a foreign crisis, it provides a good example of Washington's overall problem. Five years ago, where were the forecasters of an energy crisis? And if they were there, and doing their thing, where was their audience within the upper reaches of the government? And even if the Great Men had the time and wit to pay attention to the forecasters, what would they have done? What mechanism was there (is there) to undertake the comprehensive, across-the-board planning and implementation that would have been necessary in 1968 to avert a crisis in 1973? Or must we wait for the problem to evolve into attention-grabbing dimensions before we became seized with it and then flail around for the quick fix and the policy Band-Aids?

Henry Kissinger put this point well when he was still a college professor. There is no reason to suspect that much has changed in the intervening period. "When the bureaucracy is as large and as fragmented as it is, decisions do not get made until they appear as an administrative issue. One cannot convince a high level official that he has a problem until it appears unambiguously in the form of an administrative conflict" (*Washington Post*, 1973).

Let me conclude on a not entirely lugubrious note. It should be observed that public policy, generally, is insensitive, possibly even immune, to systematic forecasting. Most public organizations (perhaps most people) tend to identify with Micawber rather than de Jouvenel. Washington is probably no worse in this regard, and may be somewhat better, than most national capitals. Most foreign policy officials everywhere base their forecasting judgments on highly subjective considerations, frequently molded by wishes and hopes, sometimes influenced by the stake held in a given line of policy, occasionally affected by an attraction for or a phobia against a particular foreign leader or people. But, happily, there is enough slack in the process and enough resiliency in the international situation so that the consequences of being wrong are not very serious. Most countries, most of the time, seem to manage to muddle through without grave cost or risk.

But we must not be too sanguine; while many issues tend to loom very large and sharp at a particular moment only soon to be muted or overtaken by other events, there are some that are truly consequential. The margin for error has narrowed over the past two decades on questions that touch the vital interests of the Great Powers. For these questions, the consequences of a wrong guess ("estimate," "forecast") could be profound, even horrendous, and the most careful, rigorous examination and ranking of possible alternative developments or outcomes is an essential element in decision making. It is for this reason, if for no other, that my colleagues who have written the other, more methodologically oriented chapters of this book must keep plugging away. The process of policy making in international affairs can only improve.

NOTES

1. Ask a planner—any planner—when he last participated, orally or through a written contribution, in a top-level decision regarding a matter of profound importance. The odds will be high that he learned of such a decision-making session *ex post facto*.
2. One problem with in-house "essays" is that they are inevitably classified—which means, usually, that they must be read in the office and, therefore, must compete for time with telegrams, high-priority memoranda, meetings, and telephone calls. *Foreign Affairs* can be taken home and read at leisure.
3. It should be noted that the Director of Intelligence and Research, who participates in the preparation of Na-

tional Intelligence Estimates, forwards his own judgments on international problems to key Department officials. But both the present Secretary of State and his predecessor have regarded this function with massive indifference.

4. A fuller discussion of the estimative process will be found in the following chapter.

5. In 4 years of directing contract research done at the Institute for Defense Analyses on behalf of ISA during the first Nixon administration, I was unable to obtain one brief audience with the then Assistant Secretary to discuss what he wished us to do and what we were doing for him.

6. The *Armed Forces Journal* of September, 1968 discusses these outside research organizations in an article entitled, "Who Thinks for the Government?"

7. It should be emphasized again that this is very much less true in the case of studies dealing with "hardware" or "weapons systems" or "command-and-control" than it is the case of "strategic policy" or "foreign affairs" studies.

CHAPTER TWENTY-FOUR

FORECASTING OF INTERNATIONAL RELATIONS IN THE USSR

Igor V. Bestuzhev-lada & Vladimir P. Filatov

This chapter does not seek to describe all research carried on in the Soviet Union on problems of forecasting international relations. Rather, it touches upon the principal methodological characteristics of this sort of research.

Historical situations are structured in such a manner that the basic topics in the development of international relations (the inevitability of a social revolution, the possibility for the construction of socialism in one country, the strategy and tactics of foreign policy of a socialist state, the growing over of capitalism into imperialism, etc.) have already been studied in the classics of Marxism-Leninism. The basic principles of dialectical and historical materialism were formulated in these works and constitute the general methodological basis for social research in general and the study of international relations in particular. The Marxist methods

of analysis of the international situation, the knowledge of the laws of social development, and the well-informed nature of the foreign policy departments of the Soviet Union have provided the possibility for the leaders of the state to plan the foreign policy of the USSR on a scientific basis. One of the principal areas of Marxism-Leninism — concerning the unsoundness of voluntarism in politics, the defining role in a given relationship of socio-economic factors, the class nature of all policy, and the necessity in connection with these to analyze the economic, sociological, and external political conditions of the development of international relations — is to construct the foreign policy of a socialist state in coordination with the goals and tasks of the construction of socialism, and then communism. The foreign policy of the Soviet Union is formed on this theoretical basis. From this point of view scientific concepts of research also are formed on the tendencies and perspectives for development of the foreign policies of coun-

Translation by Thomas W. Robinson.

tries, and of international relations as a whole. The strengthening of Soviet work has been directed in the first instance to the solution of socio-economic and scientific-technical problems of the country. The forecasting of international relations is closely connected with the solution of national economic tasks, based on the works of V. I. Lenin and on the theory and practice of socialist planning in the USSR.

Under the influence of the ideas of V. I. Lenin in the 1920's and the beginning of the 1930's, the world's first research in the area of the theory of planned development of the national economy was carried out in the USSR. As is known, at that time the very idea of planning an economy called forth heated discussion in many countries. These were the years when Soviet scholars concerned themselves with the problem of establishing certain scientific grounds for government-wide planning, and when the scientific community of the country lived by means of the labors and successes of the first Five-Year Plan. In those years, there emerged several men with interests in prognosis: G. M. Krzhizhanovskii, S. G. Strumilin, A. V. Winter, and A. F. Joffe. Many of the prognostic efforts of K. E. Tsilokovskii are related to this time (first of all, the prediction of the further mastering of the earth's surface by man and especially his emergence into the cosmos, which was so brilliantly underscored in the 1960's).

At the end of 1935, A. M. Gor'kii came forth with the proposal to prepare a multivolume work registering the results of the first Five-Year Plan. One of these volumes would have been concerned with a prognosis of the development of the country from the 1920's and 1930's onward. The leading scholars of the country participated in this work. Unfortunately, it was not completed.

As is known, the imperialist aggression of the Fascist governments began in the 1930's. In 1935, the Italian army invaded Ethiopia, and in 1936, Germany and Italy precipitated civil war in Spain, while at the same time German troops reoccupied the Rhineland, drawing up close to the French border. The participants of the "Anti-Comintern Pact" threatened the Soviet Union, creating the "Berlin-Rome-Tokyo Axis." The Second World War was nearing.

The contemporary period in the area of forecasting is closely connected with the unfolding of communist construction in the USSR, with the stormy development of scientific-technical progress, with the appearance of demands for socialist planning, all of which presupposes an accounting of past experience, of current tendencies, and of concrete perspectives in the light of scientifically based forecasts. "Discussion of scientific forecasts should precede the working out of plans for the development of branches of the national economy," said A. N. Kosygin, Chairman of the Council of Ministers of the USSR at the March 19, 1965 session of the State Planning Commission. "We should arrange scientific forecasts according to the development of each branch of industry, in order in time to provide a path that is advanced and progressive and to know in what direction to work out the plan."

The question of a systematic heightening of the scientific foundation of socialist planning (including contributions from a number of forecasting works of a scientific-technical, socio-economic, and socio-political character) received much attention at the Twenty-third (1966) and Twenty-fourth (1971) Congresses of the Communist Party of the Soviet Union. "The necessity to modernize methods of planning has been gathering force," said L. I. Brezhnev, General Secretary of the CPSU in his speech at the Twenty-fourth Congress of the Party. "It should depend on a closer study of social demands, on an all-around analysis and evaluation of the various decision alternatives, and on their direct and their long-term consequences. In order to solve this responsible and difficult task, it is necessary to broaden the horizons of economic planning."

In connection with the directives of the Twenty-fourth Congress, a long-term plan for the development of the economy, and of cultural life of the USSR to 1990, began to be worked out. It ought to be mentioned that these sorts of long-term plans are also being worked out in other countries who are members of the Council of Mutual Economic Assistance, and also in the arena of the Program of socialist economic integration of these countries as a whole. An important place in these scientific endeavors, naturally, is occupied by problems of international relations.

In connection with these endeavors, scientific-technical, socio-economic, and socio-political forecasts in the USSR have taken on a large scope. In many scientific establishments there have appeared research groups, sectors, and sections especially created to work out forecasts of a scientific-technical, socio-economic, and socio-political character. Such scientific subdivisions are also found in the Academy of Sciences of the USSR. In particular, if one speaks of forecasting of various aspects of international relations, then such research is carried on in the Institute of Sociological Research, the Institute of Government and Law, the Institute of Geography, the Institute of the International Workers Movement, and also the Institute of World Economy and International Relations, the Institute of the USA, the Institute of Oriental Studies, the Institute of Africa, the Institute of Latin America, and a number of other academic institutes.

It goes without saying that, among these, the Institute of World Economy and International Relations, and the Institutes of the USA, of Oriental Studies, of Africa, of Latin America, and others give attention in the first instance to the analysis of foreign concepts on the development of their corresponding regions of the world and to the activities of centers for prognostication about these regions. A number of leading researchers of these institutes are specialists in the fields of methodology, methods, and practice of forecasting, and are authors of scientific works on those questions.

In the Institutes of Sociological Research, Government, and Law, the International Workers Movement, and others, primary attention is devoted to questions of working out theories of forecasting. This does not exclude the fact that some of their researchers also do forecasting work of an applied character and interest themselves in the critical generalization of foreign experience.

On the whole, in the Soviet Union several dozen scientific collectives are at work, occupied with theoretical problems of forecasting. A more significant number of research groups carry on forecasting endeavors of an applied character. This research is by no means limited to the framework of the Academy of Sciences of the USSR. Workers from many departmental scientific enterprises take part, as well as the higher schools of the country, in particular the faculties and laboratories of the Academy of Social Sciences, the State Universities at Moscow, Kiev, Leningrad, Novosibirsk, and other higher schools of the country.

The State Planning Committee of the Council of Ministers, the State Committee of the Council of Ministers for Science and Technology, the State Committee for Construction, and many other organs, including the Ministries of Foreign Affairs and of Foreign Trade, devote much attention to the topic of forecasting.

The Scientific-Technical Council on Computer Techniques and Systems of Administration under the USSR Council of Ministers' State Committee for Science and Technology, and the Presidium of the Academy of Sciences of the USSR (Chairman, Academician V. M. Glushkov), play an important role in the field of research on scientific-technical forecasting. For regular contacts between specialists in the field of optimal planning, the Academy of Sciences of the USSR has formed a section chaired by Academician N. P. Fedorenko, on national economic forecasting. In the Soviet Sociological Association (Chairman, M. N. Rutkevich), there is a section on social forecasting. These and other organization sponsor a number of scientific-technical, socio-economic, and socio-political forecasting. The enumeration of organizations and scientific centers, conferences, and symposia on questions of forecasting would occupy such a large space that the present chapter would have to be turned into a voluminous handbook. Concluding a short survey of the general condition of forecasting research in the Soviet Union, the authors consider it useful to mention the appearance in recent years of a significant number of specialist and scientific-popular works, among which the following authors stand out: V. M. Glushkov, D. M. Gvishian, A. N. Yefimov, V. V. Parin, A. M. Rumyantsev, N. N. Semenov, V. I. Siforov, S. G. Strumilin, P. N. Fyedoseev, and N. P. Fedorenko.

Soviet scientists have proceeded on the basis of the dialectical-materialist conception of the development of nature, society, and knowledge in order to solve a number of complex, general-theoretical and methodological problems of scientific-technical, socio-economic, and socio-political forecasting, and have created on this basis a significant number of special methods for working out forecasts in various fields of social relations, including the field of international relations.

Soviet scientists reject those views according to which the future should be the object of study of any sort of new science (futurology or any other). They consider that a forecast is nothing more than an integral part of each scientific discipline. But forecasts in the social sciences, as is known, form an intricate, reciprocally related complex of social forecasting. Therefore, in practice forecasting endeavors in this field take on the form of a special group of forecasts, where one direction forms the forecasting profile—that is, a special topic of research—while the other—an auxiliary direction—forms the so-called forecasting background. In relation to the latter, necessary data are prepared either on order of an adjacent, sufficiently competent scientific organization, or directly from the scientific literature. Sometimes they postulate conditions in preliminary order and are then supported or directed by scientific institutions.

A more highly developed and specialized group of forecasts in the USSR are economic forecasts, where the profiles are economic forecasts but where the forecasting background is formed by scientific-technical, demographic, sociological, socio-cultural, internal political, and external political forecasts. Profile forecasts in the forecasting of international relations are foreign policy forecasts, while forecasts in the other enumerated directions, beginning with the economic, internal political, and scientific-technical, form the forecasting background.

In such an approach, the working out of a theory of forecasting in general (general prognostics), a theory of special forecasting in particular (social prognostics), and especially a theory of forecasting of international relations (a special political prognostic) all take on paramount significance. The stormy growth of research in the field of theory of forecasting has in fact led to the birth of forecasting not as the science of the future but as the science of laws and methods of forecasting.

The theory of forecasting, in our opinion, should provide answers to such cardinal questions as the particular mechanism for outstripping the reflective activity in the human brain, the particular process of transition from ordinary to scientific consciousness concerning the development of propositions about the future, the basic methods for definition of the degree of reliability and the trustworthiness of forecasts. Complex scientific problems demanding special research stand in the way of solution of these questions.

Prognostics, as the science of laws and methods of forecasting, is called upon to provide a scientific typology of forecasts, to classify methods of fore-

casting, to reveal the actual relation between such categories as hypothesis and forecast, forecast and law, forecast and plan, forecast and decision, and so forth. First of all, however, prognostics is expected to give recommendations in the field of methodology of forecasting as it relates to concrete ways of raising the effectiveness of working out forecasts.

In their methods of working out forecasts, scientific enterprises of the Soviet Union use the most varied combination of forecasting methods. All the faster, therefore, have appeared complex combinations of various methods—forecasting systems. Here it is hardly possible or proper to look at a description or even an enumeration of the methods worked out by Soviet forecasters. In general, they all boil down to the following logical consequences of research exercises:

1. Preforecasting orientation. Making precise the task of the forecast (character, scale, object, time of prevention [of an impending military attack], and so forth). Formulation of the goal, task, subject, problem, and working hypothesis of the research. Definition of methods, structure, and organization of research.

2. Collection of data on the forecasting background according to the directives of competent scientific establishments and according to materials in the scientific literature.

3. Construction of an initial model of the subject to be forecast by using the methods of systems analysis, as far as possible with quantitative indicators, according to the basic parameters of the object. For precision of the model it is possible to utilize survey questionnaires and experts.

4. Construction of dynamic lines of development of each indicator, by means of straight-line extrapolation to the date of prevention of an impending attack as it concerns the underlying core of the future forecasting models.

5. Through methods of factor analysis, construction of a series of hypothetical (preliminary) exploratory models of the subject to be forecast, making concrete a minimal, maximal, and most probable understanding (this under the conditional assumption of the preservation of existing tendencies). The goal of this exercise is to obtain an idea of the character and scale of perspective socio-political problems.

6. Construction of a series of hypothetical normative models of the subject to be forecast,

through utilizing methods of normative forecasting (a tree of goals, graphs, matrices, scenarios, and so forth) making concrete an understanding of the absolute and the relative optimum. In the first (absolute) case, there comes into view the most desirable composition of the subject in general, unlimited by the data provided by the forecasting background. In the second (relative) case, the compromise optimum is limited by the framework of the forecasting background. In both cases the optimum is determined beforehand by definite criteria consistent with set social goals, norms, and ideals. The goal of this exercise is the appearance of desirable ways for deciding prospective sociopolitical problems.

7. Indirect verification of hypothetical models by prospective methods, first of all by methods of survey questionnaires and especially by expert opinion.

8. Construction of a final series of explorative and normative models through more precise data, approaching indirect verification of the hypothetical models.

9. Output of recommendations for planning and decision making on the basis of a comparison of the explorative and normative models. For precision of recommendations, it is possible to take one more sampling of experts.

10. A postforecasting exercise for moving to a new stage of forecasting, which ideally should be just as uninterrupted as planning or decision making.

In the international arena of the contemporary world, more and more often matters succeed one another through swift processes and events, often changing the distribution of forces within the various countries, in geographic areas, and in the whole world. The struggle for national liberation in many countries of Asia, Africa, and Latin America has begun to grow into a struggle against both feudal and capitalist relationships.

The relatively rapid changes in the international situation at times necessitate quick decisions that depend not only upon the presence of a scientifically based foreign policy strategy and flexible tactic but also upon the skill to foresee impending events, so as to react to them in good time. It is quite obvious that researchers are neither able to act as, nor should they take upon themselves the functions of, diplomats or of political and governmental actors and try to work out the strategy and tactics of behavior for the country in the inter-

national arena (this does not exclude, of course, the possibilities for scientists to make concrete, practical recommendations that on certain occasions may be of account and useful to the government). From researchers we expect, first of all, theory, methodology, and concrete methods of forecasting.

The special complexity of forecasting in international relations stems from the fact that international relations are closely connected with socioeconomic relations within each given country, with the arrangement of class forces, and with the internal policy of the ruling groups, the goals and tasks of their foreign policy, the realistic possibilities for the accomplishment of these goals, and the development of social processes inside the country. In turn, these demand knowledge and forecasts in the fields of science and technology, economics, demography, ethnography, anthropology, culture, education, and so forth.

In the Soviet Union, the solution to problems of forecasting in international relations and the creation of a corresponding theory proceeds in two special directions: (1) along the path of working out one special scientific discipline—a theory of international relations as a theoretical and methodological basis for its forecasting; and (2) along the path of working out another special scientific discipline—a theory of social forecasting (social prognostics), one of the divisions of which would be a theory of forecasting of international relations. As they often have a place in many other branches of contemporary science, the two directions are not exclusive, but rather reciprocally fulfill and are conditioned by each other. In both cases the instruments of historical, economic, juridical, philosophical, sociological, and other sciences attract the researcher. Both directions are united on the general methodological ground of dialectical and historical materialism, which is closely connected with the theory of scientific communism. The fact that just now these two reciprocally interwoven approaches predominate does not in the least exclude the possibility that in the future there will appear other approaches to researching the same object [but] on the same methodological basis.

What follows below are some of the most lively problems, in our view, of the theory of forecasting of international relations, as the latter field appears at present in the light of theoretical work in both of the indicated directions.

I. THE SUBJECT OF RESEARCH

The theory of forecasting in international relations rarely stands outside of the topic on which research is carried out (in the present instance—international relations), and includes within its bounds such elements of general sociology, the science of society, as: international relations as a subsystem of societal relations; the norms of development of direct and intermediate connections of relations among nations; and the motivating forces of international relations. As international relations emerges as a particular phenomenon in comparison with societal relations, the necessity arises to further concretize the subject of research through division into particular subjects, of which there are:

1. the participants (subjects) of international relations;

2. the environment (concrete historical conditions), in which international relations and the factors of its development grow;

3. the means (instruments) with whose aid relations between nations are made feasible.

It is possible that further research will bring forth correctives to the contents of the topic of the theory of forecasting of international relations portrayed here.

The definition of the subject not only provides us with the general trend for research but also can be looked upon as a necessary basic element in a forecasting system during that time when the indefinite nature of the subject disorients research and only rarely attains some degree of reliability of prediction. At the same time, we agree with the conclusion that in practice it is impossible to attain a high degree of reliability of a prediction with the aid of only one method, of whatever sort. The complexity of the subject of forecasting, reflecting the complexity of objective reality, weakens the systematic and complex character of the methods of its investigation.

Definition of the subject of the theory of forecasting is the first step in the creation of a theory. As is known, theory comprises the totality of knowledge of the objective world, generalized in the consciousness of human experience. Studying the essence of theory, the Soviet philosopher P. B. Kopnin came to the conclusion that in the structure of relations, every theory sets up a system of ideas, which vary with changes in knowledge. It should correspond to the level of contemporary practice and comprise a general, synthesized experience of the world and of events. In this scheme, ideas emerge in the form of a reflection of reality and are stages of knowledge of reality, developing from the simple to the complex, from the absolute to the concrete (the concept "international relations," in comparison with the concept "social relations" is more concrete).

In their content, concepts are objective and even the most abstract of them have analogues in the real world. Concepts should reflect the content of the subjects or events, that is, not its entire spontaneity but only its essential sides, characteristics, and connections. Concepts express such characteristics of abstraction as the reflection of the subjects of a phenomenon in "a pure sense." In formulating a concept, experiment, theoretical simplification (abstraction from nonexistent, external surroundings, and shading the essence of the subject), and other operations of a logical character take on much meaning. A concept is expressed in [such] terms.

These conclusions form one of the methodological bases of the theory of forecasting of international relations, as systems of defined concepts. In working out a theory, the study of the subject (or of its parts) usually begins with the most mature of its forms, that is, when essential aspects are sufficiently developed. This presents the possibility of giving working definitions that carry an abstract character and are of sufficient depth to serve as a stage of knowledge of the phenomena being studied, as a stage in the creation of a fully valued concept.

Taking the investigation laid out above as a starting point, the constituent parts of the subject of the theory of forecasting in international relations can be set up. They should be taken in the broad sense of the term, as when, for example, under international relations we include economic, political, ideological, legal, diplomatic, military, scientific, and other ties and reciprocal relations between governments, systems of governments (blocs), and basic social, economic, political forces and organizations that act in the international arena, just as in the narrow meaning of the word, when we speak concretely of Soviet-American, Anglo-French, and other bilateral relations. This is exactly why much, and in forecasting, decisive significance is attached to an exact definition of the concept (concepts) of a subject of research. The goals and the tasks of the forecast define the existence or nonexistence of one or another aspect of the subject.

Philosophies take one of two approaches to the formation of concepts: (1) they transform into animated concepts, lively contemplation (sensations, perceptions, assumptions), plus practical experience and knowledge stemming from it; or (2) they transform prior concepts into a new concept. The second approach does not result in simple summation, repetition, or multiplication of the separate elements of the prior concepts. [Rather] it looks forward to further elaborating them, and includes the transition to a new quality, wherein the entire arsenal of logical thinking is utilized, and where analysis and synthesis occupy an important place. This modification of concepts is linked with the developments of human knowledge of phenomena reflected in those concepts, and with the change in the phenomena themselves. In the process of development of knowledge a deepening of old concepts occurs in the rise of new ones.

II. INTERNATIONAL RELATIONS AS A SUBSYSTEM OF SOCIAL RELATIONS

In like manner, initiating research into the concepts of the basic components of the theory of forecasting subjects to analysis the concept of "international relations" itself (the most broad definition of this concept is given above). Various alternative definitions of the concept "international relations" worked out in the Soviet Union come down in one manner or another to the notion that relations between nations are "links," or "reciprocal links," or "reciprocal relations." In view of this, the definitions themselves turn out to be insufficient, although also quite necessary as important stages in understanding of the phenomena. Therefore, the task of research becomes the further deepening, and consequently the concretization, of the concept "international relations." In conformity with recommendations worked out by semiotics,*

---

*"Semiotics," a general theory of signs and symbolism, is usually divided into the branches of pragmatics, semantics, and syntactics [Ed.].

etymological and structural analysis were utilized as methods for resolving this problem. Etymological analysis showed that in the term "international relations" the key concept was "relations," wherein the word "international" becomes an adjective characterizing the type [specie] of relations, and indicates that of all types of relations, those arising in the external (international) arena stand out. These relations often are also termed "foreign affairs."

Structural analysis testified that the concept "relations" is a collective term and includes a differential content, extending from "reciprocal ties" of various kinds and topics to the "directiveness" of action. In the present case, [our] interest is in the contents of reciprocal "relations" (or interrelations) between one people and another. Upon further investigation, attention turned to the fact that interrelations between peoples exist as means of personal and correspondent (i.e., not face-to-face) contacts, and as sufficiently extensive, established ties and communications. The content of interrelations is always an exchange (of material things or information, or of both). In such a manner, with the aid of etymological and structural analysis, the concept "international relations" was structured, and produced three constituent parts (or components): contacts, communications, and exchange.

But it is well understood that every concept has not only a structure and a content but also a form, and that it can be understood only through the unity of content and form. International relations also has its own form, which in the most general sense is displayed as commonwealth, coexistence, colonialism, neocolonialism, and antagonism (confrontation).

Comparison of the necessary components (structure, contents, and form) allows us to create a model of the concept "international relations." It might be represented as shown in Figure 24.1. All of the components shown in the model may be saturated with concrete information and formalized as the "stuff" of social indicators, permitting evaluation and measurement. In the structure of "contacts," for instance, we include meeting and negotiations on various levels, verbal statements, diverse correspondence (notes, memoranda, protests, etc.); in the structure of "commonwealth," we include mutual aid, support, good services, additions to a treaty, agreements for cooperative

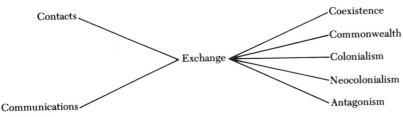

Figure 24.1 A model of the concept "International relations."

actions, etc. As a result, matrices are created in which, and on the basis of the parameters of structure, all types (kinds) of international relations are defined, as well as their intensity and level.

III. THE PARTICIPANTS OF INTERNATIONAL RELATIONS

Work on the definition of the participants in [the subjects of] international relations also has important significance. One scientist considers it sufficient to limit the understanding of the subject to research in the broadest sense; others have attempted to enumerate all possible participants in international relations. Thus, in the branch of international law of the Kiev State University, the participants in [subjects of] international relations are understood as "social communities" (classes, nations, nationalities, ethnic groups, international collectives, multiethnic communities, countries, peoples, reactionaries, and professional, youth, scientific, and other communities) (Martinenko, 1969, pp. 38–39). The Institute of World Economy and International Relations includes in its understanding peoples, governments, classes, and social, economic, and political forces and organizations (*International Relations after the Second World War*, 1962, p. xxvi).

Such a broad range of views as to the participants of international relations presents the possibility of looking at the subject of [our] research from various angles and to define the basis for a single approach for resolving the question who and what relates to the concept "participants in international relations." Further first-order analysis reveals that, of the subjects enumerated above, only a few stand out directly as playing a decisive role in the international arena. It therefore follows to separate the subjects, whose participation in international relations is important—and now and then

even decisive—and which are as a rule mediated by various social institutions, from subjects that are not direct participants in the international arena. "Social communities" belong to the first group, such as classes, peoples, and various social groups that do not take an immediate part in international affairs. To the second group belong: (1) countries, as integrated subjects; (2) governments and the state apparatus; (3) parties; (4) political and social organizations; (5) monopolies; (6) separate persons. This also provides us with a basis for considering them as direct participants in international relations, [hence] taking the term to mean contacts, communications, and exchanges between countries, governments, parties, political and social organizations, monopolies, and separate persons in the realms of economics, politics, ideology, military affairs, science, technical and cultural matters, and also various specialties. Since the preceding definition carries a structural character, it may be formulated into a system of indicators.

The opinion has been advanced above that the content of international relations is an exchange (of materials and information) and that the character of the exchange defines the form of international relations. It is not [therefore] surprising that it is urgently necessary to carry out an all-around study of the phenomenon of exchange itself. Studying capitalism, K. Marx brought forward and carefully analyzed the concepts of "trade," "money," and "cost," and on that basis drew a clear picture of the development of the capitalist economy of bourgeois society in general. In international relations, exchange is the same sort of major concept, a clearly formalized and structured definition that makes it possible to comprehend such relations correctly. Research has shown that the study of international relations, and all the more of its forecasting, is incomprehensible without an accounting and a deep knowledge of the principles of its development, and of the motivating forces that condition these principles. In other words, international relations, as a phenomenon of the superstructural order, is impossible to understand correctly without knowledge of the base upon which it rises, develops, and changes. The principles and the motivating forces in the present instance [i.e., forecasting] also stem from such a base. Marxist philosophy understands principles [in the sense of regularities] as the development of phenomena conditioned by laws, that is, the essentially necessary connections between phenomena. The concept of principles is close to the concept of a law, although it is not identical to it. In research endeavors, principles are often identified with law. Experience shows that such identification is easy and is not mistaken: a regularity always stands out as a form of the manifestation of a law. The concept of a law is close to that of essence, which is the totality of the profound (deep-rooted) bonds between those processes that define the most important parts and tendencies of the development of an object. The understanding of laws emerges through the understanding of such regularities and is (in fact) the transition from a phenomenon to its essence. This transition is always manifested by means of abstract thinking, by abstraction from a large number of individual and nonmaterial signs of the object.

There are three basic groups of laws, of regularities: (1) pan-general, or universal; (2) general; and (3) particular, or specific. The basic dialectical regularities of the world are related to universal laws and regularities, expressing ties between universal properties or tendencies in the development of the material. General laws and regularities are manifested rather broadly and reflect the connection between general properties of large totalities of objects and phenomena. Particular, specific laws and regularities express the connection between concrete phenomena and objects.

In the study of international relations, one most often deals with particular, specific regularities, and less often with general principles. As concerns universal principles, they play the role of constantly operating factors and need no special accounting in short- and medium-term forecasting. The process of coming to know the regularities of the development of international relations has special features of which the researcher must take account: there are not only objectively existing conditions but also such subjective elements as the activity of ruling groups, parties, and separate personages. This activity at times takes on a spontaneous, unpredictable character and in a definite period of time often appears to be of decisive influence on the development of relations between countries, groups of countries, parties, and so forth.

Despite these difficulties, the principles of international relations may be defined with rather great exactitude. We may take as an example the beginning of the growth of forces militating for peace and security among the peoples. There is also the principle of the gradual spread of socialism and the change in the relationship between the socialist and the capitalist worlds. Changes have not only taken place in the relations between the forces of socialism and capitalism but also within these forces. In past years, ruling groups of a number of capitalist countries have begun to come out against military adventures, for the broadening of cooperation [sotrudnichestvo] with socialist countries. In the relations between the Soviet Union and these countries, there has begun to enter into practice such forms of information exchange as political consultations, and this has turned out to be an essential aid to mutual understanding. Economic and scientific-technical ties have been significantly broadened and placed on a treaty basis.

At the same time, antagonism between the forces of social progress and the forces of reaction continued to survive as before and, as a consequence, conflicts periodically appeared.

IV. LEADING FORCES

It is not difficult to notice that each regularity is closely connected with definite material and social forces, the activity of which condition developments and changes in international relations. Regretfully, it is necessary to report that the fundamental theoretical research into these forces has still not been done, although the question has important practical significance. It is well known, for example, that the theoretical position concerning the motivating forces of the Russian Revolution, worked out by Lenin in 1905 and appearing in "Two Tactics of Social-Democracy in the Democratic Revolution," enabled the Bolsheviks to work out a correct strategy and tactics, first during the course of the bourgeois-democratic revolution [i.e., in 1905] and then during the Great October Socialist Revolution in 1917.

The motivating forces of international relations are always complex and contradictory. To define them, we start from the position that international relations is a subsystem of social relations, which enters as a constituent element into the system of production—the economic base—of social relations. At the basis of this system is production—the eternal natural condition of the life of mankind, the basis of all man's history. Production is organically and indissolubly connected with distribution, exchange, and consumption of what has been produced (as mentioned above, exchange is the content of international relations). Production possesses a social character and includes the relations between man and nature (reflected in the concept of productive forces) and between man and man (productive relations).

This brings out one of the main concepts of the Marxist science of society and reflects essential objective, material relations in any society, which are independent of the conscience of man. These relations emerge between men in the course of the production, exchange, and distribution of material goods. At the base of productive relations lies the relation between property and the means of production. Productive relations become a necessary constituent part of any mode of production: people are not able to produce without uniting through known forms for common activity and exchange through the results of their labor. The totality of productive relations makes up the economic structure, the economic base of society, and is the most important component of social relations.

The system indicated (production—economic base—social relations) is found in constant progressive development: under the influence of that process, which is termed scientific-technical progress, production is modernized; the economic base and the forms of property change; change takes place in social relations; and, finally social relations, and in the first instance productive—and hence international—relations, change.

So the classics of Marxism-Leninism demonstrate that at the base of all these changes lie processes stemming from production as a whole and the forces of production in particular. The forces of production stand out in this regard as the most active of the elements of production. Their modernization lies at the base of all historical development. The relation of man to nature is reflected in productive forces. In structural terms, they are the to-

tality and the unity of material subjects (the means of production) and man. The means of production create difficulties for man. The accumulated experience and knowledge of man materialize themselves in them. Mankind—as distinct from animals, which are satisfied for their needs with whatever is given to them by nature—produces by himself all his necessities of life. The constant growing of his demands and possibilities defines, in the last analysis, the development of the productive forces. The realization by man of his necessities (correctly or mistakenly) emerges as an interest. But mankind is not one. For many centuries he has [incorrectly] imagined himself to be a totality of most of his groups and classes. The latter differentiate themselves according to their place in the historically defined system of social production, according to their relations to the means of production, to their role in the social organization of labor, and to the distribution of its results (the social product). The existence of classes is connected with the historically defined means of production. In each sector of society, side by side with the essential classes defining the character of society, exist nonessential classes; these latter are connected either with the preservation of the remnants of the old means of production (in bourgeois society, the peasantry; in socialist society, the shallow private economy), or with the emergence of the new. The demands of classes, especially antagonistic classes, and consequently also interests, are different, and, within the same classes, are nonuniform, since classes themselves consist of social strata separate from one another. The sociohistorical activity of social strata and classes gives rise to different movements: national liberation, the workers, the youth movements, and so forth, which in the most general view emerge in the form of revolutionary, progressive, socialist forces, or reactionary forces.

In this manner, the analysis of the system of production—the economic base—of social relations permits us to enumerate such elements of the motivating forces of international relations [once again] as a subsystem of social relations, as (1) classes, (2) revolutionary, progressive, socialist, and reactionary forces, (3) necessities (or needs), and (4) interests. For forecasting international relations, the most significant, as stated, are the needs and interests of the ruling classes.

The understanding of the motivating forces and

of the principles of international relations provides us with an objective picture as to the historical path these relations will follow and what class interests will be. This understanding in turn enables us to work out a general strategy of foreign policy sufficiently exact to perceive its final goals and to evaluate the objective possibilities of its realization.

V. MEANS

This analysis of powerful changes in the international arena and of emerging conflicts demonstrates that all are the result not only of the development and the activity of the motivating forces, conditioned by definite principles, but also are the product of means, defining the sum total of factors. The study of the statistics and the dynamics of international relations provides a basis for looking at means, that is, factors, as causes, conditioning the content of international relations at a given moment and the path of its development in the near future. There is an especially close connection between such factors and the events occurring in the international arena. Therefore, it is not surprising that of the factors, most are studied under the rubric of conflict ("crisis situations"). The totality of factors, in essence, also comprises the forecasting background when investigating the perspectives for change in international relations.

Factor analysis, that is, viewing factors as reasons and consequences (actions) provides another important theoretical basis for understanding the development of international relations. It is known that the Marxist theory of knowledge presumes that cause and effect have an objective and general character. It also regards them as reciprocally tied and mutually dependent, and emphasizes that no phenomena occurs without a reason, that every cause has a consequence, and that a consequence in turn plays an active role, feeding back upon the cause. In this, Marxist theory emphasizes that the mutual action between cause and effect cannot be thought of as being out of touch with the concrete situation, and with concrete historical conditions.

Causes are of two types: (1) the full [or entire] cause; and (2) the specific cause. The full cause includes the entirety of all circumstances, under whose presence an effect necessarily follows. The appearance of a full cause is possible only in comparatively noncomplex conditions. In practice, scientific research, and especially forecasting, usually deals with specific causes, which we understand as a circumstance (a simple cause) or a number of circumstances (a complex cause), leading under definite conditions to an ensuing consequence. All this in full measure relates to means, that is, to factors that appear as simple phenomena (with one variable) or (much more often) as complex multifaceted phenomena. The more complex the factor, the more multifaceted its influence in international relations, and the more complex become the bonds between cause and effect. In the most general case, the mutual action of cause and effect often change places: if an effect appears in one guise, a cause may stand in the other.

This dialectical complexity has created and [continues to] create significant difficulties for working out applied meaning, and urgently needs a concretization of the general philosophical situation. Researchers working in the international relations field have done a lot by way of studying the principles of these relations, and also of means (instruments), with whose help those principles exist. But whenever researchers turn to concrete factors, they come up against serious difficulties.

It is well known, for instance, that the basic factor in international relations is the foreign policy of a government, which is the [basic] cause of the development of international relations and at the same time is the consequence of such factors as the type of productive relations existing in the given state, its class structure, the level of development of the economy and of military affairs, the geographic and demographic situation, ideology, and so forth. Each of these factors, in turn, is the consequence of other causes (factors): the level of economic development is defined by the stage of development of productive forces; the class structure by the type of social production; and so forth. In this evaluation, each factor takes on independent significance. As a result, foreign policy in one case deviates from the background, and in another turns into a self-sufficient subject of research.

It would appear to be worthwhile to begin one's research into factors by studying those that directly influence international relations, and to concentrate not on all but only on the most important and essential relations and dependencies. In this regard, one should adopt the view that factors possess both an objective and a subjective character, that is, one that is both constant and variable. For ease of research, we propose to divide them into political, economic, military-strategic, ideological and personality, and also geographic factors.

VI. MEANS (INSTRUMENTS)

The question of instruments, with whose help international relations are conducted, is the most well-studied sector of the field. By instruments are understood: diplomacy, economic levers, military power, foreign political propaganda, scientific and cultural exchange, tourism, and so forth. These instruments are studied for the most part as autonomous subjects of such disciplines as the history of diplomacy, world economy, military science, and others. These naturally facilitate the tasks of theoretical forecasts but do not solve them, since for forecasting what is important is not so much a detailed knowledge of these instruments individually as knowledge of the methodology of their utilization for attaining the strategic and tactical goals of the participants of international relations. The exact knowledge of the limits of possibility for utilizing these instruments, and conditions under which the greatest effect can be attained are of essential significance.

From what has been said above, it is apparent that the subject of the theory of forecasting of international relations is relatively complex. International relations is especially complicated in view of its many-sided and contradictory character, and also in view of its close connections with many social phenomena that are the subjects of research of such sciences as political economy, the theory of government and law, the history of international relations, the theory of international relations, and others. Such connections with intermingled sciences always enables [one to conduct] a mutually enriching, complex investigation.

At the same time, the process of differentiation of scientific knowledge poses problems of the methodological ordering especially sharply. In past years, the active invasion of the social sciences in general and of sociology in particular has taken place, utilizing such scientific instruments as mathematics, cybernetics, and semiotics. Without this, in the essence of the progressive process, it would be difficult to imagine the development of applied sociological, including socio-political, research.

The penetration of formal methods of knowledge into the social sciences is completely normal, since they provide the possibility to generalize the most varied material from the viewpoint of their contents, to uncover structural connections, and to operate on a more strict level of judgment. Appearing at a more recent stage in the development of knowledge, when researchers have begun to utilize categories of a rather high degree of abstraction, formal and, primarily, mathematical methods of most applications were first found in the exact sciences. Only thereafter did they spread to the social sciences.

The classics of Marxism are of enormous significance to mathematics and its methods. "For a dialectical, and hence a materialist, understanding of nature," wrote F. Engels, "an acquaintance with mathematics and natural science is necessary. Marx was thoroughly familiar with mathematics. . . ." (Marx and Engels, *Works* [in Russian], Vol. 20, pp. 10–11). He studied this science in particular and in his mathematical writings there are a significant number of interesting thoughts and conclusions.

Mathematical methods received high evaluation by a large number of Soviet scientists. The President of the Academy of Sciences of the USSR, M. V. Keldish, said:

> It seems to me that we are living through an epoch when mathematical methods are with impetuosity conquering all new fields of knowledge. Side by side with physics, the spirit of mathematical thinking is acquiring all the more significance in chemistry, biology, and geology, and broadly penetrates the social sciences, especially economics. (*Nedelya*, 1966, p. 8)

The question of the necessity of applying mathematical methods to sociology and to prognostics may be considered as solved in favor of mathematics.

Cybernetics is also thought to have exerted an influence on the methodology of forecasting of international relations, and, in its opinion, has already revolutionized and redirected social science methods and the methodological "style" of thought of social scientists. Cybernetics and the theory of forecasting of international relations have much in common: cybernetics studies complex, dynamic, self-directing systems—the subject of the theory of forecasting of international relations is a complex system of variable elements. It is for precisely this reason that the systems approach enters directly into the arsenal of the theory of forecasting. A number of useful methods may be taken from semiotics. With the help of the methods of semiotics, in particular, the structure of the concept "international relations" has been defined. But it is necessary to consider that the methods of mathematics, cybernetics, and semiotics used in forecasting should be strictly founded, circumscribed, and epistemologically defined.

The experience of Soviet forecasters testifies that the utilization of mathematical methods in forecasting international relations is far from attaining the unity of qualitative and quantitative analysis in every case. The methods of cybernetics also have their shortcomings in view of the fact that cybernetics deals with highly general and abstract concepts. The same can be said of the methods of semiotics.

The concrete nature of international relations calls for the most broad application of relevant methods of knowledge and, first of all, of the method of dialectical and historical materialism, the main principle of which is the principle of the concrete nature of truth. In these regards, such philosophical categories as content and form, cause and effect, the historical and the logical, of essence and appearance, regularity and accident, and possibility and actuality all play an important role. The experience of the development of the science of nature and society over many centuries demonstrates that no methodology of true knowlege (and forecasting without knowledge is nonsense) has ever existed beside and without philosophy. It cannot exist, since the problems of knowledge always enter into the competence of philosophy. At the base of Marxist philosophy lies dialectical and historical materialism, which also contains the theoretical and the general methodological base of the theory of social forecasting and, in particular, the forecasting of international relations.

The subject of the theory of forecasting of international relations, possessing an inexhaustible and many-sided nature, is found in constant developmental movement, and demands flexible and agile means for its cognition. Hence, broad applications in this field utilize such relevant approaches

to knowledge as analysis, hypothesis, induction, synthesis, deduction, analogy, modeling, and others. They are applied in a definite, mutually connected and mutually dependent manner (analysis and synthesis, induction and deduction, and so forth), although in separate stages of research first one, then another method comes forth, depending on the tasks that stand before the researcher.

V. I. Lenin emphasized that

> the most reliable thing in a question of social science, and one that is most necessary . . . is not to forget the underlying historical connection, to examine every question from the standpoint of how the given phenomenon arose in history and what were the principal stages in its development, and, from the standpoint of its development, to examine what it has become today. (Lenin, 1960–1970, p. 67 [Russian]; and p. 473 [English])

To this we can add: "and also, what it will become tomorrow."

But in order to give such an answer, it is still necessary to do very much.

We have shed light only in general on the general and special methodological groundwork for the construction of initial—and on its basis—explorative and normative models of the perspective for development of international relations. The details of systems analysis of international relations under the initial model, factor analysis of international relations under the explorative model, and the criteria for optimum international relations under the normative model deserve much attention. Also insufficiently worked out are theoretical questions of the limits of the utilization, for forecasting the development of international relations, of mathematical-statistical methods, and methods of modeling and the querying of experts. The question was posed of the utilization for forecasting of international relations of the survey of broad circles of the population. Finally, we conducted a special investigation into the details of the correlation between prediction and scientifically well-founded decisions in the field of international relations.

There is reason to suppose that the exchange of opinion on these questions will be of benefit to a more detailed working out of methodological problems of the theory of forecasting of international relations.

CHAPTER TWENTY-FIVE

FORECASTING IN CROSS-NATIONAL PERSPECTIVE: JAPAN

Yoshikazu Sakamoto & Hiroharu Seki

I. CULTURAL CONSTRAINTS[1]

Forecasting, though oriented to the future, is in one way or another based on information on our past experience. The question is how it is possible for us to envisage a future that will not be a repetition or a simple extension of the past.

There are three types of intellectual exercise that serve as a base for forecasting. First, one may be exposed to experiences that will reveal the future—experiences that will involve events that have clear and significant implications for what will happen. Sheer exposure to experience is sufficient to help visualize possible future developments. Through this experience, a "memory of the future" will emerge.

Second, one may take recourse to insights into and theoretical reasoning about events that are already known. A combination of imagination and qualitative, analytic power will lead to intuitive and inferential model building relevant to the future.

Third, one may establish correlations and causal relations by conducting rigorous analysis of the empirical data of the past, and build models through extrapolating these correlations and causal relations into the future.

Obviously, these three are by no means mutually exclusive. They are complementary, but of different nature. The intellectual exercise called forecasting, whether it is based on one or more of these three levels, is an art of selectively constructing images of the future. The cultural and intellectual heritage of Japan is characterized by the meagerness of such an art of intellectual construction. In fact, the art of forecasting, whether exploratory or normative, is conspicuous by its almost total absence in the history of ideas in Japan. This is due, at least, to the following three reasons.

First, humanist thinking is quite alien to the traditional ideas of Japan. The image of man exercising autonomous choice in designing and creating the future can hardly be found in the traditional culture, whether in the indigenous shamanistic notion or in such transplanted cultures as Buddhism and Confucianism. Harmony and reconciliation with the environment, natural or social, is the major theme of the Japanese cultural heritage.

Second, humanist, utopian thinking could have emerged when Japan embarked on "modernization" late in the nineteenth century by departing from the constraints of traditional ideas. For the modernizing Japan, however, future models were not something yet to be designed but either realities or future-oriented ideas that were already in existence in "Western" advanced countries including Germany and, at times, Russia. In that sense, the "future" was no longer the future. It was the past and the present. Accordingly, it is natural that not much effort was made to construct the image of the future.

Third, although there were, in the course of "modernization," some Japanese instances of forecasting designing future societies beyond the contemporary state of affairs in Western advanced societies, that effort was mostly characterized by its preoccupation with technological progress and left the fundamentals of the political and socio-economic system intact. There were recurring attempts to draw a picture of Japan, say, 50 years hence when industrialization, communication, and transportation had attained a high degree of development. But these exercises revealed the weakness in the imaginative power of the forecasters because they failed to comprehend the political and social implications of technological advancement. Moreover, most of the technological forecasts were surpassed later by the actual progress of science and technology.[2]

As a consequence of the combined effects of these intellectual and cultural traits, the predominant stand taken by the Japanese elite in their relations to international politics is, instead of freely choosing an independent future course of action, to follow the general trends in world affairs. Adaptations to international environment parallels reconciliation with natural environment.

II. THE REVEALED FUTURE

However, Japan's defeat in 1945 gave rise to a drastic change in the traditional concept and mentality. Among other changes, exposure to atomic bombs in Hiroshima and Nagasaki exerted a profound impact upon the Japanese image of the future and of international relations. The experience of atomic bombs served to stimulate the first type of intellectual exercise we referred to above. In other words, the exposure to atomic bombs indicated that the Japanese, much ahead of any other nation, had already witnessed the war of the future, that is, nuclear war. The impact of the experience of atomic bombs in 1945 was reinforced by an incident in 1954, when the United States conducted a test of hydrogen bombs in the Pacific area and a Japanese fisherman who had stayed out of the restricted danger zone was killed by radioactive fallout. In conjunction with this incident a large-scale popular movement spontaneously emerged and then grew into an international movement against nuclear bombs.

There have been several instances in the modern history of Japan when popular movements erupted over foreign policy issues. But the movement against nuclear bombs was unprecedented in the sense that it concerned not merely the national interest of Japan but also such universalistic value as the interest of the future of mankind.[3] Especially notable was the fact that there was little anti-Americanism in this movement. Opposition to nuclear weapons did not lead to opposition to the United States that dropped the bombs. One reason is that the Japanese, while deploring President Truman's decision to drop the bomb on Japan, thought that it was not so much the United States as Japan that was to blame for the outbreak of the war. A more important reason, however, concerns the future rather than the past. Many of the Japanese intuitively realized through national exposure to nuclear bombs that the nuclear weapon was a problem that unquestionably outweighed the conflict and resentment involving relations between particular sovereign states such as Japan and the United States. It was conceived as a problem that concerned the future of the sovereign state in general, not particular sovereign states. For the first time in modern history, the Japanese envisaged the future world much ahead of Western advanced nations.

Thus, one of the remarkable characteristics of postwar Japan, in comparison with the United States and USSR, was the fact that the view "there is no longer unconditional viability" and "there is no alternative to peace" was widely accepted by the general public as early as the end of 1940's.

This was illustrated by the enthusiastic support most of the Japanese gave to the "no-war clause" of the new Constitution. These reactions of the public contributed to creating favorable conditions to enhance the validity of forecasting made by Japanese intellectuals as to the future of international relations.

III. FORECAST ON COEXISTENCE

Against this background of popular intuitive understanding of the future of international relations in the nuclear age, and against the background of aggravating international tension that culminated in the Korean War, a group of approximately fifty Japanese intellectuals of various fields of specialization published, in 1949 and 1950, records of a series of symposia on the state of international relations in conjunction with the immediate issue of Japan's peace treaty. This group, the Peace Study Group (*Heiwa Mondai Danwakai*),[4] favored an "overall peace treaty" including East and West, a position in opposition to peace with Western countries alone, as espoused by the Japanese government. Their view was an outstanding example of forecasting in international relations based on those powers of insight, theoretical reasoning, and qualitative analysis that we referred to as the second type of intellectual exercise.

Noteworthy in their statement is the analysis of the trends in world politics that underlies their specific policy recommendations. Namely, it is the view that "peaceful coexistence" between East and West is possible. It may be recalled in this connection that, in 1950, neither East nor West subscribed with confidence to the principle of peaceful coexistence. In fact, there was a curious agreement between East and West in those days that, while short-term, tactical coexistence might be possible, long-range, strategic coexistence was almost inconceivable. The view of the Peace Study Group was exactly the opposite; that is, while short term, tactical conflict and confrontation might not be avoidable, long-range, strategic coexistence was quite possible.

The argument of this group was based on the following two propositions. First, there was no inevitability of war between the "two worlds." Second, there were favorable conditions for the promotion of coexistence of the "two worlds." In regard to the first, the group maintained that it was neces-sary to distinguish between three different connotations of the notion "two worlds." There were: (1) conflict between liberal democracy and communism as ideologies; (2) conflict between the bloc of West European states, with the United States and the United Kingdom as the nucleus, and the bloc of communist countries centering around the Soviet Union; and (3) conflict between the United States and the USSR. To be sure, these three are not unrelated. Nevertheless, the group stressed that it was imperative to keep the distinction in mind, since a confusion of different levels of the problem might lead to a false dichotomy that would leave no room for flexible disposition of practical issues.

Then the group pointed out that ideological conflict had not necessarily led to war between nations and, conversely, history listed many instances of war between countries upholding similar ideologies. Moreover, just as there were diverse forms of communist countries in the Eastern bloc, as illustrated by China and Yugoslavia, there was great ideological variety within the "free world," as exemplified by the United Kingdom, on the one hand, where major key industries were nationalized under the Labour Government, and the oligarchic regimes in Greece and Turkey, or the military dictatorship in many Latin American countries, on the other. Finally, major countries in the Eastern bloc and the Western bloc were not necessary opposed to one another with as much divergence and intensity as the antagonism between the United States and the Soviet Union.

Then the group went on to spell out the second proposition. First, precisely in the process of bipolarization of world politics there would be a rise of forces that would counteract the trend toward bipolarization. The recurrent move to form the "third force" was prominent particularly in Western Europe and Asia, and the desire for "nonalignment" was widespread among emerging nations. Among others, it was likely that China would take a more independent course than was commonly anticipated. These were, according to the group, manifestations of the general rule of politics that, as the power is dispersed and depolarized, there is a greater likelihood of a general equilibrium being attained.

Second, as a result of a prolonged Cold War, the political systems of both the United States and the Soviet Union would have to face a common danger.

For instance, the more intense their mutual antagonism would become, the more closely they would resemble each other by transforming themselves into "garrison-states." Since this would be a fatal blow to the opposing principles on which the two nations stood, a time would come when they would try to avoid this dilemma by reducing international tensions. Third, in the very course of reducing international tensions, the two systems would evolve toward increasing convergence, with American democracy introducing the principle of planning while Soviet communism would come to tolerate the growing scope of civil liberties. The increasing resemblance of the two systems would thus contribute to mitigating mutual distrust between the two countries.

The group stressed that they were under no illusion that the path to "peaceful coexistence" would be easy. They emphasized, however, the need to face the reality that there was no alternative to coexistence. This sober normative realism stemmed from (1) the insight, based on the experience of nuclear bombs, that nuclear war could never serve as a means to attain political ends; (2) the recognition that forecasting, including that of "peaceful coexistence," would perform the function of a self-fulfilling prophecy; and (3) the awareness that if the prophecy of doom should be fulfilled, there would be left no room for a repeated trial once an error was committed.

This group's international relations forecast proved valid in light of developments during the following decade, particularly as concerns the growing East-West consensus on the feasibility of "peaceful coexistence." It may also be noted in this connection that, while similar forecasting might have been made in those days in other parts of the world, the group published its view in 1950 when Japan was still under the Allied occupation and the group had very limited access to information on the development of international relations as perceived by intellectuals abroad.

In 1952, the Japanese government took the course of signing a peace treaty with the West, excluding the Eastern camp, and concluding an alliance with the United States. Yet, as an effective alternative for Japan's foreign policy, the group's views continued strongly to influence the mass media and public opinion. In 1960, there was a great debate in Japan on whether she should continue the alliance with the United States. Many of the intellectual leaders put forward a counter-proposal to the government position by arguing that Japan should take initiatives for reducing the tensions and therefore terminate, in due course, the alliance with the United States. This was essentially an application of the group's thesis to Asian international relations of the 1960's. The validity of this view on the possibility of "peaceful coexistence" in the East Asian context was to be demonstrated later by détente between the United States and China, and subsequently between Japan and China.

In sum, the group's forecasting on the "peaceful coexistence" turned out to be remarkably valid. It also exerted great influence over Japanese popular movements relating to foreign policy issues. The group's forecasting was based on a penetrating reading of the implications of the Hiroshima experience for the future world, and on perceptive, qualitative analysis of the structure and dynamics of the Cold War interactions. The output was a forecast of a high degree of validity.

IV. DEMISE OF FUTUROLOGY

In 1960, the popular movement seeking neutralization of Japan in light of the anticipated feasibility of peaceful coexistence and tension reduction led to the cancellation of President Eisenhower's visit to Japan and eventually to the fall of the cabinet even though popular pressure failed to end the United States-Japan alliance. In response to this neutralist intellectual current, a school of intellectual leaders called the "realist" school came to the fore around the mid-1960's. Since the "realist" school was characterized by the acceptance of the existing general pattern of international relations, and therefore by the lack of enthusiasm in the exploration of alternative futures, it showed little interest in developing positive designs or explicit forecasts concerning the future of international relations. But it had its own version of a forecast that served as implicit assumptions of its argument. First, it foresaw that the Cold War between the United States and USSR, and particularly between the United States and China in the Asian context, would not come to an end in the foreseeable future; that there was little Japan could do to mitigate international tensions; and that it served the interest of Japan to stay under the umbrella of the Cold War strategy of the United States. Second, it foresaw that, while depending strategically on the United States, Japan would be able to continue a high rate of economic growth for a long time to come. In short, the "realist" school anticipated a high degree of growth and prosperity within the framework of the United States-Japan alliance. It was a combination of surprise-free political statics on the international level and the economic dynamics of linear progress on the domestic level.

Since this school of thought stood on the premise that these two conditions would remain compatible, it failed to foresee the following four possible developments. First, it tended to underrate the danger of economic conflict between Japan and the United States that was likely to arise as a result of Japan's growth. Second, it failed to foretell the possibility of United States-China rapprochement, since it presupposed prolonged East-West Cold War in Asia. Third, it failed to anticipate in advance the mounting friction between Japan and other smaller Asian nations that were exposed to the danger of Japan's economic invasion. Fourth, it failed to foresee a serious conflict that could well arise between a high rate of economic growth and ecological balance, and between major industries and the local population in Japan whose health was affected by pollution.

Unfortunately, the introduction of futurology in Japan was promoted in the 1960's by those who had an unsophisticated belief in the myth of continuously high growth, measured in terms of GNP. Furthermore, the Japanese government, by setting "EXPO '70" as a national goal, encouraged the popular belief in economic growth for the very purpose of depoliticizing the general public, who in 1960 had been so involved in foreign policy issues. Thus, the future of Japan tended to be equated with a linear projection of rapid growth of economy and technology, and with a rosy anticipation of the advent of postindustrial Japan in the near future.

It is a reflection of this general current of thinking that in April, 1970, Japan acted as the host of the International Future Research Conference. But the time of this conference also marked a significant turning point in the development of public opinion in Japan. For instance, an international group of eminent economists such as W. W. Leontiev had met in Tokyo a month before to discuss ecological questions and issued a statement alerting the public to the danger of environmental disrup-

tion. Nevertheless, it is amazing that none of the papers prepared by the Japanese participants for the International Future Research Conference squarely dealt with the ecological problem. This is a good illustration of the extent to which futures research in Japan was then affected by ungirded optimism concerning the implications of economic growth.

April, 1970 indicated both the apex of this type of futurology and the beginning of its end. During the following year the eyes of the public were turned to pollution that was cumulatively affecting Japanese society day by day. Widespread distrust was therefore directed to the futurology that did little to alert the public to environmental issues. Futurology tended, now pejoratively, to be identified with the projection of economic growth and technological progress. Even the well-publicized "Plans for Restructuring the Japanese Archipelago" put forward in 1972 by Prime Minister Tanaka, which appeared to be a remedy for the side effects of economic growth by calling for decentralization of industrial development, was essentially an extension of the philosophy of growth (Tanaka, 1973).

Since 1972 Japan has witnessed, in addition to ever aggravating ecological crisis, increasing economic and political frictions with the United States, détente in Asia promoted by Sino-United States rapprochement, mounting Asian resentment to Japanese economic expansion, and rapidly growing awareness of the shortage of natural resources, including food, whose import was the crucial precondition for the growth of Japan's economy. It has thus become increasingly clear that the value and purpose of the two fundamental premises of the policy of the government, as well as the view of the "realist" schools, have to be questioned. That is, both the United States-Japanese alliance created during the Cold War period and continuation of high rates of economic growth have to be subject to close scrutiny, individually and in combination. The hyper-optimistic view of the future that prevailed in the past decade has made a dramatic turn into a hyper-pessimistic image of the future of Japanese society. The explosive boom in 1973 of science fiction by Sakyo Komatsu dealing with the "submersion of the Japanese archipelago" is an indication of the depressed mood of the public.[5]

Despite their sharp contrast, hyper-optimism and hyper-pessimism in regard to the future of Japan have in common the tendency to conceive the future as if it were a process of natural development. In hyper-optimism, the high rate of economic growth is viewed as a process of immutable natural growth. In hyper-pessimism, doom is viewed as a chain of natural phenomena such as the physical "submersion of the Japanese archipelago." It is not hard to detect that the Japanese intellectual heritage still hinders the development of the art of designing a humanistic, voluntaristic image of the future.

V. CONTINUING SEARCH

Because of the unfortunate initial identification of futurology with the preoccupation with economic growth, future research has failed to gain credibility in the eyes of many intellectuals in Japan. But this is not all that has been undertaken under the name of forecasting. Many of the mistakes committed by "futurology" were due to the uncritical acceptance of assumptions, the oversimplification in designing models, and the inadequate use of research methodology. In regard to forecasting Japan's economy, for instance, much more sophisticated econometrical techniques of model building and simulation have been developed. But there are not many examples of forecasting in international relations.

One example, however, is an inter-nation man-computer simulation conducted in 1969 by Seki with the collaboration of Sakamoto, Mushkoji, and others (Seki, 1970, pp. 181–239). The purpose of simulation was to identify the process of international tension reduction in Asia if that should develop in the simulated world. Besides, this simulation was intended to make a model less removed from reality. Accordingly, the model was more complex than the internation simulation designed by Harold Guetzkow. Furthermore, the students who played the role of decision makers had gone through a 3-month period of training to acquire information on the history of their respective countries so that they could also perform the role-taking function incorporated into the simulation game. The simulation consisting of twelve nations concerned with the future of the international system in Asia, with the two Koreas, the two Vietnams, and Taiwan treated as independent actors. West Europe was reduced to the United Kingdom and France; Latin American and African countries were not included in the model. There were secretaries-general of three international organizations, one universal, one for developed countries, and one for developing nations. Approximately 100 students participated in the simulation for two days. Since this was such a large-scale simulation only an interim report has been prepared. While the model was less removed from reality, variables became so numerous that it was not easy to put them within a manageable analytical framework.

The second example is a computer simulation conducted in 1969 by Isamu Miyazaki and Takashi Nakanomyo on the economic relations between the developed and developing countries in Asia (1970). Interest focused on how a change in international political conditions would affect the economic growth of developing countries. The following four cases are taken into consideration: (1) when the political situation remains unchanged; (2) when relaxation of international tensions takes place and developed countries are given priority to allocate saved resources for their own development; (3) when international tensions are eased and developed countries increase their assistance to developing countries; (4) when international tensions increase. Changes in the international political situation are operationalized in terms of changes in the amount of military expenditure and foreign aid. Based on these assumptions, a projection was made of the economic development of individual nations for the period 1965–1990, using a relatively simple model of economic growth. Despite many limitations and shortcomings, this simulation served to identify general trends, problems and opportunities involved in the changing international political climate and in the changing pattern of interaction between the developed and developing countries.

More recently, particularly in the wake of the oil crisis in the fall of 1973, a number of computer simulation models have been built to forecast the future supply and demand of natural resources and energy. While most of them concern economic and technological variables, a highly elaborate model designed by the Institute of Energy Economics incorporates political as well as techno-economic variables, such as a varying degree of restrictions on oil productions imposed by Arab countries for political reasons.[6]

Another attempt to include political variables was a system dynamics model applied by Akira

Onoshi to an analysis of the relationship between Japan's aid to Indonesia and anti-Japanese sentiment in Indonesia over the period 1966–1969. His model's forecast suggested that as long as structural variables—such as the disparities between privileged classes including the advantaged overseas Chinese on one hand and Indonesia's general populace on the other, or between the "modern" sector and the "traditional" sector—remained unaltered, anti-Japanese sentiment would grow regardless of possible increase in aid. This model was also intended to present a workable prescription for preventing unmanageable conflict in the future (Onoshi, 1974, pp. 206–230).

The normative implication of forecasting, as contained in these examples, is more pronounced in the research project undertaken by the Japanese subgroup of the Club of Rome. A simulation conducted under the direction of Yoichi Kaya on "Optimal Models of World Production," while it resembled *The Limits to Growth* in that both were aimed to be forecasts on the future world, was primarily concerned with a normative question— what is to be done in order to optimize the world production, giving priority to accelerated economic growth of less developed countries while reasonably restraining the growth of world gross product. In its paper presented to a Club of Rome symposium in Tokyo, October, 1973, Kaya's team suggested that, if optimal investment was made, that would generate "an unmistakable tendency that the ratio of food production in North America and Oceania to their gross regional product will increase, while that in Asia, including China, will decrease. In the latter area the ratio of light industry production to its gross regional product will constantly increase" (Kaya, *et al.*, 1974, p. 112).

Another research team in the Japanese subgroup of the Club of Rome pointed out, "while such models as have been developed in *The Limits to Growth* have a certain degree of usefulness in identifying and clarifying the problems, they are of little use in working out solutions or transition steps to solution. . . . Even for the purpose of identifying problems, future work has to be done on those problems that are not subject to quantifications" (Kishida, *et al.*, 1973, pp. 137ff). Among those problems is that of the heterogeneity of world society, which includes differences in historical and cultural conditions. And the team recognized the

value of *The Limits to Growth* primarily for its contribution to sensitizing the public opinion to the need for new ideas and philosophy concerning the future of mankind.

In sum, there are three notable features in the forecasting in Japan on international relations. First, while it may be said that forecasting in international relations in general remains in its infancy, this is particularly true of forecasting in Japan. Unlike the United States where simulation for forecasting has been developed as a predictive and prescriptive tool of strategic studies as well as economic analysis, Japan has been characterized by the predominance of specialists in economics and engineering as the intellectual purveyors of systematic forecasting. This has given rise to the problem that most of the models for forecasting do not readily lend themselves to forecasts in the area of international politics. Second, methods and techniques used by Japanese forecasters in international relations were almost invariably adopted with some revisions from the work of their counterparts in the United States and Western Europe. In other words, very few cumulative achievements have been registered through intranational interactions and cooperation among Japanese forecasters.

Finally, modest as their contributions have been so far, Japanese forecasters can be credited, as the examples cited above indicate, primarily with their original formulation of relevant problems and perspectives rather than methodologies. While traditional socio-cultural heritage hampered forecasting, socio-cultural conditions newly emerged in postwar Japan appear to serve as a source of intellectual inventiveness in designing the model of relevant futures.

NOTES

1. We see the value of this section on "Forecasting in Cross-National Perspective" not primarily for the information it might provide on the methods of forecasting used in countries other than the United States, because methods used are or will become more or less similar among forecasters in different countries or methods may vary within a country as much as, or even more than, among countries. Our paper will be devoted mainly to provide some ideas on the sociology of knowledge as applied to forecasting, dealing with

the question of socio-cultural preconditions for future research and forecasting.

2. This is exemplified by "Japan, A Hundred Years Hence," a special spring issue, 1920, of the then well-known journal *Japan and the Japanese (Nihon oyobi Nihonjin)* of which the editor-in-chief was Setsurei Miyake. This issue is a collection of forecasts he solicited from 463 leading intellectuals of Japan at that time, which include professors, educators, journalists, scientists, artists, writers, religious leaders, business executives, generals, and admirals. This special issue has been reproduced in book form with an introductory note by Hidetoshi Kato who observed, "Particularly intriguing is the fact that the forecasts in the area of science and technology were fairly accurate and most of them have been fulfilled in less than fifty years thenceforth" (1966, p. 28).

3. The First World Congress for Banning Nuclear Bombs, with the participation of approximately 5,000 delegates from all over Japan as well as from abroad, was convened in Hiroshima in August 1955. It adopted the "Hiroshima Appeal" that said: "If an atomic war should break out in the future, the world as a whole will be turned into Hiroshima, Nagasaki and the Bikini atoll, and the future generation will be exterminated. . . . We appeal to the people of every nation of the world to join and reinforce this movement against the nuclear bomb regardless of difference in political affiliation, religion and social system" (Hiroshima Association, 1969, pp. 367–368).

4. This Peace Study Group issued three statements successively; first, in 1949, on the problem of war and world peace, in connection with the statement issued in 1948 by eight scholars (G. W. Allport, G. Gurvitch, M. Horkheimer, *et al.*) under the auspices of UNESCO; then, in March, 1950, on the issue of Japan's peace treaty. The third and the longest, published in the December issue of the monthly journal *The World* (Sekai) (Tokyo: Iwanami Shoten) under the title of "On Peace for the Third Time," dealt extensively with the fundamental problems of war and peace in the contemporary world and provided a compelling rationale for the two preceding statements. The discussion draft of the third statement was prepared mainly by Masao Maruyama, Shigeto Tsuru, and Ikutaro Shimizu. Our following analysis of this group's view will draw on the third statement.

5. Komatsu (1973). This quasi-eschatological fiction depicts the last days of Japan that is to be submerged under the ocean due to a series of extraordinary earthquakes. This book, which topped the best sellers in 1973, sold like wildfire and achieved a circulation of 1.5 million volumes in 10 months.

6. *Interim Report of the Research Committee on Overall Energy* (Sogo Enerugi Chosakai Sogo Bukai Chukan Torimatome) and its *Reference Material* (Sanko Shiryo), Agency of National Resources and Energy (Shigen Enerugi Cho), July 25, 1974.

CHAPTER TWENTY-SIX

THE CASTE FACTOR IN SOCIAL FORECASTING: PREDICTABILITY AS A BRAHMINIC AND BOURGEOIS VALUE

Ali A. Mazrui

Predictability can be both a phenomenon and a value. In both guises it is linked to stratification systems. This is partly because the more stable a system is, the more reliable are our expectations concerning its behavior. Stability serves those who benefit from the *status quo;* but stability also serves the social forecaster by reducing the range of conceivable alternative patterns. The social forecaster finds himself sharing a vested interest with Brahminic and bourgeois beneficiaries of the *status quo.*[1]

We propose to demonstrate in this paper that the international system of stratification has the rigidity of a caste system. To that extent the white industrial nations are more like Brahmins than bourgeoisie. But to the extent that the concerns of these nations globally, and certainly in their relations with the Third World, are often capitalistic, the developed states also perform international

bourgeois functions. We might therefore look upon international stratification as a system that combines the rigidity of a caste system with the ethics of a capitalist system. International stability serves both parts of the mixture. And the global elite become a class of bourgeois Brahmins. For ease of calculation, the social forecaster shares with them a vested interest in stabilized and predictable continuities.

Yet the stability we have is that of the global system. By contrast, almost each country in the Third World is in the throes of either active, imminent, or latent instability within its own borders. We have then the paradox of a stable international system combined with acute internal dislocations in individual Third World countries.

Our illustrations in this analysis will come primarily from Africa, but the theoretical and analytical scope of the chapter is wider than that. It proposes to look at the interplay between social rigidity and societal instability in relation to problems of prediction. This is what the caste factor in social forecasting is all about.

I. CASTE AND CLASS IN INTERNATIONAL RELATIONS

Within individual societies a caste system has four major defining characteristics. The first is *heredity*, by which membership of a caste is determined by hereditary descent. The second characteristic is that of *separation*, a principle that keeps different castes exclusive from each other in social arrangements. Contact between the castes socially is minimized and intermarriage strongly discouraged if not prohibited. The third defining characteristic in domestic caste systems is *division of labor*, by which caste, either in reality or by historical definition, is associated with a particular profession or occupation. And fourthly, there is the principle of *hierarchy*, determining who is above whom in rank and status within the society.[2]

What emerges strongly from these characteristics is the element of rigidity within caste systems. And a rigid system should therefore be significantly more predictable than a flexible one. One would therefore have thought that in the whole science of forecasting, caste systems provide relatively happy arenas for accuracy.

But rigidity is not the same thing as stability. There are rigid systems that, because of that very inflexibility, are vulnerable to a sudden revolutionary upheaval. Edmund Burke was substantially right when he argued that a system entirely without means for its own reform is basically without means of its own preservation. Some responsiveness to urgent intimations for change is required if a social system is to be spared periodic ruptures.

What gives caste its stability is to some extent a tautology—it is the sanction of primordial custom over a substantial period of time. In other words, the survival of the system is partly strengthened by its prior survival, as well as by a certain degree of responsiveness to changing circumstances.

A. L. Kroeber has even seen caste as a special stage in the evolution and consolidation of classes. Kroeber enumerates the characteristics of endogamy, heredity, and relative rank, and then goes on to argue in the following terms:

Castes, therefore, are a special form of social classes, which in tendency at least are present in every society. Castes differ from social classes, however, in that they have emerged into social consciousness to the point that custom and law attempt their rigid and permanent separation from one another. Social classes are the generic soil from which caste systems have at various times and places independently grown up. (Kroeber, 1930, pp. 254b–257a)

But clearly for a class system to rigidify into a caste system special circumstances have to emerge. Preeminent among the conditions would be a special motivation by the upper castes to move in the direction of elite-closure. Another condition is the readiness of the lower castes to accept a stratification system that is so sanctioned by custom. The major difference between a class system and a caste system remains the difference in degree of social mobility. It is the endogamy and heredity within the caste system that drastically reduce, and in some cases eliminate, mobility.

But are the two concepts of caste and class applicable also to the international system? Certainly class analysis has already been applied to international relations. The division of the world between the "haves" and the "have-nots" has captured the attention of scholars and political practitioners alike. Many have portrayed that division as one of the most important issues in the last third of the twentieth century. The whole concept of a Third World is rooted in proletarian ideas. Asia, Africa, and Latin America have increasingly come to see themselves as proletarian or underprivileged continents, struggling against the power and influence of Europe and North America. The United Nations Conference on Trade and Development has increasingly become an arena reminiscent of collective bargaining between labor unions and management. The Third World is out to negotiate for better working conditions and better returns for production at the door of the global employment agency.

The nonalignment movement has also increasingly shifted its emphasis from Cold War issues to issues of economic confrontation between the developing and developed world. The movement in the days when it was dominated by Nehru of India, Nasser of Egypt, Nkrumah of Ghana, and Tito of Yugoslavia, was a movement eager to avoid entanglement in the ideological and military issues that divided the West from the communist world. Nonalignment was, at its minimum, a refusal to be tied to a military alliance with one of the major powers.

But gradually nonalignment developed into a broader concept of autonomy and the right to experiment, a reaffirmation by small powers that they were entitled to an independent say in world affairs. Issues of trade and the utilization of world resources were still substantially outside the nonalignment movement as such.

The first major economic factor to enter the movement was the issue of foreign aid. A doctrine of balanced benefaction emerged, by which it was assumed that relative independence for poor countries lay in diversifying their benefactors. A country that was heavily dependent on the United States was less autonomous than a country that managed to get foreign aid both from the United States and the Soviet Union. Nonalignment became an exercise in balanced dependency—an assumption that a client with more than one patron was freer than a uni-patronized dependent.

But by the time the nonaligned countries were assembling in Algiers in the summer of 1973 a major shift had taken place. Nonalignment was now concerned with more than just keeping out of military alliances or getting the most in foreign aid from Western and communist countries. The conconcerns of the nonaligned movement now encompassed not only issues that were previously handled only by UNCTAD but also a newly discovered capacity to use the natural resources of the poor countries as political and economic weapons against the affluent sectors of the world.

The British term "trade unionism" began to make better sense in the international domain than in domestic arrangements. What was at stake in the international domain was indeed trade, in the sense of exchanging goods on a commercial basis. The old meaning of "trade," in the sense of an occupation or skill, had been overtaken by events. Unionism within individual countries was indeed, as the Americans call it, a movement of *labor* unions. But the new unionism of the new Third World, as it has sought to use its resources for purposes of extracting economic and political concessions from the developed world, is more fittingly *trade* unionism.

And yet the very fact that Third World countries are poor and underprivileged creates legitimate comparison with domestic proletarian movements. Class analysis becomes relevant, and class interests become internationalized.

But where lies the relevance of the concept of *caste* in the international system? If Kroeber is correct in saying caste is a special stage in the consolidation of social classes, and if the issue of comparative social mobility is what ultimately differentiates caste from class, we have to examine the international system from the point of view of relative rigidity.

A simple analysis in terms of per capita income would give us at least the appearance that the international system is a class system. Where growth does occur, and per capita income rises, we might get the impression that the system permits substantial social mobility. Countries move up from much lower levels either of gross national product or of per capita income. The flexibility is reminiscent more of a class system than of a caste structure.

But the question arises whether the international system is indeed that flexible. Social mobility does not mean merely improving the lot of the poorer sections of a particular society; it must also mean the possibility of the poorest improving their position in relation to the richest. Even if the gap between the developed world and the developing countries were to remain constant, while each part of the world was at the same time improving the standards of living of its inhabitants, the situation would still not be one in which social mobility had taken place. What is at stake once again is relative deprivation—the poor must not only be earning a little more than they used to earn before; they must also have reduced the gap in income between themselves and those who are wealthier. If the gap is maintained, the sense of deprivation continues. If the gap is widened the sense of deprivation could be aggravated.

To the extent that the gap between the richer countries of the world is widening rather than narrowing, it can be argued that the international system lacks the kind of social mobility necessary to make it a class system rather than a caste structure. The rich are getting richer and, on the whole, the poor are getting less poor—but the rate of rising affluence in the United States, the Soviet Union,

Western Europe, and Japan is faster than the rate of diminishing poverty in the Third World.

If the international system was, in the first half of the twentieth century a class system, it is now moving in the direction of rigidity. We may be witnessing the consolidation and sanctification of a global caste structure.

At least to that extent, there is some latitude for relatively self-confident forecasting. The rigid stratification system that is emerging permits the stargazers to predict self-perpetuating inequalities on the world scene.

But just as there are hereditary factors in domestic castes, so there are hereditary elements in international castes. Preeminent among those factors is the issue of *race*. The most affluent societies in the world are overwhelmingly of European racial extraction. The poorest countries in the world are overwhelmingly black and African in racial extraction. Certainly those countries categorized as the poorest by the United Nations are disproportionately situated in the African continent. If people of European extraction are the Brahmins of the international caste system, the black people belong disproportionately to the caste of the Untouchables. Between the highest international caste and the lowest are other ranks and estates. There are non-white people that are honorary white men. So far these are limited to the Japanese, who do enjoy the status of honorary Caucasians in the Republic of South Africa.

There are also honorary colored people. These include white sections of Latin America. The population of Latin America is indeed a mixture consisting of European, Amerindian, Africa, and other strands. But on the whole the dominant elites of Latin America are of European extraction. To the extent that Latin America forms part of the Third World, and has shared the humiliation of being exploited and dominated by her northern neighbor, the United States, even white Latin Americans must be regarded as in some sense honorary colored people. They have shared with colored people the experience of indigence and indignity. The Latin Americans provide a foil to the Japanese. After all, the Japanese have shared with white people historically the arrogance of power, racism, and dominion of others.

The ambiguous situation of Japan and Latin America make the international caste system somewhat complex. But the main outlines are certainly there. There is an element of race in the global stratification system, and it provides a functional equivalent to heredity in domestic caste.

As for the characteristic of *separation* in the social domain that we attributed to domestic caste, the equivalent of this internationally is the imbalance in mobility as between developed and developing societies. By far the most mobile people in the world are Americans, Europeans, and the Japanese. A system of mobility that is not symmetrical creates a special kind of separation. The master can enter the hut of his slave at any time, if only to remind him of his obligation to work; but the slave has no automatic access to the house of the master. American soldiers may roam around Southeast Asia; German tourists may descend on East Africa; Japanese businessmen may conclude deals in the Middle East and Brazil. But in relative terms the flow of traffic is one way. And even when Algerians are permitted into France, or West Indians into Britain and Canada, the roles they play in the developed societies are often those that would not be touched by Frenchmen, Englishmen, or Canadians; The Third World immigrants perform "untouchable" functions.

Yet another characteristic of caste is division of labor. Again the international system betrays the characteristics of such division. There are aspects of specialization in production that are rooted in geographical conditions. Geographical conditions are themselves basically inflexible and certainly no more flexible than heredity in domestic arrangements. The sharpest factor in the global division of labor is that which separates countries heavily dependent on primary products, on the one hand, from countries that are industrialized on the other. For the time being a country whose entire economy rests on one or two agricultural products confronts hazardous fluctuations. In spite of recent shortages in certain kinds of food products in the world market, Third World countries are still engaged in an uphill struggle. There has been some improvement in the prospects for primary products in the last few years, but the improvement is not likely to be dramatic enough to transform the overall economic performance of the countries concerned. Some of these are already involved in serious attempts to diversify their economies, both in terms of producing a greater variety of primary products and in terms of inaugurating the process of serious industrialization. However, for the time being the rigidity persists in this aspect of the international caste system.

Both domestically and internationally division of labor is also connected with *hierarchy*. In some ways this is the most serious problem in human terms about caste as a social phenomenon.

But here a fundamental distinction does need to be made between a horizontal division of labor and a hierarchical division of labor. A horizontal division is one that is basically between equals. The equals may be either all underdeveloped or all developed. But the division of enterprise between them does not contain inherent disadvantage of a continuing kind to one party. Nor does it involve a relationship of submissiveness and inequity.

On the other hand, a hierarchical division of labor, when it is rigid, is the kind that leads to a caste structure. Sentencing the countries of the tropics to a life of primary production indefinitely, while the northern hemisphere continues along the path of industrial and postindustrial development, would amount to a hierarchical division of labor. Certainly the old partnership in the imperial order, of producers of raw materials in the colonies and manufacturers in the metropolitan powers amount, in terms of real disparities between the two sides, to a hierarchical order.[3]

It is because the international system shares these characteristics of heredity, separation, division of labor, and hierarchy, that the system is for the time being more like a caste structure with its rigidities than like a class system with potential social mobility. The international system is in this respect eminently congenial to the still incoherent science of forecasting.

But there is a complicating factor for that science. While the global stratification system is itself both rigid and relatively stable, the stratification systems in individual countries in the Third World, especially in Africa, are under pressure. Indeed, in a number of countries within the African continent, social classes are fluid. Domestic social mobility can be very rapid both upwards and downwards. Men rise fast to the commanding heights of the economy—and then come tumbling down with the latest political upheaval. While an individual country's prospects in the global system may be fairly accurately predictable, the precise fortunes of

its leaders or of its domestic, social, and economic system could be far from responsive to precise prior calculation. Domestic instability is thus combined with international rigidity. The science of forecasting is up against a strange and historic paradox.

Let us now look more closely at the implications of this paradox for the African states and societies.

II. THE BLACKS AND THE BRAHMINS

Of the three continents of the Third World—Asia, Africa, and Latin America—it is preeminently Africa that has most often been treated as the equivalent of a lower caste. The racial factor is particularly important in this regard.

The caste school of race relations has so far done its most penetrating analysis on the southern states of the United States, rather than in Africa itself. But the important links between caste and class have a wider validity.

We mentioned Kroeber's idea linking caste with class on a continuum. On the other hand, Lloyd Warner, in a famous article in 1936, argued that while whites and blacks in the United States made up two castes, each group in turn was stratified internally into classes. The blacks of the upper class were thus superior from the point of view of class to the poor whites, while at the same time being inferior to them from the point of view of caste (Warner, 1936, pp. 234–37).

In this article and in subsequent work, Lloyd Warner intimated a strong resemblance between the American system of race stratification and the Indian caste system. In the southern states of America the disabilities under which the blacks labored, the difficulty for them to "pass," the strong disapproval of either marriage or commensality between whites and blacks, all provided legitimate grounds for equating race relations in the American South with caste relations in India. "Therefore, for the comparative sociologist and social anthropologist there are forms of behavior which must have the same term applied to them" (Warner and Davis, 1939, p. 233).

Gunnar Myrdal also argues that "caste may thus in a sense be viewed as an extreme form of absolutely rigid class" and in the United States caste therefore constituted "a harsh deviation from the ordinary American social structure and the American Creed" (Myrdal, 1944, p. 675). "The scientifically important difference between the terms 'caste' and 'class' as we are using them is, from this point of view, *a relatively large difference in freedom of movement between groups* (Myrdal, p. 688; the emphasis is original).

The American caste system has in fact been disintegrating since Gunnar Myrdal wrote this classic, but the overall global position of the black people as a lower caste has not as yet fundamentally changed. Racial disabilities are by definition disabilities bequeathed by heredity. Separation between racial castes continues by a residual distrust of racial mixture, the relative isolation of sub-Saharan Africa from the main stream of international affairs, and the drastic imbalance in popular mobility as between the peoples of the northern hemisphere of the world and the black races south of the Sahara.

Division of labor imposes on much of the African peoples a life as "hewers of wood and drawers of water." As we indicated, the majority of the poorest nations of the world are in fact within Africa. Many of the economies are based on monoculture. As for the principle of hierarchy, that itself emerges from the economic and technological disabilities sustained by the black peoples under the cruel marching boots of history.

The unkindest cut of all are the white enclaves in Southern Africa. Within the very continent of the black races, a few hundred thousand whites in Rhodesia have so far reduced to military impotence millions of Africans not only in Rhodesia itself but also, before the 1970's, in several other black states of the continent. Technological and organizational superiority, when enjoyed either by the Israelis in the Middle East or the white Rhodesians in Southern Africa, can keep millions of technologically less sophisticated races at bay in spite of all their anger and sense of injustice.

But such situations are characterized by a latent instability. In fact, one might here distinguish between active instability, imminent instability, and latent instability. Active instability is characterized by rapid changes and severe political uncertainty. Prediction in such a situation is particularly difficult. Institutions arise and collapse, leaders emerge and are then submerged, policies fluctuate. The Congo (Zaire) was engulfed in severe active instability in the first 4 years of its independence.

Imminent instability, on the other hand, arises when one is expecting change and turbulence at any time, and yet no such change or disruption takes place. Many black African countries have an air of imminent instability even when the regime apparently in power appears to be in full control. The instability is imminent when one is not surprised upon hearing about a military coup or a similar upheaval from one day to the next, and yet the air of stability continues nevertheless. For the forecaster, such a situation is caught between the assurance of continuity and the imminence of sudden change. Will General Amin of Uganda remain in power for a few more years or will he be overthrown next week? The General has certainly lasted in power much longer than most people expected. He could conceivably be more durable than that. And yet to the extent that one would not be surprised if he were overthrown tomorrow, Uganda for the time being continues to have an air of imminent, though not active, instability.

The third kind of instability is latent instability. At first glance this looks very similar to imminent instability, and yet there are fundamental differences. While one would not be surprised if General Amin were overthrown next week, one would indeed be surprised if the apartheid system of South Africa crumbled next week. In the case of Amin, the instability is imminent to the extent that it could happen almost any time, even if it does not happen for quite a long time; but in the case of the South African racial system the instability is latent, and could be delayed for many years, and yet inherently within the system are the seeds of its own destruction.

Similarly in the Middle East, if no peace settlement is reached shortly, one could say that Israel's regional supremacy has a latent instability, while peace in the area is characterized by imminent instability. Israeli military supremacy hinges on organization and technological sophistication. But the sophistication of the Arabs in the skills of war may also increase in time and thus narrow the gap between them and the Israelis sufficiently to make Arab numerical preponderance at least relevant. The Arabs, man to man, need never catch up with the Israelis in military sophistication. All they need to do is to narrow the difference between them and Israelis sufficiently to make the vastly superior numbers of the Arab population capable of making a difference in combat.

In South Africa the difference will come partly out of a potentially widening demographic gap between whites and non-whites to the advantage of the latter; partly also because of growing political consciousness among important sectors of the black population; partly further because of potentially enhanced organizational sophistication among the non-whites in the country, and finally because of greater dependence by white industries on black labor at higher levels of skills than was previously the case. The convergence of these four factors could in time tip the scale in South Africa and convert latent instability at long last into active instability. If that were to happen, change in the direction of greater black power should indeed be well and truly underway.

An ethnic caste system in which the oppressed are a minority, as in the United States, could change into a more flexible class system without extensive violence and disruption. But an ethnic caste system like that of South Africa in which the white Brahmin class is a minority, defensively protecting its privileges against an oppressed majority, could not easily transform the caste structure into a system of adequate social mobility without violence and destruction.

Again in this case the forecaster partly has to rely on *precedent* as a basis of predicting the future. Here it is worth distinguishing between colonial systems and racial systems within Africa. The British and the French had colonial systems, and later withdrew from at least some aspects of their relationship with their former dependencies. Decolonization in the sense of withdrawal of a distant colonial power has therefore been proved feasible in Africa without resort to violence. But deracialization in the sense of ending a white minority government in a situation where the white government does not rely on the metropolitan power for survival, has so far not been accomplished nonviolently. There is for the time being no precedent of a beleaguered white community, isolated in power in a former colony, being willing to give up that power without violent struggle. What we have is the entirely different experience of colonial re-

gimes withdrawing to their metropole without violence. A number of the former British colonies and the former French colonies obtained their independence without using methods that were contrary to the spirit of passive resistance.

Even in the case of Algeria and Kenya we do not have an illustration of white settlers surrendering their power to Africans. Both Algeria and Kenya were instances of the colonial government being no longer willing to support the white settlers in maintaining themselves in power. The Algerians won their independence when De Gaulle withdrew the French commitment to the *status quo*, and gradually recalled the French army back to France. The local white Algerians were themselves furious and felt betrayed. They would never have given Algeria to Algerians if they had had the power to refuse.

Similarly, the Kenya settlers would not themselves have granted independence to black Africans but for the fact that the British government in London was no longer prepared to maintain a white settler regime in Nairobi. On the basis of these precedents, the forecaster might feel confident enough to predict that the situation in South Africa and Rhodesia would not change without a violent explosion. That explosion would end many decades of latent instability.

The case of the Portuguese colonies is somewhat different. These are indeed part of the colonial system, rather than a racial system in the South African sense. Nevertheless while no racial system in the South African sense can ever be overthrown without violence, there are also colonial systems that can only be ended in a similar manner. Not all colonial systems are responsive to Gandhian techniques. Angola and Mozambique were more like Kenya and Algeria than they are like either Nigeria or the Republic of South Africa. When Lisbon gave up the struggle to maintain the colonial system, the local white settlers in the Portuguese colonies could not successfully repeat the Rhodesian performance.

There was active instability in certain parts of the Portuguese colonies as areas changed hands back and forth between the Portuguese army and the African guerrilla fighters. The first part of the white dominated section of Africa to collapse was the Portuguese colonies. When Guinea-Bissau declared its own independence in western Africa, Portuguese colonialism in that small territory was doomed.

This fate extended to the position of the Portuguese in Angola and Mozambique before long. The only white Brahmins left in Africa were thus the white regimes of South Africa and Rhodesia, each trying to keep the latent instability of its system from finally erupting into fatal activism.

III. STABILITY AS A BOURGEOIS VALUE

But what about stratification within the black African states? Class structures in black nations at the present stage of their history are subject to substantial modifications imminently.

Africa approached independence with considerable evidence that it was evolving a power elite based on education. Some societies elsewhere may have evolved an oligarchy based on birth and ascription, as indeed some African societies have done. Other societies may have developed oligarchical systems based on wealth differentials, with the rich exercising power because they were rich. What seemed to be happening in Africa was the emergence of a class assuming critical areas of influence and prestige because it had acquired the skills of modern education.

The elite started by being, in part, the bureaucratic elite—as major positions in the civil service were rapidly Africanized. Among the criteria for such Africanization was indeed modern Western education. The emergence of an educated bureaucratic elite was accompanied by a slightly less educated political elite. The triumph of anticolonial movements had thrust leaders into the forefront of affairs—leaders who would not have attained such preeminence but for at least some basic exposure to modern schools. Indeed, many of the modern leaders, and certainly a high proportion of the politicians, were drawn from the schools where they had previously served as teachers. The modern educational system had served as a recruiting ground, and surrendered some of its own pioneer African teachers to politics as a new profession.[4]

But meanwhile Africa's new armed forces had been recruiting from the rural and less educated sections of the population. At the time the recruitments started no one had been astute enough

to forecast the power of the military in African affairs. On the contrary, many political scientists, while claiming adherence to a discipline that aspires to predict future trends, nevertheless got Africa all wrong. One Western political scientist after another discussed the great potential of political parties in Africa, and almost totally ignored the armed forces as a factor in their calculations. Some political scientists even went as far as to dismiss the armed forces of Africa explicitly as being too small to cause a real challenge to the principle of civilian supremacy in politics. James S. Coleman asserted at the time that "Except for the Sudan, none of the [sub-Saharan] African states has an army capable of exerting a political role. . . ." Coleman allowed "that the army could become a political force of increasing and perhaps decisive importance in certain countries," but the three countries he cited in this connection were South Africa, Rhodesia, and Ethiopia (Almond and Coleman, 1960, pp. 313–314).

James Coleman was among the most perceptive of all academic writers about Africa at the time, and yet even someone like him could miscalculate. Coleman was also an illustration of those who saw in political parties major media of societal transformation in Africa. Events have proved both predictions wrong. Political parties almost everywhere in Africa have turned out to be paper tigers, while the armed forces have truly emerged as effective panthers.

But precisely because the military has become a major factor in politics, the stratification system has become fluid. One army coup might favor this group; another might open doors to ethnic communities previously peripheral. In some African countries the educated class has at last been cut down to size, and a Lumpen militariat has assumed control.

For the international system, new problems arise precisely because of these fluctuations. Stability, which is so often congenial to social forecasting, is at the same time profoundly bourgeois as a value. At any rate it is a value most favored by those who have already arrived. Calls for unity in any individual society are at their most earnest when they come from those who are satisfied with the *status quo*.

In the international system those who have already arrived might not mind a certain degree of instability among the less privileged, provided the global system as a whole is left relatively undisturbed.

In fact, the world of international relations generally is dominated in its norms by the values of the middle classes and the international intelligentsia. International law itself was a product of the thinking of European middle and upper classes on how diplomacy was to be conducted and relations between states organized and controlled. There are subtleties and refinements in embassies throughout the world, and in the corridors of international organizations, which are distant from some of the bluntness and relative spontaneity of truly rural societies.

Problems arise when individual countries find themselves with a peasant for head of government. The peasants in all countries of the world are among the least sensitized to international issues. They are often the most obstinately parochial in their view of the universe. And because of that, the whole phenomenon of relations between states has remained something shaped, organized, and controlled by the values of the middle and upper classes and their respective intellectual wings.

Idi Amin, like Nikita Khrushchev before him, has brought to the refined diplomatic world of the middle and upper classes the rustic embarrassment of inadequate inhibition. Like Russia's Nikita Khrushchev in the 1950's and early 1960's, Idi Amin is today a peasant bull in the china shop of diplomatic history.

Among the middle classes one needs to have one's social arrangements fairly predictable. Appointments need to be made, and visits are often by invitation except among truly close friends or relatives. But in peasant areas one could visit even casual friends without being invited. The necessity of an invitation is a quest for stabilized social relations among middle and upper classes. Amin came into power, and proceeded to treat diplomatic visits not on the basis of bourgeois values of international diplomacy, but in relation to the more flexible and less predictable ways of rustic casualness. Israel, Britain, and France had claimed to be friends of his regime at the beginning. He visited each of these primarily at his own initiative. He also visited the German Federal Republic with the casualness of one peasant knocking on the door of his rural acquaintance. Of course, in reality arrangements had to be made in advance to receive the President of Uganda, security had to be ensured, major diplomatic banquets had to be held. The refinements of European diplomacy, so dominant in the world as a whole today, had to be extended to this visiting rural dignitary from Uganda. But the spontaneity of going there without invitation had all the bearings of the cumulative rural socialization that Amin and his kind often manifest without thinking. To that extent their casualness disturbs the canons of predictability within the refined societies.

Then there are the other surprises that Amin is capable of flinging into the international arena, ranging from the expulsion of Uganda Asians at relatively short notice to the detention of American Peace Corps volunteers.

Peasants do not normally send telegrams to each other. Amin has learned to use this particular medium, but with some rustic bluntness. And his messages have ranged from wishing Richard Nixon a quick recovery from the Watergate scandal to a reaffirmation of deep, and even dramatic affection, for Julius Nyerere, "though your hair is gray." Some of these tendencies are personal to Amin rather than to his social origins. But the very fact that he lets his personal tendencies have such free play while occupying the top office of his nation might have been influenced by the relative spontaneity of rural upbringing among the Kakwa.[5]

If Idi Amin has been a peasant ruler in charge of a relatively small developing country, Nikita Khrushchev was a peasant ruler in charge of a super power, the Soviet Union. Like Amin, Khrushchev offended the canons of refined predictability. Khrushchev basically held the initiative in international relations during most of his period in office, making surprise moves, exasperating the West, and giving the Soviet Union an image of revolutionary dynamism.

The most striking feature of West-East relations during the Fifties and early Sixties is the fact that throughout the whole period the initiative remained with the Soviet Union. The Soviet leaders pursued a dynamic policy even in unfavorable conditions; they initiated new moves, unleashed crises, published ultimatums, if necessary made sudden concessions even when the situation on the domestic front or within the Communist camp was far from stable. Western statesmen by contrast seemed lackadaisical, even lethargic; sometimes they reacted with vigor to Soviet moves, but seldom took any major initiative. (Lacqueur, 1972, p. 406)

The crises during this period ranged from Hungary and Suez in 1956 to the U2 incident in May 1960.

Khrushchev's style also offended the refined tastes of the West. He was capable of shouting loudly at another head of government or of taking off his shoe and banging it on the table at the United Nations. Like Amin he was capable of threatening the firing squad against dissenting intellectuals and students. And like Amin, Khrushchev was despised by many intellectuals in his own society, as well as abroad. "Among the intelligentsia there was a great deal of contempt for the leader who was regarded as little better than an uneducated, uncouth *mushik* . . ." (Lacqueur, p. 494).

And then the Cuban missile crisis came to pass. Eyeball to eyeball, Khrushchev and Kennedy confronted each other. The world hovered over the brink of nuclear war. Yet that peasant in charge of a super power was capable of seeing when to shrink from the brink. With astute statesmanship, Nikita Khrushchev capitulated to John F. Kennedy's challenge, promised to remove the missiles from Cuba, moved toward establishing a hot line between Washington and Moscow, and began at least to respect the canon of refined predictability of international diplomacy.

In some respects, the Cuban missile crisis was the beginning of the embourgeoisement of the Soviet Union. Khrushchev was later replaced. His successors, though in some cases descended from origins as humble as Khrushchev's, were by now bureaucrats rather than rural folk in style and temperament. The Soviet Union relinquished some of the dynamic capacity for surprising initiatives that Khrushchev had brought into the role of the socialist super power. The Soviet Union became internationally more predictable, more stable—more congenial to the science of forecasting the country's own moves. The caste factor had once again intruded to influence issues of predictability.

IV. SUMMARY

We have sought to demonstrate in this chapter that the degree to which social and political events are capable of being predicted is partly a function of caste and class. A system of rigid stratification need not always be stable. Its very rigidity could at times spell out its own doom. But there are occasions when the caste structure appears to be assured of maintaining itself for a long time to come.

We have argued that the international system of stratification is more like a caste structure than a class structure. There is considerable rigidity in the factors that determine which countries are poor and which more affluent. The burden of relative deprivation is likely to weigh heavily on the human race for quite awhile to come. The poor may get less poor, but the rich will also get considerably richer and a gap between the two could continue to widen. The international system of stratification therefore shows little sign of adequate social mobility for the peoples of the Third World. A few of those who are regarded among the more affluent may experience downward social mobility, as their economic systems decay. But those who are at the bottom of the international hierarchy are unlikely to penetrate very far into the more elevated reaches of privilege.

Africa is clearly part of the lowest caste in the international hierarchy. It has a preponderance of the least developed and poorest countries. To the extent that sub-Saharan Africa is a black region, there is also caste in the racial sense, involving generations of degradation and the continuing insult of an apartheid system within the African continent itself.

Within South Africa itself we have argued that the system has latent instability. It may be secure for one, two, or more decades, but the nature of the stratification system, and the prospects for demographic and economic change conspire to spell out a sentence of long-term doom to the system.

Within the black states of Africa there is either active instability, in the sense of turbulent changes taking place already, or imminent instability in the sense that any political disruption in any particular week would not surprise anybody *if* it occurred.

The class system within individual African societies is at the moment in a state of fluidity, as institutions arise and collapse, and leaders ascend and then disappear in a cloud of gunsmoke. Peasants stand a chance of easing out of power established aristocracies overnight. And peasant styles of diplomacy could proceed to alarm or amuse the bourgeois of world leadership.

What needs to be ultimately grasped by the science of forecasting is that while domestic stratification in individual African societies is so fluid, Africa's place at the bottom of the international hierarchy threatens to be rigid. A system of inflexible global stratification, combined with domestic instability in Third World countries, poses unique problems to the task of comprehensive social forecasting. The domestic instability bedevils the arts of prediction; the rigid international system facilitates the predictive endeavor.

But underlying our whole analysis is the simple proposition that predictability is not merely a phenomenon, it is also a value. The value of predictability presupposes stable conditions. Trends have to be capable of sustaining themselves. The *status quo* has to yield indicators for the future. To the extent that the *value* of predictability is coextensive with the value of stability, there is a profound Brahminic and bourgeois commitment involved in it all. Those who control the *status quo*, and try to make conditions constant, at once serve the forecaster and betray humanity.

This is the moral predicament of social forecasting that has to be constantly borne in mind. The task has to be undertaken, and even to predict the immutability of the international stratification system is to play to the gallery of those who have a vested interest in the *status quo*.

This chapter has attempted to exaggerate certain tensions, but in order to define the problem of caste, class, and privilege in the whole phenomenon of social prediction and moral anticipation.

NOTES

1. Although in other contexts I have distinguished between prediction and forecasting, in this chapter I shall use the two words almost interchangeably. An earlier paper of mine that drew a sharp distinction between the two was "Political Science and Political Futurology: Problems of Prediction," paper presented at the Annual Social Science Conference of the Universities of Eastern Africa, held at Makerere University, Kampala, in December, 1968.
2. Consult Celestin Bouglé, *Essais sur le régime des castes*, p. 4; English translation of the introduction in *Contributions to Indian Sociology* II, 1958. See Louis Dumont, *Homo Hierarchicus: The Caste System and Its Implications* (1972), pp. 57–58.
3. These issues are discussed in a related context in Mazrui, *A World Federation of Cultures: An African Perspective* (1974).
4. This issue is discussed in a related context in Ali A. Mazrui, "The Lumpen Proletariat and the Lumpen Militariat: African Soldiers As A New Political Class," *Political Studies* (United Kingdom) Vol. XXI, (March, 1973) No. 1.
5. This point is discussed in similar terms in Ali A. Mazrui, "Ethnic Stratification and the Military-Agrarian Complex: The Uganda Case," paper written for presentation at the Nineth Meeting of the Social Science Conference of the Universities of East Africa, Dar es Salaam, December, 1973, and at the Sixteenth Meeting of the Canadian-African Studies Association, Halifax, Nova Scotia, February-March, 1974.

CHAPTER TWENTY-SEVEN

CHANGING FRAMEWORKS OF INTERNATIONAL COLLECTIVE BEHAVIOR: ON THE COMPLEMENTARITY OF CONTRADICTORY TENDENCIES

John Gerard Ruggie

I. INTRODUCTION

Rousseau may not have been correct at the time when he wrote that the states of Europe "touch each other at so many points that no one of them can move without giving a jar to all the rest" (Waltz, 1959, p. 183), but students and practition-

This chapter is part of a larger set of "Studies on International Scientific and Technological Regimes," conducted at the Institute of International Studies, University of California at Berkeley. For comments on earlier versions of the argument, I want to thank Jonathan Aronson, Peter Cowhey, Ernst Haas, Robert Keohane, David Laitin, Henry Nau, Joseph Nye, Robert Pendley, Mary Ruggie, and Kenneth Waltz. I am also grateful to the Transnational Relations versus National Control Colloquium at Berkeley for having given me the opportunity to try out some of the thoughts elaborated below.

ers of international relations feel increasingly that his description *is* correct today—and not just for Europe but for the entire global community as well. Increasingly, we are coming to be seized by what appear to be the virtually inescapable symbols of our times: scarcities, shortages, finiteness, interdependence. Increasingly, we are looking to their institutional counterparts, the many international conferences and collective arrangements on population, food, energy, monetary relations, the environment, the seabed, and others, as indicators of political things to come: either a new world order or none.[1] And in our quest for certainty and simplicity in the face of extreme complexity, we have begun to believe in what amounts to an intellectual conspiracy theory: that all of today's "crises" are somehow interconnected—the single "crisis of crisis," or "crisis of interdependence," or "crisis of transformation," as it has been variously described.[2]

One projected outcome for the conduct of international relations is a greater degree of collectivization in the determination of the shape of the future, for better or for worse. This projection entails not only the belief that the *problematique* manifested in the current situation is one of interdependence, but also that coordinated, collaborative, collective behavior and institutional arrangements may be the only effective response to the *problematique* (cf. Kissinger, 1974, pp. 573–583; Reston, 1974). As Secretary Kissinger depicted the problem, "Our interdependence will make us thrive together or decline together. We can drift or we can decide" ("Excerpts From Kissinger's Paris Talks," 1975). And deciding, he made it clear, means creating "a structure of international cooperation," whose purpose would be nothing less than to exercise deliberate, self-conscious collective governance: "We must not regard necessity as capricious nor leave change to chance" ("Excerpts from Kissinger's Paris Talks," 1975).

Thus, the current world situation is viewed by some as historically unique. Indeed, the increase in interdependence and the emergence of "central guidance" in international politics have been interpreted as signifying the end of the very state system within which international politics has been acted out since 1648 (Falk, 1975a, pp. 969–1021 and 1971b). However, while this view is increasingly prevalent, it is by no means the only one. Its mirror image claims adherents who are no less acute in perception and offers evidence that seems just as compelling: national interdependence is challenged as a myth (Waltz, 1970, pp. 205–223); projects stressing independence accompany and outrank interdependence strategies (for a good discussion of the interplay between the two, see Nau, 1975, pp. 426–439); economic nationalism is rising to counter the transnational forces of market rationality;[3] the Third World rejects the international "structure of dependence" and opts for self-sufficiency as a model of development (see "The Cocoyoc Declaration," in Ruggie and Haas, 1975); and manifestations of "central guidance," such as the Law of the Sea Conference, barely avoid paralysis while national jurisdictions increase unilaterally and by international agreement (cf. Shap-ley, 1975, p. 918). From these illustrations it would seem that, if ours is an historical turning point, it is one at which history is forgetting to turn!

It is not my purpose here to argue that the particulars of these interpretations are right or wrong. For the purposes of the present volume the more important issue lies elsewhere. The issue raised by this debate about the current world situation is *whether, to what extent, and in what direction the international political order is changing.* I can think of no more central a problem to address in the context of forecasting in international relations. For if the international political order, the *framework* that holds international relations together, is changing, then forecasts about any particular component, problem, or trend in international relations must be modified accordingly. Thus, the issue I want to address in this chapter concerns the character and extent of long-term trends in the international political order.

Let me state my position at the outset. Below, I make a substantive and a methodological argument. Substantively, I argue what the above illustrations have already suggested: that the literature on the so-called crisis of interdependence generally foresees one of two long-term trends emerging in the international political order. The first is a tendency toward *holism*, said to result from mankind's increased impact on, exploitation of, and control over the physical environment. The second is a tendency toward *fragmentation*, said to result from an increase in the number and diversity of political claimants and a shift in the scope and character of public authority domestically. Illustrative examples of both tendencies are presented, not so much to "test" or "verify" either perspective (a task well beyond the scope of this chapter) as to more fully sketch out the trends and scenarios both project.

Methodologically, I raise the questions "What if both projections were to be equally accurate? How would one go about reconciling what are self-evidently contradictory tendencies?" My response to these questions is as follows. In my judgment, the two perspectives on the consequences of interdependence are manifestations of age-old competing views on the character of international order—one view stressing unity and the other anarchy as basic organizing principles. Traditionally, any perceived contradiction between the two has been resolved in favor of one or the other or in a new synthesis. I argue and seek to demonstrate that the relation between such opposites in the contemporary international political order is *not* one of resolution but of continued contradiction. Yet this contradiction, I contend, exhibits complementarity. By complementarity I do not mean to imply the harmony or some "ultimate" identity between contraries. I mean it in the sense that *both* opposites are inseparably and systematically accommodated at all times. It is this complementarity, I conclude, that most effectively captures emerging tendencies in the international political order.

For illustrations of both tendencies and evidence of their complementarity I look to international arrangements that have been constructed collectively by states since World War II in the attempt to come to grips with growing environmental impact and control. In the conclusion I come back to the current debate and assess it from the perspective developed in this essay. Before proceeding with this line of attack, it is necessary to spell out in some detail what I mean by the term "international political order," and how it constitutes "frameworks" of international collective behavior.

II. STRUCTURE, REGIME, AND POLICY IN THE INTERNATIONAL POLITICAL ORDER

In this discussion, "political order" indicates the principles upon which the right, competency, and ability to make collective decisions are based and the boundaries within which those decisions are held valid. That is, the concept of political order refers to the parameters and perimeters of collective choice. The international political order, then, consists of the manner in which and the range of issues over which the "community of nations" exercises collective choice. The principal actors in the international political order are national public authorities—referred to as "the state" when acting in unison, or identified separately when not. The principal basis of relations among such public authorities internationally is voluntaristic, in that no "objective" obligations exist. The principal determinants of collective choice are the international distribution of objectives and capabilities, and the constraints imposed on them. And the principal

axis of ordering relations among these actors is horizontal, in that there exist organization and authority *among* them but not above them. Any particular substantive order of relations, whether military, economic, technological, or whatever, is produced by these general principles being worked out in a particular substantive domain.

The international political order may be thought of as constituting "frameworks" of international collective behavior. By frameworks I mean patterns of institutionalization that coordinate and channel collective behavior in one direction as against all others that are theoretically and empirically possible. For purposes of analysis, one may distinguish among at least three levels of abstraction, and, thus, three sets of such frameworks: the very structure of the international political order; the regimes that are constructed within the international political order; and the policies that are enacted within international regimes.

In the discipline of international relations, the concept of *structure* has meant everything from institutions, recurrent patterns of behavior, distribution of power, to things that don't change very quickly. I will follow the standard definition of the structuralist literature: Structures are the source of the relations an observer observes, the laws governing the association and transformation of the constituent elements of a system.[4] So defined, the structure of the international political order is its "self-help" or "self-organizing" character. This structure has the consequence of making the distribution of capabilities among nations, rather than some other factor, the most basic determinant of international outcomes (Waltz, 1975; on the general characteristics of self-organizing systems, see Von Foerster and Zopf, Jr., 1971). A change in structure, then, would result in the precedence of different determinants of international outcomes. Among the possibilities traditionally considered are "objective" standards of rights and obligations, universalistic movements such as international communism, and integrated polities.[5]

Change of this sort does not appear to be frequent. "The texture of international relations remains highly constant," Kenneth Waltz has written, and prevailing relations "do not shift rapidly in type or quality" (Waltz, 1975). Generally speaking, integration, the precedence of law over political considerations, and deference to the authority of collectivities are the exceptions that attract attention, not the rule. Generally speaking, Waltz is right, in that the *self*-organizing propensities of actors are the usual bases of ordering relations.

There exist, however, other sorts of changes in the parameters and perimeters of collective choice and behavior that *do* make a difference in terms of the type and quality of prevailing international relations, and that also constitute frameworks of international collective behavior. One of these is at the level of abstraction we might call international *regimes:* institutionalized codes of conduct, mutual expectations, and collective plans, in accordance with which behavior is ordered and organizational efforts and funds allocated (a more elaborate explication of this concept is developed in Ruggie, 1975). It makes a difference, for example, whether states manage security relations by means of a system of competitive alliances, through a concert of Great Powers, or by a collective security arrangement; whether the collective management of monetary relations is exercised on the basis of international commodity reserves or by means of jointly created paper reserves; whether the collective management of nuclear technology is pursued by means of multilateral safeguards applicable to entire domestic nuclear industries or bilaterally and applicable only to those materials acquired through international assistance; and so forth. Each of these collective arrangements may be said to constitute a framework of collective behavior in the sense that each specifies and institutionalizes certain rules of international conduct for a given set of actors. What is more, these frameworks differ considerably in the parameters and perimeters of collective choice that they exhibit. With respect to parameters, collective security arrangements, jointly created paper reserves, and multilateral safeguards entail greater agreement on joint purposes and greater constraints on unilateral volition than the other arrangements mentioned. As for perimeters, an international safeguarding system applicable to entire domestic industries, for instance, marks a considerable expansion over one applicable only to those particular materials received through international assistance.

Since changes in regimes may well be commensurate with continuity in the basic structure of the international political order, we will want to differentiate between the two levels. Hence, I distinguish between the structural level and the level of institutionalized collective behavior or regimes. Change or continuity over time in the frameworks imposed on international relations by regimes may be plotted by comparing entire configurations of regimes both in terms of their functional and geographic scope and in terms of the degree to which and the manner in which they express agreement on joint purposes and constraints on unilateral volition.

There exists yet a third level at which it is possible to speak of frameworks of international collective behavior, that of international *policy.* Policy, too, constitutes a framework of action in that it specifies how the scarce resources of actors are employed by organizations and agencies in the pursuit of collective objectives. Whether a collective policy exists in a given domain, and how it was formulated, are both consequential for the type and quality of prevailing international relations. Thus, it matters which combination of whose resources are to be employed; whether the formulation of policy is dominated by ideological cleavages, by "rational" calculation based on the best available knowledge, or by *quid pro quo* bargaining; whether actors consider policies in isolation of one another or in policy bundles; whether new, nongovernmental, intergovernmental, or subnational actors are brought into the policy-making process; and so forth. Each of these possibilities constitutes a framework in that each delimits an interrelated set of actions and processes. At the same time, each of these also potentially constitutes a *different* framework, by involving different actors in the policy process, by applying different criteria to the formulation of policy, and by potentially producing very different policy outcomes.

In sum, there exist at least three meanings that the concept "framework" may assume in the context of the international political order: the structure of the international political order, configurations of international regimes, and international policy. The three levels, and the indicators by means of which one may assess change or continuity, are summarized in Table 27.1. The three levels vary in terms of how "deep" versus how

Table 27.1 The international political order.

Frameworks	Indicators of Change or Continuity
Structure	The "laws" of association and transformation among the constituent units of the international political order
Regimes	The functional and geographic scope of institutionalized collective behavior
	The degree to which and the manner in which agreement on joint purposes is expressed in and unilateral volition is constrained by institutionalized collective behavior
Policy	Issues on policy agenda
	The characteristics of the actors who are involved in the policy process
	The criteria on the basis of which policy is formulated

"concrete" they are, but each may appropriately be studied as a framework depending upon the purposes at hand. For reasons that need no elaboration, it is crucial to specify which level is being discussed when attempting to demonstrate change or continuity.

But matters are more complicated than keeping categories distinct, for students of international change have assumed at least two types of relations among these three levels. First, changes in one or in two of these levels are often used as indirect indicators of changes in the third. To cite an illustration, in his classic study of *Renaissance Diplomacy*, Garrett Mattingly observes the policies of princes in granting access to foreign emissaries, and the legal regimes of diplomatic immunities and privileges which evolved during the Renaissance, in the attempt to discern whether the basic structure of the international political order was changing. He found that the right of embassy was ceasing to be a function of social hierarchies irrespective of nationality and was becoming an attribute of

sovereignty. And he found that, whereas ambassadors could once be tried for certain crimes by the prince to whom they were accredited because that prince would try them on the basis of a universal body of law, the municipal law of each realm was beginning to take precedence and the theory of extraterritoriality was invented. Therefore, he concludes that the basic structure of the international political order was indeed changing—the modern states systems was coming to replace the Holy Roman Empire. In this structural change, formal institutions changed less than their signification, and less than the vision of society and the objects of policy from which they assumed their signification (Mattingly, 1955; see also Bryce, 1906.)[6]

Similarly, in his pioneering analysis of processes that may tend *Beyond the Nation-States*, Ernst Haas (1964) sought indicators for basic international structural change in national responses to a body of international policy. These examples raise the obvious question of how much change at one level is commensurate with continuity on another—a question of indicators, thresholds, sound judgment, and reasonable definition.

An even more complicated relation among these three levels is what we might (loosely) term "the hierarchy of causality."[7] It makes sense to argue that the structure of the international political order "causes" different kinds of regime configurations in that, once structure varies, types of regimes may become possible that are entirely different from those that existed before. The same may be argued about the relation between regimes and policy. That much is clear. It is less clear, however, how, if at all, the reverse works. Is there a certain quantum of change in policy (content or style of formulation) that "causes" a new regime to emerge; or in sets of regimes that "cause" a change in structure? Waltz, for one, would maintain that the hierarchy from structure to regime to policy clearly dominates in international relations (Waltz, 1975); neofunctionalists predicate their work on the assumption that the reverse too is possible.[8] Whatever the case, it must be remembered that this "hierarchy of causality" represents an *existential* not a *logical* condition, and that it is, therefore, subject to change.[9]

The concept of international political order and the three levels of frameworks constitute the focus of my discussion, as indicated at the outset. The above formulation by no means exhausts the range of possibility, but the general notions have been sufficiently disaggregated to allow us to proceed.[10] I turn, therefore, to an exposition of the two long-term trends identified in the introduction: that toward holism in and that forward fragmentation of the international political order.

III. ON HOLISM: TRENDS AND SCENARIOS

Diplomatic historians and political scientists have paid much more attention to the military uses of science and technology than to their nonmilitary applications and consequences. The reasons for this are easy to discern: the issue of war or peace is a recurrent and pressing one in human affairs; military technology has traditionally been associated with "high" politics—that is, with issues considered more important and more dramatic than the bases of material existence; and, more often than not, new technologies are developed first for military purposes and only subsequently find their way to civilian use.

Economic historians, on the other hand, as well as students of the so-called post industrial society, have written extensively about the relations between social organization, and modes of thought, material setting, and physical and social technologies.[11] One dominant theme about future social organization emerges from their works: there exists an irresistible tendency toward holism, communalism, or central guidance, brought on by mankind's increased impact on and control of its physical environment. Indications of this tendency are depicted on at least three levels of social reality: (1) the *cognitive*—the conceptions, metaphors, and symbolic templates on the basis of which humans organize thoughts, attitudes, and ideologies; (2) the *material*—the physical and natural setting within which human activities take place and upon which human existence depends; and (3) the *institutional*—the social-organizational arrangements and techniques through which humans act and by means of which we govern ourselves.

Below, I reconstruct some characteristic arguments as briefly but with as much fidelity as possible, and I provide some illustrative cases to more effectively sketch out what these arguments imply.

Cognitive Changes

One sort of cognitive change discussed in this literature is the potential for unhitching existing cognitive ties from the particularistic ideologies and political beliefs that now bound human vision. Two major bodies of thought concern themselves with this potential. On the one hand, there exists the belief that the methodology of science, the basis of mankind's control over the physical environment, is objective, self-correcting, and therefore equally applicable in any sort of cultural, political, or physical setting. As cause/effect relations governing the physical environment come to be even better understood, so the argument goes, questions that were previously decided on the basis of emotive or narrow normative criteria can be decided on the basis of scientific knowledge. In this scheme of things, science and technology, facilitating agreement on cause and effect, promote agreement on the ends and means of policy. Thus, science and technology, being universals, transcend particularistic ideologies and interests, and make them obsolete. International collective choice, based on objective knowledge of the laws of nature, becomes depoliticized and holistic (for a critical examination, see Haas, 1975). On the other hand, there exists a somewhat less benign interpretation of science and technology as universals—but the presumed consequence for the international political order is identical. This is the view of science and technology as representing the reduction of an increasing diversity of phenomena to instrumental rationality. Instrumental rationality, in turn, is taken to represent the increasing tyranny of means and impotence of ends. The laws of *technique* become determinative, and technique is self-augmenting, holistic, universal and autonomous. Ideologies and beliefs are not so much eliminated as they are rendered irrelevant by the "integral causality" and irreversibly collectivistic tendencies of technique.[12]

A second sort of cognitive change would go well beyond unhitching existing ties to include suggesting or even imposing new organizing metaphors on intellectual life. Presumably such organizing metaphors would come to be expressed in new patterns of social behavior too. One historical case frequently cited as an illustration is the impact of the scientific revolution of the seventeenth century upon political thought (Walzer, 1967; see also Crombie and Hoskin, 1970). The general ordering principles it entailed—that natural and social reality consist of independent units of matter in a field of continuous motion, which do not require the application of outside forces, and which are held together by laws that can be empirically discerned and inductively formulated—became a "reference map for political thought, a new source of images and analogues" (Walzer, p. 200). As C. B. MacPherson says of Hobbes' acceptance of the assumptions of the new science: it "enabled him to dispense with any postulate of moral purpose imposed from the outside, and to assume that moral values, rights, and obligations were entailed in the capacities and needs of an equally self-moving mechanism" (MacPherson, 1962, p. 78). The parallel of this cognitive reference map with the international order emerging at that time is both obvious and striking. For it is, of course, from the mid-seventeenth century that we date the modern, anarchic international system, predicated upon sovereignty and *raison d'etat*, and denying objective bases of mutual obligation and responsibility to moral purposes higher than the will of states.[13] The very opposite, according to some, is occurring today. The new scientific organizing metaphor thought to be becoming dominant stresses the finiteness of the ecosystem and the organic unity of all living things. It is captured in such notions as "spaceship earth," the "global village," and the "steady state" (for illustrations, see the contributions to Daly, 1973). Expressed in social-choice terms this metaphor implies a shift away from market rationality toward collective goods rationality, from the private to the public, from the analytic to the holistic. Again the implications for the international political order are both obvious and striking. For this metaphor entails the blueprint of an international order that is the mirror image of the one brought into being in the seventeenth century; indeed, it is most commonly expressed in a neomedieval organicism.[14]

Material Changes

Undoubtedly the most profound long-term change in the material setting of polities is the progressive socialization of the natural environment. By this I mean that what were once constants imposed by nature—distance, time, sources of energy, sources of food, the weather, the biological bases of life themselves—have progressively become objects of social choice, susceptible to manipulation and sometimes to control. Politically, this has two implications. First, it means the politicization of phenomena once entirely nonpolitical.[15] As "natural" conditions become political creations, the incidence of social conflict potentially increases, allocative and regulatory choices must be made about a new range of substantive issues, and "the cockpit of politics" becomes more decisive than ever (Bell, 1973, p. 364). A second and closely related consequence is that some of these acts, the modification of the weather and climate being an example, tend to have external costs, if not indivisible effects, associated with them: depending upon the configuration of property rights, it may not be possible to modify the weather for oneself only or without visiting adverse effects upon others (Weiss, 1975). This is taken to imply that the demand for the limitation of private choice will rise. The scope of the public sector, both domestically and internationally, would then increase as a result.

A second trend frequently discussed is the increased integration of the technological infrastructure of social, economic, and political processes. By this is meant nothing more than the impact of technologies of communication, transportation, and production on global intercourse: the instantaneous transmission of information, the increased ease of movements of people, goods, and capital, the spread of multinational enterprises, and so on. Put differently, the technological infrastructure of global processes is coming to resemble a "nondecomposable" system in which insulating space is rapidly disappearing.[16] Two implications for the international political order follow. First, in such systems of integrated technology even local and inherently unimportant acts come to be expressed as "macroscopic gesticulations," to borrow McLuhan's inimitable characterization (McLuhan and Fiore, 1968). This has the consequence of heightening awareness within the international political order. Second, Daniel Bell has argued that in such systems information and coordination become "the new scarcities," in the sense that both their necessity and their relative cost increase (1973, pp. 466ff).[17] Thus, it can be expected that the demand for the collective provision of these services too will increase.

Yet a third development in the material setting of polities has been noted. In certain United Nations circles, particularly the United Nations Environment Program, the phrase "the outer limits" of the physical integrity of the ecosystem is gaining in currency (see, for example, "The Cocoyoc Declaration," in Ruggie and Haas, 1975). By this is meant the possible limits on the carrying capacity of the planet, in terms of resource availability, absorbing wastes and pollutants, and providing for both physical and aesthetic necessities—in the face of a world population doubling over the course of the next 30 years. If such limits are indeed being approached and a pattern of the steady state comes to replace steady growth—or if such limits can be contrived, as is the case, in the short run, in the oil situation—then two sorts of choices are thrust into the international political order. First, choices about trade-offs become in part collective choices—of which the OECD-related responses to energy, balance of payments problems, inflation, and recession may be a modest illustration.[18] Second, choices about redistribution, which in a period of steady expansion were defused by the "trickle-down theory," become more pressing—as the Sixth Special Session of the UN General Assembly and the 1975 session on a "new international economic order" have indicated.[19]

Depictions of the consequences of the impact on and control of the physical environment are not limited to the images and metaphors that organize political thought or to the physical settings within which political activities take place; they also include the social-organizational arrangements and techniques that link thought and setting. I turn to the institutional level.

The Institutional

Two obvious institutional changes are associated with social control over the physical environment: a broadening of the range of issues that are the concern of foreign and international policy, and a differentiation of the international actors and institutional arrangements that deal with foreign and international policy. I briefly deal with each of these.

Issues. The concepts of "issue" and "issue-area" are much used in political studies, and it is clear that any number of typologies can be devised for them. For instance, one might examine the substantive range of concerns of policy makers, note that it now includes an array of "issues" never before on the agenda of national or international policy, and draw inference on that basis. Thus, science and technology as general categories can be said to have become "issues" in foreign and international policy, as the OECD, UNESCO, UN-ECE and European Community programs on science policy attest.[20] To this one might then add the oceans, the environment, weather modification, food, population, energy, telecommunication, nuclear proliferation, and a host of other concerns that have been placed on the policy agenda by developments in science and technology. For studies of bureaucratic politics, the outcome of specific negotiations, the problems of policy coordination, the relationship between expertise and politics in policy formulation, and so on, such a categorization of "issues" may be entirely appropriate and sufficient. For our concern here, though, it is not. For it is difficult to see what if anything about the oceans, the atmosphere, or the environment, or any of the others, is unique from the point of view of potentially leading to institutional discontinuities, except that they are *there* and are negotiated about. I propose, therefore, a simple typology of "issues" that is based on *where*, indeed, they are located in relation to the domestic policy domain, and one that cuts across substantive distinctions. We can then assess whether the substantive broadening of the policy agenda has been attended by institutional change as well.

EXTERNAL. The departments of government that deal with foreign policy were once properly called departments of "external affairs." Although there have always been exceptions, by and large the foreign policy of any given society has concerned itself with phenomena that are external to it. And, more often than not, this continues to be the case. Several aspects of the environmental science and technology field fall into this category.

Collaborative research in international laboratories, such as the CERN, is one example. A program is defined, a budget is approved, scientists come and go, experiments succeed and fail; but if the domestic policy scene is affected it is by way of indirect effect only.[21] The phenomenon that is the object of policy remains "external," and is not part of the core issues that concern governments.

INTERNATIONAL MANIFESTATIONS. A second and somewhat different circumstance exists when the object of foreign policy is the direct international manifestation of some aspect of domestic behavior. Scientific and technological problems have been prominent here, including the two oldest known cases of intergovernmental organization, the River Commissions and the Telegraphic Unions of the nineteenth century (Chamberlain, n.p., 1923 and ITU, 1965). In both of these cases international policy concerned the standardization of roles and task performance—keeping river beds clear of obstacles in the one instance, and the language, routing, and priority of telegraphic messages in the other. Contemporary illustrations include international weather observation, environmental and oceanographic monitoring, and equipment standardization and performance harmonization in civil aviation, shipbuilding, and the use of the frequency spectrum.[22] If the recommendations of the Rome Food Conference are implemented, a food production monitoring system will be added to this list. What is identical about this set of issues is that in each case the object of policy is the international manifestation of domestic behavior, and the purpose of international policy is to so arrange the confluence of the domestic behavior of several countries that, in their international manifestation, they come to constitute an integrated system. Although still "external," the link to the domestic scene is direct.

INTERNATIONAL COMMONS. Yet a third and rather different issue exists with respect to property rights in the international commons—the oceans, atmosphere, climate, and deep space. As scientific and technological developments have made the international commons exploitable, the question of property rights has become of major concern, domestically and internationally. Note, as an illustration, the ongoing Law of the Sea Conference. The issue at stake here is the precise delimitation between external and internal, and the domestic consequences of different formulae of delimitations.[23]

DOMESTIC BEHAVIOR. A fourth and final issue type is the case in which the object of foreign and international policy is domestic behavior or domestic life styles. Several modest instances of it exist in the environmental science and technology fields, including the attempt to control the use of nuclear technology and materials by means of international safeguarding and such limited international pollution standards as have been agreed to. In each case, what a society can and should do *domestically* is the issue at stake—whether it concerns the domestic use of a technology, modes of industrial production, waste disposal, or land use. At the Bucharest Population Conference reproductive habits in the Third World were added to the international policy agenda, and at the Rome Food Conference the feeding of livestock in the industrial countries joined the list too—without consequence in either case, it might be added. Nevertheless, particularly if projections of "outer limits" have any validity, then patterns of domestic behavior, consumption, and even life styles will increasingly become a direct object of foreign and international policy, and systematic societal enmeshment of this sort may, indeed, become a policy instrument as well.[24]

In sum, this typology of issues distinguishes among policy concerns in the international political order on the basis of their functional distance from the domestic domain, and it ranges along a scale of societal enmeshment. It does *not* follow that science and technology have effected a linear progression of issues along this scale. Examples of each have always existed and, as mentioned, the first instance of intergovernmental organization in the nineteenth century was a case of "international manifestations," the second category. At the same time, I think it evident that the absolute number of instances in the third and fourth categories—if not their relative weight—is increasing as a consequence of increased social control over the physical environment. So that, not only the substantive but the institutional character of the foreign and international policy agenda is changing.[25]

Actors. Much like issues, so too the character of the actors involved in policy formulation and execution may be conceptualized in a variety of ways, depending upon one's purposes. One can note whether they are economic or political entities, public or private, domestic or international, transnational or intergovernmental, and so on. Of importance here is the potential *differentiation* and reordering of international actors and institutional arrangements. These are of two types.

DIFFERENTIATION OF ACTORS/ARRANGEMENTS. The functional differentiation of institutions has long been a key focus of studies of social change: "It refers to the phenomenon that as institutions grow in size and in the functions they have to perform, specialized and distinct subsystems are created to deal with these functions" (Bell, 1973, p. 173). In the international political order this process began with the creation of specialized foreign offices in the eighteenth century. In the nineteenth century a development began that continues to this day: the managers of agencies and bureaus concerned with technological matters domestically began to establish direct relationships with their counterparts elsewhere. The international institutional arrangements that were subsequently created—like the Telegraphic Union—consisted of the institutionalization of such relationships. With time, international bureaus were created to service these arrangements. This process has continued as new areas of science and technology—for example, meteorology, aviation, shipping, oceanography, ecology—have evolved. More and more "foreign policy" is being conducted by functionally specific domestic agencies as a result. At some point a potential problem emerges: "With the growth of specialized subsystems one finds as well new, distinct problems of coordination, hierarchy, and social control" (Bell, 1973; for an illustration in the case of "food policy," see Gelb and Lake, 1974–1975, pp. 176–189). Coordination, hierarchy, and control on the basis of traditional criteria become increasingly problematic (Allison, 1971; Keohane and Nye, 1974, pp. 39–62; a good review of this literature and of the issues it raises may be found in Wagner, 1974, pp. 435–466). A potential consequence for the international political order is the subsequent *reordering* of political authority, around international, nonterritorial collective interests. This phenomenon is presumed to be most pronounced in fields such as science and technology, in which effective participation in policy making presupposes access to arcane bodies of knowledge, and in which ties of profession and training are strong.

DIFFERENTIATION AMONG ACTORS/ARRANGEMENTS. A second type of differentiation is *among* international actors and institutional arrangements. By this is meant that actors who traditionally have had nothing to do with government and institutional arrangements that are nongovernmental in character are sometimes significant international political entities. In the substantive area of concern here, the role of the International Council of Scientific Unions, the International Union for Conservation of Nature and Natural Resources, and the Friends of the Earth in preparing the agenda for the Stockholm Environment Conference is a case in point (Fararu, 1974, pp. 31–60). Furthermore, there are instances of nongovernmental actors actually and formally participating in international decision making—atmospherics, radiation standards, and the Codex Alimentarius being three illustrations.[26] Here, the potential for the holistic constructs of environmental scientists influencing the reordering of political authority is direct.

Some Conclusions

In sum, mankind's increased impact on and control of its physical environment is thought to generate an irresistible tendency toward holism, communalism, or central guidance. This tendency is depicted at the cognitive level—the images and metaphors informing thought; the material level—the physical and natural settings within which human activities take place; and the institutional level—the social arrangements that mediate thought and setting. Specifically, at the cognitive level, the increased importance of knowledge over traditional political ideologies and interests is postulated. Moreover, a shift in the basic organizing metaphor of internationalist thought, from the liberal "possessive individualism" model sustained by the metaphor of steady growth, to what we might call a "communal holism" model sustained by the metaphor of the steady state, is predicted. At the material level, it is expected that the increased politicization of the natural environment will lead to an increase in the scope of international collective choice and to the progressive constraining of the unilateral volition of states. Furthermore, increased technological integration is expected to generate the emergence of new scarcities of information and coordination, as well as an increase in the demand for their collective provision. And, were the "outer limits" of the carrying capacity of the planet to be approached, this would necessitate collective choices over the trade-offs that would maintain a balanced state. Lastly, at the institutional level, growing societal enmeshment as both an end and a means of policy, and the reordering of political authority around nonterritorial collective interests is forecast. These tendencies toward holism are summarized in Table 27.2.

The three levels of phenomena summarized in Table 27.2 bear a striking resemblance to the three levels of "frameworks" presented in Table 27.1: the cognitive changes suggesting structural change; the material changes suggesting changes at the level of regimes; and the institutional changes implying changes at the level of policy. Can we simply take such tendencies toward holism as our "independent variable" and predict changes in the international political order accordingly? To do so is to

make a mistake. For there exists a set of counter-tendencies, claiming adherents and offering evidence no less compelling than the evidence just adduced. I briefly describe this second set.

IV. ON FRAGMENTATION: TRENDS AND SCENARIOS

What appears as the progressive collectivization of international decision making looks very different when viewed from the vantage point of the scope and exercise of public authority by states. Not holism but fragmentation demands attention from this perspective. One obvious factor leading to fragmentation is that there now exist some seventy more national polities than at the close of World War II, each with its own publics, objectives, and preferred instruments of governance. A second factor is the modest but significant diffusion of power in the international system during the same period of time, particularly striking in the lessened relative position of the United States. The combination of these two factors produces a third, namely, the increased diversity of demands that polities make within the international system and, more important, the diversity of demands that have to be taken seriously. Yet a fourth factor is the changing

Table 27.2 Tendencies toward holism in the international political order.

Level	Dimension	Tendencies
Cognitive	Beliefs and ideologies	Transcendance of particularistic ideologies and interests
	Organizing metaphors	Metaphor of steady-state: holistic thinking; collective goods rationality
Material	Manipulation and control of physical environment	Increased scope of international public sector; greater constraints on unilateral choice
	Technological infrastructure	Increasingly interdependent; greater demand for information and coordination
	Carrying capacity	Collective consideration of balancing trade-offs
Institutional	International issues	Greater societal enmeshment as end and means of policy
	International actors	The reordering of political authority around nonterritorial, transnational and transgovernmental collective arrangements

scope and character of the instruments of governance in all societies. It is this fourth factor, its effects multiplied by the first three, that poses the major contradiction to the tendency toward holism. An elaboration of it follows.

The Nationalization of Society

Domestically as internationally, the nineteenth-century political order rested upon the principle of noninterference by the public sector in the private.[27] After 1815, as is well known, there emerged an unprecedented international economic order, transforming the separate national economies into a single world economy even as nationalistic tendencies came to dominate in the political realm.[28] It was, first of all, a liberal economic order, at least in theory predicated upon freedom of trade and of migration. Moreover, it was, in some instances, a multilateral order. The United Kingdom, for example, always allowed debts incurred by a country in one area to be cancelled by credits earned in another. The United Kingdom had a credit balance in its dealings with the primary producing countries, who settled their balance of indebtedness by an export surplus to the continental industrial countries, who financed their import surpluses by export surpluses to the United Kingdom (Briggs, 1968, p. 42). What made this possible, furthermore, was a single international monetary standard and fixed exchange rates, with the control of currency policies of national economies being centralized, for all practical purposes, in the City of London, and with the City providing additional requisite services such as insurance. Thus, it may also be said to have been a transnational, if not supranational, order: "The Bank of England, as custodian of the integrity of sterling, found itself—unwillingly and for the most part unwittingly—the final arbiter and court of appeal and the central executive authority of the international system of trade and finance" (Carr, 1945, pp. 14–15). In the 1870's, even though *la belle epoque* had yet to begin, the foundations of this economic order began to be undermined, with signs appearing first in the monetary realm[29] and then, in 1879, in trade as well.[30] By the time of World War I, the single world economy had been replaced, once again, by separate national economies. While attempts were made following the war to reestablish the *status quo ante bellum*—by returning to the gold standard, for example—they were unsuccessful and protectionist policies were everywhere pursued (Kindleberger, 1973). Following Smoot-Hawley, the abandonment of the gold standard, and the formulation of the Five-Year Plans in the Soviet Union, the New Deal in the United States and German planning under National Socialism,[31] as well as the collapse of the League, "by 1940 every vestige of the international system had disappeared and, apart from a few enclaves, the nations were living in an entirely new international setting" (Polanyi, 1944, p. 23).

The point at issue is not simply a decline in the magnitude of international economic transactions; that has since been reversed, at least in part.[32] The point is that a massive shift was effected from private to public power. Social relations were "nationalized" in that, first, new social classes were successively incorporated into the polity, the result being that the state became progressively an instrument of the collective welfare and standard of living of ever more broadly based publics; and in that, consequently, national political authority was reasserted over social and economic relations, domestic and international. Thus, the shift from private to public power resulted from governments creating and assuming a variety of social tasks that had not before existed, and from states appropriating for *public* management a variety of tasks that had been previously performed by a *private* economic order.

This shift affected the international political order as well. The fact that governments created and assumed new social tasks may have led to the "disappearance" of the international system in the short run; in the longer run it also meant that polities would have to attempt to *deliberately* construct the processes and structures that had managed transactions "automatically" in the past. Moreover, this deliberate, political construction of international arrangements follows certain modal patterns of design that produce fragmentation. Specifically, such arrangements tend to factor the scope of collective policy into what seem to be the most nearly independent parts; they tend to be *derivative* of domestic policy objectives; they tend to compensate for the shortcomings of national policy instruments; and they tend to be constructed *incrementally*.

Patterns of Design

Let me continue with the illustrations from the domain of economic management for the moment. The planning of post-World War II economic arrangements can be usefully traced to Article VII of the Mutual Aid Agreement between the United States and Great Britain (1942). It stressed the connectivities among the various economic and political objectives and instruments with which governments were concerned, and the necessity of approaching these multilaterally and comprehensively (Gardner, 1956). In the event, however, trade, money and redistribution were separated; a comprehensive approach to trade through the ITO was abandoned, with only the GATT remaining; and the Bretton Woods arrangement for the postwar monetary system was an unhappy compromise between a fairly comprehensive financing scheme proposed by the British and the more modest US position (Gardner, 1956). Thus, what was initially a comprehensive, broad-brush approach became successively factored into smaller and narrower units.

The derivative nature of international arrangements constructed by national public authorities may be seen by comparing the postwar monetary system with the gold standard. Once active management of domestic economies became an objective of governments, the gold standard had to be abandoned. For "strict adherence to its canons required the domestic economy to be governed by balance-of-payments considerations, regardless of how inflationary or deflationary that might be" (Cooper, 1975, p. 85). In other words, the domestic economy under the gold standard in theory was to be manipulated for the sake of an external arrangement. But with active governmental management of the domestic economy, inflationary and deflationary policies were required for the pursuit of objectives other than balance-of-payments considerations. Hence, under the Bretton Woods arrangement, "the primacy of domestic economic policy" was established, and the international arrangement subordinated to the domestic objective of full employment (Cooper, 1975).

What is more, the international arrangement constructed at Bretton Woods was designed to compensate for the inability of domestic policy instruments to fully protect the domestic economy from balance-of-payments strictures. A "double screen" was erected, as a result of which temporary imbalances could be financed, with international help if necessary, and fundamental imbalances corrected by altering the exchange rate (Cooper, 1975).

Lastly, the "go-stop" approach to revising the Bretton Woods system demonstrates the incremental character of designing international arrangements. Fred Hirsch's analysis of an alternative system based on Special Drawing Rights offers a case in point (Hirsch, 1973). Only the threat of imminent breakdown in the system generates enthusiasm for constructing a new SDR-based scheme in the first place, he argues. Thus, the SDR standard is debated only when it is seen as an unavoidable course of action. But once the imminency of the threat wanes, as it repeatedly has, the SDR standard is unfavorably compared to less demanding piecemeal reconstruction. "A comparison on this piecemeal basis is 'producer-oriented,' giving more attention to objections or resistances to change expressed by existing agencies or private operating interests than to the impact of the new arrangements on the national and international economies as a whole—as 'consumers' of the system" (Hirsch, p. 4). Thus, change in the system has been characterized by successive, "producer-oriented" incremental adjustment.

Each of these four principles of design leads, of course, to the fragmentation of policies, constituencies, institutions, and, indeed, the community of nations. Does the design of international arrangements differ in other subject areas? Specifically, does the construction of international arrangements in response to increased environmental control follow or deviate from these principles?

In the attempt to partially answer that question, consider the matrix shown in Table 27.3 (this discussion draws upon Ruggie, 1975). Its two dimensions are the *purposes* that collective arrangements in the area of environmental science and technology now perform, and the *instrumentalities* through which these purposes are performed. The three basic purposes are: (1) the acquisition of new capabilities, including research, development, and hardware construction that, once produced, may be transferred to the national level; (2) the administration or management of capabilities that already exist, including those in shipping, civil aviation, weather observation, and telecommunications, so as to make make effective use of them; and (3) the regulation or control of what national actors do with existing capabilities, or of which capabilities they will be allowed to acquire, including use of the radio frequency band, environmental pollution, and safeguarding nuclear materials. The four types of instrumentalities vary along the degree to which national behavior is integrated in the pursuit of the three purposes. Several existing international arrangements are entered into the cells to illustrate the matrix.

If the principles of design enunciated above hold, then we would expect a simple hypothesis to be confirmed. Being derivative and compensatory, it follows that these international arrangements cannot impose a greater institutional cost upon the "producers" of them than foregoing the particular objective at hand would; if they do, the continuation of the "problem" or foregoing the "opportunity" will be preferred to its institutional "solution."[33] Now imagine a diagonal in table 27.3, running from cell 1 to cell 12. It would measure the

institutional cost to the producers of constructing a given international arrangement, ranging from low (cell 1) to high (cell 12) calculated in terms of loss of autonomy and constraints on unilateral volition. Actual arrangements, then, should exhibit the attempt to limit these institutional costs.[34]

The available evidence suggests as much. First of all, a rough count of existing international arrangements in this subject area would show that the highest frequency of cases is to be found in cells 1, 2, 4, and 5. There are none, to my knowledge, in cell 12, although had Arvid Pardo's ideal of a seabed regime been realized, it would have constituted an instance. Furthermore, the two examples on either side of cell 12, the NPT safeguarding regime and Eurocontrol, are partial examples only. The safeguarding regime is applicable only to signatory nonweapon states; the Eurocontrol regime is applicable in theory only to France and Great Britain. Limiting the frequency of cases and the applicability of collective arrangements to certain members are not the only means of limiting institutional costs, however. Another is the role that national actors play in performing a collective function versus the role that international agencies play. For example, the pre-NPT

Table 27.3

Instrumentality of Collective Arrangement	Purpose of Collective Arrangement		
	Acquiring a Capability	Making Effective Use of a Capability	Coping with Consequences of Use of a Capability
A Common Framework for National Behavior	Global Atmospheric Research Program (1)	Consultative activities as per IMCO (2)	Notification and registration of use of frequencies (3)
A Joint Facility Coordinating National Behavior	European space collaboration as per ESRO (4)	Standardization as per ITU, WMO, ICAO, etc. (5)	Monitoring as per Earthwatch (6)
A Common Policy Integrating National Behavior	European collaboration in space activities as of 1 April, 1974 (7)	World Weather Watch (8)	Safeguarding as per IAEA (NPT Regime) (9)
A Common Policy Substituted for National Behavior	Euratom ideal (10)	Upper air traffic control through Eurocontrol (11)	Pardo's ideal of a seabed regime (12)

safeguarding regime of the IAEA, applicable in scope to specific installations in countries that had received international assistance of nuclear materials or technology, included considerable authority of inspection for the IAEA. The NPT regime, on the other hand, which is applicable to entire domestic nuclear industries in signatory non-weapon countries and which may, therefore, be thought to have broader scope, reduced the authority of the IAEA to verifying that national self-inspection systems are operating properly and in accordance with collectively agreed-to standards.[35] Yet a fourth means of limiting institutional costs is to proscribe the actual task that the collective arrangement executes in performing its function. To continue with the safeguarding illustration, neither the original IAEA regime nor the NPT regime is designed to prevent diversion of nuclear materials; their activities are purely *informational* in that they are to report instances of diversion to the Security Council. Still further limitations of institutional costs may be effected by manipulating the size of the collective arrangement or its voting procedures and similar techniques. (A fuller discussion of these issues may be found in Buchanan and Tullock, 1962).

Thus the hypothesis seems to hold, insofar as international arrangements in the subject area of environmental control seem to exhibit patterns similar to those described above.[36]

Some Conclusions

When viewed from the vantage point of developments in the scope and exercise of public authority domestically over the course of the past century, the central tendency in the international political order is one of fragmentation. Fragmentation is due, primarily, to three factors: the increase in the number of politics and publics; the increase in the diversity of politics and publics and, therefore, in the objectives pursued internationally; and the international implication of the changing scope and character of the instruments of domestic governance.

Evidence of this third factor may be found at both the cognitive and institutional levels, or in terms of the expectations individuals hold about state intervention and in the actual performance of states. Moreover, evidence may be found in the principles of design upon which international arrangements are constructed. These tendencies are summarized in Table 27.4.

In sum, there exist good reasons and some evidence for supporting the trend from holism toward fragmentation. As I indicated at the outset, it is not my purpose to test or verify the many particulars of these two sets of trends. I believe that, on the basis of the discussion thus far, the case can be made that the *central tendencies* projected by both coexist in the contemporary international system. I now want to raise the issue of what to do about the fact that their trajectories are contradictory, that they suggest futures that are, on the face of it, incompatible. Will one of the two trends "give"? Is one more "correct" or more "powerful"? Below, I try to show that neither gives, that neither is more correct or more powerful, but that both are inseparably and systematically accommodated in the

Table 27.4 Tendencies toward fragmentation in the international political order.

Indicator	Tendency
Number of claimants	Increase
Diversity of claimants	Increase
Scope and character of public authority	"Nationalization of society"
Patterns of design in international arrangements constructed by national public authorities	Factoring policy to most nearly independent units
	International arrangements derivative of domestic policy objectives
	International arrangements compensatory for shortcomings of domestic policy instruments
	Incremental "producer-oriented" change

construction of contemporary frameworks of international collective behavior.

V. ON COMPLEMENTARITY

Attempting to reconcile incompatible or contradictory tendencies in any system is only in part an empirical affair. More fundamentally, as Gerald Holton has suggested, it involves the role of "themata" in scientific thought (Holton, 1975, pp. 328–334).[37] "In many (perhaps most) past and present concepts, methods, and propositions or hypotheses of science, there are elements that function as themata, constraining or motivating the individual and sometimes guiding (normalizing) or polarizing the scientific community" (Holton, p. 330). Examples of such themata include symmetry, unity, continuity, synthesis, discreteness, indeterminacy, and complementarity.[38] These are, as Robert Merton describes them, "tacit cognitive imageries and preferences for or commitments to certain kinds of concepts, certain kinds of methods, certain kinds of evidence, and certain forms of solutions to deep questions and engaging puzzles" (Merton, 1975, pp. 335—338). As Holton demonstrates, the role of empirical evidence in the face of "an early, unshakable commitment" to certain kinds of themata is secondary.[39]

In the study of international orders, one will detect at least three enduring themata at work. The first is an unshakable, neomedievalist commitment to the inevitability and/or necessity of *unity*.[40] F. H. Hinsley has effectively demonstrated the origins and persistence of this themata.[41] A second is an equally unshakable commitment to the inevitable *continuity* of anarchy or to the unchanging nature of international phenomena. Superbly explicated by Rousseau, it too still informs internationalist thought today.[42] Yet a third, what we might call the Kantian themata, plays on the contradiction between holistic "needs" and anarchic system, but *resolves* this contradiction, either in favor of one or the other or by trying to effect a new synthesis between them.[43] Thus, at least three enduring themata inform internationalist thinking: unity, continuity, and resolution.

I want to propose a fourth themata: rejecting the resolution of contraries, it argues for accommodation in continued contradiction. Below I attempt to demonstrate the complementarity between holism and fragmentation at each of the three levels of frameworks of collective behavior: policy, regimes, and structure.

Policy

It is self-evident that the issues on the international policy agenda have changed and continue to change dramatically. One needs only to note Henry Kissinger's bafflement at finding himself involved in food diplomacy—"This is a new field for us. We had not in the past thought that agricultural exports required foreign policy decisions"[44]—and recall that his reaction to oil and money did not differ fundamentally. But, as argued in Section II, it is not only in substantive sense that issues are changing; they are beginning to differ institutionally as well. The issue of defining international property rights, whether in the physical space of the oceans and atmosphere or in the economic realm of collective reserve creation (SDRs), is perplexing policy makers. Confronting intersectoral and intrasocietal trade-offs on a collective basis raises more difficult problems still. And it raises problems generally not dealt with in the international political order—and order predicated upon the principle that such issues *should not* be dealt with there.

The characteristics of international *actors* too are changing, with technocrats from subgovernmental, transgovernmental, and transnational entities playing substantial roles in many of the issues discussed above. But are the criteria of policy formulation changing, as a result of the participation of these new actors in decision making in the context of new issues? Here the evidence is more murky, but I believe it is sufficient to allow us to postulate a simple "politicization threshold." By this I mean that below a certain level of political concern, new issues are dealt with by new actors in new ways.[45] Above a certain level of political concern, one of two things may happen. First, the new actors may come to be replaced by more traditional types of decision makers, acting out more traditional behavioral modalities.[46] Or second, and more interesting, new actors may in fact act in accordance with more traditional predilections.[47] In either case, new and more holistic issues are responded to, but they are responded to on the basis of traditional principles of design. Traditional principles of design expressed in a new setting will produce a new "reality," but what little evidence we have suggests that this new "reality" is not a resolution of the contradictions of the old but their reconstruction into new forms of activity.

This juxtaposition is still more effectively demonstrated at the level of regimes.

Regimes

International regimes institutionalize agreed-to rules of national conduct, mutual expectations, and norms, which are applicable to specific actors under specific circumstances. I have suggested that change or continuity in international regimes can be measured by differences over time in their functional and geographic scope and in the degree to which and the manner in which agreement on joint purposes is expressed in, and unilateral volition is constrained by, international regimes. The first of these indicators poses no difficulty. International regimes have progressively expanded since World War II, both functionally and geographically, as a direct consequence of the new tasks governments are attempting to perform domestically, and of the increase in the number of nation-states (Sewell, 1972 and Lyon, 1973, pp. 24–59). The second set of indicators requires elaboration. What it seeks to express, in essence, is (1) the type of interdependence different regimes embody, and (2) the manner in which this internal interdependence is managed.

Types of Interdependence. A glance at our matrix of international collective arrangement in Table 27.3 will remind us that they have different purposes, and that they differentially integrate national behavior in the pursuit of those purposes. They also embody different types of interdependence.

In cell 1 and in the immediately adjacent cells, we find the situation in which each actor is relatively independent from any other given actor, yet all are interdependent in the sense that unless all perform their respective tasks the success of the entire collectivity is jeopardized. The various collaborative research programs, such as the GARP, in which the actual research is carried out by na-

tional centers, constitute an example. Following J. D. Thompson, this type of interdependence is referred to as *pooled* interdependence.[48]

A different situation pertains in cell 8 and, in part, in cells 6 and 7. Here a definite order exists in the manner in which tasks have to be performed, and the output on one becomes the input for another. In the case of the World Weather Watch, for example, unless observations are made in certain locations at specified intervals, and data is transmitted in specified codes, the dynamics of weather formation cannot be detected, and the whole is rendered ineffective. This relationship is described as *sequential* interdependence.

If there were a case in cell 12, we would have an example of what Thompson calls *reciprocal* or *intensive* interdependence[49]—the situation in which each unit of a given set is penetrated by and contingent upon every other unit in that set. The examples in the two cells adjacent capture only partially this relationship, and do so for very special types of behavior only. But what of the future?

On the basis of our analysis, we can forecast the emergence of purer cases of reciprocal interdependence and more of them. How? By noting the following pattern. The relationship of pooled interdependence seems to emerge when the issue to be dealt with remains "external" to the domestic policy domain, in the sense described in Section III. On the other hand, sequential interdependence seems to be the mode in some instances in which the issue is the harmonization of the "international manifestations" of domestic behavior. However, as the issue becomes the delimitation between what is external and internal, or even the domestic behavior of lifestyles of countries, then I would argue that the realm of reciprocal interdependence is encountered. Thus, instances of international regimes embodying reciprocal interdependence will increase in like proportion to the increase in what I have called issue-types 3 and 4—the delimitation of property rights, and the collective allocation of the intersectoral and intrasocietal trade-offs.

In sum, in the types of interdependence regimes embody, we can hypothesize the emergence of at least one fundamental change toward holism.

The Management of Interdependence. J. D. Thompson has argued that for each of these three types of interdependence there exists an appropriate instrument of coordination. In the case of pooled interdependence, the instrument consists of sets of standard operating procedures, which are designed to ensure that the action of each is commensurate with the purpose of the whole. To coordinate the relationship of sequential interdependence, a plan drawing up schedules of task performance becomes necessary. Lastly, coordination by mutual adjustment, consisting of constant monitoring, negotiation, and adaptation, is required for the case of reciprocal or intensive interdependence (Thompson, 1967).

The international collective arrangements depicted in our matrix generally bear out this hypothesized pattern of association. In and around cell 1, the instrument of coordinating the interdependence among members of the collective arrangement does seem to be equivalent to standard operating procedures, whereby each pursues a task in accordance with certain agreed-to modalities so as to make the products of the behavior of each comparable and additive. In and around cell 8, however, more precise scheduling by plan takes place, the World Weather Watch once more serving as an illustration. Provisions made at the Stockholm Environment Conference, for joint consultation about environmental modification, and for compensation for trade discrimination resulting from environmental standards, may give some indication of what coordination by mutual adjustment may come to look like.[50]

Thus, these instruments of coordinating interdependencies will be issue- and actor-specific, rather than being cumulative or holistic. At the same time, each may be seen to impose a progressively higher institutional cost upon states, in the sense of constraining unilateral volition and national autonomy of action.[51] Hence, we would expect each also to be accompanied by several other instruments of coordination, the purpose of which will be to diffuse or limit these institutional costs. For example, it can be hypothesized that the more intense the level of interdependence is, the higher will be the level of government at which decisions are made, and the more directly political (as opposed to organizational or bureaucratic) decision making will be. Informal summit meetings among heads of government of the European Community, unmediated by national or international bureaucrats, offer one illustration. Thus, the scope of bu-

reaucratic politics is constrained. The summits suggest a second possibility as well—namely, that the more intense the level of interdependence among members becomes, the less will be the authority enjoyed by an international agency serving that regime. In the case of such summits, the once powerful Commission seems to serve strictly a Secretariat role. Thus, the scope of transgovernmental actors is constrained. Emerging collective arrangements in the field of oil and money suggest still two more possibilities. One is illustrated by the attempt, on the part of the United States, to limit the size of the collectivity within which the most intense types of interdependence are managed, by including only the major consumers and the single issue of oil. Thus, the scope of bargaining is kept to a set of core issues and among the most homogeneous actors. The second is illustrated by the very complicated weighted voting formula that is proposed for the OECD oil pool and financial safety net. Thus, control over the level of commitment to the collectivity is maximized by national actors.

Other examples of instruments for the management of interdependence, whose purpose is to limit the institutional costs of so doing, could be added. But enough has been said to make the point that the shift in international regimes effected by the emergence of new and more intense types of interdependencies will be attended by the construction of instruments of coordination which, while coordinating those interdependencies, will also seek to limit and diffuse them. This does not mean that the interdependencies will disappear; nor does it mean that present instruments of coordination may not be rearranged at some future point. What it does mean is that the emergence of new and more intense types of interdependencies will trigger contradictory not linear institutional change. Tendencies toward fragmentation, then, are institutionalized into the very arrangements designed to respond to holistic concerns.

Structure

As more enmeshing types of issues are dealt with collectively, as more intense forms of interdependence are embodied in international regimes, and as the management of these regimes becomes more directly political, the quality of relations among actors does exhibit a certain change. In areas in which "it counts," that is, in the newer forms of *haute politique*, the fate of individual actors is increasingly coupled within collectivities; in those instances, the viability of collectivities is no longer simply an instrument of the viability of individual actors, but becomes inseparable from it. This may be taken as a manifestation of the idea of "communal holism." At the same time, however, it is obvious that the collectivities within which this appears possible are the smallest and most homogeneous, like the European Community, and that they shift with new issues and new actors. Moreover, they are not based on a sense of mutual obligation, but held together by mutual contingencies and constraints. Lastly, they are not institutionalized in a common body of belief or law, but remain in joint orbit only as long as a certain mutuality of situation holds among a given set of managers of complex policy systems.

I briefly summarize the argument developed in this section. Those students of international futures who express the themata of unity are fond of referring to Marshall McLuhan's image of "the global village" as capturing an essential ingredient of the emerging international political order. They conveniently forget that in McLuhan's village, globalization brings on retribalization. On the other hand, those expressing the themata of continuity point to retribalization as an affirmation of their point of view. They conveniently forget that retribalization is made possible only by an increasingly complex international infrastructure. Lastly, those seeking the resolution of these contraries are forced to invent ever more convoluted intellectual systems that, in the event, predict less and less. In contradistinction, to the question "Is the international political order changing toward holism or fragmentation?" the themata of complementarity answer "yes."

VI. SUMMARY

One after another, the international orders constructed after World War II have become unstuck. We find ourselves amidst frenzied attempts to redesign and reconstruct. But as the "crisis syndromes" I mentioned at the outset indicate, we do not fully understand what is going on. At the same time, in view of the severity of the issues at stake, and given that today's acceptable order of relations

may become tomorrow's source of irresolvable conflict, the need to know and to foresee has rarely been so great. In my view, the first step toward greater understanding involves the formulation of mental imageries that effectively capture the central tendencies of the world around us. In this chapter, I have suggested what two of these tendencies are and I have sought to demonstrate the relation between them. I want to conclude by briefly pointing out some of the implications of my argument, in the context of the redesign and reconstruction of international orders.

1. The domestic public realm and the realm of international collective choice are two inseparable components of the larger set of public authority. There could be no successful theory of sovereignty, F. H. Hinsley has argued, "until the notion of the sovereign power of the individual state had been reconciled with the ethical premises and the political needs of an international community consisting of independent states (Hinsley, 1967, pp. 242—252; the citation is from p. 245). The one was literally inconceivable without the other. And so it remains to this day. Therefore, in designing future international orders, scholars and practitioners alike are well advised to abandon their quest to bring sovereignty "to bay," and to concentrate their efforts instead on exploiting the ever present tension between national and international authority.

A discussion of the Canadian approach to international environmental law illustrates this strategy pefectly (Gottlieb and Dalfen, 1973, pp. 229–258). The approach is said to begin with proposals for international regimes affirming and extending state responsibility for harm visited upon other states. If suitably stringent international rules and procedures cannot be obtained, the next step is to unilaterally extend functional and nonacquisitive *national* jurisdiction into the international realm. This has the short-term consequence of establishing a "claim" and the long-term consequence of forcing the issue onto the international agenda. Canada is then in a better position to "seek to achieve an international regime or international rules which embody both the elements of enhanced international responsibility and extended national jurisdiction . . ." (Gottlieb and Dalfen, p. 233). Advocating strong international regimes and simultaneously asserting national jurisdiction are not viewed as being contradictory, for "in the last analysis, national jurisdiction and international responsibility involve no dichotomy; they are two elements in a more complete and appropriate response" (Gottlieb and Dalfen, p. 256).[52]

2. The more "global" international problems become and the more intense international interdependencies are, the less appropriate and acceptable international orders are that involve major authoritative roles for international institutional superstructures. The reason is simply that, as this situation is approached, little can be accomplished by *adding* activities and institutions *internationally;* the "solution" increasingly involves *changing domestic* behavior. The most appropriate international strategy, then, becomes one that facilitates commensurate internal change.

Such a strategy is predicated upon three fundamental principles. The first is that effective international responses cannot be constructed without strengthening the domestic constituencies that have an interest in bringing change about. Thus, the first step toward an international "solution" is to alter bureaucratic power relations domestically. The activities of Maurice Strong and the UN Environment Program illustrate the recognition of this necessity (for a brief discussion of Strong's approach, see Engfeldt, 1973). The second principle is that effective international orders in these situations consist of an arrangement or confluence of domestic behavior that strikes a certain balance between international constraint and national flexibility.[53] Some of the proposals for "issue-linkages" now on the international agenda signal emergent international orders characterized by domestic enmeshment, minimum international institutional involvement, and a constraint-flexibility balance that one is tempted to call "managed automaticity."[54] The third and final principle upon which this international strategy is predicated is that the most appropriate role for international institutions is "interfacing" the interrelated clusters of national behavior. International institutions become the switchboards, as it were, through which connections are established and maintained, rather than being depositories of activity and authority.

In a word, the more intense and global interdependencies become, the more appropriate is the international politics of issue-linkage and the less appropriate is the politics of international institution building.[55]

3. The study and management of international conflict is increasingly inseparable from the study and management of interinternational orders in general. As a consequence of collective responses to the sorts of phenomena discussed in this chapter, the channels and instruments of international political influence are becoming increasingly numerous and diverse (see Keohane and Nye, 1973, pp. 115–179 for an excellent discussion). One may expect, therefore, that instances of international conflict will become more frequent, the variety of conflicts greater, and traditional modes of resolving them increasingly irrelevant. At the same time, if I have adequately portrayed the character of emergent international orders, then the issues over which conflict will take place and the coalitions that will form in support of different interests should also become increasingly heteronomous and shifting.

In sum, the key word in describing international futures seems to be "complexity," a condition that the crisis mongers among us bemoan and seek to resolve. The situation in which we find ourselves *is* serious; designing and constructing new international orders in the face of contradictory tendencies *is* a complicated affair. Developing appropriate mental imageries upon which to base organizational strategies is the necessary first step that has preoccupied me here. In continuing with this endeavor I think we can do not better than to repeat William Blake's prayer from time to time:

> Now I a fourfold vision see,
> And a fourfold vision is given me;
> 'Tis fourfold in my supreme delight
> And threefold in soft Beulah's night
> And twofold Always. May God us keep
> From Single Vision & Newton's sleep!

NOTES

1. This, in essence, is how Henry Kissinger posed the alternatives in an interview with James Reston (1974).
2. Most recently, this increasingly complicated descriptive nomenclature has been simplified to "The Crisis." Apparently, elaboration is no longer required. See, for example, Brzezinski (1974–1975), pp. 63–74). This synthetic appellation had, of course, already occurred to the French, as a review of the French press on the subject of "crises" makes clear: "Notes and Comment," *The New Yorker*, December 16, 1974, pp. 31–36.
3. For expressions in the Third World, see, among similar sources, "The Lima Declaration," the "Charter of

Economic Rights and Duties of States," and the "Declaration and Programme of Action on the Establishment of a New International Economic Order," as discussed, for example, in the *U.N. Monthly Chronicle* (1975). For expressions in the context of United States-Canadian relations, see the contributions to and source cited in Fox, *et al.* (1974a).

4. For a brief but useful introduction, consisting of a comparative study of structuralism in mathematics, logic, philosophy, physics, biology, psychology, linguistics, anthropology, and sociology, see Piaget (1971). A critical philosophical investigation may be found in Pettit (1975).

5. In the past, structural change has often been identified with institutional change. However, this error is no longer as prevalent as it once was. In the regional integration literature, for example, we now find the argument that the phenomenon of integration is *not* federalism, nor nationalism at a supranational level, nor functionalism, nor classical power politics (Puchala, 1972, pp. 267–284). Rather, its major attribute is said to be a "high mutual sensitivity and responsiveness" in decision making. This means that actors "tend to possess a good deal more information about one another and about one another's goals, objectives, preferences and needs than is common in more traditional diplomacy. . ." What is more, it means "some compulsion to see to it that their partners' needs as well as their own are fulfilled in decisions made and programs executed." Integration, then, is "precisely this atmosphere of shared compulsion to find mutually rewarding outcomes, this felt and shared legitimacy in concession making, and this reciprocal sensitivity to needs . . ." (Puchala, p. 282). Likewise, in recent assessments of international law we find the argument that the precedence of law over politics is *not* characterized by the emergence of adjudication mechanisms, institutions for enforcement and coercive sanctions (Gottlieb, 1972, pp. 331–383). Rather, the major attribute of such a change lies in "modes of decision making" and "procedures of reasoning" on the part of national actors: a certain quality of "principled" decision making, "guided" reasoning, constrained discretion, and consistency in application (Gottlieb, pp. 374–375). Lastly, in a discussion of the institutionalization of authority within international collectivities, I have tried to make the case that this is *not* necessarily characterized by the emergence of formal supersubordinate relations (Ruggie, 1975, pp. 557–583). Rather, I argued, authority is institutionalized insofar as there exists a growing interdependence of utility functions among national public authorities, and insofar as shared preference orderings are included in the determinants of national choice.

In sum, structural change involves such changes in the modalities of decision making, procedures of reasoning, and calculations of preference orderings that alter the quality of relations among the constituent units of the international political order, in that factors other than the distribution of national capabilities systematically become the most basic determinants of international outcomes.

6. Students of international relations generally view this complex of changes, and the attending changes recorded by the Peace of Westphalia, as constituting a major instance of international structural change. However, the view is not universally shared; Waltz, for one, disagrees.

7. I say "loosely" advisedly, for, as Piaget wisely insists, one cannot and must not assume the existence of some ultimate, absolute, terminal, or irreducible structure from which all others somehow derive. There exists no "structure of structures," he contends, only "the construction of a never completed whole" (1971, p. 140).

8. The concept "spill-over" implies this.

9. *Stability*, as Piaget makes clear, does not imply *innateness*.

10. It should now be clear why a simple "form-content" or "structure-process" distinction is insufficiently discrete. As Piaget points out, "in nature as in mathematics every form is content for 'higher' forms and every content form of what it 'contains.'" (p. 112). Cf. Lévi-Strauss (1967), especially Chapter 15.

11. An entirely new school of historiography (the "Annales" school, named after the journal in which its writings first appeared) has recently emerged, taking the structural relations among a social unit's physical setting, patterns of demography, tools of everyday existence, sources of energy, and forms of social organization as its point of departure. For a methodological discussion, see "Historical Studies Today" (1971); the leading figure of this school is Fernand Braudel. His most significant work for the purposes of this point is *Capitalism and Material Life, 1400–1800* (1974). Other significant works exploring such relations (listed in order of publication) include: Mumford (1934); Whyte, Jr. (1962); Ellul (1964); Price (1965); Galbraith (1968); Landes (1969); Ferkiss (1969 and 1974); Bell (1973); and Falk (1975).

12. The seminal work in this genre is Ellul (1964). Neo-Marxists have contended that what makes *technique* successful is that it represents a fusion of technical rationality with political domination. Cf. Marcuse (1968) and Habermas (1971); this issue is taken up in the context of international ecological politics by de Araujo Castro (1972), pp. 401–416.

13. Gross (1969), pp. 65–67. Note also W. Stark's observation in his introduction to F. Heinecke (1957): "The state is at long last accorded 'autonomy'; it is loosened from the 'heteronomous' shackles of morality" (p. xxiv).

14. Cf. Falk (1971) and the literature reviewed by Haas and Williams in their forthcoming monograph on scientists and world order.

15. For a discussion in the context of weather modification, see Weiss (1975).

16. The organizational implications of decomposability,

near decomposability and nondecomposability—terms depicting the relative complexity of systems—are explored by Simon (1969), Chapter 4.

17. Concern in Europe and in the United States about uncertainties posed by the interest sensitivity of short-term funds, brought about by the technologically based unification of short-term money markets, is a case in point.

18. Note, for instance, the creation of the International Energy Agency of the OECD, the $25 billion financial safety net for member countries in balance of payments difficulties, and promises not to pursue "beggar my neighbor" policies in the inflation-recession struggle.

19. In the Cocoyoc Declaration, future considerations of international policy in response to "outer limits" are closely linked to policy for the so-called "inner limits" of human needs. This does not imply that greater redistribution will necessarily *result*, but simply that redistributive claims become more difficult to ignore.

20. These programs consist of research on science-related problems and on science policy, and meetings of national and international officials, including ministers of science, for the purpose of developing more sophisticated and coherent national science policies. Note also, in this connection, the United Nations Conference on Science and Technology, scheduled for 1979 in Vienna.

21. In the case of CERN, one example of such an indirect effect had to do with the location of a new laboratory, and with whatever benefits accrue thereto. Germany felt it should be the site, given its level of financial contribution, but the French thought otherwise. In the end, the laboratory was built next door to the old CERN lab in Meyrin, Switzerland (Hawkes, 1971). Another indirect effect is, of course, the indirect consequences of scientific training and discoveries.

22. Examples would include the World Weather Watch of the WMO, the Earthwatch of the UN Environment Program, the Integrated Global Ocean Station System coordinated by the IOC, and the Technical Regulations of the ICAO, IMCO, and ITU.

23. A good discussion of the special problems posed by the issue of property rights in the international commons may be found in Brown and Fabian (1975).

24. One can readily conceive of such interissue bargains as a certain amount of food supplied in return for a decline in population growth rates, or a decline in per capita resource extraction and use in return for certain environmental practices, and others, becoming deliberate instruments of policy *if* a situation of "limits" were to be approached.

25. In seeking to put an end to the wars of religion for once and for all time, the Peace of Westphalia represented a deliberate attempt to so define "the rules of the game" of the international political order that domestic behavior did *not* become an issue within it. And, even though isolated exceptions have always existed, it did so rather successfully for three centuries and more.

26. Scientists have equal footing in the Global Atmospheric Research Program (WMO), and authoritative input into the UN committees on tolerable radiation levels and into the CODEX which is jointly governed by the FAO and WHO. It might also be pointed out that corporate enterprises are statutory members of certain research and development programs in the Nuclear Energy Agency on the OECD.

27. This is not to say that the private sector was not a political creation; it *was*, as Karl Polanyi aptly stated, "*Laissez-faire* was planned" (1944, p. 141).

28. "Thus the democratized nations of the 19th century went on from strength to strength proclaiming aloud, and exercising in the political sphere, the unrestricted rights of nationalism, while tacitly accepting the discipline of a supreme external arbiter of their economic destinies . . ." (Carr, 1945, pp. 16–17).

29. As Polanyi puts it, "dogmatic belief in the international gold standard continued to enlist men's stintless loyalties, while at the same time token currencies were established, based on the sovereignty of the various central banking systems. Under the aegis of international principles, impregnable bastions of a new nationalism were being unconsciously erected in the shape of the central banks of issue" (1944, p. 198).

30. "The German tariff of 1879 was long remembered as the first modern 'scientific' tariff—a piece of economic manipulation in the interests of national policy" (Carr, 1945, p. 17).

31. The impact of these attempts at national planning on international economic interdependence is analyzed by Briggs (1968).

32. Several studies of long-term patterns in international trade are reviewed by Schonfield (1965), Chapter II. They indicate, among other things, that since the establishment of the US-based economic order following World War II, the long-term decline in trade of manufactured goods was reversed and that among the industrialized countries, trade in such goods is rising considerably faster than national income. At the same time, capital flows continue to decline.

33. A more elaborate formulation of this thesis may be found in my article, "Collective Goods and Future International Collaboration" (1972, pp. 874–893). Cf. Hirsch (1973).

34. What these "costs" will be limited to will also depend, of course, on such factors as the character of the problem being responded to and the distribution of available national capabilities. Cf. Ruggie (1975).

35. An extensive comparison of the two regimes is presented in Pendley and Scheinman (1975).

36. I assume that there is no need to demonstrate the principles of factoring and incrementalism; the safeguarding regimes are perfect examples of both (Pendley and Scheinman, 1975).

37. I want to express my gratitude to Dr. Gene Rochlin for introducing me to this literature.

38. Holton (1975), p. 330. It should be noted that Holton considers themata to be more basic, less public, and much more persistent than so-called paradigms.

39. Holton (1975). One fascinating example is the case of Einstein, who accepted the empirical validity of the quantum theory but rejected one of its most essential principles, that of indeterminacy. He believed that "some day" a deterministic explanation would be found, and he was never shaken from this belief. See Cline (1963).

40. Most primitively, this themata is expressed in the belief that there exists "a progressive shifting of loyalty from smaller to larger units," and that we are now approaching "the final step on the scale of political expansion" (Brown, 1972, p. 76). A more complex version of the same argument may be found in Etzioni (1966), pp. 131–147. The most subtle contemporary representative is Falk (1975a and 1975b), who separates the condition of unity from any particular institutional form of it.

41. "That a civilization which has broken through immense barriers in almost every other direction, and which has surpassed all its predecessors on innumerable fronts, should still hold views and pursue programmes in international politics that it held and pursued when it was young—this is the outstanding failure of recent times." (Hinsley, 1967, p. 3).

42. See Hinsley (1967) for an historical review. The most forceful contemporary expression of this themata is developed in the works of Waltz (see, for instance, "Theory of International Relations," 1975).

43. See Hinsley (1967) for an historical review. The most sophisticated contemporary pursuit of this themata is to be found in the works of Ernst Haas; see his earlier studies for resolution in favor of unity (for example, *The Uniting of Europe*, 1958), and more recent statements for resolution by means of a new synthesis (for example, "The Study of Regional Integration: Reflections on the Joy and Anguish of Pretheorizing," 1970, pp. 607–646). His most recent essay, however, is closer to the fourth themata I propose below although the benefit of the doubt still goes to earlier predilections; see "Is There a Hole in the Whole? Knowledge, Technology, Interdependence, and the Construction of International Regimes" (1975), especially pp. 866–867).

44. In his Senate confirmation hearings, as cited by Rosenfeld (1974), p. 18.

45. The experience of CERN, ESRO, and the role of scientists in preparations for UNCHE come to mind.

46. This is what happened when ESRO became the European Space Agency. A similar phenomenon is noted by Russell in the monetary field (1973, pp. 431–466; cf. Dale, 1975).

47. In their study of technocrats in international policy making, Haas and Williams found that at the European level "there seems to be an inverse relationship between the potential to act meaningfully and organizational experiences which stress rationalism, consistency and scientific-technological determinism. In short, the more powerful the organization the more 'political' its modus operandi." I thank Haas and Williams for giving me access to their manuscripts while it was still in preparation.

48. This conceptualization of intraregime interdependencies is adapted from Thompson (1967), Chapter 5.

49. The term "reciprocal" has unfortunate connotations of equality that Thompson does not mean to imply. He has subsequently developed the idea of "intensive" interdependence, to replace the concept of "reciprocal" interdependence (1974, pp. 3–21).

50. Another recent example of such an arrangement is the role UNIDO would play under the Lima Declaration, in serving as the forum for negotiating industrial relocation and monitoring its progress. See *The UN Monthly Chronicle*, (April, 1975), pp. 28–30.

51. Obviously, problems existing in the environment of states also impose institutional costs upon them; for an analysis of the relationship between these two types of costs, see Ruggie (1972 and 1975).

52. One of the many case studies presented by the authors is pollution control: "Having failed to achieve international protection and then having unilaterally established a functional national jurisdiction, Canada immediately turned back to the international realms to pursue a synthesized approach to the pollution problem that would incorporate both international and national aspects in a comprehensive response" (p. 243).

53. A superb discussion of this point in the context of constructing a new international monetary system may be found in Hirsch (1973). Hirsch proposes an SDR-based system that, he feels, strikes an effective balance.

54. I am here thinking of proposed commodity agreements, particularly those proposals associated with the OPEC countries.

55. I want to acknowledge the contribution of discussions with Ernst Haas to my thinking on this point; we have further developed this thesis in Ruggie and Hass, "Environmental and Resource Interdependencies: Organizing for the Evolution of Regimes," a paper prepared for the Commission on the Organization of the Government for the Conduct of Foreign Policy, published in the Appendix of its *Report* (1975).

CHAPTER TWENTY-EIGHT

FORECASTING IN THE CONTEXT
OF INTERNATIONAL ORGANIZATIONS

Alexander Szalai

I. INTERNATIONAL ORGANIZATION AND MULTILATERALITY

There is no generally accepted definition of what constitutes an international organization. On logical grounds, one may argue for a definition stating that an international organization is an institution drawing its membership from two or more states, or having two or more states as its members, and maintaining more or less stable arrangements and facilities designed to promote periodic or continuous cooperative activities by its members (Claude, Jr., 1972).

This definition, as any other known to us, could be contested on several counts. Thus, for instance, many organizations of a typically national character have a certain number of "foreign members" or "members from abroad" and are in no way transformed by that alone into authentic international organizations. Also a closed group of individuals from different countries who have no other interest in common than to maintain arrangements and facilities for their private use (e.g., a condominium in a fashionable winter resort) would hardly qualify as an international organization.

However, quite apart from such questions of peripheral delimitation that probably could be handled by sharpening the edges of the definition, an analytically important major issue is being raised by the observation that organizations drawing their members from *two* states only, or having just *two* states as constituent members, are by no means generally recognized as genuine international organizations.

Thus, the authoritative *Yearbook of International Organizations*, issued by the Union of International Associations, will not list, by principle, any organization not having an individual or collective participation of *at least three* countries in its membership and not having the intention to cover operations in *at least three* countries. Interestingly enough, it was agreed with the United Nations Secretariat not to include in the list of intergovernmental organizations bodies arising out of bilateral agreements but only bodies "established by agreements to which three states or more are parties" (YIO, 1972, p. 15).

Of course, bilateral relations between states are all-important constituent parts of international relations in general. Nevertheless, the tendency to restrict the category of genuine international organizations to multinational organizations encompassing more than just two countries is by no means an arbitrary one. It has to be considered that the development of the contemporary complex of international organizations and of the new kind of *multilateral diplomacy* so intimately connected with certain centers of international organization (e.g., UN, EEC, CMEA, CAU) represents a *reaction* "to the extreme decentralization of the traditional system of international relations that was based to a great extent on *bilateral diplomatic activity*" and an *effort* "to adapt the mechanics of that system to the requirements posed by the constantly increasing complexity of the interdependence of states" (Claude, 1968, p. 33).

From a more pragmatic point of view, it has to be taken into account that the category of international organizations would be enormously extended and also rendered extremely inhomogeneous if it were to include the huge number and variety of essentially parochial binational organizational setups by which neighboring countries regulate traffic, transportation, communications, and trade across their common borderline, and the many kinds of binational social, cultural, professional, commercial bodies and associations that are adapted exclusively to the mutual needs of the two countries involved and normally do not play any significant role in wider international contexts.

For these and other reasons, almost all major studies on the history of international organizations and an overwhelming part of the research literature on the present set of international organizations are concentrated on organizations of a multinational character and deal at best only with certain especially relevant types of binational organizations (e.g., internationally important intergovernmental organizations to which just two states happen to be partners).

In this study we shall follow the fairly well-established practice of current international organization research and will use the term "international organizations" as a denotation of multinational organizational entities. If needed, special reference will be made to binational organizations.

Conventionally, international organizations are classified into intergovernmental organizations (IGOs) and international nongovernmental organizations (INGOs or NGOs). The category of IGOs designates organizations established by international agreements to which three or more states are parties; the category of INGOs encompasses the rest of international organizations.

Although this dichotomous classification is supported by United Nations resolutions and practices, it is neither adequate to the actual state of affairs nor particularly well suited to analytical purposes.

There are numerous major nongovernmental organizations that fulfill *de facto* intergovernmental functions but have not been established by formal international agreements. The International Criminal Police Organization (Interpol), which assures cooperation and mutual assistance among criminal police authorities in all countries of the world, is a typical example of international "nongovernmental" organizations that are *de facto* intergovernmental.

There is also a persistent trend to transform important INGOs practically into IGOs by introducing government-appointed or at least government-approved delegates into their executive bodies in place of formerly freely elected representatives. As a matter of fact, some major international scientific bodies nowadays exercise functions similar to those of typical intergovernmental authorities. The International Union of Pure and Applied Physics (IUPAP) sets, for example, binding standards for certain weights and measures that are subsequently incorporated in the national legislation of many countries. The Scientific Committee on Antarctic Research (SCAR) even exercises some of the traditionally accepted functions of sovereignty over vast areas of the Antarctic (Szalai, 1974, pp. 59–81).

Originally only nonprofit organizations, that is, organizations not attempting to make profit for distribution among their members, were regarded as qualified to be included among genuine international organizations. This position has been undermined by recent developments as more and more governments got involved by the national industries and by the establishment of various commercial state monopolies in active profit-making business. In fact, quite a number of IGOs or intergovernmentally supported INGOs (e.g., common market associations and the like) make and distribute huge profits. Furthermore, the proliferation of world-wide multinational business enterprises, multinational firms having branches and affiliations in dozens of countries and playing an increasingly important role in international politics, cannot be overlooked for long. Johan Galtung proposed the witty acronymic designation of BINGOs for this new type of "business international non-governmental organizations," which would have to be placed as a third main category of international organizations on the side of the traditional IGOs and INGOs (Galtung, 1968, pp. 12–41). Without changing its strict rules on the "accreditation" of international organizations, even the United Nations found it necessary some time ago to enter into consultations with a representative group of major multinational corporations and to recognize their special role in international developmental activities.

As we see, the whole field of international organizations is in a state of flux. Trends in the growth and development of this field are often significant indicators of certain changes going on in other parts of the international system or affecting this system as a whole. Let us put off, however, the question whether and in what way the observation and analysis of such trends might provide some foothold for forecasting in international relations and consider first certain aspects of the multilaterality of international relations embodied in the organizations we discuss.

One of the main driving forces behind the growth and the development of the field of international organizations, especially of those having an intergovernmental character, seems to be the growth of the number of nation-states active on the international scene.

As long as the set of states among which a certain amount of cooperation or reconciliation of interests has to be achieved is very small, a fairly low number of *bilateral* contacts may suffice to reach the necessary understanding. In the case of three countries (A, B, C) actually only three bilateral channels of consultation (A–B, A–C, B–C) have

to be used, may be iteratively, in order to find out about the possibilities of a consensus; in the case of four countries (A, B, C, D) the number of bilateral channels needed jumps to six (A–B, A–C, A–D, B–C, B–D, C–D). It is easy to establish by simple combinatorics that in the case of N countries $(N)(N-1)/2$ bilateral channels of consultation have to be used for the given purpose. Already in the case of twenty countries this formula leads to a rather high number of bilateral channels to be actuated, namely 190.

If we set the present number of sovereign states at $N = 150$, of which about 140 are members of the United Nations, then exactly 11,175 bilateral contacts would have to be established between pairs of states in order to reach, or to check on, any general consensus—an obviously unmanageable number and an operation of baffling complexity.

Thus, the growth of the number of nation-states active on the international scene appears to be a factor that is virtually forcing the international community to establish forums for the more or less continuous business of multilateral diplomacy (i.e., international organizations of various scope and character that may be then authorized to carry on common affairs from day to day.)

It is no wonder that the starting point of the modern history of international organizations has been conventionally set at 1815, the year of the Vienna Congress, which led to the territorial reordering of Europe by the creation of a number of new nation-states and by the restoration of many older ones that were incorporated in the Napoleonic empire.

Table 28.1 illustrates the historical parallel between the numerical growth of intergovernmental organizations and the increase in the number of independent nations within the international system.[1] As we see from Table 28.1, the number of intergovernmental organizations has grown from the last century roughly parallel with the number of independent nations (nation-states) though at a quicker pace. Major jumps in the number of independent nations after the two World Wars and during the recent decolonization period are mirrored by simultaneous or subsequent jumps in the number of international organizations. The rise of the total number of national memberships in the whole network of intergovernmental organizations can only be expressed in exponential terms: it went on over 150 years at an average yearly rate of over

Table 28.1 The growth of intergovernmental organizations (1815–1964).

Period	Number of IGOs	Number of Nations	Number of National Memberships in IGOs	Mean Number of National Memberships per IGO	Mean Number of IGO Memberships per Nation
1815–1819	1	23	6	6.0	0.3
1820–1824	1	23	6	6.0	0.3
1825–1829	1	25	6	6.0	0.2
1830–1834	1	28	6	6.0	0.2
1835–1839	2	31	18	9.0	0.6
1840–1844	2	35	18	9.0	0.5
1845–1849	2	38	18	9.0	0.5
1850–1854	2	40	18	9.0	0.5
1855–1859	3	42	24	8.0	0.6
1860–1864	3	44	21	7.0	0.5
1865–1869	6	39	54	9.0	1.4
1870–1874	7	34	65	9.3	1.9
1875–1879	9	34	106	11.8	3.1
1880–1884	11	35	136	12.4	3.9
1885–1889	17	38	203	11.9	5.3
1890–1894	21	38	267	12.7	7.0
1895–1899	23	41	299	13.0	7.3
1900–1904	30	43	412	13.7	9.6
1905–1909	44	45	639	14.5	14.2
1910–1914	49	45	753	15.4	16.7
1915–1919	53	51	826	15.6	16.2
1920–1924	72	63	1,336	18.6	21.2
1925–1929	83	65	1,528	18.4	23.5
1930–1934	87	66	1,639	18.8	24.8
1935–1939	86	67	1,697	19.7	25.3
1940–1944	82	65	1,560	19.0	24.0
1945–1949	123	75	2,284	18.6	30.5
1950–1954	144	82	2,684	18.6	32.7
1955–1959	168	90	3,338	19.9	37.1
1960–1964	195	122	4,436	22.7	36.4

4 percent leading to a 700-fold increase of the original number (6 in 1815–1819 against 4436 in 1960–1964).

Quite understandably, the size of the IGOs grew along with the number of independent nations that were, after all, potential candidates for their membership. The mean number of national memberships per IGO grew sixfold (from 23 to 122), in fairly strict parallel to the sixfold increase in the number of independent nations (from 23 to 122).

The growing need for multilateral contacts of different kinds is reflected by the fact that until 1860 the mean number of IGO-membership per nation was far below 1.0, that is only every second or third nation-state felt the need or used the oppor-

tunity to join *any* intergovernmental organization. In spite of the obvious difficulties connected with the definition and listing of "international meetings" (congresses, conferences, conventions, round tables, symposia, etc.), it may be worthwhile to mention that historical investigations set their number at 10 in 1850–1854; 602 in 1900–1904; and 4615 in 1950–1954 (YIO, 1972, p. 885).

II. TRENDS IN THE DEVELOPMENT OF INTERNATIONAL ORGANIZATIONS

The growing number of independent nations is quite obviously not the sole and not even the most important factor in the growth and development of international organizations. After all, the increasing number of sovereign nation-states is in itself a concomitant or a consequence of massive historical processes affecting the international system, such as the dissolution of empires, decolonization, the world-wide intensification of the struggle for national self-determination and independence. Empires that formerly performed to a certain extent the coordinative tasks of present-day international organizations over their own territories have been replaced by territorial groups of independent countries that still have many interests in common. For this and other reasons there is a growing need for international organizations of a regional character to take care of the interests of various territorial subsystems within the vastly expanded and ever more complex international system. Last but not least, economic, industrial, and technical developments leading to a world-wide extension and intensification of trade, traffic, and communication and to the growing recognition of global problems affecting all mankind, some of which arose as a direct consequence of those economic, industrial, and technical developments (Third World problems, exhaustion of natural resources, environmental deterioration, overpopulation, etc.)—all these and many other factors are having a powerful impact on the field of international organizations, of IGOs and INGOs alike.

This is just the reason why the observation and analysis of trends in the development of international organizations is of such a high *potential* interest to students of international affairs. We used here the term "potential interest" in order to draw the attention to the fact that the *actual* interest of political and social scientists in the study of international organizations has not yet reached any very high degree. Only a relatively small number of scholars are actively involved in research on international organizations. It may be of some interest in this context to note that no comprehensive scholarly work on the history of the United Nations is in existence. The literature on the *future* of international organizations is very limited.[2]

It is not too difficult to show that in spite of the present as yet rather underdeveloped state of statistics and data sets on the existing complex of well over 2500 international organizations—280 IGOs and 2456 INGOs as of 1972—certain *trends* in the development of this "system" can be established which throw some light on world affairs and

may provide also some ground for projections and forecasts concerning some future developments in the field of international relations. Let us look at some concrete examples.

Table 28.2 illustrates the numerical growth of IGOs and of INGOs from 1954 to 1972 in contrast to baseline data referring to 1909. The INGOs have been classified according to the main subject matter of their activities.[3] Scanning briefly the figures of Table 28.2, the following observations can be made.

1. IGOs and INGOs are both steadily growing in number. However, the numerical growth of INGOs is quicker than that of IGOs. In 1909 the number of IGOs related to the number of INGOs was about 1:5, but by 1972 the ratio was more like 1:9. There is no sign of a slowing down of this trend. It does not seem as if the creation of new intergovernmental organizations that have to be founded on formal international agreements between the member states could keep pace with the ever growing demand for the international organization of activities in a great variety of fields.

2. The most numerous INGOs belong to the class of *nongovernmental organizations associated with regional intergovernmental organizations aiming at the economic integration* (EEC and EFTA). The size of this class would appear to be much bigger if similar types of organizations associated with the Council for Mutual Economic Assistance (CMEA) and some other regional intergovernmental bodies had been taken into account. This is an entirely new species of INGOs that did not even exist 15 years ago but has grown to the largest single class of nongovernmental organizations covered by Table 28.2. It is also a species of high interest for political scientists. Whether and to what extent the intensification of mutual relations on the nongovernmental level (social and cultural contacts, travel, trade, communications, etc.) have to precede governmental measures and intergovernmental arrangements undertaken in the interest of *regional integration* and to what degree the *success* of the regional integrative process depends on such antecedents—this question was fairly central to the recent discussion about the nature of international integrative processes. Several propositions and hypotheses put forward by Karl Deutsch, Ernst Haas, and others could be tested within certain limits by a thorough analysis of time series data on the development of the IGO- and

Table 28.2　Number of international organizations by category (1909–1972).

	1972	1970	1968	1966	1964	1962	1960	1958	1956	1954	1909
IGOs	280	242	229	199	179	163	154	149	132	118	37
INGOs	2456	2281	2172	1920	1703	1540	1255	1060	973	997	176
Total	2736	2523	2401	2119	1872	1703	1409	1209	1105	1115	213
INGOs classified by main subject matter of their activities											
EEC/EFTA NGOs*	283	288	273	245	233	216	—	—	—	—	—
Health, medicine	256	225	214	173	150	133	123	104	100	101	16
Commerce, industry	251	239	233	211	168	160	163	134	123	116	5
Science	184	174	152	137	118	92	83	77	69	81	21
International relations	144	127	125	111	106	99	92	71	61	83	12
Technology	133	113	102	83	70	63	60	50	36	34	8
Professions, employees	119	112	105	93	78	76	73	67	67	56	2
Education, youth	116	106	105	91	83	71	68	62	56	54	10
Religion, ethics	112	109	103	93	87	86	87	79	70	79	21
Sport, recreation	110	99	93	90	76	72	65	55	51	67	6
Social welfare	104	95	88	76	70	64	56	53	52	52	10
Social sciences, humanistic studies	104	95	90	80	67	57	57	55	57	38	10
Arts, literature, cinema, radio, TV	89	80	75	70	65	57	57	34	34	41	6
Transport, travel	89	82	76	72	63	57	57	43	40	28	5
Agriculture	88	83	83	76	64	55	46	34	27	32	5
Press, documentation, bibliography	72	63	69	58	54	41	34	33	26	29	19
Trade unions	70	70	70	63	59	54	54	49	48	49	1
Law, administration	58	54	54	48	45	42	37	30	28	31	13
Economics, finance†	47	45	40	35	33	30	26	16	15	14	3
Politics‡	27	22	22	15	14	15	17	14	13	12	3

*It is disputed whether some of the nongovernmental organizations associated with the European Economic Community and with the European Free Trade Association are "authentic" INGOs, that is, nonprofit organizations.

†No economic and financial organizations of a profit-making character included.

‡INGOs concerned with international or world politics are classified separately under "undernational relations."

INGO-networks directly connected with the integration process, on the development of the individual and collective memberships from the countries in question in various preexisting INGOs relevant to the maintenance of social and cultural contacts, travel, trade, communications, and so forth in the region. Of course, a great amount of documentary source material would have to be studied for such a purpose because ready-made statistics and data sets suited for special investigations of this kind simply do not exist. On the other hand, the lessons of such investigations may contribute in time to a better *prediction* of the outcome of integrative processes and of international organizational measures undertaken in support of them.

3. We may assume that the proliferation of international organizations in some field of endeavor corresponds in general to a certain demand for more organized and maybe also more specialized (e.g., regionally articulated, professionally diversified) international contacts in that field. It is, therefore, rather interesting to observe how the absolute number and the numerical growth of INGOs varies over time in different fields of ac-

tivities. As Table 28.2 shows, in 1909 Science-; Religion, ethics-; and Health, medicine-INGOs formed the largest groups with 21, 21, and 16 organizations, respectively. By 1972, Science- and Health, medicine-INGOs still held their place among the numerically largest groups, but Religion, ethics-INGOs fell back to ninth place on the list, behind such relative late-starters in the domain of international nongovernmental organization as Technology and Professions, employees. Between 1954 and 1972, Technology-; Transport, travel-; and Economics, finance-INGOs *trebled* their number at an average yearly growth rate of about 6 percent and there is as yet no sign of decline in this trend. It seems that the boom of international *nongovernmental* organizational activities in certain fields often precede the creation of intergovernmental organizations in the same fields where they may have never existed before. Thus, for instance, the extremely quick growth in the number of international nongovernmental tourist organizations signaled such a growing importance of tourism in international relations that as late as 1969 the Economic and Social Council of the United Nations considered the question of transforming the International Union of Official Travel Organizations (IUOTO)—an INGO founded in 1912—into a world tourism organization of intergovernmental character. Indeed, on 5 December 1969 the General Assembly of the United Nations acknowledged in Resolution 2529 (XXIV) "the vital

contribution that international tourism is making to the *economic, social, cultural and educational progress of mankind* and in *safeguarding world peace*" and called for the conversion of IUOTO into an intergovernmental organization (World Tourism Organization) closely attached to or even incorporated into the United Nations system.

It is interesting to see how the geographical distribution of the headquarters of international organization changed in recent history. Table 28.3 sketches this global development.[4]

The figures in Table 28.3 display some trends that are well-known and others that are much less obvious without examining these data. It is surely not surprising that the upswing of decolonization that led to the creation or resurrection of many nation-states also brought about a quick increase in the number of international organizations having their headquarters on the Third World continents. The growing importance and influence of the developing countries, the needs of assistance to development, etc. induced the United Nations system and other world-wide international organizations not only to establish a number of regional organizations in the Third World but also to choose Third World metropoles as the seat of new international agencies having global responsibilities. On the other hand, there is a growing need of developing countries for the build-up of their own regional or continental networks of IGOs and INGOs.

It is not so easy to explain how Europe manages

Table 28.3 Location of international organization headquarters by continent (1850–1972).

	Europe		North America		South America and Caribbean		Africa		Asia		Pacific		Total	
	No.	%	No.	%	No.	%	No.	%	No.	%	No.	%	No.	%
1850	6	100.0	—	—	—	—	—	—	—	—	—	—	6	100.0
1870	32	94.1	2	5.9	—	—	—	—	—	—	—	—	34	100.0
1895	186	89.9	17	8.2	2	1.0	—	—	2	1.0	—	—	207	100.0
1912	417	95.4	15	3.4	3	0.7	1	0.2	1	0.2	—	—	347	100.0
1930	669	94.8	26	3.7	5	0.7	1	0.1	4	0.6	—	—	705	100.0
1954	971	81.6	145	12.2	37	3.1	13	1.1	19	1.6	6	0.5	1190	100.0
1960	1203	82.8	158	10.8	56	3.8	12	0.8	35	2.3	13	0.9	1467	100.0
1966	1986	81.0	231	9.4	107	4.4	50	2.0	71	2.9	16	0.7	2452	100.0
1972	2523	79.1	299	9.4	152	4.8	87	2.7	16	3.6	18	0.6	3187	100.0

to retain its overwhelming leadership in international organizational activities of all kinds. Still about 80 percent of all international organizations have their headquarters in Europe and this European dominance remained essentially unchanged while the total number of international organizations nearly trebled from 1954 to 1972.

Available statistics and data sets on international organizations cover among others, the evolution of the international structure of IGOs and INGOs (the rise of roof organizations, groupings, networks, etc.), the geographical and substantive distribution of international conference and meetings, the geographical extensions of the membership of IGOs and INGOs, the national representation in international organizations, etc. Part of the data material is organized in time series.

Although comprehensive and systematic data collection on international organizations is a relatively new endeavor and the field is far from being covered satisfactorily, we think that even trend analyses and projections based on the available data material can serve a useful purpose in forecasting on international relations of which international organizational activities form an important aspect.

Naturally, one has to go beyond aggregate statistics in forecasting anything about the future of international organizations and about their impact on international affairs. Hayward Alker and Bruce Russett have pioneered in the development of rather sophisticated methods for the analysis of changes in the voting patterns of the United Nations General Assembly (formulation and dissolution of voting blocs, etc.). Chadwick Alger was probably the first to carry out a regular observational "field study" on the prolonged discussions and behind-the-scenes activities of an intergovernmental committee and established analytic categories and methods that may permit a data-based evaluation and to some extent also a prediction of the outcome of certain consultative and decision-making processes in similar bodies. Kjell Skjelbaek, Kurt Jacobsen, Anthony Judge, and others produced highly interesting diachronic studies of world political trends and emerging world problems that manifest themselves in quantifiable characteristics of international organizational activities.

Thus, slowly a body of knowledge on international organizational processes is getting formed

that may provide many valuable cues for predictive studies. A methodical combination of international organizational data with events data may open up many new and promising avenues. Unfortunately, data sets embodying such a combination are still few and far between (Lopez and Stern, 1975).

Whatever hopes we put on the research of trends in international organization and on the evaluation of the findings of such research for predictive purposes, we must not forget about the limitations of our international organizational experience.

The whole complex of international organizations as we know it at present has been born and reared in a world of nation-states, and of empires built or destroyed by them. Current meanings given to the term "international," especially in the definition of international organizations, presuppose more or less the existence of the so-called nation-state system and have mostly relations among "sovereign nation-states" or "independent nations" as a referent. It would be, for instance, rather unusual to describe a colonial empire as an "international organization" although it may harbor many different dependent nations within its boundaries and organizes them in a certain way.

The most challenging questions with regard to the future of international organization transcend by far the limits of possible forecasts based on our knowledge about the existing complex of international organizations. Thus, for instance, the question whether some kind of integrated global organization (world organization, world order, world government, or the like) may arise in time out of the present set of international organizations or any subset of it—a question most often posed in the context of hopes or deceptions about the role of the United Nations in the world—involves problems the solution to which is primarily dependent on future development in the nation-state system and *not* on any predictable development within the present complex of international organizations which has the existing nation-state system as one of its most important parameters. Incidentally, at present only a relatively narrow sector of international relations is embodied in international organizations or even mediated by them.

In brief, the study of trends in the development of international organizations can contribute little to speculations, forecasts, or prophecies concerning the future of the entire international system and the possibilities of its global integration.

III. PLANNING AND FORECASTING IN INTERNATIONAL ORGANIZATIONS

We now change the subject and try to review to some extent the "status" of forecasting in the political, administrative, and operational activities of international organizations. We will be concerned not only with the actual forecasting practices of international organizations but also with the needs and possibilities for the development of these practices that may have a considerable impact on the future behavior of these organizations as actors on the international scene.

On the other hand, we have to impose certain limitations on our endeavor. Many recently created international nongovernmental organizations regard it as their main aim to provide an organizational framework for persons and institutions involved in futures research. Some of these INGOs occasionally produce quite valuable studies on various prospective developments in international affairs. Nevertheless, we shall have to concentrate our attention mainly on the pertinent activities of the major intergovernmental organizations and the United Nations system will be in the forefront of our interest.

This self-imposed limitation is not motivated by any underestimation of the importance of INGO-activities in the field of forecasting on international affairs. As a matter of fact, the achievements of the United Nations system in this field are by no means very impressive. However, for reasons that will become apparent in the course of our subsequent deliberations, we attach particular importance to the *cross-correspondence and interaction between international planning and forecasting activities,* especially to the role of forecasts in the design and administration of *world-wide programs for international action* as those developed within the United Nations family of organizations.

In order to achieve a better understanding of the intricate relations between planning and forecasting in the practice of major intergovernmental organizations that are in charge of a number of vast international programs, we have to consider some general characteristics of planning and forecasting activities and also the reasons for the wide-spread

trust in plans and the similarly widespread *mistrust in forecasts* that can be observed among international policy makers and administrators (Szalai, 1974).

Planning can be characterized as an activity intended to determine specific lines of action for reaching certain set goals. The setting of the goals may form part of the planning activity or may be exogenous to it. Planning and forecasting are akin in being both future-oriented mental activities. However, planning contains a basic volitional element—it wishes to *achieve* a future state of affairs that it regards as desirable and it gives *directives* for human action that should help to accomplish this future state of affairs. In contrast, a forecast may be concerned with the possibility of a future disaster that nobody wants and that might arise without any concerted human action contributing to it.

Planning is related to forecasting in many other ways. First, planning involves, at least tacitly or implicitly, some amount of foresight with regard to possible consequences of human action; it involves also normally the consideration of alternatives and contingencies that may arise in the course of the planned action. Both planning and forecasting tend to fulfill some preventive functions. Both serve, in different ways, to reduce uncertainty about the future.

In some cases the distinction between a "plan" and a "forecast" depends on the usage that different people may wish to make of the same set of propositions about the future. Timetables and schedules of all kinds are good examples. For the management of an airline its timetable represents a plan according to which its aircraft will have to fly certain routes at given times. Experienced passengers will regard the same timetable more like a forecast about probable departure and arrival times; moreover they will even consider, especially in winter, the probability that the plane in question may not start at all or may be forced by snow or fog to land at some airport other than the one that was foreseen originally as its destination. If airlines cared to include in their timetables the statistical probabilities of various deviations from the schedule, then their timetables would become full-fledged and well-designed probabilistic forecasts. Most airlines do have for their own internal use such probabilistically evaluated timetables because they need them for contingency planning. However, for obvious reasons this kind of information is not communicated to the public. Still, even its internal use shows how forecasting can become interwoven with the planning process—in other words, how forecasting and planning might come to represent nothing but two different strains or aspects of the very same activity.

However, we should not overlook the important fact that planning and forecasting enjoy an entirely different social status and prestige in contemporary societies. Planning has achieved a great deal of respectability and has even become an integral part of governmental policy making and administration in most countries. Consequently it has secured itself also a fairly central and well-institutionalized position in intergovernmental organizations.

On the other hand, forecasting lacks this kind of status and prestige, especially in the eyes of statesmen, administrators, diplomats, and government officials involved in the day-by-day business of politics and of international affairs. Not a few of them would still share the views of Lord Halifax who declared on the even of World War II quite openly: "I distrust anyone who foresees consequences and advocates remedies to avert them." The ill-omened policy of appeasement was conceived and defended by Lord Halifax in this spirit and nobody had to wait too long for the consequences.

There is no real contradiction between the historically well-documented disposition of political decision makers to seek the advise of soothsayers, fortune-tellers and astrologers in order to reduce uncertainty about the future and the still widespread resistance against the systematic use of contemporary methodical forecasting techniques for purposes of policy making and administration. The real contradiction lies rather in human nature itself, in the psychology of fears and anxieties. People tend to rely more on irrational hopes and feelings when fighting their uncertainty about the future than on thinking ahead and trying to face all possible consequences of their actions. In addition, fears and anxieties are themselves forecasts in a sense—they are even forecasts with a well-known tendency toward self-fulfillment. However, it would lead us too far to pursue this matter here any further.

Naturally, the mistrust of policy makers and ad-

ministrators against applications of *methodical* (i.e., methodically controlled) forecasting techniques can also be partly understood and justified on objective grounds. To date, the state of the art is by no means satisfactory and until now few forecasting methods and techniques have proved their reliability even to such an extent that they would provide on the average significantly more direct hits or at least better defined probabilities over a wider spread of alternative outcomes than reliance on traditional know-how, professional expertise, or mere intuition. Some momentous failures and blunders of recent fairly methodical future studies have been widely publicized.

But let us look at the other side of the picture. It would be a cheap argument to recount how often and in what monstrous instances eminent statesmen and diplomats were completely misled by their intuitions and guesses about the future course of events and how often the application of traditional rules of thumb led to catastrophic consequences. But what about professional expertise?

Vannevar Bush, surely one of the most outstanding science planners of our times and a high authority on technological development, declared in the late 1940's in a famous and often cited statement that intercontinental ballistic missiles are *not* feasible. At just about the same time not a single expert predicted that the computer would ever be used by business and government. Everybody agreed that the computer meant a "major revolution in science" but everybody "knew" that its main use would be in science and in warfare. As Peter Drucker reported, the most extensive market research study undertaken around that time reached the conclusion that the world computer market would, at most, be able to absorb about a thousand computers by the year 2000.

In view of the great respect and popularity that planning and programing procedures are enjoying at present in the United Nations system, it is useful to recall that the Charter of the United Nations does not contain any reference to planning or programing, does not mention it among the duties, functions, or recommended activities of any organ or body of the world organization. Neither the word "plan" nor the word "program" ever occurs in the venerable document conceived over 30 years ago.

Nevertheless, nowadays any casual visitor to the

United Nations who takes a look at the schedule of meetings for that day, at the list of documents distributed, or simply at the telephone directory of the Secretariat, must perforce become convinced that planning and programing have become one of the main and most extended activities in the world organization. There is an abundance of planning and even of program planning offices and committees; terms like "vindicative plan," "medium-term plan," "development planning," "country programing" have become household words; the United Nations maintains a number of planning centers and institutes, and so forth. The situation is by no means different in the specialized agencies of the United Nations system.

As Maurice Bertrand stated, the first so-called program budgets—the first attempts at the joint presentation of the program, and the budget (i.e., at the introduction of a modicum of systematic planning)—date from the early 1950's in the case of UNESCO and FAO, while ILO and the United Nations did not adopt program budgets until much later. The adoption of medium-term planning is of quite recent origin; it dates essentially from the early 1970's. Still the first few years of the present decade were sufficient to let the idea of medium-term planning spread like wildfire over the United Nations system; Bertrand establishes the fact that outlines of medium-term plans exist in all five major agencies of the United Nations family of organizations—the United Nations itself, FAO, ILO, UNESCO, and WHO. Even long-term (perspectivic) plans have achieved some respectability.[5]

However, it would be very wrong to think that this rapid career of systematic planning procedures was due to a particular efficiency of methodical planning procedures in reducing uncertainty about the future and in the attainment of targets set by international policy makers and administrators. Even when applying fairly compliant criteria of "plan fulfillment," one would have to come to the conclusion that only a very limited number of plans and programs launched by the United Nations system have been fulfilled in the sense of having reaching *specified* targets set in advance. (Of course, in very many cases no specified targets have been set and thus plan fulfillment cannot be checked by any objective measures.) In fact, some of the most important plans and programs of the United Nations that had well-defined and quantified goals did not come even near to their target. The history of the first development decade provides many examples. The situation improved somewhat with the increased sophistication of mathematical and computer techniques applied in methodical planning procedures. Nevertheless, this improvement would hardly suffice to explain the "planning explosion" that developed during the last decade in the United Nations and other major intergovernmental organizations.

The truth is that policy makers and administrators need planning for other purposes than just "goal attainment." First of all, methodical planning practices introduce orderly procedure in branches and sectors of decision making and implementation where traditional practices leave much to spontaneity and chance. Second, they establish scales and standards of performance with regard to managerial and administrative activities the effectiveness of which was left earlier either unmeasured or subject to individual and impressionistic assessment. Third, they involve the conscious preparatory appraisal of many more operational variables and contingencies than would otherwise be the case. Fourth, they enforce a much closer control and recording of all operational steps and phases and thus provide a much more solid basis for the evaluation of the results achieved.

The greatest service these new planning exercises did to international policy makers and administrators consisted perhaps in providing them with *a conceptual framework for ordering the tremendous amount of unaccustomed tasks and informations thrust upon them by the increased order of magnitude, the higher degree of complexity and the accelerated rate of change characterizing contemporary problems they have to cope with.*

In such an intricate and puzzling task environment as that of present-day intergovernmental organization, even the best of planning cannot provide any certitude. What it can provide is some orientation and that is something to be highly appreciated in such a situation.

Our train of thought brings us to a point where the much-belittled and disparaged stepbrother of planning, namely *methodical forecasting* comes into his right and promises to perform services that may partly enhance and partly complement those rendered by methodical planning.

IV. PARAMETERS AND VARIABLES IN CONTEMPORARY PLANNING AND FORECASTING PRACTICES

We have already made ample references to the close connection and relationship between planning and forecasting activities. We even pointed out that some elements of forecasting are inherent to planning. However, this does not mean that methodical planning as we know it today would involve *per se* an adequate portion of similarly methodical forecasting. In fact, rather the contrary is the case.

It may be helpful if we introduce at this point a somewhat technical distinction in the discussion, namely that between "parameters" and "variables." A "variable" may be defined as a value that will probably change or is to be changed within the time span of planning. A "parameter," on the other hand, is a variable that could assume many fixed values but is expected to remain stable during that same time span. For instance, if no admittance of new member-states is in sight, then the number and alphabetic seating order of delegations will be regarded as predetermined parameters in the planning of conference services for the forthcoming General Assembly of the United Nations. On the other hand, the number of speakers on various points of the agenda, the time taken up by meetings, the number of documents to be reproduced, etc. will have to be handled as variables in the course of the same planning exercise.

It is obvious that discerning between parameters and variables in this sense implies some amount of overt or covert forecasting. Planners will regard as parameters such factors that are relevant for the attainment of their targets that they do not expect to change (or to be manipulable) during the implementation of their plan. On the other hand, they will regard as variables such factors that they expect to change either spontaneously or in consequence of planned manipulations during the same time span.

In respect to the choice of parameters and variables to be taken into consideration and also in respect to the determination of the range of values, any variable might assume within the given time span, even very methodical planning operations of governmental or intergovernmental agencies relied in the past often more on guesswork implicit in traditional judgment, experience, and insight than

on conscious and explicit efforts of forecasting. In other words, their methodical planning was *not* methodical with regard to its predictive inputs and aspects.

Thus, it happened all too often that professionally well-planned projects failed because it turned out that factors "assumed" or "understood" to be parametric for the duration of the project underwent in fact very quick changes, while variables that were supposed to be manipulable (i.e., subject to deliberate upward or downward adjustments of their value) proved to be in effect immovable or, on the contrary, subject to uncontrollable oscillations and thus threw the whole project out of gear.

In brief, planners often fail to realize that parameters might well become variables over an extended period of time and variables may reach values at which they get crystallized into new parameters. Due to the present highly accelerated rate of social, economic, and technological change, "extended periods of time" tend to shrink. So-called medium-term and long-term plans involve spans of time that seem to be rather short from the point of view of forecasting (Szalai, 1974).

Of course, it would be very unrealistic to take for granted that methodical forecasting procedures built into the planning process would have safely "predicted" all such untoward developments that were unforeseen by the planners. However, they would have led at least to a systematic review and evaluation of many more possible contingencies, variations, and alternatives than planners tend to consider.

There are some governmental and communal activities in respect to which methodical medium- and long-range planning procedures have been applied for a very, very long time: public education, the development of the highway and railway network, water supply, postal services, to name only a few. Lo and behold, these are exactly those public services, facilities, and utilities that for many years happen to find themselves in a state of permanent crisis, with resources and supply lagging far behind the demand and never catching up with swiftly growing and changing requirements of contemporary society. Here again not so much the applied planning methods but rather the predictive elements involved in the planning process (assumptions about the parametric character of factors that then behave more like swiftly changing variables, etc.) seem to be at fault.

It is important to keep in mind that the contributions, the application of methodical forecasting procedures, and more generally the pursuance of systematic studies on the future can make to planning do *not* consist merely in an improvement of the estimates of relevant parameters and variables, or in the stimulation of planners to consider a greater variety of contingencies, probabilities and "alternative futures."

We may refer here to the fact that in countries where governmental economic planning became especially well developed and extended to a great variety of fields, governments soon were forced to recognize that methodical *planning* procedures would have to be complemented by methodical *forecasting* exercises (called "prognostics" in the Soviet Union). Such exercises would throw light on the possible impact of the planned achievements on political, social, and cultural value systems, social institutions and processes, collective behavior, ways of life, —in general, on domains of socioeconomic development that could not be directly considered and manipulated within the framework of governmental plans.

From the beginning, Lenin stressed the role of "scientific foresight" in socialist planning and in spite of the predominance of voluntaristic tendencies in some later periods of Soviet planning the fundamental importance of prognostics for planning was in principle always recognized. During the last decades prognostication became more and more firmly imbedded in Soviet planning practices.

In the Western world, France was among the first of those countries where the government found it necessary to establish special organs for carrying out systematic forecasting exercises and future studies of this kind within the framework of governmental administration. Even a special term, "la prospective," originally coined by Gaston Berger, has been introduced to designate this activity complementing governmental planning operations. The French Commissariat Général du Plan issues a continuous series of studies and reports under the title "Plan et Prospectives." In one of the recent volumes of this series, we find the following definition of this term:

La prospective . . . est la repérage des facteurs futurs susceptibles d'influencer les conséquences des décisions actuelles, ou d'être influencés par elles. (1972, p. 11)

The prospective . . . is the reconnoitering [or scanning] of future factors that may affect the consequences of actual decisions or that may be affected by those consequences.

(Allowance must be made in this translation for the liberty taken in using the English adjective "prospective" in a substantive sense. However, this usage is becoming more and more accepted in current English-language literature on the subject.)

It is quite clear from this definition that the establishment of prospective means in this context a forecasting operation, a kind of research on the future, intended to throw light on future factors that may affect the implementation and outcome of planning decisions or which may be affected by the fulfillment of the plan—without being included in either of these cases in the original scope of planning.

The extremely costly and sometimes deleterious side effects of the introduction of new technologies that promised to be very productive and very profitable "by themselves" has induced governmental planners and industrial managers to resort to methodical "technology assessment" as an adjunct or complement to technological planning. Essentially, technology assessment is a special variety of prospectives. It has led to the development of a number of techniques ("relevance tree analysis," "evaluation of cross-impact matrices," etc.) that are now finding increasing application to problems of nontechnological forecasting.

Technology assessment has helped a great deal to popularize modern forecasting techniques in intergovernmental bureaucracies, especially since "assessing technology for development" became a rather popular slogan. In 1970 the United Nations Economic Commission for Europe (ECE) sponsored a seminar in Warsaw on technological forecasting that considered the subject of technological assessment in its international aspects. In no time the Organization for Economic Cooperation and Development commissioned a comprehensive study on societal aspects of technology and is now developing guidelines for use by its member states on the social assessment of technology. In addressing the Second Committee of the General Assembly of the United Nations in the fall of 1973, Under Secretary General Philippe de Seynes referred to technology assessment as an already recognized though as yet insufficiently evolved discipline and urged a "truly comprehensive program for study and experimentation" for the selection of optimum technologies on a set of given social, economic, and cultural circumstances in order to eliminate guesswork from development planning which occupies at present such a central place in the activities of the United Nations system (Schieber, 1974).

V. FORECASTING AND FUTURES RESEARCH IN THE UNITED NATIONS

There has been until very recently a certain prudence or prudery in the United Nations with regard to the use of the term "forecasting." Offices of the Secretariat that were effectively involved in certain forecasting exercises or in some kinds of futures research preferred to speak of "estimates," "projections," "appraisals," "preprograming studies" they were preparing. The Center for Development Planning, Projections, and Policies in the Secretariat, which has a special branch for "review and appraisal," another one for "planning and projections," etc., produced over the years quite a number of prospective studies, short- and long-term prognoses on various aspects of socioeconomic developments that have found wide use in international futures research but no reference was ever made to the fact that the center is doing any "forecasting" works. The same applies to the Population Division that has a section for "estimates and projections," and also to the Statistical Office that has a number of branches producing a never-ending stream of most valuable "projective" information on trends in global demographic, social, economic, industrial development, international trade, and so forth. Also some of the major specialized agencies of the United Nations system, such as UNESCO, WHO, FAO, and ILO, excel in this kind of "veiled" futures research.

Nevertheless, the whole volume of such activities carried out within the United Nations family of organizations should not be overestimated. The very same factors that prompted the officers to dissimulate any forecasting or futures research activities in which they were factually involved, also prevented the systematic introduction and propagation of methodical forecasting procedures in the administration. The situation is, however, changing quickly. As Sir Robert Jackson stated in his famous "Capacity Study," the United Nations Development Program represents the one and only major

"truly cooperative and universal enterprise between the member states and the United Nations system." Furthermore, it is quite evident that *development planning* has become by far the most important *system-wide operation* within the United Nations family of organizations (UN, DP/5, 1969).

Now, development planning on the global scale, or even with regard to single world regions is an awesome task, transcending by several orders of magnitude and complexity any other planning exercise that was ever undertaken or even contemplated by intergovernmental organizations, national governments, or for that matter by multinational business enterprises. The number of parameters and variables involved in global development planning and the rate at which situations may change—and do change—by the accumulation and interaction of political, social, and economic developments in well over a hundred countries makes the task of the planner truly frightening.

It is, therefore, in the sphere of development planning that the need for the methodical application of forecasting procedures and of studies on the future came to be felt most acutely and at a relatively early date by those responsible for policy making and administration in the world organization. Any survey of futures studies within the United Nations system will show that the bulk of forecasting exercises and initiatives in the field of futures research undertaken within the United Nations family of organizations were and still are related to problems of development planning. The biggest effort of this kind is a project investigating the possible impact of measures to protect the human environment on the international development strategy. Professor Wassily Leontief has been put in charge of the United Nations–sponsored study group that is attempting to establish "alternative estimates" (the word "forecasts" is still being avoided!) of the global economic, demographic, and environmental situation in 1980, 2000, and—more speculatively—in 2050. The report of this study group was considered at the Second Biennial Review and Appraisal of the International Development Strategy in 1975. This was the first time that the results of a major comprehensive forecasting project was discussed at such a high level in the United Nations.

As of today, the situation seems to have developed to a point where a "systematic" effort to introduce methodical forecasting procedures into the planning and programing of United Nations activities cannot be delayed any more. And this is especially true with regard to the planning and programming of world-wide socio-economic development. These very acute needs for the application of methodical forecasting procedures were clearly and succinctly formulated in Maurice Bertrand's already cited "Draft Report":

The relatively general agreement that would seem to have been reached on the need to program and plan the activities of the main organizations in the United Nations system with a view to reaching common objectives, cannot however, be said to reflect any profound agreement as to what part these organizations have to play in economic and social matters. At the same time all over the world, processes of economic integration among neighboring countries in the same continent are being initiated by different methods and with varying degrees of success.

All these efforts require difficult diplomatic negotiations to define *common perspectives* in these economic and social sectors. *Only through long-term forecasting techniques, however, can the essential working hypotheses be elaborated.* National programming and planning policies which are increasingly conditioned by the data of the international situation, require for their formulation not only more precise and more comprehensive information on that situation, but a *common frame of reference* at the world and regional levels. The United Nations has admittedly offered the beginning of an answer in the form of the International Strategy for the Second Development Decade. But what many countries are asking for, at least implicitly, are perhaps far more detailed answers, providing an intellectual system of analysis, and methods and approaches much closer to the types of problem which every Government has to solve at the national level.

In these circumstances, the *need felt by Member States to develop the medium- and long-term forecasting and programming systems of the international organizations themselves, unquestionably reflects a search for clarification the significance of which, in this context, is obvious.* [Italics added.]

We think that in the last sentence Bertrand makes a very important point. The United Nations family of organizations has to develop a systematic application of forecasting procedures not only in order to improve the effectiveness of its *own* planning and programing but also because the member states need forecasts on various aspects of the international situation at the world and regional levels as a frame of reference for *their* national plans and programs.

Few, if any, of the documents issued by the world organization are so intensively studied and so continuously perused by government offices all over the world as the *Statistical Yearbook*, the *Demographic Yearbook*, the *Yearbook of International Trade Statistics*, the *Yearbook of Labor Statistics*, the UNESCO *Statistical Yearbook*, and so forth. Practically no national planning can be effectively carried out without comparing domestic and international data and without taking into account simultaneous development in other countries that are partners, competitors, or adversaries on the international scene. At the same time, no country can have all the resources, facilities, and connections needed to collect and standardize all the international data it needs to ensure the effectiveness of its own governmental planning and programing, which will always depend in some respect and to some extent on the international situation.

Very similarly, *global and regional forecasts of a systematic and methodical character will have to be produced by the United Nations system with regard to a number of international trends and developments in order to provide a frame of reference to which national governments can relate their own domestic provisions, plans, and programs.*

We may stress here again that for the time being it is of lesser importance what degree of exactitude and reliability those forecasts can achieve at the present state of the art. Their major importance lies in adding a new dimension to policy making, planning, and administration by enforcing a conscious and systematic consideration of a wide array of probabilities, alternatives, and prospectives. Moreover, very much like explicit methodical planning, explicit methodical forecasting has the advantage of providing a baseline that makes it possible to keep in evidence and to measure the deviation of factual accomplishments and developments from the expected course of events. Unfulfilled forecasts and unfulfilled plans are by no means *ipso facto* worthless. They may still have helped to ensure rational and orderly procedure and may provide very valuable data for the evaluation of past performance and for improving future action..

Nevertheless, it is, of course, a highly critical and relevant question that is being raised in this context by Bertrand and many others who advocate a system-wide application of methodical forecasting procedures in the United Nations family of organizations: To what extent, in what sectors, and by what methods is it really possible to make usable forecasts over a span of time corresponding at least to that of medium-term planning in the United Nation system, and what degree of flexibility should planning allow for in view of probabilities alternatives and prospectives established by such forecasts?

It is very difficult to give a convincing and satisfactory answer to this complex question. In some respects it touches upon problems that lie far beyond the scope of our present study. For instance, the comprehensive review of existing forecasting methods and techniques with regard to their specific applicability to various concerns and tasks of major intergovernmental organizations is in itself a topic that would have to be discussed in a whole series of separate papers.

So much can be said, however, that the best chances for the assimilation of methodical forecasting and futures research in United Nations policy making and administration offer themselves at present in connection with international problems of a not directly political character and with international plans and programs having a strong data input from fields in which prognostical and projection techniques have already achieved some currency.

It is surely not accidental that huge industrial corporations and national business firms having interests in all parts of the world took the lead in developing many new methods and techniques of forecasting in international relations in order to improve the quality of managerial decision making and of medium- or long-range policy-planning Characteristically enough, many favorite topics of this kind of "business-type" international and global forecasting do indeed have a strong "hard fact" input and involve component factors in respect to which time-series of data and sometimes even ready-made trend projections are relatively easily available.

Oscar Schachter summed up this argument in a very cogent way:

A good many international organizations of the profit-making business type promise to become foci for the development of international relations forecasting. Some of them dispose also of rather important, although as yet mostly under-used, connections and resources for this purpose. *The need for studies on the future becomes more and more conscious among international planners and administrators. Although most of the prognostic studies undertaken at present in the framework of major intergovernmental organizations are not centered around directly political problems, their methods and their finds have an import on the forecasting of international political relations.* (Schachter, 1970) [Italics added.]

There are obviously some topics and questions in respect to which no policy making or administrative organ of the United Nations would be free to resort to methodical forecasts even if the considerations involved in the forecasting process and the results of it were kept in strictest confidence. History gives evidence that in due course very great powers and empires may decline and that their end may become foreseeable quite some time ahead. Still, it is nearly unthinkable that any intergovernmental organization would be permitted to consider even as an extreme alternative of marginal probability the decline or dissolution of one of its powerful member states, or any radical shift in the world's balance of power. On a global scale, the forcible overthrow of a government is quite a customary event that presents in many cases no great surprise but may eventually give rise to grave complications on the international scene. Nevertheless, apart from very exceptional circumstances this is not a contingency that can be discussed in advance anywhere in the United Nations, save in the corridors of the General Assembly. There are also many other taboos to observe, not all of them in the sphere of peace, security, and sovereignty, though the heaviest concentration of such sensitive topics is to be found naturally in the heartland of international politics.

Interestingly enough, the Charter of the United Nations itself seems to demand in some respects a systematic scanning of possible future developments and contingencies. Article 1 of the Charter establishes as one of the main purposes of the United Nations to bring about "the adjustment or settlement of international disputes or situations that might lead to a breach of the peace." It is quite clear that the judgment about the question whether an international dispute or situation might or might not lead to a breach of the peace involves some appraisal of alternatives and probabilities in respect to the future course of events. It involves, in other words, some amount of forecasting. Whether the United Nations should or could make at least some auxiliary use of methodical forecasting procedures when striving to decide such questions in the sphere of peace and security, or whether it should continue to rely more or less exclusively on the wisdom, insight, and foresight of its own policy-making bodies—this is, of course, not a problem that could be solved merely on the basis of scholarly arguments. The present negative attitude of the majority of governmental representatives in respect to the methodical application of forecasting procedures in the international political decision making process may change in the future.

Article 14 calls for an even wider application of foresight and/or forecasting when it refers to measures for the peaceful adjustment of any situation, regardless of "origin" that the General Assembly may deem "likely to impair the general welfare or friendly relations among nations." By the inclusion of concerns about "general welfare" and all kinds of "friendly relations among nations," the whole array of not directly political problems is brought into play, to which international prospectives could be applied with some promise.

As we have stressed so much the limitations and constraints put on the application of methodical forecasting procedures in intergovernmental organizations, it is only fair if we refer now to some special advantages of doing forecasting work and futures research in an international ambience.

It can be shown, for instance, that *in respect to certain very relevant questions, intergovernmental organizations of the global type have a much better chance to arrive at correct forecasts than any national agency.* It is simply not true that local or domestic forecasts have by their narrower scope necessarily a better chance to be on target. The contrary may be the case.

Let us take as a kind of paradigm the World Weather Watch (the program launched by the World Meterological Organization that should lead to the establishment of world-wide network of interconnected meterological observation points) supplemented by a system of meteorological satellites that observe atmospheric processes that take place simultaneously in the global atmosphere.

It is quite obvious that as soon as such a comprehensive world weather watch will become operative, the reliability of meteorological prognoses and the time span over which fairly accurate weather forecasts can be established will increase to a very significant extent. First of all, many relevant atmospheric processes literally go around the world. Following them over oceans and continents and observing their interactions with other currents and forces of the natural environment permits meteorologists to see much further ahead with regard to factors influencing the weather.

Furthermore, in spite of the well-developed daily exchange of some basic domestic and local meteorological data between national meteorological services, nothing comparable to the wealth and variety of systematically ordered and evaluated informations that the world weather watch can provide could ever be obtained by any, even the richest and best equipped, national meteorological service of the world. It is also a fact that the weather does not respect national frontiers; it comes and goes as it pleases.

Finally, a host of factors external to the system of data on which present-day regional, domestic, and local forecasts are based would become internalized in global forecasts and a much more solidly established general theory of the weather could be built up in order to give better guidance to anyone having an interest in weather and weather forecasting, or even in the planned modification of the weather that is one of the great possibilities of the future.

Incidentally, this great possibility contains frightening dangers. A lot of "prospective" will have to be considered before the technology of large-scale artificial rainmaking might get accepted under tightly controlled conditions. The rain that will be drawn out of the clouds in country X might have fallen down somewhat later spontaneously in country Y. It is only too easy to imagine situations in which people would go to war for half an inch of rain diverted from their fields and pastures. Talking about the weather one day might become a highly political subject.

The United Nations system could render a very great service to national governments by providing them with *methodically elaborated and periodically revised forecasts on the development of global parameters and variables that put limiting conditions on national planning and action.* Without such a service it may easily happen—or perhaps has already happened—that the total of natural and other resources "booked" by various nations in their medium- and long-term planning exceeds everything that will be *globally* available at a given date of the commodity in question. Such an eventuality constitutes in itself a threat to future peace, security, and general welfare.

In a survey of national long-term planning, the following interesting observation was made:

> Comparison of separately expressed projections of national and regional demands for specific resources in the next ten to twenty years where they existed, showed that the *total* world availability could not accommodate the combined projections. This was found to hold true, in many cases, even where potential technological advances and new reserve discoveries might indicate some continued expansion of resource adequacy or substitution. For example, where a given country projected a requirement for approximately one third of the world's demand for some specific material by the year 1980 or 2000—and the U.S., EEC and COMECON projections were added for the same periods— the future for total world demand was, obviously, upwards of 300% of any rationally projected estimate of available world supply! (McHale, 1974, p. 4)

It is true that the United Nations and many of the specialized agencies do already publish a fairly great variety of international "estimates" and "standards" for national planning. However, relatively few of these estimates are controlled by the best available contemporary methods and techniques of forecasting; moreover, the standards issued are often more oriented on what seems to be desirable than on what may be attainable in the future. Moreover, practically no efforts have been as yet undertaken to integrate all these estimates and standards prepared by the various agencies into a coherent system that would take into account all the interdependencies and interactions between variables involved. There is no such thing at present as an interagency coordination of forecasting and standard-setting practices in the United Nations system, though its existence would enhance significantly the reliability of international esti-

mates and the applicability of international standards offered to policy makers, planners, and administrators all over the world. As of today, there is not even any guarantee that the future-oriented estimates and standards made public by the various agencies of the United Nations system—each of them with an eye to its *own* special field of concern (industrialization, education, health, food and agriculture, labor conditions, housing, or whatever else it may be)—are at all *compatible* with each other and with some not improbable alternative courses that socio-economic development may take in the future in different parts of the world.

The United Nations Institute for Training and Research took recently the initiative to create a "lookout tower for the United Nations system" that is "a program for the continuous examination of major world trends and developments that have implications for the future of mankind and may require responses from the system of international agencies" (Szalai, 1974).

As a first step in this direction, a "Project on the Future" has been launched by the Institute with the aim of probing the possibilities of "preventive forecasting." The aim is to alert the international community about evolving problems that may call for urgent international action and to stimulate such international action through the United Nations or its specialized agencies. Once again futures research on "nondirectly-political" problems, that is the forecasting of social, economic, cultural, and technological trends having a *potentially* great import on the future development of international affairs is at the time being in the foreground of the planned studies (Szalai, 1974). However, this may change rather soon. The future "politicization" of subjects that are not regarded as hotly political at present is definitely *not* under the control of forecasters and it might take place in an unforeseen way while they are still working on their forecasts.

It remains to be seen how successful this and other initiatives will be in making forecasting and futures research part and parcel of international policy making and administration in the United Nations system. To some extent even the future of the whole system may depend on the success of such initiatives. It has become only too evident that traditional methods of intergovernmental policy making and administration are not able to cope with the problems of our present and future world.

And as far as the United Nations system is concerned, it is surely not the lack of planning but the lack of *foresight* in planning that reduces the efficiency of its actions in so many fields.

As we have already said (see Szalai, 1974), Arthur Clarke's sly remark, "The future ain't as it used to be," applies also to the United Nations system. The World Organization, as it sometimes calls itself, will have to make a conscious and purposeful effort to foresee as far as possible the international future and to prepare itself for it. Only by doing so can it assure its own place in the still more complex international world of tomorrow.

NOTES

1. This table is based on Table 14 in YIO, 14th ed., p. 885. The data were derived from the following sources: Singer and Wallace (1970); Skjelsbaek, (1970 and 1971).

2. A very carefully assembled and organized international bibliography of contemporary research literature on INGOs, and also to some extent covering research on IGOs, is contained in Judge and Skjelsbaek (1971), pp. 903–919. A number of items in this bibliography, which extends to about 1970, refer to studies on the future of international organizations; also a listing of documents, statistics, data sets, relevant to forecasting is included. Bibliographies attached to the articles on "International Organization" and "International Integration" in the *International Encyclopaedia of the Social Sciences* may be used in a complementary way. More recent studies concerned with the future of international organizations that are not listed in these bibliographies, apart from those cited in the previous note, include the following: Judge (1970); Schachter (1970); Gardner (1972); Union of International Associations (1973); Jacobsen (1973); Elmandjra (1973); Swedish Royal Ministry for Foreign Affairs— Secretariat for Future Studies (1974); Szalai (1974).

3. This table presents in reorganized form the main data of Table 3 in YIO, 14th ed., p. 879.

4. This table has been calculated on the basis of Table 5 in YIO, 14th ed., p. 880.

5. Bertrand (1972) and United Nations General Assembly, Joint Inspection Unit (1974).

BIBLIOGRAPHY

Abt, Clark.
   1964   "War Gaming." *International Science and Technology,* no. 32: 29–37.

Adams, R. H. and J. L. Jenkins.
   1960   "Simulation of Air Operations with the Air Battle Model." *Operations Research* 8:600–615.

Aitken, A. C.
   1935   "On Least Squares and Linear Combination of Observations." *Proceedings of the Royal Society of Edinburgh* 55:42–48.

Alavi, Anza.
   1973   *Nuevo y Vicjo Imperialismo.* Buenos Aires: Tiempo Nuevo.

Alcock, Norman Z.
   1972   "The Prediction of War" (mimeographed). Oakville, Ontario: Canadian Peace Research Institute.

Alker, Hayward R., Jr.
   1969   "Statistics and Politics: The Need for Causal Data Analysis." In *Politics and the Social Sciences,* ed. S. M. Lipset, pp. 244–313. New York: Oxford University Press.
   1970   "Integration Logics: A Review, Extension, and Critique." *International Organization* 24:869–914.
   1973   "On Political Capabilities in a Schedule Sense: Measuring Power Integration and Development." In *Mathematical Approaches to Politics,* eds. Hayward, Alker, et al., pp. 307–373. New York: Elsevier.
   1975   "Polimetrics: Its Descriptive Foundations." In *Handbook of Political Science,* Vol. 7, eds. Fred I. Greenstein and Nelson W. Polsby, pp. 139–210. Reading, Mass.: Addison-Wesley.

Alker, Hayward R., Jr. and C. Bock.
   1972   "Propositions about International Relations." *Political Science Annual* 3:385–495.

Alker, Hayward R., Jr. and Cheryl Christensen.
   1972   "From Causal Modeling to Artificial Intelligence: The Evolution of a UN Peace-Making Simulation." In *Experimentation and Simulation in Political Science,* eds. J. A. Laponce and Paul Smoker, pp. 177–224. Toronto: University of Toronto Press.

Alker, Hayward *et al.*
1974   *Analyzing Global Interdependence.* Cambridge, Mass.: MIT Center for International Studies.

Allison, Graham T.
1969   "Conceptual Models and the Cuban Missile Crisis." *American Political Science Review* 63:689–718.

1971   *Essence of Decision.* Boston: Little, Brown.

Allison, Graham T. and Morton H. Halperin.
1972   "Bureaucratic Politics: A Paradigm and Some Policy Implications." In *Theory and Policy in International Relations*, eds. Raymond Tanter and Richard H. Ullman, pp. 40–79. Princeton, N.J.: Princeton University Press.

Allport, F. H.
1924   *Social Psychology.* Boston: Houghton Mifflin.

Almond, Gabriel A. and James S. Coleman (Editors).
1960   *The Politics of the Developing Areas.* Princeton, N.J.: Princeton University Press.

Anderson, R. L.
1942   "Distribution of the Serial Correlation Coefficient." *Annals of Mathematical Statistics* 13:1–13.

Anderson, T. W. and Leo A. Goodman.
1957   "Statistical Inference About Markov Chains." *Annals of Mathematical Statistics* 28:89–110.

Ando, Albert, *et al.* (Editors).
1963   *Essays on the Structure of Social Science Models.* Cambridge, Mass.: MIT Press.

Aronson, Elliot.
1972   *The Social Animal.* San Francisco: W. H. Freeman and Company.

Arrow, Kenneth.
1963   *Social Choice and Individual Values*, 2nd ed. New York: Wiley.

Ashley, Richard and Nazli Choucri.
1973   "Notes on Bayesian Analysis." Cambridge, Mass.: MIT Center for International Studies (unpublished).

Ashley, Richard *et al.*
1973   "Directives for Bayesian Analysis in International Relations." Cambridge, Mass.: MIT Center for International Studies (unpublished).

Averch, Harvey A. and M. M. Lavin.
1965   *Dilemmas in the Politico-Military Conduct of Escalating Crises.* Santa Monica, Calif.: The Rand Corporation, P-3204.

Ayres, Robert N.
1966   *On Technological Forecasting*, Report HI-484-DP (revised). New York: Hudson Institute.

1968   "Envelope Curve Forecasting." In *Technological Forecasting for Industry and Government*, ed. James R. Bright, pp. 77–94. Englewood Cliffs, N.J.: Prentice-Hall.

1969   *Technological Forecasting and Long-Range Planning.* New York: McGraw-Hill.

Azar, Edward E.
1970a   "Analysis of International Events." *Peace Research Review* 4:1–113.

1970b   "The Dimensionality of Violent Conflict: A Quantitative Analysis." *Peace Research Society (International) Papers* 15:122–167. Cambridge Conference.

1972   "Conflict Escalation and Conflict Reduction in an International Crisis: Suez, 1956." *Journal of Conflict Resolution* 16:183–201.

1973   *Probe for Peace: Small State Hostilities.* Minneapolis: Burgess.

1975   "Behavioral Forecasts and Policy Making: An Events Data Approach." In *International Events and the Comparative Analysis of Foreign Policy*, ed. Charles W. Kegley, Jr., pp. 215–239. Columbia: University of South Carolina Press.

Azar, Edward E., *et al.*
1972   "Making and Measuring the International Event as a Unit of Analysis." In *International Events Interaction Analysis: Some Research Considerations*, International Studies Series 1, ed. Vincent Davis, pp. 59–77. Beverly Hills, Calif.: Sage Publications.

Baier, Kurt.
1958   *The Moral Point of View.* Ithaca, N.Y.: Cornell University Press.

Balinski, M., *et al.*
1966   *Review of the TEMPER Model—Final Report.* Princeton, N.J.: MATHEMATICA Corporation.

Batelle Memorial Institute.
1971   *Trends in Western European Political, Economic and Defense Policies 1970–85,*

and Implications for United Strategy 1–4. Columbus, Ohio.

Bauer, Raymond A.
1969   *Second-Order Consequences.* Cambridge, Mass.: MIT Press.

Baumgartner, Thomas.
1975   "The Structuring of International Economic Relations" (mimeographed). International Studies Association.

Bay, Christian.
1978   *The Structure of Freedom.* Stanford, Calif.: Stanford University Press.

Bayes, Thomas.
       Philosophical Transactions of the Royal Society 53.

1958   *Biometrika* 45:293–315.

Bean, Louis H.
1969   *The Art of Forecasting.* New York: Random House.

Beardsley, Philip L.
1973   "Political Pseudo Science: Critical Essays on Behavioralism and Post-Behavioralism" (mimeographed).

Beckwith, Burnham Putnam.
1967   *The Next 500 Years: Scientific Predictions of Major Social Trends.* New York: Exposition Press.

Bell, Daniel.
1964   "Twelve Modes of Prediction." *Daedalus* 93:845–880.

1967   "Toward the Year 2000." *Daedalus* 96: 639–651.

1973   *The Coming of Post-Industrial Society.* New York: Basic Books.

Bell, Wendell and James A. Mau (Editors).
1971   *The Sociology of the Future.* New York: Russell Sage Foundation.

Bell, Wendell, *et al.*
1971   "A Paradigm for the Analysis of Time Perspectives and Images of the Future." In *The Sociology of the Future,* eds. Wendell Bell and James A. Mau, pp. 45–55. New York: Russell Sage Foundation.

Ben-Dak, Joseph D. and Michael Mihalka.
1972   "Bayesian Analysis: An Exposition and Implications for International Peace." Paper presented to the First Annual Convention of the Peace Research Society (International) Southern Section; Chapel Hill, N.C.

Beres, Louis R. (Editor).
1975   *Planning Alternative World Futures: Values, Methods, and Models.* New York: Praeger.

Berkowitz, L. and A. LePage.
1967   "Weapons as Aggression-eliciting Stimuli." *Journal of Personality and Social Psychology* 6:202–207.

Bestuzhev-lada, Igor.
1969   "Forecasting—An Approach to the Problems of the Future." *International Social Science Journal* 21:526–534.

Bhagwati, Jagdish N. (Editor).
1972   *Economics and World Order: From the 1970's to the 1990's.* New York: Macmillan.

Bick, J. H. and H. Everett.
1967   "CODE 50: A Multi-Weapon, Multi-Target Nuclear Exchange War Game." Paper presented at AMRAC Proceedings, ARPA: Project Defender (unclassified).

Billingsley, Patrick.
1961   *Statistical Inference for Markov Processes.* Chicago: University of Chicago Press.

Binder, A.
1966   "Learning and Extinction of Leadership Preferences in Small Groups." *Journal of Mathematical Psychology* 3:129–139.

Blackman, Wade A.
1972   "Forecasting Through Dynamic Modeling." *Technological Forecasting and Social Change* 3:291–307.

Blalock, Hubert M., Jr.
1960   *Social Statistics.* New York: McGraw-Hill.

1965   "Some Implication of Random Measurement Error for Causal Inferences." *American Journal of Sociology* 81:37–47.

Blalock, Hubert M., Jr. and Ann B. Blalock (Editors).
1968   *Methodology in Social Research.* New York: McGraw-Hill.

Bloomfield, Lincoln P.
1968   *Western Europe to the Mid-Seventies: Five Scenarios.* Cambridge, Mass.: MIT Center for International Studies, A/68-3.

1970   *Anticipating Conflict-Control Policies, The "CONEX" Games as a Planning Tool.* Cambridge, Mass.: MIT Center for International Studies, C/70/10.

1971 "After Neo-Isolationism, What?" *Bulletin of the Atomic Scientists* 27:9–13.

1973 *Theories of State: Analyzing the Policy Process.* Prepared for the Office of External Research, US Department of State.

1974 *The Foreign Policy Process: Making Theory Relevant.* Beverly Hills, Calif.: Sage Publications.

1977 "Policy Planning Redefined: What the Planners Really Think." *International Relations* (Canada) 32:813–828.

1978 "Planning Foreign Policy: Can It Be Done?" *Political Science Quarterly* Autumn (in press).

Bloomfield, Lincoln P. and Robert R. Beattie.
1971 "Computers and Policy-making: The CASCON Experiment." *Journal of Conflict Resolution* 15:33–53.

Bloomfield, Lincoln P. and Cornelius J. Gearin.
1973 "Games Foreign Policy Experts Play: The Political Exercise Comes of Age." ORBIS, 16:1008–1031.

Bobrow, Davis B.
1969 "International Indicators." Discussion draft paper prepared for delivery at the Annual Meeting of the American Political Science Association, New York, September 2–6.

1972a *International Relations: New Approaches.* New York: The Free Press.

1972b "The Relevance Potential of Different Products." In *Theory and Policy in International Relations,* eds. Raymond Tanter and Richard H. Ullman, pp. 204–228. Princeton, N.J.: Princeton University Press.

"Transitions to Preferred World Futures: Some Design Considerations." University of Minnesota.

1973 "Criteria for Valid Forecasting." Presented at International Forecasting Conference, MIT, Cambridge, Mass.

Bodenheimer, Susanne.
1971 "Dependency and Imperialism: The Roots of Latin American Underdevelopment." In *Readings in US Imperialism,* eds. K. T. Fann and D. Hodges. Boston: Porter Sargent.

Boorman, K.
Interview with Boorman, *et al.* In *Perspectives on Contemporary American Strategy.*

Los Angeles, Calif.: Political Research Organization, Occidental College.

Boorman, Scott A.
1969 *The Protracted Game.* London and New York: Oxford University Press.

Bouglé, Celestin.
1958 *Essais sur le régime des castes.* English translation of the introduction in *Contributions to Indian Sociology* II. Cambridge: Cambridge University Press.

Boulding, Kenneth.
1972 "The Economics of the Coming Spaceship Earth." In *The Futurists,* ed. Alvin Toffler. New York: Random House.

Box, George E. P. and Gwilyn M. Jenkins.
1970 *Time Series Analysis: Forecasting and Control.* San Francisco: Holden-Day.

Bozeman, Adda B.
1960 *Politics and Culture in International History.* Princeton, N.J.: Princeton University Press.

Brandt, Richard B.
1959 *Ethical Theory.* Englewood Cliffs, N.J.: Prentice-Hall.

Braudel, Fernand.
1974 *Capitalism and Material Life, 1400–1800.* New York: Harper Torchbooks.

Braybrooke, David and Charles E. Lindblom.
1963 *A Strategy of Decision.* New York: The Free Press.

Brewer, Garry D.
1975 "Analysis of Complex Systems: An Experiment and Its Implications for Policymaking." In *Organized Social Complexity: Challenge to Politics and Policy,* ed. Todd R. La Porte, pp. 175–219. Princeton, N.J.: Princeton University Press.

Brewer, Garry D. and Ronald D. Brunner (Editors).
1975 *Political Development and Change: A Policy Approach.* New York: The Free Press.

Briggs, Asa.
1961 "The Welfare State in Historical Perspective." *Archives Européenes de Sociologie* 2:221–258.

1968 "The World Economy: Interdependence and Planning." *New Cambridge Modern History* 12:502–528.

Bright, James (Editor).
1968 *Technological Forecasting for Industry and Government.* Englewood Cliffs, N.J.: Prentice-Hall.

Bright, James.
1973 "Forecasting by Monitoring Signals of Technological Change." In *A Guide for Practical Technological Forecasting*, eds. James Bright and Milton Schoeman, pp. 238–256. Englewood Cliffs, N.J.: Prentice-Hall.

Bright, James and Milton Schoeman (Editors).
1973 *A Guide for Practical Technological Forecasting*. Englewood Cliffs. N.J.: Prentice-Hall.

Brody, Richard A.
1963 "Some Systemic Effects of the Spread of Nuclear Weapons Technology: A Study Through Simulation of a Multi-Nuclear Future." *Journal of Conflict Resolution* 7:663–753.

Brown, Lester.
1972a *The Interdependence of Nations*. New York: Foreign Policy Association, Headline Series No. 212.

1972b "An Overview of World Trends." *The Futurist*, December, pp. 125–232.

1972c *World Without Borders*. New York: Random House.

1973a *Population and Affluence*. Overseas Development Council Paper #15.

1973b "Rich Countries and Poor in a Finite, Interdependent World." *Daedalus* 102:153–164.

1974 *In the Human Interest*. New York: W. W. Norton.

Brown, Robert Goodell.
1963 *Smoothing, Forecasting and Prediction of Discrete Time Series*. Englewood Cliffs, N.J.: Prentice-Hall.

Brown, Seyom and Larry L. Fabian.
1975 "Toward Mutual Accountability in the Nonterrestrial Realms." In *International Responses to Technology*, a special issue of *International Organization* 29, eds. John Gerard Ruggie and Ernst B. Haas, pp. 877–892.

Brunner, Ronald.
1968 "Some Comments on Simulation Theories of Political Development." In *Simulation in the Study of Politics*, ed. W. D. Coplin, pp. 329–342. Chicago: Markham.

Brunner, Ronald D. and Garry D. Brewer.
1971 *Organized Complexity: Empirical Theories of Political Development*. New York: The Free Press.

1972 *Policy and the Study of the Future*. Santa Monica, Calif.: The Rand Corporation, P-4912.

Bryce, James Vicount.
1906 *The Holy Roman Empire*. London: Macmillan.

Brzezinski, Zbigniew.
1968 "America in the Technetronic Age." *Encounter* 30:16–26.

1974–1975
"Recognizing the Crisis," *Foreign Policy* 17:63–74.

Buchan, Alastair.
1966 "Crisis Management: The New Diplomacy." *The Atlantic Papers*. Paris: The Atlantic Institute.

Buchanan, James M. and Gordon Tullock.
1962 *The Calculus of Consent*. Ann Arbor: University of Michigan Press.

Bull, Hedley.
1966 "International Theory: The Case for a Classical Approach." *World Politics* 18:361–377.

Burgess, P. and R. Lawton.
1972 *Indicators of International Behavior: An Assessment of Events Data Research*. Beverly Hills, Calif.: Sage Publications.

Burrowes, Robert and Douglas Muzzio.
1972 "Road to the Six Day War: Aspects of an Enumerative History of Four Arab States and Israel, 1965–1967," *Journal of Conflict Resolution* 16:211–226.

Burrowes, Robert, *et al.*
1974 "Mirror, Mirror on the Wall . . . A Source Comparison of Inter-Nation Event Data." In *Comparing Foreign Policy: Theories, Findings, and Methods*, ed. James N. Rosenau. New York: Halsted Press.

Butler, William F. and Robert A. Kavish.
1966 *How Business Economists Forecast*. Englewood Cliffs, N.J.: Prentice-Hall.

Cameron, John.
1973 *Which Future for the Planner: Proposals*, MIRM73-1, Strategic Studies Institute (mimeographed). Carlyle Barracks, Pa.

Campbell, Donald T. and Julian C. Stanley (Editors).
1966 *Experimental and Quasi-Experimental Designs for Research*. Chicago: Rand McNally.

Cantril, Hadley.
1961 *Human Nature and Political Systems*.

New Brunswick, N.J.: Rutgers University Press.

Caporoso, James A. and Alan L. Pelowski.
1971 "Economic and Political Integration in Europe." *American Political Science Review* 52:418–433.

Caporoso, James A. and Leslie L. Roos, Jr. (Editors).
1973 *Quasi-Experimental Approaches.* Evanston, Ill.: Northwestern University Press.

Carr, E. H.
1945 *Nationalism and After.* London: Macmillan.

Caspary, William R.
1968 "United States Public Opinion During the Onset of the Cold War." *Peace Research Society (International) Papers* 9: 25–36.

Cetron, Marvin J.
1961 *Technological Forecasting: A Practical Approach.* New York: Technology Forecasting Institute.

Chamberlain, J. P.
1923 *The Regimes of International Rivers: Danube and Rhine.* New York: n.p.

Chapman, John W.
1971 "Political Forecasting and Strategic Planning." *International Studies Quarterly* 15:317–357.

Chapman, R. L. and John L. Kennedy.
1955 *The Background and Implications of the System Research Laboratory Studies.* Santa Monica, Calif.: The Rand Corporation, P-740.

Chayes, Abram.
1972 "An Inquiry into the Workings of Arms Control Agreements." *Harvard Law Review* 84:905–969.

Choucri, Nazli.
1974a "Forecasting in International Relations: Problems and Prospects." *International Interactions* 1:63–86.

1974b *Population Dynamics and International Violence: Propositions, Insights, and Evidence.* Lexington, Mass.: D. C. Heath/Lexington Books.

1976 "From Correlation Analysis to Computer Forecasting: The Evolution of a Research Programme in International Relations." In *In Search of Global Patterns,* ed. James N. Rosenau, pp. 81–90. New York: The Free Press.

Choucri, Nazli with James P. Bennett.
1972 "Population, Resources, and Technology: Political Implications of the Environmental Crisis." In *World Eco-Crisis: International Organizations in Response,* eds. David A. Kay and Eugene B. Skolnikoff, pp. 9–46. Madison: University of Wisconsin Press.

Choucri, Nazli with Vincent Ferraro.
1974 *Energy Interdependence.* In *Analyzing Global Interdependence,* vol. 2, eds. Haywood Alker, *et al.,* pp. 1–192. Cambridge, Mass.: MIT Center for International Studies.

1976 *International Politics of Energy Interdependence: The Case of Petroleum.* Lexington, Mass.: D. C. Heath.

Choucri, Nazli, Michael Laird, and Dennis Meadows.
1972 *Resource Scarcity and Foreign Policy: A Simulation Model of International Conflict.* Cambridge, Mass.: MIT Center for International Studies.

Choucri, Nazli and Robert C. North.
1972 "Dynamics of International Conflict: Some Policy Implications of Population, Resources, and Technology." In *Theory and Policy in International Relations,* eds. Raymond Tanter and Richard H. Ullman, pp. 80–122. Princeton, N.J.: Princeton University Press.

1975 *Nations in Conflict: National Growth and International Violence.* San Francisco: W. H. Freeman and Company.

Choucri, Nazli and D. Scott Ross.
1976 *Energy Problems and International Politics: A Simulation Model of Price, Exchange, and Control.* Cambridge, Mass.: MIT Center for International Studies.

Choucri, Nazli with D. Scott Ross.
1979 *Energy Exchange and International Relations: A Simulation Model of Petroleum Price, Trade, and Payments* (in preparation).

Chow, Gregory C.
1960 "Tests of Inequality Between Sets of Coefficients in Two Linear Regressions." *Econometrica* 27:591–605.

Christ, Carl F.
1960 "A Symposium on Simultaneous Equation Estimation: Any Verdict Yet?" *Econometrica* 28:835–871.

1966 *Econometric Models and Methods.* New York: Wiley.

Churchman, C. W., *et al.*
1957 *Introduction to Operations Research.* New York: Wiley.

Ciba Foundation.
1972 *Civilization and Science: In Conflict or Collaboration?* A Ciba Foundation Symposium. The Hague: M. Nijhoff.

Claude, Inis L., Jr.
1968 "International Organization: I. The Process and the Institutions." In *International Encyclopaedia of the Social Sciences* 8: 33–40. New York: The Free Press.

1972 "International Organizations." In *Encyclopaedia Britannica* 12:428.

Cline, Barbara Levett.
1963 *Men Who Made a New Physics.* New York: Mentor Books.

Cline, V. B.
1964 "Interpersonal Perception." *Progress in Experimental Personality Research* 1, ed. B. A. Maher, pp. 221–284. New York: Academic Press.

Cockroft, James, *et al.*
1972 *Dependence and Underdevelopment.* New York: Doubleday.

Cohen, Bernard C.
1968 "Foreign Policy." In *International Encyclopaedia of the Social Sciences* 5:530–535. New York: The Free Press.

Cole, H. S. D., *et al.* (Editors).
1973 *Models of Doom: A Critique of The Limits to Growth.* New York: Universe Books.

Commissariat Général du Plan.
1972 "1985: La France face au choc du future." Paris: Colin.

Commission on the Year 2000.
1967 "The Nature and Limitations of Forecasting." *Daedalus* 96:936–947.

Coombs, Clyde H.
1964 *A Theory of Data.* New York: Wiley.

Cooper, Richard.
1968 *The Economics of Interdependence.* New York: McGraw-Hill.

Cooper, Richard N.
1975 "Prolegomena to the Choice of an International Monetary System." In *World Politics and International Economics*, a special issue of *International Organization* 29, eds. C. Fred Bergsten and Lawrence B. Krause, pp. 63–97.

Coplin, William D.
1968 *Simulation in the Study of Politics.* Chicago: Markham.

Cortes, Fernando, *et al.*
1974 *Systems Analysis for Social Scientists.* New York: Wiley.

Crombie, A. C. and M. A. Hoskin.
1970 "The Scientific Movement and Its Influence, 1610–1650." *New Cambridge Modern History* 4:132–168.

Crow, W. J.
1963 "A Study of Strategic Doctrines Using the Inter-Nation Simulation." *Journal of Conflict Resolution* 7:580–589.

Crow, W. J. and R. C. Noel.
1965 *The Valid Use of Simulation Results.* La Jolla, Calif.: Western Behavioral Sciences Institute.

Cyert, Richard M. and James G. March.
1963a *The Behavior of the Firm.* Englewood Cliffs, N.J.: Prentice-Hall.

1963b *A Behavioral Theory of the Firm.* Englewood Cliffs, N.J.: Prentice-Hall.

Dale, Edwin L.
1975 "Kissinger's Worldwide Economic Design." *New York Times*, May 28, p. 40.

Dalkey, Norman C.
1966 *Central Nuclear War Games.* Santa Monica, Calif.: The Rand Corporation, P-3437.

1969 "An Experimental Study of Group Opinion: The Delphic Method." *Futures* 1: 408–426.

Dalkey, Norman C. and Olaf Helmer.
1963 "An Experimental Application of the Delphi Method to the Use of Experts." *Management Science* 9.

Dalkey, Norman C., *et al.*
1972 *Studies in the Quality of Life: Delphi and Decision-making.* Lexington, Mass.: D. C. Heath.

Daly, Herman E.
1973 *Toward a Steady-State Economy.* San Francisco: W. H. Freeman and Company.

Davis, R. H.
1963 "Arms Control Simulation: The Search for an Acceptable Method." *Journal of Conflict Resolution* 7:590–602.

de Araujo Castro, Joao Augusto.
1972 "Environment and Development." *International Organization* 26:401–416.

de Jouvenel, Bertrand.
1967   *The Art of Conjecture.* New York: Basic Books.

1974   *Futuribles* (mimeographed). Santa Monica, Calif.: The Rand Corporation.

De Leon, Peter.
1973   *Scenario Designs: An Overview.* Santa Monica, Calif.: The Rand Corporation, R-1218-ARPA.

Dencik, Lars.
1973   "The Role of Studies of the Future in the Political Process." Paper prepared for the IXth World Congress of the International Political Science Association, Montreal, August 19–25.

Deusenberry, James S., *et al.* (Editors).
1965   *The Brookings-SSRC Quarterly Econometric Model of the United States.* Chicago: Rand McNally.

1969   *The Brookings Model: Some Further Results.* Chicago: Rand McNally.

Deutsch, Karl W.
1966   *The Nerves of Government.* New York: The Free Press.

1967   "Communication Models and Decision Systems." In *Contemporary Political Analysis,* ed. James C. Charlesworth, pp. 273–299. New York: The Free Press.

1972   "The Contribution of Experiments within the Framework of Political Theory." In *Experimentation and Simulation in Political Science,* eds. J. A. Laponce and Paul Smoker, pp. 19–35. Toronto: University of Toronto Press.

Deutsch, Karl W. and J. David Singer.
1964   "Multipolar Power Systems and International Stability." *World Politics* 16:390–406.

DeWeerd, Harvey.
1967   *Political Military Scenarios.* Santa Monica, Calif.: The Rand Corporation, P-3535.

1968   *An Israeli Scenario for a Laboratory Simulation.* Santa Monica, Calif.: System Development Corporation, SP-3139.

1973   "A Contextual Approach to Scenario Construction." Santa Monica, Calif.: The Rand Corporation, P-5084.

Doob, J. L.
1953   *Stochastic Processes.* New York: Wiley.

Dresher, Melvin.
1959   *Some Military Applications of the Theory of Games.* Santa Monica, Calif.: The Rand Corporation, P-1849.

1961   *Games of Strategy: Theory and Applications.* Englewood Cliffs, N.J.: Prentice-Hall.

Drucker, Peter F.
1973   "New Technology: Predicting Its Impact Is Perilous and Futile." *New York Times,* March 15, p. 73.

Dumont, Louis.
1972   *Homo Hierarchicus: The Caste System and Its Implications.* London: Paladin Edition.

Durbin, J. and G. S. Watson.
1950   "Testing for Serial Correlation in Least Squares Regression." I. *Biometrika* 37:409–428.

1951   "Testing for Serial Correlation in Least Squares Regression." II. *Biometrika* 38:159–178.

Eisner, Mark and Robert Pindyck.
1972   "A Generalized Approach to Estimation as Implemented in the TROLL/1 System." NBER Computer Research Center, Technology Square, Cambridge, Mass.

Ellul, Jacques.
1964   *The Technological Society.* New York: Knopf.

Elmandjra, Mahdi.
1973   *The United Nations System: An Analysis.* London: Faber and Faber.

Engfeldt, Lara-Göran.
1973   "The United Nations and the Human Environment." *International Organization* 27:393–412.

Etzioni, Amitai.
1966   "The Dialectics of Supranational Unification." *International Political Communities.* Garden City, N.Y.: Anchor Books.

1968   *The Active Society.* New York: The Free Press.

Eulau, Heinz.
1958   "H. D. Lasswell's Developmental Analysis." *Western Political Quarterly* 11:229–242.

Evans, George William, *et al.*
1967   *Simulation Using Digital Computer.* Englewood Cliffs, N.J.: Prentice-Hall.

Fair, Ray.
1970   "The Estimation of Simultaneous Equation Models with Lagged Endogenous Variables and First Order Serially Correlated Errors." *Econometrica* 38:407–516.

Falk, Richard A.
1971a "Statist Imperatives in an Era of System Overload." Paper presented to the American Association for the Advancement of Science, Philadelphia.

1971b *This Endangered Planet.* New York: Random House.

1975a "A New Paradigm for International Legal Studies: Prospects and Proposals." *Yale Law Journal* 84:969–1021.

1975b *A Study of Future Worlds.* New York: The Free Press.

Feinberg, Gerald.
1968 *The Prometheus Project.* New York: Doubleday.

Fennessey, James.
1968 "The General Linear Model: A New Perspective on Some Familiar Topics." *American Journal of Sociology* 74:1–27.

Fergenbaum, E. A. and Julian Feldman (Editors).
1963 *Computers and Thought.* New York: McGraw–Hill.

Ferkiss, Victor.
1969 *Technological Man.* New York: George Braziller.

1974 *The Future of Technological Civilization.* New York: George Braziller.

Fisher, Franklin M.
1959 "Generalization of the Rank and Order Conditions for Identifiability." *Econometrica* 27:431–447.

1966 *The Identification Problem in Econometrics.* New York: McGraw-Hill.

1970a "Simultaneous Estimation: The State of the Art." Working Paper, Department of Economics, No. 55. MIT, Cambridge, Mass.

1970b "Tests of Inequality Between Sets of Coefficients in Two Linear Regressions: An Expository Note." *Econometrica* 38:361–366.

Fishman, George S. and Philip J. Kiviat.
1967 "Digital Computer Simulation: Statistical Considerations." Prepared for United States Air Force Project RAND, Memorandum RM-5387-PR. Santa Monica, Calif.: The Rand Corporation.

1971 "The Statistics of Discrete-Event Simulation." In *Computer Simulation of Human Behavior*, eds. J. M. Dutton and W. H. Starbuck. New York: Wiley.

Flook, A.
1970 "Simulation Studies of International Conflict." *Simulations & Games* 14:181–184.

Foraru, Anne Thompson.
1974 "Transnational Political Interests and the Global Environment." *International Organization* 28:31–60.

Forrester, Jay W.
1961 *Industrial Dynamics.* Cambridge, Mass.: MIT Press.

1968 *Principles of Systems.* Cambridge, Mass.: Wright-Allen Press.

1969 *Urban Dynamics.* Cambridge, Mass.: MIT Press.

1971a "Counterintuitive Behavior of Social Systems." *ZPG National Reporter.*

1971b *World Dynamics.* Cambridge, Mass.: Wright-Allen Press.

Fox, Annette Baker, *et al.* (Editors).
1974 "The Lima Declaration," the "Charter of Economic Rights and Duties of States," and the "Declaration and Programme of Action on the Establishment of a New International Economic Order." *UN Monthly Chronicle* 12.

Franco, G. Robert.
1973 "Selecting Efficient Forecasts." *Futures* 4:383–391.

Frankena, William K.
1963 *Ethics.* Englewood Cliffs, N.J.: Prentice-Hall.

Freud, Sigmund.
1918 *Totem and Taboo,* trans. A. A. Brill. New York: Random House.

Friedlander, Saul.
1965 "Forecasting in International Relations." In *Futuribles: Studies in Conjecture*, ed. Bertrand de Jouvenel. Geneva: Librairie Droz, S. A.

Friedman, Milton.
1953 *Essays in Positive Economics.* Chicago: University of Chicago Press.

Fucks, Wilhelm.
1965 *Formeln zur Macht.* Stuttgart: Deutsche Verlags-Anstalt.

Furtado, Calso.
1973 "The Concept of External Dependence in the Study of Underdevelopment." In *The Political Economy of Development and Underdevelopment*, ed. Charles Wilbert. New York: Random House.

Gabor, Dennis.
1963   *Inventing the Future*. London: Seeker and Warburg.

Galbraith, John Kenneth.
1968   *The New Industrial State*. New York: Signet Books.

Galofre, Fernando.
1973   "Dependencia." *Economia y Politica* 4.

Galtung, Johan.
1964   "A Structural Theory of Aggression." *Journal of Peace Research* 2:95–119.

1968   "On the Future of International Systems." In *Mankind 2000*. London: Allen and Unwin.

1970   "Diachronic Correlation, Process Analysis and Causal Analysis." *Quality and Quantity* 4:55–94.

1976   *The True Worlds: A Transnational Perspective*. New York: The Free Press.

Gardner, Martin.
1969   *The Ambidextrous Universe*. New York: Mentor Books.

Gardner, Richard N.
1956   *Sterling-Dollar Diplomacy*. Oxford: Clarendon Press.

1972   "The Future of the United Nations Secretariat." *UNITAR-Institute on Man and Science*. New York.

Geisler, Murray A. and A. S. Ginsberg.
1965   *Man-Machine Experience*. Santa Monica, Calif.: The Rand Corporation, P-3214.

Gelb, Leslie H. and Anthony Lake.
1974–1975
          "Washington Dateline: Less Food, More Politics." *Foreign Policy* 17:176–189.

George, Alexander.
1959   *Propaganda Analysis: A Study of Inferences Made from Nazi Propaganda in World War II*. Evanston, Ill.: Row & Peterson.

1971   Introduction to *The Limits of Coercive Diplomacy*, ed. Alexander George, *et al.*, pp. ix–xviii. Boston: Little, Brown.

1972   "The Case for Multiple Advocacy in Making Foreign Policy." *American Political Science Review* 66:751–785.

George, Alexander and Juliette L. George.
1956   *Woodrow Wilson and Colonel House: A Personality Study*. New York: John Day.

George, Alexander L. and Richard Smoke.
1974   *Deterrence in American Foreign Policy:*

Theory and Practice. New York: Columbia University Press.

Gibbons, Jean Dickson.
1971   *Nonparametric Statistical Inference*. New York: McGraw-Hill.

Goldberger, Arthur S.
1964   *Econometric Theory*. New York: Wiley.

Goldhamer, Herbert and Hans Speier.
1959   "Some Observations on Political Gaming." *World Politics* 12:71–83.

Gordon, T. J. and H. Hayward.
1968   "Initial Experiments with the Cross Impact Matrix Method of Forecasting." *Futures* 1:100–116.

Gordon, Theodore and Olaf Helmer.
1966   "Report on a Long-Range Forecasting Study." The Rand Corporation Paper P-2982 (1964). Subsequently reprinted as an Appendix to *Social Technology*. New York: Basic Books.

Gordon, William J. J.
1961   *Synectics*. New York: Collier Books.

Gottlieb, Allan and Charles Dalfen.
1973   "National Jurisdiction and International Responsibility: New Canadian Approaches to International Law." *American Journal of International Law* 67:229–258.

Gottlieb, Gideon.
1972   "The Nature of International Law: Toward a Second Concept of Law." In *The Future of the International Legal Order* 4, eds. Cyril E. Black and Richard A. Falk, pp. 331–383. Princeton, N.J.: Princeton University Press.

Greenberg, William.
1969   "A Learning Model Simulation of UN Responses to Crises." Unpublished M.S. thesis, Department of Political Science, MIT. Cambridge, Mass.

Groennings, Sven, *et al.* (Editors).
1970   *The Study of Coalition Behavior: Theoretical Perspectives and Cases from Continents*. New York: Holt, Rinehart and Winston.

Gross, Leo.
1968   "The Peace of Westphalia, 1643–1948." In *International Law and Organization*, eds. Richard A. Falk and Wolfram F. Hanrieder, pp. 45–67. Philadelphia: Lippincott.

Guetzkow, Harold.
1950   "Long Range Research in International

Relations." *The American Perspective* 4:421–440.

1959   "A Use of Simulation in the Study of Inter-Nation Relations." *Behavioral Science* 4:183–191.

1966   "Validation Studies in the Simulation of International Processes." Paper presented at the Norman Wait Harris Conference at the University of Chicago.

1968   "Some Correspondences Between Simulations and 'Realities' in International Relations." In *New Approaches to International Relations*, ed. M. A. Kaplan, pp. 202–269. New York: St. Martin's Press.

1969   "Simulations in the Consolidation and Utilization of Knowledge About International Relations." In *Theory and Research on the Causes of War*, eds. Dean G. Pruitt and Richard C. Snyder, pp. 284–300. Englewood Cliffs, N.J.: Prentice-Hall.

Guetzkow, Harold, *et al.*
1972   *Simulation in Social and Administrative Science: Overviews and Case-Examples.* Englewood Cliffs, N.J.: Prentice-Hall.

Gurr, T.
1968   "A Causal Model of Civil Strife: A Comparative Analysis Using New Indices." *American Political Science Review* 62:1104–1124.

1970   *Why Men Rebel.* Princeton, N.J.: Princeton University Press.

Gurvitch, Georges.
1953   "Hyper-empirisme Dialectique." *Cahiers Internationaux de Sociologie* 15:3–33.

Haas, Ernst B.
1958   *The Uniting of Europe.* Stanford, Calif.: Stanford University Press.

1964   *Beyond the Nation-State: Functionalism and International Organization.* Stanford, Calif.: Stanford University Press.

1968   *Collective Security and the Future International System.* University of Denver, Monograph Series in World Affairs 5.

1970   "The Study of Regional Integration: Reflections on the Joy and Anguish of Pretheorizing." *International Organization* 24:607–646.

1975a   "An International Scientific Society?" In *International Institutions and the International Political System*, ed. G. Goodwin. London: Croom Helm.

1975b   "Is There a Hole in the Whole? Knowledge, Technology, Interdependence, and the Construction of International Regimes." In *International Responses to Technology*, a special issue of *International Organization* 29, eds. John Gerard Ruggie and Ernst B. Haas, pp. 827–875.

Habermas, Jürgen.
1968   *Knowledge and Human Interests.* Boston: Beacon Press.

1971   "Technology and Science as 'Ideology.'" In *Toward a Rational Society*, pp. 81–122. Boston: Beacon Press.

Halberstam, David.
1972   *The Best and the Brightest.* New York: Random House.

Hampden-Turner, Charles.
1970   *Radical Man.* Cambridge: Schenkman.

Hannan, E. J.
1960   *Time Series Analysis.* London: Methuen.

Hardin, Garrett.
1968   "The Tragedy of the Commons." *Science* 162:1243–1248.

1972   *Exploring Ethics for Survival.* New York: Viking Press.

Hare, Richard M.
1952   *The Language of Morals.* Oxford: Clarendon Press.

Harman, Willis W.
1969   "The New Copernican Revolution." In *Stanford Today.*

1970   *Alternative Futures and Educational Policy.* Menlo Park, Calif.: Educational Policy Research Center, Stanford Research Institute.

Harris, William R.
1974   *On Countering Strategic Deception.* Santa Monica, Calif.: The Rand Corporation, R-1230-ARPA.

Hatry, H., *et al.*
1962   *TEMPO Military Planning Game: Description and Discussion.* Santa Barbara, Calif.: G. E. TEMPO.

Hawkes, Nigel.
1968   "The World in 2020." *Nature* 218:14–16.

1971   "CERN: Final Planning Begins for Europe's Big Machine." *Science* 172:653.

Helmer, Olaf.
1966   *Social Technology.* New York: Basic Books.

1972a "Cross-Impact Gaming." *Futures* 4:149–167.

1972b "On the Future State of the Union." Institute for the Future report, R-27.

Hermann, Charles F.
1967 "Validation Problems in Games and Simulations with Special Reference to Models of International Politics." *Behavioral Science* 12:216–231.

1969 *Crises in Foreign Policy: A Simulation Analysis.* Indianapolis: Bobbs-Merrill.

Hermann, Charles F. and Margaret G. Hermann.
1967 "An Attempt to Simulate the Outbreak of World War I." *American Political Science Review* 61:400–416.

Hermann, Charles F., *et al.*
1973 *NEON: A Foreign Events Data Set.* Beverly Hills, Calif.: Sage Publications.

Hetman, François.
1973 *Society and the Assessment of Technology.* Paris: OECD.

Hewson, John and Siguke Sakakibara.
1975 *The Euro-Currency Markets and Their Implications.* Lexington, Mass.: Lexington Books.

Hibbs, Douglas A., Jr.
1972 "Problems of Statistical Estimation and Causal Inference in Dynamic, Time Series Regression Models." Prepared for the 1972 Annual Meeting of the American Political Science Association, Washington, September 5–9.

1973a *Mass Political Violence.* New York: Wiley.

1973b "Problems of Statistical Estimation and Causal Inference in Time-Series Regression Models." In *Sociological Methodology 1973*, ed. Herbert L. Costner. San Francisco: Jossey-Bass.

1974 *On Analyzing the Effects of Policy Interventions: Box-Jenkins and Box-Tiao vs. Structural Equation Models.* Cambridge, Mass.: MIT Center for International Studies.

Higgins, Benjamin.
1968 *Economic Development.* New York: W. W. Norton.

Hilsman, Roger.
1967 *To Move a Nation.* New York: Doubleday.

Hinsley, F. H.
1967a "The Concept of Sovereignty and the Relations Between States." *Journal of International Affairs* 21:242–252.

1967b *Power and the Pursuit of Peace.* New York: Cambridge University Press.

Hiroshima Association for Publication on Peace and Culture (Editor).
1969 *The Testimony of Hiroshima* (Hiroshima no Shogen). Tokyo: Nihon Hyoron Sha.

Hirsch, Fred.
1973 "An SDR Standard: Impetus, Elements, and Impediments." *Essays in International Finance* 99. International Finance Section, Department of Economics, Princeton University.

"Historical Studies Today." *Daedalus* 100. Winter 1971.

Hitchcock, D. R.
1958 *A Note on Evaluating Operational Gaming.* Santa Monica, Calif.: System Development Corporation, SP-40.

Hobson, J. A.
1938 *Imperialism.* London: Allen and Unwin.

Holsti, Ole R.
1963 "The Value of International Tension Measurement." *Journal of Conflict Resolution* 7:608–617.

1971 "Crisis, Stress, and Decision-making." *International Social Science Journal* 23:53–67.

Holsti, Ole R., *et al.*
1968 "Perception and Action in the 1914 Crisis." In *Quantitative International Politics*, ed. J. David Singer, pp. 123–158. New York: The Free Press.

1969 "The Management of International Crisis: Affect and Action in American-Soviet Relations." In *Theory and Research on the Causes of War*, eds. Dean G. Pruitt and Richard C. Snyder, pp. 62–79. Englewood Cliffs, N.J.: Prentice-Hall.

Holton, Gerald.
1975 "On the Role of Themata in Scientific Thought." *Science* 188:328–334.

Horvath, William J. and Caxton C. Foster.
1970 "Stochastic Models of War Alliances." In *Alliance in International Politics*, ed. Julian R. Friedman, *et al.*, pp. 165–174. Boston: Allyn and Bacon.

Houthakker, H. S. and S. P. Magee.
1969 "Income and Price Elasticities in World

Trade." *Review of Economics and Statistics* 51:111–125.

1972 "How Global Forces Are Reshaping Human Life." *The Futurist* 6:232–235.

Howard, R. A.
1966 "Decision Analysis: Applied Decision Theory." In *Proceedings of the Fourth International Conference on Operational Research*, eds. D. B. Hertz and J. Melese. New York: Wiley.

Huntington, Samuel.
1973 "Transnational Organizations in World Politics." *World Politics* 25:333–368.

Husserl, Edmund.
1965 *Phenomenology and the Crisis of Philosophy.* New York: Harper and Row.

Iklé, Fred C.
1964 *How Nations Negotiate.* New York: Harper and Row.

1971a *Every War Must End.* New York: Columbia University Press.

1971b "Sound Forecastings—The Problem of Changing Values." *Futures* 3:142–150.

Inbar, Michael and Clarice S. Stoll.
1972 *Simulation and Gaming in Social Science.* New York: The Free Press.

Interim Report of the Research Committee on Overall Energy.
1974 (Sogo Enerugi Chosakai Sogo Bukai Chukan Torimatome) and its *Reference Material* (Sanko Shiryo), Agency of National Resources and Energy (Shigen Enerugi Cho), July 25.

International Relations After the Second World War.
1962 State Political Literature Publishing House, l:xxvi. Moscow.

International Telecommunication Union.
1965 *From Semaphore to Satellite.* Geneva: International Telecommunication Union.

Isaacs, R.
1965 *Differential Games: A Mathematical Theory with Applications to Warfare and Pursuit, Control and Optimization.* New York: Wiley.

Ivanoff, Dmitri N., *et al.*
1967 *Structure of a Methodology for Environmental Projections.* Huntington Beach, Calif.: Douglas Aircraft.

Jackson, Robert.
1969 "A Study of the Capacity of the United Nations Development System." United Nations Document DP/5.

Jacobsen, Kurt.
1973 "The United Nations System: A Quantitative Analysis of Inequality, Conflict, and Relevance" (mimeographed.). IPRA. Oslo.

Janis, I. L. and S. Feshback.
1953 "Effects of Fear Arousing Communications." *Journal of Abnormal and Social Psychology* 48:78–92.

Jantsch, Erich.
1967a "Forecasting the Future." *Science Journal* 3, no. 10:40–45.

1967b *Technological Forecasting in Perspective.* Paris: Organization for Economic Cooperation and Development.

1972 *Technological Planning and Social Futures.* London: Cossel Associates Business Programmes.

Jeffreys, H.
1961 *Theory of Probability*, 3rd ed. Oxford: Clarendon Press.

Jensen, Lloyd.
1972 "Predicting International Events." *Peace Research Reviews* 4, no. 6:1–65.

Jervis, Robert.
1970 *The Logic of Images in International Relations.* Princeton, N.J.: Princeton University Press.

Jestice, Aaron L.
1964 *Project PATTERN—Planning Assistance Through Technical Evaluation of Relevance Numbers.* Washington, DC: Honeywell.

Johnson, Norman L. and Samuel Katz.
1969 *Distributions in Statistics: Discrete Distributions.* Boston: Houghton Mifflin.

Johnston, John.
1972 *Econometric Methods*, 2nd ed. New York: McGraw-Hill.

Journal of International Affairs 26:192–215. Summer 1972.

Judge, Anthony J.
1970 "International Organizations and the Generation of the Will to Change: The Information Systems Required." UAI Study Papers INF/5, Union of International Associations. Brussels.

Judge, Anthony J. and Kjell Skjelsbaek.
1973 "International Non-governmental Organizations as a Field of Study." *Yearbook of International Organization* 14:909–919.

Jungk, Robert.
1969 "Look-out Institutions for Shaping the Government." *Futures* 1:227–231.

Jungk, Robert and Johan Galtung.
1968 *Mankind 2000.* London: Allen and Unwin.

Kahn, Herman.
1964a "Alternative World Futures." New York: Hudson Institute, paper HI-342.

1964b *Thinking About the Unthinkable.* New York: Avon.

1965 *On Escalation, Metaphors, and Scenarios.* New York: Praeger.

1966 "On Alternative World Futures: Issues and Themes." New York: Hudson Institute.

1968 "The Alternative World Future Approaches." In *New Approaches to International Relations,* ed. Morton A. Kaplan, pp. 83–136. New York: St. Martin's Press.

1970 *The Emerging Japanese Super State.* Englewood Cliffs, N.J.: Prentice-Hall.

1974 "On Studying the Future." New York: Hudson Institute, paper HI-2101/c-P.

Kahn, Herman and B. Bruce-Briggs.
1972 *Things to Come.* New York: Macmillan.

Kahn, Herman and Anthony J. Wiener.
1967 *The Year 2000: A Framework for Speculation on the Next Thirty-Three Years.* New York: Macmillan.

Kaiser, Karl.
1969 "Interdependencies in World Politics." *International Journal* 24:726–750.

1971 "Transnational Politics: Toward a Theory of Multinational Politics." *International Organization* 25:790–817.

Kaplan, Abraham.
1964 *The Conduct of Inquiry.* San Francisco: Chandler.

Kaplan, Morton.
1957 *System and Process in International Politics.* New York: Wiley.

Kato, Hidetoshi.
1966 *The Japanese Who Forecast* (Yogen suru Nihonjin). Tokyo: Takeuchi Shoten.

Kay, David A. and Eugene B. Skolnikoff (Editors).
1972 *World Eco-Crisis: International Organizations in Response.* Madison: University of Wisconsin Press.

Kay, I.
1972 "Digital Discrete Simulation Languages: A Discussion and an Inventory." *The Proceedings of the Fifth Annual Simulation Symposium.* New York: Gordon and Breach.

Kaya, Yoichi, *et al.*
1974 "A New Design for Development." In *In Search for a New World Model* (Atarashii Sekaizo o Motomete), ed. Saburo Okita. Tokyo: Diamond Sha.

Kecskemeti, Paul.
1958 *Strategic Surrender: The Politics of Victory and Defeat.* Stanford, Calif.: Stanford University Press.

Kendall, M. G.
1954 "Note on Bias in the Estimation of Autocorrelation." *Biometrika* 41:403–404.

Kent, George.
1972 "Political Design." University of Hawaii, The Dimensionality of Nations Project, Research Report No. 63.

Keohane, Robert and Joseph Nye.
1972 *Transnational Relations and World Politics.* Cambridge, Mass.: Harvard University Press.

1973 "World Politics and the International Economic System." In *The Future of the International Economic Order,* ed. C. Fred Bergsten, pp. 115–179. Lexington, Mass.: D. C. Heath.

1974 "Transgovernmental Relations and International Organizations." *World Politics* 27:39–62.

Kishida, Junnosuke, *et al.*
1973 "A Policy-Oriented Examination of 'The Limits to Growth' Model." In *International Symposium on Social Systems Research* (Shakai System Kenkyu Kokusai Symposium). Tokyo: Japan Techno-Economic Society.

Kissinger, Henry A.
1974 "Address to the Sixth Special Session of the United Nations General Assembly." *International Organization* 28:573–583.

1975 Excerpts from the Paris talks. *New York Times,* May 29, p. 19.

Kiviat, Phillip J. and A. Alan B. Pritsker.
1969 *Simulation with GASP II.* Englewood Cliffs, N.J.: Prentice-Hall.

Kiviat, Phillip J., *et al.*
1968 *The SIMSCRIPT II Programming Language.* Englewood Cliffs, N.J.: Prentice-Hall.

Klein, Lawrence R.
1971 "Whither Econometrics?" *Journal of the American Statistical Association* 66:415–421.

Klingberg, Frank.
1961 "Studies in the Measurement of the Relations among Sovereign States." In *International Politics and Foreign Policy*, ed. James N. Rosenau. New York: The Free Press.

Knorr, Klaus.
1964 "Failures in National Intelligence Estimates." *World Politics* 16:455–467.

Komatsu, Sakyo.
1973 *The Submersion of the Japanese Archipelago* (Nihon Retto Chinbotsu). Tokyo: Kobunsha.

Kothari, Rajni.
1975 *Footsteps into the Future.* New York: The Free Press.

Kramer, Gerald H.
1971 "Short-Term Fluctuations in U.S. Voting Behavior, 1896–1964." Cowles Foundation Paper No. 344, New Haven, Conn.: Cowles Foundation for Research in Economics at Yale University.

Krech, David, *et al.*
1969 *Elements of Psychology*, 2nd ed. New York: Knopf.

Kroeber, A. L.
1930 "Caste." *International Encyclopaedia of the Social Sciences* 3:254b–257a. New York: The Free Press.

Kuh, Edwin and John R. Meyer.
1957 "How Extraneous Are Extraneous Estimates?" *Review of Economics and Statistics* 39:380–393.

Kuhn, Harold W.
1962 "Game Theory and Models of Negotiation." *Journal of Conflict Resolution* 6:1–4.

Kuhn, Thomas.
1964 *The Structure of Scientific Revolutions.* Chicago: University of Chicago Press.

Kuznets, Simon.
1951 "Statistical Trends and Historical Changes." *Economic History Review* 3:265–298.

Lakatos, Imre.
1970 "Falsification and the Methodology of Scientific Research Programmes." In *Criticism and the Growth of Knowledge*, eds. Imre Lakatos and Alan Musgrave, pp. 91–195. Cambridge: Cambridge University Press.

Landes, David S.
1969 *The Unbound Prometheus.* Cambridge: Cambridge University Press.

Laponce, J. A. and Paul Smoker (Editors).
1972 *Experimentation and Simulation in Political Science.* Toronto: University of Toronto Press.

La Porte, Todd R. (Editor).
1975 *Organized Social Complexity: Challenge to Politics and Policy.* Princeton, N.J.: Princeton University Press.

Laqueur, Walter.
1972 *Europe Since Hitler.* Hermondsworth, England: Penguin Books.

Lasswell, Harold D.
1938 "Chinese Resistance to Japanese Invasion: The Predictive Value of Precrisis Symbols." *American Journal of Sociology* 43:704–716.

1941 "The Garrison State." *American Journal of Sociology* 46:455–468.

1966 "The Changing Image of Human Nature: The Socio-cultural Aspect (Future-Oriented Man)." *American Journal of Psychoanalysis* 26:157–166.

1968 "The Future of the Comparative Method." *Comparative Politics* 1:3–18.

Lasswell, Harold D. and Daniel Lerner (Editors).
1965 *World Revolutionary Elites: Studies in Coercive Ideological Movements.* Cambridge, Mass.: MIT Press.

Leavitt, Michael.
1970 "Thoughts on Computer Simulation of International Relations." Paper delivered at Annual Meeting of the American Political Science Association, Los Angeles, Calif.

1971 "A Computer Simulation of International Alliance Behavior." Unpublished Ph.D. dissertation, Department of Political Science, Northwestern University, Evanston, Ill.

1974 "Theory, Partial Theory and Computer Simulation in the Study of International Relations." In *The Simulation of Intersocietal Relations*, ed. Joseph D. Ben-Dak. New York: Gordon and Breach.

Leites, Nathan.
1951 *The Operational Code of the Politburo*. New York: McGraw-Hill.

1953 *A Study of Bolshevism*. Glencoe, Ill.: The Free Press.

1959 *On the Game of Politics in France*. Stanford, Calif.: Stanford University Press.

Lenin, V. I.
1939 *Imperialism, the Highest Stage of Capitalism*. New York: International Publishers.

1960–1970 *Collected Works* 39:67 (Russian 5th ed.); 39:473 (English 4th ed.).

Lévi-Strauss, Claude.
1953 "Social Structure." In *Anthropology Today*, ed. Alfred L. Kroeber, pp. 524–553. Chicago: University of Chicago Press.

1963 "Social Structure." In *Structural Anthropology*, pp. 277–323. Garden City, N.Y.: Anchor Books.

Lindblom, Charles E.
1959 "The Science of Muddling Through." *Public Administration Review* 19:79–88.

Lindgren, B. W.
1971 *Elements of Decision Theory*. New York: Macmillan.

Linstone, Harold A.
1974 "Planning: Toy or Tool?" *IEEE Spectrum* 11, no. 4:42–49.

Lipset, Seymour M. and Leo Lowenthal (Editors).
1961 *Culture and Social Character*. New York: The Free Press.

Livermore, W. R.
1898 *The American Kriegspiel: A Game for Practicing the Art of War Upon a Topographical Map*. 2nd ed. Boston: W. B. Clarke.

Livingston, Dennis.
1971 "Science Fiction Models of Future World Order Systems." *International Organization* 25:254–270.

Lopez, George A. and Jean M. Stern.
1975 "A Framework for Data Collection on IGOs." Working paper prepared for the panel "The Applicability of Events Data for the Study of International Organization." Annual Meeting of the International Studies Association, Washington, DC, February.

Lyon, Peter.
1973 "New States and International Order." In *The Bases of International Order*, ed. Alan James, pp. 24–59. London: Oxford University Press.

MacPherson, Crawford B.
1962 *The Political Theory of Possessive Individualism*. New York: Oxford University Press.

Malinvaud, E.
1966 *Statistical Methods of Econometrics*. Chicago: Rand McNally.

Malthus, Thomas.
1951 *Principles of Political Economy*. New York: A. M. Kelley.

1963 *An Essay on the Principle of Population*. Homewood, Ill.: Richard D. Irwin.

Marcuse, Herbert.
1968 "Industrialization and Capitalism in the Work of Max Weber." In *Negations: Essays in Critical Theory*, pp. 201–226. Boston: Beacon Press.

Marien, Michael.
1973a "Daniel Bell and the End of Normal Science." *The Futurist* 7:262–268.

1973b "Herman Kahn's Things to Come." *The Futurist* 7:7–15.

Markley, O. W.
1971 *Alternative Futures: Contexts in Which Social Indicators Must Work*. Menlo Park, Calif.: Educational Policy Research Center, Stanford Research Institute.

Marshall, Andrew.
1966 *Problems of Estimating Military Power*. Paper read at the Annual Meeting of the American Political Science Association.

Martinenko, P. F.
1969 *The Sociology of International Relations*. Kiev.

Martino, Joseph P.
1972 *Technological Forecasting for Decision-Making*. New York: American Elsevier.

1973 "Evaluating Forecast Validity." In *A Guide to Practical Technological Forecasting*, eds. James Bright and Milton Schoeman, pp. 26–52. Englewood Cliffs, N.J.: Prentice-Hall.

Marx, Karl.
1936 *The Capital: A Critique of Political Economy*. New York: Modern Library.

Marx, Karl and Friedrich Engels.
 1948 *The Communist Manifesto.* New York: New York Labor News Co. *Works* (in Russian) 20:10–11 (no date).

Mattingly, Garrett.
 1955 *Renaissance Diplomacy.* Baltimore: Penguin Books.

Mayer, Jean.
 1975 "Management of Famine Neglect." *Science* 188:571–577.

Mazrui, Ali A.
 1973 "The Lumpen Proletariat and the Lumpen Militariat: African Soldiers as a New Political Class." *Political Studies* (United Kingdom) 21:1–12.

 1973, 1974
   "Ethnic Stratification and the Military-Agrarian Complex: The Uganda Case." Paper written for presentation at the Ninth Meeting of the Social Science Conference of the Universities of East Africa, Dar es Salaam, December 1973, and at the Sixteenth Meeting of the Canadian-African Studies Association, Halifax, Nova Scotia, February-March 1974.

 1975 *A World Federation of Cultures: An Africian Perspective.* New York: The Free Press.

McClelland, Charles.
 1961 "The Acute International Crisis." *World Politics* 41:182–204.

 1968 "Access to Berlin: The Quantity and Variety of Events, 1948–1963." In *Quantitative International Politics,* ed. J. David Singer, pp. 159–186. New York: The Free Press.

 1969 "International Interaction Analysis in the Predictive Mode." World Event/Interaction Survey Technical Report No. 3 (mimeographed). Los Angeles: University of Southern California, School of International Relations.

 1973 "Some Effects on Theory from the International Event Analysis Movement." In *International Events Interaction Analysis: Some Research Considerations,* International Studies Series 1, ed. Vincent Davis, pp. 15–43. Beverly Hills, Calif.: Sage Publications.

McClelland, D. C.
 1953 *The Achievement Motive.* New York: Appleton-Century-Crofts.

 1961 *The Achieving Society.* New York: Appleton-Century-Crofts.

McGowan, Patrick J.
 1974 "Problems in the Construction of Positive Foreign Policy Theory." In *Comparing Foreign Policies,* ed. James Rosenau, pp. 25–44. New York: Halsted.

McHale, John.
 1972 *A Continuation of the Typological Survey of Futures Research,* U.S., HSM-42-71-71. Sponsored by National Institute of Mental Health.

 1974 "Long Range National Planning: A Proposal for Comparative Analysis" (mimeographed). *UNITAR Conference on the Futures, Document CPF/BP 5.*

McHugh, Francis J.
 1966 *Fundamentals of War Gaming.* 3rd ed. Newport, R.I.: US Naval War College.

McLuhan, Marshall and Quentin Fiore.
 1968 *War and Peace in the Global Village.* New York: Bantam Books.

Mead, Margaret.
 1951 *Soviet Attitudes Toward Authority.* New York: McGraw-Hill.

Meadows, Donella H., *et al.*
 1972 *The Limits to Growth.* New York: Universe Books.

Meehl, Paul and Albert Rosen.
 1967 "Antecedent Probability and the Efficiency of Psychometric Signs, Patterns, or Cutting Scores." In *Problems in Human Assessment,* eds. D. N. Jackson and S. Messick, pp. 392–412. New York: McGraw-Hill.

Meier, Robert C., *et al.*
 1969 *Simulation in Business and Economics.* Englewood Cliffs, N.J.: Prentice-Hall.

Mendlovitz, Saul H.
 1975 *On the Creation of a Just World Order.* New York: The Free Press.

Merton, Robert K.
 1967 *Social Theory and Social Structure.* New York: The Free Press.

 1975 "Thematic Analysis in Science: Notes on Holton's Concept." *Science* 188:335–338.

Mesarović, Mihujlo.
 1974 *Mankind at the Turning Point: The Second Report to the Club of Rome.* New York: Dutton.

Milburn, T. W. and J. F. Milburn.
 1966 "Predictions of Threats and Beliefs About How to Meet Them." *The American Behavioral Scientist* 9:3–7.

Miller, David C. and Ronald L. Hunt.
1973 *Futures Studies and Research Curriculum Guide.* San Francisco: DCM Associates.

Miller, L. W., *et al.*
1967 *JUDGE: A Value-Based Tactical Command System.* Santa Monica, Calif.: The Rand Corporation, RM-5147-PR.

Mincer, Jacob and Victor Zarnowitz.
1969 "The Evaluation of Economic Forecasts." In *Economic Forecasts and Expectations: Analyses of Forecasting Behavior and Performance,* ed. Jacob Mincer, pp. 3–46. New York: National Bureau of Economic Research.

Miyake, Setsurei (Editor).
1920 "Japan, A Hundred Years Hence." In *Japan and the Japanese* (Nihon oyobi Nihonjin), ed. Lafcadio Hearn. Tokyo: Hoku Seido Press.

Miyazaki, Isamu and Takashi Nakanomyo.
1970 "An Economic Projection on Asia, 1975–90." Unpublished paper prepared for the World Order Models Project under the auspices of the Institute for World Order, New York.

Modelski, G.
1970 "Simulations, 'Realities,' and International Relations Theory." *Simulations & Games* 1:111–134.

Monin, Andrei S.
1972 *Weather Forecasting as a Problem in Physics,* trans. Paul Superak. Cambridge, Mass.: MIT Press.

Moore, Wilbert E.
1967 *Order and Change: Essays in Comparative Sociology.* New York: Wiley.

Morgenstern, Oskar, *et al.*
1973 *Long Term Projections of Power.* Cambridge, Mass.: Ballinger.

Morse, Edward.
1969 "The Politics of Interdependence." *International Organization* 23:311–326.

1972 "Crisis Diplomacy, Interdependency and the Politics of International Economic Relations." *World Politics* 24:123–150.

Moses, Lincoln E., *et al.*
1967 "Scaling Data on Inter-Nation Action." *Science* 156:1054–1059.

Moy, W. A.
1971 "Variance Reduction." In *Computer Simulation Experiments with Models of Economic Systems,* ed. Thomas H. Naylor. New York: Wiley.

Mumford, Lewis.
1934 *Technics and Civilization.* New York: Harcourt, Brace.

Myrdal, Gunnar.
1944 *An American Dilemma: The Negro Problem and Modern Democracy.* New York and London: Harper and Brothers.

Nance, R. E.
1971 "On Time Flow Mechanisms for Discrete System Simulation." *Management Science* 18:59–73.

Natanson, Maurice Alexander.
1963 *Philosophy of the Social Sciences: A Reader.* New York: Random House.

Nau, Henry R.
1974–1975 "U.S. Foreign Policy in the Energy Crisis." *The Atlantic Community Quarterly* 12:426–439.

Naylor, Thomas H. (Editor).
1969 *The Design of Computer Simulation Experiments.* Durham, N.C.: Duke University Press.

1971 *Computer Simulation Experiments with Models of Economic Systems.* New York: Wiley.

Naylor, Thomas H. and J. M. Finger.
1971 "Validation." In *Computer Simulation Experiments with Models of Economic Systems,* ed. Thomas H. Naylor. New York: Wiley.

Naylor, Thomas H., *et al.*
1966 *Computer Simulation Techniques.* New York: Wiley.

1968 "Some Methods for Evaluating the Effects of Economic Policies Using Simulation Experiments." *Review of the International Statistical Institute* 36:184–200.

Nedelya, 1966, no. 34, p. 8.

Neustadt, Richard.
1970 *Alliance Politics.* New York: Columbia University Press.

Newcombe, Alan and James Wert.
1972 *An Inter-nation Tensiometer for the Prediction of War.* Oakville, Ontario: Canadian Peace Research Institute Press.

North, Robert C.
1962 "Decision-making in Crisis: An Introduction." *Journal of Conflict Resolution* 6:197–200.

North, Robert C. and Nazli Choucri.
1972 "Population and the International System:

Some Implications for United States Policy and Planning." In *Governance and Population: The Governmental Implications of Population Change*, ed. A. E. Keir Nash, pp. 251–278. Washington, DC: US Government Printing Office, vol. 4 of Report of the Commission on Population Growth and the American Future.

"Notes and Comment." *The New Yorker*, December 16, 1974, pp. 31–36.

Nowell-Smith, P. H.
1954   *Ethics.* Baltimore: Penguin Books.

Nowotny, Helga.
1971   "The Uses of Typological Procedures in Qualitative Macro-Sociological Studies." *Quality and Quantity* 5:3–37.

Nye, Joseph.
1974   "Transnational Relations and Inter-State Conflicts: An Empirical Analysis." *International Organization* 28:961–998.

Nye, Joseph S., Jr., and Robert O. Keohane.
1971   "Transnational Relations and World Politics: An Introduction." In *International Relations and World Politics*, World Peace Foundation, 25, eds. Robert O. Keohane and Joseph Nye.

Office of Research Analysis.
1968   *Long-Range Forecasting.* Holloman Air Force Base, New Mexico.

Ogburn, W. R.
1972   *Social Change.* New York: Viking Press.

Ogden, C. K.
1932   *Bentham's Theory of Fictions.* London: Kegan-Paul.

O'Leary, Michael and D. Coplin.
1975   *Quantitative Techniques in Foreign Policy Analysis and Forecasting.* New York: Praeger.

Olson, Mancur.
1965   *The Logic of Collective Action.* Cambridge, Mass.: Harvard University Press.

Onoshi, Akira.
1974   "Analysis of Japan's Development Aid to Indonesia and the Structure of Anti-Japanism." In *Japanese Economy in the Age of Globalization* (Chikyuka Jidai no Nihon Keizai). Tokyo: Nihon Keizai Shimbun Sha.

Orcutt, Guy H.
1952   "Actions, Consequences, and Causal Relations." *Review of Economics and Statistics* 34:305–311.

Orcutt, Guy H. and Herbert S. Winokur, Jr.
1969   "First Order Autoregression: Inference, Estimation, and Prediction." *Econometrica* 37:1–14.

Ozbekhan, Hasan.
1968   "The Triumph of Technology: 'Can' Implies 'Ought.'" In *Planning for Diversity and Choice*, ed. Stanford Anderson, pp. 204–233. Cambridge, Mass.: MIT Press.

Page, William.
1973   "Population Forecasting." *Futures* 5: 179–194.

Patchen, M.
1970   "Models of Cooperation and Conflict: A Critical Review," *Journal of Conflict Resolution* 14:389–407.

Paxson, Edwin.
1963   *War Gaming.* Santa Monica, Calif.: The Rand Corporation, RM-3489-PR.

1972   "Computers and National Security." In *Computers and the Problem of Society*, eds. Harold Sackman and H. Borko, pp. 65–92. New York: American Federation of Information Processing Societies.

Peccei, Aurelio.
1969   *The Chasm Ahead.* New York: Macmillan.

Pen, J.
1969   *Modern Economics.* Baltimore: Penguin Books.

Pendley, Robert and Lawrence Scheinman.
1975   "International Safeguarding as Institutionalized Collective Behavior." In *International Responses to Technology*, a special issue of *International Organization* 29, eds. John Gerard Ruggie and Ernst B. Haas, pp. 585–616.

Perspectives on Contemporary American Strategy. Los Angeles, Calif.: Political Research Organization, Occidental College.

Pettit, Philip.
1975   *The Concept of Structuralism.* Berkeley: University of California Press.

Phillips, W. R.
"Forecasting for Planning." In *Knowledge and Diplomacy: The Interaction of Disorder and Foreign Policy*, ed. G. Hilliker. Columbus: Ohio State University Press (forthcoming).

Piaget, Jean.
1971   *Structuralism.* New York: Harper Torchbooks.

Pirages, Dennis and Paul Ehrlich.
1974 *Ark II.* San Francisco: W. H. Freeman and Company.

Platt, John.
1971 "How Men Can Shape Their Futures." *Futures* 3:32–47.

Polak, Frederick.
1961 *The Image of the Future.* New York: Oceana.

Polanyi, Karl.
1944 "*Laissez-faire* Was Planned." In *The Great Transformation.* Boston: Beacon Books.

Pool, Ithiel de Sola.
1967 "The International System in the Next Half Century." *Daedalus* 96:930–935.

Popper, Karl.
1959 *The Logic of Scientific Discovery.* New York: Basic Books.

1965 *Conjectures and Refutations: The Growth of Scientific Knowledge.* New York: Harper Torchbooks.

Powell, Charles A.
1973 "Validity in Complex Experimentation." In *Experimental Studies in Politics.*

Prebisch, Raul.
1950 *The Economic Development of Latin America and Its Principal Problems.* Lake Success: UN Dept. of Economic Affairs, UN Document E/CM.12/89/rev. 1.

Prehoda, R. W.
1967 *Designing the Future.* Philadelphia: Chilton Books.

Price, Don K.
1965 *The Scientific Estate.* Cambridge, Mass.: Harvard University Press.

Prince, George M.
1970 *The Practice of Creativity.* New York: Harper and Row.

Puchala, Donald J.
1972 "Of Blind Men, Elephants and International Integration." *Journal of Common Market Studies* 10:267–284.

Pyke, Donald.
1970 "Technological Forecasting: A Framework for Consideration." *Futures* 2:327–331.

Quade, Edward (Editor).
1964 *Analysis for Military Decisions.* Santa Monica, Calif.: The Rand Corporation.

Quade, Edward and Wayne Boucher (Editors).
1968 *Systems Analysis and Policy Planning.* New York: American Elsevier.

Raiffa, Howard.
1968 *Decision Analysis.* Reading, Mass.: Addison-Wesley.

Raiffa, Howard and Robert O. Schlaifer.
1961 *Applied Statistical Decision Theory.* Cambridge, Mass.: Harvard Business School.

Randers, Jørgen and Donella Meadows.
1973 "The Carrying Capacity of Our Global Environment." In *Toward a Steady-State Economy,* ed. Herman E. Daly. San Francisco: W. H. Freeman and Company.

Rao, Potluri and Zvi Griliches.
1969 "Small Sample Properties of Several Two-Stage Regression Methods in the Context of Auto-Correlated Errors." *Journal of the American Statistical Association* 64:253–272.

Rao, Potluri and Roger LeRoy Miller.
1971 *Applied Econometrics.* Belmont, Calif.: Wadsworth.

Rapoport, Anatol.
1960 *Fights, Games and Debates.* Ann Arbor: University of Michigan Press.

Rashevsky, Nicholas and Ernesto Trucco (Editors).
1960 *Arms and Insecurity.* Pittsburgh: Boxwood Press.

Rawls, John.
1951 "Outline of a Decision Procedure for Ethics." *Philosophical Review* 60:177–197.

1971 *A Theory of Justice.* Cambridge, Mass.: Harvard University Press.

Read, Herbert.
1971 *Anarchy and Order.* Boston: Beacon Press.

Reich, Charles A.
1970 *The Greening of America.* New York: Random House.

Reston, James.
1974 "Interview with Henry Kissinger." *New York Times,* October 13, p. 1.

Richardson, Lewis F.
1960a In *Arms and Insecurity,* eds. Nicholas Rashevsky and Ernesto Trucco. Pittsburgh: Boxwood Press.

1960b *Statistics of Deadly Quarrels.* Pittsburgh: Boxwood Press.

Riker, William and Peter Ordeshook.
1973 *An Introduction to Positive Political*

Theory. Englewood Cliffs, N.J.: Prentice-Hall.

Rivlin, Alice M.
1971   *Systematic Thinking for Social Action.* Washington, DC: The Brookings Institution.

Robinson, Thomas W.
1971   "Alternative Regime Typology: The Case of Future Domestic and Foreign Policy Choices for Mainland China." Santa Monica, Calif.: The Rand Corporation, P-4531.

Rolbiedki, Waldemar.
1970   "Prognostication and Prognoseology." In *Mankind 2000,* eds. Robert Jungk and Johan Galtung. London: Allen and Unwin.

Rosecrance, Richard N.
1963   *Action and Reaction in World Politics: International Systems in Perspective.* Boston: Little, Brown.

Rosecrance, Richard and Arthur Stein.
1973   "Interdependence: Myth or Reality." *World Politics* 26:1–27.

Rosenau, James N. (Editor).
1969a *Linkage Politics.* New York: The Free Press.

1969b *International Politics and Foreign Policy: A Reader in Research and Theory.* New York: The Free Press.

1973   "Theorizing Across Systems: Linkage Politics Revisited." In *Conflict Behavior and Linkage Politics,* ed. Jonathan Wilkenfeld, pp. 25–56. New York: David McKay.

Rosenau, James N., *et al.* (Editors).
1976   *In Search of Global Patterns.* New York: The Free Press.

Rosenfeld, Stephen S.
1974   "The Politics of Foods." *Foreign Policy* 14:17–35.

Rosenthal, Robert A. and Robert S. Weiss.
1966   "Problems of Organizational Feedback Processes." In *Social Indicators,* ed. Raymond A. Bauer, pp. 302–340. Cambridge, Mass.: MIT Press.

Rostand, Jean.
1960   *Error and Deception in Science.* New York: Basic Books.

Rothstein, Robert L.
1972   *Planning, Prediction and Policymaking in Foreign Affairs.* Boston: Little, Brown.

Rubin, T. J.
1970   *Development Status of Environmental Information Systems.* Santa Barbara, Calif.: G. E. TEMPO.

Ruggie, John Gerard.
1971   "The Structure of International Organization: Contingency, Complexity and Post-Modern Form." *Papers, Peace Research Society (International)* 18:73–91.

1972   "Collective Goods and Future International Collaboration." *The American Political Science Review* 66:874–893.

1975   "International Responses to Technology: Concepts and Trends." In *International Responses to Technology,* a special issue of *International Organization* 29, eds. John Gerard Ruggie and Ernst B. Haas, pp. 557–584.

Ruggie, John Gerard and Ernst B. Haas (Editors).
1975a "The Cocoyoc Declaration." Adopted by participants in the UNEP/UNCTAD Symposium on Patterns of Resource Use, Environment and Development Strategies. Cocoyoc, Mexico, October 8–12, 1975. In *International Responses to Technology,* a special issue of *International Organization* 29, eds. John Gerard Ruggie and Ernst B. Haas, pp. 893–902.

1975b "Environmental and Resource Interdependencies: Organizing for the Evolution of Regimes." Paper prepared for the Commission on the Organization of the Government for the Conduct of Foreign Policy, published in the Appendix of its *Report.* Washington, DC: US Government Printing Office.

Rummel, Rudolph J.
1963   "Dimensions of Conflict Behavior Within and Between Nations." *General Systems Yearbook* 8:1–50.

1966   "Dimensions of Conflict Behavior Within Nations, 1946–59." *Journal of Conflict Resolution* 10:65–73.

1969   "Forecasting International Relations: A Proposed Investigation of Three-Mode Factor Analysis." *Technological Forecasting* 1:197–216.

1972   *Dimensions of Nations.* Beverly Hills, Calif.: Sage Publications.

Russell, Edward C. (Editor).
1973   *SIMSCRIPT II.5 Programming Language.* Los Angeles, Calif.: CACI.

Russell, Robert W.
1973   "Transgovernmental Interaction in the International Monetary System, 1960–1972." *International Organization* 27:431–464.

Russett, Bruce M. (Editor).
1972   *Peace, War, and Numbers.* Beverly Hills, Calif.: Sage Publications.

Sackman, H.
1974   *Delphi Assessment: Expert Opinion, Forecasting, and Group Processes.* Santa Monica, Calif.: The Rand Corporation, R-1283-PR.

Samuelson, Paul A.
1976   *Economics*, 10th ed. New York: McGraw-Hill.

Sargent, Lyman Tower.
1974   "Images of the Future in Science Fiction." Paper for delivery at Annual Meeting of the American Political Science Association.

Savage, Leonard J.
1954   *The Foundations of Statistics.* New York: Wiley.

Schachter, Oscar.
1970   "The Future of the United Nations." *American Journal of International Law Proceedings* 64: 277–284.

Scheff, Thomas J.
1963   "Decision Rules, Types of Error, and Their Consequences in Medical Diagnosis." *Behavioral Sciences* 8:97–107.

Schelling, Thomas.
1958   "The Strategy of Conflict: Prospectus for a Reorientation of Game Theory." *Journal of Conflict Resolution* 2:203–264.

1960   *The Strategy of Conflict.* New York: Oxford University Press.

Schieber, Marc E.
1974   "Assessing Technology for Development." *UNITAR News* 6.

Schink, William A. and John S. Y. Chiu.
1966   "A Simulation Study of Effects of Multicollinearity and Autocorrelation on Estimates of Parameters." *Journal of Financial and Quantitative Analysis* 1:36–67.

Schlaifer, Robert O.
1967   *Analysis of Decisions Under Uncertainty.* New York: McGraw-Hill.

Schon, Donald.
1967   "Forecasting and Technological Forecasting." *Daedalus* 196:759–769.

Schonfield, Andrew.
1965   *Modern Capitalism: The Changing Balance of Public and Private Power.* London: Oxford University Press.

Schuessler, Karl F.
1968   "Prediction." In *International Encyclopaedia of the Social Sciences* 12:418–425. New York: The Free Press.

Schultze, Charles, *et al.*
1971   *Setting National Priorities: The 1972 Budget.* Washington, DC: The Brookings Institution.

Seki, Hiroharu.
1970   "Changing Patterns of the International Systems in Asia—An Interim Report on a Simulation." In *Political Process of International Tension Reduction, The Annals of The Japanese Political Science Association, 1969* (Nihon Seiji Gakkai Nempo). Tokyo: Iwanami Shoten.

Sewell, James Patrick.
1972   "Functional Agencies." In *The Future of the International Legal Order* 4, eds. Cyril E. Black and Richard A. Falk, pp. 480–523. Princeton, N.J.: Princeton University Press.

Shane, Harold G.
"The Educational Significance of the Future." A report prepared for Sidney P. Marland, Jr., US Commissioner of Education, Contract No. OEC-O-C-0354.

Shank, Robert and Kenneth Colby.
1973   *Computer Models of Thought and Language.* San Francisco: W. H. Freeman and Company.

Shapley, Deborah.
1975   "Now, a Draft Sea Law Treaty—But What Comes After?" *Science* 188:918.

Shubik, Martin.
1968   *Simulation of Socio-Economic Systems.* New Haven, Conn.: Cowles Foundation for Research, Yale University.

1972a   "On Gaming and Game Theory." *Management Science* 18:37–49.

1972b   "On the Scope of Gaming." *Management Science* 18:20–36.

Shubik, Martin and Garry D. Brewer.
1971   "Systems Simulation and Gaming as an Approach to Understanding Organizations." In *Symposium on Computer Simulation as Related to Manpower and Personnel Planning*, ed. by Arthur I. Siegel.

Washington, DC: Bureau of Naval Personnel.

1972a "Methodological Advances in Gaming: The One-Person Computer Interactive, Quasi-Rigid Rule Game." *Simulations & Games* 3:329–348.

1972b *Models, Simulations and Games: A Survey.* Santa Monica, Calif.: The Rand Corporation, R-1060-ARPA/RC.

1972c *The Literature of Gaming, Simulation and Model Building: Index and Critical Abstracts.* Santa Monica, Calif.: The Rand Corporation, R-620-ARPA.

Silvert, Kalman.
1970 *Man's Power.* New York: Viking Press.

Simon, Herbert.
1957 *Administrative Behavior*, 2nd ed. New York: Macmillan.

1969 *The Sciences of the Artificial.* Cambridge, Mass.: MIT Press.

Simon, Herbert and Nicholas Resher.
1966 "Cause and Counterfactual." *Philosophy of Science* 33:323–340.

Simpson, Anthony.
1962 *Anatomy of Britain.* London: Hodder and Stoughton.

Singer, J. David.
1972 *The Scientific Study of Politics: An Approach to Foreign Policy Analysis.* Morristown, N.J.: General Learning Press.

Singer, J. David and Michael Wallace.
1970 "Intergovernmental Organization in the Global System, 1815–1964: A Quantitative Description" and "Intergovernmental Organization and the Preservation of Peace, 1816–1964: Some Bivariate Relationships." *International Organization* 24:239–287.

Skinner, B. F.
1971 *Beyond Freedom and Dignity.* New York: Knopf.

Skjelbaek, Kjell.
1970 "Development of the Systems of International Organizations: A Diachronic Study." *IPRA Studies in Peace Research.*

1971 "Shared Memberships in Intergovernmental Organizations and Dyadic War, 1815–1964." In *The United Nations: Problems and Prospects*, ed. Edwin H. Fedder, pp. 31–61. St. Louis: Center for International Studies, University of Missouri.

Slovic, P. and S. Lichtenstein.
1971 "Comparison of Bayesian and Regression Approaches to the Study of Information Processing in Judgment." *Organizational Behavior and Human Performance* 6:649–744.

Smoke, Richard.
1974 *Deterrence and American Foreign Policy.* New York: Columbia University Press.

Smoke, Richard and Alexander L. George.
1973a "Theory for Policy in International Affairs." *Policy Science* 4:387–413.

1973b "Theory for Policy in International Relations." Discussion Paper No. 19, Public Policy Program, John F. Kennedy School of Government, Harvard University, Cambridge, Mass.

Smoker, Paul.
1968a "An International Processes Simulation: Theory and Description." Simulated International Processes Project, Northwestern University, Evanston, Ill.

1968b "International Processes Simulation: A Man-Computer Model." Simulated International Processes Project, Northwestern University, Evanston, Ill.

Snyder, R. C.
1962 "Some Recent Trends in International Relations Theory and Research." In *Essays on the Behavioral Study of Politics*, ed. Austin Ranney, pp. 103–171. Urbana: University of Illinois Press.

Solow, Robert M.
1957 "Technological Change and the Aggregate Production Function." *Review of Economics and Statistics* 39:312–320.

Soroos, Marvin W.
1973 "Some Methods of Futures Research for Investigating Problems Related to Population, Ecology, War, and Peace in the Global System." Paper presented to the Second Annual Convention of the Peace Society (International), Southern Division, Lake Cumberland State Park, Kentucky, April 18–21.

Staël von Holstein, Carl-Axel S.
1970 *Assessment and Evaluation of Subjective Probability Distributions.* Stockholm: The Economic Research Institute.

Stark, W.
1957 "Introduction." In F. Meinecke, *Machiavellianism*, pp. 1–22. New Haven, Conn.: Yale University Press.

Stinchcombe, Arthur L.
1968 *Constructing Social Theories.* New York: Harcourt, Brace.

Stouffer, S. A., *et al.*
1949 *The American Soldier: Adjustments During Army Life.* Vol. I of *Studies in Social Psychology in World War II.* Princeton, N.J.: Princeton University Press.

Strauch, Ralph.
1972 "Winners and Losers: A Conceptual Barrier in Our Strategic Thinking." *Air University Review* 23:33–44.

1974 *A Critical Assessment of Quantitative Methodology as a Policy Analysis Tool.* Santa Monica, Calif.: The Rand Corporation, P-5282.

Sulc, Oto.
1969 "Interactions Between Technological and Social Changes: A Forecasting Model." *Futures* 1:402–407.

Sunkel, Oswaldo.
1973 "National Development Daily and External Dependence in Latin America." In *Continuing Issues in International Politics,* ed. Yale Ferguson. Pacific Palisades, Calif.: Goodyear Publishing.

Swedish Royal Ministry for Foreign Affairs.
1974 "To Choose a Future: A Basis for Discussion and Deliberations on Future Studies in Sweden." Secretariat for Future Studies. Stockholm.

Symposium on Civilization and Science: In Conflict or Collaboration?
1972 *Civilization and Science.* New York: Elsevier.

Syracuse University Research Corporation.
1964 *The U.S. and the World in the 1985 Era.* Syracuse, N.Y.: Syracuse University Research Corporation.

Szalai, Alexander.
1974a "Forecasting in International Organizations: Needs and Possibilities." UNITAR Conference on the Futures. Document CPR/BP 4 (mimeographed).

1974b "The Future of International Organizations." In *Organizations of the Future,* ed. Harold Leavitt, *et al.,* pp. 59–82. New York: Praeger.

Tanaka, Kakuei.
1973 *Building a New Japan—A Plan for Remodeling the Japanese Archipelago.* Tokyo: The Simul Press. (English edition of *Nihon Retto Kaizo Ron.* Tokyo: Nikkan Kogyo Shimbun.)

Tanter, Raymond.
1966 "Dimensions of Conflict Behavior Within and Between Nations, 1958–1960." *Journal of Conflict Resolution* 10:41–64.

1972a "Explanation, Prediction, and Forecasting in International Politics." In *Analysis of International Politics,* ed. J. N. Rosenau, *et al.,* pp. 41–57. New York: The Free Press.

1972b "International Systems and Foreign Policy Approaches: Implications for Conflict Modeling and Management." *World Politics* 24:7–39.

Terman, L. M.
1938 *Psychological Factors in Marital Happiness.* New York: McGraw-Hill.

Theil, Henri.
1966 *Applied Economic Forecasting.* Amsterdam: North-Holland Publishing.

1970 "On Estimation of Relationships Involving Qualitative Variables." *American Journal of Sociology* 76:103–154.

Theobald, Robert.
1968 *An Alternative Future for America.* Chicago: Swallow Press.

Thevenaz, Pierre.
1962 *What is Phenomenology?* Chicago: Quadrangle Books.

Thibaut, J. W. and C. Faucheux.
1965 "The Development of Contractual Norms in a Bargaining Situation Under Two Types of Stress." *Journal of Experimental Social Psychology* 1:89–102.

Thibaut, J. W. and H. H. Kelley.
1959 *The Social Psychology of Groups.* New York: Wiley.

Thomas, Clayton J. and Walter L. Deemer.
1957 "The Role of Operational Gaming in Operations Research." *Journal of the Operations Research Society* 5:1–27.

Thompson, James D.
1967 *Organizations in Action.* New York: McGraw-Hill.

1974 "Social Interdependence, the Polity, and Public Administration." *Administration and Society* 6:3–21.

Thorson, Stuart and John Stever.
1974 "Classes of Models for Selected Axiomatic

Theories of Choice." *Journal of Mathematical Psychology* 11:15–32.

Torgerson, Warren.
1958 *Theory and Methods of Scaling.* New York: Wiley.

Toulmin, S. E.
1960 *An Examination of the Place of Reason in Ethics.* London: Cambridge University Press.

Touraine, Alain.
1971 *The Post-Industrial Society,* trans. Leonard F. X. Mayhew. New York: Random House.

Tribe, Laurence H.
1972 "Policy Science: Analysis or Ideology?" *Philosophy and Public Affairs* 2:66–110.

Triska, Jan, *et al.*
1964 *Pattern and Level of Risk in Soviet Foreign Policy-Making, 1945–1963.* Stanford, Calif.: Stanford University Press.

TROLL/1 User's Guide. Computer Research Center for Economics and Management Science. National Bureau of Economic Research, June 1972 (prepublication version).

Truman, H.
1955–1956
Truman's Memoirs. Garden City, N.Y.: Doubleday.

Union of International Associations.
1973 "The Open Society of the Future: Report of a Seminar to Reflect on the Network of International Associations." Union of International Associations. Brussels.

United Nations General Assembly, Joint Inspection Unit.
1974 "Review of the Intergovernmental and Expert Machinery Dealing with the Formulation and Review of Programs and Budgets: Report on Medium-Term Planning in the United Nations System." UN Document A/9646, June 13.

UN Monthly Chronicle.
1975 April, pp. 28–30.

US Commission on the Organization of the Government for the Conduct of Foreign Policy.
1975 *Report.* Washington, DC: US Government Printing Office.

Von Foerster, Heinz and George W. Zopf, Jr. (Editors).
1962 *Principles of Self-Organization.* Oxford: Pergamon Press.

von Wright, George.
1971 *Explanation and Understanding.* Ithaca, N.Y.: Cornell University Press.

Wagar, Warren.
1971 *Building the City of Man: Outlines of a World Civilization.* New York: Grossman Publishers.

Wagner, R. Harrison.
1974 "Dissolving the State: Three Recent Perspectives on International Relations." *International Organization* 28:435–466.

Wallich, M. A. and N. Kogan.
1965 "The Role of Information, Discussion, and Consensus in Group Risk Taking." *Journal of Experimental Social Psychology* 1:1–19.

Wallis, Kenneth N.
1967 "Lagged Dependent Variables and Serially Correlated Errors." *Review of Economics and Statistics* 49:555–567.

Waltz, Kenneth N.
1959 *Man, the State and War.* New York: Columbia University Press.

1970 "The Myth of National Interdependence." In *The International Corporation,* ed. Charles P. Kindleberger, pp. 205–223. Cambridge, Mass.: MIT Press.

1975 "Theory of International Relations." In *Handbook of Political Science,* Vol. 8, eds. Fred I. Greenstein and Nelson W. Polsby, pp. 1–85. Reading, Mass.: Addison-Wesley.

Walzer, Michael.
1967 "On the Role of Symbolism in Political Thought." *Political Science Quarterly* 82:191–204.

Wanniski, Jude.
1975 "The Mundell-Laffer Hypothesis—A New View of the World Economy." *The Public Interest* 34:31–52.

Warner, W. Lloyd.
1936 "American Caste and Class." *American Journal of Sociology* 42:234–237.

Warner, W. Lloyd and Allison Davis.
1939 "A Comparative Study of American Caste." In *Race Relations and the Race Problem,* ed. Edgar T. Thompson, pp. 219–245. Durham, N.C.: Duke University Press.

Warnock, Mary.
1960 *Ethics Since 1900.* London: Oxford University Press.

Wascow, Arthur I.
1968 "Looking Forward: 1999." In *Mankind 2000,* eds. Robert Jungk and Johan Galtung. London: Allen and Unwin.

Watson, John B.
1927 Quoted in the *Chicago Tribune,* March 6, p. 1.

Weaver, Warren.
1948 "Science and Complexity." *American Scientist* 36:536–544.

Webb, Eugene J.
1969 *Individual and Organizational Forces Influencing the Interpretation of Social and Political Indicators.* Washington, DC: Institute for Defense Analyses, P-488.

Weil, Herman and Jay McIlroy.
1975 "Stochastic Simulations of Long-Range Forecasting Models." Arlington, Va.: Consolidated Analysis Centers, Inc.

Weiner, Milton G.
1968 "Gaming." In *Systems Analysis and Policy Planning: Applications in Defense,* eds. Edward Quade and Wayne Boucher, pp. 265–278. New York: American Elsevier.

Weiss, Edith Brown.
1975 "International Responses to Weather Modification." In *International Responses to Technology,* a special issue of *International Organization* 29, eds. John Gerard Ruggie and Ernst B. Haas, pp. 805–826.

Western Europe to the Mid-Seventies: Five Scenarios. Doc. A/68-3.
Cambridge, Mass.: MIT Center for International Studies.

Whaley, Barton.
1969 *Strategem: Deception and Surprise in War.* Cambridge, Mass.: MIT Center for International Studies, CIS-C/69-9.

1973 *Codeword Barbarossa.* Cambridge, Mass.: MIT Press.

White, Morton.
1950 *Toward Reunion in Philosophy.* Cambridge, Mass.: Harvard University Press.

Whiting, Allen S.
1972 "The Scholar and the Policy-Maker." In *Theory and Policy in International Relations,* eds. Raymond Tanter and Richard

H. Ullman, pp. 229–247. Princeton, N.J.: Princeton University Press.

Whyte, Lynn, Jr.
1962 *Medieval Technology and Social Change.* New York: Oxford University Press.

Wilcox, Wayne.
1970b *Forecasting Strategic Environments for National Security Decision-making: A Proposal and a Method.* Santa Monica, Calif.: The Rand Corporation, RM-6154-PR.

Wilensky, Harold L.
1967 *Organizational Intelligence.* New York: Basic Books.

Wohlstetter, Albert.
1964 "Strategy and the National Scientists." In *Scientists and National Policy-Making,* eds. Robert Gilpin and Christopher Wright, pp. 174–239. New York: Columbia University Press.

Wohlstetter, Albert, *et al.*
1954 *Selection and Use of Strategic Air Bases.* Santa Monica, Calif.: The Rand Corporation, R-266.

Wohlstetter, Roberta.
1962 *Pearl Harbor: Warning and Decision.* Stanford, Calif.: Stanford University Press.

Wolfenstein, Martha.
1957 *Disaster: A Psychological Essay.* Glencoe, Ill.: The Free Press.

Wright, Quincy.
1965a "The Escalation of International Conflicts." *Journal of Conflict Resolution* 9: 434–439.

1965b *A Study of War.* Chicago: University of Chicago Press.

Yearbook of International Organizations, 14th ed.
1972 Union of International Associations. Brussels.

Young, Oran R.
1972 "The Perils of Odysseus: On Constructing Theories of International Relations." In *Theory and Policy in International Relations,* eds. Raymond Tanter and Richard H. Ullman, pp. 179–203. Princeton, N.J.: Princeton University Press.

Zellner, Arnold.
1971 *Introduction to Bayesian Inference in Econometrics.* New York: Wiley.

Zinnes, Dina A.
1967 "An Analytical Study of the Balance of

Power Theories." *Journal of Peace Research* 3:270–288.

1968 "The Expression and Perception of Hostility in Pre-war Crises: 1914." In *Quantitative International Politics*, ed. J. David Singer, pp. 85–119. New York: The Free Press.

Zinnes, Dina A., Douglas Van Houweling, and Richard Van Atta.
1969 "A Test of the Balance of Power Theory in a Computer Simulation." Evanston, Ill.: Northwestern University.

Zinnes, Dina A. and Jonathan Wilkenfeld.
1971 "An Analysis of Foreign Conflict Behavior of Nations." In *Comparative Foreign Policy: Theoretical Essays*, ed. Wolfram F. Hanreider, pp. 167–213. New York: David McKay.

Zwicky, Fritz.
1957 *Morphological Astronomy*. Berlin: Springer Verlag.

1962 *Morphology of Propulsive Power*. Monograph 1. Society for Morphological Research, Pasadena, Calif.

1969 *Discovery, Invention, Research*. New York: Macmillan.

INDEX